HISTORY OF MEDIEVAL INDIA

HISTORY OF MEDIEVAL INDIA

[For B.A./M.A., and other Examinations]

By

Hukam Chand

ANMOL PUBLICATIONS PVT. LTD.

NEW DELHI - 110 002 (INDIA)

ANMOL PUBLICATIONS PVT. LTD.
4374/4B, Ansari Road, Daryaganj
New Delhi - 110 002
Ph.: 23261597, 23278000
Visit us at: www.anmolpublications.com

History of Medieval India

First Published, 2005

PRINTED IN INDIA

Published by J.L. Kumar for Anmol Publications Pvt. Ltd., New Delhi - 110 002 and Printed at Mehra Offset Press, Delhi.

Contents

Preface

History of Medieval India as a paper is being taught at the graduate and post graduate level in B.A., M.A., Competitive Examinations and other History courses syllabus in almost all the Indian Universities and Institutions. The various courses conducted by institutions at the Central and State level too have been considered in respect of their syllabus, course contents and requirements. Thus the material presented here would be of interest as well as great use to the students of B.A., M.A. and other Competitive Examinations. This book will provide complete knowledge of the aspects of Mughal Administration, their Religious Policies, Decline of Mughal Empire, Rise of Maratha Power Sikh Power, The Anglo-French Conflict in India, British Conquest of Bengal, Constitutional Development, Revolt of 1857, Policies of the Associations (1851-1885), Growth of Nationalism, etc. have been discussed briefly here.

The major topics dealt in this book are—Mughal Administration and Religious Policies; The Decline fall of Mughal Empire; Rise of Maratha Power Under Peshwas; Rise of Sikh Power; Rise of Ranjit Singh; The Anglo-French Conflict in India; The British Conquest of Bengal; British Policy in India (1818-1851); Constitutional Development; Revolt of 1857; The Policies of the Associations (1851-1885); The Growth of Nationalism; India and Neighbours (1818-1885).

Hukam Chand

1

Mughal Administration and Religious Policies

According to Holy Quran the real master of the whole world is its real ruler *i.e.* Allah. It is everybody's sacred duty to obey the command of Allah. To propogate his message, the Allah has sent into the world his messengers and Muhammad is his last Prophet. To obey the Prophet is to obey the command of Allah. For the Muslims, next to Prophet is the Caliph. Following this theory of Islamic sovereignty, the Turkish Sultans in India, though practically independent, continued to consider themselves as a part of the Islami world and a representative of the Caliph and from time to time receive investiture from him. Infact the nature of the relationship between the Delhi Sultans and the Caliph was a more formal one. The Mughal rulers ended even this formality. They never declared themselves the representatives of Caliph.

The Mughal Kingship. In its early home in Arabia Islam believed in perfect democracy. People claimed equality in social as well as political affairs. Prophet Muhmmad at the time of his dearth did not declared or nominated a successor, as he did not want to encroach upon the right of the tribe to elect its own leader. Democracy, however, did not last very long. Practice soon becamc widely divergent from theory and even in Arabia it was only during the time of first four Caliphs that the realy democracy existed. After the first four Caliphs the Caliphate became hereditary and assumed the ories of monarchy. After the transference of the capital from Madina to Damascus in 661 A.H. the old idea of the political equality of all Muslims is appeared. After that where ever Islam spread monarchy followed in its way. The democratic institutions of the early Arabs were nowhere evident. The Muslims rulers established autocratic monarchies and discarded the idea of popular government. The same sprit characterized their rule in India. Indian history of the medieval period is a history of monarchs and courts rather democratic movements and political progress. The rulers during the period of Delhi Sultanates as well as during the Mughal period established a benevolent despotism in India. The Mughal emperors ruled without any effective check on their authority. In theory they were only servants of the low—the Muslim Law. They could neither supercede it, nor modify it, but in actual practice this was true of the personal law of the Muslims alone.

The founder of the Mughal dynasty in India announced his new triumph to the world by adopting high soufinding titles. After his accession to the throne of Hindustan his notion of royal dignity grew much higher than before. The title of padshal was assumed by Babur in the year 1508 as he tells us in his memoirs, *"Up to that date people had styled Taimur Beg's descendants Mirza, even when they were ruling, now ordered that people should style me Badshah'."* By doing so Babur declared over lordship above all the Chaghatais and the Mughals as well as over all Mirzas. Humayun also thought himself to be the God's representative on earth. When Askari Mirza rebelled against Humayun he said to have exclaimed one night while he was drinking wine, *"Am not I a king, God's representative on earth?"* Akbar,' Jahangir, Shahjahan and Aurangzeb all claimed to be the "shadow of God." "Waqil of God" on earth, "Khalifa of their age and country". The well known historian of Akbar's age Abul Fuzal in his preface to the Ain-i-Akbari says, *"No dignity is higher in the eyes of God than royalty and those who are wise, drink from its auspicious fountain."* Parviz addresses Jabangir as his visible God and his Lord and Kiblab (placed looked towards in worship). Jahangir says in his memoirs, *"God Almight is the guardian of all His servants, and is specially so a kings, because their existence is the cause of the contentment of the world."* Similarly the royal authority during the time of Shah Jahan was supreme and the emperor was embodiment of it. Aurangzeb was too jealous of power to share even the semblance of it with another. He kept every body at a distance. Even the princes of the blood royal were treated with suspicion. In brief we can say the Mughal emperors believed in theory of divine right of kings. Though the Mughal emperors were Sunnis yet their belief in the divine right of kings was strong as that of the Shia kings of Persia. The Persians regard their kings as Lords Paramounts, but as sons of the Prophet. They regarded themselves as the choosen representatives of God, supernaturally gifted and divinely appointed leaders, whose right to the allegance of their subjects was derived from heaven and not from any election. His jurisdiction which was all-embracing, rendered his position still stronger.

MAIN FEATURES OF MUGHAL ADMINISTRATION

1. Certain Foreign Elements of the Administration were Followed. The Mughals in the beginning readily adopted the administrative system which had been introduced by their Pathan predecessors. During the time of Babur and Akbar no major change was done in administrative system. It was during the period of Akbar that administrative system was changed but he could not altogether ignore the previous system. In this regard the well-known historian Sir Jadunath Sarkar says in his book 'Mughal Administration', "*The Mughal administration presented a combination of Indian and extra-Indian elements; or more correctly, it was the Perso-Arabic system in lndiim setting.*" In fact the principles of their governments, their Church policy, their rules of taxation, their departmental arrangements and the very title of their officials, were imported ready made from outside India. But a Compromise was affected with the older native system already in possession of the field and familiar to the people governed. They modify the foreign elements so that the Mughal administration may suit local needs.

2. New Revenue System. The entire revenue system of the Mughal empire as it was developed during the reign of Akbar was a resultant of two forces—the time honoured Hindu practice and the abstract Arabian theory. In fact the early Maslim rulers very wisely retain the old Hindu revenue system in tact employed the old Hindu revenue officials and seldom interfered with the working of this department so long as the land tax was regularly collected. But in the case of the other sources of state income the Muslim Laws and the practice of Islamic State outside India exercised their full influence. For example even during the Mughal period the Hindus paid the Jiziya from 1526 to 1563 and again from 1679 to 1707.

3. The Mughal Government was Military in its Origin. The second feature of the Mughal's government was that it was a military based government from beginning to the last. Every official of the Mughal government had to be enrolled in the army list; he was given a Mansab as the nominal commander of so many horsemen, which determined his pay and status.

4. The State as a Manufacturer. Another very important feature of the state during the Mughal period was that it was the largest manufacturer or rather the only manufacturer on a large scale in respect of several commodities. The modern practice of government buying readymade goods from the open market or giving orders for large quantities to contractors, were not in practice at that time. Therefore state was forced to manufacture the commodities of its need. The state used so maintain several factories or karkhanas of its own in the principalities of the empire where several hundered people used to work. These factories used to make carpets, harness, saddles, bridles, tents, beddings, weapons, tools, oil, cloth, etc.

5. Centralization of Power. According to Sir Jadunath Sarkar the Mughul Government was a highly centralized autocracy. The crown was the motive power of the entire administrative machinery. Where the government is absolute the supreme authority, concentrated in one man's hand. The Emperor was the head of the state and in practical his powers were unlimited.

6. High Sense of Justice: In the matter of the administration of Justice the Mughal Emperors aimed at laudable standards of fairness, and impartiality. In secular matters the law was largely the same for all and there was no pleading of privilege and peerage.

7. A Secular State. In theory Mughal like every other Muslim ruler was under the Holy Law, but that was a region of speculation and vagueness when applied to practical powers of the king. "Though he led 'the divine service and presided at the prayers of the, emperor enjoyed no spiritual functions. The Mughal emperors of India did not pay homage to any outside Caliphs as some of their Turks and Pathan predecessors did. Most of the Mughal rulers knew that the position of the monarch could be strong only if the State was securarised. Though the Mughal emperors never issued an edict formally *abolishing* Islam as the State religion, as was done in Turkey in 1928; yet for all practical purpose they kept the State and the Church separate. They did not make State offices a monopoly of the Muslims. A person before being appointed to an office was not required to take an oath admitting his faith in Islam. The various offices of State were open to all, irrespective of caste or religion, though the majority were naturally held by those professing the faith of the ruling dynasty.

THE STRUCTURE OF CENTRAL GOVERNMENT UNDER THE MUGHALS

The Emperor. The emperor was the pivot of Mughal administration. He was the fountain of all honours, the source of all administrative power, and the supreme dispenser of justice. He was the despot and the source of all authority. He was the head of the state, supreme commander of the military and the chief executive of the civil administration. Even the religious and political authority was not beyond his reach. Inspite of this, he never had his way, was not uncontrollable and did not misuse his authority. He was always anxious of the welfare of the people. He enjoyed some privileges as well which nobody in the Empire could enjoy without the permission of the Emperor, for example till Shah Jahan's time all the Mughal Emperor continued to enjoy such privileges as, Jharokha a Darshan. Taslim-I-Chowki, beating of drums, distributing titles, use of stamps on 'Firmans,' giving capital punishment, making elephants fight, weighing themselves in balance with coins and so on Some of these were given up by Aurangzeb considering them as Anti-Islamic *e.g.* 'Jharokha Darshan,'. Mughal' Emperor was also the protector of Slam and a spiritual leader of his Muslim subjects. Being a spiritual leader he levied Zakat on his Muslim subjects and used that money to construct mosques and helping Muslim saints and poor men, Mughal emperors transacted business of the state according to the importance of the problem. *(i)* If the problem was in public interest, the emperor held the court in Diwan-i-Aam or Diwan-i-Khas. In Diwan-i-Khas, only nobles, Amirs and other important persons could find their entrance, while general public was allowed in Diwan-i-Aam. *(ii)* If the problem to be discussed was confidential, the emperor held discussions either in Ghusl-Khana or his private apartments.

The Mughal government was a centralised despotism. The Emperor was the head of the State and in theory of his power's were unlimited. But in practice he often deferred to the wishes of his ministers. We have it from Monserrate that Akbar patiently listened his ministers even if they disagreed with him and sometimes even altered his opinion. Despots though the Emperors were, theirs was a benevolent despotism and in this respect they did not compare it with the benevolent despots of Europe a century later. The enlightened policy of religious toleration which Akber followed stood in striking contrast to that of Tudors and Bornbons alike with the exception of Aurangzeb the early Mughal Emperors encouraged arts and literature and in their own way sought to promote the welfare of the people.

According to Sarkar, "The Mughal Emperor had no regular Council of Ministers. The Wazir and the Diwan were the richest persons below the Emperor, but the other officers were in no sense, his colleagues. They were admittedly inferior to him and deserved rather to be called secretaries than ministers. Nearly all their work was liable to revision of the Wazir and Royal Orders were often transmitted to him through him", It was not necessary for the Emperor to consult his ministers on all occasions. He could act even without them or against them. Neither the ministers nor the Wazirs acted as a check on the authority of the Emperor. The Mughal Government was a one-man rule and Aurangzeb was his own Prime-Minister.

The Chief Departments and Their Head

1. The Exchequer and Revenue (under the High Diwan).
2. The Imperial Household (under the Khan-i-Saman or High Steward).
3. The Military Pay and Accounts Office (under the Imperial Bakhshi).
4. Canon Law, both Civil and Criminal (under the Chief Qazi.)
5. Religious Endowments and Charity (under the Chief Sadar.).
6. Censorship of Public Morals (under the Muhtasib).
7. The Artillery (under the Mir Atish or Darogha-i-Top Khanah).
8. Intelligence and Posts (under the Darogha of Oak Chauki).

The innumerable Karkhunahs (*i.e.* factories and stores) each under a darogha or superintendent were not departments. Most of them were under the Khan-i-Saman.

Central Ministers and Their Duties

1. Wakil Prime-Minister. The literal meaning of Wakil is representative. He was the representative of the State. That Minister should be called Wakil who could enjoy all rights of the Emperor on his behalf. This office continued in vogue in Akbar's, Jahangir's and Shah Jahan's reign. During their time Prime Minister was called Wakil or (Wakil-i-Mutalak); Some later emperor reviewed the office of Wakil *e.g.* Jahandar Shah appointed Asad Khan as the Wakil-i-Mutalak and appointed his very son Zulficar Khan as Wazir.

During Akbar's time till the fall of Bairam Khan this office was very important because this office was incharge of finance as, well civic administration. After the fall of Bairam Khan, Akbar let his new Wakil Munim Khan remain as political prime or chief adviser and taking away financial power from him created a separate office of Wazir or Chief Diwan, who be can the head of this financial department. After Bairam Khan the most powerful Wakil was Asaf

Khan who was given a Mansab of 9,000 Jat and 9,000 Sawar by Shah Jahan. Thus the place of Wakil became higher, that that of Diwan.

Rights and Duties of Wakil. Wakil generally had these rights and duties; *(1)* To advice the emperor or about the appointment and dismissal of Subedars, Faujdars and Diwan. *(2)* He advised the Emperor on the question of Jagirs. *(3)* In the evening he presented all the papers etc. before the Emperor. *(4)* He used to keep the royal stamp. *(5)* He had the right to acqpire one copy of all the information coming from the provinces. A copy of all the papers of the Diwan used to come to him. *(6)* His stamp and signatures were needed on all appointment letters. He had the right to have band and come in Palanquin.

2. The Wazir or Diwan. The Wazir or Diwan was the head of the Revenue Department. When Wakil had not been appointed or he was absent, all his works used to be performed by the Wazir. The office of the Wazir got revenue papers and return and despeches from the provinces and the armies in the field. On many ceremonial occasions he acted as the representative of the Emperior. All the orders of the payments had to be signed by him and all payments were made through his department only. Under the directions of the Emperor, he himself passed orders. All questions concerning revenue were settled by him and he consulted the Emperor only important cases. He had two assistant known as the Diwan-I-Am or Diwan of Salaries and the Diwan-I-Chas or Diwan of Crown-lands. After the death of Aurangzeb, Wazir became virtually the ruler of the state.

Rights and Duties of Wazir. *(1)* All the employees concerned with raising of revenue used to be under him and either he used to advise the Emperor in their appointment or sometimes himself did the appointment. *(2)* He used to acquire the description of income and expenditure from the provincial Diwan. He distributed the income from the Empire amongst various departments and kept an account of the entire income and expenditure of the Empire. *(3)* He presented the account of land revenue, imports and exports etc.

3. Mir Bakshi. After the Diwan came the Mir Bakshi. The Mir Bakshi was the chief military adviser. He worked as the Inspector General of the mausabdars contingents an their Paymaster holding annual reviews of troops and troopers. This maintained a high standard of military strength. When the review was complete he issued a certificate which enabled the mansabdar to draw his salary. He thus maintained a complete record of all the mansabdars serving in various capacities at the capital or outside, their ranks, the salaries including special awards, the way in which they drew their salaries, a complete record of their services as well as the result of the annual reviews of their troops and horses. He assigned the mansabdars present at the imperial camp or the capital to guard duty though the list so prepared had to be sent to the Diwan for final sanction. He recorded all orders of royal displeasure and saw to their enforcement; the titles and cash awards with drawn, royal presence forbidden", mounting guard on the emperor denied, all found a place in his office. As the Chief of the State, he drew up the plans of campaigns of various armies in consultation with the commanders and after discussings them with the Emperor. He had a hand in the progress of the most military expeditions, advising the Emperor when reinforcements were necessary or when the smouldering jealousies of rival commanders in an expedition rendered the recall or transfer of one of them necessary. He was usually the Emperor's chief adviser in recommending horses increments and awards following a successful campaign. He was the nerve centre of the administration.

4. Khan-i-Saman or High Steward. He was a very important officer of the Mughal times, as he was the head of the Emperor's household department and accompanied him during his journeys and campaigns. All the personal servants of the Empeor were under his control. He also supervised the Emperor's daily expenditure, food, tents, stores etc. He engoyed great true and influence and there are examples of Wazirs being appointed from among the Khan-i-Samans. He used to keep a list of requirements of the Emperor and the Harems. He was to meet the requirements and in order to do so procure things from the places where they were available. Most of the ordinary requirements were met by the imperial factories or Karkhanas. The Khana-i-Saman was incharge of all the State-owned factories and State industries. He was to see that the court was properly furnished and decorated according to the taste and instructions of the Emperor. He was to keep ready stock the 'robes of Honour' or Khataba, as at any time, the Emperor may need one. He was also to make all purchases of royal princes and princesses.

5. Muhatasib. He was appointed by the Emperor to inspect the moral of the people. He used to perform both religious and secular duties. As a secular official he saw that the shopkeepers and traders are taking right prices or not. He used to see to the cleanliness of the city. He was responsible for the inspection of the markets and their maintenance. As a religious officer he saw to it whether the people follow the rules of the Prophet. During Aurangzeb's time his principal duty was to see to the descarnation of new Hindu temples and punish those Muslims who gave up Namaz and Roza.

6. Sadar-us-Sudur. He was the Chief Sadar of the Empire. He was also called by the names of the Sadar-i-Kul and Sadr-i-Jahan. This office was filled by the persons, who had a very lofty character. Sadar-us-Sudur was the connecting, link between the Emperor and the people. He was the guardian of Islamic Law and the spokeman of the Ulema. According to the Ibn Hasan, the function of the Chief Sadar seems to have been limited to the use of his power for the award by the State of stipends and Jagirs to the Ulema and the needy. It was his duty to look into and decide cases relating to grants. He was the Almoner of the Emperor. He distributed the money for charitable purposes. There was a Sadar in every province. While sending the Provincial Sadars to their charges, the Chief Sadar acquainted them with the names of those who held rent-free lands. Each Sadar was to obey the Chief Sadar and carry out his orders.

7. Qazi-ul-Quzat. Qazi-ul-Quzat was the highest judicial officer next to the Emperor. He was responsible for the proper and efficient administration of Justice. The provincial Qazis were appointed by him. In every province, district and city there were Qazis who used to decide the cases. The duty of the Chief Qazi was to bear appeals from their courts and supervise their conduct.

PROVINCIAL ADMINISTRATION

The Mughal Empire was very vast. For administrative convenience, the Mughal Emperors had divided it into provinces or Subas—the number of the provinces was not uniform throughout. Before 1602, Akbar's Empire consisted of 12 Subas. With the conquest of three Deccan provinces the number rose to 15. In the time of Jahangir, there were 17 provinces and this number further increased in the time of Shah Jahan when it touched the higher insure of 22. In the time of Aurangzeb the number of provinces was 21. The administration in a province was mostly modelled on the pattern of the Central Government.

1. Subedar. Every province was headed by a governor who during Akbar's time was called "Sipahsalar" and in his successors time he was called "Subedar" and "Nazim." He was minister of the the Emperor in the province. He was assisted by the Diwan, Bakshi, Faujdar, Kotwal, Qazi, Sadar, Amil, Bitikchi, Potdar or Knizandar, Waqa-i-Navis Qanungo and Patwari. Provinces were divided into Sarkars and Parganas. All the administration of the province was centralised at the capital town. The Subedar possessed both civil and military authority. He was the representative of the emperor in the province. He held his court but could not sit in the Jharokha. He could not declare war or make peace without the permission of the Emperor.

2. Provincial Diwan. Dr. A.L. Srivastaya says, "He enjoyed in the early days of Mughal rule an equal status with the Subedar but not equal authority. In fact these two offers had to keep a strict and jealous watch on each other, thus continuing the earliest administrative policy and tradition of the Arabs...The Diwan was incharge of revenue administration. He was a representative of the imperial Diwan and an independent incharge of the revenues of the 'province. The revenue collected in the province was remitted to him. He received all the records of the collection, remissions, and arrears of land revenue from various parts of the province and sent them on to the imperial Diwan. He had control over the purse of the province and no payment could be made without his sanction. He was required to co-operate with the Subedar in the administration of the province. If there was a difference of opinion between the Subedar and the Diwan, the matter was referred to the Emperor.

3. Provincial Bakshi. In the province third significant official was Bakshi. He was appointed by the Central Bakshi according to the advice of the Emperor. His primary responsibility was to look after the organization of the army of the province. He managed the recruitment, discipline, training and supplies for the Provincial army. Sometimes, duties of Waqya Nawis were also handed over to him. In that case he sent news of the province to the centre. This enhanced duty also meant additional prestige to him.

4. The Waqya-i-Nawis. The Waqya-i-Nawis was very important officer of the Central Government in the Province. He recorded all the events and occurrences of the Province and submitted his letter to the Central Government. Whenever a new appointment of a Waqya-i-Nawis was made, he was given the following advice:

> "Report the truth, lest the emperor should learn the facts from another source and punish you. Your work is delicate; both sides have to be served. In the words of most of the high officers, forbidden things are done. If you report them truly the officers will be disgraced. If you do not, you yourself will be undone.......In every matter write the truth but avoid offending the bodies. Write after carefully verifying your statement." The Waqya-i-Nawis posted news-writers and spies in the offices of the Sipahsalar, Diwan, Qazi and others. They daily reported and provided him a consolidated report.

5. The Qazi. Every city of Province and even a large village had its local Qazi, who was appointed by the, Chief Qazi or the Supreme Qazi of the Empire, called the Qazi-ul-Quzat. The Qazi assisted by the Mufti and the Mir Adil administered justice to the people. The Subedar was the highest court of appeal in the province. When there was a difference of opinion among the judicial officials in the province the decision of the Central Government was final. All cases of capital punishment were to be referred to the Emperor.

THE RAJPUT AND THE RELIGIOUS POLICIES OF THE MUGHAL

1. Babur and Rajputs. Babur the founder of Mughal dynasty first of all had come to an understanding with contemporary ruler of Mewar, Rana Sanga on the question of dividing the Afghan empire between them. But with the passage of time they began to suspect each other's motives leading to a war between them. On the basis of Tuzk-i-Babri it is said that Rana Sanga invited Babur to invade India against ibrahim Lodhi, and he promised him to help in the battle field. Probably Rana Sanga invited Babur to invade India thinking that like Taimur Lange, Babur would also leave India taking wealth of booty. But Babur laid the foundation of his rule in Agra and Delhi. Babur's contention was that by not helping his against ibrahim Lodhi, at Panipat, Rana Sanga had behaved treacherously against him. The forces of the both rulers reached at Khanwa; a place about 10 mile ahead of Sikri. Babur defeated Rana Sanga. Rana Sanga escaped and wanted to renew the conflict with Babur. But he was poisoned by his own nobles, who considered such a course dangerous and suicidal. Medini Rai, a subordinate all of Rana Sanga held the fort of chanderi. He was also defeated by Babur. When Babur defeated Medini Rai and occupied Chanderi, he married Humayun to a Rajput princess but nothing more is known about her. One can conclude that this marriage had little or no political significance.

2. Humayun and Rajputs. According to a popular story it is said that the queen of Chittore offered Rakhi to Humayun when her state was invaded by Bahadur Shah, the contemporary ruler of Gujrat But the Emperor could not take advantage of it. According to some historians though Humayun marched from Agra to Gwalior to asses the true condition of the conflict. But when he came to know that Bahadur Shah was engaged with the Rajpots who were considered the enemies of the Mughals at that time. Humayun did not consider it proper to create difficulties for Bahadur Shah therefore, he waited for the war between Bahadur Shah and Rajputs to come to an end. If this argument is true, then it was a blunder on the part of Humayun. He should have taken advantage of the opportune moment and attacked Bahadur Shah. This would have resulted in a twofold advantage for him. First, a powerful enemy like Bahadur Shah would have been removed from his path for ever. Secondly, he would have got the co-operation of the loyal Rajputs. Thc cra of sympathy and secularism which started during Akbar's time would have started even in Humayun's time. Finally, Humayun repaired to the court of Shah of Persia due to Afghan pressure and perfidy of self-seeking kinsmen. It is said that Shah Tahmash told Humayun that when the Afghans and the Rajputs were rivals for power and Babur had secured sovereignty by displacing the former; wisdom and farsight demanded that all efforts should be made to rope in the support of the latter in the annihilation of Afghan power.

3. Akbar and Rajputs. Akbar allopted a policy of goodwill and friendship towards the Rajput. As against his predecessors he followed the policy inspired by a number of factors. The reasons which promoted Akbar to follow his policy can be called as the background of Akbar's Rajput policy. For convenience of study these reasons can be described under the following heads:

(i) ***For Establishment of Permanent Vast and Mighty Empire.*** Born under the roof of a Hindu Chieftain, Akbar was brought up-in a liberal society where fanilticism was unknown and religious toleration, brotherhood and friendship were the watch words. His religious policy was an indication of this very spirit. He was tolerant towards the Hindus not by the compulsion of circumstances but by his nature and nurture. He bad before him his future plans of establishing a vast and mighty empire and for that he

must have planned and planned very wisely. He had realised that the Hindus formed the majority of the population and were thus a potent force to be utilised for the establishment of a permanent rule.

(ii) ***For Establishment of Permanent Peace and Order.*** Akbar was a great politician and diplomat. A short while after his accession he had understood that in India permanent peace could not be established if the military leaders of the Hindus, the Rajputs were kept hostile. The history of the last 350 years bore ample testimony to the fact that in the land of the Hindus it was impossible to establish a stable or peaceful government without the co-operation and sympathies of the Rajputs.

(iii) ***Impressive Qualities of Rajputs.*** Bhar Mal, the ruler of Amber had come to Akbar's court at Agra immediately after his accession. He had made a favourable impression on the young king, for when people were running helter-skelter from a maddened elephant, the Rajputs under Bhar Mal had stood firm. Akbar knew of the other many good qualities of the Rajput. He knew that the Rajputs were redoubtable fighters. To the vigour of the body they combined skill in the use of arms, and in the hour of crisis feared neither death nor deserted to the enemy for lure of gold or office. Their loyalty to the salt was proverbial. Their mental qualities were superior even to their military excellencies. They regarded no sin more heinous than treachery to their master. They considered it inconsistent with their 'dignity' and family pride to the anything dishonorable. Gold and silver could nor purchase their sense of honour and chivalry. They preferred death to dishonour Akbar knew that these all good qualities of Rajputs could be utilized for imperialist expansion and making them confidential administrative advisers.

(iv) ***Influence of Some Personalities.*** Akbar's guardian and tutor Bairam Khan was follower of the Shia sect of Islam.

Under his guidance Akbár had not developed the rigidity of the Sunnis. Akbar was also influenced by his liberal teacher like Abdul Latif.

(v) ***Akbar's Gratitude and Affection for Rajputs.*** It is also said that Akbar was born under the roof of a Rajput he had a sense of gratitude and affect on for that community whole. His natural breadth of vision, liberal tendency of his family and the whole some influence of his tutors specially Abdul Latif have also been mentioned as the predisposing causes of Akbar's generous treatment of the Rajputs.

(vi) ***To Shake off the Foreign Nature of Monarchy.*** Akbar realised that co-operation with the Rajputs could help him shake of the foreign nature of his monarchy and convert it in of a national one, which in turn could win popular support and strengthen the roots of his dynasty.

Effects of Akbar's Rajput Policy

(i) Mughal Empire Consolidated. The Rajput policy of Akbar proved very beneficial to the Mughal state. As a result of Akbar's policy all the Rajput states of Northern India except for a part of Mewar passed under his suzerainty. The alliance secured to the Mughal empire the services of the bravest warriors in India. The steadfast loyalty of the Rajputs became an important factor in the consolidation and expansion of the empire. It was mainly because of Akbar's friendly policy towards the Rajputs that the foundation of Mughal Empire became so deep that even after him the Empire continued far many years. They added to the military strength of the empire and contributed to its expansion by successful wars against Afghans, Rajputs, Kashmiris, Gujaratis and others. They laid their lives in the service of the Emperor and the empire and endeared themselves to his heart by their high moral qualities. They also distinguished themselves as administrators and patrons of art and letters. Akbar's Rajput policy created a suitable atmosphere for the Hindus and Muslims to come near each other and understand each other. Though Akbar could not establish friendly relations with all the Rajputs yet he set a good example for his successors. So long as they followed Akbar's policy. Mughal empire continued to progress and prosper.

(ii) Peace and Prosperity in Country. The Hindus and particularly the Rajputs who has always opposed the Muslim regime, abandoned opposing the Mughal rulers. Akbar, because of this policy, succeeded in suppressing the different revolts and established peace and order in the country. Because of peace between the two communities (the Mughals and the Rajputs), Rajasthan escaped the unnecessary destruction due to warfare and also the turmoil. The atmosphere of peace and order helped the people of different provinces to improve their economic situation. This improved the economic position of the country.

(iii) Benefits to The Rajputs. The Rajput policy of Akbar proved beneficial to the Rajputs also. The allience ensured peace in Rajasthan, and enabled the Rajputs to serve in far flung part of the empire without worrying about the safety of their homelands. By being enrolled into the imperial service, important positions in the empire were open to the Rajput Rajas. Thus, Bhagwan Das of Ambar was appointed joint governor of Lahore, while his son, Man Singh, was placed in charged of Kabul. Later on, Man Singh was appointed the governor of Bihar and Bengal. Other Rajput Rajas were placed in charge of strategic provinces, such as Agra, Ajmer and Gujrat, at various times. As high grades of the empire, they were granted Jagirs in addition to their hereditary kingdoms thus augmenting their resources. The Rajputs were given a place of honour at the court which made them so grateful that they became firm and loyal supporters for life.

(iv) Cultural Integration. Because of the adoption of a liberal policy towards the Rajputs there was a beautiful integration of Indian and Muslim cultures in the field of art, architecture, literature and language. During Akbar's time the Rajput and Mughal artists gave birth to a national school in the fields of architecture and painting.

Religious Policy of the Mughal Emperors

Babur. Though an orthodox, Sunni, Babur was not begoted or led by the religious divines. At a time when there was a bitter sectarian feud between the Shias and the Sunnis in Iran and Turna, his court was free from theologial and sactarian conflicts. His belief in Sunni orthodoxy did not precent him from making an alliance with Shah Ismail Safavi, the Shia ruler of Persia, who was notorious for his persecution of the Sunnis in his dominion. According to A.L. Srivastava, "Babur even agreed to encourage the Shia faith in Samarqand." Babur had a strong faith in God and honesty. He believed that a prayer inspire with humanity and meekness and welling forth from a sincere heart did not go unanswered. He was careful about the Namaz and the Roza. But in many other respects his religious life was tainted with sins. He made free use of wine, opium and bhang and although on a number of occasion, he took a solemn vow before God to desist from drink in future, he forgot his vows and took to his cups again when surrounded by genial company in the pleasure garden of nature. God and religion were to him a heaven of refuge, not a bar to his happiness or progress though he declared the battle against Rana Sanga of Mewar a Jihad and assume the tile of Ghazi after the victory at Khanwa in 1527, the reasons were clearly political. He fought a holy war against Medini Rai of Chanderi too. At Ayodhya, he built a mosque on the very spot which was looked upon with great revence by the Hindus as the birth place of Lord Ram Chandra. He discriminated against the Hindu traders when he abolished the stamp duty for all Muslim traders, while allowing it to remain at the old rate for the Hindus. Some of the acts of Babur may be excused on the ground that everything is fair in love and war.

Though it was a period of war only a few instances can be found of destructions of temples. He married a Shia wife, gave her his warmest affection and made her son the heir to his throne. He does not seem to have done much to promote Islam or persecute Hindus. A.L. Srivastava writs. He fought a holy war against Medini Rai of Chanderi too. At Ayodhya, he built a mosque on the very spot which was looked upon with great reverence by the Hindus as the birth place of Lord Ram Chandra. He discriminated against the Hindu traders when he abolished the stamp duty for all Muslim traders, while allowing it to remain at the old rate for the Hindus. Some of the acts of Babur may be excused on the ground that everything is frangible and war. But in fairness to him, it may be added, that his attitude towards his new subjects in this country was not as bad as that of the most of the rulers of Sultanate period.

Humayun. Humayun was deeply religious. He carefully observed the dograms of his faith, and always tried to live like a true Muslim. Although he was a staunch Sunni but his perfound love and respect for the ahl-i-Bait (family of Prophet) shows that he was favourably inclined towards the Shia faith. His learning in favour of that faith is borne out by the fact that the entire machinery of his government was in the hands of Shias. Bairam Khan his principal adviser and *ataliq* of the heir-apparent and Shah Abul Maali, his special favourite were Shias. But he had much stronger interest in spiritual matters. While in Badakhshan, he had thought of renouncing the world and adopting the life of a *darvesh*. He was kind to the Shias but he did not extend complete religious tolerance to the Hindus, who profound the vast majority. He was definitely partial to his co-religionists and never attacked a Muslim, if he was engaged in war with the Hindus. He demolished temple and did not refrain from hurting the susceptibility of the Hindus.

4. Jahangir. Jahangir was born of a Rajput mother and had grown up in the atmosphere of Ibadat-Khan's discussions. His teacher Abdul Rahim Khan-i-Khana was under the inference of Vaishnav doctrines and it was widely believed that though he does described himself a Sunni, he was at heart a Shia. Jahangir had opportunities of coming in close contact with scholars of different religions. Because of the influence of his father, the royal household, the court and different scholars was surcharged in the atmosphere of religious toleration and rationalism. Dr. R.P Tripathi has written about Jahangir, "In his religious news he was not narrow and took delight in conversing man of other faiths. His inclination was however, more towards Sufism. None the less, he was more orthodox, than his father and less than his son, Khurram. He made practically no difference between the Hindus and the Mohammedans or the Christian subjects....." He abolished Jizia and pilgrimage tax like his father. He opened highest public services to the non Muslims, The cultural contact between the Hindus and the Muslims, sought to be established by Akbar through participation in Hindu festivals and Persianuans Nations of Hindu books continued. He patronized Surdas, the great Hindi writer. In certain directions however, Jahangir showed some backsliding. Whreas Akbar and left alone conversion to different faiths, Jahangir gave stipends to Muslim converse, tried to stop the conversion of Muslim women in Hindu in Hinduism in Mirpur and Rajori in Jammu where this was happening on a large scale. Jahangir demolished the Hindu temple of varah (Boar God) and Pushkar. The Sikhs incurred his displeasure because Guru Arjun, the fifth Sikh Guru, had blessed Khusru's banner. After the suppression of the rebellion, he was called to Lahore and awarded capital punishment as a traitor.

Jahangir, like Akbar has been accused of being a non-Muslim but, this charge is totally a baseless. He had respect for the teachings of Islam and retained this attitude till the end of his life because he too introduce no change in the organization of the Ecclesiastical Department and rewarded who got converted to Islam and penalised those who turned a way from it. He prohibited public sale of wine and set apart 25% of the net gains from escheated property for the constructions of mosques. He also prohibited sale of meat on certain days held sacred by him. We find him postponing the sacrificial slaughter of animals to the day following, the Id and the Id fell on one of the days when animals could not be openly killed. But he can by no means be described staunch or even an orthdox follower of the principles of Islam. He was himself addicted to drink and initiated his own son Khurram into the habit. Nor was he very regular in Roza and Namaz, "This is true that Jahangir was far inferior to his father in many respects and did nothing to improve upon the administrative system.

5. Shah Jaban. The well kriown historian Shri Ram Sharma writes about the religious policy of Shah Jahan, "Shah Jahan followed his grandfather's path so far as the general plan of his policy was concerned. The one short—lived change was the re-introduction of the pilgirmage tax. Religious toleration and absence of civic disabilities on religious grounds remain parts of his administrative policy in general." But according to my view in his religious policy Shah Jahan was not liberal and tolerant of other faiths like his grandfather Akbar. There was a ting of intolerance in his religious policy though he did not systematically persecute the Hindus. Orthodox Muslims did not like the views of Akbar and Jahangir and there was some resentment among them. Shah Jahan was ¾th Rajput by parentage. But from the very outset, he was more staunchly attached to the tenents of Islam. He was regular in Roza and Namaz. And as long as, he was in the capital never neglected the Roza. Mumtaz Mahal's orthodoxy influenced him and Lahori, a historian presumes him as, "the defender, of the Faith", Christians were, persecuted from 1632 A.D. to 1635 A.D. after the capture of Hughly. 'Burnier says, "The Jeusists was severly oppressed by the Emperor." Shah Jahan endeavoured to give his court an Islamic atmosphere ablished Sijda (prostration before the monarch), discontinued the Hindu practice of tuladan the cellebration of Hindu festivals like Vasant, Raksha Bandan, Dussehra etc. and restored the Hijri Aera to the state calender. He began celebrating at court the Muslim festivals of Id, Shab-i-Barat, Milad and Barawafat in orthodox Muslim fashion. The destruction of Hindu temples was stated in his reign. He for bade Hindus to keep Muslim salves, to marry Muslim wives and to live Muslim style. Those who had Muslim wives were ordered either to forsake them or marry them afresh by Anikah after their own conversion to Islam. He also assumed the role of defender and propogator of Islam. He spent Rs, 30,000/- every year in public charity, in the holy month of Ramzan, and sent Rs. 40,000/-Rs, 50,000/ for charity to Macca. He established a separate department for securing conversions to Islam. His administrative policy as a whole was just and liberal and he appointed capable Hindus to government posts. During his period of rule there was no permanent adaptation of religious persecution as an integral element of state policy. He too did not revive the Jizia. During the latter part of his reign there, is no reference to temple destruction or any other form of religious persecution. Under Shah Jahan the position of the Hindus remained unshaken in the Empire even though Khafi Khan states that Shah Jahan issued an order prohibiting employment of Hindus in the public services. At the end of the tenth year there were 76 Hindus occupying the status of 500 or above out of 419 in all. When Aurangzeb rebelled against Shah Jahap in 1658 Maharaja Jaswant Singh was the premier noble of the Empire being a 6000er. Raja Ragu Nath was the Imperial Finance Minister and Raja Jai Singh was the closest confident of the Emperior. Nor he deprive the Hindu poets, artists and scholars of state patronage, so that Sunder Das, Chintamani, Kavindracharya, Maha Kaviray Pandit Jagannath, Sukhsen and others rejoyed his favour and patronage. He permitted the renovation of the Chintamani at Ahmedabad and at the requests of the citizens of the Cambay prohibited cow slaughter there. It would thus appear that Shah Jahan had no inborn hatered for the Hindus. He considered it his duty to enable them also to live in peace and honour.

❐

2

The Decline of Mughal Empire

Party factions in the Mughal Court was one of the most important factors which sapped the vitality of the Mughal Empire. These parties sacrificed the interest of the empire for their selfish interest. There were two important parties, Hindustani Party and Turani Party.

The Turani party mainly consisted of foreign elements such as Arabs, Negroes, Afghans, Pathans and Europeans. During Aurangzeb's period they had became powerful and their important leaders were Chin Kilich Khan and Asaf Jah Nizam-ul-Mulk. The Hindustani Party mainly consisted of natives. They were Shias and so were disliked by the Sunnis. Their leaders were two Sayyid Brothers namely Syed Abdulla Ali and Syed Hussain Ali. The Hindustani party included Marathas, Rajputs and Hindu land-owners.

Sayyid Brother, the leaders of the Hindustani party played a vital role in the Mughal ploitics after the death of Aurangzeb. According to Prof. S.R. Sharma "The History of nearly ten years from the accession of Farrukh-Siyar to the discomfiture of Prince Sultan Mohammad is very largely the biography of Sayyid Brothers, at the 'king-makers' Abdulla Khan and Husain Ali Khan Barha are familiarly known is history."

Sayyid Brothers. The Sayyids claimed descent from Abdul-Farah, Sayyid adventurer from Mesopotemia, who had settled near Patiala centuries earlier. The father of Sayyid Brothers was the Subedar of Bijapur and Ajmer successively. The elder brother Abdulla Khan received an Imperial mansab and was attached with Prince

Muhammad Muszzam Shah Alam. The younger brother Hussain Ali Khan served as a Faujdar in the Subas of Ajmer and Agra. Both the brothers rose to prominence during the battle of Jajau. In 1711 Abdulla Khan by favour of Prince Azim- us- Shan was made his deputy in province of Allahabad. Sayyid Brothers also helped Farrukhsiyar in his contest for the throne in 1712. In fact Furrukhsiyar's successes was almost entirely due to them. In 1712 they had dethroned Jahandes Shah and put him to death along with his Wazir Zulfikar Khan. As a reward of their services Farrukhsiyar appointed Abdullah Khan as his Prime Minister and Hussain Ali Khan as commander-in-Chief of the Mughal army.

Sayyid Brothers played a dominant role in Mughal politics. From 1712 to 1712 they were in control of the real power and the king were more puppets in their hands.

Farrukhsiyar having atained throne with the help of sayyid Brothers tried to do away with them. His attempts to realise life object proved fatal for him. The tragedy of Farrukhsiyar's life was the fruit of his own conduct. As Khafi Khan puts it, "From the beginning of his reign he himself brought his troubles on himself: he had no will of his own, he was inexperienced in business; he was entirely dependent on the opinion of other, for he had no resolution or direction: he was not cautious in listening to the words of artful men."

Farrukhsiyar owned his throne to Sayyid Brothers and, naturally, they expected to exercise the real power of the state, Leaving to the emperor only pageantry, and such command of wealth and honours as might enable him to gratify his favourites. But the two Brothers got much below their expectations and the lion's share went to Tufani officers and Emperor's friends. And as Khafi Khan remarks "the two brothers were not inclined to bear patiently Mir Jumla's invidious and provoking interference in their affairs."

Farrukhsiyar tried to get rid of Sayyid Brothers. He started participating in plots against Sayyid Brothers. Prof. S.R. Sharma refers to the three plots in which Farrukhsiyar participated:

(a) "Sayyid Hussain Ali was sent against the Rajputs, with secret despatches to Raja Ajit Singh offering him tempting terms in the event of his getting rid of the Imperial general."

(b) "A direct attempt was made on the life of the elder Sayyid Abdullah Khan under the very nose of the emperor: at the Nauroz ceremonies the Wazir was to have been surrounded and assassinated or imprisoned. But unfortunately for Farrukhsiyar, this plot was miscarried like the rest; the Wazir caught scent and overawed the imperial muster on the occasion by a larger massing of troops in advance."

(c) "Hussain Ali Khan on the failure of the first plot was despatched to the south as Subedar of the Deccan. While at the same Daud Khan Panni was secretly incited to confront him on the way and get rid of him, if possible, on promises of giving him the viceroyalty of the Deccan in place of the Deccan in place of the Sayyid."

Under such conditions it was quite essential for the Sayyid Brothers to weaken and overawe their enemies. Sayyids joined hands with Jats and also secured the alliance of Raja Ajit Aingh. Attempt of Dand Khan to kill Hussain Ali khan was also foiled. After this plot Abdullah Khan moved to the capital and brought about a revolution. The palace was surrounded by Sayyid troops. Farrukhsiyar was deposed. He was dragged out of harem, insulted and brutally strangled.

After Farrukhsiyar two puppets were raised to the throne called Rafi-ud- Darajat and Rafi- ud- Daula. Both these kings ruled from February 1719 to September 1719. Both these kings were weak and patients of T.B. After death Sayyid Brothers raised Mohammad Shah on the throne. Mohammad Shah's original name was Roshan Akhtar and he was the son of Jahan Shah. Mohammad Shah was an inexperienced youth. So Sayyid Brothers continued to wield all the power. Mohammad Shah like his predecessor, Farrukhsiyar, tried to get rid of Sayyid Brothers.

Fall of Sayyid Brothers. With the purpose of realising his object Mohammad Shah sought the help of Nizam-ul-Mulk who was a sworn enemy of Sayyid Brothers. Nizam-ul-Mulk invaded Khandesh which formed part of the viceroyalty of Sayyid Brothers. Nizam-ul-Mulk defeated and killed the nephews of Sayyid Brothers called Dilawar Khan and Alam Ali Khan. This news perplexed Sayyid Brothers and it was decided that Abdullah Khan would remain in the capital to look after the administration while Hussain Ali would march to the south along with the emperor to reduce the Nizam. On their way a conspiracy was formed against Hassain Ali and he was assassinated. The leader of the conspiracy was Mohd. Amin Khan. He was the leader of the Turani Party. Sayyid Hussain Ali was stabbed to death in October, 1720. Thc emperor now retreated at the head of the army. He appointed Mohd. Amin Khan as his Wazir and gave him the title of Imad-ul-Daula. The Emperor now proceeded to Delhi defeated Sayyid Abdullah at Bilochpur near Agra in November 1720. He was taken prisoner and in 1722 he died in jail. And in this was the rule of king makers came to an end.

RISE OF HINDUSTANI AND TURANI PARTIES

These party factions cared more for their personal selfish interests than for the general interests of the Mughal Empire. Thus, a constant tug-of-war was going on between the rival factions with a view to gaining ascendancy in the Mughal Court and consequently the Court had come to be divided into two opposite and rival armed camps. According to Irvine, there were forty party factions at the Mughal Imperial Court, out of which two were most important. These were:

(1) **Hindustani Party.** The first was the Hindustani party under the leadership of the two Sayyid Brothers, Abdulla and Hussain Ali. Owen states, "The Sayyids of Barha, though of alleged exotic origin, were old inhabitants of Indian and prided themselves on being Hindustanees. As such, their sympathies would naturally be with the natives rather than with the Mughal conquering class of foreigners. And though they were Muslims, they were also Shias, another cause of estrangement between them and the Mughals, who were mostly Sunnis, and a strong ground

for aversion to Aurangzeb's reactionaly and persecuting policy, and for rallying what I may call nationalist sentiment to their side under the banner of toleration and political equality, as established by Akbar." Thus, the Hindustani party led by the Saiyed Brothers consisted of the Mohammedans born in India, many of whom were the decendants in their second or third generation from foreign immigrants. Men like the Sayyids of Barha, for instance, whose ancestors had settled in India many generations before, came of course, under the description of Hindustani or Indian-Born people. To this class also belonged all the Rajput and Jat chiefs, and other powerful Hindu landowners.

(2) **Turani Party.** The second party was called the Mughal, Turani or Irani party. According to Irvine, "The Turani party formed the backbone of the army of occupation. Their numbers were increased still further during the twenty- five years or more, from 1680 to 1707, during which Alamgir waged incessant wars in the Deccan, with the local Mohammedan states and then with the Marathas." In this party was also included the Afghan or Pathan element who, though discouraged under Shah Jahan, had found favour under Aurangzeb. Then, in this party, were included also the other foreign elements like the Arabs, Habshis, Rumis and Farangis (Europeans). Their leaders during the reign of Farrukhsiyar were Mir Jumla, Itikad Khan, Khan Duran, Mohanmmad Amin Khan (Itimad-ud-Daula), the mother of Mohammad Shah, and Mohammad Shah the Emperor himself.

FEATURES OF THE PARTY FRACTIONS

(i) Firstly, the Mughal Imperial Court was the centre of intrigues and counter-intrigues by one party against the other party. The palace revolutions of king- making were the work of the Hindustani party or "Wazirs' friends" under the leadership of the Sayyid Brothers, while the more effective and real revolution by which was brought about the fall of the Sayyid Brothers was the work of the Irani or

Turani party, also called the "Emperor's friends." This triumph of the kings's Friends over the "king-makers" is one of the most fascinating stories recorded in history.

(ii) Secondly, it should be remembered that none of these party factions had any solid national programme before them which should have given them the name of political parties in modern conception of the term, rather they were only pary factions which concerned themselves merely with efforts for their personal ascendancy and achievement of their selfish ends in the Court. The worst consequence of this party faction, therefore, was that the Mughal Imperial Court became a hot- bed of intrigues which produced confusion and chaos in the Court and thus resulted in corruption and inefficiency in the entire governmental machinery of the Empire. Under such circumstances, the fall of the Empire was in the logic of circumstances.

The Sayyid Regime (1712-1720)

1. The two brothers first acquired importance during Farrukhsiyar's contest for the throne. They claimed descent from Abul Farah, a Sayyid adventurer from Wasit in Mesopotamia, who had settled near Patiala centuries earlier. During the battle of Jajau (1707), they held the ranks of 3,000 and 2,000 respectively and fought for Bahadur Shah I. Abdulla was the elder and Hussain Ali was the younger brother. As has already been said before, it was by the favour of Prince Azim-us-Shan, that in 1711 Sayyid Abdulla khan was made his deputy in the province of Allahabad. Three years earlier in 1708, Hussain Ali had been appointed to the government of Bihar by the same prince. The claims of Farrukhsiyar on the gratitude and support of the Sayyids was great and, as already noticed, they did not fail him in his contest for the throne (1712). In fact, Farrukhsiyar's success was almost entirely due to them. The result was fateful. In 1712, they dethroned Jahandar Shah and ignominiously put him along with his Wazir Zulfikar Khan to death and in his place installed Farrukhsiyar on the throne. As as reward for their invaluable service to Farrukhsiyar, he appointed Abdulla Khan as his Prime Minister and Hussain Ali Khan as the Commander-in-Chief of the Mughal army. Saiyed Abdulla Khan was awarded the title of Nawab Qutb- ul- Malk,

Yamin-ud-Daula, Sayyid Abdulla Khan Bahadur, Zafarjang, Sipah Sardar, Yar-i-Wafadar. The younger brother, Husain Ali Khan, was awarded the title of Umdat-ul-Malk, Amir-ul-Umra Bahadur Firoz Jang Sipah Sardar. During this period (1712-1720), it may be noted that the emperors were mere puppets, their life being spent more inside the zenana than outside it.

Farrukhsiyar Wants to Free Himself from the Yoke of the Sayyid Brothers. The tragedy of Farrukhsiyar's life was the fruit of his own conduct. As Khafi Khan puts it, "from the beginning of his reign he himself brought his troubles on himself; he had no will of his own; he was inexperienced in business; he was entirely dependent on the openion of others, for he had no resolution of discretion; he was not cautious in listening to the words of artful men." In short, as Elphinstone has well said. "Farrukhsiyar was incapable of comprehending a great design and to irresolute to execute a small one without support. "Farrukhsiyar owed his throne to the Sayyids and, natrurally, they expected to exercise all the real power of the state, leaving to the Emperor only the pageantry, and such a command of wealth and honours as might enable him to gratify his favourites. But they received very little besides the two offices which were the price of their services, while according to Irvine, "The Emperor's friends and the Turani Chief, Mir Jumla, obtained the lion's share." Consequently, as Khafi Khan remarks, "the two brothers were not inclined to bear patiently Mir Jumla's invidious and provoking interference in their affairs." Farrukhsiyar now began his efforts to free himself from the galling yoke of the Sayyid Brothers. He, therefore, commenced taking part in a series of plots against the Sayyid Brothers. The Sayyids throughout acted with admirable restraint and tact. But human patience has its limits; and when the furies burst nemesis proved relentless."

The three plots in which Farrukhsiyar participated against the Sayyid Brothers were the following:

(1) In the words of Prof. S.R. Sharma,"Sayyid Hussain Ali was sent against the Rajputs, with secret depatches to Raja

Ajit Singh, offering him tempting terms in the event of his getting rid of the Imperial general, *i.e.*, Hussain Ali Khan."

(2) On the failure of the first plot, Sayyid Hussain Ali was despatched to the South as Subedar of the Deccan, while at the same time Daud Khan Panni was secretly incited to confront him on the way and get rid of him, if possible, on promise of receiving the viceroyalty of the Deccan in place of the Sayyid.

(3) A more dire attempt was made on the life of the Sayyid Abdulla Khan under the very nose of the Emperor. At the Nauroz ceremonies, the Wazir was to have been surrounded and assassinated or imprisoned. But unfortunately for Farrukhsiyar, this plot also miscarried like the rest; the Wazir caught scent of the trap and overawed the Imperial master on the occasion by a large massing of troops in advance.

2. Consequently, the Sayyid Brothers Got Farrukhsiyar Dethroned and Murdered (1719). As has been pointed out above, Farrukhsiyar employed very shameful measures to get rid of the Sayyid Brothers, which resulted in very fatal results for him as well as for his throne. Prof. S.R. sharma says, "In the face of such persistent dangers, the Sayyid Brothers should have been fools it they also did not make efforts to weaken, outwit or overawe their enemies. Thus, When the imperial officers were fighting against the rebellious Jats, their chieftain Churaman Jat was given surreptitious support by Abdulla Khan; Hussain Ali Khan discovered the secret messages to Raja Ajit Singh, Offered him suitable favours and finally secured his alliance; the attempt of Daud Khan resulted in Hussain Ali's victory, the death of Daud, and the discovery of further incriminating farmans; and the plot to assassinate Abdulla Khan led to the Wazir's sending for his brother from the South, who marched posthaste to the capital with all the forces he could rally and brought about a revolution.

3. The Sayyid Brothers then Raised Two More Puppet Emperors Rafi-ud-Darajat and Rafi-ud-Daula on the Throne. The end of the tragedy of Farrukhsiyar's murder has been described. After the assassination of Farrukhsyar, the Sayyid Brothers raised Rafi-ud-Darajat, a son of Rafi-us-Shan and a youth of twenty on 28th February 1719. He was very intelligent, but was badly suffering from consumption. The Emperor became a complete puppet in the hands of the Sayyid Brothers, who thus carried on the administration in his name. There was a rebellion by Niku-Siyar son of Akbar, who set himself up as Empleror in the Agra Fort with Mitra Sen, a Nagar Brahmin, as his Wazir. Consequently, Rafi-ud-Darajat was deposed on 9th June, 1719 by the Sayyid Brothers, as he was about to sink owing to the disease. He died a week after his deposition. The Sayyid Brothers then raised Rafi-ud-Daula, the elder brother of the deposed Emperor, on 6th June 1719 with the title of Shah Jahan II. He too was consumptive and a pluppet in the hands of the Sayyids.

4. Then the Sayyid Brothers Raised Mohammad Shah on the Throne. After the death of Rafi-ud-Daula, the Sayyid Brothers crowned prince Roshan Akhtar, the son of Jahan Shah, as Emperor under the title of Mohammad Shah, on 28th September, 1719. He was a weak and inexperienced prince and, as such, the Sayyids retained all powers in their hands. Mohammad Shah also, like Farrukhsiyar, attempted to get rid of the Sayyid Brothers with the active assistance of Nizam-ul-Mulk. During these days, Nizam-ul-mulk, who was appointed the governor of Malwa, left for that province. There was no love lost between the Sayyid Brothers and the Nizam. Consequently. Nizam-ul-Mulk invaded Khandesh then included in the viceroyalty of the Sayyid Hassain Ali. Dilawar Khan, the nephew of the Sayyid Brothers and Alam Ali Khan, the nephew of Hussain Ali Khan, sent against Nizam-ul-Mulk, were defeated and killed respectively by him (Nizam-ul-mulk). These news highly perplexed the Saryad Brother who then decided that while Sayyid Abdulla Khan should remain at Delhi to run the administration, Sayyid Hussain Ali should proceed to the Deccan along with the Emperor to put down Nizam-ul-Mulk. While the Emlperor was on the way, a conspiracy was formed against Sayyid Hussain Ali by one Mohammad

Amin, a persian adventurer and Hider Ali Khan, the Superintendent of Imperial artillery. Consequently, Sayyid Hussain Ali was stabbed to death in October, 1720.

The Character and Services of the Sayyid Brothers to the Mughal Empire.

(i) Character

Khafi Khan, the critical and not very sympathetic historian, remarks about the two Sayyid Brothers, "In the course of this narrative, upon some points, the pen has been used to condemn the two brothers, the martyrs of misfortune, and this cannot now be rectified; but in atonement I will now write a few words upon the excellence and beauty of character, the love of justice, and the liberality of both brothers.... Both the brothers were distinguished in their day for their generosity and leniency towards all mankind. The inhabitants of those countries which were innocent of coutumacy and selfishness made no complaints of the rule of the Sayyids. In liberalilty and kindness to the learned men and to the needy, and in protection of men of merit, Hussain Ali Khan excelled his elder brother, and was the Hatim suited to his day. Numbers owed their comforts to the cooked food and raw grain which he gave away. At the time of the scarcity at Aurangabad, he appropriated a large sum of money and a great quantity of grain to supply the wants of the poor and of widows. In their native country of Barha, they built sarais, bridges and other buildings for the public benefit. Sayyid Abdulla was remarkable for his patience, and wide sympathy."

(ii) Services to the Mughal Empire

(a) The Sayyid Brothers were like Akbar, the advocates of the spirit of tolerance in matters or religion. They were much opposed to the reactionary policy of Aurangzeb.

(b) It was under their influence and at their suggestion that the jizya was abolished at the accession of Farrukhsiyar, It was again at their suggestion that Mohammad Shah (1719-48) also abolished it and consequently, they won over the sympathies of the Rajputs. An attempt was made by their rivals at the Court a few years later to reimpose it which they did for a time, but as long as the Sayyids were in power, this could not be permanent.

(c) Likewise, the Marathas, under the influence of Hussain Ali Khan, were won over by the grant of their utmost demands of Chauth and Sardeshmukhi. If Farrukhsiyar had been tactful and wise, they could have been secured as allies of the empire. But they became the instruments of destruction in the hands of the Sayyids because of Farrukhsiyar's own inaptitude.

(d) Abdulla Shah showed his sympathy for the Jats also when the Sayyid Brothers mediated on behalf of Churaman Jat to allow him to retain his post on condition of submitting to the Emperor. Thus Jai Singh, who was besieging the Jat fort of Thuri, was directed to raise the siege. Thus Churaman visited Delhi in April 1718.

(e) They formed a Hindustani party. In order to counteract the machinations of the bigoted party at the Court, they formed a Hindustani party, which included the Hindus and the Mohammedans among its members. The Rajputs were also the chief supporters of the Sayyid Brothers on account of their conciliatory policy.

(f) It was on their suggestion that Rattan Chand, a grain merchant, was appointed as Diwan in place of Inayat Ullah Khan.

(g) Raja Ajit Singh was transformed into a strong ally from a rebel, and induced to give his daughter in marriage to Farrukhsiyar. Their alienation later was the fruit of Farrukhsiyar's own folly.

Causes of the Downful of the Sayyid Brothers

The fall of the Sayyid Brothers can be attributed to many causes which are the following:

(1) Firstly, in order to strengthen their own, party, the Sayyid Brothers had patronised many nobles with promotions and ranks. But at a later date the same elevated nobles turned against the Sayyid Brothers and began to hatch conspiracies against them. The result of their intrigues proved fatal to them.

(2) Secondly, the Sayyid Brothers had acted as "king- makers" and, as such, they had brought about the deaths of Farrukhsiyar and many other royal princes. These heinous crimes on their part had alienated the sympathies of the people from them and when they walked towards decadence, people did not come forward for their help and, consequently, they met with a great fall in life.

(3) Thirdly, the supremacy of the Sayyid Brothers in the Court meant decadence of the other nobles from power and influence. Hence they put forth every opposition to the Sayyid Brothers and their opposition due to jealousy against them had totally disgusted the other Court nobles them. Hence their fall.

(4) Fourthly, their rise to power brought about the formation of a rival party against them in the court. The members of this rival party were saadat Khan, the Governor of Oudh. and Nizam- ul- Mulk. The Nizam had been turned out of the governorship of the Deccan in 1712 by Hussain Ali Khan.

(5) Fifthly, the Emperor Mohammad Shah was chafing under the galling yoke of the Sayyid Brother. He, therefore, was anxious to get rid of the Sayyid Brothers. To achieve his end, he had to align himself with the party of opposition to the Sayyid Brothers. Thus the secret alliance of the Emperor with the party against the Sayyid Brothers was a very important cause of their downfall.

(6) Sixthly, the Sayyid Brothers were liberal in their outlook and very tolerant in their attitude towards the Hindus.

Consequently, this Hinduising policy on their part in the form of the abolition of the Jizya, the appointment of the Hindus to the various posts in the government, the marriage of Ajit Singh's daugther with the Emperor Farrukhsilyar through their mediation and, above all, their tolerance towards the Hindus in the matter of religion, were the things which were very much resented by the members of the Turani and Irani parties. Consequently, there was an open rebellion against them.

Significance of Their Work. It is presumed that if the Sayyid Brothers had been spared, they could have established a strong state on a national and tolerant basis with the support of the Indian Mohanmmedans and Hindu princes. Thus, by establishing a strong central government, they would have avoided the invasions of Nadir Shah and Ahamed Shah Abdali. They would also have checked the rapid rise of the Marathas and the English to power. They would have thus maintained the power and prestige of the Mughals quite intact. But, unfortunately, this all could not be possible on account of their execution which, in its turn, did not improve the things as was expected. The Mughal Emperor became free from the dominant influence of the Sayyid Brothers only to fall under the influence of evil counsellors and Nizam-ul-Mulk, feeling disgusted with the state of things at the Court, retired to the Deccan in disgust. Thus ended the career of the great personalities.

Rise of the Turani Parti. Another very important powerful leader of the Turani party was Nawab Saadat Khan who had also received the title of Barhan- ul- Mulk from the Emperor. In the opinion of Dr. A. L. Srivastava, "excepting Nizam-ul-Mulk Asaf Jah, Nawab Saadat Khan was undoubtedly the most powerful, great and an ambitious person out of all the nobles and the courtiers of the Mughal Court. At the time of Nadir Shah's invasion on India in 1738-39, Saaddat Khan made such a mean display of his low mentality that he most treacherously got the Emperor and Nizam-ul-Mulk both in the Camp of Nadir Shah. It was in 1748 when the Mughal Empire was on its last legs that Nawab Saddat Khan died.

Ahmed Shah, the successor of Mohammad Shah, later on appointed Safdar Jung, the nephew and successor of Nawab Saadat Khan, as his Wazir. But another important courtier. Jawed Khan, who was awarded the title of Nawab Bahadur and enjoyed the close confidence of the new Emperor, set up a new party of his own in the Court. This "junta" or clique of the eunuchs and ladies became so powerful that it assumed the virtual control over the whole of administration and stood very strongly in array against Nawab Safdar Jung and the other powerful nobles of the Court. They even went to the extent of making attempts on the life of Nawab Wazir Safdar Jung, but all their efforts failed. This tug-of-war between the two parties further widened the gulf between them. In the end, Nawab Safdar Jung got the Nawab, Bahadur Jawed Khan, murdered in 1752. This murder roused the indignation of the Emperor against Nawab Safdar Jung and then started an internal strife between the Emperor against Nawab Safdar Jang and then started an internal strife between the Emperor and Wazir.

The Emperor then appointed Intizam- ud- Daula as the new Wazir but soon the two nobles, Intizam-ud-Daula the Wazir and Imad-ud-Daula, the Mir Bakshi, came to grips with each other. The result was that the Emperor dismissed the Wazir Intizam-ud-Daula and appointed Imad-ud-Daula as the Wazir. Immediately on his elevation to the post of the Wazir, Imad-ud-Daula dethroned the Emperor and blined him and placed Alamgir Sani on the throne instead. The new Emperor was nothing more than a mere puppet in the hands of his selfish and unscrupulous Wazir. The net result of Imad- ud- Daula's elevation to the post of the Wazir was that he began to plunder the royal treasury and starve the members of the royal family.

In 1757 when Ahmed Shah Adbali invaded India for the fourth time and stayed in Delhi for some time, the Emperor Shah Alam Sani complained to Ahmed Shah Abdali against his minister, Imad-ud-Daula, for his rough and rude behaviour towards him. On this, Ahmed Shah Abdali called to his presence Najib-ud-Daula, the Rohilla governor of Saharanpur and Najibabad and appointed him as the

Emperor's Mir Bahshi and his lord protector. But, on the return of Ahmed Shah Abdali from India, Najib-ud-Daula also was forced to go back to Afghanistan. After this, the crafty and unscrupulous Wazir, Imad-ud-Daula, got Shah Alam Sani murdered and placed instead Shah Jahan III, grandson of Kam Bakhsh, on the throne, but the same day, the prince Ali Gauhar, the son of Alamgir Sani, then living as a refugee in Bihar, declared himself as the Emperor under the title of Shah Alam Sani. He appointed Shuja-ud-Daula, the new Nawab of Oudh, as his minister, but on account of a stiff opposition from Imad-ul-Mulk, he could not invade and conquer Delhi.

Najib-ud-Daula had by this time prevailed upon the new Nawab of Oudh, Shuja-ud-Daula also to his point of view. Thus these Court intrigues and counter-intrigues resulted in the thired Battle of Panipat in 1761. In this battle, Suraj Mal Jat and Wazir Imad-ud-Daula were on the side of the Marathas, but just at the last moment, there occurred serious differences on the question of war tactics and, consequently, they left the Marathas on the eve of this historic battle. As a consequence of the third Battle of Panipat, not only that the Maratha power alone was smashed to pieces but the Mughal Empire also completely came to an end. The entire Mughal Empire, the Emperor and the Mughal nobility. all lay prostrate on the feet of Ahmed Shah Abdali and the decision of their salvation and of their life and death entirely lay in the hands of this Afghan adventurer. But since Ahmed Shah Abdali was not interested to syat in India, nor was he intersted to occupy India, he appointed Shah Alam Sani as the Emperor of India with Shuja- ud- Daula as his Wazir and Naib- ud-Daula as the Deputy of Delhi in his behalf. Thereafter, no doubt up to 1858, come of the rulers of Delhi continued on ruling over India, but the truth is that the Mughal Empire had practically come to an end with the third Battle of Panipat in 1761.

In this way we can conclude that one of the most important factors which contributed towards the disintergration of the Mughal Empire was the division of the Mughal Court into two selfish party factions, the Turani and the Hindustani parties, which cared more for their own selfish ends than for the national interests of either the country as a whole or the Mughal Empire.

INVASION OF NADIR SHAH

Nadir Shah is known as the Napoleon of Iran. He was born in a poor family. To begin with, he was the leader of a gang of robbers. Throughout his early life Nadir Shah had to pass through hardships and difficulties. This had made him brave and energetic. His name was Kuli Khan Nadir. Nadir Shah overthrew the Safair dynasty and became the ruler of Persia in 1736 and assumed the title of Nadir Shah. In 1722 Persia or modern Iran was snatched away from Shah Hussain Safair, the ruler of Persia, by the Afghans. In the time of Shah Tahmasp Persia was recovered from the Afghans. Nadir Shah proved very helpful in the recovery of Persia, Thereafter Nadir Shah entered the service of Shah Tahmasp, the present ruler of Persia. That was in 1727. Tahmasp was very weak and, therefore, Nadir Shah become the defacto ruler. In 1732 Nadir Shah threw off even that nominal yoke. He deposed Tahmasp. Shortly afterwards the son and successor of Tahmasp also died. Then Nadir Shah became ruler of Peria.

Causes of the Invasion

(a) **Bad Condition of the Empire.** The Mughal empire had become weak by this time. The selfish nobles were not prepared to support the Emperor. The provincial governors were trying to grind their own axe. Internal weakness was sure to court external aggression.

(b) **Shelter to Persians.** The Mughal ruler of India, Mohammad Shah had promised that he would not give shelter to the Persian fugitives. However, later on, he violated his own promise, and gave shelter to the fugitives from Persia. Nadir Shah complained against this attitude and sent his envoy to the Delhi Court requesting the Mughal Emperor, Mohammed Shah, not to provide refuge to the Persian rebels. The agent of Nadir Shah was maltreated at the Delhi Court, envoy was detained and Mohammad Shah did nothing to please Nadir Shah or fulfil the promise he had given him earlier. This provided Nadir Shah with sufficient ground to attack India.

(c) **Fabulous Wealth of India.** Nadir Shah had heard about the fabulous wealth of India and he wanted to plunder it. The time was also opportune because the Mughal Empire had politically and militarily become too weak to defend the great wealth. Nadir's men knew about the weakness of the Empire, the inbecility of the Emperor the inattentiveness of the Ministers, the spirit of the independence which had crept among the grandees. This was enough to make Nadir Shah Pounce upon the rich and defenceless plains of India.

(d) **Neglect of the Defence.** The Mughals were very careless and slack about the border defences. The defence of North- West Frontier especially was miserably neglected. Nadir Shah made capital out of this weakness of Mughal defence machinery.

Course of Events

Capture of Kabul and Peshawar. Nadir Shah marched towards India in the early months of 1738. North- west Frontier was not properly protected at the time when Nadir Shah invaded. As a result Nadir Shah did not find it difficult to conquer the frontier regions. He entered northern Afghanistan in the month of May 1738. Towards the end of the month he easily captured Ghazni. In the month of June 1738 Kabul fell. A couple of months later, in September, Jalalabad also surrendered to Nadir Shah's forces. In the month of November Peshawar was captured, too.

Capitulation of Lahore. The Mughal forces stationed at Jamrud and Peshawar could not do anything to check the advancing forces of Nadir Shah. Nadir Shah kept on moving and attacking. In January,1739, Lahore also fell. The testimony of A. Mukhlis runs thus: "Nasir Shah was ow in possèssion of the country as far as Attock and Mohammad Shah and his advisers could no longer remain blind to the danger that threatened them. They understood that this was no ordinary foe against whom they had to contend, no mere plunderer who could be satiaed with the spoils of a province and then return to his own country, but a leader of unshakable resolution who shaped his course with his sword. How to relate the ruin and desolation that overwhelmed this beautiful country! Wazirabad, Imanabad and Gujrat town, which for their population may almost be called cities, were levelled with the earth. Nothing was respected, no sort of violence remained unpractised, property of all kinds became the spoil of the plunderer and women the prey of ravisher."

Sack of Punjab. The governor of the Punjab tried to check him near Wazirabad but was defeated. As K.K. Datta says : the whole province of the Punjab was thrown into great confusion and disorder. All this while the pleasure-loving Emperor and the carpet-kinghts of his court, whose conduct during the invasion of Nadir Shah 'forms a role of disgraceful inefficiency amounting to imbecility,' did not give any resistance to Nadir Shah's approaching forces.

Battle of Karnal. When the seriousness of the situation was realised, the imperial troops marched in a sudden frenzy and camped at Karnal. Karnal is about twenty miles from Panipat. The Mughal Emperor, Mohammad Shah, now fully realised the gravity of the situation. He decided to march personally at the head of the imperial army against the Persian forces of Nadir Shah. He made a frantic bid to check the advance of the invader. A battle was fought between the royal Mughal troops and the Persian troops in February 1739. In this battle the Mughal army was completely routed and the forces of Nadir Shah emerged vicotorious. The Mughal Amir-ul-Umara, Khan Dauran died in action in the battle.

Nadir Shah at Delhi

On the advice of Khan Dauran an attempt was made by the well- wishers of the Emperor to do something about Nadir Shah. As a result the most importantally of Mohammad Shah, Nizam-ul-Mulk gave a bribe of fifty lacs of rupees to Nadir Shah and requested him not to proceed further towards Delhi. Nadir Shah was on the point of agreeing when Saadat Khan an adversary and enemy of Nizam-ul-Mulk, convinced Nadir Shah that his going to Delhi would be much more profitable and would add to his prestige and reputation ultimately. Nadir Shah decided to march to Delhi.

Nadir Shah entered Delhi along with the defeated Mughal emperor. At first Nadir Shah's troops were kept in good check. They did no harm to the people of the capital. In all the mosques of Delhi Khutba was read in the name of Nadir Shah. Suddenly an unfortunate rumour went round that nadir Shah was dead. There upon there was a tumult among the inhabitants of Delhi. In this confusion a few Persian solders were killed. When Nadir Shah learnt of the fate of his deceased soldiers he ordered a general massacre and in about eight hours, about thirty thousand men, women and children were put to death. The city was horribly sacked. Then this carnage was stopped at the request of Mohammad Shah. Nadir Shah returned back after a stay of about two months taking with him gold, silver, jewels, etc. worth about seventy crores of rupees, including Kohinoor diamond and the Peacock throne. He also annexed the territories west of the river Indus.

Recoronation of Mohammad Shah. Nadir Shah and his men routed the Mughal army, looted the city of Delhi and the nearby villages were pillaged, Nadir Shah captured all the granaries of the city and posted guards on them. The rich people of the city were especially harassed for money. This went on for 57 or 58 days. After that Nadir Shah left for the home country, Parsia, leaving Mohammad Shah to manage his own affairs as he had promised to the Mughal Emperor before he had entered Delhi. However, before Nadir shah left for Persia he crowned Mohammad Shah again as the Mughal Emperor. On that occasion Mohammad Shah is stated to have exclaimed. "As the generosity of the Shah-in-Shah has made me a second time master of a crown and a throne and exalted me among the crowned heads of the world, I beg to offer him as my tribute the provinces of the Empire, west of the river Indus, from Kashmir to Sind, and in addition the Subans of Thatta and the forts subordinate to it."

Results of Nadir's Invasion

(1) Nadir Shah's invasion gave a severe below to the already weak Mughal Empire. The Empire's decay and downfall was quickened. The prestige of the Empire was ruined. The hollowness

and weak texture of the Mughal Empire was exposed by the invasion of Nadir Shah. Mohammad Shah was obliged to marry his daughter to the youngest son of Nadir Shah. Later in 1747, Nadir Shah was killed. As a result of Nadir Shah's invasion the provincial governments became independent. Nizam-ul- Mulk, Asaf Jah in the Deccan, Saadat Ali Khan in Oudh and Alivardi Khan in Bengal, Bihar and Orissa became virtually independent.

(2) Nadir Shah's invasion resulted in the loss of territory also. Nadir Shah took away the Mughal possessions lying to the west of river Indus. This is true that the aforesaid territories were presented to Nadir Shah by Mohammad Shah himself, after he had been crowned for the second time by Nadir Shah. All the same that territory was, in a way, lost to the Mughal Empire. There was chaos and confusion wherever eye travelled in the Empire. Western Punjab and Sind were completely lost to the Mughal Empire. Kabul was also snatched away and since then Afghanistan was virtually separated from the Indian dominions.

(3) Nadir Shah's invasion prepared the way for invasions from the north- west in two ways. Firstly, the Mughals lost all the territory to the west of river Indus. Thus natural defence on the north-west of river was lost to the Mughals. Even otherwise the defence of north-west frontier was sadly neglected by the Mughals. That is why Nadir Shah could conquer the north-west regions so easily. Secondly, the invasion clearly demonstrated the utter weakness of the Mughal Empire. Ahmad Shah Abdali commenced the attack on India within a decade of Nadir Shah's invasion. Because of the defenceless northwest frontier, the Afghans were encouraged to penetrate into India in large numbers and create confusion. After Nadir Shah's invasion in 1739 India became the target of many foreign powers for their invasions. This large series of foreign invasions, after the departure of Nadir Shah, on India can be explained by the political chaos and confusion that Nadir Shah had left and the defenceless frontiers of the north-west.

(4) Nadir Shah took away a booty worth seventy crores of repees. The financial condition of the empire was already bad. The

financial bankruptcy of the Empire further contributed to the downfall of the Empire. About the financial loss done to the empire by Nadir Shah Anandram Mukhlis says. " All the regal jewels and property and the contents of the treasury, were seized by the Persian conqueror in citadal. He thus became possessed of treasure to the tune of sixty lakhs of rupees and several thousand Asarfis; Plates of gold to the value of one crore of rupees, and the jewels, many of which were unrivalled in beauty by any in the world, were valued at about fifty crores of rupees. The Peacock Throne alone constructed at great pains in the reign of Shah Jahan, had cost one crore of rupees. In short, the accumulated wealth of 348 years changed matters in a moment."

MUGHAL EMPIRE SHRINK TO THE AREA AROUND DELHI

The Mughal empire declined rapidly after the death of Aurangzeb (1707 A. D.). All most after the death of every Mughal ruler there was a far of succession which resulted in huge destruction everytime. On Aurangzeb's death his three sons (Muazzam, Azam and Kam Bakhsh) fought among themselves for the throne. The 65 years old Muazzam succeeded and occupied the throne in the name of Bahadur Shah. There was further deterioration in the field of administration in Bahadur Shah's reign. The position of state finances worsened as a result of his reckless grants of jagirs and promotions. During his reign the remmants of the Royal treasure, amounting in 1707 to some 13 crores of rupees, were exhausted.

Bahadur Shah was grouping towards a solution of the problems besetting the Empire. Given time, he might have received the Imperial fortunes. Unfortunately, his death in 1712 plunged the Empire once again into civil war.

A new element entered the succeeding wars of succession while previously the contest of power had been between royal princes and the nobles had merly aided the aspirants to the throne, now over ambitions nobles became direct contenders for power and used princes as mere pawns to capure the seats of authority. In the civil war following Bahadur Shah's death one of his less able sons Jahandar Shah, won because he was supported by Zulfiqar Khan, the most powerful noble of the time. Jahander Shah was a weak and degenerate prince who was wholly devoted to pleasure. He lacked good manners and dignity and decency. During his reign the administration was virtually in the hands of the extremely capable and energetic Zulfiqar who had become his wazir. Many jealous nobles secretly worked against Zulfiqar Khan.

Wars still, the emperors to did not give him his trust and co-operation in full measure. The emperor's ears were poisoned against Zulfiqar Khan by unscrupulous favourities. He was told that his wazir was becoming too powerful and ambitious and might even overthrow the emperor himself. The cowardly Emperor not dismiss the powerful wazir but he began to intrigue against him secretly. Nothing could have been more destructive of healthy administration.

Jahandar Shah's inglorious reign came to an early end in January 1713 when he was defeated at Agra by Farrukh Siyar, his nephew. Farrukh Siyar owed his victory to the Sayyid brothers, Abdullah Khan and Husain Ali Khan Baraha, Who were therefore given the offices of wazir and mirbaksh respectively.The two brothers soon acquired dominant control over the affairs of the state. Farrukh Siyar lacked the capacity to rule. He was cowardly, cruel, undependable and faithless, Moreover, he allowed himself to be influenced by worthless favourites and flatterers. Inspite of his weakness, Farrukh Siyar was not willing to give the Sayyid brothers a free hand but wanted to exercise personal authority.

In the end, in 1719 the Sayyid brothers deposed him and kill him. In his place they raised to the throne in quick succession two young princes (Rafi-ud-Darajat and Rafi-ud-Daula) who died of consumption. The Sayyid brothers now made the 18 years old Muhammad Shah, the Emperor of India. The three successors of Farrukh Siyar were mere puppets in the hands of the Sayyid. Even their personal liberty to meet people and to move around was restricted. Thus, from 1713 until 1720, when they were overthrown, the Sayyid Brothers wielded the administerative power of the state.

Even though the Sayyid brothers had tried hard to conciliate and befriend all sections of the nobility, a powerful group of nobles headed by Nizam-ul-Mulk and his father's cousin Muhammad Amir Khan began to conspire against them. These nobles were jealous of the growing of the two brothers. These nobles declared that the Sayyids were following anti-Mughal and anti-Islamic policies. They thus tried to arouse the fanatical sections of the Muslim nobility against the Sayyid brothers. The anti-Sayyid nobles were supported by Emperor Muhammad Shah who wanted to free himself from the control of the two brothers.

Muhammad Shah's long reign of nearly 30 years (1719-1748) was the last chance of saving the Empire. But Muhammad Shah was not the man of the moment. He was weak-minded and frivolous and overfond of a life of ease and luxzury. He neglected the affairs of state. Instead of giving full support to able wazirs such as Nizam-ul-Mulk, he fell under the evil influence of corrupt and worthless flatterers and intrigued against his own ministers. He even shared in the bribes taken by favourite courtiers.

Disgusted with the fickle-mindedness and suspicion nature of the Emperor Nizam-ul-Mulk decided to leave the Emperor and his Empire to their fate and to strike out on his own. He relinquished his office in October 1724 and marched South to found the state of Hyderabad in the Deccan. "His departure was symbolic if the flight of loyalty and virtue from the Empire." The physical break-up of the Mughal Empire had begun. The other powerful and ambitious nobles also now began to utilise their energies for carving out semi-independent states. Hereditary nawabs owing nominal allegiance to the Emperor of Delhi arose in many parts of the country, for example, in Bengal, Hyderabad, Avadh and the Punjab. Everywhere petty zamindars, rajas and nawabs raised the banner of rebellion and independence. The Maratha sardars began their northern expansion and overran Malwa, Gujrat and Bundelkhand. Then in 1738-1739, Nadir Shah descended upon the plains of northern India. He entered Indian territory towards the end of 1738, without meeting any opposition. Hurried preparations were then made for the defence of

Delhi, but the faction ridden nobles refused to unite even in sight of the enemy. They could not agree on a plan for defence or on the commander of the defending forces. The two armies met at Karnal on 13th February 1739 and the invader inflicted a crushing defeat on the Mughal army. The Empeor Muhammad Shah was taken prisoner and Nadir Shah marched on to Delhi. He compelled Muhammad Shah to cede to him all the provinces of the Empire west of the river Indus. Nadir Shah's invasion inflicted immense damage on the Mughal Empire. Taking advantage of this weakness of the Mughal government, Ali Muhammad Khan Rohila established his control over the Province of Katehr situated to the north of the Ganga river. This province came to be known as Rohilkhand afterwards after his name. Muhammad Shah invaded Rohilkhand, defeated Ali Muhammad Rohila and took him as a prisoner but later on released him.

In 1747 A.D. Nadir Shah was assassinated and Ahmed Shah Abdali became the independent ruler of Afghanistan. On the eve of launching his first attack on India Ahmad Shah Abdali had conquered Kabul, Kandhar and Peshawar. In January 1748 he launched his first attack. There was a battle at Manpur. On the Mughal side the heir apparent, Ahmad Shah and Mir Mannu were fighting. Mir Mannu Was the son of the late Wazir Qamar- ud- Din. In this battle the Afghan invader was defeated and Ahmed Shah was sent running away. Mir Mannu was appointed Governor of the Punjab. After the death of Muhammad Shah His 21 year old son, Ahmad Shah ascended the throne. He, too, proved to be an incapable ruler. He did not possess any sort of capability to carry on the administration. He was an indulgent and debauched man and consequently, his Durbar (Court) was turned into an assembly of women and eunuchs. Ahmad Shah Abdali, the ruler of Afghanistan invaded India twice in his reign. Mir Mannu had not properly settled down as the Governor of the Punjab when Ahmad Shah Abdali launched his second invasion of Punjab in 1750. The Governor came out to give the invader a stubborn resistance but he could make little headway. He surrendered to Durrani, the invader. Ahmad Shah Abdali invaded India third time in 1752 A.D. He defeated the Punjab Governor and then proceeded towards Delhi. In Delhi the Mughal Emperor in an attempt to save

Delhi from another sack and massacre made peace with Abdali and offered him Multan and Punjab. The Abdali had also conquered Kashmir in the course of the third invasion of India. Ahmad Shah Abdali invaded India for the fourth time in 1756 A.D. He entered Delhi on January 28th 1757 A.D. He plundered Delhi and Mathura mercilessly. He carried with him untold wealths of India while returning home. Thus Ahmad Shah Abdali gave a shattering blow to the Mughal Empire which was already on its last legs and capured some of its areas. As a result of all this the Mughal Empire was confirmed to only Delhi and its surrounding areas.

The Sikh took advantage of the confusion and disorder prevalent all over the country during the reign of alamgir second and they occupied Lahore in 1758 under the leadership of Jassa Singh Kalal. The Sikhs, however had to vacate Lahore when Ahmad Shah Abdali invaded reoccupied it as soon as he left for Afghanistan.

Alamgir II was a puppet in the hands of his Wazir Imad- ul-Mulk. True, but even he was fed up with this sort of tutelage. When the emperor could tolerate no more, he started planning to get rid of the powerful Wazir. But he was no match for his wily Wazir. As a result the Emperor himself was murdered at the instigation of Imad-ul- Mulk, the Wazir. Ali Gauhar was in Bihar at the time of his father, Alamgir II's death.

Shah Alam II, who ascended the throne in 1759, spent the initial years as an Emperor wandering fron place to place far away from his capital, for he lived in mortal fear of his own Wazir. He was a man of some ability and ample courage. But the Empire was by now beyond redemption. In 1764, he joined Mir Quasim of Bengal and Shuja-ud-Daula of Avadh in declaring war upon the English East India Company. Defeated by the British at the Battle of Buxar, he lived for several years at Allahabad as a pensioner of the East India Company. He left the British shelter in 1772 and returned to Delhi under the protective arm of the Marathas. The British occupied Delhi in 1803 and from that year till 1857, when the Mughal dynasty was finally extinguished, the Mughal Emperors merely served as a political front for the English.

Steps Taken for the Protection of the Mughal Empire. Though the successors of Aurangzeb were incompetent and luxurist but they did not help in the decline of the Mughal empire intentionally. It is different that they did not have the capacity to solve the changing polictical, social economic circumstances and that is why the Mughal empire declined in no time. Rulers and high officials took the following steps for the protection of the Mughal empire:

(a) **Adoption of Friendly Policy by Bahadur Shah.** After Aurangzeb's death, his eldest son Muazzam tried to avoid the civil war. But dur to his other brothers (Azam and Kam Bakhsh) being in the war path he had to fight in which both the others were killed.

Bahadur Shah was a well-read and an able ruler. He changed the socalled policy of intolerance towards the Hindus which was in vogue and established very good terms with them. The pulling down of the Hindu temples was altogether stopped and policy of adjustment was adopted. Thus he tried to take Hindu into his confidence. There was no destruction of temples in his reign. In the beginning, he made an attempt to gain greater control over the Rajput states of Amber Marwar (Jodhpur) by replacing Jai Singh by his younger brother Vijai Singh at Amber and by forcing Ajit Singh of Marwar to Submit to Mughal authority. He also made an attempt to garrison the cities of Amber and Jodhpur. This attempt was, however, met with firm resistance. This may have made him recognise the folly of his actions for he soon arrived at a settlement with the two states, though the settlement was not magnanimous. Though their states were restored to the Rajas Jai Singh and Ajit Singh, their demand for high mansabs and the offices of subahdars of important provinces such as Malwa and Gujrat was not accepted.

Bahadur Shah had tried to conciliate the rebellions Sikhs by making peace with Guru Gobind Singh and giving him a high mansab (rank). But when, after the death of the Guru, the Sikhs once again raised the banner of revolt in the Punjab undr the leadership of Banda Bahadur, the Empeoror decided to take strong measures and himself led a campaign against the rebels, who soon controlled practically the entire territory between the Sutlej and the Jamuna, reaching the close neighbourhood of Delhi.

Bahadur Shah conciliated Chaṭarsal, the Bundela chief, who remained a loyal feudatory, and the Jat chief Churaman, who joined him in the campaign against Banda Bahadur. There was further deterioration in the field of administration in Bahadur Shah's reign. The position of state finances worsend as a result of his reckless grants of jagirs and promotions. Bahadur Shah was groping towards a solution of the problems besetting the Empire. Given time he might have revived the Imperial fortunes. Ultimately, his death in 1712 plunged the Empire once again into civlil war.

(b) Zulfiqar's Efforts During Jahangir's Regime. Zulfiqar's succeeded in the civil war which was fought among the sons of Bahadur Shah after his death in 1712 A.D. He himself was a weak and corrupt ruler but succeeded in securing the services of an able minister Zulfiquar Khan. Zulfiqar Khan was a wise and industrious man. He tried his hard to save the Mughals from Downfall. He befriended the Hindus, especially the Marathas and the policies of Aurangzeb at a fast pace. He stopped the most hated jazia tax and thus won the sympathies of Hindus. For reforming the bad economic condition of Mughal empire Jahandar Shah controlled the distribution of jagirs, appointments for different posts on a large scale and promotions. His wazir, Zulfiqar increased the central control on the Manabdars, so that the efficiency of the Mughal army could be maintained. He stressed the marking of horses and writing of description of soldiers, and checked the army very strictly. For increasing the income of the state, he restarted Izaredari system. Though this sysyem was not useful for the peasants, and long term results of this system did not prove helpful for the state enen than Zulfiqar's this step in the bad financial condition of the state.

(c) **Efforts of Sayyid Brothers.** The Sayyid brothers adopted the policy of religious tolerance. They believed that India could be ruled Harmoniously only by associating Hindu chiefs and nobles with the Muslims nobles in governing the country. Again, they sought to conciliate and use the Rajputs, the Marathas and the jats in their struggle against Farrukh Siyar and the rival nobles. The abolished the jiryah immediately after Farrukh Siyar's accession to the throne, Similarly, the pilgrim tax was abolished from a number of places. They won over to their side Ajit Singh of arwar, Jai Singh of Amber, and many other Rajput princes by giving them high positions of influence in the administration. They made an alliance with Churaman, the jay chieftain. In the later years of their adminstration they reached an agreement with king Shahu by granting him the swarajya (of Shivaji) and the right to collect the chauth and sardesh mukhi of six provinces of the Deccan. In return, Shahu agreed to support them in the Deccan with 15,000 mounted soldiers. The Sayyid brothers made a vigorous effort to contain rebellions and to save the Empire from administrative disintegration. They failed in these tasks mainly because they were faced with constant political rivalry, quarrels, and conspiracies at the court. Even though the Sayyid brothers had tried hard to conciliate and befriend all sections and of the nobility, a powerful group of noble headed by Nizam-ul-Mulk began to conspire against them. The neighbours were jealous of the growing powers of the two brothers.

(d) **Attempts of Nizam-ul-Mulk.** In 1722 he became the Wazir. He made a vigorous attempt to reform the administration. But Muhammed Shah did not co-operate him. He fell under the evil influence of corrupt and worthless flatters. Disgusted with the fickle- mindedness and suspicious nature of the emperor, Nizam-ul-Mulk decided to leave the court. He gave up his office in october 1724 and marched South to found the state of Hyderabad in the Deccan. His departure was symbolic of the flight of loyalty, and virtue from the Empire. The physical break-up of the Mughal Empire had began.

POLITICAL REVIVAL AMONG THE HINDU MARTIAL

Political Revival among the Hindu martial classes and the rise of other independent States. It is to be noted here that with the commencement of the disintegration of the Mughal Empire, political awakening had come to dawn upon the martial races of the Hindus and 'consequently' they had started asserting their claim for their separate independent regions in different parts of India, as for instance, the Rajputs in Rajasthan, the Sikhs in the Punjab, the Jats in the region round about Agra and Mathura and the Marathas in Maharashtra. But one thing which is very important to note here is that this political awakening was not a national movement, nor was it intended to set up any All India Hindu Empire; rather it was an attempt on the part of the above Hindu martial groups to set up their own respective regions. The following account about the different martial races is, therefore, necessary.

(1) The Rajputs. Immediately after the death of Aurangzeb in 1707. the most important States of Rajplutana, like Marwar, Mewar and Ambar, had commenced to assert their independence in their respective areas. It was in the reign of Bahadur Shah I that Raja Ajit Singh of Marwar (Jodhplur), Raja Jai Singh of Ambar (Jaipur) and Durga Dass Rathore, abandoned their alliance and allegiance to Bahadur Shah and entered into a mutual alliance with one another against the Mughal Emperor. On the other hand, the Sikhs also were rising in the Punjab. Consequently, Bahadur Shah made some of the serious attempts with conciliatory measures to win the Rajpluts to the cause of the Mughal Empire. He was successful to some extent in his efforts in this respect. But after Bahadur Shah's death, the Rajput became bolder than before and, as such, they became practically independent. The Emperor Farrukhsiyar sent Sayyid Hussain Ali to invade the ruler of Marwar, but the anti Sayyid party at the Mughal Imperial Court sent a secret message to Raja Ajit Singh to make an end of Hussain Ali under all circumstances, assuring him the grant of the whole of Hussain Ali's property apart from the award of the rich gifts and presents. Raja Ajit Singh paid no heed to the secret instructions, and without fighting Sayyid Hussain Ali, he concluded peace with him. After that, the rulers of Jodhpur and Jaipur began to take greater part in the Delhi politics and with the practical support of the Sayyid Brothers, attempted to strength their own party at the Court. Consequently, Raja Ajit Singh was appointed the Governor of Gujarat and Ajmer, which charge he held up to 1721, the year of the accession of Mohammad Shah to the throne of Hindustan. Similarly, Raja Jai Sing of Jaipur also was appointed as the Governor of Surat. In this way the whole region commencing at a distance of sixty miles right from Delhi and going right up to Surat on the western coast of India was entrusted to the care of the Rajputs. But it is not difficult to undrstand that it was not a safe policy to have entrusted the border regions of the Mughal Empire to these Rajputs whose dependence could not be expected to be very reliable, especially when the Mughal Empire was already well- nigh on the road to disintegration.

(2) The Sikhs. It was in 1708 that, after the death of Guru Gobind Singh, Banda Bahadur succeeded to the political and military leadership of the Sikhs. Most of the brave and warrior Sikhs gathered under his banner in obedience to the commands issued by the Guru on the eve of his death in the south. At the head of forty thousand Sikhs, Banda was able to assassinate Wazir khan, the Governor of Sirhind, who had got the two of the Guru's innocent and minor sons bricked alive in the walls of the fort of Sirhind. He was also able to occupy the entire province of Sirhind and had set up the Sikh rule there. Then he conquered the entire region lying between the Sutlej and Jumna and later on made Mukhlispur, near Sadaura, as the capital of his State. Bahadur Shah proceeded against Banda in person and after defeating Banda, expelled him from the fort of Mukhlispur. But, on the death of Bahadur Shah in 1712, Banda again appeared in the plains, occupied the fort of Lohgarh and laid waste the entire province of Sirhind. In 1715, he was besieged in the fort of Gurdas Nangal in the Gurdaspur district in the Punjab by the Mughal forces sent by Farrukhsiyar and after a very brave resistance to the Mughal forces, he was taken prisoner with about 726 of his faithful Sikh followers.

After the death of Banda, the Sikhs were left leaderless and, as such, they were subjected to great tyranny and oppression by the Mughal Government, but in spite of all this, their military powere could not be suppressed by the Mughals. During the course of invasions on India by Nadir Shah and Ahmed Shah Abdali, the Mughal government was considerably weakened and, taking advantage of the favourable circumstrances, the Sikhs reorganised themselves under the leadership of Nawab Kapur Singh. After the departure of Ahmedshah Abdali from India after his first invasion in 1748, the Sikhs came under the leadership of another Sikh warriou and organiser, Jassa Singh Ahluwalila. They built up a strong fort, Ram Rauni in Amristsar. After Ahmed Shah Abdali's fourth invasion in 1752, when he wrested away the Punjab from the Mughals, the Sikhs defeated and turned out of the Punjab his son, Timur Shah, who was appointed as the Governor of the Punjab by Ahmed Shah Abdali on the eve of his departure from India. They then occupied Lahore and struck their own coins there. Taking maximum advantage of the political disorder that following in the Punjab after the third battle of Panipat, they further increased their power in the Punjab. Very soon they took possession of Lahore and Amritsar and became the masters of the great part of the Punjab.

(3) The Jats. During the last days of Aurangzeb's reign, the Jats under the leadership of some of the daring village leaders like Raja Ram and Churaman, had commenced devastating and plundering the imperial territory lying between Agra and Delhi. Though Churaman Jat committed suicide in 1721, yet long before his death he, by taking advantage of the weakness and degenerated political condition of the Mughal Empire, had considerably increased the power of the Jats. After his death, his nephew, Badan Singh succeeded him and practically brought under his control the whole of the region round about Agra and Mathura. He was very popular among the Jats but he always enertained a strong hatred against looting and plundering depredations. On the death of Badan Singh, his adopted son, Suraj Mall became the leader of the Jats. Under his leadership, the Jats became a very strong power in India. He took a great part in the politics of the country during his life and extended the Jat jurisdiction to Aligarh, Etawah, etc. He made Bharatpur his capital which had been in the possession of the Jats from the beginning. He was the greatest fighter and a statesman amongst the Jats. He was having a large, well-equipped and strong army under him and his treasury also was full. But after 1763, when he died, the power of the Jats had considerably weakened.

(4) The Marathas. In the opinion of Prof. S.R. Sharma, "the rise of the Maratha power was not due to any specific person of a great ability; rather, it was due to the whole nation itself as one unit and depended mostly on common men. This is a historical fact which finds support from the Maratha history itself from 1707 to 1761. During this period, the Marathas, under the leadership of the Peshwas, like Balaji Vishwa Nath, Baji Rao I and Balaji Baji Rao, carried on depredations in the different parts of India. In 1719, the Peshwa Balaji Vishwa Nath obtained from the Emperor the right of collecting Chauth from the six Mughal Subas of Deccan. The second important Peshwa, Baji Rao I, conqured Malwa, Gujarat and Bundelkhand. But under the leadership of Balaji Baji Rao, the Marathas had reached the highest peack of their glory and power, Raghuji Bhonsle devastated the entire region of Bengal and Bihar, defeated Alivardi Khan and obtained from him the province of Cuttack in Orissa. In 1760, the Maratha leader Sada Shiv Bhao inflicted a terrible defeat upon the Nizam of Hyderabad at Udgir. Consequently, the Nizam had to hand over to the Marathas under Sada Shiv Bhao the places like Bijapur, Daulatabad and Asirgarh. The other Maratha leaders also, like Raghunath Rao (or Raghoba). Malrar Rao Holkar and Ranoji Sindhia devastated the whole of northern India and occuplied Delhi also. The Mughal Emperor had been reduced to the position of a mere puppet in the hands of the Marathas. Raghoba did not stop here; he occupied the Punjab also and hoisted the Maratha flag on the borders of Attack.

But, by virtue of the Maratha occupation of Delhi under Raghoba and their expansion up to the Punjab which had been wrested by the Afghans from the Mughal Emperors in 1752, the Marathas came into a direct conflict with Ahmed Shah Abdali. The ultimate result of this direct conflict between the two powers was the Third Battle of Panipat in 1761 in which the Marathas were defeated and their power was smashed by Ahmed Shah Abdali. But it will be interesting to note that in spite of the crushing defeat of the Marathas in the Third Battle of Panipat, the dying Mughal Empire could not revive itself to life. This shows the amount of its weakness. Rather on account of the disorders and anarchy that followed the Third Battle of Panipat, the Mughal Emplire stood on the point of complete dissalution, and the Hindu martial races like the Sikhs, the Marathas and European powers and the English appropriated to themselves the greater part of the Mughal Empire.

(5) The Rohillas. The Rohillas, an Afghan clan, by taking advantage of the weakness of dissolving Mughal Empire, made themselves independent masters of the rich tract of land lying to the north of the Ganges, which later on came to be known as Rohilkhand.

The Dismemberment of Other Parts

(i) The kingdom of Mysore also was gradually rising into importance and getting stronger at the expense of the Mughal Empire.

(ii) The kingdom of Arcot in the Carnatic was gradually becoming important.

(iii) Provinces beyond the Indus were annexed by the King of Persia.

(6) The Rise of European Powers. Among the European powers, the Portuguese, the Dutch and the Danes had lost their influence in India, while the English and the French were becoming powerful. The defeat of the French at Wandiwash and the complete defeat of Court de Lally in 1760 and the fall of Pondicherry in 1761, decided once for all that the French had no chance of founding an empire in India.

(7) The weakness of the Imperial government of the Mughals, besides encouraging the independence of the provincial governors, invited attacks from different quarters. The Marathas plundered the suburbs of Delhi, the Persian King Nadir Shah sacked Delhi and Ahmed Shah Abdali made his first invasion on India and in the next invasion wrested the region of the Punjab from the Mughal Emperors.

SUCCESSOR OF AURANGZEB

(1) Accession of Bahadur Shah I. Aurangzeb died in 1707 A.D. and after him there was an armed struggle for succession among his three sons (Muazzam, Muhammad Azam, Kambakhsh) Before his death Aurangzeb had drawn up a will in which he sought to divide his empire in three parts. But his sons gave a deaf ear to their father's wishes and decided to resort to the arbitration of sword. The news of Aurangzeb's death was signal for civil war. The eldest claimant, Prince Muazzam who was busy at Jamrud in Afghanistan made a dash for Delhi to participate in the scramble for the throne. Munim khan came to the assistance of Muazzam. The second son, prince Azam-us-shan, rushed to Agra and captured it. Any how Agra was the key to the situation. It held big herds of treasures. Muazzam reached Agra in June 1707 and captured the fort. He also took possession of crores of rupees and other parts of treasures. After that Muazzam and Azam both decided to contest for the throne. Prince Azam had declared himself Emperor and got coins struck in his name. The fraticidal battle that ensued between the two brothers (on 18 June 1707 A.D.) brought about Azam's defeat and death along with his two sons. Likewise, Kambakhsh wanted to try his luck. However, he too was defeated near Hyderabad in another battle on the 13th of January, 1709 A.D. He was fatally wounded in this battle. Thus, the same night his death occurred. In this war Bahadur Shah ascended the throne of Delhi at the ripe age of 65.

(2) His Relations with Marathas. It was in the year 1687 that Sambhaji, the son and successor of Shivaji, was arrested and cut to pieces. His entire family including his son, Sahu, who was still a minor, was thrown behind the bars. Aurangzeb thought that he had done away with Marathas, but very soon he realised his mistake, when he found that the entire Maratha nation had taken up arms against him. In order to create dimensions amongst the Marathas, he thought of realising Sahu from prison but this idea of his remained unrealised, because of constant warfare in the south. After his death, Bahadur Shah on the advice of Zulfiqar Khan released Sahu, thus giving a practical shape of his father's design. His policy towards the Marathas Sardars (chiefs) was that of half- hearted conciliation. While he granted them the sardeshmukhi of the Deccan, he failed to grant them the chauth and thus to satisfy them fully. He also did not recognise Sahu as the rightful Maratha King. He thus let Tara Bai and Sahu fight for supremacy over the Maratha Kingdom. The result was that Sahu and the Maratha sardars remained dissatisfied and the Deccan continued to be a prey to disorder. There could be no restoration of peace and order so long as the Maratha sardars fought one another as well as fought against the Mughal Authority.

(3) Bahadur Shah and the Rajputs. Bahadur Shah was sufficiently aged at the time of his accession. Consequently, he could not set about any firm and courageous policy. He was learned dignified and able. He followed a policy of compromise and conciliation, and there was evidence of the reversal of some of the narrow minded policies and measures adopted by Aurangzeb. He adopted a more tolerant attitude towards the Hindu chief and raja's. There was no destruction of temples in his reign. In the beginning. he made an attempt to gain greater control over the Rajput states of Amber and Marwar (Jodhpur) by replacing Jai Singh by his younger brother Vijai Singh at Amber and by forcing Ajit Singh of Marwar to submit to Mughal authority. He also made an attempt to garrison the cities of Amber and Jodhpur. This attempt was, however, met with firm resistance. This may have made him recognise the folly of his actions for he soon arrived at a settlement with the two states, though the settlement was not magnanimous. Though their states were restored to the Rajas' Jai Singh and Ajit Singh, their demand for high mansabs and the offices of subahdars of important provinces such as Malwa and Gujarat was not accepted.

(4) His Relations with the Sikhs. In 1707 Aurangzeb died and with his death the relation of Guru Gobind Singh with Bhadur Shah became cordial. So much so that Guru Gobind accompanied Bhadur Shah in Southern expedition. In 1708 Guru Gobind Singh was stabbed to death by a Pathan and the leadership of Sikhs passed into hands of a disciple of Guru Gobind Singh popularly called Banda Bhadur. Banda Bhadur had been instructed by the late Guru fight Mughal tyranny inj general and Wazir Khan in particular. He rallied round his banner thousands of Sikhs and revolted against the Mughals in the Punjab openly when Bhadur Shah had gone to the Deccan. He occupied numerous Mughal territories and put to the sword countless Mussalmans. Wazir Khan, the commander of Sirhind was attacked on 22nd May, 1710 A.D. He was defeated and killed. Banda made Sirhind his main centre and began to conquer the surrounding Mughal territories . He soon acquired Amritsar, Pathankot, Kasur, Batala, Kalanaur etc. and established his rule over them. When Bahadur Shah came to know about these events he was greatly enraged. Bahadur Shah decided to march against the Sikhs in person. Bahadur Shah was ably supported by Amin Khan. Banda was besieged at the fort of Lahgarh in Makhlispur. The Mughals were successful in capturing the fort in Nov. 1710. Benda, however, was successful in making good his escape from the fort. He retired to the hills. The Mughals recovered Sirhind and the rest of the territory, snatched away by the Sikhs, but the Sikhs continued the struggle and went on engendering trouble for the Mughals. After the Mughal victory at Lohgarh the Mughal Emperor Bahadur Shah, retired to Lahore. Bahadur Shah conciliated Chatursal, the Bundela chief, who remained a loyal feudatory, and the Jat Chief Churaman, who joined him in the campaign against Banda Bahadur. There was further deterioration in the field of administration in Bahadur Shah reign. The position of state finance worsened as a result of his reckless grants of jagirs and promotions. Bahadur Shah was groping towards a solution of the problems besetting the Empire. Given time, he might have revived the Imperial fortunes. Unfortunately, his death in 1712 plunged the Empire once again into civil war.

INVASION OF AHMED SHAH ABDALI

Ahmed Shah was a general in the army of Nadir Shah. Nadir was greatly impressed by the qualities of his general. He complimented him by saying, "I have not found in Iran, Turan or Hind any man equal to Ahmed Shah in capacity and character." Ahmed Shah was an Afghan Chief of the Abdali clan. Nadir Shah was assassinated in 1747. Thereafter Ahmed Shah became an independent ruler of Afghanistan. He declared himself King at Kandhar. He captured Kabul also. After his accession he styled himself as Durr-i-Durran or the pearl of the age. He and his successors, therefore, were known as Durrani also. That is why Ahmed Shah is known as Abdali and Durrani both.

After establishing his power and position at home, Ahmed Shah Durrani led Several expeditions to India between 1748 and 1767. In all he led seven expeditions to India during the time of Ahmed Shah and Shah Alam II. He wanted to achieve supremacy over India. The attempt of Ahmed Shah Abdali show a revival of Afghan power trying to establish supremacy over the ruins of the Mughal Empire. The invasion of Ahmed Shah Abdali were more than mere plundering raids.

Causes of the Invasions

(1) Neglected Defences. The problem of neglected defences of the border areas had become chronic with the later Mughals. What is most intriguing is that in spite of the reverses suffered by the Empire in the previous reigns, the Emperor of Delhi had still not awakened from their sleep and did nothing to improve the situation in this connection. Especially the defences of the northwest were sadly neglected. This brought about Nadir Shah's invasion and the same thing facilitated the series of Ahmed Shah's invasions.

(2) Increased Prestige at Home. By successful foreign invasions and expeditions Ahmed Shah wanted to consolidate his position at home. His foreign successes were sure to increase his prestige at home. This would have added to his reputation in international sphere too. Elphinstone says that, "Ahmed Shah Abdali must have entertained the desire of establishing political authority over at least a part of India, though there were other motive which led him to undertake these expeditions. These other motives must be financial gain, political ambitions and other."

(3) Weakness of Mughal Empire. It was a universily known fact that Mughal Empire was very weak, even before the invasion of Nadir Shah. After that the position became more precurious and pitiable. Ahmed Shah had seen it himself when he came to India with his master, Nadir Shah, during his invasion of India. He had seen the weakness of the Empire, the imbecility of the Emperor, the inattentiveness of the Ministers, the spirit of independence which had crept among the grandees. Besides of this weakness and loose organization of the Empire, Ahmad Shah thought he would be able to conquer the whole of India. He was right to some extent.

(4) Ambiton of Enhancing Strength. It is a human desire to be powerful, popular, rich and all that. Ahmed Shah Abdali was no exception, more so, because he was a very ambitious ruler. He wanted that his nobles and subordinates should keep singing poems of praises for him and should be loyal. Besides, for retaining or extending his power and territory a strong army was also necessary. Thus for enhancing his strenght it was necessary that Ahmed Shah's huge army should have been properly organised and his nobles and subordinates kept happy and loyal. But all this entailed a heavy expenditure. Ahmed Shah Abdali decided that the booty he got from the Indian campaigns sould be used in showering favours and gifts on the Afghan chiefs and the nobility. Besides, he thought that the money he would capture in India would be utilized in the reorganization of his army and towards meeting its clossal expenses. Thus his ambition of increasing his strength was to be fulfilled at Indian cost.

(5) Immediate Cause. The immediate cause of Ahmed Shah Abdali's invasion or rather invasions was that he was invited to attack India by Shah Nawaz Khan. Shah Nawaz Khan had become the Governor of the Punjab and he had invited Ahmed Shah Abdali or Durrain as such. The invitation was extended to Ahmed Shah in the year 1748. This invitation whetted the appetite of Ahmed Shah for pouncing on India and after sacking Lahore, Ahmed Shah made a dash towards Delhi like a hungry wolf.

Ahmed Shah Abdali

First Invasion (1748). On the eve of launchng his first attack on India Ahmed Shah Abdali had conquered Kabul, Kandhar and Peshawar. In January 1748 he launched his first attack. He brought with him twelve thousand veteran troops. Therc was a battle at Manpur. On the Mughal side the heir-apparent, Ahmed Shah and Mir Mannu were fighting. Mir Mannu was the son of the son of the late Wazir Qamar- ud- Din. In this battle the Afghan invader was defeated and Ahmed Shah Abdali was sent running away. Mir Mannu was appointed Governor of the punjab.

Second Invasion (1750). Mir Mannnu had not properly settled down as the Governor of the Punjab when Ahme Shah Abdali launched his second invasion of the Punjab in 1750. The Governor came out to give the idvader a stubborn resistance but he could make little headway. The reason was that the Governor did not receive any help from the Central Government at Delhi. This happened because the Delhi Court was preoccupied with the problem of Civil War which was threatening the capital. When the Governor was convinced that his single handed resistance was useless, he gave up and surrendered to the Durrani, the invader.

Some scholars are of the opinion that Ahmed Shah Durrani came the second time and attacked the Punjab. The Governor of the Punjab was defeated. The Durrani did not do much. He received a heavy indemnity and retired to his homeland.

Third Invasion (1751). Dr. V.A. Smith believes the second invasion to have occurred in 1749 and on that basis observes thus about the third invasion, "Two years later Ahmed Shah Durrani invaded India for the third time, and captured Delhi which again suffered from the horrors of massacre and pillage Mathura, too, was once more the sense of dreadful slaughter."

Some scholars believe that this third invasion of Ahmed Shah Durrani occurred in 1752. They say in the Durrani invaded the Punjab again. He gave another defeat to the Punjab Governor and then proceeded towards Delhi. In Delhi, the Mughal Emperor, in an attempt to save Delhi from another sack and massacre, made peace with the Abdali ruler and offered him Multan and the Punjab.

But the usually accepted view is like this. Ahmed Shah Abdali invaded India in December 1751, for the third time. He gave another defeat to Mir Mannu, the Punjab Governor, and compelled the Mughal Emperor, Ahmed Shah, to surrender to the invader the territory in the east upto Sarhind. This further reduced the boundaries of the already truncated Mughal Empire. Mir Mannu still remained the Governor of the Punjab. However he was now the Governor of the Durrani at Lahore. He was now to act as Governor on the dictates and directions of his new boss, Ahmed Shah Abdali. The Abdali had also conquered Kashmir in the course of his third invasion of India.

Fourth Invasion (1756). Ahmed Shah Abdali invaded India for the fourth time in November, 1756. It was during the reign of the Mughal Emperor, Alamgir the second. Mir Mannu, the Governor of Punjab and the agent of the Durrani, died in November 1753. He was succeeded by his infant son under the Regency of mother, Mughlani Begam. The infant successor of Mir Mannu also died in May, 1754. Thereafter there was the wildest chaos and confusion in the Punjab. It is believed that the Regent mother encouraged this confusion. She invited the Wazir of Delhi, Imad- ul- Mulk, for her help. Imad- ul-Mulk wanted to have some hold over the Punjab. He therefore immediately responded. He quelled the disturbance, brought the Punjab under him and appointed a reputed nobleman of Lahore whose name was Mir Munim, as Governor of the Punjab. When the Abdali learnt of this act of the regent mother and the Delhi Wazir, he was white with rage. He invaded India again, therefore, in November 1756. He arrived at Delhi in January 1757 and ordered a general sack of Delhi. Delhi was looted mercilessly again and its people were subjected to devastation and destitution. Imad-ul-Mulk begged forgiveness and got it. Thereafter the invader, Ahmed Shah Abdali, compelled the Mughal Emperor to cede the Punjab, Sind, Kashmir and the Sarhind District to him.

Fifth Invasion (1759). Ahmed Shah Abdali invaded India for the fifth time in October, 1759 From May 1757 to April 1758 there was the wildest disorder in the Punjab. Thus the rule of Timur Shah was a resounding failure. He treated a Sikh leader wrongly and as a result there were Sikh rebellions on all sides. The Governor of Jullundur, Adina Beg Khan, requested the Maratha help against the Afghans. Lahore was invaded and the Afghans expelled from there in April 1758. This included Timur Shah and expelled from there in April 1758. This included Timur Shah and his officers of course. The Marathas captured Lahore. But in October 1759, Ahmed Shah Abdali invaded India again. This time he came with frightening speed and made a furious attack on those who were responsible for the expulsion of his son, Timur Shah, and his officers. He was in the ultimate analysis successful. The Punjab was completely vanquished and conquered. The Marathas were also fighting for supremacy in India like the Afghans. It was quite obvious, therefore, that a major war between the Afghans and the Marathas was in the offing. This came about in January of the Year 1761 in the Third Battle of Panipat. In this the Marathas were crushed. Ahmed Shah then asked his chiefs in India to recognise Shah Alam II as the Emperor of India, Munir-ud-Daulah and Najib-ud-Daulah agreed to pay to Ahmed Shah Abdali a tribute of forty lacs of rupees every year, on befalf of the Mughal Emperor. After all this, towards the end of 1762 Ahmad Shah Abdali left India for his home country.

Sixth Invasion (1764). Ahmad Shah Abdali invaded India for the sixth time in March 1764. The reason was that there was trouble in Punjab again. In the intervening period of two, three years between the fifth and the sixth invasions of Ahmad Shah Abdali the Sikhs had regained strength considerably and wanted to assert themselves once again. They, therefore, made a concerted effort and were successful in capturing Lahore. They also succeeded in killing the Afghan Governor of the Punjab, Khwaja Abid, at Lahore. When this new travelled to Ahmad Shah Abdali he came rushing, trampling people on the way, to Lahore and chastised the offenders. Unfortunately, he could not stay here for long. His stay lasted only about a fortnight this time. Since his soldiers had mutinied in Afghanistan and a civil war had broken out, Ahmad Shah had to leave India in a Hurry.

Seventh Invasion (1767). Ahmad Shah Abdali had to leave India in haste because he had to put his own house in order. That was in 1764. After he had successfully completed his job at home he thought of India again. The Punjab was a running sore for Ahmad Shah Abdali. He reached here once again but was not very successful in crushing the Sikhs completely. Before long he had to retrace his steps because he perhaps had a presentiment that he would ultimately fail if he persisted in his project. The soldiers of Ahmad Shah Abdali were sore because tgey were not receiving their salaries regularly every month. There was the danger of their revolting again. Realising all this Ahmad Shah Abdali thought it best to retire from India.

Results of Invasions

1. As soon as Ahmad Shah Abdali left India to go back to Afghanistan, the Sikhs immediately captured Lahore again. The Sikhs also occupied the open country.

2. Ahmad Shah Abdali retained hold of Peshawar and the country west of Acctock, while he abandoned the Manjha District and Central Punjab including Lahore to the Sikhs, but the Sind- Sagar and Jeck Doab in the Eastern Punjab remained a debatable land which finally came into their possession in the days of his worthless successors.

3. The invasions of Ahmad Shah Abdali seriously thwarted the quickly expanding Maratha Kingdom. The Maratha imperialism was also making rapid strides. These imperialistic ambitions of the Marathas were also checked by the aforesaid invasions.

4. A modern writer has correctly observed," His career in India is very intimately a part of the Sikh struggle for independence."

5. Since the Sikhs were successful in giving constant trouble to Ahmad Shah Abdali, they cherished higher ambitions to rise as a

mighty power. In and after Ahmad Shah Abdali the Sikhs went on attaining more and more power and reputation. Thus the invasions of Ahmad Shah Abdali contributed a good deal to the rise of the Sikh power.

6. The invasions of Ahmad Shah Abdali were a source of a great restlessness to the British East India Company. The reason was that Ahmad Shah Abdali and the East India Company both were aspiring for India. The Restivcness and anxiety of the East India Company continued throughout the period of Ahmad Shah Abdali's invasions and even after he was no more.

7. This series of invasions gave another blow to the already decadent and tottering Mughal Empire. The reduced extent of Empire and the truncated power and prestige of the Mughal Empire went a long way in bringing about the disintegration and downfall of the Mughal Empire.

CRISIS OF THE JAGIRDARI SYSTEM

The history of Jagirdari system is very old. During the beginning of the medieval period of Indian history most of the Brahmins and Rasjputs were Jagirdars. Qtadars of Delhi sultanate can also be called jagirdars up to some extent in a broader sense. The founder of the Mughal dynasty, Babur, distributed jagirs on a large scale to make his friends haplpy. Umayun also gave away by jagirs. Akbar tried to control the jagirdari system to some extent, but he could also not remove jagirdari system completely. After Akbar, the jagirdari system continued during the reign of his successors. The practice of granting jagirs to officers and amirs instead of giving salaries especially after 1707, proved fatal for the Mughal Empire.

The successpors of Aurangzeb gave away jagirs on a large scale. Bahadur Shah I started Izaredari system in the place of Ryotwari system (in this system the peasant could deposit the tax directly in the royal treasury). In this system, contrators promised the goverment to pay a fixed amount as revenue. But these new jagidars (Izardars) could collect as much tax from the peasants as they wished. This increased the problems of the peasants. Poverty and dissatisfation arose among the peasant.

Fall in the Character of the Jagirdars. The Mughal Empire was mostly dependent on some sincere, able and good character nobles. These people use to control the weaknesses of the Emperors and as such they used to check the downfall of the Mughal Empire. But in the 18th century the jagirdars were morallly declined. Day by day, they were becoming luxurious and spendthrift. They also became greedy, selfish and ungrateful. They did not have thc power to save themselves from low pursuits what to talk of saving the emperor.

Demand to have Permanent Hereditary Control over the Jagirs. They started demanding more and more jagirs and asked the emperor to grant them permanently hereditary control on jagirs. First the jagirs were granted according to the abiltiy of the nobles. Therefore, of the people belonging to lower level of the society could get high posts responsibilites. Thus, they (the people of lower status of society) could bring a new blood into the nobility but due to their selfishness these high ups monopolised all the jagirs thus bolcking the way for the able people. It resulted in the deterioration of their ranks which cost the state heavily. Many jagirdars did not deposit thc share of land revenue of the state regularly. In this way the income of the state lessened as a result due to the lack of money in the treasury, officials and soldiers were not paid regularly.

Lack of the Loyalty Towards the State Among the Jagirdars. To say that all the jagirdars of the 18th century were weak and incompentent is quit wrong. Many of them as Ali Mohammad Khan, Nizam-ul-Mulk, Sadat Khan and Aliverdi Khan etc. were competent and powerful people but they used their ability in enchancing themselves instead of doing something concrete for the state. Some of them established their own independent principalities or states. This act of theirs was directly disintegration of the Mughal Empire.

Paucity of Jagirs. One of the major causes of the growing selfishness and cliquishness of the nobles was the pacucity of jagirs and reduced income of the existing jagirs at a time when the number of nobles and their expenditure was going up. So there ensured intense mutual rivalry among them for the possession of existing jagirs. The heart of the matter perhaps was that no arrangement could have been made which coluld satisfy all the nobles, for there were just not enough offices offices and jagirs for all.

Formation of Many Groups by the Jagirdar. In the 18th century most of the jagirdars joined one or the other group. The main groups were Hindustani, Irani, Turani which were further subdivided into smaller groups. Their infighting converted the Mughal court into a hot bed of conspiracies. To humilitiate one another they were alsways ready to use any means against the Emperor. They did not forget their differences and join hands even in the face of any national calamity, rather they helped the invader.

A Great Set-back to the Military Power. The different jagirdars kept lesser number of troops with them in order to save more and more of money. Consequently, the fighting force of the state got weakened and consequently it failed to check either the inernal revolts or the external incursions.

The Jagirdari System Resulted in the Economic Crises. To keep their income intact the different jardars tried to grab the government land. Thus they cause a serious situation for the Central Government and caused much decrease in its income.

CAUSES OF DOWNFALL OF MUGHAL EMPIRE

Babur founded the Mughal Empire in India in 1526 but could not find time to consolidate it. It was extended and consolidated by Akbar. It continued in its full splendour till the death of Aurangzeb in 1707, though some symptoms of weakness had started becoming apparent even before that. The decline became very rapid after his death. The causes of the downfall of the Mughal Empire may be studied under two categories ; causes attributable to Aurangzeb and causes for which he cannot be held responsible. Having rapidly and progressively expanded for a century and a half the rule of the House of Timur began to give way in India. During this long period, from its birth in about Babur's time to maturity and stage of grandeur and perfection in Shahjahan's time the Empire had acquired such solidity and power that it took about half a century to disintergrate. Even after the Empire was almost completely liquidated, nominal sovereignty of the Empire persisted for another century. It was only after the First War of Indian independence had waged and failed in 1857-58 that the last Mughal Emperor Bahadur ShahII was formally deposed. The decline and downfall of this formidable Empire came about on account of a variey of forces and factors. The working and progress of these form the subject-matter of our discussion in the present chapter.

(A) Causes Attributable to Aurangzeb

1. Reversal of Akbar's Religious Policy. Akbar had followed a liberal religious policy and therby made an attempt to make his Empire broadbased on the consent of the governed. He tried to reconcile the Hindus who formed the majority of the population. No interference was made in their affairs. Pilgrimage Tax and Jaziya were abolished. There was no discrimination in matters of Government services. Many Hindus like Birbal, Todar Mal, Man Singh held highest positions at Mughal Court in Akbar's time. But Aurangzeb had received Islamic type of education and he wanted to rule in the interests of the Muslims only. In fact Aurangzeb indentified his rule with that of Muslims states before the advent of the Mughals. The obvious result was that the broadbased Akbar's reign was repelled by religiously intolerant Muslim reigns of Pre- Akbar days. Now it was in the logic of history therefor that the State of Aurangzeb should have met the same fate as was the share of Muslim States of pre-Mughal dasys. The martial races of India were alienated and this proved suicidal for the empire. The Hindus could neither hold fairs freely nor repair or extend old temples. Many of their temples were pulied down. Pilgrims Tax and Jaziya were reimposed. Several Hindus were forcibly converted to Islam. Aurangzeb was a Sunni and wanted to set up Sunnism. He presented the non- Muslims, little realizing that his subjects were a heterogeneous population. Guru Teg Bahadur was put to death for refusing to adopt Islam. There was discrimination even in the economic sphere. The result was that the empire lost the sympathy of the Hindu majority. The Jats, the Sikhs, the Rajputs and the Marathas began to strike blows at the Mughal Empire.

2. Wide Extent of the Empire. The conquest of Bijapur and Golkunda made the empire too extensive to be properly controlled by one man. There were no good means of transport and communication in those days and it became difficult to hold the forces of disruption in check in such a big empire. The very extent of the empire contributed to its decline.

3. Long Wars in the Deccan. Aurangzeb remained in the Deccan for twenty- six years. During this period he was busy conquering the States of Bijapur and Golkunda, and fighting against the Marathas. The efficiency of army was lowered due to continuous fighting. The treasury became empty. The administrative system in Northern India began to get out of gear. The provincial governors began to care less for the Emperor. The Sikhs, the Jats and the Rajputs became turbulent. Thus the long Deccan wars of Aurangzeb contributed to decline of Mughal Empire.

4. Conquest of Bijapur and Golkunda. Aurangzeb conquered the States of Bijapur and Golkunda in 1686 and 1687 respectively. Their conquest was apparently a great triumph for Aurangzeb but really it proved a blunder and contributed to the downfall of the Mughal Empire. These two states had been a check on the rising power of the Marathas. Their conquest left the Marathas free to turn their whole attention against the Mughals. The demobilised soldiers of the armies of Bijapur and Golkunda had no means of subsistence. They either joined Maratha armies and increased their strenght or formed bands of robbers and started plundering the country. This only increased the difficulties of the Mughals in the Deccan. The Deccan was a running sore for Aurangzeb. It was a political miscalculation as well as a military failure. The distant states could not be administered properly and they behaved in an irresponsible, nay, independent manner.

5. Suspicious Nature of Aurangzeb. Aurangzeb was a man of suspicious nature and could not give his confidence to any one. He had naturally to steer the mightly ship of the State single handed. He always sent two generals to command the army. They could not often agree regarding the plan of action and precious time was wasted. Divided commands impared the efficiency of the army. Morover, it was due to the suspicious nature that he ignored the political training of his children and they were not fit to govern the big empire. He had the qualities of affection, sympathy and chivalry but lacked the qualities of a successful monarch.

His fanatical approach alienated him from the symapthies of Rajputs, Marathas, Sikhs and Jats. He indulged in wars with them. As a result the royal coffers were fast becoming empty. The soldiers of Bijapur, Golkunda and the Marathas either joined the oppostion or became pluderers. This further depleted the finances of the state. Therefore financial bankruptcy of the Mughals also contributed to the downfall of the Mughals.

This was because of the suspicious and distrustful temperament of Aurangzeb. What was more harmful was his extreme puritanism and his faith in extremes. He did not share his responsibilities with his officers or his sons. When the officials were not held in confidence, they became slack and thereby administration also became loose. And Aurangzeb, of coursc, could not carry on the huge complex of the Mughal administration single handedly.

6. Policy Against Shiyas. The two Shiya states of Bijapur and Golkunda were exercising a restraining influence on the rising Maratha power. When these were conquered by Aurangzeb they became part of the Mughal empire. Moreover, now the Marathas had nothing to fear from them. They started attacking the Mughal territories here and there. The soldiers of the Bijapur and Golkunda armies who lost their jobs, either joined the Marathas or became plunderers. Both ways they struck at the roots of the Mughal empire. The Deccan thus became a pointed thorn which was pricking the Mughal emperor all the time. The conquest of Deccan also proved nothing.

Aurangzeb was a religious fanatic. He was a Sunni and therefore wanted the whole world so be Sunni. With this notion on the back of his mind he launched a project to persecut the Syiyas. This step was a strategic miscalculation on the prestige by adding the two Shiya states to the empire, but in fact he had dug the grave of the empire. The persecution of Shiyas went a long way towards the disintegration of the empire.

7. Policy Against Rajputs. The policy of Aurangzeb towards the Rajput was just opposite to the one follwed by Akbar, the great. Akbar had enunciated a policy of matrimonial alliances with the Rajputs in order to bring them closer to him. He knew the importance of being cordial with a brave race. The Rajputs were given high offices and confidence by the Great Mughal. Before Aurangzeb the Rajputs would go to any extent in support of the Mughal empire. But things changed in the time of Aurangzeb. He alienated the Rajputs. Although Jai Singh and Jaswant Singh had helped him to attain the throne, he was blind to it and utterly forgetful of the favour, he turned against them.

Raja Jaswant Singh of Marwar or mordrn Jodhpur was in Jamrud towards the close of 1678 when he was poisoned to death on the orders of Aurangzeb. Aurangzeb thought that by killing Jaswant Singh he would have chances to abuse the Rajas and Hindus generally. Aurangzeb wanted to capture the two infant sons of Jaswant Singh. The wife of Jaswant Singh was protected by Rana Raj Singh of Marwar (Udaipur). Thereupon a war began between the imperialists and the clans of Mewar and Marwar, although Amber (Jaipur) was still supporting the imperial cause. The Rajputs thus turned against the treacherous Aurangzeb.

8. Policy Against Marathas. Besides inciting other powers, Aurangzeb roused the Mrathas also against him. As a result generation after generation the Marathas went on fighting against the Mughals. He refused to recognise the importance of befriending the Maratha chief, Shivaji, but continued to be hostile to them. This was so because he was a religious fanatic and could not tolerate, any person who was not a muslim and that too a Sunni, Shivaji and his men resorted to guerilla warfare and created hell for Aurangzeb. For twenty- five long years Aurangzeb went on struggling with the Marathas. After Shivaji, Sambhaji and then Raja Ram : from 1700, onwards Raja Ram's widow Tara Bai, administered the affairs of the state and disturbed the Mughals. In spite of the death of three Maratha kings in quick succession the Marathe confederacy was not weakened.

9. Policy Against the Sikhs. In the time of Shah Jajan good relations prevailed between the royal Mughals and the Sikh Gurus. This policy was changed in the time of Aurangzeb because he felt offended for the Sikh Guru had not helped him during the war of succession. Instead he had supported Dara, Aurangzeb's brother and rival claimant to the throne. In the time of Guru Tegh Bagadur, Aurangzeb compelled the Guru to accept Islam. This was in keeping with his policy of creating a predominant Muslim India. Tegh Bahadur refused to embrace Islam and was consequently executed in 1675. The next Guru was Gobind Sing. The Sikhs were flaired up at the behaviour of the Emperor and swore that they would take no rest until they avenged the execution of their Guru. Guru Gobind Singh created the Khalsa and stirred the Sikhs to action against the death of his father, Tegh Bahadur. Gobind Singh was adamant and he fought against the tyranny of Aurangzeb. The four sons or Gobind Sings were lost while fighting in the battlefield.

(B) Some Another Factors

1. Weak Successors of Aurangzeb and Despotic System of Government. The Mughal Emperor till the death of Aurangzeb were all competent persons but his successors were worthless rulers. This was true also because Aurangzeb kept his sons under strict control and crushed their spirit lest they should do to him what he had done to his father. He did not educate them well. Thus he himself made them incompetent. The Mughal system of government was despotic with all the powers of the Government concentrated in the hands of the Emperor. Such a system is a source of strength in the hands of competent rulers but contributes to the decline of the empire when worthless rulers come to the helm of affairs. When Aurangzeb was succeeded by weak rulers in 1707, the despotic system of government greatly contributed to the decline of empire. Aurangzeb by ignoring political training of his children had become partly responsible for this. The weak successors of Aurangzeb were merely puppets in the hands of selfish nobles.

2. Degeneration of Mughal Nobility. Mughal India had produced great nobles before 1707 and they had greatly contributed to the growth and consolidation of the empire. Some of them were Bairam Khan, Raja Man Singh, Muzaffar Khan, Abdul Rahim Khan-i-Khana, Shah Baz Khan, Todar Mal, Asaf Kahn and Saidulla Kaan. With the decline in the character of later Mughal Emperors, deterioration set in the Mughal nobility also. Great wealth encougaged luxury and the presence of many women in the harem encouraged debauchery. The law of the lapse of property of the nobles to the State at their death added to the feeling of wasting the wealth at their disposal in their life time itself. It undermined their character and love for adventure. Such nobility was no match for the tough Marathas and the Rajputs.

3. Inefficiency of the Army. The Mughal State was a military State but the army itself had become inefficient. The pomp and show adversely affected it. The weakening of the Mughal army had become apparent even in the time of Shah Jahan when it failed to retake Kandhar from the Persians in spite of three expeditions. The recruitment of the mansabdari troops was in the hands of the mansabdars and the standard of recruitment differed from mansabdar to mansabdar. The mansabdar commanded the same troops throughout life and was lookded upon by them as their chief and not merely their officer commanding. The method of payment through the mansabdars was defective because the State could not have direct control over the troops. Later on the practice of making assignments on revenues of lands, instead of cash payments, to the mansabdars was introduced. The mansabdar practically converted these assignments into jagirs. They were not generally loyal to the later Mughals and the Emperors were without a strong army to assert their authority. The Mansabdars were jealous of one another and sometimes would not co- operate on the battlefield . Towards the end of 17th century many mansabdars were in treasonable correspondence with the enemy.

4. Financial Problem. Akbar had set up a good financial system and the people had prospered. The share of the State was one- third of the produce of land and it dealt directly with the oultivators. This equitable system deteriorated in the hands of his successors. The system of framing out land revenue was gradually introduced. The share of the State was raised to one- half of the produce of land in the time of Shah Jahan and it made the condition of peasantry very bad. Land owners and officers oppressed the people a lot while realising taxes. Though the farmer was giving more, the income of the state was comparatively less. A portion of state income was misappropriated by the collectors. A lot of money was wasted on magnificence of court and costly buildings. Wars of Aurangzeb also exhausted the treasury. He was not in a position to pay the troops regularly towards the end of his reign. The financial condition became still worse under later Mughals. Constant and costly wars depleted the royal treasury.

5. Court Factions. Hostile cliques were formed at the Court in the time of later Mughals and these did not cobine even in the case of external invasions. There were two principal factions. The Turani or Central Asian Faction consisted of Sunni Muslims. Its chief leaders at the time of Nadir Shah's invasion were Nizam- ul- Mulk, Asaf Jah and Qamar- ud- Din. The other faction consisted of Persian nobles who were mostly Shias. Their leader at that time were Amir Khan, Ishaq Khan and Saadat Khan. The two factions were so hostile to each other that the interests of the empire were sacrificed. These factions proved tremendously detrimental for the competness and integrity of the Mughal empire. The Mughal Emperors were not able to control them. Asaf Jah, Safdar Jang, Saadat Khan and Sayyid Brothers were constantly plotting and planning. They consplired to place or displace kings that suited them. Everyone of the above leaders had different likings and affiliations. They even corresponded with enemies. Saadat Khan for instance flirted with the Marathas and Nadir Shah against national interests.

6. Foreign Invasions. When the Mughal Empire weakened, the foreigners felt encouraged to attack it. Nadir Shah of Persia attacked India in 1739, defeated Mohd. Shah, massacred the people of Delhi, took away booty worth about seventy crores of rupees, including the famous Peacock throne and Kohinoor diamond. He also annexed the Mughal territories lying to the west of the Indus river. After him Ahmad Shah Abdali of Afghanistan attacked India many times and futher weakened the emplire. the North-West Frontier Policy of the Mughals was a failure and they could not check invasions from that direction. In fact the weakness of the later Mughals prevented them from giving adequate attention to the defence of the north- western order. This was the convenient gateway to india in the time of later Mughals.

7. Climatic Factors. When the Mughals came to India under Babar, they were highly energetic. Within a few centuries they lost their old vigour due to the hot and moist climate of India as well as too much of wealth. That is why in the later period, the Mughals were able neither to put down rebillions nor defend the country.

8. Appearance of the Europeans. The appearance of the Europeans also contributed to the decline of the Mughal Empire. The European troops were better disciplined and had superior arms. Moreover, the English had strong navy and Mughals were not in a position to check them at sea. The English came to India as a trading company and later on usurped political power and becam masters of the destinies of the Indian people. The Mughal empire declined declined very rapidly after Aurangzeb's death in 1707. Within a few decades of that, the Emperors became merely figure- heads and the empire was simply their dignity.

9. Wars of Succession. There was no law of succession among the Mughals. The throne belonged to the successful prince. There was a war of succession almost after the death of every

Emperor. These became more frequent after the death of Aurangzeb. Within ten years after Aurangzeb's death there were as many as seven fratricidal wars of succession. The Hindustani and Turani factions of the court conspired against each other and kept on placing their candidates on the regal throne. No love for affection was left in the royal family and the royal court became a happy hunting ground for political intrigues, plots and conspiracies. Many experienced soldiers and generals were killed. Many princes of royal blood perished. A lot of money was wasted, which in its turn contributed to make the financial condition of the Government bad.

10. Defects of Despotism. The despotism that are passed from father to son are bound to fall into the hands of incompetent hands. It is always possible that an able father gives birth to a worthless son and in his time there may be rebellions, dissensions, factions and intrigues. This happened in the case of Mughal family also. Aurangzeb was succeeded by weak rulers in quick succession who also contributed to the liquidation of the empire. A despot to be successful has to be a person full of good qualities befitting a successful ruler. If he has even one defect, the results affect the character of the state. Therefor, the decay and downfall of despontiams are always there in the logic of history.

11. Attempts at Independence. In India there has never been a time when there were no leaders in any part of the country. These leaders thought that they should leave no stone unturned to secure local independence. In this connection they first tried to win the support of the local people which was not a difficult task. After doing it, it becomes difficult to suppress the desire of the people for independence. This phenomenon was not absent even in the time Akbar the great. Such people also contributed their mite in the downfall and disappearance of the Mughal empire. The Mughals were looked upon as foreigners and, therefor Rojput, Jats and others started their patriotic crusade. Akbar was wise and therefore he followed a policy of befriending the brave Indians. Later, when Aurangzeb reversed this policy, the patriotic Indians spelt the doom of the empire.

12. Impossibility of National Government. It is not possible to govern a huge country like India from a single center wherever that centre might be situated. The distant provinces begin to grumble against the centre favouring other provinces which are nearer the centre and which are in a better position to impress upon the centre the urgency of their demands. Unless there are adequate means of transport and communication, firm control over the entire country is not possible. In the Mughal period there were no efficient means of transport and communication. Therefore news was slow in travelling. It took time, for instance, to know that a particular province had revolted.

14. Lack of Maritime Period. The Later Mughal had neither the time nor perhaps the inention to developl sea- power on the military plane. Perhaps they did not realise that sea was no more an effective frontier and natural check to the enemy. On the other hand, it had become a smooth passage to the country. In the absence of naval power, the Indians could not face the Europeons on the seas. The same was the mental state of the Mughals also. The foreigners therfore, waited and attacked and started the process of wresting one territory after the other from the hands of the Indian potentates. Thus the Mughals were mainly responsible for sleeping over the fact that India was covered by seas on three sides, and, therefore they should have had a strong navy and the result was that these foreigners who had come to India as more or less visitors, became masters of our country's destinies.

13. Impact of Reformers. Besides other factors which precipitated he disintegration of the Mughal empire, one was the impact of religious reformers. In the south Ram Das emphasised the implortanse of Maharashtra Dharma and political sovereignty. He advocated that religion could be protected by power only. And the source of power, according to Ram Das, lay in orgânization. By these assertions Shivaji was encouraged to wage his war for independence. The spirit of revolt and desire for independence were enouraged by Satnamis. Roshniyas and others. In the Punjab, the Sikh Gurus emphasised the need of attaining military and political power in order to protect and promote their religion.

15. Corrupt Administration. The Later Mughals lacked vigour because they were weak profligates and debauchees. They were usually given to their harems and all their strength, energy and vivacity was sucked by the inmates of the harems. The administration was thus entrusted to the officers of the court. These officers naturally cared more for selfich inerests and naglected State affairs. Imad- ul- Mulk, Wazir of Alamgir II, deprived the royal family even of the necessary funds. The result of this chaotic atmosphere was that the administration of the country became slack and loose. Bribary was rampant in all the branches of administration and the common people had to groan under the excesses of the officers. Even the titles were exchanged for money. Huge amounts were piled up by high officials for distributing favours and titles. It is alleged that an official of Aurangzeb's court whose name was Quabli Khan, collected about 15 lakhs of rupee in a year or so. After Aurangzeb was no more, the situation became more pitiable. The later Mughals were almost lost in sensual pleasures. Sometimes the court was seen to be dominated by eunuche and women. This happened in the time of Ahmad Shah when Javid Khan dominated the court. Sometimes the emperor himself dressed like a woman and behaved in a most shameful manner before the people of the court and outside. All this went a long way in creating chaos and confusion as the order of the day. Weak rulers means loss of administration. In the circumstances the downfall and liquidation of the empire was only a matter of time.

(C) Results of the Downfall of Mughals

1. In the North Region. As the symptoms of the disintegration of the Mughal empire began to mainifest, the country began to be crowded by independent local dynasties. Punjab was a prominent place in this context. Marathas and Ahmed Shah Abdali were contending for supremacy but ultimately, both had to leave the Punjab. So the Sikhs took over Punjab which was divided under a number of subordinate principalities. In Rajasthan, Maharanas of Mewar, Jai Singh of Amber and Ajit Singh of Mewar, were no longer the Mughal vassals. They took an active part in the enthronement and deposition of the puppet rulers on the Mughal throne. But theyformally did not oppose the Mughals even now. Kabul and Ghazni passed on to the Persian control. Later, however, they were captured by Ahmad Shah Abdali. Abdali, founded an independent kingdom of Afghanistan. The boundaries of this kingdom of Abdali were almost the same as that of modern Afghanistan. Sindh and Kashmir had already declared their independence. The Baghelas and the Bundelas also asserted independence. Suraj Mal Jat and Bandan Singh founded the kingdom of Bharatpur. The principality of Bharatpur played a noteworthy part in the subsequent history of India.

2. In the South Region. Gujrat and Malwa were, for a short period, ruled over by Mughal Governors and were subordinate to the Mughals in name. However, soon afterwards they passed on to the hands of the Marathas. Under the Marathas the ruling houses of Sindhia, Holkar, Peshwa and Gaekwad were founded. Mysore was an independent Hidus kingdom which later on reached great heights under Hyder Ali and Tipu. The Nawab of Carnatic acted like an independent prince although he was supposed to be a subordinate of the Nizam. The Nizam of Hyderabad entertained the hopes of bringing the entire Deccan under his control, although he acknowledged the suzerainty of the Mughal Emperor. In the south, the Masrathas were most powerful. Under the Peshwas the Marathas reached the zenith of their glory and reputation. Orissa, Madhya Pradesh and Bombay were under their away.

The Uttar Pradesh of today was divided between the Nawabs of Oudh in the east, the Rohillas in the west and Marathas in the south. Alivardi Khan founded and independent nawabship of Bengal, Bihar and a part of Orissa. The portion of Orissa was amalgamated in the nawabship later on. Besides the states that proclaimed independence whose mention we have made in the foregoing lines there were numerous nawabs and petty rajas whoes postion was changing from time to time. Sometimes they would become subordinate to the Nizam, sometimes to the Marathas and so on. Thus this infection of independence was spreading like wildfire.

3. Advent of the English. Among the so many powers mentioned above, only the Marathas seemed to be in a postion to found an all-India empire. They made attempts towards that end also. However, the leaders could not rally around them all their subordinates and subsquently the vision of founding an all-India empire was shattered. The subordinates and vassals had a pastime in mutual quarrels. Their political attacks turned out to be plundering raids and naturally, therefore, the Rajputs and the general people had no sympathies left for the Marathas. Hyder Ali of Mysore and the Nizam of Hyderabad connued to conspire and plot against the Marathas. Their idea was to benefit from the dissensions among the Maratha ranks and have their own interests catered to. The French came in the field and started meddling with the Marathas and other powers in order to gain their own interest. Ultimately the English appeared on the scene. They gradually established their own position and built up their supremacy at the cost of the Marathas and built up their supremacy at the cost of the Marathas and other native powers of Hindustan.

❑

3

Rise of Maratha Power Under Peshwas

Aurangzeb died in 1707, the reins of the government of Maharashtra were actually in the hands of Tara Bai, the widow of Raja Ram. Her son, Shivaji II, in whose name and on whose behalf she was carrying on the administration, was only a puppet in her hands. But after the death of Aurangzeb, a new trouble arose for Tara Bai. Shahu, the son of Sambhuji, had been in a close custody of Aurangzeb for the last seventeen years, period when Aurangzeb was in the Deccan carrying on wars against the Marathas. But, on the death of Aurangzeb, a civil war commenced between the two of his sons, Azam Shah and Bahadur Shah, for the throne. Taking advantage of this civil war between the Mughal princes, Shahu somehow or other managed to escape to the Deccan. On the his arrival in Maharasthra, he was given a very warm reception and some of the leading Maratha, sardars like Parsoji Bhonsle, Balaji Vishwanath, and Nemaji Sindia, began to espouse the cause of Shahu.

Opposition of Shahu from Tara Bai. Naturally, Tara Bai could not tolerate this sudden appreance of Shahu in Maharashtra becaus it threatened her position seriously. Hence she declared that Shahu was a pretender. Her pretention was that Shahu's father, Sambhuji, had lost the whole of his kingdom to the Mughals. and that the new state of Maharashtra, as it then existed, really was the creation of her own husband, Raja Ram. As such, she said that Shahu had absolutely no right to the throne of Maharashtra. So, instead of going for a reception of Shahu, the sent a huge force under the command of Dhanji Jadav with a view to expelling shahu from

Maharashtra. Consequently, a fierce battle took place between Shahu and Tara Bai on the banks of river Bhima in 1707 in which, on account of Dhnaji Jadav's treachery, Tara Bai's forces were defeated decisively. After having achieved this glorious victory in the battle, Shahu proceeded towards Satara, where his coronation ceremony as the Chhatrapati was performed with great pomp and show in 1708.

In spite of the crushing defeat that Tara Bai received at the hands of Shahu, the internal differences in the maratha ruling family did not cease. Tara Bai remained constantly giving trouble to Shahu as long as she lived. Apart from her, Raja Ram had left another widow, Rajas Bai, who also wanted to establish her claim on the throne of Maharastra. Somehow or other, she managed to put Tara Bai into confinement and declared her son, Sambhuji, on the throne of Maharashtra at Kolhapur. Hence this prince also remained a source of thorn into the side of Shahu for a number of years afterwards because he often palyed in the hands of the Nizam of Hyderabad, who wanted to take advantage of the dissensions in the maratha ruling family and thus fish in the troubled waters. Ultimately, Shahu defeated Sambhuji in 1731 and, according to the Treaty of Warna in 1731, he handed over the entire region south of the river Warna to Sambhuji, while he kept the whole of the region north of this river to himself.

The Reign of Shahu (1708-1749). The most important achievement of Shahu was that he arrested the progress of centrifugal tendencies and gave to the state of Maharashtra strong centre under him. Prof. S.R. Sharma also recounts his achievements in glowing words, when he writes : "His private life was very pure and he was model of generosity, and this quality exercised a tremendous influence upon those who came into contact with him. The most important service that he did to the cause of his country was that.he appreciated the qualities and the services of the Peshwas and thus was able to get maximum benefit from their ability as the Peshwas to the cause of the expansion of the Maratha Empire in the Deccan."

The Prime Minister of Shivaji was called the Peshwa. The office of the Peshwa was first created by him when he set up the

Ashta Pradhan or Council of Ministers in his administrative set-up. The Peshwa was the first of the ministers and the head of the executive government of the country. The practice of having the Peshwa continued on during the reign of Raja Ram and Tara bai, the Successors of Shivaji. But the post of Peshwa was not hereditary either under Shivaji or his immediate succesors, but in the reign of Shahu this post became hereditary with the appointments of the seventh Peshwa, Balaji Vishwanath, after him his son, Baji Rao I, and then his grandson, Balaji Baji Rao. With the passage of time, the Peshwa became sole power in the Maratha state and the Chhatrapati became a mere figurehead. The Government of the country fell entirely into their hands and they ruled the country from 1714 to 1818 with, after the death of Shahu in 1749, Poona as their capital.

RISE OF THE PESHWAS

The First Peshwa, Balaji Vishwanath (1713-1720) as the founder of the Peshwa dynasty. The founder of the hereditary family of the Peshwa was Balaji Vishwanath, who was a Chipavan Bragman born on the western coast of the Janjira district. Here he was born in an obscure village named Shrivardhan. He started his career as a clerk of Sabhasad. It was in the year 1699 that he was appointed as Sar-Suba of Poona and Daulatabad. When Shahu came to acquire the government of the Maharashtra in his hands in 1708, Balaji Vishwanath was the first man who supported his cause. Within a few months, he was able to reorganise Shahu's army by virtue of which service Shahu gave him the title of "Sena-Karte". In the capacity of Sena-Karte, Balaji Vishwanath was able to crush Tara Bai's power and defeated individually and collectively all those Maratha Sardars who were espousing her cause. Having been impressed with the meritorious services of Balaji Vishwanath to his cause as well as to the Maratha State, Shahu sppointed Balaji Vishwanath on the post of the Peshwa.

Balaji Vishwanath, who was himself a great statesman, took a maximum advantage of the intrigues and counter- intrigues that were going on in the Mughal court at Delhi. Both the Saiyad Brothers. Abdulla Khan and Hussain Ali, were not having good relations with Farrukhsiyar and his successor, Rafi- ud-Darajat. Consequently,

Balaji Vishwanath took full advantage of this situation in the Mughal court at Delhi and concluded a treaty with the Mughal Emperor in 1719 according to which the Marathas obtained the following advantages:

(1) Yesu Bai, the mother of Shahu and other prisoners of the royal family, who were undergoing confinement at Delhi, were released.

(2) Shahu was recognised as the master of all those regions which were named as 'Swaraj'territories. He was also recognised as ruler of Berar and Carnatic territories, which were conquered by the Maratha Sardars and had been duly incorporated in the Maratha dominions.

(3) The Mughal Empmeror also gave legal permission to shahu to collect the Chauth and Sardeshmukhi from the six Deccan Mughal Subas, *viz.*, Khandesh, Berar, Bidar, Bijapur, Golconda and Aurangabad.

The importance of this Mughal-Maratha treaty of 1719 is of a special significance in the history of the rise of the Maratha power in the Deccan. This treaty transformed the status of the Marathas from mere marauders to that of legal representatives of the Mughal Emperors in the Deccan.

Estimate of Balaji Vishwanath's achievements. Balaji Vishwanath was not destined to live long after the conclusion of this treaty. He died in 1720. In history he enjoys his repuatation greater as a statesman than as a military general. The following are, therefore, the achievements of Balaji Vishwanath:

1. **Solved the Financial Problem of the Empire.** The most important achievement of Balaji Vishwanath was in the field of finance. He converted the processes of the collection of the Chauth and Sardeshmukhi into a regular system and thus reorganised the financial position of the Maratha state. It is for this reason that Grant Duff has highly praised the financial ability of Balaji Vishwanath in very bright words.

In his opinion, Balaji Vishwanath always encouraged the peasants to improve agriculture in their city and also increased the interests of the Maraatha Sardars in the collection of land-revenue from the peasants for the Maratha state.

2. **He Established the Superiority of the Peshwa Over Other Maratha Sardars.** Last, but not least , achievement of Balaji Vishwanath was that he established the superiority of the Peshwas over the other Maratha Sardars. This superiority of the Peshwas was not meant to establish only the superiority of the Peshwas in the state, but it was a superiority of his family and the future Peshwas also. He is, therefore, considered as the second founder of the Maratha imperialism.

3. **Won Great Maratha Sardars to Shahu's Cause.** He prevailed upon the haughty Maratha Sardars like Kanoji Angre to epouse the cause of Shahu and thus he was also able to crush Tara Bai's power which had threatened the very existence of Shahu.

4. **Secured the Right of Chauth and Sardeshmekhi in the Deccan from the Mughal Emperor.** He secured from the Mughal Emperor the legal right to collecting the Chauth and Sardeshmukhi from the six Mughal Subas in the Deccan. Sir Richard Temple has rightly said, "By virtue of his arguments and threats, he was able to wrung and establish the Maratha sovereignty in the Deccan."

BAJI RAO-I, THE FIGHTING PESHWA (1720-1740)

When Balaji Vishwanath died in 1720, Shahu apointed Balaji's eldest son, Baji Rao, as the Peshwa. He was an enterprising young man of 20 years and was having a very high ideal before him. Grant Duff writes, immediately after the assumption of power in his hands, Baji Rao spoke to Shahu,"This is the right time for us, Hindus, to turn out the Muslims from our Holy Land. We have to strike the tottering tree, *i.e.*, the Mughal Empire and the branches will themselves fall down." He wanted that Shahu should turn the whole of the Maratha power against the centre of the Mughal Empire. "He told Shahu, 'Strike, strike at the trunk and the branches will fall off themselves.' Listen but to my counsel and I shall plant the Maratha banner on the walls of Attock." Rhetoric succeeded where arguments might have failed. Shahu, completely carried away, cried with blazing eyes, "By heaven! you shall plant it on the throne of the Almighty!" Thus, according to this policy, the young Peshwa, Baji Rao, first turned towards the expansion of the Maratha power towards the North and thus established a strong Maratha Empire on the ruiens of the Mughal Empire. This was the policy of Baji Rao I.

ACHIEVEMENTS OF BAJI RAO-I

Following Were the Achievement

(A) Baji Rao I and the Nizam. But, the Peshwa's task was not so easy as it seemed to be. There were many difficulties. He had many enemies in Maharashtra itself. He had also to face the open hostility of Chin Kilich Khan, the Nizam- ul- Mulk of Hyderabad, who was the leader of the Turrai party at the Mughal Court. Professor S.R.Sharma says," Nizam- ul- Mulk was so strong that he could not be overlooked." He had checked the advance of the Marathas like a colossus giant. After the fall of the Saiyad Brother in the year 1720, he brought the Mughal Emperor, Mohammad Shah, under his control. Fortunately for him, the charge of the Deccan also was in his hands at that time and therefore, he decided from the very beginning that he would not implement the treaty of the year 1719 according to which the Marathas had got the legal right from the Mughal Emperor of collecting Chauth and Sardeshmukhi of the six Mughal Subas of the Deccan. On the other hand, the young and energetic Maratha Peshwa, Baji Rao I, was also determined to establish the Maratha emopire not only in the Deccan, but in the North also.

The Nizam tried to sow seeds of dissensions among the Marathas. But the Nizam was not desperate, bold and intrepid like Baji Rao. He was more of a statesman than of a general in the battlefield and he wanted to involve his enemies, *i.e.*, the Marathas in such a complicated net by his cleverness as to be able to sow seeds of dissensions amongst them and thus weaken them by exciting the one Sardar against the another. It was in this way that he wanted to gain his objective. In the year 1726-27, Nizam was able to bring some of the Maratha chiefs to his side against Shahu, so much so that he was able to excite the rival head of the Marathas at Kolhapur (Sambhuji) against shahu, suggesting him to become the ruler of the entire Maratha state. He told Sambhuji plainly that he recognised only him (Sambhuji) as the only and rightful ruler of the etire Magarashtra. It was on this plea that the Nizam refused to make payment of Chauth to Shahu:

1. **Defeat of the Nizam at Palkhed in 1728. The Treaty of Munji Shivgaon.** March 1728. The Peshwa, Baji Rao I, could not tolerated this oppostion from the Nizam. Consequently, he declared war against him. As a general, the Nizam was no match for Baji Rao I. A fierce battle was fought in the battlefield of Palkhed in 1728 in which the Nizam was decisively beaten by Baji Rao and was thus forced to accept the terms of the Treaty of Munji Shivgaon. According to the terms of the Treaty of Munji Shivgaon:

    (a) Shahu was recognised by the Nizam as the only king of the Marathas.

    (b) The Nizam also recognised his legal right of collecting the chauth and Sardeshmukhi which the Mughal Emperor had granted to Shahu according to the treaty of the year 1719, and

    (c) The Nizam also set free all the Maratha prisoners of war and promised not to take the side of Sambhuji in future.

2. **Second Defeat of the Nizam.** In spite of the fact that the Nizam had accepted the terms of Munji Shivgaon, he was not fully reconciled to the Marathas from his heart and, as such, he continued on with his intrigues against Baji Rao. He excited. Trimbakrao Dhabade, the Commander in Chief

of Shahu, to rebel against the authority of the king. Baji Rao lost no time and at once proceeded against the Nizam and inflicted a crushing defeat on Trimbakrao Dhabade in the Battle of Bhilapur in 1731. Trimbakrao was defeated and killed in the battle. With his death, the last great enemy of the Peshwa was removed from the path of opposition.

(B) Conquest of Malwa and Bundelkhand. The most important achievement of Baji Rao I was not his victory over the Nizam, but the expansion of the Maratha power towards the north. He sent his brother, Chimanaji Appa, for the conquest of Malwa. Gridar Bahadur, the Brahman governor of Malwa, was badly defeated by Chimnaji Appa in the battle of Amjhera in 1728 and the Marathas occupied Malwa. At last, the Mughal Emperor appointed one Rajput prince, Sawai Jai Singh, as the governor of Malwa, but he also abstained from entering into any kind of quarrei with the Marathas. Rather he allowed the three Maratha Sardars, Odhaji Pawar, Malhar Rao Holkar and Ranoji Sindhia to set up their own semi- independent Maratha states at Dhar, Indore and Gwalior. Now, Baji Rao turned his attention towards the conquest of Bundelkhand. At that time, Chhatrasal, the Bundela Sardar, was busy fighting against the Mughal governor, Mohammad Khan of Allabhabad. Chhatrasal through a secret envoy, requested Baji Rao to come to his aid. The Peshwa considered this offer as a God-sent boon and, as such, at once proceeded towards Bundelkhand. He was able to occupy the greater part of Bundelkhand.

(C) His Expedition Against Delhi. After having been able to conquer Malwa and Gujerat, Baji Rao brought about a " Grand Hidu allliance" by inviting the co-operation of the Hindu Rajas. This move on the part of Baji Rao unnerved the Mughals. Dr. Dighe writes."This tactic exhausted the very breath of the Mughal Court at Delhi." Baji Rao knew very clearly the condition of the dying Mughal Emperor and hence he was afraid of neither the Mughal Emperor nor his ministers like Saadat Khan and Nizam-ul-Mulk. Consequently, it was in 1737 that he decided to strike the tettering trunk of the Mughal Empire. Crossing the river Jumna, he suddenly appeared before Delhi and defeated the Mughal army in Talkatora. Had the Peshwa wished, he would have destroyed completely the Delhi city at that time, but he abstained from leading such a disastrous expedition and deposing the Mughal Emperor from the throne.

(D) The Battle of Bhopal, 1737. Having studied the activities of Baji Rao, the Mughal Emperor, Mohammad Shah, thought that the only person who could save Delhi from the Marathas at this critical time was the Nizam. He, therefore, sent a word to the Nizam to fasten towards the north at once. On the other hand, the Nizam also felt that was the only suitable occasion to destroy the power of the Marathas, who were his staunch enemies in the Deccan. He knew that was the right time to involve Baji Rao in a great danger when the Mughal army under Saddat Khan and his own army under himself could encircle Baji Rao I. But all the calculations of the Nizam came to nothing. He received a crushing defeat in the battle of Bhopal. Consequently, he was forced to sign a very humiliating treaty with the Peshwa in January,1738.

(E) Conquest of Selesette and Bassein. The Peshwa, Baji Rao I, also waged a successful war against the Portuguese. He had serious grievances against their behaviour and policy towards the Marathas. Consequeltly, he despatched his own brother, Chimanaji Appa, to wage a successful war against them. Within a few months of his arrival, Chimnaji was able to reduce to occupation the places like Thana, Selesette and Bassein, and the Portuguese consequently had to accept their defeat. The occupation of the Portuguese offered a stubborn resistance to the Marathas at this place, yet Baji Rao displayed marvellous cleverness, consistency of purpose and miraculous boldness.

Death of Baji Rao. The death of Baji Rao it is very closely associated with the life of a Muslim dancing girl, Mustasni by name. This pretty girl fell into the hands of Baji Rao in Bundelkhand. She was so beautiful and accomplished a girl that Baji Rao was pleased to keep her in his own palace. It is said that it was in her company that he had developed the habit of taking meat and drinking wine. The constant company of Baji Rao I with a Muslim dancing girl created a stronger stir among the leading Maratha Sardars, especially the Maratha Brahmans. At last, they got Mustani arrested in Poona and also conspired against taking her life. Baji Rao could not tolerate this separation of 28th April, 1740 on the banks of the river Narmada at a place called Rewarkhad, before he heard of the death of Mustani. On the other hand, when Mustani heard of the death of Baji Rao, she also passed away at Poona. Sir Richard Temple has named Baji Rao I as a fighting Peshwa for the incarnation of the "Hindu Power."

Estimate of Baji Rao-I. Good Points. Baji Rao-I was a great general who never knew what tiresomeness was. He had created a terror both in the Deccan as well as in the north. Raja Shahu had placed a complete faith in him and his own soldiers preferred to die for the sake of Baji Rao. Sir Richard Temple writes, "His heart was full of harred for the old enemies of the Hindu nation, that is the Muslims, and also the new rivals in the field, that is the Europeans, and consequently, he wanted to uplift Hinduism and Hindu nation by imbibing in him the spirit of nationalism in his mental frame.

Weak Points. But while Baji Rao possessed so many virtues, he had developed certain defects also in his character. He was always jealous of his enemy Maratha Sardars and sometimes would be prepared to sacrifice even the best interests of the Maratha Empire in his anxiety to take action against his enemies. He believed in the establishment of a national Hindu empire and was a very resourceful administrator. He was also able to extend the boundaries of the Maratha Empire to a great extent. But he was not able to set up such an important political organisation which would have given an immediate benefit of the Maratha nation. He was a fighting Peshwa, who waved the banner of the Marathas in the north and struck a deadly blow on the tottering Mughal imperialism. Taking all into consideration, we still have to believe that Baji Rao I was not an empire-builder like Shivaji.

EVENTS OF THE PERIOD OF BALAJI BAJI RAO

(1) Culmination of the Maratha Power. Elevation of Balaji Baji Rao to the Post of Peshwa in 1740. On the death of the fighting Peshwa, Baji Rao I in 1740, his son, Balaji Baji Rao, was appointed as the Peshwa by Shahu. He was only eighteen years of age at the time of his appointment as the Peshwa and, as such, there was some quarrel on the question of his appontment. Raghuji Bhonsle, one of the nearest relative of Shahu, opposed the appointment of Balaji Baji Rao as the Peshwa and espoused the cause of another person, Balaji Nayak, but Shahu did not allow his scheme to materialise. At the same time, Shahu did not want that there should be any friction between Bhonsle and Balaji Rao. Hence Shahu gave full liberty to Raghu Bhonsle to expand the Maratha power in the north-east and, as such, he was able to satisfy Raghuji.

(2) Permanent Establishment of the Superiority of the Peshwa (1749). By the year 1749, the superiority of the Peshwas was permanently fixed up in the administrative machinery of the Marathas. The Maratha Raja Shahu, who had been a great patron of three generations of the Peshwa, Balaji Vishwanath, Baji Rao I, and Balaji Baji Rao, expired in 1749. Shahu had desired to adopt his old enemy and relative the Kolhapur Raja, as his son and, as such, he executed a will in favour of Raja Ram II, the grandson of Tara Bai, as his successor. On the death of Shahu, Tara Bai strained every nerve to regain her lost postion of power in the state, but all her efforts proved futile in the face of Balaji Baji Rao's strength and statesmanship. Consequently, Ram Raja allowed full liberty of action to the Peshwa, Balaji Baji Rao, in the administration of the country.

(3) The Origin of the Maratha Confederacy. According to Sydney Owen it was from the time of Balaji Baji Rao that the Maratha state was transformed into the Maratha Confederacy, the real power having been divided among the various Maratha Sardars forming that Confederacy. The Peshwa had become for all practical purposes the real leader or chairman of that Confederacy. There is no doubt that the Maratha Sardars were feeling restless under the Peshwa and showed obedience to his orders only in a lukeworm way, but in spite of all that, he was the all powerful ruler of the Maratha state and was considered a superior man in the body- politic of the Marathas at that time. On the other hand, the Kolhapur branch of the Maratha Raja had only a small piece of land for his administration.

(4) Holkar and Scindia Appointed as the Wardens of the Marches. It should be noted here that Malhar Rao Holkar, Ranoji Scindia and Jaswant Rao Pawar had become semi-independent in Central India, but they were considered as the Wardens of the Marches appointed by the Peshwa and working on his behalf in that part of the country. They had been given full freedom to levy Chauth and Sardeshmukhi in Central India and consequently they were extending the Maratha power. It was at this time that Malhar Rao Holkar and Ranoji Scindia struck a deadly blow at the Rajputs and the expanded their power in Rajputana at the cost of the Rajput princes.

(5) Balaji Baji Rao antagonised the Rajputs. On the death of Raja Jai Singh of Jodhpur, there was a civil war for the throne between the two claimants, Madho Singh and Ishwar Singh. Taking advantage of this civil war, Holkar and Scindia both set aside the old traditional friendship of the Rajputs, began to conquer the Rajput territory and thus expanded the Maratha power at the cost of the Rajput princes.

(6) Raghuji Bhonsle Antagonised the Jats. Like Holkar and Scindia, Raghunath Rao, the brother of the Peshwa, also wanted to extend his personal influence in the north. Consequently, with the help of Malhar Rao Holkar, he commenced war against Suraj Mal, the Jat Raja of Bharatpur, in 1753. Though he was successful in collecting the Chouth from Bharatplur, the one great loss that the Maratha sustained from this warfare against the Jats was that the Jats were completely alienated from the Marathas from this time onwards. This adversely affected the Maratha expansion towards the north.

(7) Raghoba Occupies Delhi and the Punjab. After his warfare with the Jats was over, Holkar and Scindia both proceeded towards Delhi which they laid under contribution to a great extent. After having occupied Delhi in 1757, Raghoba and Holkar both brought Najib-ub-Daula, Ahmed Shah Abdali's deputy in Delhi, under arrest. The Mughal Emperor was forced to welcome the Marathas. Raghoba had become so strong by this time that he brought the Mughal Emperor, Alamgir Sani, under his protection. After having consolidated his position strongly in Delhi, he proceeded towards

Lohore with a view to occupying the Punjab which was a part of the Afghan monarchy. He expelled Ahmed Shah Abdali's son, Timur Khan, and his general, Jahan Khan, and occupied Lahore.

(8) Raghuji Bhonsle Occupies Cuttack. Where as Raghunath was able to expand the Maratha power to the north-west and fixed his banner on the walls of Attock, another Maratha Sardar, Raghuji Bhonsle, consolidated the Maratha position in the north-east. There is no doubt that his adversary, Alivardi Khan, was a very strongman but ultimately he was forced to hand over the whole region up to Balasore (Cuttack) to the Marathas, and he was also forced to pay to the Marathas the amount of twelve lakhs of rupees and Chauth in 1757.

(9) Sadasheorao Bhau Occupies the Carnatic. The Marathas also were able to establish their superior position in the Deccan. The most important Maratha Sardar who brought the highest glory to the Maratha power in the Deccan was Sadasheorao Bhau. He was the brave son of the brave Chimnaji Appa. It was in 1746 that he was able to consolidate the Maratha power in the Carnatic region by leading an expedition against it. In this expedition, he had to fight out a tough resistance, but within a year he was able to restore the Maratha ascendancy in the region lying between the river Krishna and Tungabhadra.

(10) Bhau Defeats the Nizam at Udgir. It was in the year 1758-59 that Bhau invaded the Nizam of Hyderabad and occupied Ahmednagar through treachery. Then he inflicted a decisive defeat on the Nizam in the battle of Udgir. According to the terms of the treaty concluded after his defeat at udgir, he was forced to part with half of Bijapur and Bihar which also included therein the forts of Asisgarh, Barhanpur and Daulatabad, in favour of the Marathas.

Estimate of the Achievements of Balaji Rao. The Maratha power at its pinnacle of glory (1760). Sydney Owen is quite correct when he says that Balaji Baji Rao's period was the period of the Maratha ascendancy. By the year 1760, the Marathas were able to humble down the pride of the Nizam and deprived him of the great part of his state. They also brought Carnatic into their empire and had also exacted a large tribute from the Raja of Mysore. Thus, they had become almost unquestionably the masters of the Deccan. In the Central as well as the Western India also, Damaji Gaikwad, Malhar Rao Holkar and Ranoji Sindhia had established their occupation very firmly. In the north eastern region, the Cuttack region in Orissa formed part of their empire and Bengal and Bihar also paid Chauth to the Peshwa. The brave Rajput also had been force to pay to the Marathas their tribute and the fighting Jats also, after a good deal of resistance, had accepted the superiority of the Marathas over them. But the most important of all of his acievements was that the Mughal Emperor had completley fallen under the Maratha protection and they were able to plant their banner in the north- west as far as the walls of Attock.

In this way, we conclude that the rise of the Peshwas as a political force in the administraive setup of the Maratha Empire was one of he most important events in the history of the expansion of the Maratha power in India during the eighteenth century. Balaji Vishwanath was a statesman of a high order, who acquired a legal status for the Marathas for the establishment of their power in the Deccan according to the terms of the treaty of 1719 that he got from Farrukhsiyar, the Mughal Emperor. Baji Rao I was the great fighting Peshwa, who conquered most of the territories like Malwa, Bundelkhand and Gujarat which formerly belonged to the Mughals. Under Balaji Rao, the third important Peshwa, the Marathas were able to expand themselves in all the corners of India, implanting their banner on the walls of Attock.

MARATHA ACTIVITIES IN DELHI AND PUNJAB

The warlike Peshwa Baji Rao I had begun the policy of expansion towards the north. It was he who stated that now the time has come, let us strike at the trunk of the withering tree, the branches will fall of themselves.' Obviouly Baji Rao wanted to uproot the Mughal Empire completely. He established his control over Gujrat, Malwa Bundelkhand, etc. In 1737 he appeared at the gates of Delhi and could have brought the Mughal Empire to an end in one stroke, but he retreated. Baji Rao's son Balaji Baji Rao followed the aggressive policy of his father. He was not content with the kingdom in South, rather he wanted to establish the Maratha domination in the north too. Ahmed Shah, Abdali, the Afghan ruler was equally ambitious. He had invaded India four times prior to the third battle of Panipat. Every time with a large booty he haa returned to his mother country.

Ahmed Shah Abdali never desired to occupy the throne of Delhi or to rule over India. He did not want to entangle himself in Indian poliltics. He simply wanted to annex Punjab upto the river Sutlej, so that he might have enough revenues to maintain an army and to feed his poor country, If Naguib Khan, Mulika Zamoni and other anti-Maratha elements had not acted with inimical intentions, perhaps a rapprochement might have been reached between Abdali and the Marathas. Whenever there seemed the likelihood of compromise, Naguib Khan impedimented it.

Maratha Activities in Delhi. In October 1756, Raghunath Rao moved from Poona. He should have reached Delhi in time so that he might have offered resistance to Abdali and might have compelled him to retreat. But Raghunath Rao moved with a slow speed. In January 1757 he reached Indore and in May 1757 the Marathas reached Agra where they were warmly received by Gazi-ud-Din. Marathas entered Doab and extended their away upto Saharanpur. After a struggle of fortnight they easily captured Delhi.

The conduct of Naguib Khan was known to every Muslim. He was full of anti-Maratha sentiments. It was he who had participated in committing atrocities on the Hindus and in polluting their temples. So it was quite essential that he must be kept in prison. Every Maratha of Delhi and north suggested Raghunath Rao to throw Naguib Khan behind the bars. But Naguib Khan somehow or the other secured the friendship of Malhar Rao Holkar. He requested Malhar Rao and pledged that if he was protected from death or disorder then he would serve the Maratha interests with all the courage, sincerity and fidelity. Ghulam Hussain, the author of Seir-ul-Mutakhrin says, "Holkar received a large bribe from Naguib Khan and he had rerquested Raghunath Rao that Naguib Khan Might be released and his services be utilised to establish Maratha authority round about Delhi." Raghunath Rao could not turn down the request of Holkar and Naguib was released without any condition. Naguib Khan had promised that he would not interfere in the affairs of Delhi and would cede all the forts in Doab to Marathas.

After the departure of Naguib Khan, Mughal Empror was beseated on the throne. Gazi-ud-Din was appointed as the Wazir asnd Ahmed Khan Bagash was appointed as the Mir Bakhshi. He further sent force to capture Doab. Raghunath Rao sent encouraging reports to Peshwa and boasted that Marathas are the masters of the area extending from Varanasi to the Sutlej and he intends to liberate Punjab from the yoke of Ahmed Shah Abdali.

Maratha Activities in the Punjab. In March 1758 the Marathas reached Sarhind where for the first time they come into contact with the Sikhs. The Sikhs were the Staunch enemies of the Pathans and they wanted to establish their independent rule in their own mother country *i.e.* Punjab. From 1755 to 1765 the Sikhs produced three leaders. *viz*., Jassa Singh Ramgarhia, Jassa Singh Ahluwalia and Ala Singh Jat, who successfully opposed Ahmed Shah Abdali. In 1751 Ahmad Shah Abdali had razed famous Amritsar temple of the Sikhs to the ground and the sacred tank was levelled to the ground. Abdali appointed his son, Timur Shah, as the governor of the Punjab and Jahan Khan as the Commander-in-Chief. At Sarhind Raghunath Rao thought over the issue whether to advance further towards the Punjab or to retreat. The Mughal Empror and Ghazi-ud-Din strongly advocated the reoccupation of Punjab. The Mughal Subedar of Jullundur, called Adina Begg, who was already waging war against Abdali seeking the help of the Sikhs. He also encouraged Raghunath Rao to carry out the plan of the conquest of Punjab. The Plan of the Marathas seemed quite amibitious as they went on extending the frontiers of their empire, while their base was still at Poona. The Marathas had no means to administer the areas upto Sindh.

Raghunath's Capture of Sarhind. Raghunath Rao besieged Sarhind. Abdus-Samed Khan was protecting the fort with 10,000 soldiers. Khan was wounded and he accepted the authority of the Marathas. He agreed to serve the Marathas as he had agreed to serve Ahmad Shah Abdali. Ala Singh Jat supported the Marathas in the capture of Sarhind. Taimur Shah and Jahan Khan were being molested by Adina Begg in Lahore.

Taimur Shah Quits Lahore. As soon as Taimur Shah and Jahan Khan learnt that the Marathas have captured Sarhind and with all their forces are advancing towards Lahore, both the chiefs in panic left Lahore and moved towards their native country. They carried with them whatever they could carry. Marathas hotly chased them, consequently they had to leave a major part of their goods on the banks of the River Chenab.

Abdus Samad Khan now offered his services to the Marathas for the protection of border areas against Ahmad Shah Abdali. Peshwa despatched Abdul Rehman from Poona and Raghunath Rao was instructed to utilise his services. Raghunath Rao thus handed over the administration of Peshawar to Abdul Rehman and Abdus Samad Khan. They were instructed to capture the areas of Kabul and Kandhar. Kabul and Kanhbar once formed parts of Mughal Empire but during the reign of Mohammad Shah Mughal Empire had lost them. Marathas in fact aimed to bring about the total disaster of Abdali. But Abdali was more intelligent than these Maratha chiefs. The Marathas were thinking that their arrangements would go undisturbed, but Abdali struck at their weakest point. He utilised Naguib Khan and got Dattaji killed.

The Marathas could not retain their hold over this vast area for more than six months. In the summer of 1759 Ahmad Shah Abdali got rid of internal troubles. In September he captured Peshawar and within a few days he captured Punjab. The establishment of Maratha authority in the Punjab was challenge to Ahmed Shah Abdali who did not want to lose Punjab. Thus Maratha imperialism came into clash with Abdali Imperialism and the finish decision was taken in the historic field of Panipat where none of the combatants could gain anything.

FEATURES OF THE CIVIL GOVERNMENT

The first part deals with the system of administration on which Shivaji laid the foundation of the Maratha Kingdom in the Deccan. The second part deals with the administrative changes which the Peshwas during their regime introduced in the administrative system of Shivaji according to the circumstances and needs of the time. As regards the system of administration set up by Shivaji, it has already been discussed by me in my "Mughal India" in the chapter on the Marathas. Here an attempt has been made in the following pages to discuss the system of administration as was set up by the Peshwas and the changes that they introduced in the already existing sysyem of administration which they inherited from Shivaji.

Important Features of the Maratha System of Administration. It will be very appropriate to note here that the Maratha system of administration was a compound of the principles laid down in the old Hindu Granths and the Muslim institutions of the Medieval Ages. This has been revealed to us by the scientific and minute studies that have been made of the Maratha system of administration under the Peshwas by the great writer like S.M. Edwards and Shri S.N. Sen. They are of the opinion that the Maratha system of administration, as existed in Maharashtra in the 18th and in the beginning of the 19th centuries, was a combination of two types of administrative principles. On the one hand, it contained the principles of Government, as laid down by Kautalya in his Arth-Shastra and other sacred Hindu Granths, which Shivaji had incorporated in his system of administration that he had actually inherited from the Muslim States of Bajipur and Golkunda and other Muslim states of the Medieval Ages. To these two categories the third category of principles may also be added and they are the changes which the Peshwas themselves introduced in their system of administration as suited their circumstasnces and conditions. Thus the Maratha system of administration was a compound of the principles drawn from three different sources:

(a) principles taken from the ancient works on Hindu policy.

(b) principles borrowed from Shivaji and his followers who, in their turn, had borrowed from the principles of Muslim policy and

(c) the modifications introduced there in later on by the Peshwas.

(2) It may also be noted here that the Maratha system of administration was not static, but dynamic. A good many big changes came to be introduced in it course of time and especially under the Peshwas. In other words, the Maratha system did not remain the same throughout the Maratha period and, as such, some sort of inefficiency and deterioration did occur in it with the gradual passage of time and by gradual introduction of fresh changes in it. The following examples of changes will be worthy of note:

(a) In the first place in the political aims and ideals, the Peshwas differd from Shivaji, the founder of the Maratha greatness. Shivaji never acknowledged the Mughal Emperor as his overlord. Shahu, the grandson of Shivaji, on the other hand, had been brought up in the Mughal Court, and as such, acknowledged the Mughal Emperor as his overlord. He accepted a Mansab of 10,000 from Farrukhsiyar. Shahu promised to pay to the imperial treasury an annual tribute "for Sardeshmukhi or ten percent of the whole revenue, and also bound himself to protect the country by keeping ready an army for the Emperor". In other words, shahu commenced his rule as the Mughal feudatory chief ruling on behalf of the Mughal Emperor. He was sincerelly belief in the legitimacy of the Mughal claim. What Shahu sincerely believed, the Peshwas found most convenient to continue. Further, they actually tried to derive what advantage they could from that policy. When Malwa was conquered by the Maratha arms, they did not hesitate to have their claims strengthened by an Imperial grant. The celebrated Mahadji Sindia simply followed this traditional policy when he obtained for his master the Peshewa, the Firmans of

Vakil-i-Mutliq. Similarly, Nana Phadnavis referred in his autobiography to the Emperor as the Prithavi-Pati, master of the world.

(b) In the days of the Maratha empire from 1674 to 1714, the Raja of Satara was the real head of the Maratha State and, as such, he enjoyed full and independent powers over the entire Maratha Goverrnment though he has also a Council of Ministers called Asht- Pardhan to assist him in the administration of the country. But, on the other hand, in the later period, *i.e.*, under the peshwas, the Rajas of Satara were deprived of all powers in the Kingdom, so much so that they enjoyed no powers even of appointing or dismissing their ordinary servants. These powers only the Peshwas enjoyed. Every item of expenditure in the palace at Satara spent by the Rajas was pre- authorised only by the Peshwas, so much so that even his domestic expenses were very strictly scrutinized by the Peshwas.

(c) The rise of the Peshwas affected the Maratha history in two ways. *(i)* In the first place, it destroyed the solidarity of the Maratha constitution which Shivaji's Asht-pradhan was expected to maintain quite intact, because the Peshwas deprived the Asht-Pradhan Council of all its powers by virtue of which it had guarded the Maratha constitution. Now all those powers of the Asht-Pradhan began to be exercise by the Peshwas themselves, whose ambition led them to establish an autocrat Government. The postion of the other members of the Asht-Pradhan became that of pure subordinates who could not express their independent opinion on any matter of the State, because they were strictly dominated by the Peshwas who were all-in-all in the State. *(ii)* In the second place, the abolition of the Asht-Pradhan Council removed the only bond of union, the only check to selfish individualism of the Maratha leaders and, as such, created another set of Maratha Sardars who also, in imitation of the exampie set by the Peshwa, aserted their independence, thus endangering the solidarity of the Maratha Government whose members they were.

(d) Shivaji was wise enough to abolish Jagirdari system because it created centrifugal tendencies in the State. But under the Peswas this Jagirdari system or Saranjams were revived. Consequently, the Saranjarndars or the feudal Sardars established their own independence in their principalities which they now held in proprietary rights as against the Raja of Satara who was before that the real and legal proprietor of the whole of the land in Maharashtra. These new Maratha Sardars, during the Peshwa period, began to exercise sovereign authority within their fiefs, although the Peshwa had the prerogative of appointing their chief officers. The Diwans of the Gaikwar, the Holkar and the Sindia were always appointed by the Peshwa, but all of them claimed uncontrolled exerices of sovereign rights without any interference from the Peshwa. At the head of the Government, was the Peshwa, who had power to act as the deputy of the Satara Raja. He was, therefore, the head of the feudal nobles and one of them at the same time. The feudal nobles rendered military service in return for their fiefs or Saranjams and were independent rulers in everything but name. The villages in Magharashtra proper, however, were managed by their own officers under the supervision of the Saranjam's agents.In fact no single term of polictical philosophy can be applied to it. Unable to call it a monarchy, aristorcracy or democracy, Tone calls it a "Military Republic". This is true only in one sense that the meanest soldier, if he had ability, could logically expect to be a Sardar of the empire. The empire itself, as Tone points out, "based as it was not upon confidence but jealousy, and incapable of a comprehensive policy of national patriotism which had been the aim of Shivaji, fell to pieces when it came into conflict with a nation which combined individual self- sacrifice with national ambition".

Another very important distinctive feature of the Maratha administration was that whereas under Shivaji the Marathas confined their activities more to the Maratha National State, under the Peshwas this policy was reversed and they turned their attention more to the establishment of an All-India Maratha empire. In other words, the main objective of the Marathas under Shivaji was the acquisition of the Maratha national independence or still, in other words, it was the establishment of the Maratha homeland for themselves in the Deccan. The main target of Shivaji's attention and activities was the Maharashtra. There is no doubt that even under Shivaji also there were some territories of Maharashtra proper called Mughal land or Maratha Samaraj- land which were subject to their indirect control exercised by them by virtue of their right of collection of the Chauth therefrom, but the Marathas paid very little attention to such distant lands during those days. But in the later period of Maratha history or under the Peshwas, this policy was completely reversed and there commenced the policy of consolidating their All-India empire or Hindu-pad-Padshahi hardly established by them at the cost of their own Maharashtrian land. This policy, as we have already discussed, cost them very dearly. In their efforts to hold under them their conquered territories in different parts of India, they were forced to neglect the administration of their own Maharashtrian cournty. This neglect weakened their home government which ultimately succumbed to the very effective onslaughts of the rising power of the English.

From the foregone discussion it will be easy to conclude that the Maratha State was not merely a robber State, but they had set up a good system of Government in their kingdom. Their system was not static, but dynamic and consequently it witnessed the introduction of many changes in it during the period of the ascendancy of the Peshwas between 1714 and 1772, so that it had not remained what it was under Shivaji. The most important change was that in their efforts to hold their imperial territories conquered by them out of Maharashtra, they overlooked the administration of Maharashtra itself. This weak administration in their own counrty could not stand before the strongly organised power of the rising British power in India.

THIRD BATTLE OF PANIPAT

The Third Battle of Panipat marks a turning point in the history of India. It dealt a fatal blow to the dominance of Maratha power in India. No doubt Marathas repaired the losses of Panipat and re-established their authority in the north, yet their recovery proved short-lived and temporary. The banner of power slowly and gradually shifted from that of the Marathas to the British.

Factors Leading to the Battle. The war between the Marathas and Ahmed Shah Abdali was inevitable. Many factors were responsible for it.

1. Commitment to the Mughal Emperor. In 1748 Mohammad Shah died and was succeeded by Ahmad Shah who was a puppet in the hands of his wazir, Safdar Jung. This new wazir had serious differences with Rohillas and Bangashes. Consequently he decided to crush them and with this aim in view invaded them. The war lasted for two years and the wazir found it difficult to crush them. The wazir now sought the help of Scindhia and Holkar. Their combined forces gave a crushing defeat to the opponents in the battle of Hussainpur in April 1751. Thus the Maratha prestige in the politics of Delhi was established. The Rohillas now looked towards Ahmad Shah Andali for help. They induced him to invade India in order to crush the power of the wazir. Ahmed Shah Abdali in 1752 invaded India and captured Punjab and Multan and these two provinces were annexed to the Afghan empire.

2. Maratha Activities in Delhi and Punjab. The loss of Punjab was greatly felt by the Mughal Emperor, who on the advice of Imad- ul- Mulk accepted Maratha protection. Ahmed Shah entered into contract with Scindhia and Holkar on the following conditions.

1. That the Peshwa should be given the right to the Chauth from the Punjab, Sindh and Doab.
2. That the Peshwa was to be appointed Governor of Agra and Ajmer.

3. That the Peshwa should defend the emperor from his internal and external affairs.

4. That the Emperor should pay fifty lakhs of rupees to the Marathas for their help.

In this way there started a perpetual hostility between the Marathas and the Afghans. The Maratha Undertaking was an open challenge to the Afghans. Having contracted this alliance both the chiefs retired to south and a big force was sent under Raghunath Rao. The Marathas turned out Naguib Khan, the Afghan representative in Delhi, from Delhi and the son of Ahmed Shah Abdali called Taimur Shah was made to run from Lahore. All this infuriated Ahmed Shah Abdali, who desired to retain Punjab as a part of his Afghan empire.

3. Ahmed Shah Accepted the Challenge. The occupation of the Punjab by the Marathas was a challenge to the authority of Ahmed Shah Abdali. He regarded Punjab as a part of his empire. Raghunath Rao had not completed all the administrative arrangements of the newly acquired areas, when he had to go to south. This was Naguib's opportunity. He entreated Abdali for an early return. The Peshwa wan not in a position to pay personal attention towards the affairs of the north as he was busy in the affairs of south. Holkar was busy in Rajputana and Dattaji was only a rash and reckless soldier, who was not capable enough to counter the intrigues of Naguib Khan. At the end of 1759, Abdali made a sudden sweep into the Punjab and having quickly affected a strong combination with the Rohilla chiefs, attacted Dattaji by crossing the river Yamuna and killed him outright in January 1760. Ahmed Shah Abdali did not return to his country and stayed in India with a view to consolidate his position and to deal a crusing blow to the power of Marathas.

The Battle. Soon the news of the death of Dattaji reached Peshwa. He immediately decided to meet the challenge. In order to offer resistance to Ahmed Shah Abdali Bhan started from Delhi in October 1760. He captured Kunjpur quite easily. Now he advanced towards Panipat. On the advice of Ibrahim Gardi Bhau decided to meet Ahmed Shah Abdali in the field of Panipat. Thus he encamped himself in the historic field of Panipat. The Third Battle of Panipat was the most sanguinary and decisive battle of Indian history. Bhau and his nephew were the central wing. To his left was stationed Ibrahim Gardi and Damaji Geikwad. On Bhau's right Jankoji Scindhia and Malhar Rao Holkar took their stand. Bhau did not keep any reserve force and this was his great mistake. On the other side Shah Wali commanded the centre. The right flank was guarded by the Rohillas. Ahmed Shah Abdali took his stand at the back of the centre with a reserve force.

The battle began at 9 a.m. For few hours Ibrahim Gardi discharged his artillery and wounded about 8 or 9 thousand persons. In the meanwhile, Bhau with his fierce attack broke three or four lines commanded by Shah Wali Khan in the centre. He dismounted his horse and cried out to his running forces " Our country is far off, my friends wither do you fly". It showed that the battle was going in favour of Marathas.

At this time Ahmed Shah Abdali threw in his reserves. This turned the balance in favour of the Afghans. At about 3 p.m. Viswas Rao received a bullet and he died on the spot. When Bhau came to know of it, he committed a mistake in dismounting the elephant to mourn over the loss of his nephew. Then in a fury he entered the rank of Ahmed Shah Abdali which was a great mistake on the part of Bhau. The leader of the army being invisible, their prevailed chaos and confusion in the army and within an hour the entire army of the Marathas was routed.

So, the Marathas suffered a great loss in this battle. The Maratha casualities were estimated at 75,000.

Reasons of Maratha Defeat in the Battle. The following were the causes which contributed towards the defeat of the Marahas in the Third Battle of Panipat:.

(1) Haughtiness of Bhau Sahib. It is believed on all hands now that main responsibility for the defeat of the Marathas in this battle falls on the character and actions of Bhau Sahib, who was haughty, proud and unyielding, By his arrogance, he alienated the sympathies of the Jats and the Rajputs who consequently had to withdraw much of their support from the Marathas. Malhar Rao Holkar and Surajmal Jat of Bharatpur advocated the use of guerrilla tactics of war in this battle against Ahmed Shah abdali. But being a man of unbending and arrogant nature, Bhau Sahib scornfully neglected their advice. Moreover, he overestimated the efficacy of Ibrahim Gardi's artillery, which estimated of his did not come out to be correct.

(2) Bhau Sahib's Dismounting the Elephant. After the death of Vishwas Rao, the fight assumed a very critical turn, and during this period he (Bhau Sahib) dismounted the elephant to mourn and weep over the loss of his nephew, Vishwas Rao. This was great mistake of his as a general for which he cannot be excused. Instead of wailing over the loss of a particular individual on such occasion and instead of supervising the combatants and keeping touch with all the division of his troops as a general, he lost his balance of mind at the death of Vishwas Rao and plunged himself into the jaws of death like a common soldier and then was not heard of any more. His disappearance in the battle-field created panic in the Maratha army and they lost all morale. This brought about their defeat.

(3) Absence of Unity Amongst the Maratha Leaders. The Maratha leaders fighting under Bhau Sahib were burning with jealousy against one another. As such, it was beyond any expectation that they would have fought with perfect unity and strength in the face of a grave national danger that they were facing in this battle. Hence, expecting sacrifice from them for a national cause was simply hoping against hope. In view of their long- standing personal jealousies and family feuds, they had lost all capaciy and ability to put in a great resistance to the enemy. For instance, Damaji Gaekwad, Jankoji Sindia and Malhar Rao Holkar were feeling extremely jealous of one another. Hence the emergence of a fatal result during the course of this battle was inevitable for the Maratha national cause. When Bhau Sahib dismounted the elephant on the death of Vishwas Rao. Malhar Rao Holkar left the battle-field along with his force.

The Jats and the Rajputs Remained Aloof. By their wanton aggression and grasping interference with the people of Northern India including the Rajput chiefs and the Jat Raja for more than ten years, the Marathas under RaghubaSindia and Malhar Rao Holkar had alienated the sympathies of the Hindus and the Muslims alike. Though some of the Rajputs and the Jats did join the battle on the side of the Marathas, yet keeping in view the Maratha aggressive activites against them during the past ten years, they fought only half-heartedly. Hence,the people in Northern India did not, therefore, raise their little finger to help Bhau Sahib in his distress.

(5) The Marathas Failed to Get the Support of the Sikhs. The Marathas did not realise the importance of the help of the Sikhs who were the best fighters in Asia. They were the deadly enemies of Ahmed Shah Abdali and were fighting out a war of independence against him to have their own homeland in the Punjab, and the Punjab was the bone of contention between Ahmed Shah Abdali and the Marathas. They should have won over the Sikhs to their cause and in that case the Marathas would have been sure of their success. Their failure to have their support of the Sikhs led to their defeat in the battle.

(6) The Marathas did not Adopt the Guerilla System of Warfare. Some of the historians attribute the defeat of the Marathas in this battle to their failure to adopt the guerilla tactics of war. Suraj Mal, the Jat Raja of Bharatpur and Malhar Rao Holkar, too, suggested to Bhau Sahib the use of this system of warfare, but Bhau Sahib, who was of an unbending nature-a defective character did not yield to this pressure, because he had already decided to fight an open battle with Ahmed Shah Abdali.

(7) Alliance of Nawab Wazir of Oudh and Rohillas with Ahmed Shah Abdali. By exciting their religious sentiments, Ahmed Shah Abdali had won over the sympaties of the Nawab Wazir of Oudh, the Rohillas and the other Muslim population in Northern India. This inflicted double injury to the Maratha cause.

Firstly, the number of Ahmed Shah's force increased heavily when more and more of Muslims came under his banner to fight for the defence of their co- religionist, Shah Abdali.

Secondly, the Indian Muslims knew the internal shortcomings of the Marathas and, as such, took maximum advantage of these to inflict good losses on them. Without the active co- operation of Najib- ud- Daula, the victory of Abdali Shah would have been very much doubtful.

(8) The Abdali's army was larger in number and more effective in fighting strength than that of the Bhau. Sir Jadu Nath Sarkar has estimated, on the basis of contemporary records, the Abdai's army at 60,000 while the Maratha combatants did not exceed 45,000. Hence the Marathas had to yield before the superior number of Abdali's forces which also included the local Muslim population and the Rohillas.

(9) There is no doubt that Bhau Shaib had a good park of artillery under an able commander, Ibrahim Gardi, but his army as a whole was out- classed in weapons and other equipments. Abdali Shah possessed many hundreds of long Swivel guns which were fired from the backs of the moving camels. Whereas the Gardi's artillery became ineffective in a hand- to hand fighting, the Swivel guns continued plying from all directions. Abdali's troops were armed with muskets as against Maratha troops equipped with lances and swords. This is also an instance of defective war strategy of the Marathas.

(10) Another cause of their defeat was that the Maratas failed to keep their line of communication intact with Delhi where he had foolishly left only a few thousands of men to hold the imperial city and allowed himself to be entrapped by the enemy. While the Shah maintained full contact with the friendly Rohilla country in the Doab, the Maratha army was completely isolated and besieged in the territory many hundred of miles from their country. This is another instance of defective military strategy of the Marathas.

(11) The Afghans were able to receive a regular supply of provisions, food and fodder for their animals from the Doab and the Delhi region and had, therefore, more than adequate provisions for themselves, their horses and other beasts of burden. The Marathas, on the other hand, suffered starvation for two months before the actual battle took place. When the battle commenced, they had to fight out with bare-stomachs. The failure of the Marathas to make arrangements for the regular supply of provisions in the battle is also an instance of a weak military strategy of the Marathas.

(12) It would be injustice to Ahmed Shah Abdali if, while recounting the causes of the Maratha defeat, we ignore his war tactics as a general of a consummate ability. He was a very experienced and a seasoned genral of his time in Asia. His towering personality as born leader of men and his genius for war and diplomacy constituted a very material cause of his succes in the Third Battle of Panipat. Thus, though Bhau Sahib was also a fearless soldier, he was eclipsed in generalship by his adversary, Ahmed Shah. He was apt to note every change in the fortune of battle and could adjust himself according to it. It is said that Ahmed Shah's orders were obeyed as they were as inevitable as death. Nobody dared to disobey or delay in their execution. Apart from this, he was always alert and never took rest until he had defeated his enemies.

In this way we conclude that the inordinate ambition of the Marathas under the three Peshwas especially under the third Peshwa, to establish the Hindu- pad- Padshahi, led them on to enter into serious conflicts with different Indian powers of the time. This ambition forced them to undertake heavy commitments which it was difficult for them to fulfil. Their commitments with the Emperor of Delhi led them on to the conquest of the Punjab which was the territory of Ahmed Shah Abdali. Hence a clash between the two powers had become inevitale. The clash burst forth in the Third Battle of Panipat in 1761 in which the Marathas suffered national defeat and dishonour..

RESULTS OF THIRD BATTLE OF PANIPAT

So far as the question of an unprecedented loss of manpower of the Marathas in the fateful Third Battle of Panipat is concerned it was considered to be a greate national disaster. On this point there is no difference of opinion amongst the historians who have written upon this subject. Sir Jadu Nath Sarkar is of the opinion that it was a national destruction like that of Flodden Field in the History of Scotland and that there was no home in Maharashtra which had not to mourn the loss of one or more of its members. Dr. V.A. Smith is of the opinion that the Third Battle of Panipat fought in 1761 was the bloodiest and the most destructive of the two battles of Panipat fought in 1526 and 1556. Another great historian, Elphinstone, is also of the opinion that the Maratha defeat in this battle was complete and the calamity that befell the Marathas was really great. It created a great panic amcgst the Marathas and the whole Maratha "nation became disspirited." Even the great Maratha historian, Sardesai, who does not attach much political significance to this battle, also admits that the destruction wrought by the Third Battle of Panipat was really a heavenly calamity which destroyed the man-power of the Marathas in one stroke.

A Great Controversy. There is a good deal of controversy over the question. "How did the Third Battle of Panipat affect the fortunes of the Maratha power." On this point the opinion of historians is divided. One of the opinions led by the great historian of the Maratha History, Sardesai, says that nothing was decided at Panipat. In other words, he says that the Battle of Panipat led to no decisive results and that the victor Ahmed Shah Abdali gained nothing and the vanquished Marathas lost nothing of political importance excepting the death of 75,000 Maratha soldiers. On the other hand, the second opinion led by Sir Jadu Nath Sasrkar says that the Battle of Panipat was turning point in Indian History, meaning there by that the battle led to many important political results not only for the organisation of the Marathas as a political power but for their country as a whole. In view of this difference of opinion, the correct situation can be known only by the study of both the view-points.

(A) First view: It Led to no Direct Political Results. In support of this contention, the following are the observations of historians are:

(1) G.S Sardesai. He says: "It is a popular mistake of long-standing to suppose that the Third Battle of Panipat destroyed the Maratha power in the North or that it essentially shook the Maratha empire of India. Notwithstanding the terrible losses in man-power suffered on that field by the Marathas, the disaster decided nothing. In fact, it pushed forward in the distant sequel two prominent members of the dominant race, Nana Phadnvis and Mahada Ji Sindia, both miraculouly escaping death on the fatal day, who resuscitated that power to its former glory. Not long after the Battle of Panipat, the Maratha power began to prosper again as before and continued to do so for forty years, until the death of Mahada Ji Sindia or until British supremacy was established early in the 19th century by the second Maratha War (in 1803). The first set-back the Maratha power received was by the premature death of their greatest Peshwa Madhavrao I which enabled the British Power to come forward so easily on the stage of history and dispute Indian supremacy with the Maratha for a quarter of a century. The disaster of Panipat was indeed like a national vistation destroying life, but leading to no decisive political consequences. To maintain that the disaster of Panipat put an end to the dreams of supremacy cherished by the Marathas, is to misunderstand the situation as recorded in contemporary documents.The truth is correctly staded by a learned scholar who assets that. "The fall of the Angrias (1756) and the disaster of Panipat (1761) freed the British from the thraldom of insidious neighbours and hastened their rise." This is indeed the indirect but important consequence of the Maratha disaster. Instead of this event crushing Maratha aspirations for good, it certainly gave them a new strenght and a fresh vigour in their efforts to establish supremacy over the Indian continent. Their mettle was severely tested and found to be as vigorous as ever before. In the midst of the extreme misery and distress of the beleaguered camp, there was absolutely no sign of panic or revolt, no wail of despair or defeat. Bhau's courage inspired every soul to supreme exertion and even after the final rout, people wrote and spoke of the events as if they were heroes. The Marathas have been a practical people possessing a temperament which never was over-enthusiased under victory or crushed under disasters. The disaster instead of damping their spirits, made them shine higher as, when a nation is on the path of advancement and progress, such ups and downs are inevitable. Such valiant soldiers as Dattaji, Jankoji, Ibrahim Khan, Sadashivrao did not die in vain. They left their mark on the fortunes of their nation and prepared it for a greater effort such as the young Peshwa Madhavrao actually put forth. Out of death cometh life is only too true. Although one generation, the older one was cut off, the younger generation soon rose to take its place and perform the nation's service as before. The disaster was felt as personal by almost every home in Maharashtra, and every soul was stirred by it to rise to the Nation's call." In another place, G.S. Sardesai writes: "The battle of Panipat is usually understood by most writers to have given a final blow to the rising power of the Marathas. This I think is far from being the case. The loss was doubtless heavy so far as man- power was concerned, but beyond this, the disaster did not materially affect the Maratha fortunes. A younger generation arose to replace quickly the losses suffered at Panipat and so far as the Afghans were concerned, they did not gain anything by their victory. Ahmed Shah, worn out by a long and harassing campaign of 18 months and not caring any longer to trust Najib-ud-Daula or his lukewarm allies, early in March, 1761 tok his leave of the Indian plains which had brought him no material profit. The Marathas made good their fortunes ten years later, when the next Peshwa and his spirited generals including Mahaddaji Sindia brought the legitimate emperor back to Delhi and installed him on his hereditary throne under Maratha protection, thus fulfilling to the latter the written understanding of 1752, and indirectly also the grand ideal of Hindu- pad- Padshai for which the Peshwas had been striving from the beginning of their regime. The declining point of Maratha fortunes began not on the day that brought upon the Marathas disaster of Panipat, but the day on which their best and most highly qualified ruler, Madhavrao I died a premature death in 1772." Thus the Third Battle of Panipat decided nothing.

(2) **Surrinder Nath Sen's View.** S.N. Sen also corroborates the view point of Sardesai when he says that the Third Battle of Panipat did not deal a death- blow to the Maratha Empire. About its ultimate result, there is no difference of opinion, but its immediate effects have been variously estimated. The victor, it may be safely asserted, hardly derived any permanent gain; he had to leave Delhi shortly afterwards and he failed to consolidate his authority in the Punjab where the Sikhs were founding a new power. The powerful confederacy of the Mohammadan potentates of Hindustan dissolved even before the departure of the Afghan leader, and they had to settle their accounts with the Marathas as best a they could. The vanquished were temporarily stunned but were not annihilated. Their supremacy survived for another forty years, and twenty-five years after the disaster of Panipat. Delhi again found a Maratha military dictator using its impotent emperor an instrument and symbol of his power. Panipat did not deal the death- blow to the Maratha empire, as it is commonly suggested; only arrested its expansion and granted the future rulers of India the respite they needed for consolidating their power in Bengal. There is no doubt their defeat in this battle stunned the Marathas but this is also true that their defeat did not completely annihilate their power and within a space of eleven years after this battle they were again able to establish their supremacy both in the North and the Deccan. In other words, G.S. Sardesai and some other Maratha historians who support this

viewpoint very proudly assert that the Third Battle of Panipat did not prove fatal to the cause of the Maratha fortunes in India. Although one generation, the older one, was cut off, the younger generation soon rose to take its place and perform the nation's service as before.

(B) Second View. But the second viewpoint says that the Third Battle of Panipat dealt a deadly blow to the Maratha power from which they never recovered after this event and that the disaster of the Third Battle of Panipat was one of the causes of their downfall later on. In support of his contention, the viewpoint of eminent historians like Sir Jadu Nath Sarkar has been discussed as:

Sarkar's View. His views are in direct contrast with those of Sardesai. Sir Jadu Nath Sarkar says, " It has become a fashion with the Maratha historians to minimise the political results of the Third Battle of Panipat. But a dispassionate survey of Indian History will sho how unfounded this (Maratha) chauvinistic claim is. A Maratha army did, no doubt, restore the exiled Mughal Emperor to the capital of his fathers in 1772, but they came then not as king-makers, but as the dominators of the Mughal Empire and the real masters of his nominal ministers and generals.

(C) Third and Correct View. After having discussed the above opinions as expressed by the two sets of historians, it is easy for us to believe that in view of the weight of historical evidence and further course of history of this country, the view as expressed by Sir Jadu Nath Sarkar duly supported by Elphinstone are reasonable and correct because of the tremendous political effects which the Third Battle of Panipat produced on the course of Indian history. It, is therefore, advisable to discuss the political and other effects of the Third Battle of Panipat in the following:

(1) Maratha army with its leaders was completely wrecked and out of over one lakh of persons only a few thousand reached Maharashtra and that too in great military power of the Marathas that for about three months the Peshwa could not get the authentic details about the caualties and the fate of the Bhau Sahib and some of the other leaders.

(2) So far as the question of the results of the Third Battle of Panipat on the future course of Maratha history is concerned, we cannot definitely assert that it brought about the complete political death of the Maratha Empire, but at the same time, we cannot consider it to be an ordinary battle. Although, after his victory, Abdali did not make India his home, ye the Muslim supremacy of Western India cosisting of the provinces of the Punjab, Multan and Delhi, the fate of which kept hanging in the balance during 1754-60, remained an accomplished fact and the Marathas hereafter made no attempt whatever to recover the Punjab and to guard the Frontier. In short, the Maratha dream for the establishment of their Hindu- pad- Padshahi or their domination over the entire country was gone for good on account of the serious consequences of their defeat at Panipat.

(3) The moral effect of the Maratha defeat was even greater. The Marathas lost their spirits. Dr. A.L. Srivastava says, "The Maratha legions which were hitherto looked upon as invincible lost their reputation, military as well as political. The Indian world after 1761 no longer thought that the Maratha friendship was worth having,"because the Marathas had clearly demonstrated during the last four years that they could not protect their dependents any more than they had been able to protect their own selves."

(4) It led to the rise of Raghunath Dada, the moist infamous character the Maratha History. Sir Jadu Nath Sarkar writes, "This battle, by removing nearly all the great Maratha captains and statesmen including the Peshwa Balaji Baji Rao, left the path absolutely open and easy to the guilty amibition of Raghunath Dada, the most infamous character in the Maratha history. Other losses time could have made good, but this was the greatest mischief done by the debacle of Panipat." In short, the internal dissensions in the Peshwa's family that brought about the down fall of the

Marathas owe their origin to the circusmstances created by the Maratha defeat at Panipat.

(5) It cleared the path for the rise of the Sikh power in the Punjab. Before the Third Battle of Panipat, there were four powers which were trying to establish themselves in the Punjab. They were *(1)* Adeena Beg, *(2)* The Sikhs, *(3)* The Marathas and *(4)* Ahmed Shah Abdali. Out of these four, Adeena Beg had already died in 1753. Out of the remaining three, the Marathas under Balaji and the Afghans under Abdali Shah exhausted themselves in this battle, thus making the path clear for the rise of the Sikh power in the Punjab. The Sikhs, who were dyed in the colour of their nationality, look advantage of the great anarchy that prevailed in the Punjab in the absence of Abdali Shah from there. And, when he was busy with the Marathas in the Battle of Panipat in 1760-61, they expelled the Afghans out of the Punjab and conquered the largest part of it and thus set up an independent Sikh State for themselves in the Punjab.

(6) After the Battle of Panipat, the Mughal empire existed in the minds of the Europeans as well as the Indians only in name and not in fact. It was there only as a tradition and not as an effective political entity after the Third Battle of Panipat. Though there was still a nominal emperor on the throne of Delhi, yet he was only a fugitive depending entirely on the mercy of the foreign power. It has, therefore, been rightly remarkded that the capital city being separated from its master, it had become a widow. The position of the Mughal emperor had become so much hopeless and pitiable that he could not come to his capital city of Delhi for a period of full eleven years from 1761-1772 and when he, after all, entered Delhi in 1772, he was the master neither of himself nor he was in possession of any territory; he was only a puppet in the hands of the foreign powers.

(7) It cleared the way for the rise of the British power in India. The crushing defeat of the Maratha and the consequent

destruction of their political aspirations "freed the British merchants in India from the thraldom of insidious neighbours and hastened their rise." Sardesai writes, "This absorbing contest of Panipat made it impossible for the Wazir and his Maratha allies to take note of the political revolution that had come over Bengal by the battle of Plassey in 1757 and its sequel. The english merchants were thus enabled to make a successful bid for the position of king-makers in Bengal and Bihar and to use the power thus acquired to cleverly throw their net of supremacy over the whole land. The ignorant and mutually-quarrelling Indian chiefs failed to realize the significance of these British activities and the meaning of their political and territorial ambition. Ali Gauhar, Shuja-ud-Daula, Suraj Mal, Ghazi-ud-Din, Najib Khan, Raghunath Rao, Malhar Rao Holkar, each and all, unaccustomed to take long views, could not appreciate the trend of the epoch- making events that were happening in Bengal and in the Karnatak. They all wasted their energies in personal wranglings at Delhi. The Third Battle of Panipat did verily prove a turning point in Indian History. In the middle of the first century there were two strong parties contending for the mastery of India, the rising Marathas and the waning Muslims. A third power, the British, was fast rising on the Indian horizon. The first two so weakened each other by their mutual struggles culminating in Panipat that the field was left clear for the third, the British power. On the next day of the battle of Panipat, the Mughal emperor Shah Alam II was defeated by the British under Carnac and had, as a result thereof, to throw himself on British protection. On 16th February, 1761, the British captured Pondicherry and smashed the French power in India. Thus the political star of the English East India Company was now on the ascendant.

In this way we can say that it is very difficult to believe in the observation of the great Maratha historian, G.S. Sardesai, that "Nothing was decided at Panipat in 1761." Rather it is to be believed that in view of the great political results that accrued out of this historic battle of Panipat in 1761, it was really a turning point in the history of India inasmuch as it cleared the path for the establishment of the British ascendancy in India on the practical effacement of the Mughal monarchy in Delhi.

CHARACTER AND ACHIEVEMENTS OF BAJI RAO-I

Balaji had rendered signal services to the Maratha nation, in general and to Sahu, in particular, Before his death, Balaji was blessed by Sahu thus: I hope in trust that you will run the administration of the state with ability....... you have my blessings. My successors will retain the post of Peshwa. This turned out to be true also. After Balaji's death in 1720 Sahu appointed his young son of twenty years as his Peshwa. But the appointment was not so simple and easy. The senior officers of the Marataha confederacy opposed bitterly this appointment. It was true also because now these senior, seasoned and experienced officers would have to serve under a boy. Sahu used his good offices to have the allegiance of all the chiefs to Baji Rao. Baji Rao had extraordinary brilliance, sagacity and thereby justified his selection. His greatest deficiency was his bubbling youth. Baji Rao had a towering personality, combined with good looks and a dignified bearing. However, he did not lack the qualities of a good Peshwa. He was a wonderful horse rider and looked upon war as a pastime only. He was thrilled at the prospects of adventure. He was an admirable warrior. Besides being good at books and arms he had received practical experience of diplomacy and statecraft. He was tactful in his dealings. Like any Maratha soldier he would not hesitate to sleep on bare ground. He would satisfy himself with very unsumptuous and frugal food without feeling anything.

Baji Rao had a magnetic personality. As a result, numerous youngmen of merit and capabilities started rallying round him. It was through the help of these young men that. Baji Rao could realise his aim and prove himself worthy of the deep faith Sahu had put in them. A few of his supporters who were noteworthy were the following:

(i) **Chimnaji Appa.** The greratest supporter of Baji Rao was his own younger brother, Chimnaji Appa. Unlike the Mughals, there was greatest of affection and regard for the brother mutually. The younger brother remained loyal and sincere to Baji Rao throughout his career. The Mughals should have taken a lesson from this example. If they had done so the course of history would have been different.

(ii) **Udaji Pawar.** We know of Udaji Pawar as the founder of the kingdom of Dhar in later course of time. Udaji thus was another young man who was of immense help to the young Peshwa, Baji Rao I.

(iii) **Malhar Rao Holkar.** Holkar was another team-mate of Baji Rao in his political amibition. We know only little about the birth and parentage of Malhar Rao Holkar. But this boy was very promising. He made a meagre beginning but rose to heights. Malhar Rao started his career as an ordinary soldier but ultimately had the honour of being the founder of the Kingdom of Indore. He proved of greate help to Baji Rao, the Peshwa.

(iv) **Ranoji Scindia.** Ranoji was another youngman who proved helpful to Baji Rao. It is said that Ranoji had made a very small beginning. Perhaps he used to carry the shoes and slippers of the Maratha King. He was, for some time, the personal attendants of Sahu. But it is creditable that in spite of the humble beginning Ranoji rose high.

(v) **Fateh Singh Bhonsle.** He was another youngeman who joined Peshwa Baji Rao in his amibitious plans for the betterment of the Marathas. Fateh Singh was almost as young as Baji Rao himself was. In fact, all his sides were about the same age and they made a good team. But Fatch Singh Bhonsle had a remarkable resemblance in age. But he was not of a low or meagre origin. He was adopted by Shu as his son. He made a good friend and comrade of Baji Rao.

Baji Rao had become the Peshwa, but his job was extremely difficult. The senior leaders were opposed to him. Besides, there were other enemies all round. Therfore he had to be very cautious and careful. Baji Rao's primary problem was to retain his Peshwaship, because that itself was in danger. So that had to be straightened out first before any other schemes could be undertaken. He knew that the slightest mistake on his part would be magnified at the hands of the jealous opponents, who were mostly working under him. The responsibilities of the Peshwaship were also fairly heavy and they required bold and broad shoulders. The Raja of Kolhapur had become almost a traditional enemy of the Peshwas. Besides, the dissatisfied Maratha leaders were posing a grave threat to the new Peshwa and could at any moment rise against him openly. They had to be put under proper control-Nizam-ul-Mulk was a formidable adversary. He was known coming back to the south once again. He was known for his anti-Maratha leanings. Every man knew what was happening in the Maratha camp and Nizam had particular experience and knowledge of Deccan politics. He was bound to use force and diplomacy against the Marathas. Thus the circumstances were very tiring and difficult and Baji Rao had to behave in a very careful manner.

AIMS OF BAJI RAO

The main aim of Baji Rao was to cleanse his land and drive the enemies out. For this he proposed to follow a vigorous policy. He believed, "this is the time when we can earn fasting glory by driving the enemies out of the land. If we direct our blows against the trunk of the pagoda tree its branches will fall to the ground by themselves. Maratha expansion in Hindustan will carry our victorious banner from the Krishna to Attock". The same is found in Grand Duff's work as, "Now is the time of drive the stranger from the country of the Hindu...... By directing our efforts to Hindustan Maratha flag shall fly from Krishna to attock." Baji Rao wanted to set up a purely Hindu state and this ideal was expressed by him as "Hindu Pad-Padshahi."

Baji Rao was dreaming of establishing an All-India Hindu Empire. He was basing his ambition on the fact that the Mughal Empire was thoroughly rotten by now. Its very foundations were shaken and it had become insubstantial and hollow. An all- India Hindu Empire was first conceived by the great Maratha King Shivaji. Now Baji Rao was sonly trying to revive that amibtion of the Marathas and carry it to completion. It was a very difficult task indeed. To achieve this, they had first to extinguish the Mughal rule from India. In this task they could reasonably hope to procure the help and co- operation of the Rajputs by appealing to their religious weakness. It is true that Baji Rao could get thē assurance of help from Hindu states, but the hurdles in their way were many, Marathas were not united. They were divided into two distinct warring factions. The Raja of Kolhapur was source of constant harassment and trouble to the Maratha King. He had to be humbled and cowed down. Then the Marathas, as a whole had to be organised in a very systematic manner so that they could rise as one man. The Mughal Viceroy of the Deccan was another source of trouble. He was also to be handled in such a way that he should not be in a position to harm the Maratha cause.

Delicacy of Situation. Baji Rao's position was very delicate. If any thing went wrong, his Peshwaship would be in danger. And there was always the likelihood of wrong news or magnified errors being conveyed to Sahu against the Peshwa. Baji Rao, therefore, was very alive and alert and took all necessary precautions. He picked up two persons and posted them ultimately near Sahu. Their job was to refute any wrong information that reached Sahu against Peshwa and thus save Sahu's ears from being poisoned. They were also required to keep the Sahu properly posted about the every day developments that were taking place in the state. For this task the two persons who were selected by Baji Rao were Amoaji Pant Purandare and Chimnaji Appa. Ambaji was the deputy to the Peshwa and was usually always present by the side of Sahu. Ambaji was alive upto 1734 and during the period he was in office, he rendered meritorious and memorable services to the peshwa. When Ambaji had to leave station and go out with any work, then this task of Ambaji was entrusted to Chimnaji Appa, the younger brother of Baji Rao. Chimnaji Appa was very loyal and helpful to his brother throughout his life. When Balaji Baji Rao, the son of Baji Rao grew up, this delicate job was alternated between Balaji Baji Rao and Chimnaji Appa.

Besides the arrangement stated above, Baji Rao took meticulous care that Sahu should be properly respected. He paid him all due courtesies and confidence. This was intended to retain the affection and confidence of Sahu. The result of this was that Sahu was impressed by Baji Rao. He instructed his personal followers to give all possible help to Baji Rao. These followers of Sahu were Khando Ballal and his son Govindrao, who actively supported Baji Rao. Fateh Singh Bhonsle, the adopted son of Sahu, also helped the Peshwa on Sahu's instructions. Although members of 'Ashta Pradhan' were not favourable to Baji Rao (among them Pratinidhi and Senapati were most notable) no harm could be done to him as the Chhatrapati himself was giving his blessings and kind eye to Baji Rao.

RELATIONS WITH NIZAM

Opportunity for Nizam. The rivalry between Sahu and Shambhaji strengthened the hand of the Nizam. The Mughal Emperor had granted a Sanad to the Marathas to levy Chauth and Sardeshmukhi in the Deccan provinces. This Sanad was ignored by Nizam, the Deccan Viceroy, on the ground that it was not certain as to whether Sahu or Shambhaji was the real successor of Shivaji. And the Marathas could not realise the taxes. The real cause of this difficulty, however was that Nizam wanted to establish an independent kingdom of his own. In fact the Sanad in question was prepared by the Sayyid Brothers. They had compelled the Emperor to sign that Sanad. Leter on, the Sayyids got the emperor murdered. But when Baji Rao met Nizam, he had to agree to honour the Sanad. However, he still wanted to evade the Sanad and instigated the supporters of Kolhapur to demand the Chhatrapati rights for Shambhaji. There ensued a war between the two factions in which Baji Rao achieved success for Sahu's faction. Then there was a meeting of Nizam and Baji Rao about the Sanad of 1719. Nizam did agree about the Sanad but avoided giving any distinct recognition to those rights.

About 1724 Gujrat and Malwa were captured by the Nizam and thus he became better equipped to subjugate the Maratha territories.

He might have achieved it, but in the meanwhile the Mughal Emperor declared him to be a rebel and ordered Mubariz Khan, the Deputy Viceroy, to be the Viceroy. That turned the tables. Mubariz wanted Maratha help and requested for it. On the other hand Baji Rao also wanted to strengthen the Maratha position against the Nizam. Unfortunately the Marathas proposed impossible terms to Mubariz Khan, which he turned done, allied hemself with Carnatic. In the war that ensued between Mubariz Khan and the Nizam, Mubariz was defeated and killed. Historians hold confliotiong views about Baji Rao's role in the aforesaid war. Some say he was neutral but Dr. Dighe says he supported the Nizam. This was perhaps because Baji Rao was inimical to Mubariz Khan. Ultimately the Nizam won the battle.

After the war, Nizam maintained friendly appearances towards the Marathas for the time being. The Maratha gained some thing from the war between the Nizam and Mubariz Khan. The Nizam admitted the claim of the Marathas to levy Chauth and Sardeshmukhi from the Deccan. He also promised to Baji Rao that the Marathas could levy Chauth and Sardeshmukhi on Malwa and Gujrat also, in due course. But on the whole victory of the Nizam-ul-Mulk proved to be a source of further troubles to the Marathas. The Nizam joined the Marathas against Carnatic, but his real object was to keep the Marathas busy there while he could consolidated his own position.

The Marahtas busied themselves in the Carnatic while the Nizam shifted his headquarters from Aurangabad to Hyderabad, and started preparing for war with the Marathas. The Marathas were successful in subjugating the Ghorapades of Gutti and the Polygars. The Raja of Tanjore and the Nawab of Arcot were subjugated for the time being. However, these decisions were not of a permanent nature. That required greater efforts and more labour to have been invested. The result of these conquests meant only loss to the Marathas, in terms of men and money and did not bring about any substantial gains to them.

Baji Rao's Strategy. Baji Rao rushed back home and consultations started at the highest level. The greatest difficulty was that Nizam had artillery and Marathas had no antidote. Baji Rao organised the strategy of the war. Accordingly Baji Rao started for Burhanpur and Sahu with Chimnaji proceeded towards Purandhar. When Baji Rao was heading towards Burhanpur after attacking Khandesh, Nizam thought that Baji Rao was running away. He therefore started chasing him. He was sure that if Baji Rao was defeatd Sahu could not be saved by anybody else. Thus he kept on chasing Baji Rao. In this hurry, the Nizam left his artillery behind. The position of Marathas became better because their real planning was not known to the Nizam. Baji Rao, during his so called flight was constantly informed about the movements of the Nizam. Baji Rao kept his subordinates well informed as to what course of action they were supposed to take. The result of all this arrangement was that the Nizam walked into the trap, as it were. A battle was fought at Palkhed near Daulatabad in which the Nizam suffered heavy losses. He was not completely vanquished but was completely nervous and unnerved. He requested Baji Rao for peace. In March, 1728 the Treaty of Mungi Shivgaon was concluded and thereby Baji Rao secured for Sahu the claim of levying Chauth and Sardeshmukhi in Deccan. He also promised that he would not help Shambhaji against Sahu. Thus the position of Sahu was made much better than before. The reason was that the centre of Sahu's opposition, Nizam-ul-Mulk, was cowed down for the first time. This was a personal victory of Baji Rao and he was rightly proud of this contribution of his to the Maratha Nation.

The Nizam remained hostile even after that. He made a plot with Trimbak Rao Mabhade but the Peshwa dafeated and killed Mabhade in 1731. Then Nizam joined hands with Mohammad Khan Bangash but was defeated by Baji Rao. Then Nizam made a secret agreement with Peshwa by which Baji Rao agreed not to molest Nizam's territory in return for Chauth and Şardeshmukhi while Nizam was to remain neutral during Baji Rao's expendition to Northern India. Nizam thus hoped to save his territory by diverting Maratha's attention to the North.

Control over Malwa and Gujrat. Baji Rao crossed the Narbada in 1724 and proceeded towards Malwa. The time was favourable because Rajput rulers of Rajasthan, particularly Jai Singh of Jaipur, were in sympathy with the Maratha ideal of extending Hindu rule. They were not likely to come and oppose him whole heartedly on behalf of the Mughals. The Peshwa met with little opposition and over-ran the whole of Malwa. He returned to Poona leaving his lieutenants Udajit Pawar. Malhar Rao Holkar and Ranaji Sindhia to collect tribute. They became the founders of the States of Dhar, Indore and Gwalior. The Maratha armies overran Gujrat also and the collection of tribute from this province was assigned to Khande Rao Dabhade. He left hehind his lieutenant Damaji Gaikwàd who became the founder of the State of Baroda. In 1728 Peshwa sent his brother, Chimnaji Appa who expelled the Muslim Governer of Malwa and the Maratha hold over the province was firmly established.

Control over Bundelkhand. Mohammad Khan Bangash, the Mughal governor of Allahabad, besieged the Bundela Chief, Chattra Sal, who requested Peshwa for help. Baji Rao personally led Maratha forces and defeated Mohammad Khan Bangash who agreed not to attack Bundelkhand in future. Thus Maratha control was established over Bundelkhand.

Battle of Bhopal. The Maratha power was increasing with a great speed. This increase of power was quite alarming. Nizam was called to Delhi by the Mughal Emperor and an attempt was made to drive out the Marathas by securing the governorship of Malwa for his own son. However, in December, 1737 Baji Rao inflicted a crushing defeat on the Nizam once again. This battle is known as the battle of Bhopal. During this war Baji Rao applied the same strategy as he had applied in the battle of Palkhed. Baji Rao then imposed his terms on the vanquished. A treaty was concluded on Januay 7, 1738 which is known as the treaty of Durai Sarai. According to the terms of the treaty the Nezam had to pay the Peshwa 50 lacs of rupees as war indemnity. Besides, the landbetween the rivers Narbada and Chambal was to be ceded to Peshwa in full sovereignty. The whole of Malwa was also given to Peshwa.

This is surprising that the Peshwa did not pursue the Nizam to honour the terms of treaty immediately. Instead, he returned to

Poona. He should have pestered the Nizam becaue he had proved undependable previously. The Peshwa was dissipating his evergies in subduing the Raja of Kota and others. What he got from them was much less than what he could have got from the Mughal Emperor.

The Nizam had assured Baji Rao that he would attain royal assent to the agreement reached at by him. Nadir's invasion created a gap and the Royal Firman from the empror could be issued to the Marathas only in 1741, when Baji Rao was no more and his son Balaji Baji Rao had become the Peshwa.

Raid on Delhi. In 1737 Baji Rao crossed the Jamuna and plundered Doab. Saadat Khan of Oudh defeated a body of Maratha troops under Malhar Rao Holkar and sent a note to Delhi boasting that he had driven the Marathas across the Chambal. Baji Rao proved the exaggeration of that report. By covering 10 day's march in two days, he appeared in the neighbourhood of Delhi and defeated a Mughal army. The Mughal Empror, Mohammad Shah, called Nizam- ul-Mulk for the help but Baji Rao defeated the forces of Nizam near Bhopal. The Mughals were forced to accept their rule over Malwa.

Capture of Bassein (1739). Peshwa's brother Chimnaji Appa, captured Salsette in 1737 and Bassein in 1739 from the Portuguese. The Peshwa's war with the Portuguese was long- drawn. The Marathas decide to conquer Salsette in March 1737, and the fighting came to an end in 1739 when the fort of Bassein was captured. The Marathas had captured Salsette and Bassein and that was perhaps the maximum they could do. This was because they did not have the courage to make an attempt on the other Portuguese possession like Goa, Daman, Diu and Chaul. When fighting was stopped and peace was concluded, the Marathas obatined from the portuguese their northern possessions iucluding four forts of strategic importance and also three hundred and forty villåges. From the aforesaid, the Marathas received more than two lacs of rupees every year. Besides, Salsette and Bassein, twenty forts and eight towns were also obtained by Marathas. The Portuguese gave to the Marathas some ammunition also but that was of a poor quality. Still, on the whole, the Marathas gained heavily from the Portuguese.

RELATIONS WITH SHAMBHAJI

The Maratha Chhatrapati, Sahu was in Mughal captivity for a long lime. The intention of this detention was to convert Sahu to Islam. However, Sahu refused point blank to be converted to Islam. But during his detention, Sahu was given luxurious bringing up and such aristorcratic retouches that he became a very docile and quiet sort of a person. For this reason, Sahu wanted to be at peace even with Sambhaji, his rival to the Maratha throne. Perhaps Sahu would have exerted himself and used the good offices of Peshwa Baji Rao to reach a settlement with Shambhaji. Unfortunately many Maratha leaders crossed over to Shambhaji. These leaders were very selfish and self-centred. They did not bother about the general Maratha interests and cared to augment their personal interests only. These Marathas had some grievances either against the Chhatrapati or the Peshwa. And mind you! these grievances were not necessarily genuine. These self-seeking Marathas instigated Shambhaji to go to war with Sahu.

Overtures of Sahu. In agreement with his masters' wishes Baji Rao thought it worthwhile that an attempt may be made that the two factions of the Marathas were brought together and the aims of Shivaji realized. In this connection, he persuaded his master to correspond with Shambhaji. Accordingly Sahu wrote a letter to Shambhaji in 1725. In this letter he asked Shambhaji to be friendly with him so that Maratha unity may not be impaired and their reputation should remain high. He therefore proposed that their spheres of influence should be divided and they should work freely in their respective spheres. Besides, they should work in unison so that their joint cause should be strengthened. Baji Rao had thought the river Krishna should be the boundary line. Sahu should operate on the north of it and Shambhaji's sphere should be on the southern side. Sahu also suggested that a portion of the area subjugated by one should be given to the other voluntarily. This will retain their separate entity and at the same time strengthen the Maratha cause as such. However, wisdom did not dawn on Shambhaji and he turned down such a reasonable offer of Sahu. Thus the hand of friendship which was extended by Sahu, on Baji Rao's instance, was not warmly accepted. The pro- Sahu group was officially led by Baji Rao I. These people were sincerely interested in augmenting the prestige and dignity of the Maratha Chhatrapati Sahu and the Chhatrapati confided in them. The anti- Sahu group, naturally did not enjoy the confidence of the Maratha king. The reason was that these people were allegedly plotting to dethrone Sahu and enthrone some other person on the Maratha throne perhaps Shambhaji.

Growth of Peshwa's Power. Baji Rao was joined by many capable and hold officers, with the result that he became very powerful. He had organised the realization of Chauth from Malwa in a very scientific, Systematic and successful manner. This success enhanced the reputation of Peshwa Baji Rao I. With this success the whole of Malwa came almost directly under the control of Peshwa Baji Rao I and his followers. In due course, it was given a legal shape by an order of the Maratha King. Besides Peshwa Baji Rao, other Maratha chiefs were also gaining more and more power every day. These chiefs were mainly the Pawars, the Scindhias and the Holkars.

Round about the year 1736, Sahu conferred on his Peshwa. Baji Rao, the honourable and uncommon mansab of 7000 (Saat Hazaari). This was a rare honour and the prestige of the Peshwa immediatly shot up. Besides the Peshwa, his brother Chimnaji was also honoured by the king. King Sahu conferred the mansab of 5000 (Paanch Hazaari) on Chimnaji and thus acknowledged the services rendered by him to the Maratha nation. In the year 1736 Sahu agreed with Baji Rao and it was decided that unless the Sahu acquired real control over the provinces of Deccan, he should not be given the stipulated six lacs of rupees which were to be given to him in place of the right of levying Chauth and Sardesmukhi on the Deccan provinces. It was further agreed that Baji Rao I would be granted a sum of thirteen lacs of rupees as an allowance for his expenditure. To give this arrangement about realization of taxes a real shape, it was agreed by Chhatrapati that Baji Rao should be made governor of Malwa besides his normal duties. Thus by the agreements stated above the postion of the Peshwa became of paramount importance.

Incidentally this was the pinnacle of Peshwaship's glory in the Maratha history. In the same context of the letter Baji Rao launched an attack on Carnatic. And the idea was exactly what was incorporated in Sahu's letter to Shambhaji. But Shambhaji got apprehensive and he thought perhaps he and his territories were not secure. He apprehended that perhaps Baji Rao might attack Shambhaji next, which was absolutely hypothetical and far from reality. All the same in order to guard himself against this Shambhaji aligned himself with the Nizam-ul-Mulk.

Lemency with Nizam. Thinking that perhaps Baji Rao was thinking of attacking Shambhaji and his territories, Shambhaji entered into a secret agreement with the Nizam- ul- Mulk. The central idea of this agreement was that with the help of Nizam, Shambhaji would make an attempt to throw Sahu away from the throne and become the Chhatrapati himself. The result of this agreement was that Nizam attacked Poona in 1727. We have already discussed that Baji Rao had compelled the Nizam to acknowledge the power and position of Sahu after he had defeated the Nizam at Palkhed. And Sahu was immensely pleased with this arrangement of Peshwa Baji Rao. Now, after the developments stated above had taken place, Baji Rao, made an attempt to neutralise the Nizam's power and further, Baji Rao actually attacked Shambhaji. In the battle that ensued between Shambhaji and Baji Rao, Shambhaji was defeated and captured. No harm was done to Shambhaji's person but was compelled to acknowledge the overlordship of Sahu. This achievement of Baji Rao of 1731 was another bright feather to his cap. The result was that Sahu's position as Chhatrapati was established after all. His postion became unchallenged. Automatically, the Nizam-ul-Mulk was isolated. Nizam and other powers of the Deccan were all placed in such a postion that they could not raise their head against the Chhatrapati. This was a very significant contribution to the golry of the Marathas and dignity of his master Chhatrapati Sahu.

Opinions of Historians. However, there are some other historians who firmly believe that the reasons were somewhat different than those stated above. They bellieve that Sahu was slightly unsure of Baji Rao's success against the Nizam. It was very clear that if Baji Rao was defeated or captured by Nizam, Sahu would be nowhere. He would be completely ruined. These fears of Sahu were however, unfounded and were not borne out by facts. At the battle of Palkhed the strategy of Baji Rao completetly checkmated the designs of the Nizam and he was entrapped by Baji Rao. This was in spite of Nizam's being powerful, experienced, tactful and resourceful. This policy of Baji Rao was followed in subsequent wars against Nizam also. And thus Nizam was completely subdued. He had to acknowledge the position of Sahu and to accept his right to levy Chauth and Sardeshmukhi. This was all due to Baji Rao. They also thought that as Sahu's policy was timid and submissive by temperament so he also did not want to endanger his position and rights as far as possible. He thought that the safest course would be to follow a friendly policy with Nizam. After 1731, when Shambhaji was defeated and was made to accept the overlordship of Sahu there was nothing to fear from Nizam or from any body else.

There are still other historians who give their own arguments regarding why Sahu was followed a friendly policy towards Nizam-ul-Mulk. When Balaji Vishwanath had gone to Delhi, at that stage Nizam had given him his support to enhance his claims and arguments. Since then Sahu was grateful to Nizam- ul- Mulk. He could not easily forget his debt to the Nizam. In fact, he did not want to act against anyone wanted to be friendly with every one for one reason or the other. He did not want to act against the Mughals, against Shambhaji and against Nizam for different reasons, of course. Historians say that the Marathas had a soft corner for Nizam and therefore, also he had to follow an accommodative policy. Ultimately when Nizam was defeated and finally when Shambhaji was also defeated and acknowledged Sahu as the Chhatrapati the whole unpleasant episode came to an end.

ESTIMATE OF BAJI RAO I

Fighting Peshwa. The fighting Peshwa,as Baji Rao was popularly known, made a gigantic contribution towards the consolidation and expansion of Maratha reputation and power. The good qualities of a ruler, diplomat and warrior were pleasantly blended in him. He stormed Rajputana and Delhi and got what he wanted. Bundelkhand and Gujrat were also overrun by him. Wherever he went he made his impact felt by laymen and noblemen. He wonderfully executed the plan of subjugating Malwa and realizing Chuath and Sardeshmukhi from there. The job was especially assigned to him by the Chhatrapati. He was given money to cover his expenses and was made the Governor of Malwa. His success over Malwa was complete and Malwa became permanently under the Marathas. His relations with the Nizam- ul- Mulk form an interesting study. Nizam was very powerful and had other qualities of statemanship and diplomacy. He was known for his anti Maratha propensities. Baji Rao succeeded in crushing the Nizam in a way. Nizam was outwardly friendly with Baji Rao and his master but secretly expoused Shambhaji's cause. He did so becasue it was in his interest. If Sahu and Shambhaji were quarrelling Nizam would benefit. But Baji Rao forestalled the Nizam everywhere. He entrapped the Nizam and humbled him in the battle of Palkhed and later in the other battles. He (Nizam) was eventually compelled to accept defeat against Baji Rao and acknowledge the rights of Chhatrapati for Sahu . Nizam's defeat was a great landmark in the history of Baji Rao's success.

Baji Rao and Chhatrapati's Dignity. In spite of every thing, the position of Chhatrapati did not improve substantially during the Peshwaship of Baji Rao. The evils of feudalism were as much prevalent as at any time. Disagreements, Plottings, intrigues and jealousness did not cease. The Marathas could not be bound into a simple unit. Despite the efforts and the apparent successes of Baji Rao, there was no real cohesion of the Marathas, no real bonds of unity. Baji Rao made no efforts whatsoever to remove the defects that flow naturally from the war of liberation. His father, Balaji Vishwanath, left no stone unturned to remove the defects of the war of liberation waged among the Marathas. But still the achievements of Baji Rao were great. However, his achievements enhanced his own prestige more than that of his master, the Chhatrapati. As far as personal power, revenues and jagirs and the family reputation was concerned. Baji Rao's position was about the best among the Marathas.

The Pratinidhi, the Sumant and the Senapati were nowhere near the Peshwa in power, position reputation and pre- eminence. The achievements of Baji Rao were really great. But then, that does not mean that Baji Rao was on the same level as that of Shivaji. After Shivaji , there was no statesaman or officer in the Maratha confederacy who could be placed by his side. Baji Rao was the first after Shivaji who was a great patriot who contributed substantially to the cause of Maratha solidarity and reputation.

End of Baji Rao I. Baji Rao died in the year 1740. He was not even forty years old when the end came. Baji Rao was born in the year 1700. Thus he was only in the fortieth year when he died. Baji Rao died a natural death. Before death overtook him, Baji Rao was taken ill. The Maratha empire which was recently formed after reorganization under Sahu, received a thunderous shock by the untimely death of the valiant and the brilliant Peshwa who was fairly young throughout his tenure of office. Another reason which made the absence of Baji Rao felt was that his son and successor, Balaji Baji Rao, was not as able and dashing as Baji Rao. Baji Rao was a real jewel of a man and a real patriot who did a lot for the Marathas.

PESHWA BALAJI BAJI RAO (1740-61)

After the death of Baji Rao I his son, Nana Sahib popularly known as Balaji Baji Rao was apponited as the Peshwa. Balaji Baji Rao at the time of his apointement was only eighteen years old. He did not succeed to his father's office without opposition. He was opposed by Raghuji Bhonsle, one of the near relatives of Sahu. He stressed that Balaji Naik should be appointed as the Peshwa.Sahu paid no heed to the plans of Raghuji Bhonsle and without hesitation appointed Balaji Baji Rao as the Peshwa. Sahu did not allow the differences of Balaji Baji Rao and Raghuji Bhonsle to persist and sought a compromise in them. He permitted Raghuji Bhonsle to extend his dominions independently towards the north-east.

The office of the Peshwa reached its high water mark during the period of Balaji Baji Rao. The year 1749 witnessed the death of Sahu. Sahu had no son, who might have succeeded him, and it was his desire that he should adopt his rival, the Raja of Kolhapur as his son. He also signed a will in the name of Raja Ram II, the grandson of Tara Bai.After the death of Sahu. Tara Bai tried to regain her lost position, but she found Balaji Baji Rao more than a match to her. Raja Ram II gave full liberty to the Peshwa to handle the affairs of the state. Raja Ram II concluded a traty with Peshwa called 'Sangola Treaty ' according to which the king handed over the real power to the Peshwas. From this time onwards Poona, the residence of the Peshwa, became the capital of the Maratha Empire. Satara became the residing place of a phantom king. Raja Ram II was corrupt and inefficient. If he descended from Shivaji was also doubtful.

Birth of Maratha Confederacy. According to Sydney Owen, "It was during the period of Balaji Baji Rao that Maratha state was transformed into Maratha confederacy. The Peshwa had become for all practical purposes the real leader of the Maratha confederacy. His orders were obeyed, through loosely or jealously. This position he had attained by the dint of his own power. Raja Ram II, had only a small tract of land under his administration and he virtually lost his influence in the Maratha State.

Pinnacle of Maratha Power. The observation of Elphinstone runs thus," The Maratha power was now at its zenith. Their frontier extended on the north to the Indus and Himalayas, and on the south nearly to the extremity of the peninsula, all the territory within those limits that was not their own paid tribute, The whole of this great power was wielded by one hand...... and all pretentions of every description were concentrated in the Peshwa." Dr. V.A. Smith writes " Elphinstone's statement requires correction in so far that the one hand, which directed the Maratha Government was that of Sada Sheo (Sadasiva) Bhao, the Peshwa's first cousin, and was not that of Balaji himself, who was addicted to sensual indulgence and left the entire management of all the affairs of government to his cousin, a man well trained in the conduct of business and accustomed to steady work." "Sadasheo Bhao, having organized a regular well- paid army including a large train of artillery and 10,000 infantry, disciplined more or less completely after the European manner and under the command of a Mohammedan general, named Ibrahim Khan Gardi, believed himself qualified to dispute the sovereignty of India with the Durrani. Mohammad Shah, the nominal emperor of Delhi, was not taken into serious account."

Defects of his Policy. The new Peshwa followed a forward policy like his father but, according to Maratha historian Sardesai, he made two fatal mistakes. Firstly, he rejected his father's idea of "Hindu Pad Padshahi" or bringing all Hindu chief under one flag. The Marathas began to look to their interests only and ignored the interests of the rest of Hindus. The depredations of his chiefs alinated the Rajputs and destroyed all possibility of the combination of Hindu States against Indian Muslim powers of foreign Muslim invaders. Secondly, he made a revolutionary change in the military organization of army. Now it came to consists not only of light infantry and cavalry as in the days of Shivaji, but also foreign artillerymen and mercenaries of all types. Such an army could not have the desperation and dashing spirit of a national army.

Extension of Maratha Power. In spite of these defects of policy, the Maratha empire expanded in the North as well as in the South.

(1) In 1740-41 Raghuji Bhonsle raided Carnatic, defeated and killed its Nawab, Dost Ali, and made peace with his son, Safdar Ali. Dost Ali's son- in- law, Chanda Sahib, was sent as a prisoner to Satara. The Nawab had to pay two lacs of rupees to the Marathas.

(2) The Marathas exacted Chauth even from the principalities lying to the south of the river Krishna.

(3) They helped the English under Clive and Watson to reduce the pirate Angira.

(4) Balaji Baji Rao invaded Mysore and levied Chauth.

(5) Raghuji Bhonsle defeated Ali Vardi Khan, conquered the greater part of Orissa and forced him to give twelve lacs

of rupees a year as Chauth for the provinces of Bengal and Bihar.

(6) They defeated Nizam Ali of Hyderabad and got Bijapore, Aurangabad, part of Bihar and the strong fort of Daultabad.

(7) In 1758 Peshwa sent his brother Raghuba to help Emperor Alamgir II against his enemies. Raghuba took Delhi and expelled the son of Ahmed Shah Abdali from the Punjab.

Thus the Maratha power was at its zenith by 1760. Nearly the whole of Western India from the Himalayas and the Indus to the extreme south of the Deccan was now dominated by the Marathas. With Delhi in their hands and Durrani Afghans expelled from the Punjab, it seemed likely that they were destined to bring the whole country under their complete subjection. But in 1761 the Maratha power received a crushing blow at the Third Battle of Panipat and their dream of founding an empire was shattered. The unity of Marathas disappeared with the weakening of the power of the Peshwa. He died a broken- hearted man within a few months of the defeat.

Positioin of Peshwa. Sahu had directed Raja Ram in his will that the office of Peshwa should be retained. He had also advised the next Chhatrapati to retain Balaji Baji Rao I as Peshwa. The positions of the Peshwa was very distinguished and towering. The only positions of any moment in the Maratha court were those of Senapati, Sumant and Pritinidhi besides the Peshwa, of course. These officers were somewhat important but as compared to the Peshwa they were completely insignificant. The predominance of the Peshwa was thus established over the other Maratha chiefs and officers. In this way, this Chitpawan Brahmin family of Konkan continued to dominate the Maratha court as it had been doing so for the last three generations.

Balaji's Tact. As far as possible, Balaji Baji Rao always behaved a subordinate and servant of the Chhatrapati. He made no attempts to boss over the weak Chhatrapati Raja Ram. He was very tactful in dealing with the dignitaries of the royal family Balaji was firmly of the opinion that nothing should be done in the Maratha camp which may encourage the enemies of the Marathas to cast their evil eyes on the Maratha kingdom. In the time of Balaji Bajirao, regular bouts were going on between Raja Ram and Tara Bai for political supremacy in the Maratha camp. In this political scramble for power, Balaji was obviously with the Chhatrapati, Raja Ram.

The Peshwa wanted to handle Tara Bai with tact and diplomacy. He did not want to harm the person of Tara Bai. The reason was that Tara Bai belonged to the royal family of the Marathas and she was renowned and talented too. He did not want to be disrespectful towards her. He himself said that he could have imprisoned Tara Bai and completely crushed her along with her followers but he did not do it because he wanted to avoid the oreation of circumstances which would jeopardise the interests of the Marathas. In fact, Balaji Baji Rao did not believe in magnifying the internal quarrels or disagreements between the Marathas and publishing them or making them a political issue, because that would help the enemies. Therefore, he thought of a different course to handle Tara Bai.

CAUSES OF MARATHA'S FAIL TO ESTABLISH STRONG EMPIRE

After the death of Aurangzeb, the Marathas expanded their stated into a vast empire. During the frirst Peshwa Balaji Vishwanath's period, the Maratha union was founded and grandually the whole of Deccan and many areas of Northern India came under the control of the Marathas. But after some years only in 1761, in third battle of Panipat, the Marathas were defeated and day by day their power and influence declined. The following were the causes for their decline:-

(1) Weak Successors of Shivaji. Shivaji was a great leader and a nation builder. He gave a new life, to the Maratha race by his example and qualities. He not only created a vast empire by conquests but consolidated it and founded an admirable administrative system which was a clear proof of his great statesmanship and constructive genius. The Maratha power so ably founded and organised by Shivaji became some what disorganised under his weak successors though it was again reviewed in the beginning of the 18th century under the guidance of the first three Peshwas.

(2) Lack of Strong Finances. The Marathas did not pay any particular attention to the strengthening of their financial position and consequently they always suffered from financial stringency. The whole affairs of their income and expenditure was unsystematic and their resources were altogerher disorderly. Their taxation was also not based on any system. In the words of Dr. K.KDutta," Another drawback of the Maratha state was its lack of sound economic policy and satisfactory financial arrangements, without which the political development of a nation becomes impossible."

(3) The Mutual Distrust and Jealousy Among the Different Members of the Maratha Confederacy. The diiferent members of the Maratha confederacy *i.e.* the Peshwa, Holkar, Gaekwad, Bhonsle, Sindhia etc. Indulged in fighting resulting in the wastage of their power and energy which they could otherwise use against a common enemy. This mutual distrust and jealously among themselves could not make them stand in the face of clever politicians like the Britishers.

(4) Out of- Date Methods of Warfare. Shivaji had adopted the policy of guerilla warfare and as his field was a hilly one he succeded, but when the Maratha rule extended to the plains also this type of warfare failed and the Marathas had to fight face to face in which they got defeated. Their fighting techniques were old and hence could not stand against the Britishers who were conversant with the latest methodology.

(5) Weaknesses in the Political System. The fundamental cause for decline of the Marathas was that their political system did not help in strengthening and establishing permanent system of administration in the captured areas. Actually, the same policy helped them in increasing their power that itself destroyed them. The areas that the Marathas conquered, they got Chauth and Sardeshmukhi. A fixed amount of the total sum had to be sent to the central government in Satara by the Maratha chiefs and the rest, the Maratha chiefs kept for himself. The chief maintained a separate army from the income of the conquered areas. Though, principally, the Maratha chiefs were the representatives of the central Maratha government and Peshwa but practically, they had their independent authority. The selfishness and ambitiousness the Marahta Chiefs did not help them in having respect for the Satara government. Because of this, by the mid 18th century five separate powers of the Marathas came into existence. First, in Pune the Peshwa had their powers and other four powers were Bhonslas in Nagpûr, Holkars in Indore, Scindhiyas in Gawalior and Gaikwads in Baroda. The five-power unity came to end after the third battle of Panipat. In this war, the unhappy people, because of their (the Marathas) plundring and exploitatioin, did not favour them. After the death of thousands of soldiers and ablset commanders, the Maratha confederacy grew many dissensions among the chiefs.

(6) Apotion of the Narrow Ideal of the Maratha Rule. Shivaji had thought of establishing Hindu rule. His treatment even of the Muslims was good, though he plundered Mughal territories. This idea of Hindu rule was substituted by that of the Marathas rule in the time of Peshwas. The result was that they began to ill- treat non-Marathas. They even lost the sympathies of the Rajputs and the Jats.

(7) Marathas not Good Diplomats. The Marathas were not good diplomats. The English, on the other hand, were masters in the art of diplomacy. The Marathas did not realise in time that their real rivals were the English. They co- operated with the English against Tipu Sultan in the Third Mysore War. It greatly weakened Tipu, the greatest foe of the English in the South. The Marathas resented the subsidiary alliance made by wellesley with the Nizam since it deprived them of their plundering preserve. Even then they did not help Tipu Sultan against the English in the Forth Mysore War. Even after that the English were able to keep the Marathas divided and defeated them one by one. Thus poor dilomacy of the Marathas contributed to their downfall.

(8) Role of the Britishers in Their Decline. The European powers and especially the Britishers Played an important role in the decline of the Marathas. After 1773, the Britihsers started paraticipating in the internal disputes of the Marathas. They fought with the Marathas four times. After the wars the Britishers captured many states of the Marathas as well as money and in this way, they helped in the decline of the Marathas Power.

(9) Neglect of the Sea-Power. The Marahtas too like the Mughals neglected the sea power. It is true that a fleet of ships alone could not have saved the Maratha from the dowfall of their power butn even then it could be of great help to them in facing the Englich to a considerable extent. The neglect of this sea- power brought their fall still nearer.

(10) Disaster of Panipat. Prior to 1761 the Maratha fame spread for and wide so much so that even the Mughal Emperor was in their hands (power). The saffron flag was flying over the fort of Attack and the dreams of a Hindu Empire had been realized but just at that time this Marathas empire received a fatal blow when Ahmad Shah Abdali, the ruler of Afghanistan gave them a crushing defeat in the third battle of Panipat. On the one hand, this defeat damaged the Maratha honour utterly and their hollowness was exposed to everyone, on the other hand, the Marathas and the Muslims rendered themselves so weak by their mutual fighting that the way for the rise of a third power,that is, the English was opened.

CHARACTER OF TIPU SULTAN

Tipu Sultan was son of Hyder Ali's the Sultan of Mysore. He himself remained the Sultan of Mysore from the year 1782 A.D., when his father died, to the year 1799 A.D. He was an able son of an able father. But some historians have pointed him as one, who was unjust, cruel and fanatic ruler. For example Kirkpatrick says.- "He (Tipu) was the cruel and relentless enemy....... the opressive and unjust ruler and what not." But an objective study of history prove the falsity of the above charges. Many of the modern as well as the contemporary historians have testified that he was learned, tolerant and a man of high character. He knew Persian, Urdu and Telgu, besides other languages. He was the conscientious ruler who left no stone unturned in bringing prosperity to his people.

Tipu as a Ruler. Tipu Sultan ruled Mysore till his death in 1799. He was, for one, an innovator. His desire to change with the times was symbolised in the introduction of a new calendar, a new system of coinage and new scales of weights and measures. His personal library contained books on such diverse subjects as religion, history, military science, medicine and mathemetics. He showed a keen interest in the French Revolution. He planted a 'Tree of Liberty' at Sringapatam and became a member of a Jacobin Club. His organisational capacity is borne out by the fact that in those days of general indiscipline among Indian armies his troops remained disciplined and loyal to him to the last. He tried to do away with the custom of giving jagirs, and thus increase state income. He also made an attempt to reduce the hereditary possessions of the poligars. However his land revenue was as high as that of other contemporary rulers=it charged up to 1/3rd of the gross produce. But he checked the collection of illegal cesses, and he was liberal in granting remissions.

Love for the Country. Tipu had a great and deep love for his country. He never joined a foreign power or the Britishers against any Indian ruler. He adopted the policy of struggle for ousting the Britishers from India. Though he was unsuccessful in his task, he was very much influenced by the revolutionary ideas, their love for freedom and nationalism of French.

Tipu as an Able Army Organiser. Tipu Sultan had the capacity to organise his army well. His army was organised on western style. They were always equipped with guns and arms. He manufactured weapons in large numbers in Mysore. He also tried to organise his navy well. The main proof of his organisational ability was that during that period when indiscipline in the army of almost all the states of India was an ordinary thing, his soldiers remained discipleined and loyal to the last. He prepared himself the models for the shape of the ship. He was an able commander.

Far Sighted Politicians. He showed keen interest in the French Revolution and planted the 'Tree of Liberty' at Sringapatam. He understood the danger because of the British interference in the

Indian politics. He sent his men to other countries (Afghanistan, Arabia, Turkey and France) to seek help against the British. He tried to make the best use of the war going on between the British and French. Perhaps due to this very reason the French general Napolean had come upto Egypt.

A Man of High Character. He was a man of very high character. He was free from all vices in his personal life and was miles away from the lavish life. He was far head of his contemporaries from this point of view.

A Great Economist. Though not free from contemporary economic backwardness, Mysore flourished economically under Tipu, especially when seen in contrast with its immediate past or with the rest of the country. When the British occupied Mysore after defeating and killing Tipu in 1799, they were completely surprised to find that the Mysore preasant was much more prosperous than Madras, Sir Johan Shore, Governor General from 1793 to 1798, wrote later that "the peasantry of his dominions are protected and their labour encouraged and rewarded." Tipu also seems to have grasped the importance of modern trade and industrry. In fact, alone among the Indian rulers, he understood the importance of economic strength. He made some attempts to introduce modern industries in India by importing foreign worksmen as experts and extending state support to many industries. He sent ambassadors to France, Turkey, Iran and Pegu to develop foreign trade. He also trade with China. He even tried to set up a trading company on the pattern of European companies.

A Religious Man. Some British historians have described Tipu as a religous fanatic. But this is not borne out by facts. Though a staunch Muslim, he was not fanatic. His Shringeri letters testify that he had apponited Hindu on many high positioins and even contributed financially to the constructuion of the Hindu temples. In the words of Historrian Sen- " Tipu knew how to placate the Hindu opinion and religious intolerance was not the real causes of ruin."

ACHIEVEMENTS OF TIPU

(1) In the Industrial Sphere. Among the contemporary Indian rulers, Tipu Sultan was the first Sultan who tried for industrial progress after understanding the importance of economic power. He invited foriegn experts to India. He gave government help to many industries. He also tried to establish modern industries.

(2) In the Sphere of Trade. Tipu Sultan thought it necessasry to increase economic power for progress of trade as well as industries. He tried to establish a company for trade on European sryle. He sent his ambassadors to France, Turky, Pegu and Iran in order to develop trade with these countries.

(3) In the Administrative Sphere. Tipu Sultan tried his best to give good administration to his people. He made many reforms in land revenue and military sphere. He gave protection to the farmers and encouraged the workers.

Tipu Sultan's character had many qualities and he got achievement in many fields but he had a very bad quality in his character. He was very quick in every work. He attacked Travancore frequently. The English governor Cornwallis sent him the message from Madras that his attack on Travancore would be understood as an attack on the Britishers. War between the two again began in 1789 and ended in Tipu's defeat in 1792. Even though Tipu fought with exemplary bravery. Lord Conwallis, the then Governor-General had succeeded through shrewd diplomacy in isolating him by winning over the Marathas, the Nizam and the rulers of Travancose and Coorg. This war again revealed that the Indian powers were shortsighted enough to aid the foreigner against another Indian power for the sake of temporary advantages.

The Third Mysore war came to an end by the treaty of Seringapatam in March, 1792. Following were the main provisions of this treaty:

(a) Tipu had to surrender half of his dominion which were divided among the English, the Marathas and the Nizam.

(b) Moreover, Tipu had to pay £30,00,000 as war indeminity.

(c) Tipu had to agree to an independent state of Coorg which lates on came under the British protection.

(d) He had also to surrender, his two sons as hostages to the English.

Tipu Sultan had lost half of his territory as a result of Third Mysore War and was burning with revenge. He wanted to get back his territory and to achieve that object, was carrying on negotations with the French and Zanuan Shah of Kabul. Tipu wanted to have allies to expel the English. Wellasley was not prepared to tolerate this. After making Subsidiary Alliance with the Nizam, he asked Tipu Sultan to accept the same but he refused. This led to war. Mysore was attacked from two sides. The main army under general Harris supported by Nizam's subsidiary force under Arthur Wallesely attacked Mysore from the east, while another army advanced from Bombay. Tipu was at first defeated by the Bombay army and was later on defeated by the general Harris at Mallavalli. Then he was besieged in Seringapatam. He was offered peace on payment of £2,000,000 and surrender of half of his kingdom. He refused these harsh terms. He fell fighting and his capital was capured.

❐

4

Rise of Sikhs Power

The Sikhs were persecuted by the Mughals after the execution of Banda Bahadur. Later on another complicated factor was added to Punjab politics by the Afghan invasions of Ahmad Shah Abdali. The Sikhs organised themselves to meet this double danger of Mughal persecution and Afghan invasions. They organised themselves into small military bands, about sixty-five in number, which pooled their resources in times of danger under leaders like Nawab Kapur Singh and Jassa Singh Ahluwalia. The collective strength of these bands was called Dal Khalsa. It was completely organised in 1748. In course of time these were combined into a number of bigger units, about twelve in number which came to be called Misls. These held practically the whole of Punjab between 1767 A.D. and 1799 A.D. These Misls were not deliberately created but gradually developed to meet the exigencies of the time.

The word Misl in Arabic language means equal. These were so called because all of these, irrespective of their size and strength, were considered equal. Moreover, in Sikhs religion all Sikhs are equal. Hence all members of a Misl considered themselves equal to one another including the Chief.

The twelve Sikh Misls were Singhpuria (Faizalpuria), Ahluwalia, Ramgarhia Bhangi, Kanheyia, Sukarchakyia, Phulkian, Dullewalia, Nakkais, Shahids, Karorsinghia (Panjgarhia) and Nishanwalia.

HISTORY OF MISLS

1. Singhpuria of Faizalpuria Misl. This Misl was founded by Kapur Singh, the son of a Jat Peasant. He was held in great esteem by the Sikhs and was practicaly their leader in religious and political affiairs from 1734 to 1748. He was a great warrior and had participated in many battles. At the same time, he was a great devotee of Guru Nanak and converted many people. The Mughals tried to conciliate him and gave him the title of Nawab but still he continued to fight for freedom. He was the organiser of Dal Khalsa. He gave its control to his Deputy, Jassa Singh Ahluwalia, in 1748.

Kapur Singh died in 1753 and was succeeded by his nephew, Khushal Singh. He was also a great warrior and extended the territories of the Misl. He was succeeded by his eldest son, Budh Singh, in 1796. Ranjit Singh annexed the territories of this Misls west of the Sutlej River in 1816.

2. Ahluwalia Misl. This Misl was founded by Jassa Singh Ahluwalia, who belonged to the low caste of Kalals. He was born in 1718 and lost his father at the age of five. He was brought up by his mother and she secured for him the blessing of Mata Sundri Nawab Kapur Singh took him under his charge at an early age.

Jassa Singh came into prominence after the invasion of Nadir Shah and began to lead Sikh bands. In 1747 he plundered Kasur. This was, followed by the looting of Jullundur Doab. Nawab Kapur Singh was growing old and he appointed Jassa Singh as the leader of Dal Khalsa. Kapur Singh died in 1753 and Jassa Singh became the real leader of the Sikhs.

Jassa Singh fought against the Afghans in many battles. Khwaja Obed, the Afghan Faujdar of Lahore, attacked Gujranwala which was held by Charat Singh, but Jassa Singh joined Charat Singh and drove back Khwaja obed. In 1761 Jassa Singh even occupied Lahore and issued coins. In 1762 Ahmad Shah inflicted a crushing defeat on the Sikhs under Jassa Singh at Kup. The Sikhs suffered terrible losses and it is known as Ghallughara. The Sikhs under Jassa Singh recovered very soon. They defeated and killed the Afghan Faujdar of Sarhind, Zain Khan.

Ahmad Shah Abdali did not attack Punjab after 1767. Jassa Singh took advantage of it and extended his power. He captured

Rajkot and Kapurthala from the Muslims. He joined the coalition formed by Bhangis. Kanheyias and Sukurchakiyas. The allies captured Ramgarhia territories. Jassa Singh was a brave and tolerant ruler. He died in 1783 and was succeeded by his cousin Bhagh Singh. In 1801 he died and was succeeded by his son Fathe Singh Ahluwalia. The new ruler was a great warrior and even Ranjit Singh exchanged trubans with him.

3. Bhangi Misl. It was founded by Hari Singh, a Dhillon Jat of Hung. He was addicted to bhang and this Misl came to be called Bhangi Misl. It was the strongest Misl and included in its territories the two biggest cities of the Punjab, Lahore and Amritsar. He extended his territories up to Pakpattan. Amritsar was the headquarters of Bhangi Misl. He had a large army of about 15,000 and his revenue was about 15 lacs of rupees. He was killed in a battle in 1770 A.D. The next ruler was Jhanda Singh. He forced the ruler of Jammu to pay tributes. He also forced the Chief of Kasur to pay tribute. The Faujdar of Sarhind was also defeated. He was assassinated by a hired assassin of Jai Singh Kanheiya. He was succeeded by his brother, Ganda Singh.

4. Kanheyia Misl. It was founded by Jai Singh. It included the territories of Hajipur, Mukerian, Pathankot and Gurdaspur. He fought against the Bhangi Chief, Jhanda Singh and Jassa Singh Ramgarhia. Thus he increased his territories. After this he conqured Kangra. In alliance with Jassa Singh Ahluwalia and Tara Singh Gheba, he plundered Kasur.

Jai Singh married his grand daughter (Mehtab Kaur) to Ranjit Singh, son a Sukurchakia chief, Mahan Singh. After the death of Jai Singh affairs of Kahneyia Misl were controlled by Mai Sada Kaur. After consolidating his position, Ranjit Singh annexed Kanheiya Misl territories.

5. Ramgarhia Misl. Its founder was Jassa Singh Ramgarhia. He was the son of a carpenter. He took to fighting career and became famous as a great warrior. In 1734 Zakriya Khan, the Governor of Lahore, stopped persecution of the Sikhs for some time and tried to win over Sikhs in a peaceful manner. He took Jassa Singh Ramgarhia into service and gave him five villages as Jagir. Later on he joined Adina Beg. When Mir Manu and Abina Beg besieged the Sikhs in the fortress of Ram Rauni, he changed sides and joined the besieged.

Jassa Singh Ramgarhia, with the help of Amar Singh Phulkian, became the master of some territory near Sirsa in Hissar. He plundered the territories upto Delhi. He made the Muslim Chief of Meerut pay heavy tribute. He punished the Muslim governor of Hissar who had maltreated two Hindu girls.

Jassa Singh Ahluwalia died in 1783. Taking advantage of that Jassa Singh Ramgarhia came back and recovered all the lost territories. His Misl included Kalanpur. Qadian, Ghuman etc. He made alliance with the Bhangi Chief, Gulab Singh, to check the rising power of Ranjit Singh but was defeated at Bhasin. He died in 1803 and was succeeded by his son, Jodh Singh. Ranjit Singh maintained friendly relations with him. Jodh Singh died in 1814 and then Ranjit Singh annexed Ramgarhia territories.

6. Sukurchakiya Misl. It was founded by Charat Singh. He carved out a small principality between the Ravi and the Chenab rivers. He captured Eminabad and Sialkot. He made Gujranwala his headquarters. Khwaja Obed, Ahmed Shah's Faujdar of Lahore, marched against him but was defeated. When Ahmad Shah attacked Punjab in 1762 (6th invasion). Charat Singh harassed him a good deali. After Ahmad Shah's return, he plundered Wazirabad and the territory as far as Rohtas. In 1774 he marched against Jammu but was accidentally killed.

Charat Singh was succeeded by his son, Mahan Singh. He was a minor and the affairs for the next six years were controlled by his mother, Mai Desan. In 1780 he became a major and took power in his own hands. He was also a great warrior. He conquered Rasulnagar and Alipur which came to be called Ramnagar and Akalgarh. He plundered the territory of Jammu. Jai Singh Kanheyia became jealous of his rising power. Mahan Singh got help from Jassa Singh Ramgarhia and they defeated Jai Singh. Peace was made and Jai Singh married his grand-daughter, Mahtab Kaur, to Ranjit Singh. Mahan Singh died in 1793 and was succeeded by his son, Ranjit Singh.

7. Phulkian Misl. The founder of Phulkian Misl was Ala Singh. Taking advantage of the confusion about the middle of 18th century, he greatly increased his territories. His headquarters was Barnala. In 1762 Ahmed Shah appointed him his deputy in Malwa for a heavy annual tribute. In 1764 he joined Sikh Sardars who defeated and killed Zain Khan, Ahmad Shah's Faujdar of Sarhind. He was a deeply religious man.

In 1765 Ala Singh was succeeded by his grandson, Amar Singh. In his time Patiala became the strongest State in Malwa. He annexed Kot Kapura, Saifabad, Bhatinda, Hansi, Hissar and Rohtak.

Amar Singh was succeeded by his seven-year old minor son, Sahib Singh. He was a weak ruler and Patiala was attacked by the Marathas. His sister Sahib Kaur drove them away. Taking advantage of the quarrel between Sahib Singh and his queen Aus Kaur. Ranjit Singh attacked Malwa territory. The rulers of Malwa region appealed to the English for protection. By the treaty of Amritsar of 1809, the Sutlej River became the boundary line between the territories of the Company and Maharaja Ranjit Singh.

8. Karor Singhia Misl. It was also called Panjgarhia Misl and was founded by Bhagat Singh. Its territories-were absorbed either by the rulers of Kalsia State or by Ranjit Singh.

9. Dallewalia Misl. It was founded by Gulab Singh. The most important Chief produced by this Misl was Tara Singh Gheba. He was a great warrior and had participated in the Sikh attacks on Sarhind and Kasur. After his death the territories of the Misl were annexed by Ranjit Singh.

10. Nishanwalia Misl. It was not a powerful Misl. It was founded by Sangat Singh and Mohar Singh, who had been the standard-bears of Dal Khalsa. They possessed Ambala and Shahbad. When Malwa passed under the protection of the Company, the English took away Ambala and Shahbad became and dependant State.

11. Shahidi Misl. It was founded by Baba Dip Singh. After him Karam Singh and Gurbaksh Singh were its chiefs. Their followers were Akalis and had territory to the east of the Sutlej.

12. Nakai Misl. Its founder was Hira Singh and his territory lay between Lahore and Multan. Its most important Chief was Ram Singh. The Misl became weak after his death and its territories were annexed by Ranjit Singh.

In this way we find that there was no strong kingdom in the Punjab in the second half of the eighteenth century. The Sikh Sardars or the Chiefs of Misls were often fighting against each other, though they often cambined to face the Afghan invasions. This made it easy for Ranjit Singh to establish his kingdom.

CAUSES OF THE RISE AND FALL OF THE SIKH POWER

Whereas it was all anarchy and chaos in the Punjab during the Misl rule before him, it was Ranjit Singh who, by virtue of his statesmanship and industry, had established a strong Sikh Kingdom in the Punjab. But, though outwardly, this Kingdom seemed great and wide, yet internally its weaknesses were eating into it like a worm in the wood. But the greatest pity is that this Kingdom vanished within a period of ten years of its founder Ranjit Singh's death, whereas in view of its vitality ana strength, it should logically have continued on strongly and efficiently for a long time even after his death. It is strange that the Punjab state fell like a ripe fruit into the lap of the British Government within a very short time after Ranjit Singh's death. Hence it is necessary to discuss the causes which brought about its speedy end. The Sikh state collapsed due to the following:

1. Ranjit Singh had concentrated all the powers of the state in his own hands. He was the source and centre of all the power of the state. He was the pivot of the governmental administrative machinery which revolved round his person. His word was law. As a matter of fact it was one man's show. There is no denying the fact that he was a benevolent despot who considered the welfare of his subjects as his

paramount duty, but he had concentrated all the powers in his own hands without allowing anybody else to share them. Though he had set up a Council of Ministers to get their advice on the matter of administration of the state, yet he seldom consulted them. It all depended upon his whether to consult the Council of Ministers or not. In short, the whole of the administration of the Punjab state depended upon one head, which was really a difficult task to carry on for an unlimited amount of time. He should have realized the importance of decentralization of powers and, as such, he should have also kept in view the incapability of a single one, as he was, to carry on the administration of such a vast empire single-handed.

2. Ranjit Singh's government was a military government. We know that a big state was created out of the combination of disjointed atoms. For this he had to pass the whole of his life in constant warfare. Hence he could not devote much of his time towards the improvement of his civil administration and the consolidation of his Kingdom, both of which consequently remained in a hopless and in an imperfect condition. Even in civil administration, Ranjit Singh devoted more attention towards the revenue and finacial aspects. He gave to the country neither any sound constitution, nor established any regular institutions which would have given efficiency and stability to his system of administration. He must have realized that his administration was imperfect, and, as such, an incomplete system of administration could endure only during his life-time under his strong thumb. This came out to be true. The moment the Maharaja. slept the sleep of death, his administration collapsed at once. It is to be noted here that there was no systematic arrangement for the maintenance of government records in the early days of his rule and whatever departments were established by him were established only in the closing years of his rule, when the civil and military departments were enstrusted to his officers.

3. One of the most significant features fo Ranjit Singh's Court was its cosmopolitan character. But this proved its weakness also. His Court consisted of the people of various nationalities and they were employed on the basis of merit. But the presence of people of diverse elements was also a weakness in itself and this ultimately resulted in the collapse of the Kingdom. The reason is obvious to explain. By the presence of people of different nationalities in the Court, the Court lost all unity, cohesion and oneness of prupose which are a source of strength to an empire. As long as the Maharaja himself remained alive at the helm of affairs in the Court, all these variegated elements dared not raise their heads, but the moment he closed his eyes in death, all these self-seeking parties, with a view to gaining their own selfish ends, stood up in the Court ready to sacrifice the larger interests of the state at the altar of their own sordid interests. On the death of the Maharaja, the three selfish parties that arose were: *(a)* the Sindhanwalia party, *(b)* the Dogra party, and *(c)* the Court party. The motives of each of these parties were their own self-preservation more than the preservation of the Sikh state. Even during the life-time of the Maharaja these parties were sharply divided against each other in cliques based on personal animosities and jealousies, as a result of which each of them looked at the other with feelings of enmity and harted, but they were helpless before the domineering personality of the Maharaja. After the death of the Maharaja, the hidden hatred became open against each other. Accordingly, the mutual hatred towards the Dogra party, Sindhanwalia party and the Court party together with their hatred towards the British Government began to show its results and in an instant the Lahore Court became the scene of those diabolical intrigues, revolts and murders which at once sapped the energy of the State and brought about its speedy fall. The successors of the Maharaja were too incompetent to arrest the disintegrating forces that had been let loose by these parties in the Court, much less to control these parties.

4. The most serious blunder committed by the Maharaja was the grant of too much of ascendancy in his Court to the Dogra party which consisted of Rajas Dhian Singh, Gulab Singh, Suchet Singh and Hera Singh, the son of Raja Dhian Singh. They had created for themselves so much of political influence in Ranjit Singh's Court that they had become practically all in all there. By virtue of their close proximity to the royal house, they had become conversant with the weaknesses of the royal house and the rulers, and, as such, wanted to take full advantage of the knowledge of these weaknesses, so much so that they had secretly decided to divide the Sikh Kingdom between the two brothers. According to General Gardener, "both the Jammu brothers, Rajas Dhian Singh and Gulab Singh, were determined to set up their independent Dogra state in Jammu and Kashmir." This view has been collaborated by General Charles Gough also says that they had decided upon the partition of the Sikh Empire between themselves, Jammu-Kashmir and North-western region of the Punjab going to Raja Gulab Singh, while the entire Southern Punjab with Lahore as its capital going to Raja Dhian Singh. With a view to materializing their this policy, it was necessary for them to lay their hands, after Ranjit Singh's death, on the lives of the princes of the royal family one after the other in quick succession. Accordingly, because of their presence in the Sikh Court, they started a network of mean intrigues and created strong obstruction in the smooth running of the administration. They soon murdered many princes of the royal blood and got finished many great nobles of the Court. In short, whatever amount of anarchy and chaos spread in the Punjab after the death of Ranjit Singh, a lion's share in creating it was that of the Dogra party. They acted as traitors to the Sikh state and became an effective instrument in its downfall. Hence much of the responsibility for the downfall of the Sikh Empire falls on the Dogra party.

5. During his life time, Ranjit Singh created such a strong army that the parallel of which was nowhere in existence with any local power in India at the time. The ability to keep such a strong army under him was in the possession only of Ranjit Singh and of nobody else. After Ranjit Singh's death, the Khalsa Army gradually began to assert its independence from the Central Government. The weak successors of Ranjit Singh could not keep it under their control. Moreover, most of the faithful and patriotic generals like Hari Singh Nalwa, Diwan Mohkan Chand, Misser Diwan Chand, Diwan Ram Dayal. etc. had died one after the other, and now there were no such faithful and patriotic generals in the army who would have controlled this army and thus had saved the Sikh Kingdom from its collapse. The weak successors of the Maharaja also could not control this strong Khalsa Army. The result of its strength was that the Khalsa Army began to dream of complete independence from the Central Government and, as such, it assumed the form of a turbulent body of soldiers. After Ranjit Singh's death, whatever generals were left, they were either weak or traitors. They were the real leaders of the Khalsa Army at this time. Now the Khalsa Army had become so uncontrollable that it decided to wield political control in the state now. Consequently, it became a "king-maker", elevating to throne anybody they liked and deposing or murdering any prince they liked, according to their sweet choice. The same policy they adopted towards the ministers of the state also, making and unmaking ministers according to their sweet wishes. The Khalsa Army became so strong in the state after the execution of Sardar Jawahar Singh that none dared become the Prime Minister.

6. Maharja Ranjit Singh proved no exception to this fact. Amongst the successors of Ranjit Singh, both Maharajas Kharak Singh and Sher Singh were incompetent. Both of them indulged themselves in the pleasures and comforts of life and entrusted the affairs of the state to their traitor and

faithless ministers. On the other hand, Kanwar Nau-Nihal Singh got no opportunity to show his work and worth as a ruler. Maharja Daleep Singh, who was elevated to the throne in 1843, was only a minor. The result of the incompetence of Ranjit Singh's successors was that they could neither control the turbulent Khalsa Army nor could they control the Central Court which infortunately consisted of elements of various types. Ranjit Singh had concentrated all the state powers in his own hands and had not given to his successors a proper training in politics, which was so very necessary for their becoming competent rulers. Hence, because of their inexperience in the art of government, they could not carry on the administration of the country satisfactorily, rather they entrusted it to the care of their traitorious friends, who, in the their own turn, took advantage of the weakness of the Central Government and set on foot worst type of intrigues and anarchy in the court. This anarchy and confusion put an end to the Sikh state very soon. Moreover, whenever Ranjit Singh sent military expeditions he would issue so minute instructions to the generals on the spot regarding military operations that they could not act according to their own initiative and according to the circumstances of the time on the spot. This kept them inexperienced both in the civil and military administration of the state. Hence they developed no self-confidence in their own ability and efficiency.

7. The most potent cause of the downfall of the Sikh Kingdom was the annexation policy and the gradual encirclement policy of the Punjab by the British Government. Whatever measures the British Government adopted towards the Punjab right from the time of Ranjit Singh up to its annexation in 1849 explain the facts that the British Government was determined on the annexation of the Punjab partly on account of commercial reasons and partly on account of political reasons. The British Government

never wished to see the establishment of so strong, united and independent Sikh state in their close proximity as would foil the attempts of the British Government to annex it. It is for this reason that the British Government setting aside the existing promises with Ranjit Singh, put in their best efforts to lay their hands on his Kingdom and at last they succeeded in their attempts. They concluded the treaty of Amritsår with Ranjit Singh in 1809, but whereas the Maharaja always remained faithful to his treaty in letter and spirit, the British cared little for it and broke it so many times. They encircled the Sikh Kingdom by the construction of the forts and contonments all round it. They bowed Ranjit Singh down on the questions of Ludhiana, the Cis-Sutlej territory, Ferozepore, Shikarpur and Sindh. they completed the Punjab's encirclement and began to look forward to some opportunity for its annexation at some convenient time. On the other hand, the Maharaja showd a different attitude towards the British Government. He yielded before them on every occasion. The fact is that the Maharaja was conscious of his weakness against the British Government and he was convinced of the fact that the British Government would be successful in swallowing up the Punjab one day or the other. Hence it was this consciousness of his weakness that forced him to avert war with the British Government every time. Under these circumstances, it is easy for us to conclude that in the policy of postponing war with the British Government Ranjit Singh committed a great political blunder.

8. The First and the Second Anglo-Sikh Wars broke the very backbone of the Sikhs and cleared the way for the annexation of the Punjab by the Britishers. This can be said with the least doubt that had the Sikh generals not proved traitors in the battles, the Sikhs would never have got defeated in the First Anglo-Sikh War. Mr. Sinha says in this connection that "the Sikhs were defeated in the battles of Sabroan and

Ferozeshah through the treachery of their generals and in the battles of Gujrat and Chillianwala, they got defeated through the incompetency of their generals. The Khalsa Army was in no way inferior to the British army in points of bravery and war tactics. After the conclusion of the First Anglo-Sikh War, the British Government did not annex the Punjab because they were conscious of the strength of the Sikhs, otherwise they would have found themselves involved in serious complications on account of its annexation at that time. They annexed it only after the termination of the Second Anglo-Sikh War, and Maharaja Daleep Singh was pensioned off and the Khalsa Army was disbanded. Their defeat in the Second Sikh War had broken their backbone.

It was the work only of Maharaja Ranjit Singh to unite and transform into a powerful Sikh Kingdom the twelve Misls which were always at war with one another and which presented very great difficulties in the way of the establishment of a great kingdom in the Punjab. To him alone goes the credit of such a great achievement. It was this man who saved India's honour by permanently checking all the invasions on India from the North-west corner of India. The Maharaja had tried to establish a national government in the Punjab with himself as its head, broadbased upon the willing consent of all the sections and people without any distinction of caste, creed and colour. Though his administrative setup was not so complete and so exemplary, yet he gave a solid proof of his statesmanship and his natural efficiency by establishing a liberal and strong kingdom in the Punjab. Yet he gave law and order to his state and created a strong state out of nothingness. For all these brilliant achievements, the Maharaja deserves all praise. It is for this reason that India in general and the Punjab in particular feel proud of him. But according to the maxim "whosoever rises must after all fall" the Maharaja's Kingdom also had a downfall. But for this Ranjit Singh personally was also responsible to a great extent.

CAUSES OF THE FIRST SIKH WAR

Following are the causes of First Sikh War:

(1) Policy of Encirclement. The British had been following a policy of encirclement since 1830. The Sikhs had occupied Shikarpur and the British had forced Maharaja to withdraw his troops from there. The Amirs of Sind were forced to have a British Resident at Hyderabad in 1838.

The British were following the policy of encirclement from Punjab side also. They occupied Ferozepore in 1835 and established a cantonment in 1838. The Sikhs felt that this policy of encirlcement was being followed by the British with the ultimate idea of conquering Punjab.

(2) Annexation of Sind (1843). The British had annexed Sind in 1843. The Sikhs began to fear that their next target would be Punjab itself. Even strategic considerations would induce them to attempt its conquest, because Sind could not be effectively controlled without the occupation of the Punjab. The Sikhs began to fear the designs of the British all the more after the annexation of Sind.

(3) Military Preparations. The British thought of taking advantage of anarchy in the Punjab after the death of Ranjit Singh and began to increase the strength of their forces near the River Sutlej. They increased the number of their forces from 2,500 in 1836 to 14,000 in 1843. They began to prepare boats at Bombay which could be used for military pontoon bridges across the Sutlej.

(4) The British Wanted to Recover Prestige. The British had suffered setbacks in the First Afghan War, though they had recovered their position later. The spell of their invincibility had been shattered. They wanted to re-established their military prestige. The conquest of Punjab could serve the desired purpose. The task had become easier in view of the fact that their troops and their convoys had passed through Punjab during the First Afghan War, and they had become familiar with the geography of the Punjab.

(5) Appointment of Broadfoot at Ludhiana. Clark was succeeded by Major Broadfoot as the British Resident at Ludhiana. He was a hot-headed man and declared that the territories of the Sikhs on the left bank of the Sutlej were under the protction of the Company. the Sikhs were irritated and felt that war with the British was inevitable.

(6) Anarchy in the Punjab and the Policy of Sikh Durbar. There was anarchy in the Punjab after the death of Maharaja Ranjit Singh in 1839. He was succeeded by his son, Kharak Singh. He died in 1840 and was succeeded by his son, Kharak Singh. He died in 1840 and was succeeded by his son, Nau Nihal Singh. He was crushed as a result of the fall of a gateway of Lahore fort within five days. There was some difficulty regarding succession to the throne and ultimately it was decided that Mai Chand Kaur (widow of Kharak Singh) should become the regent for the expected son of Nau Nihal Singh. Sher Singh, another son of Ranjit Singh, got the throne with the help of the Khalsa army and got Chand Kaur murdered. Wazir Dhian Singh also met the same fate. It was during the time of Sher Singh that the British troops and convoys were permitted to pass through Punjab to Afghanistan. Sher Singh was shot in 1843 by Ajit Singh, one of the supporters of late Mai Chand Kaur. Dalip singh, youngest son of Ranjit Singh then became the ruler and his mother Rani Jindan was appointed guardian. Lal Singh and Teja Singh became ministers. The Khalsa army had become very powerful and Lahore Durbar feared it. The Sikh sardars incited it against the English. They thought that the victory of Khalsa army would mean expansion of territory and its attention would be diverted from politics. In case of defeat, its strength would be reduced and it would become less dangerous. The Khalsa army, encouraged by Lahore Durbar, crossed the River Sutlej near Kasur, Thereupon. Lord Hardinge declared war and proclaimed the annexation of Sikh territories on the left bank of the Sutlej.

EVENTS

(1) Battle of Mudki. The Khalsa army threatend Ferozepore and the British forces under Hugh Gough advanced from Ludhiana to save Ferozepore. They unexpectedly came in contact with the Sikh army at night after a march of about 20 miles. The battle was fought at Mudki. Teja Singh left the Sikh forces at a critical time and the English were victorious.

(2) Battle of Aliwal. A Sikh army under Ranjit Singh Majithia crossed the Sutlej and dashed towards Ludhiana. The English suffered a setback in a skirmish at Buddewal but soon they got reinforcements and defeated the Sikh army in the battle of Aliwal. The Sikhs fled across the Sutlej and many of them were drowned.

(3) Battle of Ferozeshah. The division of Sir John Litter joined Sir Hugh Gough and a terrible battle was fought at Ferozeshah. The British Commander-in-chief, Sir Hugh Gough said, "During that night we were in a critical and perilous state." The Sikhs were again defeated due to the treachery of their commanders.

(4) Battle of Subraon. Another Sikh army crossed the Sutlej under Teja Singh and constructed a bridge of boats to retreat in case of defeat. The Sikh commanders, with the exception of Sham Singh Atariwala, did not properly lead the Sikhs. Cuningham has rightly remarked. "Hearts to dare and hands to execute were numerous, but there was no mind to guide and animate the whole." The Sikhs were defeated and the bridge of boats collapsed as they were retreating. Many of them were drowned and many more shot dead by the British forces.

TREATY OF LAHORE (1846)

The war came to an end by the Treaty of Lahore which was signed on 9th Murch, 1846. Its terms were:

(1) The English were given all the territory lying between the Sutlej and the Beas rivers.

(2) Lahore Durbar was to pay an indemnity of one and a half crores of rupees. The Sikhs had only fifty lakhs of ruppees. They gave the State of Jammu and Kashmir to Maharaja Gulab Singh for one crore of rupees.

(3) The Maharaja renounced all claims to the Sikh territories on the left bank of the River Sutlej.

(4) A limit was placed on Khalsa army. It was not to exceed 22,000 infantry and 12,000 cavalry. The Sikhs had to surrender all the guns used by them against the English.

(5) The Lahore government was not to employ any European without the consent of the English.

(6) The British troops were to be given passage through the Punjab whenever required.

(7) A British force was to remain at Lahore till the end of the year. Henry Lawrence was appointed Resident at Lahore.

Things did not work smoothly after the Treaty of Lahore. Lal Singh and other Sikh leaders were opposed to the handing over of Jammu and Kashmir to Gulab Singh. They encouraged its Muslim Governor, Shaeik Imam-ud-din, to rise against Gulab Singh. The relvolt was put down by the British forces. Lal Singh was removed from ministership and deported to Banaras. Thus Gulab Singh got the State of Jammu and Kashmir.

TREATY OF BHAIROWAL (1846)

The Sikh Durbar feard that there would be anarchy again after the withdrawal of British troops. In this connection Lord Hardinge wrote a letter saying. "The coyness of the Durbar is very natural. But is very important that the proposals should originate with them and in any document proceeding from them this admission must be stated in clear and unqualified terms. Our reluctance to undertake a heavy responsibility cannot be set forth." Hence it made the treaty of Bhairowal with the British Government in December, 1846. Its clauses were:

(1) A council consisting of 8 pro-British Sikh chiefs was the administer the affairs of Lahore kingdom during the minority of Dalip Singh. It was to act under the advice of the British Resident.

(2) A British force was to be kept at Lahore and the Sikh Government was to pay Rs. 22 lacs a year for its expenses.

The arrangement was to continue till 1854 when Maharaja Dalip Singh was to become major.

The treaty made the English virtually masters of the Punjab. Criticising the Treaty Mahajan says. "In Bhairowal Treaty the duplicity practised by the British Government in India registered another great triumph since the anxious desire of the Governor-General was adroitly manouvred to have the apperance of a request emanating from the leading Sirdars of the realm."

REASONS FOR NOT ANNEXING PUNJAB

Lord Hardinge did not annex Punjab due to four reasons:

(1) The existence of a Hindu State between Afghanistan and British India would have been advantageous to the Company.

(2) A lot of money was required for spending on the newlyacquired province.

(3) Lord Hardinge doubted the strength of English to occupy and keep under control the whole of Punjab at this stage.

(4) The English had some regard for the memory of Maharaja Ranjit Singh who had been faithful throughout.

❐

5

Rise of Ranjit Singh

Ranjit Singh was born at Gujranwala in 1780. He was the son of Mahan Singh and grandson of Charat Singh of Sukarchakia Misl. His mother, Raj Kaur, was the daughter of the Chief of Jind. She was popularly known as Mai Malwin, since she belonged to Malwa region of the Punjab. Ranjit Singh remained illiterate. He spent his time in hunting and indulge in every kind of excess. He was betrothed at the age of six to Mahtab Kaur, grand-daughter of Jai Singh of Kanheiya Misl. He had a several attack of smallpox which left marks on his face and resulted in the loss of the left eye. He started accompanying his father to the battle-fields at the age of ten.

Mahan Singh died in 1792 and Ranjit Singh became the ruler at the age of twelve. The affairs were controlled by his mother and her favourite. Diwan Lakhpat Rai. In 1796 he was married to Mahtab Kaur and his mother-in-law, Sada Kaur, also began to take part in managing the affairs. Ranjit Singh ended the influence of all the three in 1797 and took power in his own hands. Burnes calls him "A despot without cruelty."

The time now was favourable for Ranjit Singh to expand his territory. Many of the Sikh Misls had become weak. The English had not even acquired Delhi at that time. The Afghans were about to be weakened by internal troubles. Ranjit Singh's conquests can be divided into two.

A. Conquests of Consolidation

(1) Conquest of Lahore 1799. Lahore was held by the Chiefs of Bhangi Misl. In 1798 it was captured by Zaman Shah of Kabul but he had to go back to Afghanistan due to internal troubles and Lahore was reoccupied by the Bhangi Chiefs. Zaman Shah on his way back lost some guns in the River Jhelum due to sudden floods. Ranjit Singh got those guns taken out of the river and sent those to Zaman Shah. Zaman Shah was much pleased. He sent a Khilat to Ranjit Singh and made him the governor of the Punjab. He permitted Ranjit Singh to occupy Lahore. Ranjit Singh with the help of his mother-in-law captured Lahore in 1799. He was welcomed by the people who were sick of the misrule of the Bhangis.

(2) Battle of Bhasin (1800). The rising power of Ranjit Singh was an eyesore to the neighbouring Chiefs. A confederacy consisting of Gulab Singh Bhangi of Amritsar, Sahib Singh Bhangi of Gujrat, Jodh Singh of Wazirabad, Jassa Singh Ramgarhia and the Pathan Chief, Nizam-ud-Din, of Kasur was formed. Ranjit Singh got help from his mother-in-law. The confederates due to internal differences could not take timely action. Their leader Gulab Singh died and they were dispersed in the irregular fight of Bhasin. It greatly raised the prestige of Ranjit Singh.

(3) Conquest of Akalgarh and Gujrat. Sahib Singh Bhangi had fought against Ranjit Singh at Bhasin and now his territory was attacked. He received help from Dul Singh of Akalgarh. Ranjit Singh defeated them and captured Akalgarh in 1803. Gujrat was finally annexed in 1809.

(4) Capture of Amritsar. In 1805 Ranjit Singh captured Amritsar from the widow of Gulab Singh of Bhangi Misl. It became his religious capital.

(5) Coquest of Dallewalia Misl. Tara Singh Gheba died in 1807. Ranjit Singh attacked his territory soon after his death. His widow fought but was defeated at Rahon in 1807 and the territory of this Misl was annexed.

(6) End of Karor-Singhia Misl. Ranjit Singh attacked Bhagat Singh of Karor-Singhia Misl in 1810 and annexed his territory.

(7) Conquest of Faizalpuria Misl. Faizalpuria Misl had territories on both sides of the Sutlej river. Ranjit Singh asked their

Chief, Budh Singh, To submit and, on his refusal to do so, annexed his territories on the right bank of the Sutlej in 1811.

Expeditions Into Malwa. Ranjit Singh wanted to be the ruler of all the Sikhs and to achieve that object he wanted to bring the territory of Malwa under control. The greater part of this territory was held by the Chiefs of the Phulkian Misl. The most important States of this region were Patiala, Nabha and Jind.

(1) First Expedition (1806). There was a dispute between the rulers of Patiala and Nabha for the small town of Doladhi. The rulers of Nabha and Jind sought the help of Ranjit Singh. He was already on the look out for such an opportunity and in 1806 he crossed the Sutlej with 20,000 troops. Ranjit Singh captured Doladhi and forced Sahib Singh to pay heavy tribute. On his way back he conquered Ludhiana, Raikot and Jagraon. These places were not annexed but given to friendly chiefs (Fathe Singh Ahluwalia and Gurdit Singh) who had accompanied him.

(2) Second Expedition (1807). There was querrel between Sahib Singh of Patiala and his queen, Aus Kaur. She invited Ranjit Singh. He crossed the Sutlej a second time in 1807. After settling the dispute he forced the rulers of Ambala, Kaithal, Kalsia and other chiefs of the region to pay tribute. He occupied Wadni, Zira and Kot Kapura.

(3) Treaty of Amritsar (1809). The second expedition alarmed the Chiefs of Malwa and they approached Mr. Seton, the British Resident at Delhi, for protection. He was not prepared to make a definite commitment as he had instructions to follow the policy of non-interference. The Sikhs were thus frustrated and most of them accepted Ranjit Singh as their overlord. The British soon decided to check the growing power of Ranjit Singh. Sir Charles Metcalf was sent and after a good deal of haggling, the Treaty of Amritsar was signed in 1809. The Sutlej River became the boundary line between the company's possession and the kingdom of Maharaja Ranjit Singh. Thus Ranjit Singh's idea of ruling over Malwa did not materialise and his ambition to become the sole leader of the entire

Khalsa nation remained unrealised. (The Treaty of Amritsar has been discussed in detail in the question on Anglo-Sikh Relations.)

B. Conquest of Imperialism

(1) Conquest of Kasur. Nizam-ud-Din of Kasur had joined the confederacy against Ranjit Singh, and afterwards had been forced to submit. He died in 1801 and was succeeded by his son Qutb-ud-Din. He tried to recover independence and made a secret treaty with Nawab Muzaffar Khan of Multan. Ranjit Singh sent an expedition and the Nawab surrendered after offering resistence. Kasur was annexed and its Nawab was given Mamdot by way of Jagir.

(2) Conquest of Jhang Chiniot. Ranjit Singh sent expeditions against Ahmad Khan of Jhang and Chiniot to exact tributes in 1803 and 1805. The latter made a secret alliance with Nawab Muzaffar Khan in 1807. Ranjit Singh sent an army against Jhang. Ahmad Khan was defeated and his possessions were annexed in 1807.

(3) Conquest of Kangra. Kangra was the most powerful of the hill States at this time and was ruled by Sansar Chand Katoch. He tried to capture Hoshiarpur but was defeated by the Sikhs. Then he began to expand at the cost of neighbouring hill States. The Raja of Kahlur of Bilaspur sought the protection of Gurkhas of Nepal. They besieged Kangra. The Raja of Kangra (Sansar Chand) shught the help of Ranjit Singh even by agreecing to give the fort of Kangra. The Gurkhas withdrew on the approach of Sikh army and Ranjit Singh got the fort of Kangra in 1809. The whole State was annexed in 1829.

Conquest of Multan. Multan occupied a position of commercial and strategic importance. It was ruled by Nawab Muzaffar Khan, Ranjit Singh sent six expeditions:

Expeditions to Multan

(a) The first expedition was sent in 1802 and the Nawab agreed to pay tribute.

(b) The second expedition was sent in 1805. The Maharaja came within 20 miles of Multan but came on hearing that

Holkar, hotly pursued by General Lake, had come to the the Punjab.

(c) In 1807 Ranjit Singh came to know that Muzaffar Khan was carrying on intrigues with Ahmad Khan of Jhang and Qutab-ud-Din of Kasur. He marched to the vicinity of Multan but could not capture the fort. He exacted tribute and then returned.

(d) In 1810 Ranjit Singh sent Diwan Mohkam Chand to conquer Multan. The city of Multan was captured but the fort was bravely defended by the troops of the Nawab. The parties came to terms after two months. The Nawab agreed to pay tribute and to supply troops.

(e) In 1816 and 1817 Ranjit Singh again made an attack but the fort of Multan could not be captured.

(f) In 1818 a large army was sent under the command of Kharak Singh and Misl Diwan Chand. The fort of Multan was besieged. The Nawab and his forces put up a very stiff resistance. Muzaffar Khan and his eight sons fought bravely. He was killed with five of his sons and Multan was captured. Two sons of the late Nawab were given jagirs. This conquest greatly increased the prestige of Ranjit Singh and added to his resources.

Career and Achievements of Maharaja Ranjit Singh

Ranjit Singh was born at Gujranwala on 2 November, 1780 in the house of Mohan Singh the leader of the Sukal Chakiya Misl which controlled the territory between the Ravi and the Chenab. His father died when Ranjit Singh was a mere boy of 12. His military career started at the age of 16. Within a few years he made himself strong by annexing the neighbouring territories. Ranjit Singh was a man of ambition and stamina and the political situaion at that time was eminently suited for his rise. His aim was to bring all the Sikhs into a compact body under his own command. He wanted to establish an independent Sikh national kingdom under his own banner. Luckily for Ranjit Singh, the important misls were in a state of disintegration towards the close of the 18th century. The struggle for power politics also engulfed Afghanistan in a civil war from which the country did not recover for three decades. Ranjit Singh fully exploited the political situation to his advantage and by following a ruthless policy of 'blood and iron' carved out for himself a kingdom in the central Punjab.

In return for the services rendered to Zaman Shah Adbali during the latter's invasion of the Punjab (1798), the Afghan ruler authorised Ranjit Singh to occupy Lahore and rule it on behalf of the Sirdars from Lahore, which he occupied in 1799. The occupation of Lahore considerably enhanced the prestige of Ranjit Singh. In 1805 he made himself the master of Amritsar. By and by, he brought under his control the Sikh Misls or fraternities west of Sutlej. Ranjit Singh was encouraged by the policy of non intervention followed by Sir George Barlow (1805-1807). He intended to extend his authority over the territory know as the Cis-Sutlej Malwa states. These Sikh states were formly under Scindhia, but when the latter was turned out from there, they informally came under British protection. In 1806, some Sikh chiefs of these states quaralled among themselves and asked for the intervention of Ranjit Singh. The later accepted the invitation, crossed the Sutlej and occupied Ludhiana. When this happened , the Sikh cheifs were alarmed and they appealed to the British Government for protection. At that time, Lord Minto was the Governor-General and he was determined to keep the power of Ranjit Singh to the west of the Sutlej. The British Government declared that they would not allow Ranjit Singh to establish his control over the Cis-Sutlej states and there was every possibility of war between the two power. At this time, Ranjit Singh hesitated. Negotiations were started and Charles Metcalfe was sent for that purpose. After many delays, the Treaty of Amritsar was signed in 1809.

The Relations of Maharaja Ranjit Singh with the British. It was very difficult for the British and Ranjit Singh to flourish side by side in the country, especially when the British were determined to establish their supremacy in India. But their engagement in Europe in the French Revolution (from 1793 to 1815) made it possible for the two powers to live in peace and to make progress side by side.

(1) The British Mission of 1800. The idea of a French attack on India always haunted the English espcially when their struggle with France had started in 1793. The English were afraid lest Zaman Shah, the ruler of Afghanistan, should invade India in coalition with Napoleon. So, in 1800 they sent a British representative (Yusuf Ali) to Ranjit Singh. As a result of this mission it was agreed that in case of any foreign attack both the sides would act unitedly.

(2) Treaty of Lahore (1806). In 1805, the Maratha chief Holkar, after his defeat from the British, reached Punjab to seek Ranjit Singh's help. But fully knowing the might of the English, he very cleverly evaded the Maratha chief. At this, the English were much pleased and they concluded a treaty with Ranjit Singh. According to Treaty of Lahore (1st January, 1806) both the sides agreed not to give shelter to each other's enemies and also to interfere in each others affairs.

(3) The Treaty of Amritsar. The following were the terms of the treaty:

(1) River Sutlej became the boundary the territories of the English and Ranjit Singh.

(2) Both the parties agreed not to interfere in the internal affairs of others.

(3) Both the parties agreed to remain friendly with each other.

(4) Ranjit Singh promised not to invade areas south of Sutlej.

(5) The two parties also agreed to help each other in case of danger from any third party.

Criticism of the Treaty

(1) Maharja Ranjit Singh honourably observed the terms of the treaty and remained a constant and loyal ally of the British. He temporarily saved his kingdom from English encroachment. But he

could not remove the threat permanently, he only left it over to his successors.

(2) Besides, the treaty gave the British a degree of control over Ranjit Singh's relations with the neighbouring States of Sind, Bahawalpur and Afghanistan.

(3) In fact this treaty was a great diplomatic achievement of the British because without firing a single shot they got their frontiers pushed from the Jamuna to the Sutlej.

(4) The treaty helped the Britishers to make conquests elsewhere. They defeated the furkhas of Nepal and won the Fourth Maratha war.

(5) According to some historians it greatly lowered the prestige of Maharaja Ranjit Singh.

His Administration. Maharaja Ranjit Singh was a good administrator. He reformed the administration in so many ways–

(1) Provincial Administration. Ranjit Singh divided his empire into four subas (provinces) for the convenience of administration. These four subas were Lahore, Peshawar, Multan and Kashmir. The head of the suba was known as Nizam, provinces were divided into many districts. The head of the district was known as Kaadar. He was responsible for law and order in the district.

(2) Village Administration. Village was the smallest unit in Ranjit Singh's administration. Gram Panchayats were responsible for the village administration. These Panchayats arranged for all the works of the village. Gram Panchayats also worked for justice.

(3) The Central Administration. He also believed in centralized administration. All the military or civil powers vested in him. But he did not believe in one-man-rule. Used to consult his ministers who belonged to all the relegions. He wanted welfare of all the people. To give a clean administration he had divided the whole administration into different departments which were being looked after by different ministers.

(4) Land and Revenue System. The main source of income of the state in Ranjit Singh's period was land revenue. Peasants gave 1/3rd to 2/5th part of their crops as land tax. The head of the district, Kaardar, was responsible for collecting the tax from the peasants and for depositing the amount in Government treasury. He was helped by Mukaddam, Patwari and Kanungo in this work. Each of them was a servant of the state who used to get salary in cash. These officials did not exploit the peasants. Peasants were given financial aid by the state at the time of natural calamities.

Custom duty, fines, Estate Duty etc. were the other sources of income of the state other than the land-revenue.

(5) Military System. Maharaja Ranjit Singh built up a powerful, disciplined and well-equiped army along European lines with the help of European instructors. His new army was not confined to the Sikhs. He also recruited Gurkhas, Biharis, Oriyas, Pathans, Dogras and Punjabi Muslims. He set up modern foundries to manufacture cannon at Lahore and employed Muslim gunners to handle them. It is said that he possessed the second best army in Asia, the first being the army of the English East India Company.

(6) Law and Judicial System. Laws were not strict. Generally, fines were paid by the wrong-doers. But if any person made a mistake again and again, then an organ of the body was cut. Death penalty was not given. Laws were not written. King himself was the supreme judge. He had all the judicial rights. The last appeal was sent to his court of all the important cases. Gram Panchyats in villages, Kaardars in districts, Nazims in the provinces and king in the centre used to do justice. There was one Supreme Court in Lahore. Apeals against Nazims and Kaardars could be made in this court. In the case of justice, Maharaja Ranjit Singh never made difference on any base.

(7) His Religious Policy. Ranjit Singh had great capacity for choosing his ministers and officials. His court was tudded with outstanding men. He was torlerant and liberal in religions matters. While a denont Sikh he was "known to step down from his throne to wipe the dust off the feet of Muslim mandicants with his long grey beared." Many important ministers and commanders were Muslims and Hindus. The most prominent and trusted of his ministers was Fakir Azizuddin, while his finance minister was Dewan Dina Nath. In fact, in no sense was the Punjab, ruled by Ranjit Singh was a Sikh State. Political power was not used for exclusive Sikh benefit. On the other hand, the sikh peasant was as much oppressed by sikh chiefs as was the Hindu or the Muslim peasant.

Ranjit Singh's Personality and Character

(1) As a Ruler. Ranjit Singh was a good administrator. Though he was an absolute monarch and believed in centralization of administrative powers, but he never ignored the welfare of the people. He used to consult his minister who belonged to all the religions. He administered both the civil and military wings to the entire satisfaction of his subjects. It is said that a box was affixed outside his palace in which his subjects could lodge their complaints. He also paid personal visits to various parts of the state to acquiant himself with the real state of affairs. Above all, he gave to the people of Punjab the blessings of peace, the like of which they had not seen in the past one hundred years.

(2) As a Man. Regarding the physical features of Maharaja Ranjit Singh Baron Hugal has written," I must call him the most ugly and unprepossessing man I saw throughout the Punjab. The scars of small ox on his face form so many dark pit in his greyish brown skin his short straight nose, the skinning lips do not impress anyone". Though his physical features were ugly yet he commanded a great popularity among his people. He was very much loved by his subjects both civilians and military men. He had a strong physique, a powerful will, wounderful memory and great personal courage. In spite of his being a ruler of a vast empire he used to lead a simple life and wore very simple clothes. He never appropriated to himself the high sounding titles nor did he run the government in his own name. His government was named as Sarkar-i-Khalsa. On his coins there was the inscription of Nanak Sahai or Govind Sahai. He was very intelligent. He had the capacity to judge people at first sight. Though illiterate, yet he impressed those who came in his contact. He possed a remarkable memory. Whenever a foreigner came to his court he asked a 'hundred thousand question about India, Europe, Nepolean Bonaparte, this world and the next world. Jacquemont says," His prodigious memory knew the name, position and history of from ten to twelve thousand villages in his kingdom." He was a very liberal and Kind-hearted man.

(3) As a Brave Soldier and Conqueror. Ranjit Singh was a great brave, courageous, fearless, an able soldier and commander. He is called rightly the 'Lion of Punjab'. He fought several wars but never suffered a defeat. He led his armies and often fought in the forefront like a common soldiers. He was thoroughly conversant with various arts of war. Probably he was the first modern Indian ruler who proceeded towards Afghanistan and succeeded in capturing it. Victor Jacquemont, a French visiter to the Court of Ranjit Singh, compares him with Nepolean Bonaparte. "Brave and war like" remarks. Dr. Ishwari Prasad, "He dashed against dangers with conquerable heroism."

(4) As a Patron of Learing and Literature. Though Maharaja Ranjit Singh was illiterate, like Akbar, yet he did much for the spread of learning. He was a great patron of learning and encouraged education. He patronised scholars, Zafarnama, Fathenama, Guru Khalsaji Ka etc. were written at his instance. He used to give great honour to scholars and men of literature. Historians like Munshi Mohan Lal, Shah Muhammad, Ganeshdas, Diwan Amar Nath, etc. were famous scholars of his court.

(5) As a Politician and Siplomat. Maharaja Ranjit Singh was also a great politician and diplomat. In the beginning of his career he gave a solid proof of his diplomacy by sending after the Amir of Afghanistan his canon, and secured Lahore in return for the same. His political wisdom enabled him to maintain friendly and good relations with the British and the neighbouring states. Dr. Bipan Chanda writes correctly," When the British forbade Ranjit Singh in 1809 to cross the Sutlej and took the Sikh State east of the river no match for the British." Thus by his diplomatic realism he saved his kingdom from English encroachment. True, Ranjit Singh used

Machiavellian methods, the policy of 'force and fraud' to gain his ends, but he was not cruel and blood-thirsty.

(6) As a Man of Religion. Ranjit Singh was a devoted Sikh and always submitted to the religious codes and practices. He always regarded himself a servant of Khalsa. He spent money out of his own pocket to build the golden dome of the Golden Temple at Amritsar. He offered gifts before the Durbar Sahib after every victory. He had fixed a certain portion of the income from the custom duties of Amritsar for 'Karah Prashad' to be offered at the Durbar Sahib.

No doubt Ranjit Singh was a staunch Sikh and true follower of Sikhism, yet he did not bear any sort of contempt for other religions. He kept religion apart from policies. In making appointments he cared more for the merits tham for the religion. Most of his ministers were non-Sikhs. His foreign minister was a Muslim named Fakir Aziz-ud-Din. some of his generals like Misr Diwan Chand and Mohkam Chand were Hindus. He never discriminated in the grounds of religion, race or creed in providing Government jobs. The Sikhs, the Hindus and the Muslims were equl sharers in the blessings of his rule. The establishment of a secular State was a great achievement of Ranjit Singh.

(7) Some Defects of his Character. There were, some defects in Ranjit Singhs' character.

(1) He cannot be called a constructive statesman. The kingdom he had so assiduously built up disintegrated within a decade of his death. It is pointed out that like all other autocrats, Ranjit Singh kept all the state powers in his own hands and did make any provision for the training of his successors.

(2) He followed too mild a policy towards the British. Historian N.K. Sinha says, "In this Anglo-Sikh alliance, the British Government was the rider and Ranjit Singh was the horse. He must have felt that they would sooner or later occupy Punjab. Once while seeing the map of India in which all but the Punjab had been shown red which was the colour of the British Empire, Ranjit Singh said : "Sab lal ho jaiga"

meaning that the time would come when whole of this map would be marked red. In other words, Ranjit Singh knew that the English were bound to annex the Punjab after his death, and there was the bound to be a war between the two powers on this score.

(3) He failed to subordinate the army to the civil authority so long as he lived his personal influence kept the army under control, but after him the army; got out of control.

(4) He was addicated to wine and used to lead a luxurions life. He had only eighteen wives. He was too gready. He got Kohinoor (well-known diamond) from the ruler of Afghanistan by treachery. He snatched a beautiful mare, named Lailli, from an Afghan governor of Punjab and gave proof of his gready nature.

Inspite of the above mentioned defects, he was a great ruler of his time. He occupies a high place in Indian history. The memory of this great hero is still cherished by the people of the Punjab. He was a human being, he was unfortunate too, in the respect that almost all his loyal and brave generals such as Hari Singh Nalwa, Mohkam Chand, Diwan Chand etc. had died before he himself left this mortal world. Summing up his achievements Cunninghan writes, "He consolidate the numerous petty states into a kingdom, he wrested from Kabul the fairest of its provinces and he gave the potent British no cause of interference." Ranjit Singh ruled on the principles of secular State and established a fair and liberal civil administration though it was not of an advanced type.

Weak Successors of Maharaja Ranjit Singh. His sons Khund Singh, Sher Singh and Naunihal Singh fought for the succession. They sought help of the Sikh chiefs, but were killed one by one. The Sikh kingdom of Ranjit Singh became weak. The state of disorder lasted till 1845. During this period, the Khalsa organisation entrenched itself strongly and every aspirant of the throne tried to enlist its support. The discipline of the army fell apart. It became disorganised. It was feared that if it was not put to some use, it could start ransacking and looting the people. The army was ordered to cross Sutlej. The English watched the political conditions of the Punjab and to a greater extent had a hand in worsening it. They wished to bring Punjab into the area of their control. On the crossing of the Sutlej by the Sikh troops, the English declared war in December, 1845.

The Metcalfe Mission and the Treaty of Amritsar, 1809

(1) In the treaty that was signed between Ranjit Singh and Lord Lake, after the departure of Holkar from the Punjab, there was no mention of the exact eastern boundary line of Ranjit Singh's kingdom. Hene a golden opportunity offered itself to him in the expansion of his kingdom towards the east. Ranjit Singh was a very ambitious ruler whose one aim in life was to bring all the Sikhs under his banner, no matter whether they were living to the north or the south of the river Sutlej. He, therefore, desired to take advantage of any opportunity which would enable him to occupy not only the Trans Sutlej region but the Cis-Sutlej territory also which was then being rule over by the three Phulkian rulers of Patiala, Nabhas and Jindh States. It was only with the conquest of the Cis-Sutlej territory that he could unite all the Sikhs under him. Luckily, an opportunity fell into his hands at this time which he utilised to extend his kingdom in the Cis-Sutlej region. On the queston of resolving a dispute between Sahib Singh, the Raja of Patiala, and Jaswant Singh, the Raja of Nabha, over a village, Doladhi, Raja Jaswant Singh of Nagha in collaboration with Raja Bhag Singh of Jindh invited Maharaja Ranjit Singh to Malwa region to settle the dispute as an arbitrator between the two parties. Ranjit Singh who was already in the look-out of an opportunity at once accepted the invitation and entered into the Malwa territory at the head of an army more than necessary. After some resistence, Raja Sahib Singh of Patiala submitted and accepted the decision of Ranjit Singh regarding the dispute. Raja Sahib Singh paid also a heavy amount as a present to Ranjit Singh.

(2) Ranjit Singh sent his second expedition against the Malwa territory in 1807 when he got another golden opportunity to do it on the invitation of Rani Aas Kaur, the Rani of Raja Sahib Singh of Patiala, to settle a family dispute between the Rani and her husband.

The Rani promised to hand over to Ranjit Singh a gun Kara Khan and a jewelled necklace also. Ranjit Singh advanced towards Patiala but before he reached Patiala the dispute between the husband and the wife had already been over. But Ranjit Singh did obtain the gun Kara Khan and the jewelled necklace as promised by the Rani. Ranjit Singh obtained a good amount as present from Raja Bhag Singh also. On his way back to Lahore, Ranjit Singh conquered Narain-Garh which he handed over to Fatch Singh Ahluwalia for an annual tribute. He conquered Zera also which he handed over to Diwan Mohkam Chand for annual tribute. Then he conquered Wadni which he gave to his mother-in-law, Rani Sada Kaur, for an annual tribute. Ranjit Singh conqured Ferozepur also. During the course of Ranjit Singh's two Malwa expeditions, he obtained presents from Raja Sahib Singh of Patiala and Jaswant Singh of Nabha, the Afghan rulers of Malerkotla, Bhai Lal Singh of Kaithal, Gurdit Singh and Karam Singh of Shahabad. Rani Daya Kaur of Ambala, Bhagwant Singh of Buria and Jodh Singh Kalsia. Ranjit Singh subjected many of the Zamindars of the Cis-Sutlej territory also to tribute.

The above two expeditions of Ranjit Singh into the Malwa territory considerably harassed all the rulers and Sardars of this region, since they had come to know about the sinister motives of Ranjit Singh against their territories. Thus with a view to avoiding increasing danger from Ranjit Singh, a deputation consisting of Raja Bhag of Jindh, Bhai Lal Singh of Kaithal, the Diwan of Patiala and the Wakil of Nabha waited upon the British Resident, Mr. Seton, at Delhi in March, 1808, and complained to him against the aggressive attacks of Ranjit Singh on their territories. They requested the Resident to help them against Ranjit Singh, who in the words of Cunningham "laboured with more or less of intelligent design to give unity and coherence to diverse atoms and scattered elements; to mould the increasing Sikh nation into a well ordered state or commonwealth as Gobind had developed a sect into a people. But all had become jealous of him and perhaps he was alone in the policy of excluding the British strangers from confines of the Punjab." Mr. Seton really wanted to help the deputationsits but failed to find any way out of the difficulty. Since Mr. Seton had no instructions from his Calcutta Government, the Cis-Sutlej Chiefs could not get any encouragement from the British at this stage. Consequently, in view of this discouraging reply from the British Resident, the Cis-Sutlej Chiefs found their safety and that of their territories only in their submission to Ranjit Singh by entering into separate and individual treaties with him and to stop him from his further attempts to swallow up their territories.

With the despatch of Metcalfe Mission to the Court of Lahore, a new chapter opens in Anglo-Sikh relations to understand which it is necessary to understand the background of European politics at this time. In the post-French Revolutionary period, Napoleon was busy in conquring the entire continent of Europe. During the intervening period of three years from 1798 to 1801, Napoleon had conqured a good deal of European Continent and, as such, he was dreaming of a universal Empire like Alexander the Great. He was preparing himself for an invasion on India on the invitation of Tipu Sultan. Though, by defeating him in Syria and Egypt, the English had ended all chances of his invasion of India at the time, yet, in view of his achievements in Europe, it was presumed that Napoleon might try to invade India at any time in the future. The Russian Czar Paul I and France had already made preparations for a joint attack on India, so much so that it was decided that the Russian army should advance towards India by way of Bokhara and Kheva, while the French army should join the Russian army at Astrakhan after crossing the River Danube. But their programme came to a sudden end on account of the pre-mature death of Czar Paul I at this time. But the atmosphere created by Napoleon in 1806-1807 produced a real situation of danger for the English. The King of Persia, after sustaining a defeat from Russia, was busy making an alliance with France, which resulted in a traty between the two in 1806, according to which the ruler of Persia promised to extend a number of facilities to France in the event of their contemplated invasion on India. On the other hand, the English were growing apprehensive of Ranjit Singh's aggressive activities also in the Cis-Sutlej region and, as such, did not consider their interests and rights there out of danger at the hands of Ranjit Singh. But because Ranjit Singh was the ruler of a frontier state, the English did not like to offend him on any ground. Under these circumstances, Lord Minto, the then Governor-General, tried to control the dangerous situation, thus existing at the time, very diplomatically. At this time, two great problems that faced him were: *(a)* To arrest the advance of Ranjit Singh towards the Cis-Sutlej territory; *(b)* Making friends with Ranjit Singh in order to jointly face the possible invasion of France on India. It was, therefore, with a view to achieving these objects that Lord Minto despatched Sir Charles Metcalfe to Ranjit Singh at Lahore to negotiate for a friendly aliance with the Maharaja.

Ranjit Singh's Third Expedition Against Malwa, September 1808 December 1808. At this time begins the second phase of Metcalfe's negotiations with Ranjit Singh. It has already been noted above that in the course of Metcalfe's negotiations with him, Ranjit Singh had tried to take advantage of the British proposal for friendly alliance with him. Thinking that the British really felt the need of his friendship he had made an attempt to extort as much advantage as possible from them, but in vain. Stopping all negotiations, he now conquered as much of the Cis-Sutlej region as possibly he could do. Sir Lepel Griffen says, "there was some genius in his policy that deserved success." Consequently, in his third expedition, he conquered Faridkot and Maler Kotla. Proceeding further he also occupied Ambala and Shahabad. Mehtab Singh, the ruler of Thaneswar, also paid his tribute to the Maharaja. The Raja of Patiala entered into a friendship with him and both of them promised to help each other. Metcalfe did protest against the Maharaja's aggressive expeditions against the Malwa territory but the Maharaja did not at all care for it. Ranjit Singh returned to Lahore from his third expedition at the beginning of Decemeber 1808.

British Towards Ranjit Singh. At this time an important event took place in the politics of Europe which eliminated all chances of any French invasion on India. A rebellion broke out in Spain against Napoleon. Sir Arthur Wellesley had defeated the French at many places. Cordial relations had been established between England and Turkey. In other words, in Europe Napoleon was getting defeats and, as such, there was no danger of any French invasion on India now.

The political situation in Europe completely changed the nature of policy of the British Government towards Ranjit Singh. As long as the British entertained danger from the French invasion, they remained in favour of concluding a friendly treaty with Ranjit Singh, and really if the danger had increased, it was very probable that they would have definitely accepted Ranjit Singh's demand that he sould be recognised as the independent ruler of Cisterritory also. But now when all danger from any French invasion on India had vanished, they began to give scant care to the Maharaja's freindly alliance. The Government now wanted to check the rising Sikh power "to oppose the extension on the Indian side of the Sutlej of an ambitious military power which would be substituted upon our frontier for a confederacy of friendly chiefs rendered grateful by our protection and interested in our cause." So, when Ranjit Singh returned to Lahore from his third Malwa expedition, Metcalfe gave on 10th December, 1808 at Amritsar a note to Ranjit Singh from the Governor-General and two days later sent him another note. It was argued : "His lordship has learnt with great surprise and concern that the Maharaja aims at the subjugation of chiefs who have long been considered under the protection of the power ruling in the north of Hindustan. The British Government sent an envoy to the Maharaja to give him information of a great danger. The Maharaja did not receive these propositions with the same confidence and cordinality with which they were made, but in reply brought forward a demand for the assent of the Government to the subjugation of chiefs connected with it....instead of wating for a reply proceeded to excute his intention of subjugating the chiefs... In making the reference the Maharaja showed that he well knew that without the consent of the British Government, he had no right to invade the country between the Sutlej and the Jumna...The Britsh Government cannot acknowledge any right in the Maharaja to any territories that he may have taken possession of situated between the Sutlej and the Jumna since the first reference of this question to the British Government....The Government-General expects that the Maharaja will restore all the places he has taken possession of since that period to the former possessors and will confine his army to the right bank of the Sutlej....In expressing these sentiments the British

Government is desirous of maintaining the most amicable relations wth his Government." Thus with a view to enforcing the British demand the Governor-General sent General David Ochterlony who reached Ludhiana on the 19th February to back the British demand by a military demonstration. Metcalfe again met Ranjit Singh and asked him to abandon all his rights on the Cis-Sutlej territory, but Ranjit Singh was not prepared to accept the proposal which stood in opposition to the most cherished ideal of his life. uniting the Sikh of Trans-Sutlej and Malwa territories under him. Ranjit Singh evacuated all his recent acuisitions, withdrew his own troops from Ambala, gave up Saniwal but strove to retain Faridkot which he later on abandoned on April 2, 1809. Moorcroft says, "at one stage of the negotiations Ranjit Singh seriously thought of going to war with the English. Metcalfe also reported the same thing to the English. A great part of his army was collected under his best general, Diwan Mohkam Chand, in the Kangra country. He was posted at Philaur. His artillery and infantry were also kept in readiness. Besides, he summoned back the old chiefs from their homes and hastened the completion of the new fort at Amritsar.

In 1809 commences the third phase of negotinations between Ranjit Singh and Metcalfe Mission. In this round of negotiations with Metcalfe, Ranjit Singh felt that with the occupation of Cis-Sutlej territory by the British, their northern boundary had reached the banks of the river Sutlej and that the establishment of the British dominion in his very close proximity was an indication of a great danger to him. Hence it was now he who became impartient of a friendly treaty with the British Government so that by taking advantage of the British friendship, he might be spared the necessity of keeping his army in the east and use it effectively for the subjugation and consolidation of the other parts of the unconquered Punjab. Metcalfe also expressed the need of a friendly treaty between the two powers, since the establishment of a freindly power in the Punjab would be more useful to the British than an unfriedly power. Thus partly on account of the above consideration but mainly on account of the following factors, Ranjit Singh was forced to sign treaty of Amritsar:

(1) **Firm Policy of the British Government.** When the British Government felt fully convinced with the defeats of Napoleon in Europe that chances of a French invasion on India had become very remote, they felt themselves now quite secure and, as such, they adopted a firm policy towards Ranjit Singh. They knew their own strength and were conscious of Ranjit Singh's weakness and, therefore, addressed to him with a firm attitude. Ranjit Singh rightly realized that to fight against the British when he was not militarily so strong then would produce serious consequences for him. Hence he was obliged by the circumstances to sign the treaty.

(2) **The Defeat of the Akalis.** It was during the course of Metcalfe-Ranjit Singh negotiations that once a clash of arms occurred between the Akalis and a small military continugent of Metcalfe in which the Akalis were badly defeated. Ranjit Singh had placed much of his dependence on the strength and religious enthusiasm of the Akalis. But the defeat of a good number of Akalis at the hands of a handful of the English forces convinced him that the trained English army was far better than the untrained army that he had under him at the time and, as such, his success against the British in case of a war would be impossible.

(3) **The fear of Cis-Sutlej Rulers Joinging the British Government.** Ranjit Singh knew that the bone of contention between the British and himself was the Cis-Sutlej region ruled over by his Sikh co-religionist rulers of Patiala. Nabha and Jindh whom he wanted to subjugate and bring under his control. He also knew that by being hard-pressed by his domination, they had many times expressed their desire to come under the protection of the British Government as against his protection. Under these circumstances Ranjit Singh realized that if he did not sign the treaty there would be a war between himself and the

British and in case of a war the Sikh rulers of Cis-Sutlej territory would definitely fight in favour of the British against him.

(4) **The Idea of no Danger from the British in Case of a Treaty.** Ranjit Singh had correctly realized that the strength of the British was definitely far superior to that of his and that they had now securely established themselves in the close proximity of his kingdom. He, therefore, rightly came to the conclusion that in order invade his kingdom or to interfere into his affairs, they would always try to find out one pretext or the other and since he was weaker than them, it would be better to make friends with them, so that there should be no danger from their side to his kingdom and he should be able to consolidate his dominions completely. Thus it was in view of this advantage rightly understood by him that Ranjit Singh signed the treaty of Amritsar.

The Treaty of Amritsar and its Terms

(1) The Lahore Government was placed "on the footing of the most favoured powers"–the British Government having no concern with the territories and subjects of the Raja to the northward of the river Sutlej.

(2) Ranjit Singh retained the territory he had possessed on the left bank of the Sutlej before the coming of Metcalfe but he was not to "maintain in the territory of the river Sutlej more troops than are necessary for internal law and order of that territory" and he was not to encroach on others' possessions and rights.

(3) In the event of the violation of any of the preceding articles or of departure from the rules of friendship, the treaty shall be considered null and void.

(4) This clause was ordinary and bore the names of the signatories of the treaty.

Significance of the Treaty of Amritsar. The Treaty of Amritsar produced consequences of a lastig nature and, therefore, it was a great landmark in the Anglo-Sikh relations. The following were the advantages and disadvantages to the parties concerned:

Disadvantages to Ranjit Singh

(1) Failed to realize the chief ambition. The chief ambition of Ranjit Singh's life was to unite all the Sikhs under his banner no matter they were living to the south or the north of the river Sutlej. But this treaty divided the Sikh people into two distinct parts by fixing the Sutlej as the boundary line between the Sikh people, one living to the north of the Sutlej being governed by Ranjit Singh himself and the other living to the south of this river, called the Malwa territory, which came under the possession of the English by the Treaty of Amritsar. Thus Ranjit Singh suffered a diplomatic defeat and had to put his pride in his pocket and eat the humble pie. His ignorance of the turn of the events in Europe brought about this discomfiture. We are reminded, as we read this history of his failure of the truism–"If you wish to obtain your objectives by force you must be strong, if you want to obtain them by negotiations you must be stronger still. N.K. Sinha has rightly said, "His failure to absorb the Cis-Sultej States was a tragedy of Sikh militant nationalism and the success of the Cis-Sutlej Sikhs with the aid of the British Government marked the disruption of the great creation of Guru Gobind Singh." Thus, Ranjit Singh got a great disgrace and, as such, he never though of becoming the unopposed leader and ruler of the Sikh people.

(2) Lowered down the prestige. This treaty considerably enhanced the prestige of the British Government while it struck an effective blow at Ranjit Singh's prestige and honour. Though Ranjit Singh remained an independent ruler of the Punjab state, yet there existed no equality between the British and the Maharaja. The very fact that Ranjit Singh agreed to maintain a fixed number of forces and to be treated as one of the "the most favoured powers" by the British shows that the British were to play the role of a Paramount Power and the Lahore Chief that of a subordinate.

(3) This treaty brought the British boundary line very close to that of Ranjit Singh's kingdom and, as such, exercised a great effect on the politics of Ranjit Singh's his Government and his foreign policy. This treaty brought the English in the centre of the Punjab, whereform they now began to devise ways and means of the conquest of the Punjab. They obtained a complete knowledge of the geography of the Punjab. Not only this but they also obtained a complete knowledge of the politics of the Punjab state, and when Ranjit Singh died, they took a full advantage of the geographical and polictical conditons of the Punjab and effected its conquests which had become one of their chief ambitions since the treaty of Amritsar was first concluded in 1809.

Advantages to the British Government

(1) The English made Ranjit Singh thier permanent friend and ally and Ranjit Singh, in his turn, never abandoned their friendship. Consequently, being perfectly immune from any danger from a strong ruler on their northwestern frontiers, the English obtained a golden opportunity to conquer the other parts of India with Great facility.

(2) This treaty gave to the British a diplomatic and military victory over Ranjit Singh. The British influence was fully established in the hearts of the people and they far exceeded Ranjit Singh's influence and prestige. In a way, the British Government became a paramount power and Ranjit Singh subordinate to this power. The boundary line of the British dominions now reached the river Sutlej, on the left bank of which they were now entitled to establish their military cantonments like Ludhiana.

(3) Ranjit Singh was a ruler of the Punjab state and, as such, was in possession of a north-western frontier. India was always fearing a Russian invasion on India during the reign of Ranjit Singh. Even on the termination of the French Revolutionary period there was a danger of Napoleon's invasion on India with the help of Russia. But the presence of a strong and faithful friend in the person of Ranjit Singh on the border state of the Punjab gave a tremendous

advantage to the English. His presence stopped all chances of any invasion from the north-weastern frontiers, and in case of an invasion both would have faced the external menace jointly.

Advantages to Ranjit Singh

(1) This treaty brought the three Phulkian Sikh states of Patiala, Nabha and Jind under the British protection. They carried on their aministration in an independent way. If the Maharaja had obtained the occupation of these states, as he had desired to do in 1809, they would have also been annexed to the British dominons on the termination of the Second Anglo-Sikh War when the entire Punjab of Ranjit Singh up to Peshwar was annexed by the British in 1849. In other words, the independence which they got in 1809 during this treaty and which they kept for a period of one hundred and fifty years (1809-1956) would have come to an end in 1849 with the annexation of the Punjab. Hence this treaty gave a good deal of advantage to the Sikhs. And now when the first stage of the formation of states on lingustic basis has been achieved the formation of the Punjabi Suba if allowed would make states the centre of Punjabi culture and literature and as such, would find full chances of their development.

(2) This treaty gave a great advantage to Ranjit Singh also. The treatuy strengthened Ranjit Singh's eastern boundary line very much, because he had now only freinds–the English–on his eastern frontiers. Consequently, he did not feel the necessity of maintaining the whole of his army on the eastern boundaries; rather he kept only a part of his army here. Hence he was able to spare the whole of his army to be utilised in the conquest of different regions, Attock, Kashmir, Dera-jats, Bannu, Kohat and Peshawar and, as such, he was successful in that. If there had been no treaty of Amritsar with the British, Ranjit Singh would never have been able to wrest away so many territories from the afghan rulers nor would he have been able to conquer and consolidate his position in the Punjab. Cunningham, is, therefore, correct when he says, "One of the indirect results of the treaty of Amritsar was that Ranjit Singh had become the master of the Punjab almost unheeded by the British."

(3) If Ranjit Singh had not acted wisely to conclude the treaty of Amristar, the outbreak of a war between Ranjit Singh and the British Government would have been certain, and in that eventuality the defeat of Ranjit Singh, who was not sufficiently strong at that time from military point of view, would also have been sure. In that case the infant Sikh state would have easily fallen into the British hands in 1809. But acting with wisdom and forethought Ranjit Singh signed the treaty of Amritsar and entered into friendship with the English. In other words, he saved the infant Sikh state from destruction at the time when it was very weak. This grant of lease of life enabled this infant Sikh state later on to develop into a big strong Sikh Kingdom in the Punjab.

In this we conclude that the greatest aim of the Maharaja was to unite all the Sikhs, both living to the north and south of the river Sutlej, under his banner. But this ambition of his failed to materialize because of the opposition of the British who had become a dominant power in Delhi.

VARIOUS STAGES IN THE UNIFICATION

Ranjit Singh's aim in life was to bring all the Sikhs into a compact body under his own banner. The Sikhs at the time were living in two regions, some were living to the north of the River Sutlej where, except the members of the Phulkian Misl, all the other Misls were in occupation of the northern Punjab, called Majha. Ranjit Singh wanted to bring the territories of all such Misldars under his own rule with a view to establishing an independent Sikh national kingdom with himself as its national king. The other part of the Sikh population was residing to the south of the river Sutlej, called Malwa territory, ruled over by the rulers of Phulkian Misl. Ranjit Singh held that all the Sikhs, wherever they were living whether to the north or the south of the river Sutlej formed a part and parcel of the Sikh Commonwealth.

The First Stage in the Conquest of the Territories of The Sikh Misls

(1) The first stage of Ranjit Singh's conquests begins with the conquest of the territories of various Misldars living to the north of

the river Sutlej. In connection with his conquests, it can be conveniently said that the most important and significaant event in the career of Ranjit Singh's conquests was the conquet and occupation of Lahore. The civil administration of Lahore those days was in the hands of three Bhangi Sardars,. Chet Singh, Mohar Singh and Sahib Singh. The population of Lahore was very much fed up with their rule and, as such, they were always desirous of a change of masters. In their eyes, none looked better than Ranjit Singh whom they wanted to be their new ruler. Consequently, most of the inhabitants of Lahore, the Hindus, the Muslims, and the Sikhs, sent a joint invitation to Ranjit Singh to attack and occupy Lahore, they themselves promising their full support to him. Ranjit Singh was already waiting for some opportunity to occupy Lahore. He also requested his mother-in-law, Rani Sada Kaur, to help him with men and money as much as she could do. Accordingly, the joint forces of Ranjit Singh and Rani Sada Kaur invaded Lahore. Of the three Bhangi Sardars, Chet Singh alone resisted for some time but he also ultimately fled.

Effect of the Occupation of Lahore. The occupation of Lahore by Ranjit Singh filled all the other rulers of the Punjab with great jealousy. Especially the Sikh Misldars and Nizam-ud-din, the Nawab of Qasur, could not tolerate Ranjit Singh's hold established in Lahore. Hence, all of them joined hands together and formed a coalition against Ranjit Singh under the leadership of Sardar Gulab Singh Bhangi of Amritsar. This coalition comprised on Sardar Gulab Singh Bhangi of Amritsar, Sardar Sahib Singh of Gujrat, Jodh Singh Bhangi of Wazirabad, Jassa Singh Ramgarhia and Nizam-ud-din, the Pathan ruler of Qasur. With Ranjit Singh also there was no other alternative but war. Hence he also made strong preparations to meet the coalition successfully, at the same time calling Rani Sada Kaur, his mother-in-law, with all her troops to his help. The joint forces of Rani Sada Kaur and Ranjit Singh left for Lahore. Both the armies encamped against each other in a small village, Bhasin, at a distance of 12 miles from Lahore, but no battle was actually fought because both the parties over-estimated the strength of the other, and also because there was no unity and cohesion amongst the members of the coalition on account of their mutual jealousies that did not allow them to fight against Ranjit Singh jointly. In this way, both the armies remained facing each other in the field of battle for a period of two months. At last one night, Gulab Singh Bhangi the leader of the coalition, died of excessive drinking. With his death departed all the courage and spirit with which members of the coalition had come to meet Ranjit Singh. Hence they were forced to retire to their own place without doing any harm to Ranjit Singh. It was a very easy conquest of a valuable prize. The importance of the Battlc of Bhasin lies in the fact that Ranjit Singh got rid of a danger. After this the Sikh chieftains never had a chance of uniting and far less of overthrowing him.

Significance of the Battle of Bhasin. The Battle of Bhasin has a special significance in Ranjit Singh's career of conquests. In this battle all the staunch enemies of Ranjit Singh like Gulab Singh Bhangi, Jassa Singh Ramgarhia and his neighbour Nizam-ud-Din, the Nawab of Qasur, had united against him. And had there been no disunity and mutual jealousies amongst them against one another, the battle would have been fought by his enemies with great intensity and with onenes of purpose and in that case it might have proved a great stumbling block in his carrer of conquest. But fortunately failure of the coalition resulted in the success of Ranjit Singh. And according to Sinha, "Ranjit Singh got rid of a great danger. After this, the Sikh chieftains never had a chance of uniting and far less of overthrowing him."

(2) Conquest of Akalgrah and Gujrat, 1809. Ranjit Singh did not take the offensive against the great cheifs at this stage. He went in for easier victims first. He resorted to aggression and without any provocation from them he picked up quarrel with them and annexed their territories to his kingdom. Immediately after the Battle of

Bhasin, the Misldars who fell victim to his aggression were Sardar Sahib Singh Bhangi of Gujrat and Dul Singh of Akalgarh. Sahib Singh Bhangi of Gujrat was blamed because he had participated in the Battle of Bhasin in 1800 against Ranjit Singh. Hence Ranjit Singh attacked Gujrat. Ranjit Singh defeated him and took him prisoner but released him later on, on the mediation of a Sikh holyman, Baba Keshra Singh. Dul Singh of Akalgarh who was one of the right-hand-men of Ranjit Singh's father, Mahal Singh, came to the help of Sahib Singh. Ranjit Singh defeated both of them and took them prisoners but released both of them later on. After this, Ranjit Singh went to Akalgarh and annexed it, leaving to Dul Singh's widow two villages for her subsistence.

(3) Capture of Amritsar and the Battle of Lohgarh, 1805. Another of Ranjit Singh's important conquests was the conquest of Amritsar about which the historians have given different dates. Cunningham and Lateef say that it was the 1802, but Sohan Lal, the court diarist of Ranjit Singh, says that it was in 1805 that Ranjit Singh conquered Amritsar. Anyhow, the events of the conquest go like this. Sahib Singh Bhangi of Amritsar was succeeded after his death by his minor son, Gurdit Singh, as the ruler of Amritsar, with his mother Mai Sukhan as his guardian. In view of the close proximity of Amritsar to his own independent capital of Lahore, there was a natural desire in Ranjit Singh to conquer Amritsar, the spiritual capital of the Sikhs. He only wanted a pretext which he conveniently found. He demanded of Mai Sikhan the famous gun Zamzama which, said Ranjit Singh, was confiscated from Ahmed Shah Abdali by the Sikhs in 1764 and in this confiscation his Sukerchakya forefathers also had a share. Mai Sukhan refused to hand over this gun to Ranjit Singh. On this refusal, Ranjit Singh invaded Amritsar and besieged Lohgarh. Fateh Singh Ahluwalia with whom Ranjit Singh had exchanged turbans was also present by the side of Ranjit Singh. The battle lasted for two hours only. Both Mai Sukhan and Gurdit Singh fled away from Amritsar, but afterwards submitted to Ranjit Singh. Ranjit Singh annexed Amritsar and its surrounding territory to his kingdom allotting a jagir for the sub sistence of Mai Sukhan and Gurdit Singh.

Singnificance of the Occupation of Amritsar. Like the conquest of Lahore, the conquest of Amritsar also had a special significance in Ranjit Singh's career of conquests. The conquest of Lahore had placed the political capital of the Punjab in the hands of Ranjit Singh, and now the conquest of Amritsar placed the spiritual and religous capital of the Sikhs in his hands. With the occupation of Lahore and Amritsar, equality between Ranjit Singh and other misldars came to an end and Ranjit Singh's Prestige and honour definitely became superior to those of the other Misldars, who now began to realize the enhanced status of Ranjit Singh in the Sikh population of the Punjab.

(4) Conquest of Dallewala Possessious and the Battle of Rahon, 1807. The most important leader of this Misl was Tara Singh Gheba who was a very powerful noble, but, in view of his great strength, Ranjit Singh never looked at the former's possessions with covetous eyes as long as Tara Singh lived. But when Tara Singh died in 1807 in the siege of Narain Garh undertaken by Ranjit Singh with the help of Tara Singh, Ranjit Singh lost no time in invading the Dallewal territories. The widow of Tara Singh resisted for some time at Rahon, but in vain. At last the territories of the Dallewala Misl were annexed to the Lahore state.

(5) The Conquest of Karorsinghia Territories, 1810. Sardar Baghel Singh, whose territory lay to the south of the river Sutlej, had many exploits to his credit to the south of river Sutlej. He had no male issue. On his death, Ranjit Singh invaded the former's territories in the Jullundur Doab like Hariana and its neighbouring territories without any kind of provocation by the former. His widows, Raj Kaur and Ram Kaur, could not withstand Ranjit Singh's attack and, consequently, their territories were annexed to Lahore state.

(6) Conquest of Faizalpuria Territory, 1811. The territories of Faizalpuria Misl lay on both sides of the river Sutlej. Its greatest leader was Budh Singh. Ranjit Singh asked him to submit to him but Budh Singh refused to do it. Consequently, Ranjit Singh prepared a strong force under the leadership of Dewan Mohkam Chand and ordered the great general to invade Faizalpuria territories. Jodh Sinh Ramgarhia and Fatch Singh Ahluwalia with whom Ranjit Singh had made friendship, also joined Diwan Mohkam Chand in this expedition. The Jullundur and Philaur territories were easily occupied, but Budh Singh with a great cleverness crossed over to the south of river Sutlej and was safe in his territories.

(7) The Annexation of the Territories of the Other Misls, 1811-12. In 1811, Ranjit Singh occupied the territory belonging to Nakkai Misl which included Pakpatan in it. Similarly when Jaimal Singh of Kanehya Misl died in 1812. Ranjit Singh occupied his territory which consistted to Taragarh, Fatchpore and Mirthal.

(8) Annexation of Ramgarhia Misl 1815. After the Battle of Bhasin, Ranjit Singh turned his attention towards his enemy, Jodh Singh Ramgarhia. Ranjit Singh applied force in the case of weak Misls, but he did not touch the strong Misldars; rather he moved very diplomatically towards them and made friendship with them. Jassa Singh Ramgarhia was 75 years of age at the time when he died in 1803. He was succeeded by Jodh Singh Ramgarhia. Ranjit Singh made friends with Jodh Singh, and used to call him "Babaji" as a mark of respect for him. Ranjit Singh was clever enough not even to look at the territories of Jodh Singh as long as the latter lived. But when Jodh Singh died in 1815, Ranjit Singh lost no time in invading and taking possession of Ramgarhia territory. The annual income from Ramgarhia territory to about 6½ lakhs of rupees.

(9) Ranjit Singh and Fatch Singh Ahluwalia. Thus all the Trans-Sutlej Misls were gradually absorbed. An exception was, however, made in the case of Fatch Singh Ahluwalia, who was perhaps regarded as a safe friend. His relations with Ranjit Singh were peculiar. In youth there was a position of complete equality between the two. In 1802, there was a romantic exchänge of turbans and the formal establishment of friendship. At the time the possession of Fatch Singh were equal if not greater in extent than those of Ranjit Singh. They together entered into a "treaty of Friendship and Unity" with the East India Company in 1809. From this complete equality he gradually sank into the position of a dependent ally and the instrument of Ranjit Singh's aggrandisement. As the Maharaja's power increased, the territory of Fathe Singh Ahluwalia was also very considerably extended by him. But even at this stage the show of equality was kept up. As Metcalfe wrote, "One of the ministers of Fatch Singh was employed in common with the ministers of Ranjit Singh in 1808-1809." No person was employed on behalf of any other Sikh Chief. But he sank into the position of a subordinate chief without any very formal acknowledgement of subjection. In 1810, we find the Lahore Chief dictating to him in matters that the Ahluwalia Sardar regarded as his own concern. He was compelled to profess that he would abide by the orders of the Maharaja and though very reluctant to release Amar Das Singh, whom he had put under restraint, he had to do it. In 1813 Ranjit Singh ascertained from reliable persons how many troops Fatch Singh Ahluwalia had and on learning that he kept 3,500 horse and foot, the Lahore Chief said that he should inspect the Ahluwalia detachment on the Dussera Day. Faithfully, the Ahluwalia Chief served his erstwhile comrade until 1826. when all at once he crossed the Sutlej and threw himself on the protection of the English.

Till as early as 1809, if Metcalfe is to be believed, he had reasons to be apprehensive after the absorption of the Ramgarhia and Kankeya Misls. But the immediate reasons for this hasty decision are not wellknown the English, true to their terms of the treaty with Ranjit Singh, could not concern themselves with the territory on the other sides of the Sutlej. Ranjit Singh was, however, anxious for an amicable adjustment with his turban brother. He was brought back with marked honour. He said that his evil councillors had led him astray. He was reinstated to more than half his Trans-Sutlej lands and the full exercise of the rights he possessed in them. It is relevant to note than on Fathe Singh's death in 1826, Ranjit Singh demanded a heavy Nazrana from his son. It was in this way that Ranjit Singh was able to absorb the territories of all the Misldars one by one.

Criticism of Ranjit Singh's Policy Towards the Sikh Misls

(1) Abolition of Gurmatta. Ranjit Singh also abolished the institution of Gurmatta in 1805 A.D. Gurmatta was the Central Diet of the Sikh Misls and used to meet at Akal Takhat (Amritsar) to formulate a common programme against their enemies who were generally the Muslim Governors and invaders. So long as this instititution of Gurmatta existed, all the Sikh Sardars of the Misls considered themselves as equals and asserted their equality at the annual meetings of the Gurmatta. but with the abolition of this institution the Sikh Sardars ceased to meet together and, consequently, they were deprived of all opportunities to claim and emphasise equality with one another. Thus, Ranjit Singh, after the abolition of Gurmatta, assumed the role of the Chief of the entire Sikh community.

(2) Use of Force and Diplomacy. As described elsewhere, the greatest desire of Ranjit Singh was to become the ruler of the whole Sikh nation with himself as the national King of the Sikhs. In order to achieve this, he had contracted friendship with those who could give him a tough fight and subdued by force those who were weak. This policy of Ranjit Singh towards the Misls has been summed up by Latif in the following words :–

"The old Sikh confederacies had either all been swept away by his systematic usurpations and grasping policy or like the Phulkians and the Nahiangs had sought the protection of a power greater than his by settling themselves in the east of the Sutlej. The Kanhayia and Ahluwalia Misls ranged themselves under his banner and took pride in following him to the battlefield."

(3) Aggressive. This policy of Ranjit Singh towards the Misls, particularity towards those who were weak, has been described as aggressive and unscrupulous. When he wanted to attack a Misl, he would not even wait to find out a pretext in order to justify his aggression. Most of his wars against the Misls were fought without any provocation and without even any justification. Tara Singh Gheba had died and his body had not yet been burnt when Ranjit Singh invaded his territory and annexed it. Similarly, his wars against the Bhangis, the Faizalpurias and the Karor-Singhas were fought without any provocation given by them. Latif, writing about the policy of Ranjit Singh regarding his wars against the Misls, says, "With him (Ranjit Singh) the weak were sure to go to the wall and their ruin was the foundation upon which was built his greatness." Thus while fighting against the weak. Ranjit Singh was not moved by any feelings of pity and compassion; rather, he held, like Bismarck, that "bursts of sentiments are out of place in politics."

(4) Unscrupulous. Even with those powerful Sikh Misldars with whom Ranjit Singh had contracted friendship he was not sincere. By entering into friendship with them, he was simply gaining time to attack and annex their possessions at some convenient time. His treatment of Sada Kaur, head of the Kanheyia Misl, who is generally described as the ladder through which Ranjit Singh rose to power, bears out clearly how aggressive and unscrupulous Ranjit Singh was while dealing with the Sikh Misls. In 1821, all her possession except Wadni were annexed. Similarly as soon as Jodh Singh, the Ramgarhia Sardar, died in 1815, his possessions were annexed.

(5) Policy was Most Successful. Most of the Sardars, who were even friendly to the Lahore Chief had realised during their lifetime the aggressive intentions of Ranjit Singh. The following incident clearly illustrates this. Once Ranjit Singh wanted to give some presents to the Ramgarhia Sardar, Baba Jodh Singh, but the latter declined and said, "A man is fortunate in these times, if he is allowed to retain his turban on his own head." The only Sardar who escaped his aggression was Fathe Singh, the leader of the Ahluwalia Misl. But it must be remembered that Ranjit Singh's policy of consolidation of the territories wrested from the Sikh Sardars was highly successful because of the following reasons:

(a) The Sikh Chiefs, whom he dispossessed, found to their satisfaction that their conqueror was generous and forgiving. Whenever he annexed the territories of a Sardar, he would offer him a handsome jagir for his maintenance, if, of course, he was willing to serve him (Ranjit Singh). Gurdit Singh Bhangi of Amritsar, Sahib Singh of Gujrat and a number of other Sikh Sardars who agreed to acknowledge Ranjit Singh's suzerainty, were given jagirs and so within a short time, they got themselves reconciled to the new situation.

(b) Similarly those soldiers who were in the service of the Sikh Misldars were recruited by Ranjit Singh in his irregular cavalry the "Ghorcharas" and thus ceased to be a source of trouble to him any longer.

(c) During the years 1797-1823. Sikh Military monarchy was created and consolidated. This was the work of one man. During all this time his work consisted of conquering territories over territories. To use the language of Hugel he "joined together a multitude of disjointed materials." Political parochialism and local dynasticism were almost insuperable barriers. There was no current of popular enthusiasm to sweep these away. No triumphant militarism, no dramtic scene as in the Glarie des Glacis at Versailles on January 18, 1871, was to help the creation here of a majestic fabric. There was also no high-bred courtesy to help his diplomacy to lose half its grossness. Yet this architect, skilful in his own way, worked out a scheme, the inevitability of whose success seems surprising. He was as inexorable as fate, unmoved by feelings of pite or compasion. Bismarck told Jules Favre, the tearful suppliant for the fate of his conquered country, that "bursts of sentiment are out of place in politics." The same attitude of mind must be associated with the creative work of his great organiser. Cautious, discerning, conciliatory, depending more on diplomacy than on force, he was "more unscrupulous than cruel." Most of those chiefs whom he dispossessed. and the list is very long. found to their relief that their conqueror was willing to give them sufficient jagir to maintain them in comfort and even high rank in state service if they were willing to serve him. Qutb-ud-Din of Kasur, Ahmed Khan of Jhang, Sarfraz Khan of Multan, Sultan Khan of Bhimbur,

Sahib Singh of Gujrat, his Gulab Singh, Ranbir Chand of Katoch (grandson of Sansar Chand) and many other persistent enemies of the Lahore Chief, found to their great relief that this erstwhile foe was forgiving and generous within limits.

In this way we conclude that the highest aim of Ranjit Singh's life was the establishment of Sikh Kingdom in the Punjab with himself as the national King of all the Sikhs under his banner, no matter whether they lived to the South or the North of the river Sutlej. This he did by annexing the territories of all the Sikh Misldars. But in doing so, he used forced as well as diplomacy, diplomacy in the case of strong and force in the case of weak Misldars. Thus he was unscrupulous. He was unscrupulous also in his dealings with the Misldars. But in his dealings with his relations he acted like Bismarck who used to say, "bursts of sentiments are out of question in politics." He ultimately succeeded in uniting the Punjab under him amd and thus setting up the Sikh Kingdom. This was the greatest achievement of Ranjit Singh.

❐

6

The Anglo-French Conflict in India

STRUGGLE OF ANGLO-FRENCH FOR THE POLITICAL SUPERMACY OF THE DECCAN

For nearly 20 years from 1744 to 1763 the French and the English were to wage three bitterwars for control over the trade, wealth, and territory of India. These wars are generally known as the Carnatic wars in Indian history. Many causes were responsible for this struggle which can be discussed under the following heads.

The First Carnatic war 1744-48 A.D.. The first war between the English and the French started in India in 1744 A.D. and continued till 1748. This war is known as the First Carnetic war.

Causes

(1) War of the French and the English in Europe. In 1742, war broke out in Europe between French and England. One of the major causes of the war was rivalry over colonies in America. The war in Europe between England and France soon spreah to India where the two companies clashed with each other.

(2) Ambition of Dupleix. In Dupleix came to India as a governor of the French East India company. He was very ambitious. He wanted to establish a French State in India. For the fulfilment of this aim, he belived that the English were the main obstacle. Because of his ambitions also the struggle between the two companies took place in India.

(3) **The Political Conditions of India.** Lack of powerful central authorites in India also encouraged the struggle between the French and the English. After the death of Aurangzeb (1707 A.D.), the Mughal empire continuously declined. The invasion of Nadir Shah (1739) gave a powerful blow to disintegrating Mughal empire. The weak political condition encouraged these foreign compaines to interfere in the political life of the Indians and it was natural to have struggle between these two powers.

(4) **Trade Rivalries.** The second cause of the war between the English and the French was their rivalry in trade. Either of the two desired to out do the other in financial matters. Under such circumstances how long could a war between the two be avoided? As one scabbard can sheath only one sword it was quite impossible for these two great European powers to carry on their trade side by side in India.

Events. Due to above four reasons the two East India Companies clashed with each other. When the news of outbreak of the Austrian was of Succession (in which England and France took part against each other in Europe) arrived in India in 1744 A.D. the governor of the French settlement of Pondicheerry was Dupleix while the governor of the English settlement was Morse. Being well-aware, of his feable sea-power, Dupleix sent this proposal to the English governor that the English and the French in India should follow the policy of remaining neutral. However, the English Governor had already received the intimation that an English fleet of sea-ships had set for India for his help from England under commander Barnett. Morse, therefore, reported to give Dupleix any sort of assurance. Dupleix had, therefore to request the Nawab of Carnatic Anwar-ud-Din in whose state both the ports of Madras and Pondichery were situated that he should not permit any party to wage a war in his state. Consequently the

English stayed their war activities for time being at the suggestion of the Nawab because they did not desire to incur his displeasure. On the other hand, Dupleix had written to the Governor of another French settlement, Mauritius, La Bourdonnis to send him the naval help. This fleet arrived at the Coromandal coast of India in July 1744. He defeated Peyton, the successor of Barnett, who was an incapable officer and put him to flight towards Ceylon. Now there was no obstacle left in the way of the English to start a war against the French. In 1745, the English navy captured French ships off the south east coast of India and threatened Pondicherry. Dupleix asked the French to invade Madras. Under his brilliant leadership, the French retaliatred and occupied Madras on 21st September, 1746 A.D. This led to a very important event of the war. The British appealed to the Nawab of Carnatic, in those territory Madras was situated, to save their settlement from the French. The Nawab agreed to intervene as he wanted to convince the foreign merchants that he was still the master of his territories. He sent an army against the French to stop the two foreign trading companies from fighting on his soil. And so the 10,000 strong army of the nawab clashed with a small French forces consisting of 230 Europeans and 700 Indian soldiers trained along Western lines, at St. Thome on the banks of the Adyar river. The Nawab was decisivelydefeated. This battle of Adyar is considered as one of the Important events of the Indian history. This battle revealed the immense superiority of Western armies over Indian armies because of their better equipment and organisation. The Indian pike was no match for the Western musket and bayonet, nor the India cavalry for the Wester artillary. The large but ill disciplined and unwieldy for territorial expansion in Indian armies could not stand up against the smaller but better desciplined western armies.

In 1748, the general war between England and French ended and, as part of the peace settlement, Madras was resorted to the English (by the Treaty of Aix-la-Chapelle). Though the first Carnetic war ended, the rivalry in trade and over the possessions in India continued and had to be decided one way or the other. Moreover the war had revealed to the full the weakness of Indian government and armies and thereby fully aroused the cupidity of both the Companies for territorial expansion in India.

The Second Carnetic War 1748-1754 A.D.. Only a few months had elapsed since the end of the Frist Carinetic War when the English and the French had to get themselves involved into another war in 1748 A.D. It is known as the Second Carnetic War.

Causes

(1) **Struggle for the Succession of the Throne of Tanjore.** The English openly supported the claim of Shahji to the throne of Tanjore in 1748 as against Pratap Singh. They agreed to support him with the army. Shahji agreed to give away Devi Kota to the English for this help. The company's armies captured Tanjore. Pratap Singh entered into an alliance with the English who retired Shahji on pension. The success frightened the French.

(2) **Disputed Succession at Hyderabad and Carnatic.** The First Carnatic war had established a tradition to interfere in the affairs of the Indian Princes and thus to make the maximum of the rotten India political state of affairs. The opportunity come when in 1748 the aged Nizam, Asaf Jah, the ruler of Hyderabad in Deccan, died. Two persons now claimed the throne- Nasir Jang, the second son of the Nizam and Muzaffar Jang, the grandson of the Nizam (daughter's son),

There was a similar contest for the throne in the Carnatic. The Nawab of Carnatic dies and the throne became a bone of contention between Chanda Sahub, the son-in-law of the deceased Nawab and Anwar-Asaf Jah. Now this was a time when by meddling in Indian affairs a supplementary in Deccan could be achieved for which both were ready but Dupleix took the initiative and on a request from Chanda Sahib, he immediately agreed to come to his help. He took the side of Chanda Sahib and Muzaffar Jang. The English could not tolelrate that the French should come soon to them with puppet on the throne and that they may be threatened at each and every moment they supported the opposite parties.

Events. Chanda Sahib, with the help of the French, defeated and killed Anwar-ud-din. On accession to the throne of Carnatic, Chanda Sahib gave a very fertile and rich area to the French. On the other side there was a confrontation between Muzaffar Jang and Nasir Jang, the main claimants to the throne of Hyderabad. When both were dead, the French General Bussy installed Salabat Jang, a younger brother of Nasir Jang on the throne of Hyderabad. The new ruler gave to the French, as a result of their help, the territory of Northern Circars. In this way, by 1750 A.D. the whole of the south came under the influence of the French.

The English were upset by the increasing French influence. The estblishment of Chanda Sahib, the ally of the French, on the throne of Carnatic was bound to have adverse effect on English trade since the hinterland of Madras would be in the hands of their enemies. Governor Saunders decided to take vigorous pleasures. Clive was sent with 200 European and 300 Indian soldiers. He captured Arcot, the capital of Carnatic,Chanda Sahib sent about half of his army under his son Raja Sahib to take back Arcot and Clive was besieged there. The timely arrival of Murari Rao, a Maratha chief, enabled Clive to defeate Raja Sahib. Then Chanda Sahib was forced by Major Lawrence to raise the seige of Trichinopoly. He fled away and was put to death by the Raja of Tanjore. Thus Muhammad Ali became the Nawab of Carnatic. Dupleix tried to recover his position but could not do anything. He was recalled in 1754. His successor, Godheau, soon after his arrival, began to negotiate for peaceful relations with the English and ended warfare with them in 1754 A.D. and he signed the Treaty of Pondicherry.

Treaty of Pondicherry, 1754 A.D.

According to this treaty both the companies promised that they would not interfere in the internal affairs of the Indian rulers. Secondly, Bussy's stay at Hyderabad was accepted by both the sides. Thirdly, both the companies promised to give up all the posts and privileges granted to them by the Indian rulers. Fourthly, both the parites returned the conquered parts of each other and they were left with those portions alone which were with them before the beginning of the hostilities. Fifthly, it was also agreed between both the companies that this treaty might be considered temporary until approved by their respective governments at home.

Criticism of the Treat. It has been pointed out that by the treaty of 1755, Godheau sacrificed everything for which Dupleix had fought. According to Dupleix himself," Godheau had signed the ruin of the country and the dishonour of the nation". The French agreed to give away all that they had captured so far. Whether the treaty was wise or not, one thing is certain. It made the English stronger. It also gave them mugh needed rest before embarking upon the Third Carnatic War.

Third Carnatic War (1756-1763)

Causes. The peace between the French and the English in India proved very short-lived. In 1756, there broke out the well know Seven Years' War in Europe and before long the two nations began to fight in India also. Thus the third Carnatic War was merely an echo of the Seven Years' War in Europe.

Events. When there ensued a war between the British and the French in Europe, the French Government sent a powerful army under the command of Count-de-Lally to mitigate the influence of the British in India. As soon as he came to India in 1758 he captured Fort St. George and decided to attack Madras, but by this time the English had won name and fame by winning the Battle of Plassey in 1757 A.D. But still Lally proceeded further. He asked de-Ache,the naval commander, to give him naval protection which he refused to do. Lally then made a political and military bluder. He called Bussy from Deccan. Taking advantage of the situation Clive sent his armies to Deccan which captured Northern Circasrs. Nawab Salabt Jang immediately changed his affiliation and joined the English. Lally then attacked Madras but failed to take that also. He was defeated in the battle of Wandiwash (1760)and Bussy was made prisoner. In 1761 the English armies conquered Pondicherry, Karikal and manny other French possessions.

Effects or Results of Anglo-French struggle. The war ended in 1763 with the signing of the treaty of Paris. The French factories in India were restored but they could no longer be fortified or even adequately garrisoned with troops. They could serve only as centres of trade; and now the French lived in India under British protection. Their dream of Empire in India was at an end. The English, on the other hand, ruled the Indian sea, Freed of all European rivals, they could now set about the task of conquering India.

During their struggle with the French and their India allies, the English learnt a few important and valiable lessons. Firstly, that in the absence of nationalism in the country, they could advance their political schemes by taking advantage of the mutual quarrels of the India rulers. Secondly, the Western trained infantry, European or Indian, armed with modern weapons and backed by artillery could defeat the old-style Indian armies with ease in pitched battles. Thirdly, it was proved that the Indian soldier trained and armed in the European manner made as good a soldier as the European. And since the Indian soldier too lacked a feeling of nationalism, he could be hired and employed by anyone who was willing to pay him well. The

English now set out to create a powerful army consisting of Indian soldiers, called sepoys, and officered by Englishmen. With this army as its chief"instrument and the vast resources of Indian trade and territories under its command, the English East India Company embarked on an era of wars and territorial expansion.

The Causes of Failure of the French. The French East India Company made efforts to establish monopoly of trade and political authority in India. The struggle between two companies continued from 1744 to 1763. During that period many wars took place between the two and the French power in India declined because of continuous defeat, and by 1770 the French East India Company ended. For this defest of the French in this struggle some historians make responsible the French governors. Dupleix and Lally. But there were many causes for the success of the English. These can be discussed under the following headings:

(1) **Policy of William Pitt.** The credit of the English success in India is also due to their War Minister, Pitt who kept Franch so involved in warfare in Europe by his policy that she could not pay her attention to India at all. As soon as Pitt the Younger became the War Minister in 1758 he introduced such powerful changes that France remained involved in European affairs only. He helped Fredrick the Great of Prussia to keep French busy fighting in Europe. Thus France could not send adequate help to India and America while England sent the needed help to India.

(2) **Excessive Interference of the French Government.** The French East India Company was heavily dependent on the French Government which helped it by giving it treasury grants, subsidies, and loans, and in various other ways. Consequently, it was largely controlled by the Government which appointed its directors after 1723. Moreover, big shares in the company were held by the nobles and other rentiers who were more interested in quick dividends than in making the company a lasting commerical success. So long as the loans and subsidies from the Government

enabled the directors to declare dividends, they did not care much about the success of soundness of its commercial ventures. State control of the company proved harmful to it in another way. The French state of the time was autocratic, semi-feudal, and unpopular and suffered from corruption, inafficiency and instability. Instead of being forward-looking it was decadent, bound by tradition, and in general unsuited to the times, control by such a state could not but be injurious to the interests of the company.

(3) **Entry from Wrong Side by the French.** The French entered India from the wrong quarter. The Deccan was not fertile. It was absolutely unproductive. The result was that the military conquest of the Deccan by the French did not compensate them. Their enterprise was a failure. On the other hand, the English entered India from the right quarter. They started from Bengal. It had a very productive soil, There was a lot of gold with the people and consequently the English got a lot of money after the conquest. Moveover, through the Ganges River, the English could penetrate into the interior of the country from Bengal. In the absence of good roads, the river provided an easy means of communication and transport at that time.

(4) **Appreciation of the Work of Company's Employees by the English Government.** The English Government appreciated the work of the able employees of the company. It was a great encouragement to them. This appreciation became a source of great incentive even to other employees. It created great zeal and initiative in its staff. The work of Clive was highly appreciated. The French government did not treat its employees in the same spirit. The treatment meted out to Dupleix and La Bourdonnais was definitely bad. All the services of Dupleix were forgotten and he died a penniless person.

(5) **Economic Reasons.** The economy of the French Company was not sond. The reason for this poor economy are:

(i) Their trade with India was neither progressive nor profitable.

(ii) Dupleix nursed the ambition to establish a French empire in India. He had to entangle himself into the politics of the native rulers, and sacrificed the interests of the trade. This worsened the financial condition of the French company.

(iii) Dupleix spent money beyond the means sof the Company. The directors did not support him for the reasons.

On the other hand, the British East India Company had a strong financial base. Its resources were many and the trade avenues were extensive. They had a profitable trade in the northern India and Bengal. The French had confined themselves to the south which was not so much profitable in terms of trade.

(6) **Stronger Sea-power of the English.** During the Austrian War of succession Frech maritime strength was so greatly reduced that, according to Voltaire, she was left with no worships during the Seven Years' War. Pitt the Elder made the maximum use of the superiority of England on the high seas. Superior naval force enabled the English East India Company to keep open her communications with Europe, cover her operations on land in the Carnatic by supplying reinforcements from Bombay and Calcutta and cut off and isolate French force in the Carnatic from the rest of the world. Superior maritime strength proved to be England's most powerful weapon in the struggle for colonial supermacy.

(7) **Success of the Britishers in a Prosperous Province as Bengal.** In 1757, after defeating the Nawab of Bengal in the battle of Plassey, the English established their supremacy there. The Allahabad Treaty, which was signed after the success of the battle of Buxor, gave them the right to

collect Diwani of Bengal, Bihar, and Orissa. This helped them in strengthening their economic position. They used the revenue amount in purchasing Indian goods which increased the profit of the company in trade. The French did not get an economic resource like Bengal.

(8) **Superior Position of the English Company.** The English Company enjoyed superiority against the French company in many respects from the very start of their struggle. The English company was a private company and mostly remained free from the interference of the British government. Therefore, its financial position largely remained sound. The financial disparity between the two companies increased further when the English captured political power in Bengal. Thus, the English company was superior to the French Company in its finances and organisation. The English company also possessed better straitegic and trade centers in India. On the south-east coast, Pondicherry was certainly a good settlement of the French but Madras under the British was equally good.

(9) **Efficient Generals.** The British were quite lucky to have foresighted generals like Clive, Forde, Sirl Eyro Coote and Lawrence with them. On the contrary, the French had no able generals with them except Dupleix. But Dupleix as per Dr. V.A. Smith's versian was not a good general, because throughout his life he had been a businessman.

(10) **The Recall of Dupleix.** The recall of such a brilliant tractician as Dupleix when his presence was so badly needed in India to safeguard the French interests was a fatal mistake of the French Government. The French Government further made a serious mistake in abandoning the policy pursued by Dupleix. With his recall the French influence and power which he had so patiently built rapidly came to naught. The appointment of such-headed and incapable generals like Count Lally was another factor in weakening the position of the French in India.

POLICY OF DUPLEIX

Dupleix was the most competent of all the French Governors sent to India., He was at first Governor of Chandernagar in Bengal. In 1742 he was made Governor of Pondicherry. During the First Carnatic War he captured Madras from the English but had to return it when peace was made in Europe by the Treaty of Aix-la-Chapelie in 1748. He brought about a great change in the policy of the French in India. The aim of his policy was to extend French influence and power. He grasped several facts very clearly. Firstly, the political condition in India was rotten. The Mughal Empire had decayed and independent States, which arose on its ruins, were often at war with each other. India was thus internally weak. Secondly, the Indian system of warfare was out of cate. The large indisciplined levies of Indian rulers were not able to stand before the well trained infantry of Europeans. Thirdly, Indian recruits could be trained in European methods of warfare, and could be grerat assets under the command of European officers. Fourthly in the disturbed political condition of India the French could not be sure of their trade. Hence they must arm themselves to protect their trade. They must extend their political influence and power further their commercial interests. To achieve these objects he began to interfere in the quarrels of native States.

In 1748 Nizam-ul-Mulk Asaf Jah died and there started a dispute between his son Nasir Jung and grandson (daughter's son) Muzaffar Jung. About the same time started a dispute for the throne of Carnatic between Nawab Anwar-ud-Din and Chanda Shahib, son-in-law of a former Nawab, Dost Ali. Dupleix took up the cause of Mazaffar Jung and Chanda Sahib. Their combined forces defeated Anwar-ud-Din at Amber and he was killed. His son Muhammad Ali was besieged in Trichinopoly. In case of Hyderabad both Nasir Jung and Muzaffar Jung were killed. Then the French Officer Bussy placed Asaf Jah's youngest son, Salabat Jung, on the throne and himself stayed at Hyderabad to help him. The English realised the gravity of the situation and gave help to Muhammad Ali. Clive captured Arcot, the capital of Carnatic. Chanda Sahib sent a part of his army under his son Raja Sahib to recapture it and Clive was besieged. when reinforcements arrived, Clive defeated this army. Then the English defeated Chanda Sahib at Trichinopoly and Muhammdad Ali was made Nawab of Carnatic. Dupleix's policy was successful at Hyderabad where Saladat Jung was made the Nizam but it failed in Carinatic where Muhammad Ali, the friend of the English, became the Nawab. The French Government did not like Dupleix's policy and recalled him. He was tried on his return and died a penniless person.

Dupleix was certainly ambitious but his motive were patriotic. His countrymen did not understand him and he was not given that good treatment which he well deserved. He was a genius and a far-sighted politician.

There is difference of opinion regarding the achievement of Dupleix. Historian like Malleson and Hamont consider him a hero. In spite of controversy it must be admitted that Dupleix did not succeed in his ultimate designs yet he achieved much. He made the French cause proper in India, raised their military prestige, cenceived of praiseworthy goal of them and pointed out the right way to reach the goal. It is even said that he would have recovered the lost position with the help of troops brought by Goldehu, if he had not been recalled. Dupleix was certainly the greatest man sent by the French of India, though he failed and was misunderstood by him countrymen.

Dupleix as a Statesman

As a statesman, it was Dupleix who for the first time rightly grasped the real rotten political situation in India. He rightly realised that the position of the French trade was precarious so long as it depended on the pleasure and caprice of Indian rulers. He was the first to make the two important discoveries-that the native armies were weak against the European soldiers and a handful of native soldiers disciplined in European fashion and officered by Frenchmen whould be more than a match for the vast indisciplined hordes of native rulers. This discovery he had made during the first Anglo-French conflict when an incident occurred which had great influence on the subsequent history of India. Dupleix had secured the sanction of Nawab Anwar-ud-Din in his attack upon Madras by promosing to make over the ciry to him after its capture. When Madras fell into his hands he refused to keep his promise and so Anwar-ud-din sent a large force to enforce his claim. But to the surprise of all, a handful of French troops completely routed his vast army at Mailapur or St. Thome in 1746. The importance of the battle lies in the fact that it revealed the helplessness of the Indian army against a small body of trained Europeans. Dupleix profited by this manner and his ambitions began to soar high as soon as the war with the English came to a close. He perceived that in the rivalries of the local princes his small but well-disciplined army might play a decisive part. This would ensure French supremacy in the courts of the Indian princes whose influence he might utilise in ousting the English from India. This was the grand idea which he began to cherish. Henceforth, he began to look forth for opportunities to extend French influence by calculated interference in the internal quarrels of the Indian States. The second discovery that he made was the inabiliy of the political dynasties in India and the constant quarrels between the native rulers. First of all he intended to drive the British out of India. Then one by one, he hoped that the Indian States would fall into his own hands since they were weak and disorganised Sir Alfred Lyall pays tribute to the statesmanship of Dupleix when he writes: "Dupleix was a man of original and energetic political instincts, of an imperious and morally intrepid disposition, who embarked upon wide and somewhat audacious schemes of oriental dominion, and lost the stakes for which he played more through want of strength and support than want of skill. He saw that so long as an European Comany held their possessions or carried on trade at the pleasure of capricious and ephemeral Indian Governments, the position was in the highest degree precarious. The right method, he argued, was to assert independence, to strike for mastery and to strike down any European rival who crossed his path; and if the English had not been too strong for him he might have succeeded. He made the common-place mistake of effecting ostentatious display and resorting to astute intrigues in his dealings with the Indians; whereas a European should meet orientals not with their weapons but with his own. His claim to be recognised as Nawab of the Carnatic under patents of doubtful authenticity, was a grave political blunder, since it was quite impossible for the English to acquiesce in a position that would have placed their settlements in perpetual jeopardy." Again we may regard him, nevertheless, as the most striking figure in the Indian episode of that long and arduous contest for transmarine dominion which was fought out between France and India in the 18th Century, although it was far beyond his power to influence the ultimate destiny of either nation in India, and although the result of his plans was that "we accomplish for ourselves against the French exactly everthing that the French intended to accomplish for themselves against us." It is certain moreover, that the conception of an Indian Empire had already been formed by others beside Dupleix and that more than one clear- headed observer had perceived how easily the whole country might be subduced by an European power.

Dupleix as an Administrator

According to Malleson, "Dupleix was great administrator and diplomat with a wonderful capacity of organisation and great persistence and tenacity of purpose. He was an adventurer of a very high order, not only endowed with a restless genius, a deep imagination but also given to ostentatious display. Successful as an administrator and an organiser, he took the delicate pursuit of intriguing with the native princes with the ultimate object of building up a French Empire in India, but he sought to promote the glory and honour of his country with inadequate means and support. Though a past-master in the intricate game of oriental politics, all his ambitious schemes were miscarried and when at last he went back he left only a wreck of them all behind him. Like a meteor he passed away from the horizon of India with all his dreams dashed to dust and claiming only a twilight of glimmer as his glory."

Growth of the French Power Under Dupleix

According to P.E. Roberts, "Dupleix was a striking and brilliant figure in Indian history. For even if we give up the old uncritical estimate we need not deny his real claims to greatness. His political conceptions were daring and imaginative. He raised the prestige of France in the East for some years to an amazing height; he won the reputation amongst Indian princes and leaders that has never been surpassed and he aroused a dread in his English contemporaries which is at once a tribute to his personal power and a testimony to his sagacity." His claim to honour cannot justly be denied. P.E. Roberts says, "Dupleix was a real founder of European ascendancy in India." When he came to India, he rightly studied the political rotten condition of the country. He was the first Frenchman who conceived a practical scheme to found a French colonial empire in India. When the First Carnatic War broke out, Dupleix refused to confirm the treaty made by La Boundonnais and carried away the English Governor and officers as prisoners of war to Pondicherry. He thus raised his nation very high in the estimation of the natives. The death of Nizam-ul-Mulk in 1748 led to important results both in Hyderabad and in the Carnatic. Dupleix, by his able diplomacy, succeeded in placing Muzaffar Jung on the throne of Carnatic. He himself became Governor of Southern India and founded the town of Dupleix Fatehabad in commemoration of his triumph. Thus by his policy of tactful and calculated interference in the affairs of rival Indian princes, he succeeded in making French influence supreme in Southern India. Dupleix had a strong faith in the righteousness of his cause and also an earnest desire to serve his country's interests. It was again due to diplomacy of Dupleix that on the eve of the First Carnatic War he could threaten the British Governor at Madras, Mr. Morse, through Nawab Anwar-ud-din and by this he could avoid his invasion which was quite imminent till he could invite La Bourdonnais.

Dr. V.A. Smiths's Remarks Falsified. He was sent to India as the Governor of Chandernagore, but in 1742 he was made the head of the French establishments in India. He was in power up to 1754 and during the 13 years he strengthened the French prestige and power. As a true nationalist the great aim and ambition of his life was to oust the English from India and to establish a French colonial empire here. To fulfil his schemes he trained and disciplined Indian sepoys on European lines and made it a part of his policy to interfere in the disputes of rival Indian princes and take advantage of the situation. Dupleix's triumph was for a time complete. He defeated, as has already been pointed out above, the English in the First and the Second Carnatic Wars, succeeded in getting the Northern Circars and assumed the title of Nawab so that he made the French influence supreme in the Deccan and the French came to be regarded as the gratest nation of Europe. The growing prestige and power of France was mostly due to the efforts, foresight, patriotic spirit and strong determination of this great man. His country's interest was always dearest to him and he never allowed himself to be carried away by designs of present game. But if he failed to realise his ambition of setting up a French colonial empire in India. It was in a very large measure due to the mistakes and lack of support and co-operation on the part of the French Government and the offcers under him and several other causes beyond his control. The English breathed a sigh of relidf when they succeeded in getting rid of him by persuading the French Government to recall him to France at the time of peace negotiations that opened after the Second Carnatic War. His English contemporaries regarded him as a dreadful foe of the English interests in India. Maj. Lawrence says, "It is my opinion that there can never be any peace while Dupleix stays in India. He neither values man nor money nor anything but what can gratify his own ambitions. The continued ill-success of his troops would have made any body but him reflect and be glad of the terms offered, but he talks not like the Governor of Pondicherry but as the Prince of the Province." Under these circumstances, no blunder of the French Government was greater than the recall of this great man to Franch when his absence in India could prove most ruinous to the French interests in India. The above achievements of Dupleix falsify the remarks made by Dr. V.A. Smith that "The character and merits of Dupleix hardly merit the admiration which they have generally received". On the other hand, the truth is that if he had a little more of favourable circumstances, he would have surely succeeded in establishing a French Empire in India. Unfortunately, finance was always his stumbling block from the first to the last. Dupleix was never finacially supported by the Home authorities. A Company's support was never enough to ensure the success of the French sheme of building the French Empire in India.

He Spent Money Out of his Own Pocket to Finance the French Wars Against the English. He spent £3 lakhs from his personal pocket to advance the interests of his country and patiently contiuned his work though the French Government did not support him. Dupleix will always remain a tragic figure in Indian history. He was let down both by his fortune and by the countrymen. He rightly pointed out that " He had sacrificed his youth, his fortune and his life for the sake of the enhancement of the prestige and glory of the French nation in India. He had spent money out of his own pocket to finance the wars which he waged in India against the Brithish with a view to establishing the French Empire in this country." This was not a mean achievement on the part of Dupleix. When we consider that he formed the plan of conquest and dominion at a time when all other Europeans entertained the highest opinion of the strength of the Mughal Government, we cannot refrain from acknowledging and admiring the sagacity of his genius." Even the rivals, who profited by his recall, place him on a pedestal scarcely scarcely, if at all, lower than the pedestals upon which stand Clive, Warren Hastings and Wellesley in grandness of conception and his wide scope of projects of empire; he was their fore runner and their inspirer."

Causes of Dupleix's Failure to Establish French Empire in India. There is no doubt that Dupleix was wise statesman and he was ambitious and farsighted. He wanted to estasblish the French empire in India by ousting the English who were their only rivals in India. But certain circumstances and difficulties continued to make it difficult for him to realise his great ambition of founding the French Empire in this country. The responsibility of the failure of Dupleix to realise his ambtions in India falls party on the French government and partly on himself. The following, therefore, were the causes of his failure to estasblish French Empire in India:

Causes for which Dupleix was Personally Responsible

(1) Dupleix Flung his Nets Too Far. *(a)* Firstly, it has rightly been said that the Frenchmen will ever regret that Dupleix flung his nets too far and that he did not confine his efforts to the Carnatic. This is quite correct. Unfortunately, Dupleix did not care to see the limitations under which he was carrying on his political activities in India. He carried his conquest very far inland without a powerful navy to guard French interests on the Indian coast. The control of the sea was a fundamental factor for the success of the people who, from a distance of thousands of miles, wanted to carve a kingdom in far off lands. The English had the advantage over the French in two respects: *(1)* They had better ships and command of the sea routes; *(2)* The English had their possessions more favourably placed than the French. The French had no settlements on the West coast as compared with Bombay, while Calcutta, the richest part of the country, quite easily over-shadowed Chandernagore which was under French occupation. Dupleix had carried his conquests far into the interior of the country without either having strong points on the coasts or efficient means of keeping open communication with Europe. Naval supremacy of the English steed them in good stead. The British navy, which was quite supreme on the high seas, could proceed any way in order to help the British Company. This could not be done by the success of the English in the Anglo-French conflict for supremacy. The other great handicap in the way of the French navy was that it was so much engaged in wars in Europe and America that it was not posible for it to attend to the needs of the French in India.

(b) Secondly, he failed because his ambition was not restrained by a consideration of what was possible for him to do. He attempted too much at one and the same time, regardless of the limited resources at his command. He would at oncé dominate the Carnatic and the Deccan although he had not sufficient men and money for such a big project. Had he first concentrated upon the Carnatic and reduced Trichinopoly, he might have gained his object. The services of Bussy, the ablest of the Fremch generals then in India, might have turned the scale in his favour at

Trichinopoly, but he kept him at Hyderabad to maintain influence in the Nizam's Court. In the reuslt, he lost his hold on the Carnatic and subsequent developments there led to Bussy's recall and the consequent collapse of the French influence at Hyderabad.

(2) Another cause of Dupleix's failure in India was that he made a mistake in sending away Bussy to Hyderabad and thus dividing the strength of the French in two directions. It is true that Bussy maintained the position and influence of the French in Hyderabad till 1758. But if the united forces of the French had worked together in the Carnatic, it would have been very difficult for the English to overwhelm the French there. It was because of this divison in the French stength that ultimately proved fatal to the French cause. With the depature of Bussy from Hyderabad, all French influence that was established in Hyderabad also disappeared.

(3) Another handicap from which Dupleix suffered was that he was not a great general and, as such, lacked personal courage. On the other hand, the person with whom he was matched was Clive, a great diplomat as well as a great general. No wonder while Dupleix failed, Clive succeeded.

(4) Dupleix as a statesman failed in one respect and failed grandly. He focussed his whole attention to the Deccan politics alone and did not do anything to establish the French influence in Bengal where, on the other hand, the English were very busy strongly establishing their political influence. The province of Bengal was definitely more prosperous than the Deccan and its occupation by the English gave them a great power by virtue of which they were in a position to crush the power of the French in the Deccan. If, like the English, Dupleix also had tried to penetrate into Bengal province too, he would have been able not only to create many difficulties by creating a diversion in the attention of the English in Bengal, but in the Deccan also, at the same time.

(5) Another serious handicap from which Dupleix personally suffered was that he was vain and quarrelsome. He would pick up quarrel even with the subordinates from whom he would have expected co-operation. He may also be charged with duplicity. But it should, however, be noted here that nobody is perfect on this earth. That he failed is no fault of his. V.A. Smith says, "It is futile to lay stress upon the personal frailties of Dupleix, Lally or lesser men in order to explain the French failure. Neither Alexander the Great, nor Napoleon could have won the Empire of India by starting from Pondicherry as a base and contending with the power which held Bengal and the command of the sea-the English."

(6) As has already been pointed out above, Dupleix studied the real politically rotten situation in India and, as such, wanted to take advantage of it. He saw that India was divided into a number of states and, therefore, by involving one prince against the other in quarrel he would be able to finish them all one by one and turn by turn. Consequently, he busied himself in the internal quarrels of the Indian rulers so much that he forgot all about himeself. This too much interference in the affairs of the Indian prices irritated them very much and he became very unpopular in their eyes. This also was one of the causes of his failure in India.

(7) **Lack of Support from the French Government.** Another great handicap which failed Dupleix in India was his failure to receive a whole hearted support from the Home Government. The Home Government was so busy in wars with England in Europe and America that she could not properly attend to the affairs of the French in India. Dupleix was anxious to promote the glory and honour of his country but his resources were most inadequate. Critics have rightly pointed out that the masters of Dupleix looked

more to the dividends and not to the future French Empire in India. It is true that Dupleix was also partly to be blamed because he did not unfold his plans and their prospects to the Home Govyernmets, but evern when he did so, nobody felt enthusiastic about them. The only result was that he was called back.

(8) **Non-co-operation.** Unfortunately for Dupleix, He was placed in a very delicate postion. His subordinates, both of high and low ranks, did not supports him whole-heartedly. They did not carry out his instruction faithfully. Instead, they were fighting among themselves for selfish ends. They sacrificed the general interest of their own country for their sordid interests. In these circumstance, Dupleix failed to realise his amibitons which otherwise he would have done if he had received full co-operation from his subordinates as a team working under his leadership whole-heatedly for the common cause of their country's glory.

(9) **Incompetence of the French Generals.** Another cause that prevented Dupleix from permanently estasblishing the French empire in India was the hopeless incompetence of the French generals. "It is idle to deny the fact that the subsequent course of events was determined to a large extent by personalities rather than circumstances. The brilliant genius and dash of Clive, on the one hand, and the indecision and the lack of energy displayed by Lally and his colleagues, on the other, determined the issue. Had Dupleix at his disposal a military genius like that of Clive, the history of French in India might have been altogether different.

(10) **Financial Resources.** Dupleix's resources in India were small and slender. His grand designs could not be carried into practice without adequate finance. It has rightly been said that finance was always the stumbling block in his way. If he had enough of money he could have recruited a number of soldiers form the Indians but the paucity of

funds did not allow him to do so. It was impossible for anybody to fight with those soldiers whose salaries had been promised but had not been paid. The result was that the schemes of Dupleix could not be carried out. Therefore, Dupleix will ever remain a tragic figure in the history, thwarted by destiny and let down by his countrymen to enrich whom he wrote, "he had sacrificed his youth, his fortune and his life." He had spent all his fortune, some £ 2,40,000 in providing the sinews of war. These facts alone speak volumes for his sincerity and devotion to his country.

(11) Another serious handicap from which Dupleix suffered was that the French East India Company was a concern of the Government and all appointments were made by the Government. Hence the servants of the company did not care for their officers in India, because they depended more for patronage of the appointing authorities at home than for Dupleix or his officers in this country. Moreover, the Company being a Government concern could not get as much of attention from the Home Government as it should have done because the Government was busy in other engagements in their activities in Europe and America.

(12) According to Dodwell," The Policy of Dupleix indeed lacked the elements of permanent success and could never have survived an European war. Had he never been recalled, Coote or some other English leaders would nonetheless have besieged, Captured and ruined Pondicherry. The indipensable condition of political expansion in the East lay in the 18th century as it had lain in the 16th and 17th, in the predominance at sea. But this condition, as events were to prove, was not possessed by Frence. Dupleix's success was only obtained under temporary conditions of a most favourable nature. He launched his campaign after the war of the Austrian succession. The most powerful weapon of the English, their naval power, was for moment out of action. They could not pursue, intercept, or destroy the vessels which carried the Pondicherry recruits and munitions. Without this advantage it is unlikely that Dupleix would have obtained as high a degree of success as he in fact secured."

In this we find that Dupleix was after all a man and he his limitations. He had to face a number of serious problems, some of them being created by his own countrymen. His political projects were daring and brilliant and if the French Government and his officers had thoroughly co-operated with him and if he had been given the right type of men and timely financial help, he could have realised his great ambition of life. His works,achievements and character amply justify the truth of the statement, "but in spite of his final failure, Dupleix is striking and brilliant figure in English history." For a time he raised the prestige of France in India to an amazing height and his interference in the Deccan would have shattered to English hopes there, if only the French Government had supported him. He was a capable administrator otherwise,and his political conceptions were daring and imaginative. His grand scheme failed because unsupported by the Home Government, he could not adjust them to the limited resources at his command.He wad indeed prone to tortuous intrigue and unscrupulousness in money matters but in these respects his conduct was not worse than that of his European contemporaries in India. His successful and largelly praised rival. Clive, was equally unscrupulous in money matters. He was more greedy and extortionate.

CAUSES THAT LED TO THE DEFEAT OF THE FRENCH

The English and the French had properly established their settlements in India by 1740 and had bcome serious rivals of each other. They forght three wars in India known as the Carnatic Wars and by 1763 the English had completely crushed the French military and political power in this country. Several factors contributed to the ultimated success of the English:-

(1) Commercial Superiority. The English Company carried on much more trade than the French Company. According to Moreliet, the value of the sale of Indian goods in England between 1736 and 1756 was £ 41,200,000 while that of the French goods was £11,450,000. In other words the receipts of the English Company from the sale of Indian goods were about three and a half times more than the receipt of the French Company. Flourishing business is essential to the prosperity of a trading company, whatever its administrative and military successses may be. Due to the superiority in trade, the financial position of the English Company was better than that of the French Company.

The English Company carried on trade on a large scale even during war and its financial position continued to be good. It was in a position to finance its wars properly. The French neglected trade during the war and their financial condition became bad. They were not able to pay their troops regularly during the closing years of the Third Carnatic War.

(2) The English Company was a private concern but the British Government took great interest in its affairs. The Company had advanced loans to the Government and thus placed it under obligation. Moreover, some of the director of the Company were memberes of Parliament and could thereby exercise some influence on the Government. They could make the Government take interest in the affairs of the Company. The French Company was a Government concern but the French Government did not take keen interest in its affairs because of entanglements in European affairs.

(3) The English Company was a private concern and its employees possessed greate initiative and enterprise. Their fortunes were linked with the prosperity of the Company and they took great interest in its affairs. The French Company became a governmet concern and its shasre

holders had been granted a fixed dividend. Its employees did not have that zest and initiative which was possessed by the employees of the English Company.

(4) The English Government appreciated the work of the able employees of the Company. It was a greast encouragement to them. This appreciation became a source of great incentive even to other employees. It created great zest and initiative in its staff. The work of Clive was highly appreciated. The French Government did not treat its employees in the same spirit. The treatment meted out to Dupleix and La Bourdonnais was definitelybad. All the services of Dupleix were forgotten and he died a penniless person. This must have crushed incentive in other emplyees. It contributed to the downfall of French power to some extent.

(5) The French Government recalled Dupliex in 1754. It was blunder. He had not been reponsible for the French setbacks in the Second Carnatic war. He was a competent person and had done much to further French interests. He might have still done something to retrieve the position of the French. His unjust recall created a vacuum which could not be filled. There was no competent person to take his place. Moreover, his policy was given up by his successors. His recall greatly contributed to French failure in India.

(6) The settlements of the English in India were superior to French settlements. On the Western Coast Bombay was far superior to Mahe. Madras on the Eastern Coast was as good as Pondicherry. Calcutta in Bengal surpassed Chandernagar in prosperity. If the Englsih lost one of their settlements, they could hold out in others. If the French lost Pondicherry, they lost everything, since other French settlements could be easily captured. It placed the English in an advantageous position.

(7) There was the fullest co-operation among the officers of the English Company and it greatly contributed to its

success. There was lack of co-operation among the French Officers. They sometimes quarrelled in times of crisis and it adversely affected the interests of the company. Dupleix and La Bourdonnais quarrelled with each other after capturing Madras and the latter left for Mauritius.

The generals of the English Company were also superior to the French generals in India. Dupleix was no match for Clive and Lawrence. Even Bussy was not their equal. Lally was for inferior in generalship to Sir Eyre Coote.

(8) Mistakes of Lally. Count de Lally was sent as Governor General and Commander-in-Chief during the Third Carnatic War. He was a daring man and an incorruptible person, but at the same time he was hot-headed and obstinate fellow. After capturing Fort St. David, he decided to attack Madras and for his help called Bussy from Hyderabad. It was political and military blunder. The moment Bussy left Hyderabad, the English captured Northern Circars and Nixam Salabat Jung joined the English. Thus the French influence at Hyderabad came to an end and Lally did not have the satisfaction of capturing Madras. Even Pondicherry was lost in 1761. Thus Lally's mistakes also contributed to French failure.

(9) Conquest of Bengal. The English conquered Bengal in 1757. It was rich and populous province. Its conquest greatly increased their resources in men and money which were used against the French in the Third Carnatic War. Clive sent Colforde from Bengal and he captured Northern Circars. The Bengal troops took an important part in defeating the French at Wandiwash in 1760 and in capturing Pondicherry in 1761. Thus the capture of Bengal enable the English to win victors in the Deccan.

(10) Wrong French base. The French started the conquest of India from a wrong direction. The Deccan was not the proper base for attempting the conquest of India. It was

not fertile and its conquest at the very outset did not pay. The French conquests in the Deccan naturally did not properly pay them. The English were wiser in attaching grater importance to Bengal. It was a rich province and lucrative for its conquerors. Moveover, the English could conquer the Gangetic Valley. In the absence of good roads, rivers provided a good means of communication and transport.

(11) The English had their naval base at Bombay. They could keep and repair their ships in that port. They could being these into action any time. The French had their naval base in the Isle of France which was very far off. Hence they could not bring their navy into action at proper time.

(12) The policy of William Pitt the Elder became a decisive factor. He became war Minister of England in 1758 when she was faring badly everywhere during Seven Years War. He revolutioniesed her war policy. He gave liberal subsidies to Frederick the Great of Prussia so that he might raise troops and keep the French busy fighting in Europe. Naturally the French would not be in a position to send help to India and America. England would be free to send help there. His massterly war policy had the desired effect. Frederick kept the French busy in Europe and they could not send much help to India. England could send reinforcements and thereby turned the scales asgainst the French. The defeat of the French in the Third Carnatic har was to a great extent due to Pitt's wise policy.

(13) France is situated on the continent of Europe and she was dragged almost into every Europeasn war. It kept her attention pinned on Europeon affairs only and she could not properly attend to Indian affairs. Moreover her resources in men and money were exhausted on Europeon battle-fields. Hence she could not spare enough money and soldiers for India. England is an island and she took part in comparatively fewer Europeon wars. She could conserve

her financial and manpower resources which she profitably used in India. No wonder the English succeeded and the French failed in their bid for supremacy in India.

SUCCESS OF THE BRITISH AGAINST FRENCH RIVALS

The Anglo-French struggle in India was but a part of the larger struggle between England and France for colonies and markets that dominated the 18th century. Out of their struggle England came out victorious. Her victories in Europe decided the fate of France both in America and India. With the causes of the French failure in that larger struggle we are not for the present concerned. What is important to note is the fact of that failure and its ruinous effects upon French ambitions in India." The following, therefore, are the causes to which the failure of the French and the success of British can be attributed:

(1) The administrative system, financial condition and stability of the French Company were inferior to those of the British East India Company. In all these, the French Company was definitely inferior to the British company. The French Company from the very beginning, was a state deparment and, as such, it was being run, managed and controlled by the state. Consequently, in its basic structure, there were certain serious flaws. Lethargy, inefficiency and weakness, which played a very important part in bringing about its failure, were rampant and, as such, were the basic features of the administrative system of Louis XV, the emperor ofFrance (1715-1776). Sir Alfred Lyall says, "India was not lost by the French because Dupleix was recalled, or because La Bourdonnais and D'Ache both left the coast at critical moments, or Lally was a headstrong national. All power was in the hands of the royal commissariat, the proprietors of the company taking no interest on their capital, and this interesrt had since 1733 been guaranteed them by the state. The ministers of Louis XV were, no doubt, lethargic and unenterprising. But it must in all fairness to them be remembered that European complications necessarily limited the amount of attention they could devote to Eastern affairs; also it is quite clear from the early history of the French Company that individual energy and initiative in France

were sadly lacking in matters of foreign trade. The state, under Louis IV and Colbert, had galvanised the French Company into life, and when the vigorous hands of the patrons were withdrawn, its energy evaporated." During the days of Louis XIV, who took a maximum interest in the affairs of the Company the company did progress very mush, but after his death nobody from his administration was in a position to devote any amount of his attention towards the Eastern affairs because of the European complications. This resulted in the defeats and failurs of the French East India Company in India.

(2) On the other hand, the English Company still was a vigorous, self-reliant commercial body, managed by a private corporation, and far from being dependent upon state support. It had long been a creditor of the Government for large sums. Its constitution enabled it to wield no inconsiderable influence in matters of public policy while at the same time it escaped the deadening effect of detailed state interference. Its members knew that if they worked hard, they would be able to get profit and if they slackened, they were to be ruined. The result was that the English Company became prosperous.

(3) The English were lucky in having Bombay as their naval base. This enabled them to keep their ships in safety at Bombay and to also start their operations at once as soon as an opportunity demanded. Another asdvantage they got out of this possession was that they could repair their ships also very easily in the harbour of Bombay. On the other hand, the French, unfortunately, had their naval base in the Isle of France which was really a distant place from the soil of India. Hence they could not take any speedy action that was necessary in connection with various situations which arose from time to time during the entire couse of the Carnatic Wars.

(4) Another cause of English success was their naval supremacy. The naval supremacy of the English enable them to send help to India whenever necessary and whenever they pleased. On the way, they faced no obstructions. On the other hand, the French East India Company had not control on the seas and, as such, it was this factor that cut off the link between the French possession in India and France. The French, while coming to India, had to avoid Englishmen

on the way and could not reach India when they were badly needed and hence they ran short of provisions and army. Sometimes, the French vessels were delayed for months and years on the way. The instance of count de Lally is sufficient to clear the point. Although he had left his country at a very early time, he actually reached India very late on account of forced hardship on his way on acount of the British supremacy on the sea. While the English received supplies of food and money frôm Bengal, recruits of men from Europe, grain from their northern settlements, the French could receive nothing but what came to them laborioulsy by land.

(5) The English again had another very, fortunate position in having three important places in India,*i.e.*, Calcutta, Madrass and Bombay. The result of this situation was that if one of these places was conquered by the French, the other two places still remained in the hands of the English and, even if the two places fell into the hands of the French at a time, the English had still third place with them, because of the reason that the French were not in a position to conqer the three British places simultaneously since these were situated at a great distance from each other. On the other hand, the French had only one place and that also could be conquered with one stroke. That place was pondicherry. There is no doubt that the French had two other places on the West Coast, *viz.*, Mahi and Karikal, but they were liable to be conquered any time by the Britishers and were always at the mercy of the English.

(6) It was just by accident that the French had entered into India From a wrong quarter. They had made their entry into India through the Deccan which was not fertile, rather it was unproductive. As a consequence of this factor, the military conquest of the Deccan by the French did not compensate them, because their expenditure exceeded their income from the Deccan. Hence their enterprise from the Deccan was a failure. As against it, the English were fortunate to have made their entry into India through one of the rechest provinces of this country, *i.e.*, Bengal. It was very productive and fertile. The people were rich and prosperous and they had plenty of gold with them. The result was that immediately after their conquest

of Bengal, the English laid their hands on a sufficient quantity of gold in Bengal.

(7) The French Company made another very serious mistake in as much as they subordinated their commercial interests to their territorial ambitions. This made the French Company poor by their entanglements in the Indian wars in which the whole of their funds was wasted. Moreover, the Frendh Government at home was very busy in wars in Europe and America at that time and as such, was not in a position to send men and money for the help of the French East India Company in India. The failure of Dupleix to receive sufficient aid from the Home Government led to his failure as well as the Failure of the French East India Company in this country. On the other hand, the English devoted enough of their attention to commerce and trade from the very beginning; rather they always kept their eye on the sea, because they had sufficiently realised the importance of commerce and trade through seas. Whatever letters the directors of the English East India Company sent to the Company in India, they emphasized not on the territorial conquests but on the importance of increasing trade. This commercial superiority of the English East India Company over the French East India Company in India was definitely a very great factor responsible for giving the success to the English and failure to the French.

(8) Through Bengal the English could easily penetrate into the interior of the country. Another very important thing worthy of note is that Bengal and the interior of the land, being under the possessing of the English, they could penetrate into the interior of the country from Bengal through the valley of the Ganges river. There is no doubt the means of transport and communication were not developed and there were no good roads those days, but the rivers provided an easy means of communication and transport to the company people at that time. This was a great advantage with the English, while the French had no such advantage. So, they fail in India.

(9) Another very important cause of the French failure and the success of the British was that the english were very lucky in having very able and great men in their service at that time. Lord Clive was

a soldier and a statesmen also at the same time. On the other hand, Dupleix was obly a statesman, and not a soldier at all. Consequently, Dupleix was no match to Clive. There were other able Englishmen in the service of the East India Company like Lawrence and Sir Eyre Coote. As compared to these neither Count de Lally nor Bussy was a match for Sir Eyre Coote. They were suffering from lack of co-operation with one another. Hence, nothing but disaster fell to their lot. The quarrel between Dupleix and La Boundonnais on the question of Madras is an instance that can be quoted to show that the servants of the French East India Company did not co-operate with one another in this country. Consequently, La Bourdonnais had left India and the latter situation had to be handled by Dupleix alone. As against this, there was a very great co-operation existing amongst the servants of the East India Company, who helped one another very much and that was really the fundamental cause of their success.

(10) Policy of William Pitt the elder. William Pitt the elder, also called the 'Great Commoner', one of the greatest war ministers of England, followed a vigorous foreign policy. During the Seven Years' War (1757-63) which was going on between the English and the French in Europe and America simultaneously, the English won splendid vicotories through. Pitt's genius tact and enthusiasm. Pitt, by liberally helping Purssia against France in Europe, kept France so mush engaged in the European fight that it could send no hellp to India and America simultaneously. Her inability to send men and money to India and America in time was one of the most important causes of defeat of the French in both the countries. "During the Third Carnatic War, England had the ablest war minister she had ever had, whereas the Government of Louis was incompetent in the extreme. It was in the hands of Court favourites. The whole English nation was interested in the struggle and was using all its energy to win it, whereas the French Government was autocratic and had little sympathy for the common people."

(11) Recall of Dupleix. The recall of such a brilliant tactician as Dupleix, when his presence was so badly needed in India to safeguard the French interests, was a fatal mistake of the French

Government. The French further made a serious mistake in abandoning the policy pursued by Dupleix. With his recall, the French influence and power, which he had so patiently built up, rapidly came to nought. The appointment of such hot-headed and incompetent generals as Count de Lally was another factor in weakening the position of the French in India.

(12) Too much interference from the French Ministry. Dutta andSarkar say, "Lastly owing to the fact that the majority of the French East India Company's shasres were held by the French Crown, the Company was liabale to be ill advised and capticious instrucions from the French courts and Ministers, which deprived the men on the spot in the French serttlements in India of the advantage they won by dint of their own policy and endeavours.

Now it can be concluded that though the mistakes of the French officers in India were also to a great extent responsible for the failure of the French East India company in this country, yet, as sir Alfred Lyall has said, "the bankruptcy of the French East India company, their bad administration, at home and abroad, their policy of sacrificing their commercial and colonial interests in favour of participating in very disastrous wars in Europe and, above all, the weakness of their supremacy at sea, were some of the causes of their failure." Dr. Ishwari Prashad also speaks in the same strain when he writes, "the postition of the French Company as a department of State, the pre-occupation of the State with American colonies and its consequent neglect of India, the harshness of Lally in creating a spirit of insubordination, the misfortune of Dupleix in having no better men to execute his plans, then the Med and Gouty D' Duteisel and the feeble Law and the coo! resolute spirit of Launders, Lawrence and Clive. all were weak in finance and on the seas."

❐

7

The British Conquest of Begal

The beginnings of British political away over India may be traced to the Battle of Plassey in 1757, when the English East India Company's forces defeated Sirajud-Daula, the Nawab of Bengal. The earlier British struggle with the French in South India had been but a dress reheasal. The lessons learnt there were profitably applied in Bingal. At that time, the kingdom of Bengal included the provinces of Bengal, Bihar and Orissa. It was the most fertile and one of the richest kingdoms in India. Its industries and commerce were well developed. As has been noted earlier, the East India Company and its servants had highly profitable trading interests in the province.

CAUSES OF THE BATTLE OF PLASSEY

(1) Misuse of the Royal Farman of 1717. The company had secured valuable privileges in 1717 under a royal farman by the Mughal Emperor, Furrikh Siyaar which had granted the company the freedom to export and import their goods in Bengal without paying taxes and the right to issue passes or dastaks for the movement of such goods. The Complany's servants were also permitted to trade but were not covered by this farman. They were required to pay the same taxes as Indian merchants. This farman was a perpetual source of conflict between the Company and the Nawabs of Bengal. For one,it meant loss of revenue to the Bengal government. Secondly, the power to issue dastaks for the Company's goods was misused by the Company's servants to evade taxes on their private trade. All the Nawabs of Bengal,from Musshid Qualikhan to Alivardi Khan had objected to the English interperation of the farman of 1717. They had compelled the company to pay lump sums to their treasury, and firmly suppressed the misuse of dastaks. The company had been compelled to accept the authority of the Nawabs in the matter, but its servants had taken every opportunity to evade and defy this authority. Matters came to a head in 1756 when the young and quick-tempwred Suraj-ud-Daula succeeded his grandfather, Alivardi Khan. He demanded of the English that they should trade on the same bases as in the times of Mussid Quli Khan.

(2) Knowledge of the Political and Military Weakness of Indians to the English. The Anglo-French wars continued from 1744 to 1763. During that period, three Carnatic wars took place, the English came to know about the political and military weakness of Tanjore, Karnatka and Hyderabad. After realising these weakness, they tried to get profit in Bengal with the left of their emperience in the Deccan India, so that they could strengthen their power. Now they increased their activities, as a result of which this struggle was necessary. For example, instead of agreeing to pay taxes on their goods to the Nawab, they levied heavy duties on Indian goods entering Calcutta which was under their control. All this naturally annoyed and angered the young Nawab who also suspected that the Company was hostile to him and was favouring his rivals for the throne of Bengal.

(3) Fortification of Calcutta. The breaking point came when, without taking the Nawab's permission, the company began to fortify Calcutta in expectaion of the coming struggle with the French, who were stationed at this time at Chandernagore Siraj rightly interpreted this attack as an attack upon his sovereignty. How could an independent ruler permit a private company of merchants to build forts or to carry on private wars on his land? Moreover he feared that if he permitted the English and the French to fight each other on the soil of Bengal, he too would meet the fate of the Carnatic Nawabs. In other words, Siraj was willing to let the Europeans remain as merchant but not as master. He ordered both the English and the French to demolish their fortifications at Calcutta and Chandernagore and to desist from fighting each other. While the French Company obeyed his orders the

English refused to do so, for its ambition had been whetted and its confidence enhanced by its victories in the Carnatic. The English not only refused to obey the command of the Nawab, on the contrary, some impertinent english officer is reported to have spoken to the officers of the Nawab that "the ditch shall be filled up, provided it be with the head of the Moors." This enraged the Nawab who eventually decided to punish the English. He had certainly good reasons for it.

(4) Political Reasons. Siraj-ud-Daula succeded his grandfather Alivardi Khan, to the Nawabship of Bengal in 1756. He desired to use his powers as a ruler as effectively as were used by his predecessors while the English, emboldened by their success against the French in South India, decided to engage him in a fresh adventures and, therfore, refused to accept his authority. The English did not give presents to him at the time of his coronation. At one time, the English refused him permission to visit their factory.

(5) Krishan Das Affairs. A rich Bengali merchant named Krishan Das had incurred the displeasure use of the Nawab. He had fled to Calcutta with his family and treasure. The Nawab asked the English to hand over Krishan Das to him but they did not agree becuase they knew it well that Diwan Rajballabh and his son Krishan Das could prove to be very useful in their anticipated struggle with the Nawab. In the words of Sarkar and Dutta,"Thus was born a mutual suspicion which made the conflict inevitable."

(6) Capture of the Kothis at the Kassim Bazar and Calcutta. Acting with great energy but with undue haste and inadequate preparation, Siraj-ud-Daula seized the English factory at Kasim Bazar, marched on the Calcutta, and occupied the Fort William on 20 June 1756. He then retired from Calcutta to celebrate his easy victory, letting the English escape with their ships. This was a mistake for he had underestimated the strength of his enemy.

(7) Black-Hole Tragedy. It is said that Siraj-ud-Daula ordered to keep 145 Britishers, including woman and small children in a small room after his victory over Calclutta. According to the English historians almost all of them died of suffocation. This incident is known as Black Hole Tragedy in History. About this incident, whether it actually took place or not, the historians have conflicting views. Most people say that the Nawab did not have any hand in this incident. Any how, after conqueing Calcutta, the Nawab left it to celebrate this victory. The Britishers took refuge in Fulta, on the bank of occean, reaching there by ship. They were protected there because of their mastery over sea-power. There they waited for the help of their company in Madras.

(8) Activities of the English Against the Nawab. When the Britishers in Madras came to know about their defeat at Kasim bazar and Calcutta they immediately sent their army under the leadership of Clive and navy under the leadership of Watson for recapturing Calcutta. This combined force recaptured Calcutta in 1757. Siraj-ud-Daula opposed them for sometime but later on he signed a treaty forcible with Clive. This treaty is known as the Treaty of Alinagar in history. By this tready, the English got back all their forts. They also got the right of fortification and miniting coins.

(9) Direct Challenge to Nawab's Sovereignty by the English. The East India Company was now determined to remain in Bengal even against the wishes of the Nawab and to trade here on its own terms. Nevertheless the English Company demanded the absolute right to trade in Bengal irrespective of the Bengal Nawab's orders. This amounted to a direct challenge to the Nawab's sovererignty. No ruler could possibly accept this positon. Siraj-ud-Daula had the statesmanship to see the long- term implications of the English designs. He decided to make them obey the laws of the land.

(10) Conspiracy Against the Nawab. The wheel had gone a full circle. Now the English were on the offensive. Taking advantage of the disaffection among the Nawab's officers, Clive arranged a conspiracy in which Mir Jafar (the commander-in-Chief of the Nawab's army), Rai Durlabh Jagat Seth (an influential banker of Bengal) and Ami Chand an intermediary, joined. It was planned to make Mir Jafar the Nawab who in turn was to reward the services of the Company and pay compensation for the losses suffered by them earlier.

In this way, the traitor Mir Jafar, sold the independence of his country to the English for fulfillment of his country selfish ends. Ami Chand, the mediator (intercessor) demanded 30 lakhs of rupees for keeping this treaty a secret. In such a situation, Clive got prepared two copies of the treaty-one on red paper and the other on white paper. The red one was fictions and there was a mention of the provision of payment of 30 lakhs rupees to Ami Chand but in the genuine copy of the treaty on white paper no mention of Ami Chand was deliberately made. When Watson refused to sign the false draft Clive himself forged his signatures on it. From the moral point of view, whatever Clive did was improper, but it was just in keeping with the commonly repeated proverb," Everything is fair in love and war."

Events. Having joined a conspiracy organised by the enemies of the young Nawab to place Mir Jafar on the throne of Bengal, they presented the youthful Nawab with an impossible set of demands. Both sides realised that a war to the finish would have to be fought between them. They met for battle on the field of Plassey, 20 miles from Murshidabad, on 23rd June 1757 the fateful battle of Plassey was a battle only in name. In all, the English lost 29men while the Nawab lost nearly 500. The major part of the Nawab's army, led by the traitors Mir Jafar and Rai Durlabh, took no part in fighting. Only a small group of Nawab's soldiers led by Mir Madan and Mohan Lal fought bravely and well. The Nawab was forced to flee and was captured and put to death by Mir Jafar's son Miran.

Results. The Company was granted undisputed right to free trade in Bengal, Bihar and Orissa. It also received the zamindari of the 24 Parganas near Calcutta. Mir Jafar Paid a sum of Rs. 17,700,000 as compensation for attack on Calcutta to the company and the traders of the city. In addition he paid large sums as 'gifts' or bribes to the high officials of the Company. Clive, for example received over two million rupees, Watts over one million. Clive later estimated that the Company and its servants had collected more than 30 million rupees from the puppet Nawab. Moreover, it was understood that the British merchants and officials would no longer be asked to pay any taxes on their private trade.

Historical Significance of the Battle of Plassey. The battle of plassey was hardly important from the military viewpoint. It was a mere skirmish. The Battle of Plassey is important because of the events that followed it. The statement of Admiral Wattson,"the Battle of Plassey was not a very important incident for the company only, but also for the British nation seems true." Sir J.N. Sarkar clearly mentions its significance by saying," On 23rd June 1757 the medieval period of India ended and the modern period started." For the British the Battle was important from the following points of view:

(1) Political Important. *(a)* It made the British the masters of Bengal. The nawabs of Bengal became merely puppet in their hands. *(b)* The conquest of Bengal made it possible for the British to attempt the conquest of whole India. *(c)* It added to the company's prestige and a single stroke raised them to the status of major contender for the Indian Empire.

(2) Military Importance. *(a)* An English army of 6,000 troops was maintained in Bengal to assist the Nawab to maintain his position. As Bengal was situated near the ocean it was very easy for the English to move their troops and they could get the full benefit of their navy. *(b)* The vast resources of Bengal helped the English to conquer the wars of the Deccan and extend their influence over Northern India. Their victory in Bengal also filled them with great enthusiasm to fight against the French, the Marathas and Sikhs and rout them.

(3) Moral Importance. *(a)* The evernts and results of the battle showed that the British did not give any importance to moral values. They believed in conspiracy, deceit, greed, bribery, dishonesty and immoral acts. *(b)* The English kipt morality aside and started economic exploitation of Bengal as they could. *(c)* Mir jafar had got the Nawabship of Bengal through treachry. His greed and misact inspired traitors, loyalty vainshed and treachery prevailed everywhere.

(4) Economic Importance. *(a)* this helped in strengthening the financial position of the English East India Company. The English received a huge amount. Clive, for example, received over two miliion rupees, Wattson over one million. *(b)* The Company had got monopoly over the trade of Bengal. It was understood that the British merchants and officials would no longer be asked to pay any taxes on their private trade. *(c)* The Nawab (Mir Jafar) could not make the stipulated payments and always fell in arrears. *(d)* The decline of Indian industries started rapidly after this battle.

MIR JAFFAR AND MIR KASIM

Mir Jaffar was made Nawab of Bengal after the battle of Plassey in 1757. This is called the First Revolution in Bengal. He remained on the throne so long as Clive was in India. Things changed after the departure of Clive. The administration of the Nawab was inefficient. He played into the hands of worthless favourites and the condition of the people was becoming bad. His treasury was empty and payments due to the Company were getting into arrears. Moreover, he had nothing to grease the palms of the officers of the Company. The members of the Calcutta Council thought that a change of Nawab would bring them money. Hence they decided to replace Mir Jaffar by his son-in-law, Mir Kasim. They made a treaty with him in September, 1760. He was to give to the Company the districts of Burdwan, Midnapore and Chittagong. He was to pay all arears due from Mir Jaffar to the Company. He was to pay five lakhs of rupees for the Carnatic wars. The retiring Nawab, Mir Jaffar, was to be given a befitting pension. It was verbally agreed that he would pay £50,000 to Vansittarte, £27,000 to Holwell and £ 25,000 to other members of the Calcutta Council. Mir Jaffar was then removed from Nawabship and he went away to Calcutta. The deposition of Mir Jaffar was the breach of a treaty founded on the most solemn oath Even some members of the Council protested against it and described it as an indelible stain upon the national honour of the English.

The new Nawab Mir Kasim was far more competent person than his predecessor, Mir jaffar. He gave the districts of Burdwan,

Midnapore and Chittagong to the Company. The arrears were cleared. The sums promised to the members of the Calcutta council were paid. Ram Narain, Deputy Governor of Bihar, was removed and deprived of his treasures. Worthless favourites of Mir Jaffar were dismissed and they were deprived of their ill-gotten money. The rebellious Zamindars, who had challenged the authority of the previous Nawab, were suppressed. Army was strengthened and Armenian Officers were employed to train it. Factories for the manufacture of arms were started.

Mir Kasim then transferred his capital from Murshidabad to Monghyr, a place near the border of Bihar. There were several reasons for this. Firstly, he wanted to have his capital as a strongly fortified place. Secondly, Murshidabad had been associated with the capital of previous worthless Nawabs. It had been the centre of intrigues and corruptions. Monghyr as the new capital would have no such antecedents. He wanted to associate his new regime with a new capital. Thirdly he feared that Mir Jaffar would be restored sooner or later. The hostile attitude of some members of the Calcutta Council like Ellis made him feel that all the more. He wanted to have his capital at a safe distance from Calcutta so that in case of reappointment of Mir Jaffar, he might ebin a position to offer resistance or to escape to Oudh. Fourthly, there would be less interference at Monghyr because of its great distance from distance from Calcutta.

Then the Nawab turned his attention to the question of private trade. By a firman of the Mughal Empror issued in 1717 the Company had been permitted to carry its goods duty-free in the provinces of Bengal, Bihar and Orissa. This applied to the goods of the Company meant for export by sea and protected by the 'dustak' or permit of the President of the Calcutta Council. The privilege came to be greatly misused in course of time. The servants of the Company carried on a lot of private trade and they claimed exemption from all payments. This too much adversely affected the position of the Nawab. His revenues were reduced too much. Moreover, the native merchants of the Company paid no duties while the Indian merchants had to pay these. Thus the Indian merchants were not able to withstand this unfair competition and were being ruined. The Nawab requsted the Calcutta Council again and again to check this abuse but no attention was paid. The Nawab then abolished duties on the goods of all. It put the English and the Indian merchants on an equal footing in matters of trade. The Nawab could not impose duties on the goods of the Company but he was certainly free to abolish duties on the goods of all. His action cannot be criticised because he had done so after repeated requests to the Calcutta Council that they should stop the misuse of dustaks.

Towards Battle of Buxar (1764). Ellis, the agent of the Company at Patna, suddenly seized that city but it was immedately recaptured by the Nawab's troop. Ellis and other Englishmen were thrown in to the prison. Every Englishman in the territories of the Nawab was ordered to be seized. The Calcutta Council issued a proclamation dethroning Mir Kasim and reinstating Mir Jaffar. The Nawab refused to care for it. The English army marched towards Nawab's Capital. A severe battle was fought at Geriah in which the Nawab was defeated. The English captured his capital Monghyr and the Nawab fled to Patna. The Nawab declared that he would put to death all the English prisoners if advance towards Patna was not stopped. The English army continued its march and Mir Kasim got all the Englishmen in his custody murdered by a German named Walter Rheinbardt popularly know as Samru. The English forces captured Patna also.

Mir Kasim fled away and took shelter with Nawab Shuja-ud-Daula of Oudh where the Mughal Emperor Shah Alam II was also staying. All the three made a common cause and attacked Patna but were repulsed. Then they took up position at Buxar. Sir Hector Monroe advanced with Company's troops and defeated them at the battle of Buxar in 1764. Shuja-ud-Duala made one more attempt but was defeated at Kara. Mir Kasim fled away while Shuja-ud-Daula and Empror Shah Alam II surrendered to the English.

The Battle of Buxar. The first attack launched by the three Muhammadan leaders was against Patna. It was repulsed by the English who had already occupied it on the flight of Mir Qasim from that place. They then encamped themselves at Buxar. Sir Hector Munro inflicted on them a crushing defeat at Buxar. The Nawab Wazir of Oudh made one more effort to retrieve his fortune, but was defeated at Karah. Mir Qasim fought with great courage, but in vain, his defeat being due to the lukewarm support of his allies. Of them, Shuja-ud-Daula and Shah Alam surrendered to the Britishers. It was in this way that the schemes of Shuja-ud-Daula for the conquest of Hindustan and the hopes of Mir Qasim to take vengeance of English foes were frustrated for ever.

The Results of the Battle. Shah Alam and Shuja-ud-Daula entered into a treaty of Allahabad (1765)with the Company, whose terms were the following:- *(1)* Shuja-ud-Daula received back the province of Oudh minus the Districts of Allahabad and Karah, but he had to pay 50 lakhs of rupees as war indemnity. In other words, the power of the Nawab Wazir of Oudh was broken. *(2)* Shuja-ud-Daula had to keep English troops for the protection of his frontiers and bear their expenses. *(3)* Shah Alam, the Mughal Emperor, granted the English the right to collect revenue in Bengal, Bihar and Orissa. This is known as the grant of Diwani. Shah Alam received an annual pension of 26 lakhs of rupees and the Districrts of Allahabad and Karah which had been taken away from the Nawab-Wazir of Oudh. *(4)* Mir Qasim fled from the field of battle to an unknown place. Mir Jafar, the old man of 72, was confirmed as Nawab of Bengal. This is called the third revolution in Bengal. Mir Jafar was to acknowledge the sole monopoly of the English on salt on payment of a duty of not more than 2 1/2%. The Nawab's forces were limited. He was to receive a permanent British Resident at his Court, to make good all the losses incurred by the English in the war with Mir Qasim. Mir Jafar also promised to re-impose all the old transit duties against his own people and to restore to the Company's servants all their former concessions.

EFFECTS OF THE BATTLE OF BUXAR

(1) Mir Jafar was made a puppet in the hands of the Company. Mir Qasim who had had been dethroned was replaced by Mir Jafar as the Nawab of Bengal, as pointed out above. The conditions

imposed upon him according to the treaty of Allahabad reduced his powers to such an extent that soon after he began to feel that he had no real powers and that he had fallen at the mercy of the English people. The reduction of his army, the stationing of a British Resident at his Court, his permission to the servants of the Company to enjoy all those privileges and concessions in free- trade that they had enjoyed before their abolition by Mir Quasim and finally, the compulsion of the Nawab by the Company to pay to it all the losses that the English had suffered during the war with Mir Qasim, had made the Nawab a real took in the hands of the English. The next year, *i.e.* in 1765, Mir Jafar died and he was succeeded by his son Nizammudin as the Nawab. According to the terms of the treaty of February, 1765, the new Nawab agreed to maintain troops only for the support of his dignity and maintenance of internal peace and the collection of revenues. The English got the right of controlling the appointment of the officers of the Nawab. At this time the condition of Bengal was chaotic.

(2) The power of Nawab-Wazir of Oudh was broken and henceforward Oudh was at the mercy of the Company. The Nawab-Wazir was very much humbled by his defeat. He was confirmed in his kingdom with the exception of the disctricts of Karah and Allahabad, Chunar and the Zamindari of Benares including Ghazipur. The Nawab-Wazir also agreed to pay Rs. 15 lakhs to the Company as war indemnity. He also entered into a defensive alliance with the East Indian Company by which the latter agreed to help him for the defence of his frontiers and the former promised to pay the cost of maintenance of the forces. The Nawab-Wazir also agreed to allow the Company to carry on the trade duty-free throughout his dominions. The result of the above provisions was that Oudh was created into a buffer state between Bengal and North- Western India.

(3) According to P.E. Roberts,"It was not merely the Nawb of Bengal as at Plassey, but the Emperor of all India and his titular Prime Minister who were defeated." According to Ramasy Muir."It finally riveted the shackles of Company's rule upon Bengal. It announced not only the defeat of Bengal, but that of the Emperor as well as of

Nawab-Wazir of Oudh. The Emperor passed into the hands of the Company and Oudh lay at its feet." According to the treaty of Allahabad made by Clive with Shah Alam, the latter was given the districts of Karah and Allahabad which were secured from the Nawab-Wazir of Oudh. The English Company also promised to pay Rs. 26 lakh as tribute. In return for all this, the Mughal Emperor granted the Diwani of Bengal, Bihar and Orissa to the English Company.

(4) The Victory at Buxar Completed the Work of Plassey. According to the British victory in the Battle of Plassey in 1757. The English had got the standing place in India and now by their victory over the Nawab of Bengal they had become the real masters of the situation. Their supremacy was ensured in Bengal, Bihar and Orissa. There was complete transformation in the position of the British in India, because the supremacy they had attained in Bengal by their victory at Plassey was legally confirmed by their victory at Buxar. The East India Company had not remained now the mere trading Company; rather it had now become the sovereign power in India. Consequently, its prestige rose very high in the estimation of the people and princes in India.

(5) The Relative Importance of Plassey and Buxar Viewed.

(a) First View: The Battle of Plassey More Important. Some historians regard the Battle of Plassey more important than the Battle of Buxar. It was Plassey, they say, that brought a complete transformation in the position of the British in India. It change them from a body of merchants to king makers and laid the foundation of the British supremacy in India. The Battle of Buxar only won the legal sanction for the position that had already been won and which made the British the de-jure power as well. This was, of course, an important change in itself, but the former step was more difficult to accomplish and, therefore more important. In short, it may be stated that had there been no Battle of Plassey, there would have been no Battle of Buxar. The Battle of Buxar was simply an attempt by the

Indian powers to challenge the position that had already been won by the foreigners and it only confirmed that usurpation.

(b) **Second View. The Battle of Buxar More Important.** On the other hand, the second view is that Clive's victory at Plassey was not comparable to the Battle of Buxar. Plassey may almost be said to have had no direct or immediate result beyond the palace revolution. It was Buxar, which coming after the dazzling success of Adams, conferred upon the Company and its officers the legitimate status as servants and successors of the Mughal Empire and virtually the masters of Bengal, Bihar and Orissa by Imperial grant, though Orissa really remained subject to the Marathas for many years. (Keene). The Battle of Buxar confirmed as legal what was considered as usurpation by the victory of Plassey. It was no longer a usurpation; hence forth it was recognised to be legal power. It made the Company position at Plassey as legal, whereas formerly it was that of only a usurpation. It completed the work of Plassey.

Third View and Conclusion: Both Important for the Growth of British in India. These are the two sides of the same question. But in conclusion we can say that both the victories had important effects on the growth of the British power in India. The fact is that Buxar completed the work of Plassey and legally confirmed the British in Position and power which they had achieved by Plassey. Plassey gave them the standing place, and Buxar made them the masters of the situation. The latter closed the story of the military conquest of Bengal, Bihar and Orissa by the British. It finally riveted the shackles of the Company's rule upon Bengal.

CHARACTER AND ACHIEVEMENTS OF LORD CLIVE

Clive was the son of a clergyman and was born in 1725. He was a restless boy at school and often created troubles. He often organised gangs of boys and troubled the shopkeepers. His teachers thought that he would not be successful in life. He joined the service of East India Company as a writer clerk in 1743 and reached Madras in 1744. He felt gloomy and tried to shoot himself but was not successful. He thought that God probably wanted to keep him alive for a higher destiny. He exchanged aword for the pen during the First Carnatic War. He was taken prisoner when Madras was captured by the French in 1746. He was released when this war came to an end in 1748.

Part in the Second Carnatic War. The turning point in his career came during the Second Carnatic War. The fortunes of the English appeared to have fallen very low. The French had set up Salabat Jung as the Nizam of Hyderabad and secured Northern Sircars from him. The French officer Bussy was staying there to support him on the throne. In Carnatic also Chanda Sahib backed by the French was successful and Muhammad Ali, the friend of the English, was besiged in Treichinopoly. It was Clive's plan and dash which upset French plans in the Carnatic. He suggested to the Governor of Madras that he should be given some troops and he would be able to capture Arcot, since Chanda Sahib's army was besienging Muhammad Ali at Trichinopoly. He went 200 European and 300 Indian troops and captured Arcot. "Chanda Sahib sent some army and it besieged Clive in Arcot. Reinforcements arrived and Chanda Sahib's army was defeated at Arcot. Then the English attacked Chanda Sahib's forces at Trichinopoly and put him to flight. Muhammad Ali was relieved and placed on the throne of Carnatic. Thus the English were able to place their nominee Muhammad Ali on the throne of Carnatic. All this was the work of Clive. He went back to England in 1753.

The Conquest of Bengal. Clive was again sent to India as Governor of Fort St. David in 1755 and made Lt. Colonel. He reached India in 1756. Nawab Siraj-ud-Daula of Bengal had got annoyed with the English and captured Calcutta. Clive and Admiral Watson were sent and they recovered Calcutta. Peace was made with the Nawab. He returned all the English factories and promised to pay compensation for all their losses at Calcutta. Clive then learn that the dissatisfied nobles of Nawab and his commander-in-Chief, Mir Jaffar, wanted to remove him. Clive joined this conspiracy through a Bengali Brahman named Amin Chand. Sirajud-Daula was to be deposed and Mir Jaffar was to be made Nawab. The new Nawab was to give huge sums of money and some territory to the Company. When this conspiracy had been made, Amin Chand threatened to disclose the whole conspiracy to the Nawab unless he was promised payment of thirty lakhs of rupees. Clive paid him back in his own coin. He made two copies of the Treaty.The genuine one was on white paper and contained no mention of payment to Amin Chand. The fictitious one was on red paper and contained a clause regarding payment of 30 lakhs of rupees to Amin Chand. Watson refused to sign and Clive forged his signatures. He has been bitterly criticised for this.

Clive felt encouraged and wrote to the Nawab that he would place his complaints against him before his durbar at Murshidabad and marched to Plassey. The Nawab also reached there with his troops. The battle was fought at Plassey. The traitor, Mir Jaffar did not bring the main part of Nawab's army into action. The Nawab was defeated, fled away, was captured and put to death by the order of Miran, son of Mir Jaffar.

Mir Jaffar was now made Nawab. He gave a lot of money to the Company and its senior employees including Clive. The battle of Plassey was not a hotly contested battle but its results were momentous and lasting. Firstly, the new Nawab Mir Jaffar was a mere puppet in the hands of the Company. Real power was in the hands of the Company. It made the Company the de facto masters of Bengal and Bihar. Secondly, it increased the resourses of the English which enabled them to defeat the French in the Deccan during the Third Carnatic War. Thirdly, it later on facilitated the conquest of India by the Company by placing at its disposal the rich provinces of Bengal and Bihar. Morover, they could sail up the River Ganges.

First Governorship of Bengal. Clive was the Governor of Bengal from 1757 to 1760. This is called his First Governorship of Bengal. He had three ahievements to his credit during this period. Firstly, the Mughal EmperorAlamgir II conferred upon his son the

Viceroyalty of the provinces of Bengal. Bihar and Orissa. The Shahzada, who later on became Shah Alam II, attacked these provinces with the help of Shuja-ud-Daula, Nawab Wazir of Oudh. They besieged Ram Narain, the Deputy Governor of Bihar in Patna. Clive repulsed the invaders and the Nawab out of greatfulness granted a jagir to Clive. Secondly, Nizam Salabat Jung had given the territory of Northern Circars to the French. During the Third Carnatic War the French Governor, Gerarai Lally, recalled Bussy from Hyderabad in order to attack Madras. Clive took advantage of it. He sent Col. Fode from Bengal, who captured Northern Circars from the French (1759). Thirdly, Nawab Mir Jaffar feared the power of his English patrons and began to intrigue with the Dutch at Chinsura. Seven large Dutch ships arrived in Hugli from Java with 1500 soldiers. Though England and Holland were at peace in Europe, Clive attacked the Dutch by sea and land. Their ships were destroyed. The Dutch at Chinsura made peace. They agreed not to fortify their settlement and to keep only that number of armed men which was essential for police purposes. Thus, during three years' period of his first Governorship, Clive repulsed the invasion of Bihar by the Shahzada and the Nawab Wazier of Oudh, captured Northern Circars from the French and broke the military power of the Dutch in Bengal. He went back in 1760.

Second Governorship of Bengal. Clive was away from India from 1760 to 1765. During this period the Calcutta Council replaced Mir Jaffar by son-in-law Mir Kasim. The Calcutta Council fell out with Mir Kasim and decided tc make Mir Jaffar Nawab once more. This led to war. Mir Kasim was driven away from Bengal and Bihar. He made an alliance with Nawab Shuja-ud-Daula of Oudh and the Mughal Emperor Shah Alam II. They attacked Bihar but were defeated by the English Commander Munroe at Buxar. The Nawab of Oudh was once more defeated at Kara. Soon after this Clive again arrived as Governor and Commander-in-Chief of Bengal in 1765 and held that position till 1767. This is called his second Governorship of Bengal. He had been authorised to work with the existing Council, if possible: otherwise he could form a select committee of four.

Treaty of Allahabad. The first and foremost problem before Clive immediately after arrival was of making settlement with Nawab Shuja-ud-Daula of Oudh and the Mughal Emperor Shah Alam II. This was done by the Treaty of Allahabad of 1765. Its terms were:-

(1) Shuja-ud-Daula got back his kingdom of Oudh except the districts of Kara and Allahabad on payment of fifty lakhs of rupees.

(2) There was to be an English force in Oudh for the protection of its frontiers and its expenses were to be paid by the Nawab.

(3) The Mughal Emperor Shah Alam II was given the districts of Kara and Allahabad.

(4) He was to be paid Rs. 26 lakhs a year by the Company.

(5) The Mughal Emperor granted the Diwani of Bengal, Bihar and Orissa to the Company.

The treaty of Allahabad is very important for several reasons. Firstly, the grant of Diwani by the Mughal Emperor made the position of the Company legal in the provinces of Bengal and Bihar. Since 1757 they had been de facto masters of Bengal but now they became its dejure masters. Secondly, the Nawab of Oudh became a dependent ally of the Company. Thirdly, Oudh became a friendly buffer State between the Company's possessions in northern India and other powers in northern India (like Marathas). It meant the introduction of the policy of ring fence in Northern India. Fourthly, the titular Mughal Emperor became a prisoner of the Company.

Men like Sir Eyre Coote were of the opinion that Oudh should be annexed. The company was at that time in a position to annex Oudh from the military point of view. Clive, however, decided not to annex Oudh for several reasons. Firstly, the policy of aquiring new large territories and looking after them would engage the attention of the Company. It would not be in a position to give full attention to trade and this would result in financial loss. Secondly, the acquistion of a big province like Oudh would rouse jealousy of European powers and they might make common cause against the English in India. Thirdly, the Directors of the Company were against the policy of acquiring new territories. Fourthly, the annexation of Oudh would bring territories of the Company in direct touch with the Marasthas and might lead to war with them. Clive wanted to avoid this. Lastly, the Company did not have enough administrators even for Bengal and Bihar. It was not in a position to spare a large number of administrators for Oudh.

REFORMS

Civil Reforms. The next task before Clive was to make improvement in administration. The whole administrative system was characterised by corruption in the highest degree. He took several steps to clean the Augean stables. Firstly, he forced the servants of the Company to sign a covenant against the receipt of presents. Secondly, the servants of the Company were carrying on private trade on a large scale. It resulted in the neglect of company's work. The employees of the Company were ordered not to carry on private trade. Thirdly, Clive felt that the salaries of the servants of the Company were low. He wrote to the directors of the Company to increase their salaries but they did not agree. He began to grant monopoly of salt trade and began to distribute its profits among the senior officers of the Company in a graduated scale, so that the Governor was to get £17,000 a year and a Colonel in the army or a member of the Council £7,000 a year. The directors did not like this system. It was abolished two years later and they substituted for it commissions on the revenues of the provinces.

Military Reforms. Clive dealt with the military side of administration also. The most important of his military measures was the abolition of double Bhatta or field allowance of the military officers. It was to cover the extra cost of living on the battle field as compared to living in the garrison in peace time. Its origin lay in the Carnatic wars when Chanda Sahib and Muhammad Ali used to pay this field allowance to the French and the English combatants respectively. Its payments in Bengal was started on the eve of the battle of Plassey. Mir Iaffar and Mir Kasim had paid it to English combatant. The English company acquired Diwani of Bengal, Bihar and Orissa in 1765 and after that the duty of the payment of double bhatta fell on the shoulders of the Company. It was now decided to this expenditure. The military officers were to get half bhatta in Bengal and Bihar in peace time. They were to have bhatta if they took the field. Double bhatta was to be given if they were sent to Oudh.

Dual Government. Another administrative measures of Clive was the setting up of Dual Government. The Company acquired Diwani of Bengal, Bihar and Orissa as a result of the Treaty of Allahabad in 1765. Thus it came to have control over the revenues of Bengal, Bihar and Orissa. The work of administation was theoretically in the hands of the Nawab but actually it was in the hands of two deputy Nawab, Muhammad Raza Khan for Bengal and Shitab Rai for Bihar. These two deputy Nawabs were appointed by the Nawab on the advice of the Company . The company collected revenue and paid fixed annual sums of 32 lakhs of rupees for the expenses of the Nizamat. The Company performed revenue functions but the work of administration was not assumed by it. This system of dividing the functions of Government has been called Clive's system of Dual Government. The real power was in the hands of the Company because deputy Nawabs, who excercised Nizamat functions in actual practice, were appointed by the Nawab on the advice of the Company.

There were several reasons for adopting this system of Dual Government. Firstly, the directors of the Company feared that a sumption of responsibiliy would consume profits. Secondly, the Company did not have sufficient number of administrators for Bengal, Bihar and Orissa. Thirdly, foreign powers could be told that the Company was not extending territories and thus their jealousy was not likely to be roused. In other words dust could be thrown in the eyes of the European powers.

The system of Dual Government proved most defective in many ways Firstly, power was divorced from responsibility. Nawab was responsible for administration but he had no real power. The deputy Nawabs carried on the administration but in practice they were under the control of the Company. The Company controlled the revenues as well as the army. The Nawab had responsibility without power. Under these circumstances the administration began to grow bad. The zamindars, the officials and the Complany's servants tyrannised over the people. It was selfish contrivance for enjoying the spoils of office, without taking over its fundamental obligations. In 1769-70 there was a severe famine in Bengal and about one third population died. The Company remained a passive spectator and did nothing to ameliorate condition of the starving masses. Rather its employees used the occasion to make profits. The second defect was that the Company itself did not gain much. The Company had acquired the right of collecting revenue but its financial position had become very bad in spite of this. The revenue was collected through the native agents and the directors felt that a good deal of it was misappropriated by the native agents. English supervisors were appointed in 1769 but this also did not improve matters. The cultivators paid beyond their capacity but the Company did not grow rich. Thus the system of Dual Government was a total failure.

Clive went back in 1767. He was tried for accepting bribes but was honourably acquitted. He committed suicide in 1774 due to bad health.

Estimate of Clive. Clive was one of the greatest Englishmen who came to India. He combined in hinself the qualities of a soldier and a statesman in a high degree. During the second Carnatic war he displayed qualities of a great general. It was Clive's policy which resulted in the capturer of Arcot and the subsequent defeat of Chanda Sahib at Trichinopoly. Thus Clive became responsible for establishing Muhammed Ali on the throne of Carnatic. It established British influence over Carnatic. In 1756 Clive and Admiral Watson recovered Calcutta from Siraj-ud-Daula. Then he captured Chander Nagar. He made an alliance with the dissastisfied nobles of the Nawab and won the victory of Plassey. This was a great military achievement of Clive. He broke the power of the Dutch at Chinsura during his first Governorship. Col. Forde was sent from Bengal and he captured Nothern Circars from the French. The invasion of Mughal Emperor's son was repulsed. This shows that Clive was a great general.

As an Administrator. Clive showed his talents as an administrator during his Second Governorship of Bengal from 1765 to 1767. The servants of the Company were asked not to carry on privted trade or to get presents. Double Bhatta of the army in Bengal and Bihar was stopped. Many officers threatened to resign on bloc. He dealt with the situation firmly and the ring leaders were sent to England. His system of Dual Government did not prove good but it was meant to be only a temporary measure. He never meant to make it permanent.

As a Statesman. Clive was also good statesman. This is clear from the Treaty of Allahabad of 1765. As a result of it, Oudh became a friendly buffer State between Company's possessions of Bengal and Bihar and the Maratha territories in Northern India. The Mughal Emperor Shah Alam II was given 26 lakhs of rupees a year and he thus became a pensioner of the Company. Moreover, Clive secured the Diwani of Bengal, Bihar and Orissa which made the position of the English legal in those provinces. Their position became de jure. He showed great wisdom in not annexing Oudh but making it only a dependent State. This shows that he was a great statesman also.

Clive had the other side of his character also. His acceptance of bribes during his first Governorship of Bengal is a stain on his career. His method of dealing with Amin Chand by forging the signatures of Watson cannot be commended. In spite of this he must be considered a great man. He laid the foundation of the British Empire in India which in course of time came to include the whole of Indian sub-continent and lasted till 15th August 1947.

DUAL SYSTEM OF LORD CLIVE

The Dual System. It was during the period of his second governorship that Lord Clive set up a system of government in Bengal, Bihar and Orissa, which is popularly known as the Dual or Double System of government. Under this system, the Government was divided into two parts. According to this division the actual work of civil, criminal and police administration was carried on by the Nawab of Bengal, who received 53 lakhs of rupees a years from the

Company for the purpose, while the real and ultimate authority rested with the Company. The Company not only directed the Nawab in his work of administration, but also maintained a large army for the defence of the said provinces of Bengal, Bihar and Orissa. Not only this, but the authority of the Company became still more supreme when it received the Diwani *i.e.*, (the right to collect and administer the revenue) of Bengal, Bihar and Orissa in 1765, from Shah Alam, the Mughal Emperor, in return for the payment of a tribute of 26 lakhs of rupees a year.

But the System Failed After Some Time. Thus the power of military defence from the Nawab of Bengal and the grant of Diwani from the mughal Emperor Shah Alam both in 1765 made the Company the supreme authority in the kingdom, but the administration was in the hands of the Company and the Nawab was only a formal ruler. So far the position was clear. But the servants of the Company did not actually undertake the work of the Nizamat and act as the Diwan in their person. The nominal head of the adminstration was the Deputy-Naib or Nawab whom the Nawab appointed with the permission of the Company, and the work of sole administration was carried on by the native servants. But the system failed in 1772 after a period of five years from 1765, because it failed to improve matters.

The Two Stages in the Establishment of the Double Government. The frequency of revolutions in Bengal and war with Mir Qasim had impressed upon Lord Clive the necessity of ending the "perpetual struggle for superiority"going on between the Company and the Nawab of Bengal. Even before he took over the charge of his office, he had written to the Directors that "we must indeed become Nawabs ourselves, in fact, if not in name." So, it was during his second governorhipe of Bengal that he earnestly started giving a tangible shape to his idea. His ideas materialized and in a short time he acquired both the Nizamat and Diwani. The Nizamat he obtained from the Nawab of Bengal and Diwani from the Mughal Emperor, Shah Alam. By the Nizamat he obtained the executive authority with the criminal jurisdiction, while by the Diwani he obtained the authority to collect revenue and to administer civil law. These two authorities were previously enjoyed by the Nawab of Bengal. The following two stages are noteworthy:

(a) **Acquisition of Nizamat from the New Nawab, Nizam-ud-Daula, 1765.** On the death of Nawab Mir Jafar of Bengal in 1765, his son, Nizam-ud-Daula, succeeded to the Masnad of Bengal. The new Nawab was a weak man. He was elevated to the Masnad with the help of the Company according to a specific treaty between the two parties to the effect that the new Nawab on his elevation to the Masnad would receive fifty lakhs of rupees annually to run the actual administration of Bengal, while all his authority would be wielded by the officers deputed by the Company. Thus, it was according to this treaty that Raja Shatab Rai and Mohammad Reza Khan were nominated as the Deputies of the Company. Thus they were made responsible to the Company and not to the Nawab. The Comapany had already kept under it a huge force for the protection of the provinces of Bengal and Orissa.

(b) **Acquisition of Diwani from Shah Alam.** At this time, Lord Clive had a meeting with the Mughal Emperor, Shah Alam, at Allahabad. He obtained from the Emperor the Diwani of Bengal, Bihar and Orissa in return for the annual payment of tribute of twenty-six lakhs of rupees. The Diwani was the right to collect revenues and administer Civil Law. Thus by the Treaty of February, 1765 with Nawab Nizam-ud-Din and the Treaty of Allahabad in 1765 with Shah Alam, respectively, Lord Clive acquired for the company both the Nizamat and the Diwani, so very essential for the Comapny's supremacy in Bengal.

The Character of the Double Government. Thus, according to the above two measures, Lord Clive set up Double or Dual Government in Bengal, by virtue of which the Company got the real control of the province of Bengal, both civil and military, while he left the actual work of administration in the hands of the native agency, *i.e.*, the Nawab of Bengal. The Nawab and his native servants continued to conduct the affairs of the Government of the province of Bengal as heretofore. The old system of the administration of justice and Government was also retained quite intact. The native Amils, Faujdars, Kanungos and Patwaries were allowed to work as before.

Motive of Clive in Setting up the Double Government. It might be asked as to why it was that Clive hesitated to take over the administrtion of the province when he could have done that so easily. Nawab was merely a puppet in the hands of the British. As a matter of fact, all power was in the hands of the British. He was their creature and depended upon them for his existence. Clive would have rendered a great service by abolishing his office and assuming the control of the Government directly, rather than agree to play the role of the wire-puller from behind the scene. But it should be noted firstly that Clive's object in maintaining a show of Double Government was to disguise the real position of the Company and thereby disarm the jealousy of the rival European powers. Open assumption of Real Government by the Comapny would have caused a breach with other European powers. Secondly, there was another consideration. It was impossible for the company to have taken over the full Government of Bengal owing to the limited number of Company's servants and their ignorance of the task of administration.

Merits of the Dual System

In spite of some defects in the Double Government, the system definitely bespeaks of Clive's statesmanship and ability. It was suitable reply to the exigencies for which it was devised and, as such, the following points are worthy of note to show the justification for the introduction of the Double Government in Bengal by Lord Clive:

(1) It put an end to the frequent revolutions and struggle for supremacy between the Nawab and the Comapny. What has already been pointed out above show that it was in view of the frequent revolutions in Bengal and the perpetual struggle for superiority between the Company and the

Nawab that Clive had set up the Dual System of Government. This Double Government clearly defined the respective positions of the Company and the Nawab and, therefore, it left on room for future conflicts between the two. Hitherto, the Nawab claimed as much of authority and power for himself in Bengal as was claimed by the East India Company, but now with the introduction of the Double Government, the Nawab was actually reduced to a position of subordination which he had in fact acquired before, but which had not so far been legalised. In other words, the Nawab had become subordinate to and dependent upon the company, and with the establishment of this Dual System, his subordinate position was legalised now. Similarly, the Comapny also got its legal position confirmed.

(2) It removed the suspicion of the Europeans. In this connection, Clive's own observations are significant. He says, "The first point in politics which I offer to your consideration is the form of Government. We are sensible that since the acquisiton of the Diwani, the power formally belonging to the people of this province is totally, in fact, vested in the East India Comapny. Nothing remains to him, but the name and shadow of authority. This name-this shadow, however,- it is indispensably necessary, we should seem to venerate under the sanction of the Nawab. Every encroachment that may be attempted by foreign powers can be effectively crushed without any apparent inter-position of our own authority and all real grievances complained of by them can through the same channel be examined into a redress. Be it, therefore, always remembered that there is a Nawab and though the revenues belong to the Company, the territorial jurisdiction must still rest in the chiefs of the country, acting under him and this Presidency in conjunction." Thus, it was with a view to removing the suspicion from amongst the minds of Europeans powers that the system was devised by Lord

Clive. This system threw dust into the eyes of the foreigners. Direct assumption of the Government must have roused the jealousy and opposition of the European powers.

(3) It enabled Clive to satisfy or deceive the Directors of the Company also. It further satisfied-or rather deceived-the Directors at home by keeping intact the "name and shadow" of the authority of the Nawab. It is also admitted that it was not possible for the Company to assume the direct administration of government affairs at this time on account of their ignorance and insufficient numbers in the country.

(4) It also threw dust into the eyes of the natives. The discarding of all veils and covers would have caused a breach with other Europeasn powers which would have added to the difficulty of the English. The maintenance of the shadow and the name of the Nawab was "indispensably believed necessary" to keep the changes of 1765 a silent revolution. This Dual System greatly suited the idea. It nicely camouflaged the transfer of power from the Nawab to the Company by entrusting the former with the administration and the latter with the real authority.

(5) Absence of experienced and trained Englishmen with the Comapny. The running of the direct administration of Bengal was also difficult from another point of view. It was impossible and unwise for the Company to have taken over the administration at a time when it had no trained and experienced Englishmen to run the administrative work. They did not fully understand the Indian languages nor were they well-versed in native laws and revenue affairs. So Clive had no alternative but allow the continuance of the existing native machinery.

(6) It avoided all possibility of Anglo-Maratha clash.The Dual System gave a great advantage to the British, because it attempted to eliminate every possibility of Anglo-Maratha struggle. At this time, the Marathas were a rising power

and the direct assumption of the government of Bengal by the East India Company would have brought about a clash betweem the Company and the Marathas. Clive rightly believed that sudden and dramatic assumption of government by the Company would bring them into conflict with the Marathas, a great power in India. This thing he feared the most. So, by concealing the company's real position in the cover of "Dual Government", Clive wisely avoided the possibility of a fatal struggle with the Marathas. This served the British interests in India very well.

(7) The Directors of the Company refused to take direct responsibility of administration. Clive's refusal to own up direct responsibility of administration had also some valid reason behind it. The Directors at home refused to assume this heavy responsibility. Pitt, the Elder, the then Prime Minister, had also accepted such suggestion of Clive to take up the direct responsibility of the administration by the Company. Naturally when such was the attitude of higher authorities in England, Clive found no other alternative but to introduce his celebrated Dual system in Bengal.

(8) It may be stated that at this time the Company was not so much interested in the territorial aggrandisement as in commerce and finance. This system ensured the betterment of the financial condition of the Company without any increase in its burden of responsibiliy.

(9) In spite of its grave defects it can be justified on the ground that it was never regarded as a final settlement, even by its own creator. Lord Clive, nor was it an ideal system of Government. But it cannot be denied that it was a good attempt to grapple with the realities of the situation. From its very nature it could not be but a make-shift arrangement. Thus its justification may be found in the fact that it led to more open an assumption of responsibility by the Company during the regimes of Warren Hastings and Cornwallis.

(b) Defects or Demerits of the Dual System of Government. Thus, we find that the Double Government of Bengal was an adroit measure to mask the real position of the Company. Its object was to delude the European rivals of the Company into the idea that the Nawab was still the de facto ruler of Bengal. But it would be very important to note here that the Double System of Goverment was really an anomalous plan. It contemplated a curious combination of the commercial and political interests, the interests which operated in direct opposition and were destructive of each other. The division of administration into two unnatural divisions as envisaged by the system was faulty and fantastic. The Nawab was saddled with reponsibility without power; the Company had the power, but could not undertake responibility. Hence, such illogical and an impolitic division in the words of Kaye, "made confusion more confounded and corruption more corrupt." The Dual, System, in short, possessed all the defects that can come under a system where there is an 'unfortunate divorce of power from responsibility' and, as such, left the people helpless against oppression. The following were the chief defects of the Dual System of Clive in Bengal:

(1) It was Illogical and Unworkable. According to Dr. Nandlal Chaterjee,"the Double Government which Clive established was both illogical and unworkable. He forgot that the division of powers was impossible without creating anarchy and confusion. The assumption of the Diwani of Bengal exhibited the single adroitness of an astute schemer, rather than the foresight of a responsible administrator. It was a sure contrivance for enjoying the spoils of past without taking over its fundamental complications. It was avowedly a device for hoodwinking the country powers and the foreign nations, whom Clive did not want to give umbrage. He frankly justified it as an excellent scheme for concealing the political revolution in Bengal. The Nawab was now a visionary head of the state and had nothing but the name and shadow of authority. But Clive insisted that this name and shadow must be preserved.

(2) It resulted in the complete breakdown of the administration. Dr. Nandlal Chatterjee again writes, "But the tragic inhumanity of the Dual System resulted naturally in complete breakdown of the internal administration. The Nawab had no power to enforce law and justice, while the English on their part disowned the reponsibility of government. The result was disorder in the country. The villainy of the zamindars and the rapaciousness of the Nawab's officials and the Company's servants knew no bounds and the business weavers and merchants were intimidated and fleeced to the utmost. People were left virtually without appeal and many were compelled to leave their huts and homes in despair and become vagrants or freebooters. The Country was, in short, reduced to a state of miserable desolution. At no period in the chequered annals of Bengal did the province suffer such flagrant spoliation as it did in the era of Clive."

(3) Indian merchants and industries also suffered. Another serious defect of the Dual Sustem was that the Indian merchants and industies also suffered a lot during this period. The Indian traders suffered a lot under new conditions because they could not compete with the British merchants who enjoyed vast privileges and sold their goods under favourable circumstances in India. Besides, the Company's servants harmed the India industries by forcing the Indian artisans to work only in the Company's factories. They also forbade them to manufacture certain commodities like fine cloth, silken cloth, etc., the manufacture of which was detrimental to their personal interests.

(4) Abuses of private trade increased. Ramsay Muir has much emphasized the defects of the Dual Government when he says,"under this system of Government, abuses of private trade reached a greater height. The Company's servants indulged themselves recklessly into the private trade. They

cared little for the native administration. They only cared for the huge wealth that began to pour into their pockets by their indulgence in the private trade at the cost of the company. They claimed exemption from all levies and traded in favourable circumstances. Consequently, the income of the servants of the Company increased while that of the Company decreased. So, from Company's point of view also, the system was a complete failure. The evil of the system thus was that while the Company itself was in serious financial difficulties, its servanst were returning to England with big fortunes.

(5) It encouraged misgovernment and oppression of the peasantry. The Dual Government was defective in as much as it encouraged misgovernment in general and oppression of the peasantry in particular in Bengal. The Company cared only for the collection of the revenue and had nothing to do with the internal administration which remained in the hands of the Nawab. Amirs and Zamindars too neglected the welfare of the people. They concerned themselves only with the collection of excessive revenue with a heavy hand with no check whatsoever from above. Under these conditions. the well-being of the people was seriously neglected and, as such, their condition became miserable. Becher has rightly remarked, "Bengal was verging towards its ruin." The Collectors appointed by the Company exercised great power concentrated in their hands and abused these powers mostly for their personal aggrandisement and, as such became the tyrants of the districts. In fact everything went wrong. Robbers infested the province. Life, honour and property of the people were unsafe.

(6) Another serious defect of the Dual System was that the Company's income from lands seriously suffered. In 1765 the Home Government estimated the revenues of Bengal, Bihar and a part of Orissa at 36.0 lakhs per annum. It was

also expected that land revenue might rise to over thirty-six lakhs pounds if properly managed. But, unfortunately, they were exhausted by plunder and oppression. Bolts had rightly remarked that "while the nation was gazing after the fruit, the Company and their substitutes were suffered to be rooting up the tree." Besides, the land was given to the highest bidder and it changed hands very often. This frequent change of hands resulted in no improvement of land. Hence there could be no increase in land revenue, as outgoing peasants took little interest in it.

(7) The Dual System of Government also meant the complete breakdown of the native judicial system in Bengal. The Nawab's judges and functionaries could not discharge their judicial functions properly because of the constant interference of the country's official. The interference corrupted justice. The Nawab's tribunals of justice were converted by the Company's servants into instruments for their greed and capacity, with the result that there was miscarriage of justice and bad administration.

(8) Interference in the Nawab's administration. The nawab did not possess adequate funds to carry on the administration efficiently. On the other hand, the result of this absurd system was that there was a constant interfrerence on the part of the Company's servants in the internal administration of the Nawab. He was given the responsibility of administration, but had no funds or powers to run the administration smoothly. The interference made by the servants of the Company created an embarrassing situation for the Nawab and, as such, he was unable to carry on the internal administration smoothly.

Political Significance of the Double Government. The political mastery of the Company over Bengal was now an accomplished fact by this time and they were placed in such a position of advantage that it was natural for them to accept greater political power, though the Court of Directors might not have liked it at that time. The Emperor came under their control. The Nawab of Oudh became a dependant ally and the Nwab of Bengal became, in fact, their pensioner, but from various considerations, Clive shrank from accepting the formal responsibility for the administration of the province. The civil, criminal and police function were left in the hands of the Nawab, who was to be paid out of the revenues a fixed sum to cover expenses. Thus was introduced the dyarchy in 1765 and the administration carried on, in name, by the Nawab, but, in reality, by the Company. according to Prof. Mukerjee,"the policy which Clive adopted towards Emperor Shah Alam, the Nawab-Wazir of Oudh and the Nawab of Bengal reveals a good deal of political wisdom and practical commonsense. He invoked the shadow of a great name and used the fiction of the Mughal sovereignty in order to regularise the Company's position in Bengal. By receiving the Diwani from the Emperor he consolidated. British authority in Bengal and placed it on a legal basis. But he wisely refrained from trying to rehabilitate the Emperor and to make him a took in the hands of the Company. Such a course would have involved the Company in endless wars. On the contrary, he chose the safar course of making Oudh a buffer state and bound its ruler by ties of material interests. He therefore, ensured the safety of Bengal and Bihar. In those troubled times the safty of Bengal was a far greater consideration than a precarious hold on Delhi. Lastly, his "Double Government"of Bengal, although marked by serious defects, was an adroit measure to mask the real position of the Company. Its object was to delude the European rivals of the Company into the idea that the Nawab was still the de-facto ruler of Bengal."

❐

8

British Policy in India (1818-1851)

POLITICAL CONDITION OF INDIA IN 1813

The area of British influence had by now extended; roughly speaking, over the whole of Hindustan except the large tracts now known as the Centrol India. The following were the enemies of the English in India at the time:

(1) **Holkar.** Jaswant Rao Holkar died in 1811. His successor was a minor whose custody and power had become the bone of contention between the widowed mother and the Pathan Chief, Amir Khan. The struggle ended in favour of the latter who, thereupon, became at once the prop and burden of the throne. The government of the country was now virtually dissolved and the people fell a prey to all the evils of chronic disorder.

(2) **Bhonsle.** The Bhonsle Raja brooded over the losses he had sustained in the last Maratha War and maintained an attitude of reserve and distress towards the English. Since 1812, the English had been endeavouring to induce him to accept the Subsidiary Alliance, but he had rejected all overtures on the subject.

(3) **Scindia.** Scindia who had been allowed a free hand in Rajputana had utilised his opportunity to the full. In 1813 he had made an alliance with the Bhonsle Raja and the two were now engaged in attacking Bhopal, an important Mohammedan state, connecting British territory with Bundelkhand and Berar.

(4) **The Peshwa.** The Peshwa, Baji Rao II, was extremely distrustful of the English. He had claims on the Gaikwad of Baroda, which were still unsettled and which, according to the Treaty of Bassien, had been left to the arbitration of the British. He now keenly felt the loss of his position which prevented him to deal directly with the subordinate chiefs.

(5) **The Pindaris.** The Pindari chiefs-Chitu, Wasil Mohammed and Karim Khan—had brought devastation from Mysore to the banks of the Jumna and baffled all attempts to overtake them. The centre of their power was in the valley of Narmada.

Lord Moria's Policy of Non-intervention Abandoned. As pointed out above. Lord Moira had been an opponent of Lord Wellesley's policy of aggrandisement and he came to India with a fixed determination to pursue the policy of non-intervention, but the peculiar condition of India, as discussed above, forced him to revise his views and he found himself constrained to act on the lines of Wellesley and to complete his work. The policy of non-intervention, as pursued by Lord Cornwallis and Sir George Barlow and which Lord Minto also was forced to adopt in deference to the strict instructions from the home government, had given rise to grave internal disorders and encouraged aggression on the British territory. The policy was looked upon as a sign of weakness and the Gurkhas and the Burmese assumed an aggressive attitude towards the British power. But what discredited the policy of non-intervention the most was the ravages of the Pindaris, whose devastations inflicted untold misery on the people of Central India. This disorder forced Lord Hastings to give up the policy of non-intervention, "When he took over charge, he found seven different quarrels likely to demand the decision of arms."

The Wars of Lord Hastings' Period. The following wars attracted the attention of Lord Hastings during the period of his Governor-Generalship. Dr. Ishwari Prasad Writes, "It has always been the curse of aggressive imperialism that by riding roughshod over the independence of others, it generates feeling of hostility, leading to a cycle of wars which acquire an air of being defensive against states that rise to win back what they had lost. The wars of Hastings were the sequel to those of Wellesley."

1. The First Nepal War (1814-1816). It was in the time of Lord Hastings that Nepal, lying amidst the southern slopes of the Himalayan ranges, came under British influence. But before Lord Hastings could muster his forces in a final attempt to crush the spirit of independence which lurked in the Maratha state, his attention was drawn to the growing extension of the Gurkhas and the kingdom of Nepal in the interior of the Himalayas the acquisition of Gorakhpur 180 to from the Nawab- Wazir of Oudh brought the English dominions into contact with the kingdom of Nepal. About the early inhabitants of Nepal, not much is known. In the fourteenth century, the country was occupied by the Mallas, who established themselves in the valley independent principalities for themselves. Constant warfare between the principalities ultimately led to the dominance of the Gurkhas, whose chief, Prithvi Narayan, founded a dynasty of his own name in 1767. With a well-disciplined army, the Gurkha kingdom expanded rapidly until it extended to Sikkim in the east and the river Sutlej in the west. According to Princep, "When Lord Hastings took over as the Governor-General, this nation was then in actual possession of the strong country which skirts the northern frontier of Hindustan."

Causes of the First Nepal War

(1) In the process of their expansion eastwards as well as westwards, Nepal had annexed more than 200 villages from Darjeeling to Simla in spite of various protests lodged with their Government by Sir George Barlow and Lord Minto. This could not be tolerated by the British Government any more.

(2) The peaceful atmosphere in India of this time further encouraged them to invade Gorakhpur in Oudh and annex it. This was another instance of aggression on the part of the Nepalis on the British territory.

(3) Lord Minto sent an uitimatum for its restoration which was answered in the negative. This answer was received by Marquess of Hastings as Lord Minto had left India by that time.

(4) Hastings annexed the district and established police stations which were burnt down by the Gurkhas.

(5) Border disputes between the English and the Gurkhas date from 1801 when the English occupation of Gorakhpur made their frontiers conterminous with those of Nepal. The Gurkhas could not but view with alarm the growing extension of the Company's territories towards lands which they considered as falling within their sphere of influence. The undefined frontier between the Company's possessions and those of Nepal made matters complicated. The English regarded each step of extension in the Terai region as an encroachment by the Gurkhas on their dominions.

(6) The Nepali aggression reached ahead when they occupied the district of Butwal and Sheoraj. On their refusal to restore the districts, Lord Hastings declared war in 1814.

Events of the War. The English made elaborate arrangements with regard to the successful conduct of the war. All military strategists agree that Nepal is a very difficult country from the military point of view to approach. It is true that elaborate plans were made in advance, but most of them were ill executed. The Governor-General borrowed a crore of rupees from the Nawab of Oudh. Four armies were despatched under four generals, out of which two armies under General Ochterlony and Gillespie were to enter Nepal and the other two under Morley and Wood were to enter Kathmandu, the Capital of Nepal. But unfortunately, General Gillespie was killed in a premature assault on the mountain fort of Kulunga by Balabhadra, the nephew of the Nepalis to accept the following terms:

(1) The Gurkhas were to acknowledge the independence of the Raja of Sikkim.

(2) A resident was to live at Kathmandu.

(3) The territory between the river Sutlej and the river Kali was to be given to the British. Amar Singh and his party did not accept these terms and resolved to make war. Ochterlony marched a second time and defeated the Nepalese in no time. On their defeat, they surrendered and were forced to sign the Treaty of Sagauli (1826). The First Nepal War came to a close by the Treaty of Sagauli, signed by the two parties in 1826.

The Effects of the First Nepal War

(1) These annexations of the British Government proved of the highest value. The climate of these places was temperate and, therefore, led to the growth of large "hill-stations", *viz.* Simla, Kasauli, Nainital, Almora, etc.

(2) The peace proved to be of immense value because the Nepalese remained loyal to the British Government during the Indian Mutiny and even later on.

(3) The Gurkha soldiers began to join the Company's service. They proved very efficient and trustworthy soldiers.

(4) A pathway was opened to the regions of Central Asia.

THE FOURTH MARATHA WAR (1817-1818)

Causes of the Fourth Maratha War. The Peshwa, Baji Rao II, was under the influence of his minister. Trimbakji, and was intriguing once more to become the real head of the Maratha Confederacy, the position which he had lost before. In 1815, the minister of the Gaikwad of Baroda was basely murdered, on a visit to settle some dispute between the two Maratha Governments. Trimbakji was suspected of complicity in the crime. Elphinstone, the Resident, consequently demanded at once his arrest, He was delivered to the British authorities, but he escaped. The Peshwas being suspected of his complicity in this escape, was, however, threatened with war and was forced to sign a subsidiary treaty and an explicitly renunciation of his claims to the headship of the Maratha Confederacy (1817).

This was too much for Baji Rao II. He rose in rebellion, attacked and burnt the British Residency at Poona.

Events of the War. The British Resident had moved out to Kirkee, a few miles outside Poona, where the Peshwa was decisively beaten and driven as a fugitive from his capital in 1817. On January 1818, the Peshwa again suffered another defeat at Koregaon and, a few days later, another at Ashti, whereupon he surrendered to Sir John Malcolm on condition that he was paid an yearly pension of 8 lakhs. Lord Hastings followed the Mysore precedent, sought out a descendant of Shivaji and made him the ruler of Satara. The rest of the country was annexed and it now forms part of the Bombay Presidency. The attack of Poona acted as a signal to Holkar and the Bhonsle Raja to rise simultaneously. At Nagpur, the British Residency was attacked, but the enemy was beaten at Sitabaldi and Holkar was, routed at Mahidpore in 1817. In this revolt, Apa Sahib the Raja of Nagpur gave up Berar and other territory in the neighbourhood of the river Narmada.

RESULTS OF THE WAR

1. This war brought the whole country ruled over by Indian princes under the control of the British Government.
2. The power of Scindia was paralysed.
3. The power of Holkar was broken.
4. The Peshwa was a fugitive and the Pindaris had disappeared.
5. The Pathan parties of Amir Khan and Ghaffur Khan had ceased to exist.
6. The Raja of Nagpur became a captive.
7. It finally extinguished the Mmatha empire at which Lord Wellesley struck the first blow. Mr. Marshman, remarks, "The war subdued not only the native army, but the native mind and taught the princes and people of India to regard the supreme command in India as undisputably transferred

to a foreign power. In placed the Company with a more absolute authority than Akbar or Aurangzeb had ever enjoyed."

Establishment of British Supremacy in Rajputana

It was during the administration of Lord Hastings that the British influence was established over Rajputana and Central India. In the eighteenth century, the Rajput states had became a spent-up force. They had been weakened by internal faction and dynastic quarrels and so were exposed to the terrible depredations of the Marathas, the Pathans and the Pindaris. In particular, Scindia dominated them. They had sought British protection, but failed to secure it because of the policy of non-intervention pursued by Sir George Barlow and Lord Minto. Lord Hastings, on the other hand, realised the importance of an alliance with the Rajput states. It would give the Company immense strategic advantages and place at its disposal the resources of Rajputana for defensive and offensive purposes. Besides, the help of the Rajputs would be of great value in rounding up the Pindaris whom Hastings was determined to crush. Hence he forced Scindia to renounce his claim to Rajput states and then got a free hand to deal with them. The Rajput princes welcomed the sheltering arm of British protection and concluded subsidiary treaties by which they acknowledged their recognition of British paramountcy in return for protection against external enemies. Metcalfe concluded treaties with nineteen Rajput states, including Jaipur, Udaipur, Jodhpur and Boondi. Datta and Sarkar write, "This extension of political influence over the 'Rajput states makes an important step in the advance of British paramountcy in India. But Lord Hastings' Rajput policy has not escaped criticism. The Rajput states had never manifested any hostility towards the British and were, as Hastings himself expressed, the "natural allies." However, the treaties which they were led to accept subjected them to subordinate positions like other hostile states and entailed a less of their independence. All proposals, which came forward later on to improve their relations with the British, were never put into force. It may be very well asked if the Rajput states could not be protected from misrule and external aggressions by being attached with the English in a tie of the "friendly co-operation" instead of "subordinate alliance." It should also be noted that the "good and tranquillity" of the country was not "the exclusive aim" of the company's interference, as Princep holds but they were guided by considerations of political "expediency and convenience" to themselves. Lord Hastings has also been more severely criticised for continuing the tributes from the Rajput states. There was some justification for this and Mr. Princep's arguments in defence are, firstly, that the British Government by undertaking to protect the states from external foes could legitimately realize from them the cost thereof; secondly, that these were retained as a mark of supremacy over them; thirdly, that "by the immediate operation of the treaties" and by the establishment of regular govemment there was an increase of their revenues "of which it would have been an act of wanton profusion to make a distribution purely gratuitous."

Establishment of British Supremacy in Central India

As a result of the suppression of the Pindaris, British authority was extended to Central India. The Nawab of Bhopal entered into a treaty of "defensive and subordinate alliance" with the Company. Some minor states, *e.g.*, Malwa and Bundelkhand, also concluded similar treaties and acknowledged British paramountcy.

The Suppression of Revolts in Orissa and Bareilly

Hastings suppressed the disturbances in Orissa where the people were driven to revolt by over-assessment, under enhancement of the salt tax and general mis-government. The revolt was put down and the grievances of the people retrieved. The outbreak of the Mussalmans at Bareilly caused by the imposition of a municipal tax and other grievances was put down. The Zamindars of Hathras, who had shown an insubordinate spirit, refused to dismantle his fort. Hastings made suitable military preparations and bombarded the fort with success.

"Thus", write Datta and Sarkar, "the Indian powers, who had struggled so long for political supremacy on the ruins of the Mughal Empire fell before the pressure of British arms and diplomacy; all the principal Indian states now acknowledged the British way and by a series of Political and military transactions effective supremacy of the British became fully established from the Himalayas to the Cape Comorin and from the Brahmaputra to the Sutlej across which the rising Sikh power stood in friendship and alliance. Lord Hastings completed the work which Clive had begun and Wellesley had pushed forward. British sovereignty over India became an accomplished fact in his time. Princep hoped at that time, "The struggle which has thus ended in the universal establishment of British influence, is particularly important and worthy of attention, as it promises to be the last we shall ever have to maintain with the native powers of India." As subsequent events show this last struggle was yet to come."

POLITICAL CONDITIONS OF INDIA IN 1818 AND 1823

Before an attempt is made to discuss the works and achievements of Lord Hastings, it is desirable to point out that the works and achievements of Lord Hastings can be judged from two points of view, *viz.*, *(A)* His internal reforms and the task of consolidation, and *(B)* his conquests and the annexation or the expansion of the British power under him.

(A) His achievements. Marquess of Hastings was not only a great conqueror, but was also a great administrator. In spite of a great opposition that he had to face from his countrymen, he tried his level best for the social, economic and political welfare of the people of India. Fortunately, Lord Hastings was able to get the service of the best administrators available to him in India at that time. These best officers were John Malcolm, Sir Thomas Munroe, Mount Stuart Elphinstone, and Sir Charles Metcalfe. Hastings him self was a hard worker on the side of administration and tried to remove the various defects which had crept in due to the reforms of Lord Cornwallis. Each one of his best administrative officers has left impress of his personality in the history of India. But, the most important legacies left by these officers were:

(1) establishment of law, order and peace by Elphinstone, the British Resident in the territory given to the Company by the Peshwa, and;

(2) the introduction of revenue settlement in Madras by Sir Thomas Munroe.

(I) Judicial Reforms

(a) During the term of office of Lord Hastings, many reforms were introduced in the country. The problem facing the country was the evergrowing number of undecided cases in the courts of justice. As the cases were not disposed of for years together, the parties were forced to take law into their own hands in many cases. The problem could be solved by increasing the number of courts, but the Company was not willing to increase the number of courts because it involved an additional expenditure. Consequently, the Company's miserliness was attacked by publicists like Mill.

(b) In 1814, Lord Hastings provided that there was to be a Munsiff in every thana. These Munsiffs got the appointment from the judges of the Diwani Adalat, though the power of approval of their appointment was left with the Provincial Court of Appeal. According to the powers given to the Munsiffs, they were to try cases up to the value of Rs. 64, their decisions being subject to confirmation by the judges of the Diwani Adalat. Appeals could be made to the Diwani Adalat against the decisions made by the Munsiffs. If the Munsiffs were guilty of misconduct or incapacity or neglect of duty, they were subject to removal. In addition to the Munsiffs appointed to try cases, Sadr Amins were also appointed in every Zila or City. The number of the Sadr Amins depended upon the amount and nature of work to be done in that year. Though the appointments were made by the judges of the Dewani Adalat of such Sadr Amins, yet the approval of their appointments rested in the hands of the Provincial Court of Appeal. These Sadr Amins were empowered to try cases up to the value of Rs. 150. But one distinction was made in the case of their functions.

(c) Hastings also increased the powers of the registrars to whom the cases up to the value of Rs. 50 were sent for disposal. In special cases, the Diwani Adalats could also refer cases involving more than Rs. 500 to the registrars. It was also provided that appeals could be taken to the Provincial Court of Appeal against the decision of the registrars.

(d) In certain cases, the right of appeal was abolished with a view to decreasing the arrears of work. Generally, only one appeal was allowed. It was provided in 1814 that appeals were to be taken from the Diwani Adalat to the Provincial Court of Appeal. However, if the latter tried a case in its original jurisdiction, the appeal could be taken to the Sadr Diwani Adalat.

(e) It was also provided in 1821 that if one Munsiff was considered inadequate for the discharge of the work that he had in his hand at that time, more Munsiffs could be appointed for the purpose. These Munsiffs were appointed to try cases up to the value of Rs.150. Similarly, Sadr Amins also were empowered to try cases up to Rs. 500.

(f) It was also provided that in future all cases involving an amount of more than Rs. 5,000 could be instituted in the city Diwani Adalat or Zila Diwani Adalat. The Sadr Diwani Adalat was given powers to transfer cases from the district or city Diwani Adalat to the Provincial Court of Appeal. If the amount involved was more than Rs. 5,000, provision was made for the institution of these cases directly in the Provincial Court Appeal. Sometimes, these cases could be transferred to Sadr Diwani Adalat also.

(g) In 1815, it was provided that no person was to be considered as qualified for the appointment to the post of a judge of the Sadr Diwani Adalat unless he had previously officiated as a judge of the Provincial Court of Appeal for a period of not less than three years or had worked for not less than nine years in a judicial capacity.

(h) In 1818, Lord Hastings also provided that the magistrates were to be given powers to give punishment of imprisonment with hard labour up to two years and corporal punishment of more than thirty stripes.

(i) Another regulation of 1821 provided that it should becompetent for the Governor-General-in-Council to authorise the Collector of Revenue or other officers employed in the management or superintendents of any branch of the territorial revenues to exercise whole or any portion of the powers and duties vested in the magistrate or to employ a magistrate in the collection of public revenue and also to invest the person so employed with the whole or any portion of the powers of the Collector of Revenue. The powers of the Collectors were considerably increased.

(II) Revenue Reforms

(a) Lord Hastings made a final appeal to the Directors for the measure of the Permanent Settlement which had been solemnly promised by his predecessor, but the Directors rejected his request with curtness. Accordingly, arrangements were made with the representatives of each village community for the adjustment of the share of each individual cultivator, and allowing an appeal to the civil courts in case of a dispute. The system is known as the Mahalwari System.

(b) Bengal Tenancy Act of 1822. The Government Settlement of Bengal had left the rights of the peasantry to the mercy of Zamindars. This mistake was rectified. A new Act was passed by which tenants or cultivators having a hereditary and prescriptive right of occupancy were not to be dispossessed as long as they paid the rents previously settled and their rents were not be augmented except under specified circumstances.

(c) Bombay. In Bombay, Mr. Elphinstone combined the Ryotwari and Mahalwari system, fixing the ryots and the lands of each ryot by survey and entrusting farming of the village for a certain number of years to the Patel.

(d) Madras. Sir Thomas Munroe, who became the Governor of Madras in 1820, introduced in his Presidency the Ryotwari system. This system was in vague there by which the ryots became the direct payers of revenue without the intervention of either the Zamindars or the village community.

(III) Promotion of Education. The Governor-General promoted the cause of education by every means in his power and establish schools from his own private means. A college was opened at Calcutta under his patronage for the spread of English language. His wife also assisted him in this work. The Governments of Bombay and Madras likewise encouraged and assisted with funds the various schemes that were set on foot for the improvement of Indian education.

(IV) Liberty of the Press. Lord Hastings removed one harassing restraint to which the Indian press had been subjected by Lord Wellesley. During the regime of the latter, every journal was submitted on the eve of its issue to a Government Censor, who had the power to strike out matter which he considered objectionable. This censorship was now abolished. At the same time, the press was by no means left to its own guidance: it was still subject to many restrictions. "The editors were to be restrained from publishing any mad versions, strictures on the proceedings or Indian authorities in England, disquisitions on the political transactions of the local administration, or offensive remarks on the public conduct of the members of the Council, the judges or the Bishop of Calcutta, discussions having tendency to create alarm or suspicion among the parties as to any intended interference with the religion, the republication from any English or other newspapers, of passages coming under the preceding heads or otherwise calculated to affect British power of reputation in India and private scandal or personal remarks on envoys tending to excite dissensions in society."

Hasting's Resignation (1823). After him, Sir Charles Metcalfe became the Resident. On his complaints to the Governor General-in-Council, the permission was cancelled. This matter went against Lord Hastings and he was suspected by the Home authorities of supporting the corrupt financial dealings of the Company. In view of this attitude of the home Government, Lord Hastings resigned in 1823.

His Achievements

1. Marquess of Hastings followed a "forward" policy, *i.e.*, the policy of war, conquests and annexations and placed the British on the pinncle of glory and power. This forward policy he had adopted on his arrival in India when he found that the situation warranted the adoption of such a policy. The following measures which he adopted for the extension of the British power in India are worthy of note:

(a) **Subsidiary Alliances.** He made the Indian rulers enter into Subsidiary alliances with the British Government with a view to getting the protection from the Company and owning allegiance to the British power in India as the paramount power. This measure went a long way in extending the influence of the Company in the courts of the various Indian rulers.

(b) **The First Nepal War.** He defeated the Gurkhas of Nepal who, thereafter, became a valuable support to the British power in India. By the Treaty of Sagauli, the Gurkhas ceded some territories of their frontier, including Simla, Mussoorie and Nainital and agreed to have a British Resident at their court.

(c) **He Increased the British Territory by Defeating the Marathas in the Fourth Maratha War.** The war with the Marathas made a considerable increase in the British territory: The Peshwa had become rebellious and had appealed to all the Maratha chiefs to make their last bid to win back their lost prestige and territories. He himself was defeated at Kirkee. Appa Sahib Bhonsle was defeated at Sitabaldi and Holkar's army was routed at Mahidpur, The Peshwa was disposed of and given a pension and his kingdom was annexed and made a part of the Bombay Presidency. Holkar also ceded some territories in Khandesh. The Maratha chiefs were all brought under control and the Maratha power was completely liquidated.

(d) **Suppression of the Pindaris.** Lord Hastings undertook to suppress the Pindaris in Central India, where their outrages had grown intolerable. These men were either the disbonded soldiers or were the fragments of the Mughals, the Marathas and the Pathans. They carried on their plundering expeditions after the rains subsided and threatened the people with fire and sword, making the whole of Central India a hell upon earth. By defeating and destroying the Pindaris root and branch, he made the country free from lawlessness and robbery. Hastings freed India from the terrible bandits, whose ravages had devastated the country in many places. The menace of Pindaris disappeared. Within four years, they were broken and beaten back everywhere. General tranquillity took the place of general violence under the guarantee of a power willing and able to maintain it.

(e) **Establishment of British Supremacy in Rajputana.** It was during the administration of Lord Hastings that the British influence and supremacy was established over Rajputana. In the eighteenth century, the Rajput states had become a spent-up force. They had been weakened by internal factions and dynastic feuds and, as such, were exposed to the terrible depredations of the Marathas, the Pathans and the Pindaris. In particular, Scindia dominated the entire Rajputanastates. They had sought British protection, but failed to secure it because of the policy of non-intervention, pursued by Barlow and Lord Minto. Lord Hastings, on the other hand, realised the importance of an alliance with the Rajput states. It would give the Company immense strategic advantages and place at its disposal the resources of Rajputana for defensive and offensive purposes. Besides, the help of the Rajputs would be of great value in rounding up the Pindaris whom Hastings was determined to crush root and branch.

(f) **British Supremacy in Central India.** As a result of the suppression of Pindaris. British authority was extended to

Central India also. The Nawab of Bhopal entered into a treaty of "defensive and subordinate alliance with the company." The minor states of Malwa and Bundelkhand also concluded smaller treaties and acknowledged British paramounty.

(g) **Revolts in Orissa and Bareilly Put Down.** Hastings was also able to suppress the disturbances that had cropped up in Orissa where the people were forced to revolt by over assessment, undue enhancement of the salt tax and general misgovernment. The revolt was put down with a heavy hand and the grievances of the people were redressed. At Bareilly also, an outbreak of the Muslims occurred on account of the imposition of municipal tax and other grievances. But the outbreak was put down. Similarly, the Zamindar of Hathras had also shown an insubordinate attitude when he refused to dismantle his fort that he was asked to do. Hastings made suitable military preparations and bombarded the fort with success.

Results of Lord Hastings' Internal Administration and Conquests

(a) Created Order Out of Chaos. It should be noted here that the political condition of India is 1818 turned out to be quite different from the political conditions which prevailed in the country in 1813. By his bold and vigorous policy, he established perfect peace and order in India and saved the country from anarchy and confusion. Similarly, when he left Indian 1823, the political condition had gone many steps forward in favour of the East-India Company. He will always be remembered as the Governor-General who carried out the policy of Lord Wellesley to its legimate conclusion and firmly established the British government as the paramount power in India.

(b) Finished all Opposition from the Native Powers. Smith says, "In October 1817, Lord Hastings was confronted with force of more than 150,000 men - Pindaris, Marathas and Pathans with five hundred guns. Four months later, the power of Scindia was paralysed, that of Holkar broken, the Pathan armies of Amir Khan and Ghaffur

Khan had ceased to exist, the Raja of Nagpur was a captive, the Peshwa was a fugitive and the Pindaris had disappeared.

(c) Made all the Native Powers Acknowledge the British Supremacy. Thus, the Indian powers who had struggled so long for political supremacy on the-ruins of the Mughal Empire fell before the British armies and the principal Indian states now acknowledged the British sway and by a series of political and military transactions effective supremacy of the British became fully established from the Himalayas to the Cape Comorin and from the Brahmaputra to the Sutlej, across which the rising Sikh power stood in friendship and alliance. Lord Hastings completed the work which Clive had begun and Wellesley had pushed forward.

(d) Proved a Great Administrator. Lord Hastings established peace and order in the country, and removed most of the irregularities in the Company's territories. Its possessions were consolidated and the paramount position of England assured. His work of internal reforms and consolidation and extension of conquests amply prove the truth of the statement that Lord Hastings was not only an administrator, but a great conqueror as well.

(e) Completed the Work of Conquests Started by Wellesly. Lord Hastings was one of the ablest and most vigorous of the Governor-General sent to India. He completed the work left unfinished by Lord Wellesley and, thus, the British power became supreme in India. "He received and carried through the grandest strategic operations ever undertaken in India in the course of which twenty-eight actions were fought and a hundred and twenty fortresses taken without a single reverse. He was less precipitated than Wellesley, less harsh to errant native rulers and he did not proceed against them till his case was very strong.

(f) Made British as Paramount Power in India. This great political settlement of Central India in 1818—when he crushed the power of the Marathas in the Fourth Maratha War, the disarmament and pacification of the military chiefs and the adjustment of distinct relations of supremacy and subordination established the universal recognition of the British power in India. It completed and consolidated the policy of Lord Wellesley. The last shade of interference by any European rival had now faded away. The contest with the native states for ascendancy was finally decided. The largest and most important and by far the most valuable portion of this region was now under the Company's control. The rest of the region was under its sovereign influence. By the end of Lord Moira's period of office, British territory in India was taking its modern shape. Nagpur (Bhonsle's territory) and Oudh were not annexed until the time of Lord Dalhousie and British power had not been extended to Sind and Punjab in the north-west, nor to Assam and Burma to the east. In other respects, the map of political India was not unlike that of today. The defeat of the Maratha Confederacy in 1818 made the British the only sovereign and supreme power in Hindustan and the Deccan, Sind and the Punjab were the only provinces left unfinished.

POLICIES OF LORD HASTINGS

Lord Minto resigned the post of Governor General in 1813 AD. He was succeeded by Lord Hastings. He had bitterly criticized the Imperialist Policy of Lord Wallesley while he was in the Parliament of England. On reaching he found that the policy adopted by Lord Wellesley was the best. 'He, therefore, himself adopted the same imperialist policy.

Among the Indian states, when Lord Hastings arrived in India there were three categories of states with each the British had a different type of relations one was the category of those states with which the British had concluded subsidiary alliances, under which the English, undertook the responsibility of internal as well as the external protection; while the state concerned agreed to receive a subsidiary force' to be maintained at the State's own expense. Under this type of alliance a state almost completely sold away its political independence to the British. The second category was of those states which had almost a similar dependence on the British as above but these states did not have to receive any subsidiary force. And the last category was of these states, the independence of which recognised by the British, the relations here being conducted by ordinary treaties.

During the period of Lord Wellesley, a large number of the Indian princely had been brought under the first two categories. The Nizam of Hyderabad had been brought under the subsidiary system; Carnatak had been annexed; while the ruling dynasty in Mysore having been changed, it was reduced completely dependent on the British. Lord Wallesley had also tried to deal with the Maratha's, but before he was able to bring the into complete subjection he had been recalled. And it was here that one of the real troubles for Lord Hardings lay.

(1) The Nepal War (1814-1816)

(a) Causes. The Gurkhas had succeeded in establishing a strong kingdom in Nepal by the time the British became a strong power in India. Their boundary in the south nearly touched the boundary of the English empire. In 1814, when the Gurkhas captured the two districts of Butwal and Sheroaj" which the English regarded under their own protection, the latter declared war against the Gurkhas in 1814.

(b) Events. The British officials had expected an easy walk-over especially as their army attacked all along the 600 mile frontier. But the Gurkhas defended themselves with vigour and bravery. The British armies were defeated again and again. In the long run, however, the Gurkhas could not survive. The British were far superior in men, money and materials. In April 1815 they occupied Kumaon, and on 15th May they forced the brilliant Gurkha Commander Amer Singh Thapa to surrender. The Government of Nepal was now compelled to sue for peace. But the negotiations for peace soon broke down. The Government of Nepal would not accept the British codemand for the stationing of a Resident at Kathmandu, Nepal's captial. It realised fully well that to accept a subsidiary alliance with the British amounted to singing away Nepal's independence. Fighting was resumed early in 1816. The British forces won important victories and reached with in 50 miles of Kathmandu.

(c) **Results.** Nepal Government accepted a British Resident. It ceded the districts of Garhwal and Kumaon and abandonad claims to the Tarai areas. It also withdrew from Sikkim. The agreement held many advantages for the British. Their Indian Empire now reached the Himalayas. They gained greater facilities for trade with Central Asia. They also obtained sites for import hilstations such as Simla, Mussoorie and Nainital.

The relations of the British with Nepal were quite friendly thereafter. Both parties to the War of 1814 had learnt to respect each other's fighting capacity and preferred to live at peace with each other.

(2) The Pindari War. The Pindaris, were spreading terror and destruction all around. Lord Hastings very seriously desired to crush their predatory system once for all. But killing of the dogs was bound to provoke poachers, for any such attempt was bound to involve the British simultaneously into a war with Marathas who supported the Pindaris, and who would definitely try to take the advantage to pay off there old scores. The home authorities, therefore, still convinced of the wisdom of the policy of non-intervention, strictly cautioned Hastings about any "offensive operations against the Pindaris, either with a view to their Utter extirpation, or in anticipation of expected danger." Nor were they in favour of risking a war in extending protection to the victims of the Pandari raids and the Maratha plunders. Lord Hastings thus was helpless about taking any action against the Pindaris. But the circumstances soon changed. The Pindaris were becoming bolder as a result of the British indifference towards their predatory pursuits. In 1815 they plundered the dominions of the Nizam, and carried their raid even beyond the river Kishna, into the Madras Presidency, carrying away a huge body. In February 1816 they took their predatory incursion into the Northern Circars, another British territory, and subjected it to an utter devastation, carrying away huge booty and every young girl they could lay their hands upon. In the meanwhile in March 1816, Wazir Muhammad, the Nawab of Bhopal, to whom Hastings had extended protection against

Scindia and Bhonsle in October 1814, died. His son Nasir Muhammad succeeded him, and being still surrounded by serious troubles at the hands of the Marathas and others, he appealed to Hastings for protection. But the latter could do nothing beyond expressing sentiments of good will towards the new Nawab. Besides, as Hastings reported, there was a conclusive evidence that Pindaris, the Peshwas and other Maratha chiefs had formed a wide conspiracy "for the explosion of the British from India." If the British did not act on time, their very existence in India could become problematical. It was therefore not long before the Board of Control in England understood that the Pindris had to be dealt with and the British prestige in the eyes of the Indian princes saved, by extending them protection when applied for.

Events. Hastings moblised a strong army of 113,000 soldiers and 300 canons. The army was devided into two parts, the one to guard' against any trouble from the side of the Marathas and the other to exterminate the Pindaris. The Pindaris were encircled on all sides by the British forces. By diplomacy, Hastings detached the Marathas from the side of the Pindaris. The British forces ruthlessly chased the Pindaris and completely destroyed some of them. Their Chief Karim Khan surrendered on condition of being made the Nawab of Tonk. Wasll Muhammad, the second chief poisoned himself to death in the Ghazipur jail. Chitu, the third chief fled to the jungles and was devoused by a tiger.

(3) Lord Hastings and Marathas. Peshwa had signed the subsidiary alliance during the reign of Wellesley but now he wanted to break that. Holkar Scindia, Gaikwad, Bhonsle etc. all wanted to see their leader Peshwa free from the dutches of the British. On the other hand, Lord Hastings had concluded that without crushing the power of Marathas, no sound British empire will be possible here.

(i) **Lord Hastings and Bhonsle.** Hastings first of all turned his attention towards Bhonsle. He was the ruler of Nagpur and there was some trouble going on. On March 22, 1816 died Raghoji Bhonsle II. His son Parsoji was both physically and mentally unfit. Hence there arose a difference between

Raghoji's widow Bukabai and Appa Sahib. Hastings sided Appaji as he entered in Subsidiary Alliance with him. No doubt it was the most fortunate thing. After the death of Parsoji, Appaji himself sat on the throne. But in the heart of hearts he was against the English. On November 26, 1817 he got an opportunity and attacked Residency. In the battle of Sitawal Qiand Nagpur, he was badly defeated. All the territory in the north of the Narbada was annexed by the English. The rest of the territory was given to the grandson of Raghoji. An English Resident was kept to look after the administration as the ruler was a mere child.

(ii) Hastings and Peshwa. In 18 15 Ram Shastri, the Minister of Gaikwad of Baroda, was murdered at Poona, where he had gone under British safe conduct to settle some claims and counter-claims of Gaikwad of Baroda and Peshwa Baji Rao II. It was certain that Trimbakji was responsible for this murder and Peshwa's complicity was suspected. The British Resident Elphinstone, demanded that the guilty minister should be surrendered and Peshwa surrendered him after a good deal of procrastination. The guilty minister escaped from the British custody a year later in 1816. He was not traced but it was generally thought that the Peshwa was in communication with him. Peshwa was collecting troops also. Elphinstove forced him to sign a new treaty of Poona in June, 1817. The terms of the treaty were:

(a) Peshwa ceded some important positions of his territory to the English.

(b) He promised to capture Trimbakji and hand him over to the English. But that time his family was kept as hostage by the English.

(c) He left all his claims over the Gaikwad and agreed to take an annual sum of rupees four lakhs from him in lieu of the disputed territory.

(d) He renounced his claim as head of the Maratha chiefs and also agreed not to have any negotiations with other powers except through the English resident.

(e) He surrendered to the' English the Fort of Ahmednagar and relinquished his right over Malwa, Bundelkhand and North India.

One historian has rightly said, "The severity of these terms of the treaty drove the Peshwa to war with the English."

(iii) Hastings and Scindia. The English proved themselves to be very clever and shrewd by entering into a new treaty with the ruler of Gwalior, Daulat Rao Scindia on 5th Nov. 1817. They encircled him from all the four sides in such away that he was redered powerless to take any special part in the future war against the English. Moreover, the English obtained the right of making direct treaties with the Rajput states like Udaipur, Jodhpur, Kota, Bundi etc.

(iv) Hastings and Gaikwad. The English renewed their treaty with the Gaikwad as well. By that, he reduced the strength of his own army, accepted an increase ill the subsidiary force and for its expanses ceded some more districts to the English. Thus, he was made more dependent on the English.

(v) Hastings and Holkar. The famous Maratha chief Jaswant Rao Holkar died in 1817. After his death confusion and disorder prevailed in the Indore state. Taking advantage of this, the English won over the two friends, Amir Khan and Gafur Khan, of the decesed Holkar. These two Muslim Chiefs were entrusted with two Jagirs within the Indore state. In return of this they promised to be faithful to the English. This weakened the claims of Holkar as he disbanded the army of the plunderers.

(vi) Fourth Maratha War (1817-18). This was the last war which was fought between the Marathas and the English from 181710 1818 AD.

Causes

(a) The Fourth Maratha War was an outcome to the feelings of humiliation, which the Marathas had received earlier during the days of Wellesley.

(b) The Peshwa (Baji Rao II) had no doubt, himself entered into the Treaty of Bassein in 1802, but since then he was experiencing a feeling of suffocation. In order to free himself from the English yoke he was busy intriguing with the other Maratha chiefs.

(c) In 1815, Trimbakji, a minister of the Peshwa, got murdered the Brahmin envoy (Gangadhar Shastri) of Gaikwad of Baroda, when the latter came to Poona, under British security, to settle the dispute about the payment of tribute on behalf of his master with the Peshwa. The English suspected a foul play and asked the Peshwa to surrender his minister. When he did not oblige them, the British Resident arrested his minister and also compelled him to sign a new treaty by which he was forced to cede some more territories and to renounce his leadership of the Maratha confederacy.

Events. The Fourth Maratha War started with the attack of Peshwa Baji Rao on the English residency at—Kirkee. The day the Scindia signed the treaty of Gwalior, the Peshwa attacked the residency and burnt it. But his attack was soon repulsed. The same time, Appa Sahib at Nagpur and Malhar Rao II at Indore rose in arms against the English. But, the success of the English was quick. Appa Sahib was defeated at the battle of Sitabaldi on Nov. 27, 1817 and Holkar was defeated at Mahidpur on Dec.21. Appa Sahib fled to hills and the Holkar accepted the treaty of Mandasoron January 6, 1818. On the other hand, as many as 2,800 British troops had in the meanwhile gathered at Kirkee, about three miles away from the town. The Resident also reached that place and before the Peshwa could fall upon them. The British took the initiative, advanced and attacked the 26,000 strong Marathas. The battle was brilliantly fought by the

British, and the Peshwa's forces were forced to fall back upon Poona, losing about 500 of their number in the field, as against the British loss of only 86 The British waited for sometime for a reinforcement to arrive. But on 16th November, when they marched on Poona, they discovered to their surprise that the Peshwa had fled southwards. The British pursued and defeated him in several engagements, but the Peshwa himself could not be captured. He doubled back on a twisted course, eluding the British and trying vainly to break through into Berar.

Results

(a) Holkar agreed with the terms of the Subsidiary Alliance. He also agreed to keep the English Army. He promised not to keep any kind of contact with any foreign country and was also obliged to give a position of his empire to the English.

(b) The whole of Peshwa's territory was annexed to the British empire, and Peshwaship was abolished. However, the Peshwa was awarded a pension of 8 lakhs of rupees annually and was deported to Bittur near Kanpur where he passed his last days of life peacefully.

(c) Scindia had taken no part in these was, even then the English compelled him to sign a new treaty. Thus being forced he signed a new treaty in 1818. According to this treaty, the English got control over Ajmer. He promised to recognise his boundaries. In other words, by this treaty his rights and empire both were curtailed and limited to a very great extent.

(d) Appa Sahib Bhonsle was deposed from the throne and all the parts of his state situated to the north of Narbada river were annexed to the British empire. The remaining parts of his state were placed under a ruler of the Bhonsle family under the patronage of the British Government.

(4) Hastings and Rajput States. It was during the administration of Hastings that the British influence was established over Rajputana and central India. In the 18th century the Rajput states had became a spent force. They had been weakened by internal factions and dynastic quarrels and so were exposed to the terrible depredations of the Marathas, the Pathans, and the Pindaris. In particular Scindia dominated them. They had sought British protection but failed to secure it because of the policy of non-intervention pursued by Barlow and Lord Minto. Lord Hastings on the other hand, realised the importance of an alliance with the Rajput states. It would give the Company immense strategic advantages and place at its disposal the resources of Rajputana for defensive and offensive purposes. Besides, the help of the Rajputs would be great value in rounding up the Pindaris whom Hastings was determined to crush. Hence he forced Scindia to renounce his claims upon the Rajput Princes and thus got a free 'hand to deal with them. The Rajput Princes welcomed the sheltering arms of British protection and concluded subsidiary treaties by which they acknowledged British paramountcy in return for protection, against external enemies.

(5) British Supremacy in Central India. As a result of the suppression of the Pindaris British authority was extended to Central India. The Nawab of Bhopal entered into a treaty of "defensive and subordinate alliance" with the Company. The minor states of Malwa and Bundelkhand also concluded similar treaties and acknowledged British Paramountcy.

(6) Suppression of Revolts in Orissa and Bareilly-Hastings suppressed the disturbances in Orissa where the people were driven to revolt by over assessment. Undue enhancement of the salt tax and general misgovernment. The revolt was put down and the grievances of the people were redressed. An out break of the Mussalmans at Bareilly, caused by the imposition of a municipal tax and other grievances, was put down. The zamindars of Hathras (U.P.) who had shown an insubordinate spirit refused to dismantel his fort. Hastings made suitable military preparation and bombarded the fort with success.

REFORMS OF LORD HASTINGS

(A) Administrative Reforms. Lord Hastings was a great administrator. Though his hands were bound with one war or the other, yet he carried out many useful reforms:

(i) Firstly, he gave high jobs of responsibility to Indians thereby doing away with the injustice that was being done with them since the days of Cornwallis;

(ii) He also relaxed various restrictions which bore heavily on the press. It was during his resign that the first Vernacular newspaper "Samachar Patrika" began to be published.

(iii) Many bridges and roads were constructed to improve the means of communication.

(B) Judicial Reforms. The judicial system had many defects. The number of cases pending for disposal was increasing day by day. Therefore, Lord Hastings made following reforms in the contemporary judical system:

(1) He cought permission from the Directors of the Company to appoint a munsif at every thana (Police Station). The Munsif was empowered to hear cases involving the property or the claim up to Rs. 64/-. The Diwani Adalats were empowered other to confirm the decisions of the Munsifs or to hear appeal against their decisions.

(2) Besides the Munsifs, the Diwani Adalat was also authorised to appoint with the approval of the Provincial Courts of Appeal, Sadar Amins in every district or a city: their number depending on the requirements of a particular area. These Sadar Amins could hear cases up to the value of Rs. 150, but enjoyed no powers to try the cases of Europeans and Americans. The appeals from their courts also by in the Diwani Adalat.

(3) Hastings deserves our appreciation for the simplification and curtailment of procedure in civil cases, which removed the existing trouble to some extent.

(4) From the Diwani Adalat, as provided in 1814, the appeal could be taken to the provincial court of appeal if a case had come from some lower court, but for the cases originating in the Diwani Adalat itself the appeal lay rather

in the Sadar Diwani Adalat. To Simplify the procedure and avoid arrears of work, however it was provided that in certain cases there was no appeal, while in many of the rest only one appeal was permitted.

(5) The powers of the Registrars were increased. Now the Diwani Adalats were entitled to send to him cases up to Rs. 50/- and in extra-ordinary cases up to Rs 500/-. It was provided that appeals against the decisions of the Registrars could be filed direct in the Provincial Courts.

(6) Certain further changes were introduced in 1821 where by a Munsif could try a case upto the value of Rs. 150, while a Sadar Armin could go upto the value of Rs. 500. And where one Munsif was not sufficient, two or more could be appointed.

(7) From Rs. 500 upwards, the cases were instituted in the city or zilla (District) Diwani Adalat, while above Rs. 5,000 the cases went direct to the Provincial Court of Appeal, or incertain cases to the Sadar Diwani Adalat. The latter was also empowered to transfer cases from the city or Zilla Diwani Adalat to the Provincial Court of Appeal.

(C) Educational Reforms. The East India company was required to spend one lakh of rupees on education by the Charter Act of 1813. This was the beginning of a systematic plan to encourage learning. Vernacular schools were established and in 1817 the first college for higher education was founded in Calcutta. His wife was an active supporter of female education. Christian misionaries first appeared in Bengal, set up schools and began to edit and print books.

(D) Revenue Reforms. Hastings then turned to the problems of revenue collection. The existing system was unsatisfactory as it placed excessive power in the hands of the English officials, the so called supervisors. Hastings could see but one satisfactory solution that of withdrawing all Europeans from the country districts, leaving the work of local administration in the hands of native officials.

ADMINISTRATION OF WILLIAM BENTINCK

Lord Macaulay, who has written a good deal in praise of Lord William Bentinck. He says, "His seven years' rule in India is marked with eminent prudence, integrity and benevolence. He infused into oriental despotism the spirit of British freedom, who never forgot that the end of government is the welfare of the governed, who abolished cruel rites and effaced humiliating distinctions, who allowed the principle of the expression of public opinion, whose constant study it was to elevate the moral and intellectual character of the government committed to his charge; the men of all caste and creed cherished with equal veneration and gratitude the memory of his wise, upright and paternal administration."

A close study of the works and achievement of Bentinck in India reveals that the remark as given above by Macaulary is slightly overdrawn. It only represents the viewpoint of the cultured type of Indians and Europeans like Macaulay. There is no doubt that before Bentinck, the British administration in India was the adoption of Mughal system which was despotic in nature and structure. The employees of the East India Company were as despotic as the machinery of the Mughal administration. Their only object, like that of the Mughal rulers, was to care for the interests of the rulers and subordinate those of the ruled. The moral, educational and social welfare of the people was not looked upon both as their duty. The people had no share in the administration. In short, the East India Company cared more for its dividends than for the good of its people. But, though Lord William Bentinck was to a great extent the first man to attend to this question, yet he also failed in a very important respecting this policy. Whereas he was responsible for introducing social, educational and moral reforms to benefit the people under his charge, he never allowed them a share in the formulation or determination of the policy of the Government. It is in view of this drawback in his system of Government and policy that the above remark of Lord Macaulay appears to be slightly overdrawn. It would have been prudent for him to train the subject races for self-Government by inculcating in them obedience to law and a sense of discipline which comes through a close association of the people with the work of policy-making of the country.

Both the above views seem to be extreme views. The truth, probably lies somewhere between the two. But one thing does the greatest credit to the memory of Bentinck for the work that he did in India is that he never forgot that "the end of Government is the welfare of the governed." and, as such, he applied himself heart and soul in bringing about the moral, educational and social uplift of the Indians by introducing various reforms towards the achievement of that objective. The following reforms, therefore, are worthy of discussion to show that the work of William Bentinck in India in these fields went a long way in the consolidation of the British dominions, on one hand, and moral, social and educational uplift of the Indians, on the other. Taken in a humanitarian spirit, his reign was surely to be one of consolidation as Bentinck represented the liberal feelings of his country which had become predominant since the passing of the First Reform Bill of 1832 in England. He was distinctions true liberal of his day and was thoroughly in accord with the ideals that inspired the era of Catholic Emancipation and Parliamentary reforms. It is alleged that the attitude of the liberal regarding India was that:

1. Britain, and not East India Company was responsible for the administration of the country,
2. the best men in the country felt that "British influence must be founded on Indian happiness,"
3. Macaulay's view was that "we have to engraft on despotism those blessings which are the natural fruits of liberty,", and
4. as a result of the Methodist Movement, there came into existence two new movements—Evangelical and Humanitarian spirit. The advocates of these movements were supporting the causes of the weak against the strong. It was in view of the above circumstances that Lord William Bentinck's reign was maked by many beneficent

reforms in India which were conceived in enlightened and humance spirit. His reforms can be discussed under the following headings:

I. Financial Reforms

(1) William Bentinck appointed two committees to inquire into the expenditure on civil and military affairs of the Company and made recommendations for its reduction accordingly. The committees went into the whole matter and made their recommendations which, on their acceptance by him, Lord William Bentinck abolished many sinecure jobs, cut down the allowances and reduced the salary of the civil servants. But in the case of the military establishment nothing much could he achieved. However, he reduced the Double Batta at once, reduced allowance by 50 percent at all stations within 400 miles of Calcutta. This Double Batta allowance was formerly paid in full to the military personnel. Even long before William Bentinck, efforts were made by the Directors of the East India Company to reduce the allowances, but they had faild. Now they ordered William Bentinck to reduce the Double Batta at once which he did. There was a good deal of agitation on the part of military personnel against the Govemor-General, who was openly insulted and condemned by the Anglo-Indian members.

(2) In order to increase the revenues of the Company. William Bentinck regulated the opium trade. He evolved the system of licences for the direct conveyance of opium from Malwa to Bombay and thereby added to the revenues of the Company.

(3) Another important financial reform introduced by Lord William Bentinck which went along way in reducing unnecessary expenditure on the British Exchequer was the abolition of the Provincial Court of Appeal and the Circuit by his. Lord William Bentinck considered that these courts served as a 'resting place' for those members of the servants who were deemed unfit for higher responsibilities.

(4) The East India Company had obtained the Diwani from the Mughal Emperor in 1765. But long before that many grants of

revenue free lands were made and individuals and institutions got them. They were enjoying the income from such lands without doing any work to the state. The English company had also to confirm these grants. In 1793 and then in 1819, a Regulation was issued by the Governor which empowered the Collectors to examine the validity of the grants being enjoyed by the individuals and institutions. In 1828, another Regulation was issued which directed the Collectors to look into the legality or otherwise of these grants. In order to avoid miscarriage of justice, special commissioners were appointed to hear appeals from the decisions of the Collectors appointed to probe into the legality of the grants. The parties concerned pleaded that they could not produce their documents on account of the passage of time. But the Government did not accept this plea. Consequently, the Government resumed many revenue-free grant lands.

(5) The Governor-General also insisted at this time upon carrying out the revenue settlement in the North-western province. He was very particular about it when he had arrived in India as the Governor-General. Consequently, he personally had made tours of the provinces and also consulted the best opinions on the subject with a view to carrying out the settlement. Ultimately, he evolved a plan of settlement which later on became law in 1833. According to this, the land was surveyed and classification of the soil was made and the settlement made for 30 years. It was made either with the ryots or the Zamindars of the village community.

(6) The administration of East India Company had become top-heavy and even the petty clerks coming from England got very fat salaries. Lord William Bentinck thought out of a plan by which he recruited the Indians in the serve of the Company. These Indians were paid salaries much lower than those paid to the Europeans. It was in this way that he was able to save a good deal of amount which before his time was not attempted.

Results of his financial reforms. The results of the financial reforms were that the finances of the Company were rehabilitated and instead of deficit, Bentinck showed a surplus of two million.

II. Judicial Reforms

There were many defects in the judicial administration of the Company before Lord William Bentinck, which he tried to remove now. The three evils were, *(1)* delay, *(2)* expense, and *(3)* uncertainty. Calcutta had become too distant for the newly acquired territories and, as such, justice had become inaccessible to the common people. In the work of judicial reforms, Bentinck got the assistance of Sir Charles Metcalfe, Butterworth, Bayley and Holt Mckenzies. The following judicial reforms are worthy of note:

(1) Abolished provincial Court of Appeal and the Circuit. As has already been pointed out before, these courts were doing no work enthusiastically and, consequently, their' work was falling in arrears. The judges also had not acquired any knowledge in law and acquaintance with the people of the country. They could not save people from tyranny. Under trials had to rot in the jails for months together before their cases here heard and disposed off. These evils decided Bentinck to abolish these courts. Instead, he appointed Commissioners of revenue and Circuit. Bengal Presidency was divided into twenty divisions and a Commissioner was appointed for each division. These Commissioners were required to perform the same duties which were formerly performed by the judges of the Provincial Court of Appeal and the Circuit.

(2) According to a Regulation passed in the year 1831, it was provided therein to appoint respectable Indians to the Zila Courts and the City Courts. The Indian judges were empowered to try cases up to the value of Rs. 300. These Indian judges were called Munsiffs, and got fixed salaries from the Government.

(3) In 1831, a Regulation was passed which provided for the summary disposal of cases relating to rent. The Collectors were to act expeditiously to dispose of the cases in a summary fashion. These decisions were to be final and no appeals could be made against them. These decisions could be reversed only by civillaw courts by a regular process of instituting suits in the courts of law.

(4) In 1829, a Regulation was issued by the Governor that the Magistrates were to exercise the power of awarding punishments to the offenders up to two years with labour. Appeals against decisions of the magistrates were taken to the commissioners.

(5) Another Regulation of 1831 provided the appointment of principal Sadr Amins by the Governor-General-in-Council from respectable Indians who held this office. These Indian Sadr Amins were to get regular salaries from the Government. Appeals against their decisions could be taken to the Zila or City Courts. But one loophole that was kept, probably intentionally, was that neither the Amins nor the Munsiffs, who always happened to be Indians were empowed to try cases in which the Americans. Europeans and British subjects were involved.

(6) Bentinck also decided to set up a separate Sadr Diwani Adalat and Sadr Nizamat Adalat at Allahabad. It was from the beginning of 1832 that these courts started their regular work.

(7) William Bentinck also abolished the use of Persian as court language which was used in the offices before that time. He placed the vernacular as a substitute for that purpose to be utilised in the courts. This was definitely a great boon to the litigants who were thus able to express their grievances in their own language very conveniently. The value of his judicial reforms was that the defects of yearly expense and uncertainty in the administration of justice were removed and the Indians began to be appointed as judges.

III. Administrative Reforms

1. Lord William Bentinck deserve the credit of reversing the policy of Lord Cornwallis with regard to the employment of Indians in the service of the East India Company. Cornwallis had no faith in the efficiency and honesty of the Indians and, consequently, he had kept them out of office so long as he remained the Governor-General of India. He had insisted on the appointment of only Europeans in the Administration. But Lord William Bentinck found that the employment of Europeans in the administration was very expensive, while Indians may be employed on cheaper wages if he attempted to employ them.

Indians were available for clerical jobs on account of the spread of English in Bengal. Consequently, Bentinck introduced three grades of Indian judges and the highest of them, called Sadr Amins, were given a salary of Rs.750 p.m. This new policy adopted by Lord William Bentinck was in keeping with the principles laid down in the Charter Act of 1833 which provided employment of Indians also in the administration of the Company. The Act said, "No native of India, nor any natural born subject of His Majesty, should be disabled from holding any place, office of employment by reason of his religion, place of birth descent, or colour." In this work, William Bentinck was helped by Sir Charles Metcalfe who was of the opinion that "Native functionaries, in the first instance, of all departments. European Superintendents, uniting the legal powers of judicature, police and revenue in all their branches, through the districts over which they preside.

2. William Bentinck also appointed a Board of Revenue at Allahabad for the administration of revenue department in North-western Province.

IV. Educational Reforms

(1) The Charter Act, as has already been pointed out in another connection, made a provision for a sum of a lakh of rupees every year of the "revival and promotion of a knowledge of the sciences among the inhabitants of the British territories." The Government did not know how to spend this money and consequently the amount used to lapse every year. But in 1823, Mr. Adams appointed a Committee of Public Instruction to make suggestions for the promotion of education in India, which could not be done earlier on account of the preoccupation of the British Government with the first Burmese War. This work was later on taken by Lord Bentinck himself when he became the Governor-General. There were two schools of thought on this question, which became a great controversy between the Anglicists and the Orientalists: Mr. H.H. Wilson was the leader of the Orientalists and Sir Charles Trevelyan was the leader of the Anglicists. The arrival of Lord Macaulay as Law Member strengthened the hands of those who stood for the expenditure of money on English

education. This controversy later on was solved with a clear-cut decision in favour of English being taught and read in India, as against the Oriental Languages in India. This decision was primarily based on practical considerations. Regarding the British administration in India, it was felt, and rightly so, that not only the Government would get cheap clerks but there would be greater demand for English goods also. A Resolution was passed in March, 1835 by which William Bentinck declared that the "great object of British Government ought to be the promotion of literature and sciences among the natives and that the funds proposed for education should be best employed on English education alone."

2. The English education gave the Indians a lingua franca and thereby helped the cause of nationalism in the country. Not only this but the Indians were also introduced to the treasures of western sciences.

3. In 1835, the British Government established a medical college at Calcutta for the benefit of the Indians. Thus, for the first time, the knowledge of the western theory of medicine began to be given to the students in India.

V. Social Reforms

1. One of the greatest acts of humanity for which Lord William Bentinck deserves external honour is the abolition of Suttee. A widow, who burnt herself voluntarily at the funeral pyre of her lord as her last act of devotion, was called a Sati. The word "Sat" is probable derived from Sanskrit, the equivalent English of which is "truth". In course of time, the word, Suttee, began to be applied to the act of self-immolation. How and when the practice originated is hidden in obscurity. But it has a long tradition and references to it found in ancient books gave it the colour of a religious ceremony. The custom, however, was not universal, but was confined to the higher castes. Suttee should in no case be mixed with the custom prevalent in certain parts of Central and Western Asia and Eastern Europe of burying alive widows and slave girls at the death of their masters in their graves. Suttee was a voluntary act, a privilege and

an honour, accompanied by the recitation of sacred verses and involving the burning of the widowed women on the funeral pyre. The former was an act of compulsion, having its origin, Probably, in the jealousy of the dead master rather than in the devotion of the living widow. The custom had prevailed in India abolish this evil system, but no attempt proved fruitful. This evil custom was mostly prevalent in Bengal and Northern India. In 1818, there were no less than 839 cases of Suttee in Bengal Presidency. There were 722 such cases in 1829. Bentinck abolished the practice of Suttee, declaring the burning or burying alive of a widow a crime punishable as culpable homicide. When violence or compulsion was used or drugs were administered to influence the free will of victim, the offenders were guilty of murder to be punished with death. This was done by a regulation of December 1829 which declared the practice of Suttee illegal. Except the orthodox section, the prohibition found favour among the enlightened Hindus, the chief supported among them being Raja Ram Mohan Roy, who encouraged William Bentinck on the plea that no serious consequences would follow the legal prohibition.

2. Another measure which freed the society from a great pest was the establishment of a separate department for the detention and punishment of Thugs. Thugs, as we know, means cheat, and Thugee was a profession prevalent alike among the Hindus and Muslims. The Thugs moved about in gangs, strangled their victims and fleeced them of all their property. The lack of sufficient police force encouraged their notorious activities. Travelling became absolutely insecure Bentinck was the first to make determined efforts on a large scale to break up this system. The new department which he created was placed in charge of Sir William Sleeman, whose strenuous labours in course of time succeeded in breaking up the gangs with the help of approvers. The Thugs were pursued from place to place, eventually caught and punished. Consequently, in 1829, one of the Thugs turned approver and disclosed the secrets of the organisation. During the years 1831-1837, 3,266 Thugs were disposed of, 412 were hanged, and 483 admitted as approvers. The whole organisation was broken up and the country thus was saved from this pest.

3. In some parts of the country, particularly in the south, some savage tribes used to offer human sacrifices to the Earth goddess. This cruel rite was also stopped.

4. In certain parts of Rajputana the evil practice of killing their daughters as soon as they were born was prevalent among the higher sections of the Rajput society. Lord William Bentinck ordered this Inhuman practice to be stopped and, consequently, a considerable improvement in society took place.

5. The rule of Hindu law by which a convert to any other religion forfeited his claim to paternal property was abrogated by a new regulation. Bentinck's Zeal for reform was not shared by many. Even Raja Ram Mohan Ray advised caution, believing that immediate abolition might cause discontent and excitement. 'Bentinck, an ardent reformer, however, brooked no delay. (RC. Majumdarf) Sir T. Wellesley has said, "This was the most daring interference with religious and social customs undertaken by the Company's Government."

VI. Public Works

A Grand Trunk Road from Delhi to Calcutta was built and another from Bombay to Agra was started. In this way, roads were improved and trade and commerce of the country received a great impetus. The irrigation schemes started in the time of Lord Minto were also taken up in the time of William Bentinck. Canals were dug for the distribution of water in the Northwestern Province.

VII. Industrial Reforms

He encouraged steal communication between England and India via the Red Sea. He was the first to introduce steamship navigation with commendable results.

Achievements of Bentinck

(1) His reforms were eminently successful, for the public extended him full co-operation. Public-spirited persons and zealous reformers like Raja Ram Mohan Ray and Dwarka Nath Tagore gave

him active support. His economic reforms made the finances of the Government sound and ultimately made it efficient. The administrative and judicial reforms made justice cheaper, swifter and surer. The educational reforms of Bentinck gave the people a new outlook on life. The suppression of Thuggee made travelling secure and life safe.

(2) A perusal of the events of his reign amply illustrates the truth of the remark, that "Lord William Bentinck's period of Governor-Generalship may be regarded as one of consolidation rather than of expansion." Except in one or two cases, and that too out of sheer necessity, he followed the policy of non intervention. His reign was surely to be one of consolidation, as he represented the liberal feelings of his country which had become predominant due to the passing of the First Reform Bill of 1832 in England. It is alleged that the attitude of the liberals regarding India was *(a)* that Britain, and not the East India Company, was responsible for the administration of the country, *(b)* the best men in the country felt that "British greatness must be founded on Indian happiness," *(c)* Macaulay's view was "we have to engraft on despotism those blessings which are the natural fruits of liberty," and *(d)* as a result of the Methodist Movement, there came into existence two new movements Evangelical, and Humanitarian.

(3) Whatever may be said of Bentinck, it is undoubtedly true that his administration is a period of transition in the history of British rule in India. His period certainly marks the beginning of material and intellectual progress. "Bentinck ruled India with prudence, integrity and benevolence, and historians still remember his "wise, upright, and paternal administration." His work in India was a work of consolidation. "Whilst the administration of the Marquess of Hastings was marked by triumphs of war, that of William Bentinck will always be remembered for the triumphs of peace." The eager aim of Bentinck was to found "British greatness upon Indian Happiness." On account of his various useful reforms, he has earned a high place in Indian history and he deserves the "everlasting gratitude of the Indian people."

SOCIAL REFORMS DONE BY WILLIAM BENTINCK

Most of the English Governor-Generals in India were busy in wars and in exploiting the Indian sources, but Lord William Bentinck took great interest in welfare works for the Indian society. He did not do anything for war and extension of the empire. Well known historian AL. Srivastava had said, "William Bentinck was the first Governor-General in India to have carried out important reforms for the benefit of the people." The reforms made by him can be described into the following headings :

(1) The Financial Reforms. Shortly, after assuming the charge of administration, Lord William Bentinck appointed two committe as for requiring into civil and military expenditure of the Government, and recommand measures for their reduction. The committees held a comprehensive enquiry into the matter, and under their recommendations Bentinck adopted measures to introduce the following financial reforms:

(i) **Abolition of Sinecure Jobs.** He abolished many sinecure jobs. The salary and allowance of Civil Servants of the Company were also reduced.

(ii) **Reduction of Bhatta by Half.** The bhatta or allowance of the military personel posted within 400 miles of Calcutta was reduced by half. There was a lot of apposition to this measure from the side of the officers, but he did not care.

(iii) **Reduce the Expenses.** William Bentinck first of all turned his attention to and state royal expenditure. On certain items company was obliged to incur heavy expenditure.

(iv) **Indians were Included in Services.** Indians; who were so far excluded from higher appointments, were now declared eligible for them. This meant a great deal or reduction in the cost of administration, for Indians officials were conent with lower salaries.

(v) **Abolishing the Parasitical Courts.** Many parasitical courts that served no useful purpose, were abolished to achieve economy. These courts included the Provincial Courts of Appeal and Circuit, set up by Lord Cornwallis, which had negligible business compared to the expenditure incurred on them.

(vi) **Seizure of the Tax Free Land.** The native rulers had given lands to many people by way of rewards or charity during their period of rule. As these lands were gift-lands, no revenue was charged from their owners. Bentinck ordered verification of the claim of these land holders. The lands of all those who could not prove their ownership were confiscated and the rest of them were asked to pay revenue to the state. Many people suffered from this measure because they were deprived of their lands. But the measure certainly helped in increasing the income of the Company.

(vii) **Regulation of Opium Trade of Malwa.** The opium trade of Malwa was properly regulated. The system of issuing licences to carry opium from Malwa to Bombay was introduced. It considerably added to the revenues of the Company.

(viii) **Revenue Settlement of North West Province.** After proper survey and classification the land settlement of North West Province was made for 30 years in 1833. This led to the improvement of soil and the government became sure of fixed revenue from this province.

(ix) **Classification of Land on the Basis of Production.** Lord William tried to give a definite shape to the revenue system. For this purpose lands were classified according to their production and the rates of revenue were accordingly fixed according to productivity.

The net result of these economies was that the deficit of one crore that Bentinck inherited was converted into a surplus of 2 crores by 1835. He had also stimulated the economy by encouraging iron and coal production, tea and coffee plantations and irrigation schemes.

(2) Judicial Reforms

(i) The Provincial Courts of Appeal and Circuit set up by Cornwallis were burdened with excessive duties and usually arrears accumulated. The judicial procedure followed in these courts was cumbersome and often resulted in delays and uncertainites. William Bentinck abolished these courts, transferring their duties to magistrates and collectors under the supervision of commissioners of Revenue and Circuit.

(ii) **Appointment of Indian Judges.** By the Charter of 1833 it was laid down that Indians were employed in Government service according to qualification. Histherto it had been the policy of the government not to employ the natives on any responsible public post. He liberally adopted this policy and appointed native judges with jurisdiction over civil suits.

(iii) **Powers of Magistrates Increased.** A regulation was issued in 1829 which empowered magistrates to award punishments up to two years rigorous imprisonment. Appeals against their decisions could be taken to the Commissioners.

(iv) **Summary of Disposal Rent Cases.** The Regulation of 1831 empowered the collectors to decide summarily the cases relating to rent. In these cases no appeal lay to any higher court, the only remedy granted against the decision of a collector being a regular suit against him in a civil court.

(v) **Setting up Separate Sadr Diwani Adalat and Sadr Nizamat Adalat at Allahabad (1872).** The British dominion in India had become very extensive by this time and people from distant places had to go to Calcutta to file the appeals. Hence a separate Sadr Diwani Adalat and a Sadr Nizamat Adalt was set up at Allahabad. These started functioning in 1832.

(vi) **Replacement of Persian by Vernaculars as Court Language.** Centuries had passed since the Mughal rule breathed its last but Persian was still used as the court language. But as it was Greek to both the dispensers and the seekers of justice so Persian was replaced by Vernaculars as the court language. Because of this action Dr. Ishwari Parshad has recorded his praise for William Bentinck in the following words. "The change greatly benefitted the people and enabled them to express the grievances in a language known to them."

(vii) **Begining of the Codification of Laws.** A begining was made in the direction of the codification of laws. It enabled the lawyers to know more exactly what the law was. It helped in improving the judicial system.

(viii) In human punishments like cutting of arms or legs were abolished.

(3) Administrative Reforms

(i) **Liberal Policy Towards the Indian Press.** Bentinck adoped a liberal policy towards the Indian Press, Excepting that he did not permit the government officials to misuse the Press against the government, he allowed free functioning to the Press.

(ii) **Public Welfare Works.** Some other reforms carried out during the time of Bentinck, related to the Public Works Department. The construction of a road from Bombay to Agra was commenced. Digging up of irrigation canals in North-West provinces was undertaken, and the Grand Trunk Road between Calcutta and Delhi was put under repair. Canal system of Northwest province was improved. Steam ship navigation was introduced on the Ganges.

(iii) Lord Bentinck dissolved those Appeal Courts which were started by Cornwallis. These courts used to give justice by moving them from one place to another.

(iv) For efficiency various reforms were introduced in the army. Bentinck himself assumed the charge of the Commander-in-Chief in addition to his being the Governor-General of India.

(v) Creating the New Post of law Member. The post of a law member was created in the Executive Council of the Governor General, Lord Mecaulay was made the first law Member.

(vi) Setting up Separate Board of Revenue at Allahabad. The territories of the Company had become extensive and a single Board of Revenue located at Calcutta could not function efficiently. Hence he set up a separate Board of Revenue at Allahabad for North-West-Province. This had the effect of increasing efficiency in revenue matters.

(4) Social Reforms-Hindu society was ridden with a number of social abuses that was mostly inhuman and harsh. He, therefore, set himself to work seriously in this direction.

(i) Abolition of Sati. On of the greatest acts of humanity for which Lord Bentinck deserves alternal honour is the abolition of 'Sati'. The custom had prevailed in India from early time. Several Muslim and British rulers had attempted to abolish the evil custom but no attempt proved faithful. In 1829 Bentinck abolished the practice of sati, declaring the burning or burying allive of a widow a crime, punishable as culapble homicide. When violence or compulsion was used or drugs were administered to influence the free will of the victim, the offenders were guilty of murder to be punished with death.

(ii) Suppression of Thugee. The Thugs were an all-India association of robbers who moved in bands of three hundred or even more and could collect in large numbers at the time of emergency. They committed organised crime in secret convenience with the local chieftains, zamindars and officials and accompained the travellers for miles till a proper spot for the crime was reached. It was an assential trait of their system that they strangled the victim before robbing him. In 1829 Bentinck instructed his agent in the Narbada territories to take serious action against the miscreants wherever found. Captain Sleeman, who had gathered a vast knowledge on the subject, was appointed to assist him. Besides this, the officers of the Government all over the country were issued a special order to report all the cases and further information regarding their practices. The entire Governmental machinery was alerted on the subject. A Regulation was passed in 1830 whereby a mere association of person with a robber, even if he had not committed a crime, could lead to his arrest. The enactment of this measure made it now possible to take up the matter more seriously, and within a few years after this thousands of these robbers were arrested and punished by death, transportation for life, or were sent to the reformatory at Jabalpur.

(iii) **Restriction on Infanticide.** In some tribes of India, specially in some illiterate Rajput, there existed a system of killing their own daughters. The people threw the girls in a river or ocean immediately after their birth. By passing the Bengal Regulation Act, Lord Bentinck restricted and banned these killings.

(iv) **Restriction on Human Sacrifice.** In some parts of South India human sacrifice was made to make gods and goddesses happy. This system was also very cruel and Bentinck restricted this also by making new and progressive laws.

(v) **Reform in the Hindu Law of Inheritance.** Under the Hindu Law anyone fore so of his religion was desprived of his ancestral property. Now this law was changed and it was declared that any person who embraced any other religion would have full rights to his share in the ancestral property. This law encouraged conversions to Christinity.

(vi) Education Reforms. During Bentinck's administration a great controversy was raised regarding the medium of imparting education to people as well as the nature of education to be impected in India. Macaulay, the historian who was then Law Member, threw the weight of his great influence in favour of English which thenceforth became the medium of higher education. In 1835, a resolution was adopted that the funds granted by the government for education should be devoted solely to the instruction of the natives of India in the English language and in western sciences. Bentinck established the Calcutta Medical College and the Elphinstone Institution of Bombay.

This modern education had the required effect upon the Indian mind. By and by Indians began to hate Indians goods. They were now after foreign goods. These educated people also considered themselves superior to other Indians. Thus a class within a class was created. History bears witness that with the help of this very class the handful of Britishers succeeded in riding over the back of millions and millions of Indians who had not the courage even to groan.

Inspite of the above defects, these are many used of it also which cannot be ignored. *(i)* It widened their knowledge and outlook which reminded them of their weakness. They saw how backward they were in comparison to other countries of the world. *(ii)* They now decided to remove these evils. It resulted in a number of reforms which were now introduced from time to time. *(iii)* Moreover the study of English literature also infused a new spirit of patriotism in them. *(iv)* Now they began to think in terms of liberty, equality and fraternity. Hence forward they started working for their freedom.

EVENTS OF THE REIGN OF LORD AMHERST

When Hastings left India, Mr. John Adam, a senior member of the Council acted as Governor-General till the arrival of Lord Amherst who took charge of his office on coming to India in August, 1823. Before this he had proved his ability in a mission to China. But he failed to solve the Indian problems. Instead of consolidating the empire built by his predecessors, he gave birth to the problem of eastern border. His reign was also full of wars. The most important event of the new Governor-General's regime was the First Burmese war.

First Burmese War (1824-26). Burma was a big independent country on the eastern border of India. In 18th century a Tibetan Chinese tribe had established its rule in Burma. Its founder Anlompa and his successors started extending their empire and in 1768 captured Tenasserim and Arakan. When Burma was trying to extend her frontiers the English company was buy in laying the foundation of British Empire in India. Now the frontiers of Burma and India were in close proximity with each other and hence a conflict between them had become inevitable.

Causes and the events of the First Burmese War-The English had trade relations with Burma since seventeenth century and many British families were living in Rangoon, the Capital of Burma.

During the Governor-Generalship of Lord Wellesley a large number of Burmese had settled in Chittagong, a British Indian out post. The Burmese laid claim to Chittagong, Dacca and Murshidabad. In 1822 the Burmese overran. Assam and in the next year they began open hostilities. The Burmese King asked Wellesley to send back the Burmese from Chittagong. On Wellesley's refusal to do so, he was annoyed. The British were also suspicious of the Burmese because often they made plundering raids on the frontier provinces. When they captured Tenasserim, Pegu and Arakan, the British started thinking seriously to take some action to check the menace of the Burmese. In 1817-18 the Burmese forces threatened Assam and sent a letter to the Indian Government in which they demanded the surrender of Chittagong, Dacca, Murshidabad and Kassim bazar. For the time being the danger was avoided as the burmese were defeated by the Siamese. But in 1822 the Burmese conqured Siam. In 1823, they attacked Shahpuri, a small Island near Chittagong. This became unbearable to the British and Lord Amherst declared war against the Burmese in Feburary, 1824. The 47th native infantry at Barrackpore refused to cross the sea and fight for the British. They had also cause of discontent because their pay was low. Lord Amherst sent orders for shooting.

Lord Amherst sent the British forces both through the land as well as sea route. The Burmese Commander in Chief Mahe Bandula, also mobilised a big army and attacked Bengal. The Burmese were successful in defeating the English army near Chittagong. But in the meantime the British fleet advanced towards Rangoon and captured it, Mahe Bandula was forced to return to his Country. After the capture of Rangoon, the British forces marched towards Prome and gave a crushing defeat to the Burmese. Mahe Bandula, the Burmese Commander-in-Chief died of a random shot at Prome and his army fled away.

The Burmese war which dragged on for two years and cost thirteen crores of rupees. The Company's troops got the worst of it in many small engagements because of the mismanagement, forests and morasses of Burma. Their progress was also checked owing to rains. The troops suffered from rotten provisions and disease.

Result of the Burmese War. The British emerged victorious in the First Burmese war. Treaty of Yandoboo was concluded in 1826. According to the terms of the treaty Assam, Arakan and the coast of Tenassarim were ceded to the English Company. A British Resident was appointed at Rangoon, the Capital of Burma. The Burmese recognised the independence of Manipur state and entered into a commercial treaty with the British. The Burmese withdrew from Assam and Kachar. The Burmese King also agreed to pay a crore of rupees as war indemnity. No Resident was sent to Ava till 1830. In this Burmese war, the British for the first time employed steam ships in the Indian seas.

Significance of the Treaty of Yandoboo. This treaty enabled the English to seal up and secure the Indian Eastern frontier. However, the war proved to be very costly because for lack of adequate preparations by the British the war unduly prolonged. The heavy expenditure led to a big deficit in the finances of the Company.

Capture of Bharatpur. The early reverses and difficulties of the British in Burma gave rise to a conviction in certain quarters that the British dominion was faced with impending ruin. This resulted in risings in some places. In Bharatpur the claim of the minor son of a deceased ruler who had been placed on the throne with the consent of Sir David Ochterlony, the British Resident at Delhi was contested by his cousin Durjan Sal. Lord Amherst at first followed the policy of non-intervention and disapproved of the conduct of Sir David Ochterlony in trying to enforce his decision at the point of the sword which led to the latter's resignation and the appointment of Sir Charles Metcalfin his place.

After the death of Bhandar Singh the Raja of Bharatpur 1823 there were two claimants to the throne his brother Baldev Singh and his nephew Durjan Sal. The British availed this opportunity and started making interference in the internal affairs of Bharatpur. The British Government took the side of Baldev Singh and recognised him as the real claimant. But Baldev Singh died with in a month. Durjan Sal the other claimant seized the fort and imprisoned the young son of Baldev Singh. This annoyed the British. An expedition was eventually sent under Lord Cambermere who in January 1826 stormed the fortress of Bharatpur which had resisted the attacks of Lord Lake in 1805. Durjan Sal was departed. The British placed the minor son of Baldev Singh on the throne of Bharatpur and plundered the State. Lord Amherst has been criticised for the plunder of Bharatpur. A large number of native people were made captive.

Barrackpore Mutiny (1824). The Mutiny of Barrackpore is also an important event of the Governor-Generalship of Lord Amherst. While the Burmese war was going on, the Soldiers mutinied in the military cantonement of Barrackpore.

Causes of the Barrackpore Mutiny

1. The English and Indian soldiers were not treated alike. The Indian soldiers were asked to pay for the transport charges of their own luggage.

2. The English defeat at the hands of Burmese had frightened the soldiers.

3. The Indian soldiers were ordered to go to Burma via sea on account of the fear of being ostracised from the society, the Indian soldiers refused to obey the orders when they were ordered to surrender their arms, they openly revolted against their officers.

The mutiny was ruthlessly and mercilessly suppressed. The fire was opened and many soldiers were shot down. The parade ground was turned into a scene of massacre. The ring leaders were hanged. Lord Amherst has been severely criticised for his ruthless and merciless treatment with the soldiers but it may be noted he had no other alternative.

FIRST AFGHAN WAR

Lord Auckland reached Indian in 1836. Dost Mohammad Khan wanted to establish friendly relations with the East India Company. Consequently to achieve his objective he sent congratulatory letters on the arrival of the new Governor-General in India, Lord Auckland. In this letter he also made a reference to the Sikh occupation of Peshawar which was previously in his dominions. He also narrated therein the relations that existed between the Sikhs and the Afghans, the high-handed policy of the Sikhs towards him and their attempt to violate the treaty obligations between the Sikhs and Afghanistan. In this letter he, therefore, requested the Governor-General to guide him for finding out a solution of all these complicated problems which had arisen between the Sikhs and the Afghans. Dost Mohammad Khan expected that the English would help him in the recovery of Peshawar from the Sikhs. But he was simply disappointed in his expectations because Lord Auckland replied that the British Government would remain neutral in any kind of conflic between the native rulers of India. Lord Auckland said that it was the policy of the British Government in India to make no kind of interference in the affairs of independent rulers in this country. Even then Lord Auckland told Dost Mohammad that he would send a mission to his Court, which will also be directed by him to bring about a patch-up, cover differences and also bring about an exchange of views between the two Governments.

2. Lord Auckland sent Captain Burnes to Kabul ostensibly on a commercial mission but internally his aim was to find out the amount of influence that Russia was exercising over Afghanistan. On his arrival at Kabul, Burnes wrote back to Lord Auckland that Amir was fully in favour of the British Government in India but he wanted to enter into a friendly alliance with the British Government on the condition only of their prevailing upon Maharaja Ranjit Singh to hand over Peshawar to him. Personally Burnes was in favour of a political pressure being exercised by the East India Company on the Maharaja to hand over Peshawar to him, but Lord Auckland rightly thought that with a view to checking any contemplated attack of Russia on India, the friendship of Dost Mohammad would prove much of importances as that of Maharaja Ranjit Singh.. But whereas the friendship of Maharaja Ranjit Singh had already been tried as worthy of maintenance, that of Dost Mohammad Khan was yet to be tried. It was a question of giving preference to the friendship of either Ranjit Singh or Dost Mohammad Khan. Ultimately Auckland gave more importance to the friendship of Ranjit Singh over that of Dost Mohammad Khan. The Governor-General wrote to Dost Mohammad Khan asking him to give up the hope of regaining Peshawar from Ranjit Singh with their help. He also told him that he would be doing more service to him by maintaining friendly relations between Kabul and Lahore than bringing about a clash between the two powers. Lord Auckland, therefore, suggested to Dost Mohammad Khan through Captain Burnes that, in view of his assurances to him, he should not make any sort of alliance with any outside power excepting the British, otherwise he would incur displeasure of the British Government in India. It was at this time that Russian Agent reached Kabul and assured Dost Mohammad Khan of Russian full support in his bid for the conquest of Peshawar from the Sikhs. As a result of this assurance on the part of the Russian Agent, Dost Mohammad Khan felt inclined towards Russia. Consequently, he accorded a great respect to the Russian agent.

3. During the first 40 years of the 19th century, the English in India were always feeling a great anxiety regarding any Russian attack any time on British Indian Empire. They were looking at the Russian activities in Constantinople and Persia with a great anxiety and suspicion. Specially the British Foreign Minister, Palmerston, was very much dreading the Russian danger to the internal tranquility of India. The experts of the Far Eastern affairs also declared that India was in danger. It was in view of these circumstances that the British Government became more serious about the defence of the Western passes in the Suleman Mountains through which invaders had been entering into India from time immemorial. The policy of the British Government was to keep Afghanistan in the hands of some friendly power. The political and strategical position of Herat was explained to the British Government and the experts felt that in case the Persians succeeded in occupying Herat, the approach to Delhi from the point of view of geography and politics would become very easy, specially when the last obstacle of Herat vanished away. In 1836, the British Ambassador stationed in Persia, Mr. Macneil, informed the Governor-General that Russia was busy in mobilizing her troops on the Western coast of the Caspian Sea with a great speed and, consequently, it would be easier for the Russian army to reach Lahore than to reach St. Petersburg.

4. In view of these dangers, Lord Auckland decided to replace Amir Dost Mohammad Khan by Shah Shuja on the throne of Kabul because of his friendly leanings towards the British Govemment. Consequently, with a view to achieving this object the British Government concluded the Tripartite Treaty between the East India Company, Ranjit Singh and Shah Shuja, by virtue of which it was decided to replace Dost Mohammad Khan by Shah Shuja with all their military strength. Shah Shuja, on his part, promised to pay 2 lakhs of rupees a year to his helpers. He also assured that he would not keep any relations with any foreign power without the consent of the East India Company and the Maharaja.

5. It was on the instigation of Russia that the Shah of Persia laid siege to Herat on November 23, 1837. The British Ambassador

in Persia, Mr. Macneil, protested with the Shah of his besieging Herat, but no heed was paid by the Shah to the protests .of the British Ambassador. The British also feared that after conquering Herat, the Persians might attack Afghanistan with the help of the Russians, because the Persians were said to have been dreaming of the reconquest of those regions which once formed part and parcel of Nadir Shah's empire.

Events of the First Afghan War (1835-42). In spite of this sudden change of circumstances at Herat, Lorq Auckland continued to act upon his decision of an attack on Afghanistan. He based his decision on the argument that in his scheme of the replacement of Dost Mohammad Khan by Shah Shuja, he had too much advanced and, as such, it was very difficult for him to withdraw from the course that he had adopted in his relations with Afghanistan. His next argument for this attack on Afghanistan was that he wanted to make some permanent arrangement in order to avoid any risk of any attack on India from that side and he said that that opportunity was the best opportunity to implement his scheme in the context of the then existing circumstances, specially when Afghanistan had no friend at that time to resist their attack. Consequently, the British forces entered into Afghanistan and straightaway occupied Kabul and Kandhar. Up to August 1838, Dost Mohammad Khan had fallen into the hands of the British as a prisoner.

The Revolt of the Afghans Against the British. In 1811, Burnes and Macnaughton were murdered; and there was a general rising in Afghanistan owing to the following reasons:

(1) The unpopularity of Shah Shuja.

(2) The withdrawal of subsidies which had kept the Afghans loyal up to this time.

(3) the wild hilly tribes desired to return to the life of riot and rapine.

(4) the misconduct of some of the Englishmen at Kabul, especially that of Captain Burnes.

(5) the Afghans resisted the interference of foreigners in their affairs.

(6) the Mullas did not acknowledge Shah Shuja as the Amir and the Amir himself smarted under the control of the British envoy.

The Treaty of Kabul. The rising at first was local but it became national under Akbar Khan, the eldest son of Dost Mohammad Khan. General Elphinstone, the Commander-in-Chief of the British forces at Kabul, made a treaty with Akbar Khan and thus commenced the British army's retreat from Kabul. According to that treaty, the hostages were given, money and guns were supplied and 6½ lakhs of rupees more were promised.

Elphinstone's Retreat. The retreat began under the promised assistance from Akbar Khan, who proved quite unwilling or unable to protect them from the attacks of Ghilzais and other tribesmen who swarmed round the line of route. The party struggled on in misery and privation through snowstorms and a hail of bullets. The retreat became a rout, the rout a massacre. On the way, all the 16,000 men perished at the hands of the Afghans except Dr. Brydon, who escaped on a pony and reached Jalalabad to give information about the sad news. Kandhar was now under General Nott, and Jalalabad under Sir Robert Sale.

Causes of British Failure in Afghanistan

(1) The nature of the country rendered the task of maintaining Shah Shuja, in the teeth of national opposition; hopless.

(2) It was foolish for the English to have relied on the loyalty of the Afghans, who were by nature restless, fanatical, lawless and patriotically suspicious of foreigners.

(3) The position of encampment at Kabul was worst.

(4) The economy and retrenchment in military expenditure under the instructions of the Court of Directors hastened the catastrophe.

(5) The irresolution and cowardice of General Elphinstone, an old and utterly incompetent man, allowed the local rising of the Afghans to develop into a national rising.

Results of the War

(1) The war proved extremely disastrous, 20,000 lives were sacrificed and 15 million sterling were spent.

(2) Dost Mohammad was set freel and allowed to go back to Afghanistan as its ruler.

(3) It paved the way for the conquest of Sindh.

(4) It led to the establishment of goodwill between both the nations and in future each began to have respect for the other.

(5) The gates of Somnath were recovered.

End of the War. When the news of the disaster of Afghanistan reached India and England, at once a demand for the recall of Lord Auckland as Viceroy of India was made. Consequently, he was replaced by Lord Ellenborough in February, 1842. Ellenborough declared forthwith on his arrival in India that the British Government will not endanger its army and the Empire for the purpose of supporting the Tripartite Treaty only that course would be adopted which was dictated by military considerations. The reputation of the British army was to be re-established by the inflection of some single and decisive blow on Afghanistan. When he got the news of the defeat of General Elphinstone and surrender of Ghazni by Palmer, he issued orders for the evacuation of Kabul and Kandhar. Many military officers protested against the orders of Lord Ellenborough.

Pollock won a decisive victory over Akbar Khan near the Pass of Khurd Kabul. He entered Kabul and hoisted the British flag at the Fort Bala Hissar. General Nott also joined him. In order to avenge wrongs done to the Englishmen the British army blew up the great Bazar of Kabul with the help of gunpowder. After that the British forces left Afghanistan.

In October. 1842, Lord Ellenborough made the following Declaration- "The Governor-General will willingly recognise any Government approved by the Afghans themselves which shall appear desirous and capable of maintaining friendly relations with neighbouring states. Content with the limits which nature appears to have assigned to its empire, the Government of India will devote its efforts to the establishment and maintenance of general peace, to the protection of the sovereigns and chiefs its allies and the prosperity and happiness of its own faithfull subjects." Dost Mohammad was released from Calcutta and was allowed to go back to Kabul as its ruler.

P. E. Roberts Says. "The Afghan policy of Lord Auckland has met with practically universal condemnation, at the hands of the historians and every reading of the evidence deepends and strengthens the conviction that the war was politically one of the disastrous, and morally one of the least justifiable ever waged by the British in India. Of that verdict there can be no reversal." The following points of criticism against Lord Auckland's Afghan policy will be worthy of note:

1. A Complete Failure. That the First Afghan War was a complete failure goes without saying. Although 20,000 lives were sacrificed and 15 million sterling were spent, neither the Government of Indian or the British Government gained anything. The same Dost Mohammad Khan who was ousted by the British armies from the throne of Kabul had to be reinstated. This was done because there was no other alternative. Moreover, the Government of India could not maintain its control on any part of Afghanistan. Lord Ellenborough boastfully said that the victorious English army brought to India from Ghazni those gates of Somnath which were taken away by Mahmood of Ghazni during the 11th century. He claimed that "the insult of 800 years is at least revenged." According to Kaye, the "Proclamation was past all denial. It was a folly too of the most senseless kind for it was calculated to please none and to offend many."

2. English Policy in Afghanistan was Unrightous. According to Kaye, "the English policy in Afghanistan was unrighteous" and "the wisdom of our statesmen is but foolishnes and the might of our armies is but weakness, sitting heavily upon an unholy cause." According to Trotter, "the utter collapse of Auckland's policy, baneful, lawless and blundering as it was, sprung mainly from the choice of generals ill-fitted for their work. Macnaughton's cheery truthfulness, Elphinstone's bodily and mental decay, Shelton's stupid wilfulness, chronic dissensions between civil and military powers, Sale's withholding of timely succour, all conspired with Lord Auckland's half-measures and ill-timed economics to work out the dramatic nemesis of an enterprise begun in folly and wrong doing."

3. A Calamitous War. Kaye has made the following observations in connection with the failure of Lord Auckland's policy towards the First Afghan War: "no failure so total and so overwhelming as this is recorded in the pages of history. No lesson so grand and impressive is to be found in all the annals of the world. It is upon record that this calamitous war cost the natives of India whose stewards we are, some 15 millions of money. All this enormous burden fell upon the revenue of India, and the country for long years afterwards groaned under the weight." In spite of these heavy sacrifices the British Government failed to have the friendly powers on its borders. After an enormous waste of money and loss of human blood, the Englishmen left "every town and village of Afghanistan bristling with their enemies of the English while the British disaster that country encouraged new the aggressions of the Persians and intrigues of the Muscovite ally."

4. War was Morally Unjustifiable. Some of the critics have rightly pointed our that there was absolutely no justice for Lord Auckland to have sent the British troops to Afghanistan in November, 1838. The British objection was to the siege of Herat by the Persians aided by the Rusians. But as has already been pointed out before, the Russians who had been prevailed upon by the British/Government in London, had raised the siege of Herat in September 1838. In other words, the circumstances which justified the commencement of the war by Lord Auckland had ceased to exist and after the siege had been raised by the Russians and Persians it was nothing but highhandedness and aggressiveness on the part of Lord Auckland to have sent the troops against Afghanistan.

5. It may, however, be noted that Dost Mohammad Khan was the ruler of Afghanistan which was an independent state. As such, he had the option of making friends either with the English or with the Russians. He was under no obligation to make friends with only the English and, as such, the British Government had no valid reason to protest against Dost Mohammad's favourable inclination towards the Russians. Dost Mohammad Khan had given no cause of provocation of the British. Moreover, under pressure from the British Government at Home. The Russians had withdrawn their agents from the Court of Kabul. All this had been accomplished before the beginning of the war. Can Lord Auckland explain as to why he started war when the circumstances which justified the commencement of the war against Dost Mohammad Khan had ceased to exist in November, 1838. The fact is that the Russian danger was only bug-bear. It had become only imaginary, and the First Afghan War was a wild parrying of an imagined stroke, by Russia. The reasons are two, namely, that in the first instance the Persians who were aided by the Russians had raised the siege of Herat in September, 1838 and, as such, there was no cause to fear the Russians after the above date and, secondly, the fear of a Russian attack on India was only imaginary and miscalculated because there were vast territories between Russia and India—the Punjab, Afghanistan, Bahawalpur, Rajputan a and Sindh. Russia's outposts were at least a thousand miles away from the Indian boundary line.

8. Passing the British Forces Through Sindh was the Violation of the Treaty Obligations. It is pointed out that the British Government had no right to pass their troops through Sindh. Not only the British troops passed through Sindh, that territory was made the base of operations also against Afghanistan against the treaty obligations with the Amirs of Sindh. It was this act which facilitated the annexation of Sindh latest on in the time of Lord Ellenborough, because the British refused to vacate the territory of Simth which they had occupied only temporarily during the First Mghan War.

BRITISH CONQUEST OF SINDH

Lord Ellenborough was a man of considerable experience and was familiar with Indian affairs. He had acted as the President of the Bord of Control before coming to India. He was capable of taking prompt decisions. He was the Governor-General of India from 1842 to 1844 AD. His period is known for the end of the First Afghan War, annexation of Sindh to the British Empire and the British intervention in Gwalior.

1. End of First Afghan War. The First Afghan War was fought from 1839 to 1842 AD. When Lord Ellenborough was appointed the Governor-General of India in 1842 the condition of the British India was very critical an account of the First Afghan War. The first thing he did after taking over charge was to successfully end the First Afghan War.

Importance of Sindh. Sindh occupies a strategic position of great importance. It is situated on the lower banks of the Indu River and extends down to the sea, It is mostly a desert. It lay on the route from British India to Afghanistan through the Bolan Pass. During the opening years of the 19th centruy, it was ruled by a number of tribes who had come from Baluchistan. Their most important states were Khairpur, Mirpur and Hyderabad. The Amir of Khairpur claimed nominal sovereignty over the other two kingdoms.

Relations Before the Time of Lord Auckland. The politcal relation of the British with the Amirs of Sindh began in 1809 by a treaty when a mission was sent there by Lord Minto in order to create Sindh into a friendly power for fear of the growing power of France. This treaty brought about friendly relations between the English and the Amirs of Sindh and they agreed to oust the French from Sindh. This treaty was renewed in 1820 and then in 1832 and one of the terms of the treaty was that no armed vessels or military stores shall pass through Sindh. Lord Auckland had flagrantly broken the terms of the treaty by marching the English troops through Sindh on the one of the First Afghan War. The Amir were also required to contribute, "by a new treaty, three lakhs of rupees a year for the maintenance of a subsidiary force. Sindh was made the British base of operation during the Afghan War. The Amirs remained loyal throughout and humbly submitted to the British demands.

Lord Ellenborough who replaced Lord Auckland as the Governor-General of the Company felt the desirability of annexing Sindh with a view to boost the moral of the English and impress the natives of the superiority of the British arms. Mr. Qutram, the resident was asked to frame charges against the Amirs which duty he loyally performed. Then in 1842, Sir Charles Napier was deputed to Sindh with complete civil and military authority. Napier was not only accepted the charged framed by Qutram against the Amir's but also blamed them for disloyalty against the English. He demanded from the Amirs that:

(i) They should hand over the right to mint coins to the English.

(ii) They should supply coal to the English ships passing through the river Indus.

(iii) They should surrender Thatta, Sakhar, Bakhar, Karanchi, Rohri and all the territories adjoining these places to the English.

Meantime a succession dispute at Khairpur gave Napier the opportunity to interfere. Napier supported the claims of Ali Murad, brother of the old Mir Rustum in preference to the claims of Mir Rustum's son. Napier's intention was to have only one governing chief in each province, instead of many. This would simplify the Company's politcal dealings with the princes. Mir Rustum, however, abdicated in favours of his son and took to flight. From the flight of Mir Rustum may be dated the commencement of the Sindhian war. The Amir of upper Sindh fled to the desert and to lower Sindh, there to raise the banner of revolt in conjunction with their cousins of Hyderabad. The Amirs had reluctantly accepted the new treaties, but Napier suspected that the Amirs were preparing for war. When Napier repeated the Governor-General's order to disband the armed and the Amirs replied, "There are no bands, we are all submission."

Napier was not convinced and was eager to commence hostilities in winter, fearing the rigours of the hot weather ahead. He proceeded to capture Imamgarh situated in the heart of the desert and approached only by vague uncertain Tracks.

Still, however, Qutram was able to persuade the Amirs to sign the treaty so that the worst could be avoided. The Amirs warned Napier to vacate Hyderabad, lest the British should be harmed by their countrymen who could not be controlled under the circumstance. Yet the warning was not heeded, and in three days the Baluchis, excited by the high-handedness of Napier attacked Qutram's residence, who after a gallant defence was able to escape to take refuge on a steamer.

On 17 February 1843 Napier gave a brilliant battle, an able General as he was, to 30,000 men of the Amirs at Miani and was able to defeat them completely and destroy 5,000 of their number by a mere force of less than 3,000 men under his command. Hyderabad was occupied, on 27 March 1843 Mirpur fell, and Napier wrote to Ellenborough: Paccavi, I have Sindh," Sindh was annexed, and the Amirs were exiled. Napier got £70,000 out of the plunder of Hyderabad, while Qutram was offered £3,000 which he, however, refused to keep and disturbed in charity, saying "I am sick of Policy."

Annexation of Sindh by the Company can in no sense by justified. Even Napier said that it was wrong to capture Sindh. In his own words, 'We have no right to seize Sindh yet we shall do so, and a very advantageious, useful and human piece of rascality it will be," On this Dr. Marshman remarked, The rascality is more apprent than the advantage." The treaty signed by the Amirs was dishonoured by the English. Ramsay Muir says, ' Sindh is the only British acquisition in India of which it may fairly be said that it was not necessitated by circumstances, and that it was therefore an act of aggression."

The Directors themselves disapproved of Napier's Sindh policy and Lord Ellenborough's silent annexation of it though they had no courage to restore Sindh to the Amirs. It is useless to repeat too often that the Amirs were innocent, that they had given absolutely no provocation to the British, and that they remaind perfectly loyal to their engagements with the British during and after the Afghan War.

War with Gwalior. Jankoji Scindhia of Gwalior died in 1843. He was succeeded by his adopted minor son. A regent was appointed with the permission of the Governor-General. The regent was dismissed for not working properly. There was the danger of Civil war in the State and it was feared that Scindhia's army might revolt. The Governor-General demanded the reducation of troops. There upon Scindhia's army revolted but was defeated in the battles of Maharajpur and Paniar. A new treaty was made by which Schindhia's army was not to exceed 9,000. The affairs of the State, during the minority of the ruler, were to be carried on by a Council of Regency, and it was to act on the advice of the British Resident.

Recall of Ellenborough. Lord Ellenborough's relations with the Board of Directors deteriorated and he was recalled in 1844 A.D.

ANGLO-SIKH RELATIONS

For the sake of convenience of study, the Anglo-Sikh relations from 1809 to 1839 can be conveniently divided into the following two parts:

1. Anglo-Sikh Relations from 1809 to 1828. The treaty of Amritsar (1809) had inflicted a terrible blow on Ranjit Singh and the Sikhs and this they could never forget. By this treaty, the English gave him a diplomatic and military defeat. This treaty, had also rendered Ranjit Singh's high ambition of life a failure and his dream of uniting all the Sikh people, both living to the south and the north of Sutlej, came to nothing. This treaty fixed the river Sutlej as the boundary line between the, Sikhs and English and place the entire Cis-Sutlej territory under the protection of the English. They considered the consequences of the treaty of Amritsar as their national dishonour and humiliation, but Ranjit Singh had been forced by the circumstances to sign this treaty. Hence he had to keep quite. In other words, the treaty of Amritsar did not and could not establish real friendly relations between the two powers, the Sikhs and the British. Doubt suspicion and district, however, lingered on for some time. But taking advantage of his diplomacy and also by adjusting his nature according to the existing circumstances, he tried to forget this humiliation and national disgrace. During this period of doubt and suspicion, Ranjit Singh even raised a small fort at Phillaur on the opposite bank of the Sutlej to serve as a watch tower under Diwan Mohkam Chand. The deserters from the British army were also given protection. It is said that Ranjit Singh, at one stage, even entered into secret negotiations against the British with Amir Khan, Begun Samru and Holkar. But after 1812 their relations began to improve. Accordingly, Ranjit Singh many times made offers of military aid to the British. David Ochterloney was invited from Ludhiana to attend the marriage of prince Kharak Singh and on that occasion both sides professed sincerity and friendship. In 1815, Ranjit Singh went so far as to offer help to the British against Nepal and in 1821, when Appa Sahib sought the assistance of the Maharaja at Amritsar against the British, he declined. During the Governor-Generalship of Lord Amherst, ambassadors were exchanged by the two states. Though in 1822, their relations were again reshuffled for some time over the question of Wadni, yet very soon cordiality was restored and in 1826 when Ranjit Singh fell ill. Dr. Murray was sent by the British to attend him. In 1827, the claims of Ranjit Singh over Wadni Anandpur, Makhowal and Chamkaur were also admited. Thus during this period neither of the two parties did anything which might estrange their mutual relations. Thus, from 1812 to 1828 their relations were on the whole quite friendly and cordial.

2. The Anglo-Sikh Relations from 1828 to 1839. Though during this period, both the powers kept up an outward show of friendship established by the treaty of Amritsar, yet their relations became strained to a very great extent, as the discussion of the following events will show:

A great estrangement occurred in the Anglo-Sikh relations on the question of Sindh, which ultimately Ranjit Singh failed to occupy whereas the English succeeded in occupying it. The events briefly run like this. Ranjit Singh was very much interested in the occupation of Sindh on account of many reasons.

Firstly, Ranjit Singh wanted to extend his territory. This he could do only in Sindh and not in the east or the south where he was stopped to cross the river Sutlej by the treaty of Amritsar only on the occupation of Sindh, he could reach the ocean where from he wanted to establish his friendly relations with other independent foreign powers. In that case, the hold of the British over Ranjit Singh also would become loose.

Secondly, just as Bengal and Bihar are considered to be the provinces of the river Ganges, similarly the Punjab and Sindh also are considered as the provinces of the river Indus. As such, he considered himself as much right and justified in occupying Sindh as the British.

Thirdly, Sindh was in the weak hands at the time and, as such, Ranjit Singh thought he would be able to conquer it very easily.

On the other hand, the British were also very much interested in the occupation of the Sindh on account of many reasons.

Firstly, the commercial importance of Sindh was very great. In the event of the occupation of Sindh, the British hoped to get a maximum advantage of their trade with Sindh valley and the surrounding regions.

Secondly, they realized the political importance also of Sindh to be of a great value to them. By occupying Sindh, they could bring about the encirclement of the Punjab on the one hand, which aim they had already in view ever since the treaty of Amritsar (1809) and, on the other hand, they could, by being in close proximity to Afghanistan, bring Afghanistan also under their political sphere of influence to check the growing Russian danger to India from that quarter. Thus in view of these factors, Lord William Bentinck ordered Captain Burnes, the Political Agent at Cutch, to proceed via the Sindh Valley to Lahore to make delivery of the five horses and a coach which William IV, the King of England, had sent for Ranjit Singh. Outwardly, the Burnes Mission aimed at delivering the presents to the Maharaja but inwardly the Mission was sent to get an authenticated and comprehensive commercial report on the commercial importance of Sindh with a view to taking some practical measures to occupy it.

Thus was taken the decision by the British Government in the light of the Burnes' report to take possession of Sindh.

The Rupper Meeting between Ranjit Singh and William Bentinck, 1831. As already said above, William Bentinck how decided to establish British control on Sindh, but he also wanted to allay the fears of Ranjit Singh in such a way that he should be able to occupy Sindh without irritating the Maharaja. Rumours also were in air those days about a Russian invasion on India. Hence Bentinck wanted to establish personal friendly relations with Ranjit Singh to counter act Russian design in India jointly with Ranjit Singh. Under these circumstances, Bentinck arranged, through Captain Wade, the political Agent at Ludhiana, a meeting with the Maharaja at Rupar. This meeting had two objectives—one to court personal friendship with the Maharaja and second to keep the Maharaja in dark about Sindh and then to occupy it himself. On the bank of the river Jamuna, the Maharaja met the Governor-General. Great decorations were made in honour of the Governor-General at Rupar, which thus became a "veritable cloth of gold."

Ranjit Singh Failed to Occupy Sindh. It has already been pointed out above that both the parties—Ranjit Singh and Bentinck-were anxious to occupy Sindh. By this meeting the Governor-General wanted to show to the world that they were cordial friends. On the other hand, Ranjit Singh also wanted to show to the Sikh Chiefs that the British acknowledged only his dynasty as the proper head of the Khalsa. But these pretensions were only an outward show and real motives of both the Governor-General and Ranjit Singh were much deeper. Both wanted to steal a march upon Sindh, of course, in their own ways. But Ranjit Singh failed before the British diplomacy. When the Rupar meeting was going on, Col. Pottinger, the British Agent, was on his way to Sindh to negotiate a commercial treaty with the Amirs of Sindh, or as Abdal Quadir says. "William Bentinck was then lulling Ranjit Singh to sleep at Rupar so that he may steal a march upon Sindh and bring Sindh under the British sphere of influence." Ranjit Singh had come to Rupar to know the mind of the Governor-General about the Sindh question. The result of the meeting, however, was that Bentinck eventually succeeded in his real motive and forestalled Ranjit Singh by establishing British supremacy in Sindh. Some time after, the British concluded a commercial treaty with the Amirs in 1832. In 1838 they imposed a British Resident also in Sindh. Some time after, the British concluded a commercial treaty with the Amirs in 1832. In 1838 they imposed a British Resident also in Sindh quite contrary to the wishes of the Amirs. At that time Ranjit Singh realized how the conclusion of a commercial treaty of the British with Amirs of Sindh meant the establishment of a virtual British control in Sindh. It was another bitter pill for Ranjit Singh to swallow but weak as he was, he swallowed it, as he had already swallowed the first bitter pill in 1809.

The Shikarpur Affair. Shikarpur in Sindh was a beautiful city and a commercial centre. It was also the key to the Bolan Pass and at the time of any necessity it was very easy to invade Ghazni and Kandhar through this city. Ranjit Singh was very much interested in the occupation of this place and, as such, he was always on the look-out of some opportunity to do that. This opportunity came to him when a Sindhi tribe occupied a military outpost of the Maharaja's kingdom. The Maharaja led an expedition against this tribe and defeated it. Then he advanced towards Shikarpur with a view to occupying it, but the British were against Ranjit. Singh's occupation of Shikarpur. They were bent upon humiliating the Maharaja down on the question of Shikarpur too. Consequently, Captain Wade, the Political Agent at Ludhiana proceeded towards Shikarpur at the head of a huge army and forced Ranjit Singh to withdraw his forces from the place and he withdrew. It is said at that time several Sikh Sardars including Raja Dhian Singh grew angry with the Maharaja. Some of them even waved their swords and wished the Maharaja to fight. But Ranjit Singh silenced them by reminding them of how two lakhs of Maratha forces had been defeated by the British force.

The Question of Ferozepur. After conquering the Ferozepur territory, Ranjit Singh had handed it over to one of his relatives for administration for annual tribute. In view of its geographical situation, the British were thinking of occupying this also. They knew that a conflict with the Sikhs would be inevitable one day and, as such, they were trying to bring the Punjab under their encirclement. They were thus setting up military cantonments and forts round the Punjab with a view to conquering it. Ferozepur was only forty miles distant from Lahore. Consequently they forcibly occupied it in 1835 and converted it into a military cantonment in 1838. This action of the British was greatly provocative to Ranjit Singh, who in vain fretted and even protested.

In 1836, the circumstances in Europe and Asia reacted on the Anglo-Sikh relationship in India. After having been pushed back in Europe, Russians were bury expanding themselves towards Asia. Their designs aimed at an invasion of India. Amir Dost Mohammad Khan was the ruler of Kabul those days and the English were anxious to develop friendly relations with him in view of the advancing Russian danger from that quarter. Consequently, the Governor-General despatched captain Burnes to Kabul to conduct negotiations for a friendly alliance with Amir Dost Mohammad Khan. When the question of a friendly alliance between the Amir and the British came up for discussion. Amir Dost Mohammad Khan told the Captain that he was ready for a friendly alliance provided the British exerted their diplomatic pressure on Ranjit Singh to hand over to Kabul the territory had wrested away from his hands in 1834. Captain Burnes was not prepared to consider such a proposal because the British realized that to counteract the designs of proposal because the British realized that to counteract the designs of Russia the friendship of Ranjit Singh was as much useful as that of Amir Dost Mohammad Khan, and the friendship of Ranjit Singh had already been tried whereas that of the Amir was yet to be tried. Under these circumstances, the British did not want to spoil the friendly relations with a strong ruler Ranjit Singh in preference to the friendship of Dost Mohammad Khan. Hence when they failed to sign a treaty of friendship, the British decided to cement more their friendship with the Maharaja. At Ludhiana was sitting Shah Shuja, the British pensioner. They now decided to put Shah Shuja on the Kabul throne after throwing Dost Mohammad Khan out of Kabul, with a view to setting up the rule of a friendly power at Kabul. At first Ranjit Singh refused to sign the Tripartite Treaty because he though that the elevation of Shah Shuja on the Kabul throne would in no way prove advantageous to him; rather the friendship of Shah Shuja and the British could prove dangerous of him at any time. But the threats of Macnaughton forced Ranjit Singh to sign even the Tripartite Treaty in 1839. Though he signed the Tripartite Treaty, yet the distrust and suspicion of Ranjit Singh at this time became so strong that he did not agree to one of the proposals of this treaty to give passage to the British soldiers through his territory in the event of an attack on Kabul. This distrust and suspicion of the Maharaja increased so much towards the close of his reign that we find him taking even active measures against the British. In 1837, he welcomed the Nepali Mission which implied that Ranjit Singh and Nepal might jointly take a spirited action against the British.

Criticism of Ranjit Singh's Relations with the British. It would be profitable to discuss here the attitude of both the parties towards each other in order to have a clear idea about the Anglo-Sikh relations under Ranjit Singh. This is being done in the following lines:

1. **The Attitude of the British Government Towards Ranjit Singh.** The attitude of the British Government towards the Sikhs of the Punjab was aggressive and unjust. Whenever any opportunity offered itself to them, they made capital out of Ranjit Singh's weakness and their own strength. They always tried to maintain outward appearances, but internally they were always very anxious to curb down the rising power of Ranjit Singh whenever possible with a view to checking at once the rising power of the Sikhs represented by the Maharaja. When the Cis-Sutlej Sikh states approached the English for protection of the British against the Maharaja, they did not let slip this opportunity of giving them protection and as long as the danger of French menace to India existed, they tried to establish and maintain friendly relations with the Maharaja. But the moment the danger of the French menace ceased to exist, they changed their attitude and forced Ranjit Singh to sign

the treaty of Amritsar, according to which they fixed the river Sutlej as the boundary line between the two kingdoms. In other words, the English somehow or the other were anxious to swallow up the Punjab and were seriously acting upon the policy of disallowing him to expand. For instance, when the Maharaja decided to occupy Sindh, the English became a stumbling block in his way. And in order to keep up appearances before the Maharaja, William Bentinck held a meeting with him at Rupar and thus tried to hoodwink him by themselves occupying Sindh in 1838. The more they became stronger in India with the gradual passage of time, the more aggressive and unjust was the policy that the British adopted towards Ranjit Singh. When Ranjit Singh occupied Sikarpur, they treated him with war and forced him to withdraw from the place. Again, the British extorted with threats the signatures of the Maharaja on the Tripartite Treaty in 1838, though Ranjit Singh had absolutely no advantage to gain on the elevation of Shah Shuja on the Kabul throne. On the other hand, it was the British Government which had a definite advantage from this scheme, but they forcibly imposed forced partnership of the Maharaja in this treaty by making a display of threats and force. All these acts of highhandedness show that the policy of the British Government towards Ranjit Singh was justified in no way and that they were from the very beginning giving only a scant heed to the obligations of the treaty which they considered as mere sheets of paper. In short, their policy towards Ranjit Singh was unjust, aggressive and cruel. The fact is that the British knew that they had become very powerful and that there was no power in India then that could stand before them in point of strength and, as such, they went on trampling under their feet the sentiments and feelings of Indians and based their policy on no principle or any moral code of conduct.

2. **Ranjit Singh's Attitude Towards the British Government.** As to Ranjit Singh's own attitude towards

the British Government, it may be said that he rigidly observed all the treaty obligations which were enjoined upon him by the treaty of Amritsar and others. Every time that he was treated aggressively and unjustly, he on his part never tried to break his friendship with the British, rather he kept himself bound to the treaty obligations in letter as well as in spirit. The British occupied Sindh at the cost of his ambitions, he was forced to withdraw his forces from Shikarpur, they forcibly occupied Ferozepur which legally belonged to him, they forcibly extorted his signature on the treaties of Amritsar and Tripartite Treaty—in all these cases Ranjit Singh received humiliations over humilitations from the British, but he bore all these humiliations and kept quiet. The truth is that he did all this because he was conscious of his own weakness and the strength of the British Government and that is why he did not want to involve himself in a conflict with them under any circumstances.

Criticism on Ranjit Singh's Policy Towards the British. Two opinions of a diametrically opposite nature have been expressed on Ranjit Singh's policy towards the British, the one justifying it and the other condemning it. It is, therefore, necessary to discuss both the view-points before giving a final verdict, as has been done in the following lines:

(a) **The First Opinion.** The first opinion justifies his policy and says that as long as the Maharaja lived, he never tried to fight against the British; rather he acted on the treaty obligations in letter and spirit. This policy of friendship enabled him to build a strong and great empire in the Punjab. If he had acted merely on the basis of his sentiments a war with the British would have been inevitable. In the eventuality of a war the maintenance of the Sikh Empire would have been very difficult, if not impossible. This goes to his credit, that as a statesman he had rightly understood the strength of the British and his own weakness and adopted a policy of peace and quiet towards them as long as he lived.

(b) The Second Opinion. The second opinion which does not appreciate, rather condemns, Ranjit Singh's policy towards the British Government says that Ranjit Singh received diplomatic defeats from the British Government on many occasions. All his ambitions that he cherished to expand his Empire further were frustrated by the evil designs of the British, for instance, their occupation of Sindh, Shikarpur, etc., and their forcible occupation of his legal territory, as for instance, Ferozepur. In all these affairs, the Maharaja put up with the humiliations and insulsts with quietness, a conduct unworthy of a ruler of Ranjit Singh's calibre. This policy, therefore, shows that the Maharaja had either lost all sense of honour to such an extent that despite his innumerable humiliations at the hands of the British he could not open his mouth against them or he was so much afraid of the strength of the British arms as compared with his that he did not dare fight against the British arms as compared with his that he did not dare fight against the British. In both the cases, however, his policy cannot be styled other than that of cowardice. That is the reason why almost all the historians have held Ranjit Singh also responsible for the downfall of the Sikh Kingdom to a great extent. And this is a fact which cannot be denied. He had rightly understood that the English were determined to conquer the Punjab sooner or later. We know that the Maharaja had a strong efficient army in no way inferior to that of the British, he had the best military generals of his time; he had all the resources in men and money required to conduct a successful war. In spite of all this if he did not fight against the British in his life-time when he could do it. It was his great political blunder for which he cannot be excused. Unfortunately, he postponed the issue of the war to the times of his incompetent and weak successors, when the best and the most faithful of his generals had already died, when he was no more on the scene and lastly when there was no strong ruler in the Punjab to be able to control his mighty Khalsa army. Under these circumstances, the defeat of the Sikhs was a foregone conclusion and for this Ranjit Singh was also personally responsible to a great extent. If Ranjit Singh had tried to measure his strength with the British Government in his life-time, he would have definitely had, apart from his own mighty army, the military help from rebel army of Gwalior, Nepal and other Indian powers, which were feeling discontented with the British Government. In such an eventuality, it would have been very difficult for the Britishers not only to maintain themselves in the Punjab only but in India also. There is no doubt that there were many other causes also of the downfall of the Sikh Kingdom in the Punjab but the hesitant an cowardly policy of Ranjit Singh also had a chief hand in its downfall because it was this type of policy which encouraged the British to encircle the Punjab and then to conquer it. In spite of the fact that he saw with his own eyes that a day would come when the Punjab would fall into the hands of the British, he made no satisfactory arrangements to save his Kingdom. He should have acted on the policy of "Takht or Takhta" or victory or defeat his own life-time when he had the will and capacity to act. Yielding every time to the aggression of a tyrant and not facing it boldly is not becoming on the part of a statesman; rather it be speaks of his cowardice and weakness. Perhaps, Ranjit Singh adopted this week-kneed policy towards the British in order to save his Empire from the untimely destruction at the hands of the British whose mighty strength he had already recognized. The English were too strong even for a nation of warriors like the Sikhs. But Ranjit had made his Kingdom too powerful to be regarded by the British as a safe buffer state. He himself does not seem to have any erroneous, exaggerated estimate of his own power and resources. But the English would tolerate only another Patiala or Jind. In his relations with the English Government Ranjit Singh appears to be superior to the contemporary underlings of the British power in India. But he does not show any courage or statesmanship that deserve our applause. A statesman must be judged on his actual achievement. War with British Govemment would have come sooner or later. Instead of postponing it to some future period, he could if, necessary, have boldly met the British demands with regard to Sindh by declaring war, though that would have been at that time, as it proved subsequently, hopeless contest.

ACHIEVEMENTS OF RANJIT SINGH

Ranjit Singh, the lion of the Punjab, was very much loved by his subjects. Since his treatment towards all, without the least consideration of caste, creed and colour, was fair and patronising, he was very popular amongst all his subjects. Sir Lepel Griffin, writing fifty years after the death of Ranjit Singh, says, "Although half a century has passed since his death, his name is still a household word in the province; his portrait is still preserved ill castel and cottage. It is a favourite subject with the ivory painters of Amritsar and Delhi." His justice was proverbial and the people of the province of the Punjab remember him by narrating anecdotes of his justice in every house.

Ranjit Singh enjoyed a great popularity amongst his subjects and possessed a good many talents, but unluckily he was not handsome by appearance. Baron Hugel, who was a contemporary to the Maharaja, writes about the physical features of the Maharaja. His left eye which is quite closed disfigures him less than the other, which is always rolling about wide open and is much distorted by discase. The scars of the small pox on his face do not run into one another but form so many dark pits in his greyish brown skin, his short straight nose is swollen at the tip, the skinny lips are stretched right over his teeth which are still goods. He has a thick muscular neck, thin arms and legs, the left foot and the left arm drooping, and small well-formed hands, But though the Maharaja was not handsome, yet he commanded great respect amongst his subjects and subordinate officials and officers. Though disfigured and short-statured, he exercised a complete control over his subjects including his court officers and turbulent chiefs. It is said, once a court officer in the reign of William Bentinck asked Faqir-ud-Din, the foreign minister of Ranjit Singh, as to of which eye was his master blind.

3. He was very active and hard working. He was always busy in the state business right from morning to evening and always acted on Sher Shah's maxim, "it always behaves the great to be active." He has been described as the very exbodiment of practical sagacity despite unlettered ignorance. Though himself unlettered, yet he would go deep into every detail of the state work and with his indefatigable capacity for work, he would give suggestion or guidance on minute points. He personally guided his secretaries in writing out important state papers in open Durbar.

4. Ranjit Singh was possessed of a remarkable retentive memory. Jacqueont tells us that this great ruler with his prodigious memory knew the names, position and history of from ten to twelve thousand villages in his kingdom. In course of discussion with Wade on the terms of the navigation of the Sutlej, Ranjit Singh himself counted his different districts along the right bank of the Sutlej from Harikepattan to Mithankot together with the names of his local officials and forces stationed in each. The precision with which he did this showed how much he depended on himself for regulating his administration. William Macnaughton, Auckland's Chief Secretary, wrote in May 1838 that the Maharaja "passed from war to wine, and from learning to hunting with breathless rapidity."

Ranjit Singh has been described as the very embodiment of practical sagacity despite unlettered ignorance. He was a great statesman. It was his political sagacity which enabled him to know that the British were safe friends but dangerous enemies and, as such, he never tired to expose his kingdom to the consequences of a war with the British whom he considered definately stronger than himself. Hence he always kept up good relations with the British Government and citied to focus his attention to the Narth-western region as the field of his conquests at the cast of the Afghanistan monarchy. Thus he made use of the friendship of the British as much as he could and did not strain his relations with them to the breaking paint. Moreover, Ranjit Singh was a good judge of men and always chose his officials and ministers wisely an according to merits.

The Maharaja had developed a special foundness for hunting expeditions, military riding feats and numerous other out-door feats of valour and exercises. He was a good swordsman and knew well the art of warfare. He had a great fondness far a good breed of hourses and guns also and, as such, was prepared to pay any price to get them. He was also a lover of Nature and took pleasure in being amidst natural scenery. The care he took for the maintenance of the Shalimar and Nihat Gardens at Lahore bears a testimony to his taste and fondness for natural scenery.

The Maharaja himself was unlettered and took very little care to develop his taste for bookish education, but he was fond of manly feats and exercises. He did whatever he could do to promote the cause of education in his kingdom. He set up schools with jagirs attached to them far their maintenance. Once he encouraged the Christian missionaries to set up a school at Lahore for study of the Bible, but the scheme did not mature. Apart from this, the Maharaja showed a great deal of patronage to the learned and wise. His court was a galaxy of the educated and the learned whom he patranised with scholarships and other monetary help. Mian Shah Mahammad, Munshi Sohan Lal, Munshi Mohan Lal, Amar Nath, Ganesh Dass, etc., were the writers in the court of Ranjit Singh. Munshi Sohan Lal, the author of Umatul-Tawarikh in Persian, was the court historian of the Maharaja.

Another praiseworthy trait in the Maharaja's characters was that he was a devout Sikh what considered it his duty to be guided by religious code of conduct in everything he did. According to Shahmat Ali, "the Maharaja had set apart same time in his daily routine in the morning to hear the verses of the Holy Granth. On the eve of his military expeditions, he would have the orders from the Holy. Granth as well as go to holymen like Baba Sahib Singh Bedi and get his blessings. After obtaining signal victories over his adversaries, he would always make rich offerings at the Golden Temple, Amritsar. In Order to show his political supremacy, he would always regard himself as the drum of the Sikh Commonwealth and whatever he did, he did in the name of the Khalsa Panth. On his coins and seals he had gat inscribed the wards "Akal Shahi," Once when in the course of his visit to the Golden Temple at Amritsar, he violated certain Sikh rules of conduct, he hapily offered himself far punishment as he always regarded himself as the servant of the Khalsa. He had allotted a fixed amount from the octroi dutie of Amritsar city for the "sweet pudding" distributed at the Golden Temple everyday.

The Maharaja was far above any kind of religious bigotry. Though a devout Sikh, he was very liberal and generous in religious matters and, as such, he fallowed the policy of religious toleration towards the people of other religions. His aim was to bring all the people of different shades of opinion and creeds an one platform. He treated all of them alike. In the matter of recruitment to Government services, he would always apply merit as the only criterion, so that people of all religions, provided they were qualified, could be appointed in the state departments. In his employ were the people of different religions, the Brahmins, the Kshatriyas, the Rajputs, the Muslims and Christians. Some of his closest associates were not Sikhs. The Faqir Brothers, the Dogra Rajas and Brahmin. Khush Lal Singh and Tej Singh occupied more trusted positions than the persons of his awn community. Griffin, however, says that "the tolerance of the Maharaja was due rather to indifference and selfishness than to any enlightened sentiment." But whatever the origin, continues the same author, "the liberalism of the Maharaja had an excellent effect upon his administration." He never gave religion any preference over politics. Though himself a devout Sikh, Ranjit Singh respected the Brahmins, visited the tombs of Muslim Faqirs and had attached jagirs to the tombs of Muslim places of pilgrimage.

Almost a unanimous opinion has been expressed by the historians that the Maharaja was always kind-hearted and generous at heart. He never shed unnecessary blood on any occasion. After his victories in a field of battle, he never ordered the slaughter or destruction of the vanquished, as is done by those conquerors and kings who found great empires on the ruin of the old ones. He was not harsh by nature, nor was he in favour of unnecessary bloodshed. Mr. Murrar says, "He has never taken life even under circumstances of most aggravate offence." Most of those chiefs whom he dispossessed: and the list is very long, found to their relief that there conqueror was willing to give them sufficient jagir to maintain them in comfort and even high rank in state service if they were willing to serve him.

Another good trait in the Maharaja's character was his simplicity. He used his throne to sit on very few and special occasions one the contrary, he would always sit on an ordinary silver chair. He himself wore a simple dress though his courtiers always dressed themselves in gorgeous and rich costumes. His durbar was a grand Durbar reminding one of the Mughal court in point of its grandeur. The Maharaja had in his possession very coslty jewels and diamonds the most precious of which was Kohinoor, but he never wore it.

Ranjit Singh was the beau-ideal of a soldier-strong, square, active, courageous and enduring. He took pleasure in taking field against his adversaries and would take rest only when he had overcome all difficulties. Even more arduous and the greatest difficulties never disheartened him. He had natural qualities of ruling over his soldiers, like Julius Caesar, Napoleon and Alexander. At the time of his meeting with William Bentinck at Rupar in 1831, he struck dump the spectators who saw his military feats. He very successfuly competed the Spinner's Horse in tent-pegging in such a manner as to excite the applause of the Governor-General and the British military generals present there. Another of his feats is worth-mentioning. A brass vasel was laid on the ground and three times the Maharaja lifted it with the tip of his drawn sword, the horse going at full speed. In his military expeditions, Ranjit Singh was accustomed to issue instructions to his officers in such details that little or no initiative was left to them. A good general, who showed conspicuous personal bravery at No shehra and remarkable tenacity at Mankera, he was more conspicuous in the organisational than in operational part of compaigns one of his French Officers described him as a man without passions. This remark, however true, of Ranjit Singh, is certainly inapplicable to him as a soldier. He was seen to weep as some of his old soldiers approached his with petitions and showed him their wounds. The personal devotion and loyalty that he inspired smoothed the path of duty.

Maharaja Ranjit Singh was one of those few and best rulers who set up a splendid government by virtue of their intellect and ability and tried to consolidate it by means of better laws, institutions and other means. He knew that the Punjab before the Maharaja was divided into many-petty states under Misl regime and the entire system of government was in utter confusion and chaos. This state of affairs continued on for about a century. But the Maharaja gets the credit of rebuilding the Punjab and re-establishing peace, law and order in the country. No doubt he was a despot, but he was an enlightened despot who had always before him the welfare of the people under his charge. He had a sympathetic heart for his subjects. He was the source of all power in the state, and, as such, no one dared criticise his action. He was very popular amongst his subjects and, as such, commanded respect amongst them to an unprecedented degree. All his nobles and subordinates ever showed their faithfulness and fidelity towards him. He had such an attraction in his personality and a good quality in his character that none dared defy him. The best of his achievements was thc establishment of a secular state in, the Punjab and its maintenance in the same form as long as he lived.

Ranjit Singh was a human being and, as such, had certain flaws in his character. He was addicted to opium, wine and women. He had a special weakness for dancing girls and Gul Begum and Moran had a special temptation for him. Another flaw in his character was that he was unscrupulous. This is clear from the way in which he extorted Kohinoor from Shah Shujah and Laili .from its masters and also the way in which he broke his plighted words to gain his political objectives.

But despite these flaws in him, Ranjit Singh was a born ruler of men, and, as such, he is considered amongst the most striking personalities of India—a natural leader of men, with inflexible will, clever but salfish, pastmaster in strategy and cunning but master of iron will and courage, brave but greedy—these were the qualities and shortcomings which were strangely blended together in his character and constitution. Griffin says, "Men obeyed him by instinct and because they had no power to disobey. The control which he exercised, even in the closing years of his life, over the whole Sikh people, nobles and priests, was the measure of his greatness." Griffin against says, "He (Ranjit Singh) was great because he possessed in an extraordinary degree the qualities without which the highest success cannot be attained, and the absence of the common place virtues which belong to the average citizen neither diminished nor affected, in any way, the distinction of his character." It is really sad that in spite of his being a great ruler, he left no ruler behind him on his death, who would have saved his kingdom and his people from the inevitable.

His Achievements

1. It was after 1799 that Ranjit Singh started subjugating all the Misldars one by one. Their subjugation was facilitated by the internal jealousies of the Misldars towards one another, but at the time of some emergency they fought against their common enemy also. But in the Punjab of those days there was no such strong centralized government as would have put an end to all the disturbances and confusion that prevailed there. It was Ranjit Singh alone who subjugated the Misls into one unified Sikh Kingdom. Not only this but with the gradual passage of time when his resources and powers increased. He transferred the Sikh people into a strong fighting machine and for the first time' in the Sikh history enabled them to emerge a strong and unified Sikh nation under him. He was a born ruler who succeeded in bringing the discordant Sikh elements under his national monarchy. This achievement of his entitles him a very high place in history. There is no doubt that in point of their numerical strength the Sikhs were not much but by the transformation that he brought about in them, he raised them to the status of the strongest of all the Indian nationalists.

2. Ranjit Singh is considered as one of the great builders of empires. When he came of age, he was the ruler of small territory of the Sukerchakya Misk, but since he was endowed by nature with the qualities like bravery, determination and daring required of great conquerors, he rose from an ordinary position to be the master of the Punjab, Kashmir and the whole region up to Peshwar. Mr. N.R. Sinha says. "During the years 1797-1823 Sikh military monarchy was created and consolidated. This was the work of one man. His career was naturally one long appropriation clause as is the career of empire-builders in all times and in all ages. Baron Hugel writes. "The Mallaraja never shed anybody's blood unnecessarily and no person has up to this time created such a magnificent Kingdom in such a short time as Ranjit Singh did." It is on account of these reasons that he is considered as one of the great builders of empires and that is why he will be remembered in history as a great empire-builder. According to Cunningham, "Ranjit Singh found the Punjab a waning confederation a prey to the factions of its chief, pressed by the Afghans and the Marathas, and ready to submit to English supremacy. He consolidated the numerous petty states into a Kingdom; he wrested from Kabul the fairest of its provinces, and he gave the omnipotent English no cause for interference. He found the military array of his country a mass of horsemen, brave indeed but ignorant of War as an art, and he left it mustering fifty thousand disciplined soldiers, fifty thousand well armed yeomantry and militia, and more than three hundred pieces of cannon for the field.

3. The successful battles that the Sikhs fought against the Afghans in the North-west where they (the Sikhs) defeated the Afghans in many battles, disspirited them (the Afghans) very much and ultimately they had to submit to Ranjit Singh's rule, Even today, Hari Singh Nalwa and Akali Phula Singh's names are a terror to the Afghans and especially to the Afghan mothers who utter the name "Nalwa to silence to the Afghan mothers who utter the name "Nalwa" to silence their uncontrolable children. By defeating Raja Anang Pall, the ruler of the Punjab in Northwest in 1008 AD. Sultan Mahmud of Ghazni had paved the way for the future invasions on India through the North-west. Consequently the Turks, the Afghans

and the Mughals—all invaded India turn by turn through the North-western region, the last invader being Zaman Shah. By defeating the Afghans in many battles in their own homes and thus occupying their territory, Ranjit Singh showed to the world that the Indians were stronger than even the stout Afghans or other strong foreign nations. Ranjit Singh permanently saved the honour of India by liberting the Punjab from the Afghan Kings. This was not a mean achievement on his part and that is why in the annals of India the name of Ranjit Singh will always shine. N.K. Sinha writes, "Among Ranjit Singh's principal achievements we must count his very successful defence of his Kingdom against the Afghans. We know that Afghanistan was at one time a part of India. But India lost it once for all. She would also have lost the North-western Frontier region, the Punjab and Kashmir but for the rise of the Sikhs and consolidation of Ranjit Singh's sway in these regions. It is certain that if the disorganised Misls had retained their hold over the Punjab, at least the North-western Fronter region and Kashmir would have become a part of Afghanistan under the Barakazais.

4. Another very important achievement of Ranjit Singh was his setting up a national government and a secular state in the Punjab. Ranjit Singh was far above communalism and religious fanaticism and, as such, persons of different castes, creed and colour found employment under him. The services were thrown open only to merit. Though Ranjit Singh himself was a Sikh, yet his treatment towards the people of different religions was very praise-worthy. His one aim was to become the national King of all the Panjabees and, as such, he never put religion over politics. In other words, he gets the credit of setting up a secular state in the Punjab for the first time a century ago and thus set a noble example before the Government of India that in a country like India a home of many religions—a secular type of state which can secure sympathy of her people. This point of view also entitles Ranjit Singh to a high place in history.

An Empire-Builder

He failed to found an enduring state. A very important question arises here as to why Ranjit Singh, who was endowed with great qualities of head and heart, faile to build up an enduring state. There were many reasons for his failure as given below:

(1) In the first place, Ranjit Singh is generally described as a "supreme example of an intellect without a conscience." Through force, strategem and political sagacity, he certainly built up a state. But he did not breathe into the hearts of the people any noble sentiment that would have held then together after his death.

(2) In the second place, Ranjit Singh had concentrated all the powers of the Government in his own hands, and, as such, when death removed him from the scene "not a vacancy but a void was caused" and in this void perished the fabric of Ranjit Singh.

(3) Besides, all his great generals—Misser Diwan Chand, Mohkam Chand and Hari Singh Nalwa, died during his life-time. Sinha says, "only crafty and undeserving men, either weaklings or traitors, survived to command his forces. Naturally, the army grew out of control and the Punjab became a scene of the wildeest disorder."

(4) In the third place, Ranjit Singh did not subordinate the military authority to the civil authority. Sinha says, "He left the jagirdars weak and the army too powerful for his weak successors to control."

(5) But the most important cause of the failure of Ranjit Singh in founding an enduring state lies in his relations with the British Government. Ranjit Singh had realised that war with the British was certain. Instead of postponing it to some future date he should have acted boldly. In his relations with the British he "was all hesitancy and indecision." Ranjit, in his relations with the British played the role of a horse while the British Government acted as the rider and this was his fundamental mistake. When he died and the crash came, there was no strong man to keep the British away.

In this way we conclude that Ranjit Singh was one of the greatest personalities of India. Amongst his achievements a few important were that he welded the Sikh Misls under him, that he set up a grand Sikh Kingdom in the Punjab, that be finished all chances of invasions-from the North-west and, last of all, that by setting up a secular state in the Punjab a century ago, he set an example before the Indian government that in a country like India—a country of so many religions—only a secular state could suit the people. But in spite of all his achievements he failed to build up an enduring state in the Punjab, because he could not give any meassage of love or noble sentiment to his people. He centralised everything and left no able successor.

CAUSES OF SECOND ANGLO-SIKH WAR

The causes of the Second Anglo-Sikh War (1848-1849):

1. In spite of the fact that they had sustained a very strong defeat at the hands of the English, the Sikhs had not lost their heart. They thought that if they were defeated in the First Anglo Sikh War, it was due to the treachery of their leaders like Tej Singh and Lal Singh and not due to the superiority of the British forces or their own weakness in any way. The Khalsa nation had a full confidence in their own, powers and, as such, they were prepared once again to try their luck against the British in order to regain their independence.

2. The treatment meted out by the British Government to Wazir Lal Singh was not proper, especially his subsequent death due to the enquiry initiated by the British against him went a long way in creating strong feelings of hatred in the minds of the Sikhs against the British. The removal of Rani Jindan from the Regency Council and sending her away first to Sheikhupura and then to Benares in a state of confinement could not be tolerated by the Sikhs. They thought that this humiliation inflicted by the British on their respectable Sikh personalities was a national disgrace. Hence they were looked for an opportunity to take some solid steps against the British. As a matter of fact all these steps of the British began to be considered as acts of high handedness by the Sikhs.

3. The way the British had commenced ruling over the Punjab was very objectionable and irriating to the entire population. This was so specially when Sir Henry Lawrence tried to introduce certain changes in the social life of the Punjab. This was not liked by the Punjabees. Some changes in the land tenure or Zamindari system were introduced and these changes were strange and novel to the Punjabees and as such, they were not liked by them. The prohibition of Sati and infanticide were considered as a challenge to their cherished social ideals. Under these circumstances, the Punjabees could not tolerate the interference of the foreign Government in their internal affairs.

4. As has already been pointed out above, in the new Council that was set up Rani Jindan was deprived of the rights that she exercised as Regent of the Maharaja and as the Chairman of the First Regency Council. Now all these rights fell into the hands of Sir Henry Lawrence, and it was he who was carrying on the administration according to his own views, through the new Regency Council. As a matter of fact, the new Regency was only in name, the real authority behind being Sir Henry Lawrence himself who had appointed Englishmen on all the important posts in the administration of the country and who had given to the Sikhs only a nominal share in the administration. The English were treating the Sikhs very badly, thinking that they were defeated people.

5. According to the treaty of Lahore, an unscientfic and a strange type of Government had been established by the British in the Punjab. It is to be pointed out that the British had not annexed the Punjab to the British dominion after the First Anglo Sikh War but the nature of control that they were exercising over the Sikhs was so tight that they (the Sikhs) had no occasion to breathe the atmosphere of independence. A strict control over the Sikhs without a regular annexation was unscientific in nature Hence such conditions could not continue on for a long time in the Punjab.

6. According to the second treaty of Lahore, a considerable reduction had been brought about in the Khalsa Army, now the srength of the Khalsa Army being fixed at 20,000 inffantry and

12,000 cavalry. Not only this but their salaries were also considerably reduced. The Sikhs considered all these measures as a great humiliation to them.

7. The revolt of Dewan Mool Raj became the immediate cause of the commencement of hostilities between the Sikhs and the English. The Lahore Government asked him for the submission of the arrears that were accumulating against him for a long time past. Instead of submitting the accounts, he expressed his willingness to resign from the post of the Governorship of Multan. His resignation was accepted and he was replaced by Sardar Kahan Singh as the Governor of Multan. Consequently, the British sent Sardar Kahan Singh to take over the charge of Multan fort duly accompanied by two English officers, Agnew and Anderson, with a view to facilitating the taking over of the charge. Dewan Mool Raj at once handed over the Fort of Multan to Sardar Kahan Singh, but soon after the two English officers were murdered at Multan by an unidentified person. But Dewan Mool Raj was doubted to have incited this murder. After some time Dewan Mool Raj raised the standard of rebellion against the Lahore Government on 28th April, 1848 and reoccupied the Multan fort. It is very important to note here that the Second Anglo-Sikh War did not really begin with this small revolt on the part of Dewan Mool Raj because in this rebellion neither the Sikh nobles had taken any part nor the Khalsa Army. Their policy was to allow it to assume greater proportions so that it should assume the colour of the rebellion of the entire Sikh population and then to send the whole of the Indian army into the Punjab and occupy the entire country by defeating the Sikhs. This policy of theirs was successful and the British did not intentionally suppress the small local revolt of Dew an Mool Raj. The fact is that no steps were taken to suppress it from April, 1846 to the month of September of the same year.

8. As has been pointed out above, the policy of Lord Dalhousie was not to suppress the local Sikh revolt at Multan so that it should assume a general revolt of the entire Punjab and then to throw the whole of the Indian army into the Punjab. This policy succeeded and the Sikh local revolt at Multan did ultimately assume the revolt of the

entire Punjab. When he saw that by his policy a great war had been started against them in the Punjab and, as such; the annexation of the Punjab had become inevitable, on 10th. October, 1848 he declared, "Unwarned by precedents, uninfluenced by example, the Sikh nation has called for war and, on my words, Sirs, they shall have it with a vengeance."

9. When the revolt at Multan broke out. Rani Jindan was in the custody of the English at Sheikhupura as an exile. This also had created a lot of resentment amongst the Sikhs against the British Government. But the British Government accused the Rani of a conspiracy with the Punjabees with a view to expelling the English from the Punjab. Accordingly, a mock enquiry was instituted against the Rani and in the course of enquiry their doubts were confined that the said Rani did excite the Sikhs against them. Consequently, she was removed from Sheikhupura to Benares as a prisoner. Seeing this fate of Rani Jindan, a greater portion of the Khalsa Army at once got flared up against the British and the Khalsa Army joined Sardar Chattar Singh and . Sardar Sher Singh against the British Government. The moment the Khalsa Army joined the local revolt at Multan, it became a revolt of the entire Punjab.

10. As has already been pointed out above, the English were already determined to annex the Punjab and, as such, they were only looking forward to some pretext to do that. Their policy was to fight a war once again against the Sikhs and by throwing the entire Indian army in the Punjab to annex it. With this policy in view, the began to provoke the Sikh nation and the Khalsa Army directly or indirectly so that the Sikhs should first start the war and look aggressors in the eyes of the world and so that they should be considered as justified in fighting against the Sikhs. Accordingly, by giving capital punishment to Wazir Lal Singh and banishing Rani Jindan they inflicted a terrible national disgrace on the entire Sikh population of the Punjab. Under these circumstances, the Sikhs were forced to start the war against the British. The English gave all the big and responsible posts to the English alone and deprived the Sikhs of any share in the administration of their country. This was considered by the Sikhs to be a step

motherly treatment which excited them against the British Government. Not only that the Sikh army was considerably reduced by a heavy reduction in their salaries also was effected. The greatest responsibility for the starting of the war falls on the British Government on the ground that they did not suppress the ordinary revolts of the Sikhs at Multan under Dewan Mool Raj in its early stages when they could very easily do it. Their policy was to allow it to assume a general Sikh war and then occupy the Punjab by employing the whole of the Indian army at one stroke against the Punjab. Under these circumstances, there remains the least doubt that the British deliberately imposed the Second Sikh War over the Sikhs, with the result that they were provoked to start it.

RESULTS OF THE SECOND ANGLO-SIKH WAR

1. As we know, in spite of their defeat in the First Anglo-Sikh War, the Sikhs had not lost their herts. It was plain that their defeat in that war was not due to their weakness but was due to the treachery of their leaders. Hence even after their defeat in the First Anglo-Sikh War, they still hoped to win against the British. But in their defeat in the Second Anglo-Sikh War their backbone of resistance was completely broken and they lost all heart. Now they had no hope of success against the British as they had hoped after the conclusion of the First Anglo-Sikh War.

2. As has already been discussed above the English had already set up their rule in the Punjab after the termination of the First Anglo-Sikh War but they had not annexed it. But Lord Dalhousie felt after the termination of the Second Anglo-Sikh war that Lord Hardinge's policy of not annexing the Punjab after the First Anglo-Sikh War was wrong in principle and that is Why it had failed. Hence Lord Dalhousie now decided to annex the Punjab. Accordingly, it was on 29th March, 1849 that a proclamation regarding the annexation of the Punjab was read out in an open Durbar held at Lahore. Maharaja Daleep Singh was deprived of all the rights and privileges to rule over the Punjab Kingdom.

3. The entire Khalsa Army was deprived of their arms which they surrendered to the British. Jagirs of Sardr Chattar Singh, the Governor of Hazara, and those of his sons, Sardar Sher Singh and Sardar Autar Singh were also confiscated. They were made to surrender their arms to the British. The rest of the Sardars also were given suitable punishments and their Jagirs were confiscated. Many of them were imprisoned in the st. Fort William.

4. Dewan Mool Raj was tried by the British in a military court and he was proved quality of having brought about the murder of Anderson and Agnew. Consequently, he was ordered to be sentenced to death but later on this death sentence was converted to life iprisonment. It was in this way that Dewan Mool Raj also was suitably punished.

5. Maharaja Dalip Singh was sent to stay in a place in V.P. where he became a convert to Christianity. After that he went to London where his mother Rani Jindan also joined him. He died in Paris in 1893.

In this way we find that many factors contributed towards bringing about a clash between the Sikhs and the British within 10 years of the death of Maharaja Ranjit Singh. Consequently, two Anglo-Sikh Wars were fought between the two parties in both of which the Sikhs were defeated and the Punjab was annexed to British Indian in 1844.

CAUSES OF THE DOWNFALL OF THE KINGDOM

The greatest pity is that this Kingdom vanished within a period of ten years of its founder Ranjit Singh's death whereas in view of its vitality and strength, it should logically have continued on strongly and efficiently for along time even after his death. It is strange that the Punjab state fell like a ripe fruit into the lap of the British Government within a very short time after Ranjit Singh's death. Hence it is necessary to discuss the causes which brought about it speedy end. Following are the points of collapse of Sikh power:

1. Ranjit Singh had concentrated all the powers of the state in his own hands. He was the source and centre of all the powers of the state. He was the pivot of the governmental administrative machinery which revolved round his person. His word was law. As a matte or fact it was one man's show. There is no denying the fact that he was a benevolent despot who considered the welfare of his subjects as his paramount duty, but he had concentrated all the powers in his own hands without allowing anybody else to share them. Though he had set up a Council of Ministers to get their advice on the matter of administration of the state, yet he seldom consulted them. It all depended upon him whether to consult the Council of Ministers or not. In short, the whole of the administration of the Punjab state depended upon one head, which was really a difficult task to carry on for an unlimited amount of time.

2. We know that a big state was created out of the combination of disjointed atoms. For this he had to pass the whole of his life in constant warfare. Hence he could not devote much of his time towards the improvement of his civil administration and the consolidation of his Kingdom, both of which consequently remained in a hopeless and in an imperfect condition. Even in civil administration, Ranjit Singh devoted more attention towards the revenue and financial aspects. He gave to the country neither any sound constitution, nor established any regular institutions which would have given efficiency and stability to his system of administration. He must have realized that his administration could endure only during his life-time under his strong thumb. This came out to be true. The moment the Maharaja slept the sleep of death, his administration collapsed at once. It is to be noted here that there was no systematic arrangement for the maintenance of government records in the early days of his rule and whatever departments were established by him were established only in the closing years of his rule, when the civil and military departments were entrusted to his officers.

3. One of the most significant features of Ranjit Singh's Court was its cosmopolitan character. His, Court consisted of the people of various nationalities and they were employed on the basis of merit.

But the presence of people of diverse elements was also a weakness in itself and this ultimately resulted in the collapse of the Kingdom. The reason is obvious to explain. By the presence of people of different nationalities in the Court, the Court lost all unity, cohesion and oneness of purpose which are a source of strength to an empire. As long as the Maharaja himself remained alive at the helm of affairs in the Court, all these variegated elements dared not raise their head but the moment he closed his eyes in death, all these self-seeking parties, with a view to gaining their own selfish ends, stood up in the Court ready to sacrifice the larger interests of the state at the altar of their own sordid interests. On the death of the Maharaja, the three selfish parties that arose were: *(1)* the Sindhanwalia party, *(2)* the Dogra party, and *(3)* the Court party. The motives of each of these parties were their own self-preservation more than the preservation of the Sikh state. Even during the life time of the Maharaja these parties were sharply divided against each other in cliques based on personal animosities and jealousies, as a result of which each of them looked at the other with feelings of enmity and harted, but they were helpless before the dominering personality of the Maharaja. After the death of the Maharaja, the hidden hatred became open against each other. Accordingly, the mutual hatred towards the Dogra party. Sindhanwalia party and the court party together with their hatred towards the British Government began to show its result and in an instant the Lahore Court became the scene of those diabolical intrigues, revolts and murders which at once sapped the energy of the State and brought about is speedy fall.

4. The most serious blunder committed by the Maharaja was the grant of too much of ascendancy in his Court to the Dogra pary which consisted of Rajas Dhian Singh, Gulab Singh, Suchet Singh and Hera Singh, the son of Raja Dhian Singh. They had created for themselves so much of political influence in Ranjit Singh's Court that they had become practically all in all there. By virtue of their close proximity to the royalhouse, they had become conversant with the weaknesses of the royal house, and the rulers, and, as such, wanted to take full advantage of the knowledge of these weaknesses, so much so that they had secretly decided to divide the Sikh Kingdom

between the two brothers. This view has been collaborated by General Charles Gough also who says that they had decided upon the partition of the Sikh Empire between themselves, Jammu-Kashmir and North-western region of the Punjab going to Raja Gulab Singh, while the entire Southern Punjab with Lahore as its capital going to Raja Dhain Singh. With aview to materializing their this policy, it was necessary for them to lay their hands, after Ranjit Singh's death, on the lives of the princes of the royal family one after the other in quick succession. Accordingly, because of their presence in the Sikh Court, they started a net work of mean intrigues and created strong obstruction in the smooth running of the administration. They soon murdered many princes of the royal blood and got finished many great nobles of the Court. In short, whatever amount of anarchy and chaos spread in the Punjab after the death of Ranjit Singh, a lion's share in creating it was that of the Dogra party. They acted as traitors to the Sikh state and became and effective instrument in its downfall.

5. History of the World stands witness to the fact that very few competent monarchs have left competent sons behind them to succeed them. Maharaja Ranjit Singh proved no exception to this fact. Amongst the successors of Ranjit Singh, both Maharaja Kharak Singh and Sher Singh were incompetent. Both of them indulged themselves in the pleasures and comforts of life and entrusted the affairs of the state to their traitor and faithless ministers. On the other hand, Kanwar Nau-Nihal Singh got no opportunity to show his work and worth as a ruler. Maharaja Daleep Singh, who was elevated to the throne in 1843, was only a minor. The result of the incompetence of Ranjit Singh's successors was that they could neither control the turbulent Khalsa Army nor could they control the Central Court which unfortunately consisted of elements of various types. Ranjit Singh had concentrated all the state powers in his own hands and had not given to his successors a proper training in politics, which was so very necessary for their becoming competent rulers. Moreover, whenever Ranjit Singh sent military expeditions he would issue so minute instructions to the generals on the spot regarding military operations that they could not act according to their own initiative and according to the circumstances of the time on the spot. This kept

them inexperienced both in the civil and military administration of the state. Hence they developed no self-confidence in their own ability and efficiency.

6. The most potent cause of the downfall of the Sikh Kingdom was the annexation policy and the gradual encirclement policy of the Punjab by the British Government. Whatever measures the British Government adopted towards the Punjab right from the time of Ranjit Singh up to its annexation in 1849 explain the facts that the British Government was determined on the annexation of the Punjab partly on account of commercial reasons and partly on account of political reasons. The British Government never wished to see the establishment of so strong united and independent Sikh state in their close proximity as would foil the attempts of the British Government to annex it. It is for this reason that the British Government, setting aside the existing promises with Ranjit Singh, put in their best efforts to lay their hands on his Kingdom and at last they succeeded in their attempts. They concluded the treaty of Amritsar with Ranjit Singh in 1809, out whereas the Maharaja always remained faithful to his treaty in letter and spirit, the British cared little for it and broke it so many times. They completed the Punjab's encirclement and began to look forward to some opportunity for its annexation at some convenient time. On the other hand, the Maharaja showed a different attitude towards the British Government. He yielded before them on every occasion. The fact is that the Maharaja was convinced of his weakness against the British Government and he was convinced of the fact that the British Government would be successful in swallowing up the Punjab one day or the other. Hence it was this consciousness of his weakness that forced him to avert war with the British Government every time. Under these circumstances, it is easy for us to conclude that in the policy of postponing war with the British Government Ranjit Singh committed a great political blunder. If he had fought a war with the British Government in his life-time when he was competent enough on the basis of the strength of his efficient army, he would have disabled the Britishers to cross over into the territory of the Punjab so soon after his death as they did. Moreover, all the Indian princes were harassed and had become panicky by the

policy of the British Government towards the Indian states and, as such, Ranjit Singh could, in collaboration with them all, wages successful war against the Britishers. But Ranjit Singh did not prove himself a good statesman on this point and did not fight the war with the Britishers during his life-time; rather he postponed the Anglo Sikh wars to be fought during the times of his weak successors, who were too weak to fight them out successfully.

7. The First and the Second Anglo-Sikh Wars broke the very backbone of the Sikhs and cleared they way for the annexation of the Punjab by the Britishers. This can be said with the least doubt that had the Sikh generals not proved traitors in the battles, the Sikhs would, never have got deleated in the First Anglo-Sikh War. Mr. Sinha says in this connection that "the Sikhs were defeated in the battles of Sabroan and Ferozeshah through the treachery of their generals and in the battles of Gujrat and Chillianwala, they got defeated through the incometency of their generals. The Khalsa Army was in no way inferior to the British army in points of bravery and war tactics. After the conclusion of the First Anglo-Sikh War, the British Government did not annex the Punjab because they were conscious of the strength of the Sikhs, otherwise they would have found themselves involved in serious complications on accountants annexation at that time.

(B) Ranjit Singh's Responsibility in the Downfall of the Sikh Kingdom. It was the work only of Mahraja Ranjit Singh to unite and transform into a powerful Sikh Kingdom one twelve Misls which were always at war with one another and which presented very great difficulties in the way of the establishment of a great kingdom in the Punjab. To him alone goes the credit of such a great achievement. It was this man who saved India's honour by permanently checking all the invasions on India from the North-west corner of India. The Mahraja had tried to establish a national government in the Punjab with himself as its head, broadbased upon the willing consent of all the sections and people without any distinction of caste, creed and colour. Though his administrative setup was not so complete and so exemplary, yet he gave a solid proof of his statesanship and his natural efficiency by establishing a liberal and strong kingdom in the Punjab. So far as the question of the period preceding him, i.e., the Misl regime is concerned, the administrative machinery was simply hopeless and the social and political conditions of those times also were not satisfactory. Yet he gave law and order to his state and created a strong state out of nothingness. For all these brilliant achievements, the Maharaja deserves all praise. His responsibility can be gleamed through the study of the following points, the points which prove him to be a very short-sighted statesmen and which prove him to be mostly responsible for the downfall of the Sikh Kingdom:

1. "The most important factor contributing towards the failure of Ranjit Singh was his adoption of a weak and vacillating policy towards the British Government. There was a political treaty at Amritsar in 1809 between him and the British. Government but according to, Bismarck a political treaty means a rider and a horse. As regards the Anglo-Sikh relations, the British acted as a rider while Ranjit acted as a horse. In other words, just as a rider takes the horse to whatever direction he liked similarly the British people took Ranjit Singh to whatever direction they liked. The British Government encircled Ranjit Singh's Kingdom from all sides, the east, the west, the south and, if possible, they would have encircled it from the west also. Under these circumstances a clash between the two powers had become inevitable and sure. Ranjit Singh also was now fully convinced that the British Government was determined to swallow it up sooner or later, but adopted a weak and vacillating policy towards them, overlooking a very important fact that time is not on the side of defensive both in war and politics. Every time when the British maltreated him, he took every insult or rebuff as lying down and tried to avoid that clash which actually took place between the two powers after his death, his successors proving too weak to successfully stand before the Britisher who were very clever, intriguing and opportunists. Ranjit Singh was a competent match for the Brtishers. It was a great political blunder on the part of Ranjit Singh to have postponed the inevitable war. Hence he was to a great extent responsible for the annexation of the Punjab which came later on. If

Ranjit Singh ever proved a failure in his life, it was in his relations with the British Government. Hence according to History, Ranjit Singh cannot be excused for the weak policy that he followed towards the British and which ultimately paved the way for its annexation. We, therefore, cannot but fix much of the responsibility for the downfall of the Sikh Empire on Ranjit Singh. In the case of Anglo-Sikh relations under Ranjit Singh the British Government was the rider and Ranjit Singh was the horse. He never grandly dared. He was all hesitancy and indecision." In fact, he had killed the Sikh state before it seemed to have actually died.

2. The nature of monarchy that had been established by Ranjit Singh in the Punjab was a "Military Monarchy." In other words, the basis of Ranjit Singh's rule was force and, as such, only a very strong king could rule the Punjab with a strong army as the Khalsa Army. Ranjit Singh had set up a very strong rule which was based purely on "force", hence its failure after the death was a foregone conclusion. Ranjit Singh can be favourably compared to Cromwell of the British History, a great military general who had founded a very strong military dictatorship in England. Hence, just as Cromwell's military dictatorship failed because it was based upon pure force similarly Ranjit Singh's Kingdom also collapsed because it was based on "force", pure and simple. As long as Ranjit Singh lived, he efficiently controlled the Khalsa Army and used it in right channels, but as soon as he closed his eyes in death, the Khalsa Army went out of control and began to aspire for political power in the state. In its efforts as gaining political ascendancy, it began to act as king makers, placing and removing many of the princes and ministers in quick succession according to its own sweet wish. In short, it was the Khalsa Army which created anarchy and chaos in the Punjab and at last the Punjab state was involved in a clash with the British Government. Ranjit Singh did create a very strong Khalsa Army but he left no competent government machinery or any strong and competent successor to control this turbulent Khalsa Army. He had already finished the power of the great nobles and jagirdars who could control to some extent the rising power of the Khalsa Army.

3. There is one other charge from which Ranjit Singh has no escape for being considered responsible for the downfall of the Sikh empire. It was really a critical period through which the Punjab was passing at the time. As a farsighted statesman, he should have foreseen that it was very necessary for him to have given a very sound political training to his sons and successors, so that after his death they should have controlled the country and the Khalsa Army quite efficiently, During those days, only competent and able rulers alone could rule over turbulent people of the turbulent countries like the Punjab and Afghanistan. But the Maharaja fell short of his responsibility to train his sons in the art of government and herein lies the greatest of his political blunders.

4. Ranjit Singh believed in conducting all alone and independently the affairs of the state. He personally looked into the details of all the affairs of the administration great and small. Under these circumstances, officers, Sardars and his successors had been allowed a negligible initiative to do anything in the state business according to their own initiative. Hence they could not develop that self-confidence and efficiency which come only through a practical experience of state business. It was very seldom that Ranjit Singh consulted his ministers and that also only when he himself felt interested in any affairs. He had concentrated all the powers in his own hands but he should have taken a serious note a this thing that for a single man to carry on the administration of such a vast empire, it was a very difficult affair if not an impossibility. Hence in the absence of his able officers and successors, the Governmental machinery became weak and inefficient. Hence for this Ranjit Singh himself also was personally responsible to a great extent. Dr. Chopra also points out that the despotic and personal character of Maharaja's rule was also responsible for the ultimate decline of the Sikh power. Hence his death was certain to bring a rapid paralysis of the central authority in the Kingdom. His court also, as has already been discussed in the previous chapter, was composed of diverse elements and conflicting interests; and the harmonious cooperation of its members was only possible under his own unifying authority. His ministers were mostly favourites and adventurers, who had never been allowed to exercise

much personal initiative, and were always taught to reflect in their actions the sole will of their monarch.

5. Ranjit Singh has been held responsible for the ultimate decline of his Kingdom. It is generally said that he committed the grave blunder of allowing the acquisition of vast territorial power and influence by the Dogra Chiefs. This view, on the whole, has a substantial element of truth. Nevertheless, it must not be supposed that the Maharaja was blind to the dangers of his policy. We have already seen how he whittled down the possessions of his Sardars, even to the point of incurring blame for ingratitude to his servants. In the consistent pursuit of such a policy, however, the Maharaja felt a characteristic difficulty of destroying vested interests, which he had himself once created. It is, indeed, very difficult, if not almost impossible for a despot, much of whose power depends on the maintenance of a semi-feudal nobility, to curtail the size of their holdings. Thus Ranjit Singh failed to follow consistently the policy of reducing the people of the Punjab to a more or less uniform political level; the most glaring example of such a failure was the grant of an expensive and continguous territory to a single Dogra family."

BURMES WAR

The British Indian Government thrice came in conflict with the Burmese Government in the nineteenth century. These three conflicts resulted in the defects of the Burmese and the whole of Burma passed into British hands.

First Burmese War (1824-26)

It was in the year 1823 that Lord Amherst landed on the soil of India as Governor-General. He had not yet made himself familiar with the political conditions of India that he was compelled by the force of circumstances to wage war against Burma.

A Government of India has to take into account the political importance of the North-Eastern frontier as well Mughal Imperialism especially in the times of Aurangzeb, tried to push its limits towards these eastern frontiers; and the British Empire in India was, in the course of its territorial expansion, also drawn towards it.

The eastern boundary of Bengal, in which was included the district of Chittagong, for long remained 'very ill-defined, and variable'. Immediately south of Chittagong lay the Kingdom of Akakan, south of that Pegu and south of that again the coastland of Tenasserim. In the latter half of eighteenth century the history rapidly brought Arakan, Pegu, Tenasserin and the whole basin of the Burma underwent dramatic changes.

The region of Pegu was conquered by a Burman chief, named Alampora, from the Talaings in the dalta of the Irrawaddy, and thus was established a strong monarchy in about 1750 AD.' In 1766, Burmese attacked Siam and captured Tenasserim. In 1784, Alampora captured the independent State of Arakan and thus the Burmese established their control equally over upper and lower Burma, by 1793, and next pushed on close to Surma valley in 1813. These Burmese conquests made it necessary for the English to open political intercourse wit'ı the Burmese; and their Government in Calcutta accordingly sent envoys to Burma—Captain Symes in 1795 and 1802; Captain Cox in 1797, Captain Canning in 1803, 1809, 1811.

The advance of Burmese on the Chittagong frontier made an ultimate collision with the British inevitable. Fugitives flying from the territories conquered by the Burmese took shelter in the British border and used their new quarters as a base of inroads into the conquered provinces. The British Government steadily declined to surrender them to the Burmese in spite of repeated demands to this effect on the part of the latter. So, when the British were engaged in the large-scale campaign against the Pindaris, the king of Ava in 1818 sent a letter to Lord Hastings demanding the surrender of Chittagong, Dacca, Murshidabad and Kassim Bazar on the ground of these being ancient dependencies of Arakan, and hence part of the Burmese dominions. But before the letter reached Calcutta, the British had been relieved of pressures from other quarters, and the Governor-General returned the communication to the king of Burma with the remark that it was perhaps forgery.

After a temporary respite the Burmese resumed their role of conquest and annexation. In 1822 their able general Mahabandu captured Assam which brought Burmese into contact with the whole of north -eastern frontier of British India. Manipur was also captured by the Burmese.

In 1823, the Burmese captured Shahpuri and small island near Chittagong and the Burmese threatened and invasion of interior Bengal. Lord Amherst tried to establish peace with the Burmese, but the Burmese replied by turning out the British forces from an outpost near Shahpuri. War now could no longer be averted and Lord Amherst declared it on 24th February, 1824.

P.E. Roberts has pointed out, "The physical features of Burma which was one vast expanse of forest and morass, laced longitudinally by mountain ranges and the vallyes of the Irrawaddy. Sittang and Salween", afforded the best defence to the Burmese. As a military force in open fighting the Burmese could not be certainly compared with the British troops of that time, but the former possessed considerable skill in building stickades of timer with great rapidity, or in throwing up earth works and sinking rifle pits.

Organizing the plan of operation against the Burmese, the British Government decided that on the frontier, "operation should be in a great measure defensive; but not so exclusively as to preclude the expulsion of the Burmese from territories in which they had recently established themselves by usurpation." The main blow was to be struck through an expedition by sea to Rangoon with the idea that it could then proceed up the Irrawaddy, Bengal Presidency supplied a pait of the force required for the expedition, the remaining part was chiefly recruited from Madars.

Capture of Rangoon. The British Armeda under the command of Major-General Sir Archibald Campbell occupied Rangoon on 11th May, 1824. But the entire population had disappeared into the jungles of Pegu leaving Rangoon denuded of every kind of supplies. The expedition had been undertaken in a wrong season and without any satisfactory arrangement for securing supplies. Soon after the occupation of Rangoon, the rains started and with them fever and dysentery; while their troops had to depend on the provisions supplied irregularly by the Calcutta contractors.

Bandula proceeded to invade Bengal in the month of May. He repelled a British detachment at Ramu on the Chittagong frontier; but now he was recalled for meeting the counterinvasion of Pegu. On 1st December, 1824, the Burmese Army, 60,000 in number, appeared in front of the British position at Rangoon and threw up entrenchments with great rapidity. After several skirmishes, the Burmese were signally defeated on 15th December.

Sir Archibald Campbell then decided to advance upon Prome, the second city of the Burmese Empire, and after whiling away some time in dilatory preparations, he commenced his march on February 13, 1825. But Bandula held out bravely for a month before the column sent against him, and the general advance was delayed till 1st April, when Bandula was killed by a rocket and his troops consequently demoralised beat a hasty retreat during the night abandoning every thing including a store of grain. Three weeks later Campbell occupied Prome, the capital of Lower Burma, on 25th April without any resistance, but as the rains started further operations had to be stopped.

Negotiations for peace started which proved futile hostilities were resumed. But all the attempts of the Burmese to repulse the British troops remained unsuccessful. The Burmese now opened negotiations for peace. The last and desperate attempt was made by the Burmese with a force of 10,000 men, but they were repulsed. The British forces now advanced upto Yandaboo within sixty miles of their capital.

Terms of the Treaty of Yandaboo

(1) He agreed not to interfere in Cachar and Jaintia and to recognise Manipur as an independent State.

(2) He agreed to pay heavy war indemnity amounting to a million sterling.

(3) The king of Ava agreed to surrender Arakan and Tenaserim to the British.

(4) He also agreed not interfere in any way in Assam.

(5) The king of Burma also agreed to enter into a commercial treaty upon principles of reciprocal advantage. Accordingly a commercial treaty was signed in November.

(6) The king of Burma did not accept a British Resident upto 1830.

The first Burmese war has been criticised for the manner in which it was conducted. The expedition had been dispatched on almost entire ignorance of the circumstances of the country to which it was to proceed, and without any adequate preparations for securing supplies, it meant a grossly needless waste of life and wealth.

But this fact cannot be denied that this war proved advantageous for the British. With Bengal and Assam they got the princeless sea-coast and Cachar and Manipur. But this war proved quite costly. In spite of this Lord Amherst was honoured as Eart of Arakan.

Results. The Burmese made peace by the Treaty of Yandaboo in 1826. Its most important provisions were the following:

(1) The Burmese were not to interfere in Assam, Cachar, Jaintia and Manipur. These places thus passed under the control of the Company.

(2) A commercial treaty was to be concluded between the Company and the Burmese Government.

(3) The Burmese Government had to pay indemnity of one crore of rupees.

(4) The Burmese gave the provinces of Arakan and Tenasserim to the Company.

(5) A British Resident was to be posted at Ava, the Burmese Capital.

The First Burmese War put an end to Burmese aggression. The rich provinces of Arakan and Tenasserim were secured. Assam, Cachar, Jaintia and Manipur passed under Company's control. Thus the War gave valuable territories to the Company.

Second Burmese War (1852)

Cause. The Second Burmese War was fought in the time of Lord Dalhousie in 1852. The following were its important causes:

(1) Lord Dalhousie feared that France or some other European power might not establish itself in Burma. In order to root out such a possibility, he wanted to bring Burma under his control. This was the real and underlying cause and he wanted and excuse the go to war with Burma.

(2) By the Treaty of Yandoboo, the English merchants had been permitted to settle in Burma and carry on trade. Their commercial rights were not clearly defined and each party interpreted these in its own way. The English merchants were ill-treated but they continued to trade because of high profits. They complained to Lord Dalhousie about the bad treatment meted out to them by the Burmese Government. Dalhousie wanted an excuse to go to war with Burma and he seriously took up the cause of the English traders. He wrote to the Government of Burma that it had violated the Treaty of Yandoboo and must pay damages to the English merchants for the wrongs done to them. Commodore Lambert was sent to Rangoon. He captured a ship belonging to the Burmese King.

Events. The British forces were sent under General Godwin Martaban and Rangoon were captured. This was followed by the occupation of Prome. Thus the whole of Lower Burma fell into the hands of the British. The Burmese Government refused to negotiate a treaty and Lower Burma was then annexed by a Proclamation.

Results. The Second Burmese War resulted in the annexation of Lower Burma. It brough great commercial advantages to the British. The war reduced the possibility of the occupation of Burma by a European power because Upper Burma was now cut of from the sea.

The annexation of Lower Burma by Lord Dalhousie was not a just act. The British had not right to trade with Burma if the Burmese Government did not like it. The English merchants were staying there because of huge profits.

Third Burmese War (1885)

Causes. The Third Burmese War was fought in the time of Lord Dufferin. The following were its most important caüses:

(1) Lower Burma had passed into the hands of the British in a result of Second Burmese War but Upper Burma was still independent. The baw, the new king of Burma, did not like that the British should trade with Upper Burma and adopted a stern attitude. The English merchants complained to the Governor-General that they were ill-treated.

(2) The baw the king of Burma, began to negotiate commercial treaties with Germany. Italy, and specially with France whose possessions in Indo-Cnina were near his eastern frontier. A Burmese Misson went to Paris in 1868 and a French envoy proceeded to Mandalay in 1885. He made arrangement to establish a French bank there. The French Government disclaimed all knowledge of his proceedings and recalled him, but Lord Dufferin wanted to root out any possibility of French influence by occupying Upper Burma and wanted an excuse to do so.

(3) The king of Burma imposed heavy fine on the Bombay and Burma Trading Company and ordered the arrest of its officials Dufferin insisted an inquiry into the matter but the Burmese refused to reopen the question. The Governor-General sent in ultimatum that the king should admit a British envoy at Mandalay suspend proceedings against the Company till the arrival of the envoy, have no relations with any power except on the advice of the Government of India and permit the British to trade with the Chinese through his dominions.

Events. The British had already collected troops in Lower Burma and a swift attack was made. The Burmese got to time to prepare and were taken by surprise. Upper Burma was overron and the Burmese king was sent to India. The Burmese continued guerrilla warfare for about two years.

Results. Upper Burma was now annexed and that completed the conquest of the whole of Burma. The Burmese policy of Lord Dufferin has been criticised on several grounds. Firstly, it was said that King The baw was a tyrant. It was an internal affair of Burma and was no concern of the British. Secondly, it has been said in defence of the British that the English merchants were not properly treated. This, however, was no justification for war. If they could not put up with the treatment, they were free to stop trade with Burma. Thirdly, the principal grievance of the British was that the king was in communication with the French. This was no justification for interference and annexation. The Burmese king was a sovereign prince and was free to have relations with any foreign power.

LORD DALHOUSIE'S POLICY

Lord Dalhousie's conquests and annexations which brought the whole sub-continent of India under one control and his many-sided and beneficent reforms on modern lines show that he was more than any other man "the maker of Modern India" and one of the consolidators of the British Empire in India. Hence, he is to be remembered not merely for his wars, conquests and annexations, but also for his many and useful reforms and development schemes. Sir Richard Temple syas "As an imperial administrator, he has never been surpassed and seldom equalled by any of the illustrious men whom England has sent forth to govern India." He laid practically all the foundations of modern India.

The achievements of Lord Dalhousie can be discussed under the following heading:

(A) Dalhousie as an Empire-Builder

He extended the frontiers of British India almost to its modern limits. He annexed the Punjab by means of conquest and, as such, extended the boundary line of the British India up to its natural frontiers. He also annexed Sikkim, a part of Cachar, Lower Burma,

Satara, Oudh, the Central Provinces, Bhagat, Sambhalpur, Jaitpur, Jhansi, Berar, and a part of Khandesh, which he brought under British sway in his time. Thus, he was responsible for a considerable enlargement of the British territory. Almost the whole country came under one uniform rule and this uniformity helped to produce feeling of oneness, unity and integrity among the Indains. The British Empire of India under Dalhousie reached its zenith of peace, power and prosperity. Thus, he deserves being considered as one of the greatest Empire-builders whom Great Britain sent as Governor-General to India for the purposes of establishing their rule in this country. It is also the culmination of the marvellous history of the East India Company" because it as after this that wars and conquests were mostly abandoned by the East India Company.

(B) Dalhousie as an Administrator

1. Administrative Reforms. One thing that is very important to note here is that the key-note of Dalhousie's reforms which touched almost all the spheres of life and administration in the country, was centralisation. These reforms were devised with a view to gathering the threads of power into the hands of the Governor-General. Past conquests of territory which he effected created the need of some organisation which would take the place of the destroyed administrative structure of the conquered provinces and "Non-Regulation" system was the organisation devised by Dalhousie to meet this need. According to this system, the administration was presided over by a Commissioner, directly responsible to the Governor-General-in-Council. These Commissioners were appointed in various division or units throughout British India. Its chief aim was the maintenance of peace, the collection of revenue and the administration of a crude form of criminal justice. This system did not much concern itself with the improvement of the lot of the common man. The only merit it had was the economy of personnel. According to this system, no distinction was made between the civil and military perosnnel. The District Officer combined in himself all the powers of the judicial, executive and revenue functions. Since there were no laws to guide his caprice and there was none to check his whims except the Governor-General to whom he was directly responsible, the District Officer was the most important figure in his area. Those who support Lord Dalhousie for his initiating this system defend him by saying that it was a temporary measure. It has its defects also in as such as while it listed the demoralised people, it produced disastrous results. As has been pointed out above, Lord Dalhousie made a beginning in framing the system of administration on modern lines. The distribution of the work of administration among distinct departments.was begun. This made the machinery of the Government more workable and efficient. Simla became the seat of Government. The Governor-General was relieved of his duties as the head of the Bengal Presidency by the appointment of a Lieutenant Governor of Bengal. The Punjab, Burma, the Central provinces and Oudh were administratered by both civil and military officials and were called "Non-Regulation Provinces," the system by which Commissioners were appointed to carry on the administration in their areas working directly under the supervision and control of the Governor-General himself.

2. Military and Strategic Reforms. It has already been pointed out above that with the extensive conquests and annexations by Lord Dalhousie, especially in the case of Punjab, the frontiers of British India had extended to India's natural boundary lines. This addition of territory created new problems of imperial defence as well as internal security. According to the practice that prevailed before this, the army was, more or less, concentrated in Bengal, but now with the extension of the territory, this method of keeping huge armies in Bengal alone became out of date. The reason was that the political gravity had shifted from Bengal to Central and Northern India. In the North, the Company's boundary lines had gone so far as to touch the boundary lines of Afghanistan, beyond which there was the power of Russia busy in expanding itself to the West in Europe as well as to the South towards India. This changed condition of India's defence necessitated the initiation of a series of military reforms which were essential for the external as well as the enternal safety of India and consequently he shifted the headquarters of military from Calcutta to Meerut, which was set up as a very important military cantonment in the North. The army headquarters was also shifted to Simila where the Governor-General and his Counsellors use to reside. Then, there were the dangers from regular native army of India also and this danger he wanted to ward off by means of adopting a policy of reduction, disintegration and distribution with a view to de capacitating the native soldiers to organise themselves against the Government. Not only this, but he also took further measure of keeping India secure from Indian troops. He encouraged the formation of Gurkha regiments and a now irregular force in the Punjab, apart from increasing the number of British troops to be stationed in this country. Personally, he was not satisfied with the military changes that he introduced. His only anxiety was the fear from the Indian troops and this fear remained his constant companion. He knew that the work of 'army in India was not yet over and that is why he recommended for the importation of more and more British troops from England to be stationed in India. He made a series of proposals designed to strengthen the Company's military hold on the Indian territories contained in the nine-military minutes which have been regarded by the apologists as a monument of his wisdom and farsightedness. But these minutes remained uncared for by the Home authorities, but it is said by his apoogists that if he had been allowed to implement these reforms, the Mutiny of 1857 would have been averted. He thought that the British troops were an essential element of their strength and on this strength he placed the security and stability of their position in the East.

3. Dalhousie's military reforms have got a close bearing with the introduction of telegraph system in the country and the construction of railways began during his time. He organised these departments from military point of view as quick mean of transport and communications, but their commercial value was equally great because these means of transport and communications were an outlet for British capital; but to the Indian minds, who believed in self-preservation, these means of communication appeared as iron-bonds of slavery. To encourage the construction of railways, contracts were entered into with English Corporations to whom Dalhosie gave all facilities and in Additions guaranteed them interest for which the

Government became liable irrespective of the profits which the Corporation may make themselves. According to Dr. Ishwari Prasad, "As an instrument of imperialism, the state guarantee was ingenious. As a business proposition, it was fraudulent to the tax-payer. A few strategic lines were laid at enormous cost to India and extreme profits of English capitalists. Railway development in India after Dalhousie has been largely based on Dalhousie's proposal contained in his railway minute. To judge them by the integration of Indian society to which they have led, or by the growth of common consciousness, which frequent intercourse between people lead to, is to judge them by indirect and unforeseen results." In pursuit of his policy for opening railways, Lord Dalhousie opened the first Indian railway and set up the first telegraph wire. Railways were introduced with manifold objects in view to enable the government to send troops and war material at short notice to any province to suppress any popular rebellion and thus keep an effective control over the vast Indian Empire which had practically grown up to its present dimensions. The second object in view was to enable free flow of trade between England and India and to provide cheap and rapid means of travel. Consequently, the first railway line opened was the one from Bombay to Thana in 1853 and a more important one was between Calcutta and Raniganj coal area, in 1854. It is, therefore, on this account that Dalhousie is rightly called the father of the railway and telegraph systems which now cover the country like a network, for the introduction of both was entirely his work. This has modernised India. Apart from this, Dalhousie also introduced the electric telegraph system.

4. Dr. Ishwari Prasad Says. "The aim of Dalhousie to introduce commercial reforms was to throw open the produce and market of India to the exploitation of the English capital. In this he was successful beyond his expectations. His reforms were inlets through which economic imperialism riveted its whole upon India. They reflect the evolution of military imperialism into economic imperialism. The doctrine of 'free trade' was introduced and proclaimed as one of the maxims of trade applicable to every country and every clime. All ports of India were declared free. The necessary improvements in lighthouses and harbour accommodations were undertaken. All checks and hindrances that impeded the flow of goods and capital were removed. The result was that all the coasting industries of India slipped into the hands of English capitalists. Indian capital and enterprise, already shy due to the constant wars of British aggression, were blighted by Dalhousie's commercial and trade innovations. Their results, however, were more far-reaching and they are writ much upon the face of India-industrial poverty, extreme dependence on agriculture and an unbalanced economy. The following figures quoted by Sir W.W. Hunter, one of his apologists, as indicating the success of Dalhousie's commercial reforms, tell their own tale of economic exploitation from the Indian point of view.

5. "Before Lord Dalhousie came to India as the Governor General, the Public Works Department was under the charge of the over-worked Military Board and, as such, the result was that the public works, other than the military, were neglected. Dalhousie was not in favour of the Boards and consequently believed in individual responsibility as the secret of success. He abolished the Military Board and, in accordance with the orders of the Court of Directors, a Commission Was appointed in each of the Presidencies, on whose report, public works were withdrawn from the control of the Military Board, and a separate Public Works Department was set up in each of the Presidencies. At the head was the Chief Engineer assisted by executive officers and subordinates, all imported from England. An engineering service was begun and indigenous talent was sought to be developed by the encouragement of engineering colleges established at Roorkee and the Presidencies. This reorganised departments took in hand the construction of roads, irrigation works like canals, bridges and every other works of public utility. It short, material improvements of every kind were designed and executed under his guidance and supervision. The Grand Trunk Road was begun. Old canals were repaired and the new Ganges Canal and the Doab Canal were built for watermg the Upper Ganges districts. "Lord Dalhousie organised a Public Works Department, made Macadamised roads such as the Grand Trunk Road, and a road from Dacca to Aracan, whereby it became possible for the sepoys to march from Bengal to

Burma without crossing the 'backwater', induced English companies to undertake construction of railways by giving them a government guarantee of five per cent per annum on the outlay, extended telegraph, promoted irrigation by digging the Ganges Canal for watering the Upper Ganges district, and introduced cheap and uniform rate of postage for the whole of India in lieu of the old system of heavy charges. Steamers were also multiplied in the Hoogly, the Indus and the Irravaddy."

6. "The postal system as organised before Lord Dalhousie had some serious defects in it. There was no uniform rate, the fee being realised from the receiver of the letter in cash with the result that the receivers scarcely got the letter, without being relieved of something in excess of the fee. Dalhousie appointed a Commission on whose report the whole system was reorganised. The old inefficient postal arrangements were discarded. Post Offices were opened throughout the country directly under the Government of India. Lord Dalhousie established a cheap and uniform half-anna postage service throughout the length and breadth of the country. Before he set right the postal system, it took one rupee to send a letter from Calcutta to Bombay.

7. In the year 1853, the Charter of the Company was renewed for another period of twenty years. Now, as the time for its renewal approached, the authorities at home and in India were attracted towards the education and moral progress of Indians committed to their charge. The progress of education since the days of Macaulay had been very little and expenditure on it was negligible. Vernacular education ceased to be the concern of the Government ever since Macaulay burst out his propaganda against vernacular education. On the other hand, English education also suffered because of lack of funds. The filtration theory which aimed at certain education from upward downward also failed. A Committee was appointed to make recommendations with regard to the reorganisation of the whole system of education in the country. These recommendations are contained in Wood's Despatch of 1854. "This famous intellectual Charter of India embraced vernacular schools throughout the districts, the Government colleges of a high character, a University at each

Presidency. All educational establishments, supported by the state, or by the societies or by individuals might be affiliated and, above all, the glorious measures of grants-in-aid to all schools without reference to caste or creed." The Wood's Despatch of 1854 said: "Along many subjects of importance, none can have a stronger claim than that of education. It is one of our most sacred duties to be the means, and as far as in us lies of conferring upon the natives of India those vast moral blessings which flow from the diffusion of useful knowledge. By the recommendations contained in the report of the Commission, each province was to have a Department of Public Instruction in each Presidency town, there was to be a university. Training institutions in vernacular schools were to be established. The system of grants-in-aid to schools privately maintained was to be introduced. Government colleges of a higher grade were to be established. Great emphasis was to be laid on vernacular education. It was in his way that Lord Dalhousie gave effect to the Education Despatch of 1854.

8. Lord Dalhousie gets the credit of devising ways and methods for the preservation of old historical monuments found all over the country. It was during this period that regular departments of preservation of old buildings and monuments were instituted and we find old and historical buildings and monuments existing amongst us in the country.

9. He tried to supress the abominable and barbarous practices like Suttee and Thugee that still existed in some out of-the way parts of India. He passed an act which sanctioned the marriage of Hindu widows. He passed an enactment by which a person, who had changed his religion, had still the right to all share in his family property.

(10) *(a)* The British Parliament refused to renew the Company's Charter for another period of twenty years as it was done in the past, but declined as yet to abolish the Company. *(b)* The new Act placed the Indian Civil Service on a national basis by abolishing the system of nomination by the Court of Directors and introducing the system of competitive examinations by which the services were thrown open to all English subjects irrespective of colour, caste or creed.

(c) It created a new Legislative Council by the addition of two judges and representative members of the already existing Executive Council the Governor General and the Executive Council were given the power of vetoing any bill. *(d)* A Lieutenant-Governor was appointed for Bengal to relieve the Governor-General of some work. *(e)* The Act of 1853 very clearly declared that the Company held the political power of India "in trust" for the Crown until the Parliament provided otherwise.

Effects of his reforms. He extended the frontier of British India almost up to it modern limits. He broke down the various distinct in land boundaries and removed landmarks that stood in the way of the unification of the country and placed the people under the protection of one all pervading rule. This, in turn, helped to produce a feeling of oneness, unity and integrity among the Indians. The consciousness of this was quickened by the beneficent reforms introduced by him. The spread of education, the establishment of easy means of communication, regular and efficient administrative machinery widening of the Indian outlook and the advent of peace, prosperity and progress—all signs of modern India—can be traced to his benign administration. It may, therefore, be said that "the distinctive features of modern India have been far more deeply influenced by Dalhousie's work than by the Mutiny itself or by the constitutional adjustments that followed it."

11. His responsibility for the outbreak of Mutiny of 1857 or shortcomings of his imperial policy.

(a) His annexations and reforms created resentment. His annexations right and left and the 'Doctrine of Lapse' Which he applied with a view to annexing various states to the British dominions in India, gave rise to a serious discontent and resentment in the country against him. The people failed to appreciate his reforms. Therefore, his annexations and the .introduction of reforms and western innovations were, to a large extent, responsible for the uprising of 1857.

(b) The too-rapid introduction of reforms did not appeal to the deep-rooted conservatism of the Indian minds. Dalhousie's regime was one of relentless activity that comprised reforms-material, moral and economic. But their introduction was, perhaps, too rapid for the deep-rooted conservatism of the Indians to appreciate them and this may be held to explain, among other causes, the outbreak of the India Mutiny which soon after broke out in the country.

(c) While introducing reforms, Dalhousie did not appreciate the feelings and prejudices of the Indian mind. The changes were drastic and too sudden and consequent tension required only a tiny spark to produce a big explosion. While making changes, Dalhousie did not sufficiently appreciate the feelings, the prejudices and the religious traditions of those whom he ruled. He could not feel its cumulative effect on the Indian mind. He could not see his work as it appeared to others. Even measures of a decidedly beneficent nature added to the general distrust. The conservatives found their world turned upside down. This served only to increase the feeling of instability. The changes made so suddenly and so thoroughly produced just that temper which required only a trivial cause for an ouburst. The upheaval of the Mutiny was the price of progress. No explanation can absolve Lord Dalhousie of the responsibility of having created so much explosive material. He can be rightly blamed for pouring new wine into old bottle rather too hastily. Dalhousie had failed to understand human feelings and he had also failed to realise the deep resentment of the Indian rulers because of the policy of Lord Wellesley and his indiscreet application of the 'Doctrine of Lapse'. The minds of the people were full of so much discontent and uneasiness that even a slight pretext or provocation was enough to set ablaze the long smouldering fire. Dalhousie's action in the annexation of the states was most hasty and uncalled for. It appears as if Dalhousie had lost all feelings of human symapthy and he was bent upon achieving his object by means, right or wrong. Sir John Kaye says: "But in neither way did Dalhousie even come to understand the genius of the people with whom his lot was cast...His advisers insisted upon the duty of universal usurpation... .The sight of the dark section sealed their sympathies." Speaking about Lord Dalhousie's responsibility for the Mutiny of 1857 P.E. Roberts says, "Dalhousie had very well prepared the ground and now only a pretext was required for the great upheaval. The greased cartridges served as the immediate cause for the outbreak of the great rising and naturally precipitated the crisis; the discontent and resentment which were really responsible for the trouble were already in stock as the result of wrong and misguided policy of Dalhousie. It was not for nothig that Lucknow, Jhansi and Kanpur became the chief centre of mutineers. Each explosive material for discontent was ready. It needed but to be ignited. The terrible blunder of greased cartridges fanned into a fierce and devouring flame all this smouldering discontent and served as a match to a magazine." Dr. Ishwari Prasad writes about the responsibility of Lord Dalhousie for the mutiny. "There has been a greeat controversy regarding the exact responsiblity of Dalhousie for the event of 1857. Dalhousie was neither responsible for the mutiny, nor could he have averted it. The mutiny was the natural reaction of a people against foreign rule. Dalhousie's responsibility was in accelerating the outburst of that reaction. His breathless conquests galvanised the latent spirit of the people, gave unity to those who before had been divided by being placed under different systems of administration. His onslaughts on ancient royalties spread a wave of rebellion which culminated in the events of 1857.

FEATURES OF THE ADMINISTRATIVE ORGANISATION OF INDIA

The Fundamental Characteristics of the Administrative Organisation of India Under the East India Company. From 1606 the East India Company came to India originally to trade but the contemporary unstable political circumstances and their selfish purposes encouraged them to participate in India politics. Very soon they succeeded in establishing political authority in India. The successes in the Battle of Plassey and the Battle of Buxor helped them in getting the Diwani of Bengal, Bihar and Orissa and during to period of Lord Wellesley the empire of the Company continuously increased because of the Subsidiary Alliance and other methods. A new administrative organisation's necessity was soon realised to strengthen that empire because the commercial officers of the Company failed as administrative officials.

By 1784 the East India Company's administration of India had been brought under its control by the British Government and its economic policies were being determined by the needs of the British economy. We will now discuss the organisation through which the Company administered its recently acquired dominions.

In the beginning the Company left the administration of its possessions in India hands, confining its activities to supervision. But it soon found that British aims were not adequately served by following old methods of administration. Consequently, the Company took all aspects of administration in its own hand. Under Warren Hasting and Cornwallis, the administration of Bengal was completely overhauled and the foundations of a new system based on the English pattern laid. The spread of British power to new areas, new problems, new needs, new experiences and new ideas led to changes in the system of administration But the overall objectives of imperialism were never forgotten. The fundamental objectives of the British administrative organisation were:

(1) only to protect the interest of England.

(2) to take the help of forces only instead of the sysmpathy of the people and their favour to control India.

(3) only to depend on three pillars viz. civil services, army and police.

Administration. In matters of administration the British Parliament was made the supreme authority. It enforced its control through the Governor-General. The British rule stood on three pillars the civil service, the army and the police. This was so for two reasons. For one, the chief aim of British Indian administration was the maintenance of law and order and the perpetuation of British rule. Without law and order British merchants and British manufactures could not hope to sell their goods in every nook and corner of India. Again, the British, being foreigners, could not hope to win the affections of the Indian people they, therefore, relief on superior force rather than on public support for the maintenance of their control over India. During the rule of the Company, the Governor-General was the actual ruler of India. He was controlled by the Parliament of England. He fulfilled his administrative duty with the help of army. Police and Civilians and with the assistance of judiciary. The work of all three organisation in India was to protect and extend the British empire', to maintain law and order in the country; to collect revenue and to administer the country. Many Governor-General made reforms in the three pillars from time to time to maintain the administration well. The main characteristics of the three pillars of the administrative organisation during the rule of the Company are given in detail below.

(1) Civil Services

(a) **Establishment.** The actual founder of the Civil Service in India was Cornwallis (1786-1793). He divide the departments of commerce and revenue of the administration. He arranged or sufficient salary for the company servants. For stopping corruption, he restricted the private trade and taking gifts by the servants. During his period, the district officer (Collector) was given 1% of the amount of the revenue besides 1500 rupees per month. Actually the officers of the Company working as Civil servants were getting maximum salary in the world. He decided to give promotion on the basis of seniority in civil services so that the officers could remain free from the external influence due to the attractive and higher salaries.

(b) **Training.** Wellesley established college Fort William in Calcutta for the education of young recruits to the Civil Service so that they could be given training for administration work. The directors of the Company arranged for the training of the Civil Servants in East India college of Haileybury in England in 1806 instead of this college of Calcutta.

(c) **Appointment.** Till 1853, all the appointments of the civil services were made by Directors of the Company. Later on, the members of the Board of Control were also made partners for these appointment. But by the Charter Act (1853) all the appointments for civil services were made through the competitive examination.

(d) **Indians and the Civil Service.** Because of different causes, Cornwallis and his successor Governor-General did not allow any Indian to be a civil servants. Actually, according to a law of 1793, for sometime, they could not be appointed for the posts of 500 pounds or more than that. Secondly, they did not have a good opinion of the ability of the Indians and their loyality towards the Government. Those Britishers, who were in Civil Services, They never came closer to the ordinary Indian society. They used to think about the welfare of England than the Indians.

(2) Army. The second powerful and important pillar of the British empire in India was army. The army played an important role in the extension of the British empire. It maintained the superiority of the Britishers in India, and suppressed the revolts of native rulers after ending all the European power as the rivals of the Britishers. The maximum number in the army of the company was of Indian soldiers. Gradually the company tried to increase the number of the English soldiers. By 1857 their number could not increase more than one-third of Indian soldiers to all the officers of the army of the company were English. It is said that in 1856, there was only one Indian Subedar in the English army and there were only three Indians who used to get 300 rupees per month, as salary. The number of the English in the army of the company was less because they must be given higher salary. Due to this the army used to become expensive. When the maximum number of soldiers in the English army were Indians and their number was very less as compared to the number of soldiers maintained by the Indian rulers, then how did they rule us for about two hundred years? There were two reasons for this. First of all these was total lack of national feeling and patriotism and secondly, during that period the Indian soldiers did not want to be called as traitor 'Namak Haram' by showing disloyalty towards their master (the English). The Company continuously had loyal soldiers by paying regular salary to the soldiers and by giving better salalry than the Indian rulers and by giving them new weapons. The generally used to appreciate the ability of the Indian rulers. But the reality was that they were the soldiers at rent only. They did not have any respect like the soldiers of a national army. No promotions in the army were there for them.

(3) Police. After army, there was the place of policy in the administration. Cornwallis gave it a well-organised from during his period. It became the third pillar of the British administration because of his reforms..Before him, only the Zamindars maintained peace and order by keeping a police. First of all Cornwallis formed a permant police of the Company. He gave modern form to the Police Stations. A Police Station was kept under one Daroga. There were many police station in one district. One Superintendent of the district was appointed. In cities, the police officer was known as Kotwal. In village the traditional village protector was known as Chaukidar. He used to work as policeman in the village. The villagers used to look after him. Though, the police played an important role in maintaining law and order but the English police never got popularity because they generally used to take bribes. In police also a policy of discrimination towards the Indians was adopted like the army.

(4) Judicial Administration. The English followed for some years, after getting the administration of India. The Contemporary India law and judicial system. Before them, the law of each religion and social group was based on the traditions, the shastras and the customs. The cases of revenue and the customs. The cases of revenue and same other cases were decided by the king or the judges or officials appointed by him. In the village, the justice was imparted by the Gram Panchayats.

During the Company rule first of all, Warren Hastings started a new system of imparting justice. He established a Supreme Court in Calcutta (in 1774). The English judges decided cases for sometime as the basis of English laws. But it was not liked by both the Company as well as the Indians. In 1781, by a law, the English laws became limited to the Britishers only. But by this also, when all the problems of justice were not solved, then in 1793 Cornwallis gave it stability. He established small Diwani courts in big cities, who got the right to decide the cases of up to 200 rupees. Above them were one Diwani court in every district, whose head was a district judge and who was a member of the Civil services. Earlier these courts were under the district collectors and used to collect revenue also. Now the only work of the collectors was to collect revenue. In this way, Cornwallis separated the posts of Diwani Judge and collector. Appeal against the district Court could be made in provincial courts. The final appeal of the Diwani and Faujdari cases could be made in Sadar-e-Diwani court and Sadar Nizamat court respectively. Both these supreme courts were in Calcutta. A new punishment rules book was punished after taking into consideration and collecting the laws of the Hindus, the Muslims and the traditional laws. It was published in English and Indian languages.

In 1831, William Bentinck came and provincial courts, and regional courts were abolished and the work was first given to the commission and then to the district judges and district collectors. Three high courts (1855) were established in Calcutta, Madras and Bombay in the place of Sadar Diwani Court and Sadar Nizamat Court. The Government established in 1833, under the leadership of Lord Macnalary an Indian Law Commission. By preparing Indian Penal Code this Commission established universal law and courts in whole of the country. In this way, the company tried to make the Indian people believe through law and judicial system that rule of law was establishing in the rule of the company. But in practice, every one was not equal before law. There were separate courts and separate laws for the Europeans and their relatives only the European judges had the right to decide the Faujdari cases against them. As a result, generally a true decision was neglected. During the period of the Company, the justice became very expensive because now the people had to go to distant courts. They had to appoint a lawyer for themselves and had to pay court fees. The old and good agency of law, *i.e.* Gram Panchayats lost their importance in British India. The expensive judicial system made it generally impossible for the poor to go to the courts for justice. The new sovereign whom the Indians designated as "Company Bahadur" was not a ruler in flesh and blood and its laws were framed and order were exercised by persons who could stay in their post temporarily.

The Rule of Law and the British Government (1757-1857). The British introduced the modern concept of the rule of law. This meant that their administration was to be carried out, atleast in theory, in obedience to laws, which clearly defined the right, privileges, and obligations of the subjects and not according to the caprior or personal discretion of the ruler. Whim or fancy of any individual could in no-way influence the administration of country. The special feature of the rule of law that a government official, however, big to might be could be tried in a court of law for breach of officials duty or administrative excesses. In practice, of course, the bureaucracy and the police enjoyed arbitrary powers and interfered with the rights and liberties of the people. The rule of law, to a great extent, guaranteed freedom to the individual. The English, by and large, tried to carry out their administration in obedience to the interpretation of laws as made by the courts. It is true that previous rulers of India had been in general bound by tradition and custom. But they always had the legal right to take any administrative steps they wanted and there existed no other authority before whom their act could be questioned.

But the laws were not clear and healthy in every respect. These laws were made by the alien rulers whose selfish interest they were meant to serve. The British laws were not framed keeping in mind the interest, needs, requirements etc., of the Indian people, that was why they often did not suit well the Indian conditions. Though the laws were often defective, were made not by the people through a democratic process but autocratically by the foreign rulers and left a great deal of power in the hands of the civil servants an the police. But that was perhaps inviable in a foreign regime that could not in the very nature of things be democratic or libertarian. No foreign ruling power would be so foolish as to make laws that might expel its own doom. In fact the British laws seldom served the common Indians and their sentiments.

The rule of law envisages the sense of equality which the British government failed to deliver as it had set up separate court headed by English judges to try the English accused. Even when charged with the murder of a native on Eglishman was allowed to let of after paying nominal fine. It should be kept in mind that an accused was never allowed to be tried by the Indian judges. All this was a blot an the integrity of the Indian judges. Thus we may conclude that the British government gave us a practice of written codes of laws but these laws lacked equality.

Equality before law and the British Government. Theoretically the Indian legal system under the British rule was based on the concept of Equality before law. This meant that in the eyes of law all men were equal irrespective of their caste, creed, sex, religion or birth of place. The same law applied to all persons rich or poor. Before the advent of the English, justice in India was dispensed with keeping view of the caste of accused and had differentiated between the so called high born and low born. For the same crime lighter punishment was awarded to a Brahmin that a non-Brahmain. Similarly, in practice land lords, zamindars nobles, such merchants and very high officials were not judged as harshly as the commoner. In fact, very often they would be brought to justice at all for their wrong action and deeds. But the English law did not recognise any distractions. There a criminal was a criminal and that was all. Now the humble could also move the machinery of justice. The case was heard by the court of law and criminal was given punishment according to his crime and not according to his caste or status.

There was, however, one exception to this excellent principle of equality before law. The Europeans and their descendants had separate courts and even law. In criminal cases they could be tried only by European judges. A European considered it below his dignity to face trial before an Indian judge. Many English officials, military officer, planters, and merchants behaved with Indians in a haughtily, harsh and even brutal manner. When efforts were made to bring them to justice, they were given indirect an undue protection by the British Government and they were let off with light or no punishments. It was nothing but mockery of the law.

In practice, there emerged another type of legal inequality. Justice became quite expensive as court fees had to be payed, lawyers engaged and the expenses of witnesses met. Courts were often situated in distant towns. Law suits dragged on for years. The complicated law were beyond the grasp of the illiterate and ignorant peasants and other common people of India. A rich or resourceful men could buy justice, while a poor man would be completely ruined because of the long, cumbersome process of appeals from the lower courts to the highest court. They were mostly compiled accept a nominal compensation and with draw the suit. Moreover, the widespread prevalence of corruption in the ranks of the police and the rest of the administrative machinery led to the denail of justice. Officials often favoured the rich. The zamindars oppressed the ryots without fear of officials action. On the contrary, before the arrival of the British in India justice was easy, less expensive, less complicated and within the common man's reach, cases were decided on the spot. Thus, while the new judicial system marked a great step forward in so far as it was based on the laudable principles of the rule of law and equality before law and an rational and human man-made laws, it was a retrograde step in some other respects; it was now costlier and involved long delays. Now the justice was arguments dominated. By arguing a case well even a criminal could be proved innocent and vice versa. If arguments were weak in innocent person could go to the gallows. To engage a good lawyer that can argue a case competently one had to pay an exorbitant fee which was generally out of a poor man reach.

❐

9

Constitutional Development

The Regulating Act was passed by the British Parliament in 1773 to improve the affairs of the English East India Company. The passing of the Act was necessitated by several factors.

Circumstances Leading to The Passing of the Act

(1) The Company had been established to carry on trade with India and had acquired considerable territories by 1773. In other words, the Company from the position of mere traders had become a governing body. Thus the character of the Company had undergone a change. The British Parliament now wanted to have a hand in supervising Company's affairs.

(2) The condition of the people under the rule of the Company had become very bad. Clive's system of Dual Government had proved a total failure. Power was in the hands of the Company but the responsibility for administration was of the Nawab. Thus power was divorced fram responsibility. The servants of the Company tyrannised over the people. The appearance of Europeans in the villages was sufficient to create panic among the people. There was a severe famine in Bengal in 1769-70 and the servants of the Company hoarded grain. They sold it at exorbitant prices. About one-third of the population of Bengal perished. It shocked the conscience of many Englishmen.

(3) The servants of the Company made huge profits. They were generally poor when they came and, in spite of their low salaries were rich by the time they went back to England. This was due to their getting costly presents from Indians and carryig on private trade. They lived like petty princes on returning to England and were poularly

known as Indian Nawabs. They purchased rotten boroughs and began to get themselves elected to the House of Commons. All this roused the jealousy of Englishmen and the members of Parliament.

(4) The covetousness of British Parliament. The covetousness of the British Parliament was no less important a factor for the interference of Parliament. Since the acquisition of Dewani, the British statesmen at the helm of affaris were desirous of sharing the huge profits of the Company so that the financial burden of the British subjects could be relieved. They took every opportunity of taxing the Company. In 1767 an Act had also been passed according which the company was to pay the exchequer an annual sum of £ 4,00.000 for the privilege of retaining their territorial acquisitions. The friends of the company described it as blackmail.

(5) The servants of the Company were rich but the financial position of the Company was very bad. It became worse as a result of the First Mysore War. The Company was at last forced to apply to the Government of Lord North for a loan in order to escape bankruptcy. A Secret Committee was appointed and it reported that the financial conditions of the Company was really most deplorable. The British Parliament then passed two Acts. The first Act sanctioned a loan of £ 1,400,000 to the Company. The other Act was the Regulating Act of 1773 and it came into force in 1774.

Provisions of The Regulating Act

The Regulating Act made changes in the constitution of the in England and in India.

(A) Changes in England

(1) The qualification for vote in the Court of Proprietors was raised. Formerly persons holding shares worth £ 500 for a period that of six months were entitled to have a vote. Now it was laid down that a person for having a vote in the Court of Proprietors must hold shares of the Company worth £ 1,000 for one year at least.

(2) The Directors of the Company were formerly elected by the Court of Proprietors for one year, This short tenure was obviously defective. The Directors after election spent the first six months in discharging their obligations to their supporters and the next six months in preparing for the coming elections. Thus they could not take much interest in the affairs of the Company. Moreover, there could not be continuity in policy.

(B) Changes in India

(1) The Governor of Bengal was made Governor-General of Bengal.

(2) The civil and military control of Bengal was vested in the Governor-General of Bengal and four Councillors whose names were mentioned in the Act in the first instance. Warren Hastings was made Governor-General of Bengal and the other members of the Council were Francis, Clavering, Monson and Barwell. They were to hold office for five years and could be removed before the expiry of the term only by the King on a representation by the Court of Directors.

(3) The Governor-General of Bengal was bound by the decision of the majority of the Council. He was given a casting vote in case of a tie.

(4) The status of the Governor of Bengal was raised. He was to be called Governor-General of Bengal and was given the Power to superintend, direct and control the Presidencies of Madras and Bombay. They were to forward all rules and regulations to the Governor-General-in-Council. If they did not carry out the orders of the Governor-General of Bengal-in-Council or did not perform their duties properly, they could be suspended by the Governor-General-in-Council.

(5) The Governor-General-in-Council could issue regulations but these had to be registered in the newly-created Supreme Court. These could be disallowed by the King-in-Council within two years.

(6) The Act created a Supreme Court consisting of the Chief Justice and three puisne judges. Sir Elijah Impey was its Chief Justice. It could try civil, criminal, admiralty and ecclesiastical cases. It had jurisdiction over the British subjects in India.

(7) The Judges were to be the barristers of England and Ireland of not less than five years standing.

(8) The Court possessed both original and appellate jurisdiction.

(9) The Chief Justice and his councillors were to hold office at the pleasure of the Crown.

Criticism of the Act

The Regulating Act was meant to improve Company's administration but it had serious shortcomings. The following were its most glaring defects:

(1) The Act did not define the relations of the newly created Supreme Court with the Company's Courts. The Supreme Court took the view that the Company's Courts were subordinate to it but this claim was denied by the latter. There were frequent tussels between the two judicial authorities. The Supreme Court awarded heavy damages to Indian plaintiffs against the judges of Company's Proviacial Courts for acts done by them in their official capacity.

(2) The Act did not clearly define the relations of the Supreme Court with the Governor-General-in-Council. The Supreme Court took the view that the Governor-General and the members of his Council were subject to its jurisdiction.

The latter took the view that the Supreme Court had no jurisdiction over them.

(3) The Act did not state as to who the British subjects were for the purposes of Supreme Court's jurisdiction. It claimed authority over all Company's subjects in India. It claimed jurisdiction over the zamindars but the Governor-General-in-Council denied it. It led to open conflict in Cossijurah case.

Case. The Supreme Court issued a Writ of Capius against the Raja of Cossijurah for his arrest. He Court have avoided arrest only by furnishing security. The Raja concealed himself to avoid the service of the writ. The result was that the Collector could not realise the revenue and reported to the Governor-General that the revenue could not be realised because the Raja was concealing himself due to the writ issued by the Supreme Court. Warren Hastings after consulting the Advocate General directed the Raja not to appear before the Supreme Court.

The Supreme Court then issued another writ to sequester the land and property of the Raja. The Raja complained that the persons deputed by the Supreme Court entered his house, beat the servants, entered the apartment of ladies and places of worship and asked his tenants not to pay the rent to him. The Governor-General sent Company's troops. They intercepted the court party and brought them to Calcutta. The Supreme Court took action against the Advocate General and those officers who had intercepted the court party. The Advocate General was imprisoned.

(4) It was not stated in the Act as to which law was to be administered by the Supreme Court; Was it to be Hindu law, Muslim Law or the English Law? Was it to be the law of the defendant or of the plaintiff ? The judges had come from England and applied the English law indiscriminately. Nand Kumar was hanged on a charge of forgery. No

consideration was shown for the customs of the people. The employees of the Supreme Court entered the apartments of women and places of worship to enforce the decrees of the Supreme Court.

(5) The Governor-General was bound by the majority opinion of his Council. This created difficulties, Three out of four members were against the Governor-General from the very outset. They were Francies, Clavering and Monson. Only Barwell sided with him, Warren Hastings had generally to carry out the wishes of a hostile majority.

(6) The Governor-General was given the control over the Presidencies of Bombay and Madras, and yet an exception was made to it. The Governors of Bombay and Madras could act without consulting the Governor-General-in-Council in times of emergency. This created complications with the Marathas when Bombay Government made the Treaty of Surat with Raghoba without consulting the Bengal Government while the hostile majority of the Council forced the Governor-General to make the Treaty of Purandhar with party of infant Peshwa Madhav Rao Narayan led by Nana Fadnavis.

(7) The Act was vague on another point. The titular authority of the Nawab of Bengal was left in tact by implication because no assertion was made of the sovereignty of the Crown or the Company in India.

(8) The Act raised the qualification for vote in the Court of Proprietors. Thus the ultimate control of the affairs of the Company passed ito the hands of rich persons. The constitution of the Company at home thuse assumed more or less an oligarchic character.

(9) The Parliamentary control over the Company was also inadequate. The Act no doubt provided that the copies of all civil and military despatches received by the Directors

from Governor-General-in-Council in India be forwarded to the Ministry within a fortnight, yet it set up no effective machinery to study and scrutinise those reports and then urge the Government for necessary action. Thus the Parliamentary control over the company and its affairs in India remained inadequate and ineffective.

(10) The changes introduced in the company's constitution also failed to attain their object. According to G.N. Singh, the alterations in the voting qualifications of the General Court did not improve the exiristing state of affairs because the laudable object of preventing the retired Company's servants from gaining an excessive influence in the counsels of the Company was not realised. On the other hand the court of Directors was transformed into a more or less permanent oligarchy. Thus the Act was highly defective.

Merits of the Act. It may be said in favour of the Act that it marked the beginning of a written Constitution for India and asserted the right of Parliament to legislate for this country. It was also the first attempt to apply regular law to India.

The Removal of Defects
(The Amending Act of 1781)

Many of the defects of the Regulating Act were removed by the Amending Act of 1781. This is clear from the following clauses of the Amending Act.

(1) The Governor-General and members of his Council were not to be subject to the jurisdiction of Supreme Court for all acts one in their public capacity.

(2) The employees of the Company were exempted from the jurisdiction of Supreme Court for acts done by them in their official capacity.

(3) The matters concerning collection of revenues were declared beyond the jurisdiction of Supreme Court. The revenue

collectors and the judicial officers of the Company were not be subject to the authority of Supreme Court for their official acts.

(4) The question of the jurisdiction of the Supreme Court was settled. Its jurisdiction was to extend over all the inhabitants of Calcutta. It was to apply the personal law of the defendant.

(5) The Supreme Court was to take into consideration the religious and social customs and usages of the people in enforcing its decrees. Appeals against the decision of the provincial courts were not to be heard by the Supreme Court. These were to be heard by Governor-General-in-Council. Appeals could be taken to King-in-Council, if the amount in question was 5,000 rupees or more.

(6) The rules and regulations made by Governor-General-in-Council were not to be registered in the Supreme Court.

Criticism of The Act

(1) The Act did not define the relations of Supreme Court with Governor-General-in-Council and it claimed jurisdiction over them.

(2) The relations of the Supreme Court with Company's Courts were not defined.

(3) The Supreme Court claimed jurisdiction over the zamindars and other revenue collectors but it was denied by Governor-General-in-Council.

(4) It was not clear as to which law was to be applied by the Supreme Court.

(5) The titular authority of the Nawab of Bengal was not ended.

(6) The Governor-General had no power to over-rule the hostile majority in the Council.

(7) The Governor-General-of-Bengal-in-Council was given control over thePresidencies of Bombay and Madras but the Governors of these Presidencies could act without consulting the former in case of emergency.

(8) The raising of voting qualifications in the Court of Proprietors made it a sort of oligarchy.

(9) The Parliamentary control was inadequate and inefective.

(10) The changes introduced in the company's constitution also failed to achieve their object.

The Act, however marked the beginning of a written Constitution for India and asserted the right of the Parliament to interfere in Indian affairs and to legislate for India. It was also the first attempt to apply regular law to the Indians.

The Removal of Defects
(Amending Act of 1781)

Many of the defects of the Regulating Act were removed by the Amending Act of 1781.

(1) The Governor-General and members of his Council were not subject to the authority of Supreme Court for the acts done by them in their public capacity.

(2) The servants of the company were not to be subject to the authority of Supreme Court for their official acts.

(3) Matters concerning revenue collection were declared outside the jurisdiction of Supreme Court.

(4) The Supreme Court was to have jurisdiction over all persons residing at Calcutta. It was to apply personal law of the defendant.

(5) The Supreme Court was to take into consideration the religious and social customs of the people in enforcing its decrees.

(6) Appeals against the decision of the Company's Provincial Courts could be taken to Governor-General-in-Council.

(7) The rules and regulations issued by Governor-General-in-Council were not to be registered in the Supreme Court.

PITT INDIA ACT OF 1784

The Pitt's India Act. Pitt the younger, the Prime Minister of England got passed a new Act in 1784 A.D. with a view to improve the administration of the Company in India. It was called the Pitt's India Act.

Causes for Pitt's India Act. To remove the weaknesses of the Regulating Act (1773) and to reform the administration of the company, this Act also passed so that England could not loose her right in India like America. After the passing of the Regulating Act, enquiries about the activities of the Company were made in next ten years, and the Parliament of England took many steps to control the Company.

Main Articles of the Act

(1) The Company's political work was separated from its commercial work. The commercial work remained in the hands of the Directors of the Company but the political work was entrusted to a board of six members which was called the Board of Control. This included the Secretary of State, the Finance Minister, and four members of the Privy Council as commissioners. The Board had extensive powers. It supervised the civil, military, revenue, and administrative affairs of the Company. If the directors of the Company happened to disobey the orders of the Board of control, it could directly order the Governor-General.

(2) The Act placed the government of India in the hands of Governor-General and a council of three, so that if the Governor-General could get the support of ever one member, he could have his way. The Act clearly subordinated the Bombay and Madras Presidencies to

Bengal in the questions of war, diplomacy, and revenges. With this Act began a new phase of the British conquest of India.

(3) While these appointments of the Governor-General and the Governor were to be made by the Court of Directors, they could be recalled and dismissed by the Directors as well as by the Crown.

(4) The Governor-General-in-Council was given the power and authority 'to superintend, direct and control' the governments of the Presidencies in matters of wars, peace, treaties, and revenue and in such other matters as may specially be referred to by the Court of Directors.

(5) The Governor-General-in-Council could suspend the members of the Bombay and Madras governments, if they failed to give obedience to instructions of Bengal in matters of war and peace.

(6) The Governments of Bombay and Madras were to supply copies of all rules and regulations made by them to the Governor-General-in-Council.

(7) To ensure an honest administration, the Act provided strict punishment of public servants in India for receiving of demanding gifts. That Company could not pardon a public servant so punished, or could it retain him in service.

Importance or Effects of Pitt's India Act or how it improved the system of Government and remedies the defects of the Regulating Act of 1773 Most of the major defects of Regulating Act, 1773 were removed by it. The general effects of the Act were these:

(1) It virtually transferred the political management of the Indian possessions from the Company to the Crown.

(2) It preserved the commercial character of the Company by requiring the Directors to pay their best attention to trade affairs.

(3) It aimed at encouraging a peaceful policy by enjoining the strictest neutrality, except in self defence; but the clause in reference to it soon became a dead letter.

(4) It rectified the mistake in the Regulating Act by enhancing the power of the Governor-General.

(5) It introduced what is known as the system of dual government control from Englan. The President and the Board were destined to be the future Secretary of State for India and his Council. The Act helped the unification of India by making the Governor-General supreme over the Govenors of the other presidencies.

(6) The British Parliament claimed supremacy over the possessions of the Company in India. The new provision for trying persons of British descent committing offence in India was a novel one. The Proprietors lost their original importance and position. The Committee of Secrecy was given independent powers as apart from the Court of Directors.

(7) The deletion of one member from the Executive Council of the Governor-General made his position stronger. He could act according to his judgement by using his casting vote. The same was the case with the Governors.

(8) With this Act began a new phase of the British conquest of India. While the East India Company became the instrument of British national policy. India was to be made to serve the interests of all sections of the ruling classes of Britain. The Company having saved its monopoly of the Indian and Chinese trade was satisfied. Its Directors retained the profitable right of appointing and dismissing its British officials in India.

(9) While Pitt's India Act laid down the general framework in which the government of India was to be carried on till 1857, later enactments brought about several important

changes which gradually diminished the powers and privileges of the Company. In 1786, the Governor-General was given the authority to over rule his council in matters of importance affecting safety, peace, or the interests of the Empire in India.

We can conclude with the words of Prof. Keith "The Act altered the constitution of the Company at home, changed the structure of the Company in India subjected in some degree the whole of territory India, and provided in a very efficient manner for the supervision of the Company by the ministry.

ACT OF 1786

Sir John Macpherson officiated as Governor-General for some months after the departure of Warren Hastings. Then it was decided to send Lord Cornwallis. He clearly realised that it would be difficult to work under the provisions of the Regulating Act which bound the Governor-General by the majority decision of his Council. He was not keen to be the Governor-General but William Pitt the Younger, Prime Minister of England, and Dundas, the President of the Board of Control, were impressed by his integrity, character, honesty and straight-forwardness. They wanted to send him as Governor-General of Bengal and passeed the Act of 1786.

This Act authorised Lord Cornwallis to override the majority of his Council on his responsibility. He was also given the post of Commander-in-Chief. This Act gave these privileges to Lord Cornwallis personally.

CHARTER ACT OF 1793

Circumstances Leading to Passing of the Act. The East India Company was granted the monopoly of Eastern trade in 1773 for 20 years. It was to expire in 1793 and hence it had become necessary to renew the Charter. There were two factors favourable to the renewal of the Charter. Firstly, the condition of the Company had improved after 1773 and the ministers in England were favourably inclined to the renewal of the Charter. Secondly, England had got involved in a life-

and-death struggle with Revolutionary France and the attention of the nation was pinned upon the struggle. Hence there was not much opposition to the renewal of the Charter.

PROVISIONS OF THE CHARTER

The Charter did not contain any new provisions. Most of these were repetition of the clauses of previous Acts. The most important provisions of this Act were the following :

(1) The Company was to have the monopoly of carrying on trade with the East for twenty years.

(2) The payment of the members of the Board of Control and their staff was to be made out of Indian revenues.

(3) The Governor-General of Bengal and the Governors of Bombay and Madras were to have only three members in their Councils. Each of the members must have resided in India for at least twelve year before appointment.

(4) The Commander-in-Chief was not to be a member of the Council, unless specially appointed its member by the Court of Directors.

(5) No leave of absence out of India was to be given to the Governor-General, Governor, Commander-in-Chief and a few other high officials during their tenure of office.

(6) The Governor-General-in-Council could appoint justices of peace in any Presidency.

(7) The admiralty jurisdiction of the Calcutta Supreme Court was to extend to high seas.

(8) The policy of non-intervention was emphasised again.

(9) The Governor-General and the Governors could override their Councils on their responsibility.

(10) The control of the Governor-General over the Presidencies of Madras and Bombay was emphasised. When the

Governor-General went to the Presidency of Bombay and Madras, he was to supersede the Governor.

(11) The Governor-General was authorised to appoint a Vice-President of the Executive Council from amongst its members to preside during his absence.

(12) Two junior members of the Board of Control need not necessarily be members of Privy Council.

(13) The receiving of gifts by the servants of the Company was declared an act of misdemeanour.

(14) Length of service was to be considered in matters of promotion.

(15) The sale of liquor was made subject to the grant of a licence.

(16) The Act laid down that a part of the profits of the company was to be utilised to clear the debts of the Company and a part of it was to be used to raise the dividend from 1 per cent to 10 per cent.

POINTS FOR REVISION
ACT OF 1786

(1) Lord Cornwallis as a special case was authorised to override his Council.

(2) He was authorised to act as Commander-in-Chief also as a special case.

CHARTER ACT OF 1793

It had empowered the governors to act against the wishes of their Councils in certain circumstances and kept secure the monopoly of trade of the Company in India for another twenty years. But it brought no change in the governance of India. Therefore, in 1813 some efforts were made in this direction.

The Charter Act of 1793 was passed without much controversy but the Charter Act of 1813 was passed after a great deal of controversy. This was due to several reasons. Firstly there was a great demand for abolishing the trade monopoly of this Company. According to Prof. Sri Ram Sharma, the Company's territories in India had expanded so much that it was found difficult for it to continue both as commercial body and a political sovereign. This was partly due to the prevalence of Adam Smith's theory of free trade. Secondly, England was at war with Napoleon. The Continental System had adversely affected England's trade because it had closed most of the European markets to English merchants. The trading classes of England now clamoured that the Company's monopoly of trade with India should come to an end and they also should be allowed to rade with India. Thirdly, while the British people wanted free entry into India the British missionaries also demanded permission to preach Christianity among the Indian people. But the Company opposed any such move fearing that such a step would offend the Indian people. Nevertheless, the British opinion was in favour of the charter being revised to ensure an easy entry on the India soil.

Provisions of this Act. Following were the provisions of Act:

(1) By the charter of 1813 the Company was deprived of its monopoly of trade with India but it still enjoyed its monopoly of trade with Clive and trade in tea. Subjects to this the Indian trade was thrown open to all Englishmen. The shareholders of the Company, naturally enough, opposed tooth and nail this move though they did not stand to lose much by this decision as they were granted a dividend of 10½% out of the revenues of India, if the commercial account failed to provide that amount.

(2) The Act continued to the Company for a further period of twenty years the possession of the territories and revenues. "Without prejudice to the undoubted soverignty of the Crown......in and over the same." It is to be noted that the constitutional position of the British territories in India was thus explicitly defined for the first time.

(3) The Company was required to maintain its commercial accounts distinct from territorial ones. In the use of the Indian revenues it was clearly laid down that the first consideration would be given to the maintenanec of forces and the payment of interest, second to civil and commercial establishments and third to the charges on the revenues of the Company.

(4) Expect in a case of special requisition, the maximum number of troops the Crown could now send to India at the Company's cost, was to be 20,000. The Company could keep a maximum number of 29,000 Indian troops to be paid from the Indian revenues. For those troops it could make laws and regulation and hold Court Martials.

(5) The dividend was fixed at the rate of 10½% fifth-sixths of a surplus going to the State. No other payment were to be made from the Company's commercial profits unless the payments of dividends had been made. In order to provide for failure, when there was a surplus in revenues, the Company set aside £1,000,000 for the purpose.

(6) The local Government in India were empowered to impose taxes on persons, and punish those who did not pay them. These powers were to be exercised by the local Governments subjects to the jurisdiction of the Supreme Court.

(7) The Act provided for the religious learning and education of the people in India. A sum of Rs. 100,000 a year was to be set "apart and applied to the servival and to the improvement of literature and the encouragement of the learned natives of India and for the introduction and promotion of a knowledge of the sciences among the inhabitants of British Territories in India.

(8) Christain missionaries were permitted to came to India for propaganda work by securing a licnce from the Directors.

They were to reside in India with in certain limits and were subject to the regulations of Local Governments. British merchants were also allowed to go to India and settle there under licence.

(7) The church establishment was placed under the superintendence of a Bishop and three Archdeacons. Handsome salaries were provided for them out of the revenues of India. This was the beginning of the ecclesiastical department in India.

These were the important provisions of the Act which clearly proclaimed the sovereignty of the Crown over the Company's territorial acquisitions of India. The powers of the Board of Control being considerably enlarged the company was made more subservient to the Crown and Parliament and the clear establishment of the Boards control over the institutions for civil and military training to the Company servants was portent of considerable significance.

Significance of the Act. Though the Charter Act of 1813 retained the old constitution without any modification, yet it was significant for various other reasons.

(1) It abolished the Company's monopoly of trade with India, which had been for long a target of vehement criticism. Trade with India, except trade in tea, was now thrown open to all British subjects. The East India Company, as a result of it, became one of the many commercial competitiors. This was indeed, a great achievement of the Company's opponents, who had secured the freedom of trade with-India for every person in England.

(2) Soon the British trade with India increased manifolds and the British traders struck upon another market for their goods. In 1813 A.D. the company had only 1,3,00,000 worth of trade with India which rose upto 10,000,000 by 1860 A.D.

(3) It was the first charter that recognised the social aspect of the administration. The Company now undertook to spend Rs. 1,00,000 an education in India every year. The Company also under took for the first time to move for the welfare of her Indian subjects.

(4) Fourthly, a large number of missionaries began to come to India and they also started schools and colleges.

CHARATER ACT OF 1833

The Charter Act of 1833 was passed after a good deal of controversy. Strong voices were raised against the Company. Mr. Buckingham, the chief critic of Company's Government, remarked that it looked preposterous to level of administration of an immense empire in the hands of a joint stock company. The Company had many defendants also, the most important of them being Macaulay. He argued that the House of Commons owing to lack of time and necessary knowledge could not be expected to take proper care of India. He further argued that the ending of the governing powers of the Company would lead to increased nepotism and favouritism in England. It would give power of Indian patronage to the party in power in England and it would use it in its own interest. Thus the interests of India would be ignored and the British politics would come to be characterised by increased curruption, The arguments of Macaulay had their effect and the Charter Act of 1833 was passed.

PROVISIONS OF THE ACT

(1) Changes in England

(a) The Company was deprived of its commercial privileges. Its debts were to be charged on the revenues of India and was to have dividend on its capital at the rate of 10½ per cent, for 40 years. The State could pay double the amount at the end of this period in full and final settlement of the claims of the Company. Company's monopoly of trade with China came to an end.

(b) The territories and the revenues of India were granted to the Company for twenty years.

(2) Changes in India

(a) The Act changed the designation of the Governor-General of Bengal to Governor-General of India. It was symbolic of the centralising tendency of the Act. He was given greater control over the Presidencies of Bombay and Madras.

(b) Each Presidency Council was to consist of the Governor and two members instead of three.

(c) The laws were not modified so far. There was English law, rules and regulations issued by the Governor-General-in-Council, rules and regulations made by the Presidencies of Bombay, Madras etc. The Charter Act of 1833 provided for the codification of laws in India. A Law Commission was appointed under Macaulay. It submitted many reports, the most important of which was the Penal Code. It was mostly drawn up by Lord Macaulay. It remained in draft from for a long time. It was revised by his successors and enacted into law in 1860.

The Act increased the legislative powers of the Central Government. Formerly, the supreme Government of Bengal could not make laws for the whole of India. It is true that the regulations made by Madras and Bombay Governments had to be confirmed by the Governor General-in-Council, but this power had not been asserted. Hence there could not be uniformity in the regulations prevailing in the three Presidencies. Moreover, these were drawn up without proper legal advice.

(D) The Charter Act of 1833 empowered the Governor General-in-Council to make laws for all the people living in India. The subordinate Governments were deprived of the power of making regulations. The utmost they could do was to draw up drafts for regulations and send these to the Governor-General-In-Council together with the reasons for proposing these.

There were, however, certain limitations on the power of the Governor-General-in-Council to make the regulations. He could not make regulations affecting any past, present or future Acts of Parliament. The previous sanction of the Directors was necessary to empower any non-chartered court to sentence of European British subject to death. All regulations made by the Governor-General-in-Council were subject to disallowance by the Court of Directors acting under Board of Control.

(e) A fifth member, the Law Member, was added to Governor General's Council. While the other three members were to be covenanted servants of the Company of at least ten years' service, the Law Member could be a non-covenanted employee. He was not to attend or vote in the Council, except at meetings for making laws and regulations. He was to devote his whole time to the work of law-making. There were to be Governor-General three members for making laws but Governor-General and two members were to carry on executive' work. Herein lay the faint beginnings of distinction between Legislative and Executive Councils.

(f) The old licence system for the coming of the British European subjects to India was abolished.

(g) There were to be bishops at Culcutta, Bombay and Madras. The Bishop was Calcutta at to be the Metropolitan Bishop of India.

(h) The Act threw open Government services to all irrespective of religion, place of birth, descent or colour. Fitness was to be the sole criterion of eligibility.

Merits. The Charter Act of 1833 had the following important merits:

(1) It tightened the control of the Central Government over the Presidencies of Bombay and Madra's. It brought about centralisation in place of too much of local autonomy.

(2) The Governor-General-in-Council was to make regulations for the whole of India and it made uniformity in legislation possible.

(3) The codification of laws proved a blessing for the people.

(4) The Act contained the faint beginnings of the separation of the Legislative and the Executive work of the Governer General's Council.

(5) Services were thrown open to all irrespective of caste, creed and colour.

Demerits. The Act had a few demerits also. There were the following:

(1) The Presidency Governments lost all legislative powers. The Act introduced over-centralisation.

(2) The services were thrown open to the Indians but the standards were not within their easy reach.

SIGNIFICANCE OF THE ACT

The Charter Act of 1833 is regarded to be the most important Act enacted by the Parliament. It introduced far reaching changes in the Government of India. Lord Morley has described it the 'most important Act passed by the Parliament till 1906'. The other Acts sink into insignificance when compared with it. It contained humanitarian principles, lofty motives and noble ideals.

The Charter Act of 1813 simply threw open the trade with India to the British subjects. But it did not introduce any changes in the old constitution. The Charter Act of 1853 also merely simplified the administration of India. The provisions of the Charter Act of 1858 simply transferred the Company's Government to the Crown. But the Charter Act of 1833 made certain important changes in the

Government of India. It was this Act which declared "No native of India shall by reason of his religion, place of birth , descent or colour be disabled from holding any office under the Company". This declaration found appreciation in various quarters. Ramsay Muir described it as an 'unparalleled declaration which a ruling class can announce in regard to its recently conquered subjects'. Macaulay styled it as a wise, benevolent and noble clause of the Act.

But this clause of the Act was more an assurance than a reality. According to Prof. Sri Ram Sharma, "It was grandiose gesture worthy of the first reformed Parliament." But the actual progress towards the declared policy was 'heart-breakingly slow and insipid.' According to Dr. Ishwari Prasad "the declaration was more honoured in the breach than in the observance by those who were entrusted with the governance of India."

The Charter Act of 1833 in also significant in so far as it marked beginning of the Indian legislature.

The Act also abolished Company's monoply of tea trade and trade with China. It was deprived of all its commercial privileges which were left to it by the Charter Act of 1813.

The huge ingress of Europeans in India while on the one hand brought Indians into closer contacts with the Europeans, which contributed to their general improvement and prosperity, on the other hand the Europeans also exploited the Indian masses.

Besides due to this Act Indian Penal Code and the Codes of Civil and Criminal Procedure came into existence.

This Act was also a definite step towards the unification of British possessions in India and the establishment of a strong Central Government in this country.

Circumstances

The crities of the Company opposed the renewal of the Charter on the ground that the governance of a big country like India should not be in the hands of a trading company. Mill pleaded for the renewal of the Charter on two grounds. Firstly, the Company, and not the English Government, possessed the knowledge of Indian affairs, Secondly, the patronage of India would be used by the party in power in England. The Charter was renewed by the Parliament.

CHARTER ACT OF 1853

I. The Charter Act of 1853 was the last of its kind. Five years later the crown assumed the sovereignty over Indian possessions directly.

II. Factors Leading to the Charter. The following factors led to the passage of the charter:

(1) The Act of 1833 had placed the Presidencies under the Governor-General-in-Council, thus depriving ,them of their independence which they clamoured to obtain again.

(2) The Charter Act of 1833 had thrown open jobs to the Indians but the new policy was honoured more in form than in spirit. The Indians got no jobs other than the categories of jobs held by them before 1833. Punniah has rightly remarked that this clause "remained for long in the tantalising realm of unfulfilled aspiration." It gave legitimate cause of grievance to many Indians.

(3) There was also an ever growing demand that the dual government at Home should he abolished; as the Court of Directors had lived their purpose, and this institution coupled with the authority of the Board of Control made the handling of the Indian problems only more difficult, involving unnecessary delay and expenditure. An application to this effect was actually received from the Indian Presidencies which demanded the appointment of a Secretary of State with an Indian Council to handle of business.

III. Provisions of the Act, 1853

(A) Changes in the Company. (1) The Charter of 1853 was renewed and the Company was allowed retain the Government of

British India in trust for Her Majesty. No definite terms of years was fixed for the continence of the Company. Formerly each Charter was reviewed for twenty years but this time Parliament was left free to assume control of Indian Affairs for any time it liked.

(2) The number of Directors was reduced from 24 to 18, six of whom were to be appointed by the Crown.

(3) The necessary quorum for the Court of Directors was also reduced from 13 to 10 so as to ensure the Company's control by the Board of Control.

(4) The patronage of the Court of Directors was taken away. In future, vacancies were to be filled up by competitive examination. A committee was appointed in 1854 with Lord Macaulay as President for that purpose.

(5) The salary of the President of the Board of Control was not to be less than that of a Secretary of State.

(B) Changes in India

(1) The Act created for the first time a separate Legislative Council for India. This Council was to consists of 12 members *viz.* the Governor-General, the Commander-in-Chief, 4 members of the Governor-Generals Council and 6 additional members or legislative councillor. The six legislative councillors were to be chief justice of Bengal, one judge of the Calcutta Supreme Court and four Civil servants with two years standing appointed one each by the Governments of Bengal, Madras, Bombay and the N.W.P. (Agra). The judges were appointed to strengthen legal element in the Legislative Council.

(2) A Separate Lieutenant-Governor was appointed for the administration of Bengal.

(3) The Law Commission appointed under the provisions of the 1833 Act had come to an end. The Act authorised the Crown to establish a Law Commission in England to examine and put into shape the reports made by the Indian Law Commission and to recommend the necessary legislation.

(4) To manage the newly acquired territories in India, the Court of Directors were empowered to constitute a new Presidency, or the alter the boundaries of the existing ones. This enabled the Punjab to be created into a separate Lieutenant Governorship.

IV. Significance of the Act. (1) The Charter Act of 1853 is of great importance. It gave indications of the fact that the Company's rule would not last long time. The Charter was not reviewed for a definite period. The Company was to hold the territory as trust for his Majesty till parliament should direct otherwise. The Act was a compromise between two conflicting views. Those who favoured the retention of the Company's territorial authority was satisfied by the provision that the Company should continue to govern in trust for the Crown until Parliament should otherwise direct. Those who wanted the substitution of Crown control for that of the Company found to their satisfaction that the number of Directors was rereduced to 18 of whome 6 were to be nominees of the Crown and that the quorum was fixed at 10 so that when the meetings of the Court were thinly attended, the nominees of the Crown were able to have a majority. The directors lost their patronage.

(2) The Position and prestige of the President of the Board of Control were enhanced. Regarding emoluments, he was to enjoy a status equal to that of any principal Secretary of State and therefore his office now became one of the most conveted offices of the Government.

(3) Nor was the establishment of the principle of legislative power separate from the execution less significant. Legislation in this Act, commented the Montford report, "Was, for the first time, treated as a special function of the government requiring special machinery and special process. Under this Act, as Cowell remarked," Discussion became oral instead of in writing, bills were referred to Select committees instead of a single member, and legislative business was conducted in public instead of in secret." In short, a beginning of the parliamentary system was made.

(4) This Act acquired much significance by affecting complete codification of all the Civil and Criminal laws. This measure broughts uniformity in the country's legal system.

V. Main Defects in Act. (1) The Governor-General's Legislative Council did not represent Indian opinion and as such it violated the fundamental principle the laws must be made by those who were affected by them.

(2) The Councils of Madras and Bombay were left without any significant powers. They were not allowed to function independently even in their own respective spheres.

GOVT. OF INDIA ACT OF 1858

The rule of the English East India Company came to an end in 1858 by Government of India Act of 1858. There were several factors responsible for the passing of this Act.

Circumstances Leading to the Passing of the Act

(a) The dual system of Government established by the Pitt's India Act of 1784 was defective. There were frequent bickerings between the Board of Control and the Court of Directors. These caused delays in arriving at decisions and hampered efficiency. In July 1857 even Lord Palmerston had represented to the Queen about inconveniences caused by the system of double Government.

(b) The Charter Acts had also been preparing the ground for the change. The Parliament in these Acts had been laying emphasis on the Company's position as a trustee for the Crown. This was clearly stressed by the Charter Act of 1853 which stated that the Company was to hold Indian territories as a trust for Her Majesty until the Parliament should direct otherwise.

(c) The Mutiny of 1857 totally discredited the Company, the Act of 1858 was passed by the British Parliament.

(d) A feeling had developed among the British people and British Parliament that it was an anachronism to leave India in the hands of a trading company. The Queen was herself of the same opinion.

Provisions

(a) The Board of Control and the Court of Proprietors were abolished. Their powers were transferred to the Secretary of State for India and his Council.

(b) The territories of India were transferred from the Company to the Crown. The Governor-General of India was also to be called Viceroy. The armed forces of the Company were transferred to the Crown. Its employees became the employees of the Crown.

(c) The Secretary of State for India was to have the power of superintendence, direction and control over the Indian affairs. He was to be a member of Parliament and was to be assisted by a Parliamentary Under-Secretary. He was a member of the British Cabinet but his salary and allowances were chargeable on the Indian revenues.

(d) The strength of the India Council was fixed at fifteen. Seven out of these were to be elected by the Court of Directors in the first instance and afterwards were to be elected by the Council itself. The remaining eight were to be nominated by the Crown. They were to hold office during good behaviour but the Act of 1869 fixed their term at ten years and it could be renewed, if the Secretary of State for India liked. The members must have lived in India for ten years and must not have left the country more than ten years before the date of appointment.

(e) The Secretary of State for India was declared a corporate body who could sue and could be sued in India as well as in England.

(f) The Secretary of State for India was given the power of sending to and receiving secret messages and despatches from Governor-General and was not expected to communicate these to the India Council.

(g) The Secretary of State for India was to preside at the meetings of the India Council. He had a vote and a casting vote in case of a tie. He could override the Council by giving reasons but was bound by its advice in matters of services and the appropriations of Indian revenues. The members of the Councils of the Governor-General and of the Governors were to be appointed by the India Council.

(h) The Parliament got control over Indian affairs. Its members could ask questions from the Secretary of State regarding Indian administration. The whole of Indian administration could be discussed at the time of submitting report on Indian revenues to the British Parliament.

(i) The assumption of the Government of India by the Crown was to be announced to the princes and the people of India by Queen's Proclamation. The Queen's Proclamation was read at a Durbar held at Allahabad by Lord Canning, the first Viceroy of India. The territories of India were declared to have passed on to the British Crown. The civil and, military employees of the Company now automatically became the employees of the Crown. All treaties and agreements made by the East India Company with the Indian rulers were to be honoured by the Crown. The policy of Lapse and Annexation was discarded and the ruling princes were assured that their States would not be annexed. Their rights and dignity were to be maintained. There was to be no interference in the religion and the religious usages of the Indians. Equality before law was proclaimed.

The Government of India Act of 1858 has great significance in the history of modern India in many ways.

(a) The Act ended the dual system of government established by the Pitt's India Act in 1784. Voices had frequently been raised against this system but the final discrediting blow was given by the Mutiny of 1857.

(b) The territories of India were transferred to the Crown. According to G.N. Singh, the Act closed one great period of Indian history and ushered in another great era—the era of direct rule of the Crown. Marshman is of the opinion that the Act transferred from the Company to the Crown an empire more magnificent than that of Rome.

(c) The control of Secretary of State for India and his India Council increased over Indian administration. This increased control was due to several factors. Firstly, the Secretaries of State were generally abler than the President of the Board of Control. Secondly, the Act gave many powers of control over Indian administration to the Secretary of State and his Council. Thirdly, means of communication had improved and it was possible to send instructions quickly from England to India.

(d) A new policy was inaugurated towards the Indian States. The Policy of Lapse and Annexation was discarded. 'The policy of Subordinate Isolation was replaced by the policy of Subordinate Union.

(e) The Act had its dark side also. The control of the Secretary of State and his India Council was frequently bureaucratic in nature. Secondly, payment to the Secretary of State and India Council remained a burden on the Indian Exchequer till the inauguration of the Reforms of 1919.

Sir H.C. Cunningham was of the opinion that the assumption of the Government of India by the Crown was "rather a formal than a substantial change the power had already passed from the hands of the Directors to the Board of Control. The Court of Directors had already been reduced more or less to the position of an advisory body of the Board of Control, though it had enjoyed some powers of initiation. This position of the Court of Directors had further been weakened by the Charter Act of 1833. It had deprived them of patronage, the number of Directors was reduced from 24 to 18. Out of the members, 6 were to be appointed by the Crown. The Charter was renewed not for 20 years but till the Parliament directed otherwise. Thus the Charter Act of 1853 prepared the ground for the transference of Indian territories from the Company to the Crown. The act of 1858 completed this process.

INDIAN COUNCILS ACT 1861

The Indian Councils Act of 1861 was the first Act which made constitutional changes in India after the transference of territory from the Company to the Crown. Several factors necessitated the passing of the Act:

(a) The Government itself was feeling dissatisfied with the working of the Legislative Council. It had adopted all the formalities of the legislative procedure. It was impeding business and causing .delays by its long discussions. It was causing great inconvenience to the Government by demanding information on matters which could not be disclosed. It was showing too much of independence by non-compliance with the wishes of the home authorities to make certain enactments.

(b) The existing legislative arrangement in India was defective. The Legislative Council of Governor-General had to legislate for the whole of India. The Legislative centralisation had been introduced by the Charter Act of 1833 but it had proved highly defective. It was not possible for the Central Government to know about the conditions and needs of the Presidencies in detail. It was to remove this defect that the Charter Act of 1853 had laid down that the Government of each Presidency and Province was to nominate one member to the Legislative Council of the Governor-General. This was definitely an improvement but even this was not a satisfactory solution of the problem.

(c) It was said that non-association of Indians with the work of Government had been one of the causes of the upheaval of 1857. Loyalists like Sir Syed Ahmad pointed out in 1858 that the outbreak of the previous year would not have occurred if the natives had been associated with the legislative work. Under the existing system, it was not possible for the Government to know about the desirability or otherwise of passing any law.

(d) The Government began to feel the need of non-official advice on legislative matters after the Mutiny. The rising had put an end to sympathy and goodwill between the officials and the people. The growing exclusiveness made it still more difficult for the Government to know about the feelings and opinions of the people.

Provisions

(a) The Executive Council of the Governor-General was enlarged by the addition of a fifth member. It was now to Council of Governor-General and four other members.

(b) Legislative Councils were re-established for Madras, Bombay and Bengal.

(c) Governor-General in Council was empowered in his discretion to establish similar councils for North-West Province and the Punjab. These two bodies were created in 1886 and 1897 respectively.

(d) The members, in case of Provincial Councils, were to be nominated by the Governor, subject to the approval of the Governor-General. At least half of these members were to be non-officials.

(e) Governor-General's Legislative Council was expanded for purposes of making laws and regulations by the addition of not less than six and not more than twelve members. At least half of these were to be non-officials.

(f) The powers of the Legislative Councils were strictly limited to legislation. No motion was to be introduced or entertained by the Council, unless it was for leave to introduce a measure or had reference to some measure already introduced in it.

(g) All previous rules and regulations made in the executive capacity by the Governor-General-in-Council or by Governor-in Council in executive capacity were to be enforced as laws.

(h) The need for emergency legislation had been left during the Mutiny. This Act empowered the Governor-General, in case of emergency, to issue ordinances for the peace and good government of British India or any part of it. It was to have the force of-law for a period of six months, unless disallowed earlier by Her Majesty or superseded by an Act of legislature.

(i) Every bill passed by Governor-General's Legislative Council required his assent to become an Act. All measures passed by the

Legislative Council of a Presidency or a province required the assent of the Governor and the subsequent assent of the Governor-General. Any Act passed by any legislature in India could be subsequently disallowed by Her Majesty acting through the Secretary of State-in-Council.

Merits and Demerits

The Indian Councils Act of 1861 is very important in the constitutional history of India. It had following merits and demerits:

(a) The Indians were associated with the legislative work, though the persons nominated were princes, diwans and big landlords.

(b) It furnished a complete framework of governmental structure which, with some changes lasted till the end of British rule in India.

(c) Legislative powers were restored in case of Bombay and Madras. Thus it was a return to the system of legislative devolution. G.N. Singh has rightly remarked, "The Indian Councils Act, 1861, is important in the constitutional history of India for two reasons. Firstly, it enabled the Governor-General to associate the people of the land with the work of legislation, and secondly by vesting legislative powers in the Government of Bombay and Madras and by making provision for the institution of similar legislative councils in other provinces, it laid the foundations of the policy of legislative devolution which resulted in the grant of almost complete internal autonomy to the provinces in 1937.

❐

10

Revolt of 1857

British historians have only considered it as a "Sepoy Mutiny," they consider its immediate cause the greased cartridges only. Some other foreign historians hold it to be a "Muslim Conspiracy" against the British and its aim was to re-establish the Mughal Empire under the leadership of Bahadur Shah Zafar. The opinion of some historians is that it was feudal in nature because by means of this revolt all those discontented native rulers and landlords wanted to regain their jagirs and pensions which the various governor-generals had confiscated. But according to majority of Indian historians this was the first war of independence or first national movement. He is a brief review of each opinion is presented below:

First View. Sir John Lawrence, Marshman, Seelay and many other European historians are of the view that it was military rising which was triggered by the use of the greased cartridges. According to them the Indian soldiers attempted to uproot the established English Government in India by revolting against it. A few native rulers also supported them but it were only those who were deprived of their kingdoms by Lord Dalhousie. The rebels however, did not get any support from the Indian Civil population.

To substantiate their opinion they put forward several arguments which are as follows:

(1) It is stated that the revolt was restricted only to Northern India and most of the remaining country remained unaffected. Even in the North several states including the Punjab stood aloof. Therefore, such a revolt that was confined to quite a small part of the country, could not be called a National Rising.

(2) Only a few Europen troops were sufficient to suppress this revolt. It is enough to prove that the Indian people were not moved by the sentiments of freedom or nationalism.

(3) Except a few rulers like Bahadur Shah II, Nana Sahib and Laxmi Bai, the Rani of Jhansi etc. no other Indian rulers took part in the revolt.

(4) The common people and the peasants remained wholly peaceful and did not take part in the revolt in large numbers.

(5) The revolt was confined to the few urban areas without its echo being heard in the villages.

But the contention of John Lawrence and Seelay is not accepted by the majority of the historians. They argue that the revolt was started by the Indian Sepoys. But not all were a party to it. Many Sepoys fought from the side of the English. Further, the rebels could enlist the support of a large section of Indian civilian population.

Second View. Since scholars do not accept the view expressed above. Some writers are of the view that the revolt of 1857 was in fact the Hindu-Muslim conspiracy to replace to British Government by national one. This view is supported by General Outram who says, "the great rebellion was the outcome of Muhammadan conspiracy making out capital of the Hindu grievances. The cartridge incident merely precipitated the mutiny before it had been throughly organised and before adequate arrangements had been made for making the mutiny the first step towards the popular insurrection." It was in accordance with a carefully prepared plan that Bahadur Shah Zafar was declared the Emperor of India. We will have to accept the fact that Bahadur Shah was a strong pillar of the revolution even though in the earlier stages he showed a little slackness. Bahadur Shah's indifference in the beginning was a political trick which he wanted to play upon the English through which he wanted to trap them. The feeling of nationalism developed among the Indian quite later. Secondly, there is no evidence to show that there was a deep rooted Hindu-Muslim conspiracy on national lines to replace the British Government by a national One. As remarked by P.E. Roberts;

"Fortunately for British dominion in India there was no single national cause to which the agitators could appear."

Third View. As per the opinion of Mr. L.E.R. Reese that it was a religious war against the Christians' is also not accepted by the majority of the historians. One of the causes of the revolt was certainly religious. But the Indians revolted not to uproot Christianity but to defend their religion. And afterwards, the rebels forgot their religious motive. Besides, a large number of Hindu and Muslim sepoys fought under the command of the English.

Fourth View. As per the views of some historians it was a revolt against the British only by those discontented native rulers and nawabs whose territory, jagirs, pensions or allowances had been taken away by Dalhousie or other British Governor-Generals. But those scholars who do not subscribe to this view say that neither all discontented feudal elements nor all the rulers had taken part in this revolt. For example, many of the Jagirdars in Punjab had to become victim of British ambitious but some of them lend their support to the rebels. Likewise, the jagirdards of Rajputana and South India did not join the mutiny. Secondly, in this revolt many of the peasants participated who could not have had to much sympathy with the feudal lords that they jumped in the conflict to get back the lost insterests of the feudal lords.

Fifth View. As per the views of some English historians the revolt of 1857 was a racial struggle for supremacy between the Black and the White. But nowadays this view is also not accepted. Certainly all whites were on one side but all the Blacks were not on the other side. Many blacks fought from the side of the British. To be more correct, it was a war between the Black rebels on one side and the White rulers supported by other Blacks on the other side.

Sixth View. Some English historians led by T.R. Holmes described the revolt as a conflict between civilisation and barbarism. But this view is also wrong. The atrocities were committed both by the English and the Indians against each other during the period of the revolt.

Seventh View. A majority of Indian historians are of the view that the Mutiny was a war of Indian national independence. Vir Savarkar, Ashok Mehta, Pt. Jawahar Lal Nehru, Shri Jai Chandra Vidyalankar all hold the view that the Mutiny was a war of Indian national independence. Pt. Jawahar Lal Nehru writes :" It was much more than a military mutiny, and it spread rapidly and assumed the charecter of a popular rebellion and a war of Indian independence." The letter which was written by Emperor Bahadur Shah to the Rajput chiefs of Rajputana clearly proves this fact. Bahadur Shah had written in that letter, "It is my hearty wish that the Frank should be turned out of India and the whole of India should be freed of foreigners and become an independent country. But the war which is being waged to achieve success in that aim cannot be won so long as there does not appear on the scene such a worthy and talented man who may lead the revolution, gather together all the people, organise them and conduct the war under his able direct. If all the India chiefs make a determined bid to drive the English out of Indian then I am fully prepared to hand over all my royal power and authority to any of the concord of the Indian rulers which may be formed."

Among modern Indian historians, Dr. Tara Chand in his book 'History of Freedom Movement in India' has described it as a war for national independence. Dr. Bisheshwar Prasad had adhered to these views. He writes: The end of alien rule was the essential object, the chief purpose and in this sense the revolt of 1857 may be termed a national war for freedom, though the sentiment of nationalism in the modern sense had not taken deep roots in the soil of India at that moment." These Indian authors have written volumes to support their view that the great Rising of 1857 was the First War of Indian Independence. They say that:

(1) This revolt could not spread so rapidly if it had not been supported by the people.

(2) Both the Hindus and the Muslims took part in this revolt unitedly moved by national sentiments that they had buried their religious differences.

(3) The women, too, took part in this revolution on a wide scale. Some of them even wore men's uniforms to fight in this war. Therefore this 'Rising' was no merely a Sepoy Mutiny.

(4) Quite a large number of common people took part in this revolt and supported whole-heartedly the soldires who were determined to throwout the English. Who can forget the sacrifice of that Indian boatman who refused to ferry General Havelock and his troops across the river.

(5) The English annexed several of the native states on the accusation that their rulers were pleasure seekers incapable of ruling their states. Had such an accusation been true people would never have supported Bahadur Shah or Nana Sahib.

According to some critics, this revolt did have a few such factors that disprove it to be a national war. Firstly, this revolt was confired to a limited part of the country. Secondly, a national was anticipates wholesome participation of all the people of the land. But a large number of people even in those parts, where it spread, remained aloof. Thirdly, it is also maintained that if it were a National Rising it could not have been suppressed so easily.

We can very well conclude that. It was neither wholly a war of National Independence nor merely a mutiny' revolt. Recently two distinguished Indian historians Dr. R.C. Majumdar and Dr. S.N. Sen, have made an exhaustive study of all available records, official as well as non-official. The two scholars differ in their interpretation of the events of 1857-58. Both the scholars, however, agree that the uprising of 1857 was not the result of careful planning nor was there any master-minds behind it. The mere fact that Nana Sahib went to Lucknow and Ambala in March-April 1857 and the struggle started in May the same year cannot be regarded as evidence that he planned it. The view that Munshi Azim Ullah Khan and Rango Bapuji prepared the plans for the uprising is unternable. Azim Ullah Khan had gone to London to plead before the Court of Directors the right of Nana Sahib for the pension paid to Baji Rao II. On his way back he visited Turkey and met Omar Pasha on the battle field of Crimea. Rango Bapuji was sent to London to secure the rendition of Satara. The fact that both had been London on missions cannot be regarded as pointing to their participation in the conspiracy. Even the story of the circulation of messages through chapatis or lotus flowers does not prove anything. No leader of the revolt said anything at any place and at any time which could justify that they were inspired by national spirit.

Yet, Dr. Sen contends that even in the absence of national feelings among the Indians, the revolt was a war of independence. He argues that in every revolution it is only the minor it which is active with or without the popular support. It was the case with the American War of Independence and the French Revolution. The same was the case with Indians during the period of the revolt. Many Indians did not participate in it and many others actively supported the English. Therefore, the revolt cannot be accepted as a national rising. Yet, it was a war of Indian independence because both the soldiers and citizens, though only a minority among them, tried to turn out the English from India.

CAUSES OF THE GREAT REBELLION OF 1857

While writing about the Rebellion of 1857, the English historians have attributed this Rebellion to the use of greased cartridge and other things which created discontentment amongst the Indian soldiers against the British Government. But the fact is that the causes of the Great Mutiny of 1857 were deep-rooted. They are to be found in those hundred years of British rule in India to which the greased cartridges were the proverbial ignition which set the whole mine ablaze. The Revolt of 1857 was the revolt of a combination of political, economic and socio-religious causes. It was a semi-national and religious war which had for its object freedom from the English bondage and the establishment of the Mughal Empire with Emperor Bahadur Shah at the head although the latter objective was not so common as the former. Following were the causes of the revolt:

(1) Economic and Administrative Reasons

(a) Economic Unrest After the Annexation of the Native States. The annexation of native Indian states produced very serious and fatal economic and social consequences for the East India Company. The Indian aristocrates who once enjoyed privileges, both economic and social, were now deprived of such privileges by the annexation policy of the East India Company. In the new administrative machinery that was set up, they lost all hope of regaining their old influence and privileges because almost all the jobs, both in civil as well as in military departments, were kept reserved for the English people to the exclusion of the Indians. The highest rank that an Indian could get in the army department was that of a Subedar, whose monthly salary did not exceed Rs. 60 or Rs. 70, and, similarly, the highest job that an Indian could get in the civil department was that of the Amin, whose monthly pay did not exceed Rs. 50. Consequently, all the chances for the promotion of the Indians were very much limited. The Indians developed a sort of conception that it was a deliberate policy of the part of the Britishers to reduce them to the position of the hewers of saw and the drawers of water. Under these circumstances, the resentment of the Indians burst for the in the form of the Mutiny. Apart from administrative handicaps from which the Indians suffered, there was also the economic exploitation of the Indians by the East Indian Company. "The political changes prior to the advent of the British, the rise and fall of Empires in Delhi, had little or no effect upon the economic structure and life of the people. The reason for this was that the wealth remained in the country, and whatever power ruled in Delhi, it had no sympathies beyond the boundaries of India. With the English, however, it was different. Indian wealth flew out of the country. Indian economy began to be fashioned to meet the needs of Industrial England. With the Industrial Revolution of the early 19th century, England ceased to be

a mere commercial nation and was transformed into a manufactory of the world. Raw material for her factories and markets for her finished goods became England's prime needs. British policy in India was developed to meet those needs. The once famous Indian industry died of English competition and neglect; the burden on agriculture increased; and India became a land exporting raw materials and importing finished goods. English capital flowed into the country and as it carried away both interest and profits, the results were ruinous, India became a milch cow to feed England while her own sons were gradually pushed to the starvation wage."

(b) ***Hatred of the English People Towards the Indians.*** The recial distinction between the two communities living in India, *i.e.*, the English and the Indians was also getting wider day by day with all its bickerings and jealousies attendant upon it, in the minds of both of them. The British officers living in India were considering themselves as next to God and, as such, had developed a sort of hatred for the Indians. They considered the Indians as their social inferiors and behaved towards them in an autocratic and insolent way. They called the Indians as "Black people" and, sometimes, used bad names, like "swine", the word whose utterance could not be tolerated especially by the Muslims of India. Even, some of the wise British officers like Bird and Thompson were hurling disgrace after disgrace upon the Indians. While advocating the cause of the Indians for their recruitment in Indian administration. There is no doubt that the Charter Act of 1833 had provided for the absorption of Indians in the administration. But this provision of the Charter remained unimplemented for a long time to come. This thing also created a very bad feeling in the minds of the Indians and, consequently, formed one of the causes for the Mutiny.

(e) ***New Land Revenue System.*** The administrative system of the East India Company was most defective and full of flaws. Their land revenue system was very unpopular amongst newly conquered states and as such, troops had to be sent with view to the collection of land revenue in them. For instance, for the purpose of land revenue collection in the district of Panipat, 136 horsemen were stationed, whereas for police action the stationing of 20 policemen was sufficient. It is said that on the outbreak of the Mutiny, Sir Henry Lawrence had openly said, "It is Jackson, John Lawrence, Thompson, and Admonston, who had brought India to such a pitch." By the introduction of new land revenue system in the newly-acquired states, the English administrators had brought the peasants as well as the British Government into direct contact with one another, thus eliminating the middlemen between the two parties. In this way, the great Talukdars and Zamindars, who used to collect land revenue before that, were deprived of their income as well as their position. These who enjoyed freeships of land were required to submit to the Government the letters of grant given to them in order to prove the validity of their proprietary rights in that land. But those who failed to produce there documentary proof to prove their proprietary rights, were deprived of their proprietary rights. The big jagirs were confiscated and were sold to the highest bidders. These lands were purchased by speculators who had absolutely no sympathy for the peasants and who, consequently, fleeced the peasants to their hearts' content. The policy of Jackson of turning out the Indian soldiers from the army and the strict insistence of the British Government demanding the documentary proof to prove their proprietary rights in the soil made Oudh the center of rebellion against the Britishers. The newly introduced land revenue system in the newly-acquired territories reduced the aristocratic families to an adject poverty, but this measure did not improve the economic position of the peasants, because they were still groaning under the yoke of exorbitant land revenue and other taxes levied upon them. The peasants for whose benefit the land revenue system was introduced, were very slow in giving up the old method. They had fallen a victim into the hands of unscrupulous money-lenders. These peasants used to go to their old Zamindars and, with tears in their eyes, would move their sentiments by expressing their sympathies on the helplessness to which they were reduced by the English. This created a great bitterness in the minds of the Zamindars against the East India Company. The greatest blow that anybody sustained from the new land revenue system was the group of Talukdars and Zamindars of Oudh who were deprived of half of their lands as jagirs. Still, there were many Zamindars who were deprived of all of their lands. The cruelty which the East India Company practised with reference to the Talukdars and the Zamindars is clear from the fact that the villages which enjoyed freeship in land revenue for the Lakshmi Temple of Jhansi, were again subjected to the contribution of land revenue. This could not be tolerated by the Hindu population and the Zamindars and the Talukdars. They later on became the leaders of the revolt.

(d) ***Defective Judicial System.*** The East India Company was feeling boastful that they had introduced and were acting upon the principle of equality amongst the citizens in the judicial administration in India. However, it was found that the principle of civil equality was not applied to Europeans. Also, when a peasant to happened to go to a Court of Law against a Zamindar, the Zamindar had to present himself before the Court and, sometimes, he was sent to jail also. Sometimes, the decisions of the cases pending in the Court took an unduly long time to be decided and justice had become very expensive. The Indians thought that it was a deliberate attempt on the part of the English to reduce the Indians to poverty and humiliation. On the other hand, the Courts had become instruments of tyranny and oppression in the hands of clever and rich people, because the latter could manage to produce false evidence to prove false cases. When the system of flogging for civil offences was abolished, periods of imprisonment were substituted for them. These were not approved of by the people. Hence it resulted in a lot of discontent against the Britishers and, as such, formed another cause of the Great Mutiny.

II. Political Reasons

(a) ***Political Corruption.*** In addition, common people were hard hit by the prevalence of corruption at the lower levels of administration. The police, petty officials, and lower law-courts were notouriously corrupt. William Edward, British official, wrote in 1859 while discussing the causes of the Revolt that the police were "a sourage to the people" and that "their oppersions and exactions formed one of the chief grounds of dissatisfaction with our government". The petty officials lost no opportunity of enriching themselves at the cost of the royots and zamindars.

(b) ***Alien Nature.*** Another basic cause of the unpopularity of British rule was its very foreigness. The British remained perpetual foreigners in the country. For one, there was no social think or communication between them and the Indians. Unlike foreign conquerors before them, they did not mix socially even with the upper classes or Indians, instead they had a feeling of racial superiority and treated Indians with contempt and arrogance. As Sir Sayyid Ahmed Khan wrote later:" Even natives of the highest rank never came into the presence of officials but with and inward fear an trembling." Most of all, the English did not come to settle in India and make it their home. Their main aim was to enrich themselves and then go back to Britain alongwith their wealth. The people of India were aware of this basically foreign character of the new rulers.

(c) ***Imperialist Policy of the English.*** The English wanted to expand their empire in India. They followed the policy of

Imperialism and Dalhouise propounded a new policy to achieve this aim. He introduced the policy of Doctrine of Lapse. Those rulers who had no issue used to adopt someone as their son and successor. Lord Dalhousie refused to acknowledge them and annexed their states into the British Empire. This created great dissatisfaction among the Indian rulers. This enraged the Marathas, Nawab of Avadh, Rani Laxmi Bai etc. Those states which were left untouched were afraid that their states would be annexed any moment. Thus due to unjust policy of Lord Dalhousie there was such a great dissatisfaction that at last it burst out in the shape of the revolt of 1857 A.D.

(d) ***Discontent Amongst Indian Rulers.*** The expansionist policies of the British Governors general, Lord Wellesley and Lord Dalhousie, gave rise to discontent amongst the older rulers of India. Whatever treaties the British officials made used to twist them into whatever way liked. The annexation of Avadh by Lord Dalhousie in 1856 was widely resented in India in general and in Avadh in particular. More specifically it created an atmosphere of rebellion in Avadh and in the company's army. The sepoys possess regional and local patriotism and did not like that their home-land should come the foreigner's sway.

The annexation of Avadh, along with the other annexations of Dalhousie created panic among rulers of the native states. They now discovered that their most grovelling loyalty to the British had failed to satisfy the British greed for territory. The big state of Nagpur was declared lapsed. The Punjab was annexed, and Satara Jhansi, Sambhalpur and other went the same way. The titles and pensions of Nana Saheb, the adopted son of Peshwa Baji Rao II, of the Nawab of Carnatic and of Tanjore, were swept away. Fuel was added to the fire of discontentment as a result of the utterness of some irresponsible officers like Sir Charles Napier, who declared: "Were I the Emperor of India for twelve years, no Indian prince should exist. The Nizam should be no more heard of Nepal would be ours." What is of even greater importance, the political prestige of the British suffered a great deal because of the manner in which they had repeatedly broken their written and oral pledges and treaties with the Indian powers and reduced them to subordination while pretending and claiming to be their friends and protectors.

(e) ***Certain Political Events Effect.*** The period of the growth of discontent among the people coincided with certain political events which shattered the general belief in the invincibility of British arms and encouraged the people to believe that the days of the British regime were numbered. The British army suffered major reverses in the First Afghan War (1838-42), and the Punjab Wars (1845-49) and the Crimean War (1854-56). In 1855-56 the Santhal tribes men of Bihar and Bengal rose up armed with axes and bows and arrows and revealed the potentialities of a popular uprising by temporarily sweeping away British rule from their area. Though the British ultimately won these wars and supressed the Santhal uprising: the disasters they suffered in major battles revealed that the British army could be defeated by determined fighting, even by an Asian Army.

(f) ***Policy of Racial Arrogance and Discrimination.*** The British considered Indians as low and hatred them. They were not in favour of giving higher and high-paid posts to the Indians. In fact they excluded the Indians from all high civil and Inilitary jobs. In the army the highest post in the civil services for which an Indian could get was that of a Subedar while the hightest post in the civil services for which an Indian could qualify was that of a Sadaramin. It dissatisfied the educated Indians who expected to get gainful employment in the service of the company. These grievances were dilated upon by Sir Sayyid Ahmed Khan in 1860 A.D. who declared that the most important cause of the Mutiny had been the non-admittance of the Indians into the legislative and the administrative branches of the Government because of which it failed to understand the Indian grievances in time. The muslims were perhaps the most dissatisfied lot in this respect. They had till recently occupied almost all the important civil and military posts in the Government, and had been the most privileged community of this country. Their old position having vanished, they now started lagging behind the other communities.

(III) Religious Causes

(a) Englishmen, the Indians irritated the Indians, both the Hindus and the Muslims. It was easy for the Indians to tolerate political and administrative injustice but it was beyond their power to tolerate religious and spiritual injustice. The orthodox Hindus regarded the English as great iconoclast and feared that their own religion would be destroyed by Christianity. One of the chief aims of the English people in India seems to have been to convert the Indians to Christianity. Both the army and civil population were under the fear that the Government intended to make every Indian a Christian. Missionary activity was extended by the Englishmen to all parts of the country. On many occasions the meetings of the missionaries were held at the headquarters of the districts under the chairmanship of the Collectors. Once, Mr. Mangles, the Chairman of the Court of Directors of the East India Company, made the following statement in the House of Commons: "Providence has entrusted the extensive empire of Hindustan to England in order than the banner of Christ should wave triumphant from one end of India to the other. Everyone must exert all his strength that there may be no dilatoriness on any account in continuing in the country the grand work of making all Indians Christians." Major Edwards had openly

declared. "The conversion of all Indians to Christianity was the ultimate aim of our occupation of India." To the same effect wrote Rev. Kennedy, "whatever misfortune come on us, as long as our Empire in India continues, so long let us not forget that our chief work is the propagation of Christianity in the land until Hindustan from Cape Comorin to the Himalayas, embraces the religion of Christ and until it condemns the Hindu and Muslim religions, our efforts must continue persistently. Vir Savarkar has gone so far as to say that the military and civil officers of the East India Company used to abuse Ram and Mohammed and used to put pressure on the Indian citizens to embrace Christianity. The soldiers were tempted with the offer of promotions in case of their embracing Christianity. The Christian missionaries were given many privileges for their activities. American Missionary Society set up a big printing press at Agra and the books which it printed strongly condemned the idol worship, ridiculed the Hindu gods and goddesses, and called the Hindu superstitions as foolishness and ignorance. Thus English attempts at conversion of the people to Christianity were as systematic and sustained as their policy of territorial aggression. The Indians felt a great concern over the prohibition of Suttee and permission of widow remarriage because they considered these measures of the British East India Company as a direct challenge to their religion and society. Hence discontent against the British Government.

(b) ***Danger from the Englishmen to End Civilisation.*** In 1856 was passed the Religious Disabilities Act by the East India Company, according to which the Hindu law of property was changed with a view to facilitating the conversion of Hindus to Christianity. Formerly, a convert from Hinduism was not allowed to inherit his ancestral property, but this hurdle was now removed. The English made no secret of their intentions to convert the Hindus to Christianity when by this Act they declared that even on the conversion of a Hindu to Christianity, he could still inherit the property of his father. It was a strong rumour set afloat at the time in India that Lord Canning was specifically appointed as the Governor-General of India to convert the Indians to Christianity. In this inflammatory atmosphere, the introduction of the railways and the telegraph system was regarded by the Indians as an attempt to Europeanise them. The same suspicion was attached to the postal system. In the new schools, boys of all castes and religions sat together and this was considered to be an attempt to interfere with the religion of the people. The activity of the Christian missionaries and the introduction of female education amongst Indians by Dalhousie convinced them that under the pretext of introducing western system of education in India, the English were really trying to put an end to the Indian civilisation and culture. Dr. Ishwari Prasad says, "The English, happy in their ignorance of Indian philosophy, attempted to introduce Western notions of inheritance, marriage and succession and thereby consciously and unconsciously trampled upon the most sensitive portions of a Hindu's life. This was a great degradation and was the result of a well-settled policy. It has been a common belief of all imperialisms that to degrade the conquered, to disrupt their social system, to make them forget heir past, to impoverish them and then to lure them to the religion of the conqueror is a better guarantee of stability than mere military strength. In its application to Indian Society, however, the policy recoiled on its promoters. It stirred the people, brought back to them the reminiscences of their glorious past and cemented the causes of rebellion."

IV Military Causes

The revolt of 1857 'started with the military of company's sepoys. We have therefore to examine why the sepoys, who had by their devoted service enabled the company to conquer India, sudden by became rebellions. The following were the main military causes of the Mutiny of 1857:

(a) ***Loss of British Prestige in the First Afghan War.*** The defeat suffered by the English in the First Afghan War shattered the myth of the invincibility of the British arms. This defeat had quite an adverse effect on the Indian soldiers and they acquired the belief that the English were not invincible. It gave them courage to take arms against the English.

(b) ***The Indian Soldiers Indifferently Treated.*** The English did not give a good treatment to the Indian salaries. The soldiars and emoluments of the British soldiers were much higher than those of the Indian soldier. The higher posts in the army were exclusively reserved for the English and the Indians were not thought fit and competent for them. Due to these glaring examples of discrimination the Indian soldiers sometimes revolted.

(c) ***The Annexation of Avadh.*** The annexation of Avadh by Lord Dalhousie in 1856 was widely resented in India in general and in Avadh in particular. More specifically, it created an atmosphere of rebellion in Avadh and in the company's army. Dalhousie's action angered the Company's sepoys, most of whom came from Avadh. Lacking an all-India feeling, these sepoys had helped the British conquer the rest of India. But they did possess regional and local patriotism, and did not like that their homelands should come under the foreigner's sway. Moreover, the annexation of Avadh adversely affected the sepoy's purse. He had to pay higher taxes on the land his family held in Avadh.

(d) ***To Stop Foreign Allowance.*** When the Company's soldiers went to fight in other parts of India or in a foreign country, they were given additional allowance. After the war the conquered area was annexed to the Company's empire and" the additional allowance payable to the soldiers was stopped. A new instruction was issued according to which the allowance of the soldiers working in Sind and Punjab was discontinued.

(e) ***Rules.*** The contemporary military rules were based on the Western systems and the Indian soldiers hated these rules. For example, the Hindus could not have a Tilak on their forehead; could not wear caps not keep moustaches and beards. It was an affront on their religious feelings.

(f) ***Border Security.*** The Indian soldiers in the Company's employ were part of the broader society. They saw everywhere the discontentment prevailing against the corrupt economic, commercial and financial policies of the British. Like the other people even they had this feeling that the British were only exploiting India and were bent upon destroying their religion. Like the other sections of the society even they were dissatisfied with the British policies and activities.

(g) ***General Service Enlistment Act.*** The changes introduced by Lord Canning, the successor of Lord Dalhousie added fuel to the fire, The General Service Enlistment Act, that he passed spread a wave of indignation among the Indian soldiers, for now they could be sent to fight anywhere, in or outside the country. It confirmed their suspicion towards the intention of the British because, in that case, they were liable to undergo sea travelling which would have meant loss of their caste.

(h) ***Transference of Jobs.*** The morale of the army, especially of Bengal division, had deteriorated and discipline had become lax. The Company itself was largely responsible for this. Many able British officers had been transferred from regimental duties to civilians posts. Promotions were by seniority alone and many old officers, who had lost vigour, commanded the troops. General Godwin commanded the troops during the Second Burmese War at the age of seventy.

(i) ***Disparity in Soldiers.*** A large number of British soldiers were sent to Europe, Middle Asia and China in wars and hence the number of British soldiers in India had diminished considerably. Under such circumstances the Indian soldiers got the right opportunity for which they had been waiting for a long time.

V. Social Causes

Besides the political, economic and religious causes social causes as well spread discontentment and resentment among the people. A few of these causes are given below:

(a) ***Ill-Treatment of the Hindus.*** The English who belonged to the ruling class treated the Indian very contemptuously and sometimes crossed all limits of decency. They called Indians 'niggars' and swines' and humiliated them like anything. Whenever an Englishman appeared on the road every Indian had to stand up or bow to him. Undoubtedly the Indians resented such a practice.

(b) ***Discontent Because of the Social Reforms Carried on by the British.*** Lord William Bentinck and other Governor-generals passed Acts to remove many of the evils in India. They declared Sati system to be a legal offence. They gave consent to widow remarriage. Efforts were made to encourage the education of women like the West. Railways and other means of communications were started. The conservative people viewed these reforms of the British with suspicion. They thought that the British wanted put an end to our old institution like family, caste system and other social bonds. The conservative people therefore opposed these reforms: They made this propaganda among the people that the British were wanting to destroy Indian society.

(c) ***Lack of Social Relations and no Care for Social Status.*** The British did not maintain any social relations with the Indians in general: They even removed the Indians of aristrocratic families from high posts and had destroyed their social status and respect. This was, therefore, natural to create discontent among the Indians.

(d) ***No Due Place to Indian Literature and languages.*** Besides disregarding the Indian customs and traditions, the British did not give due place to Indian literature and languages. Instead of encouraging them, they tried to impose European literature and language upon the native inhabitants. This created a great discontent among the native inhabitants.

VI. Psychological Causes

A propesy had been made that the British rule would last for a century. The British had become masters of Bengal, Bihar and Orissa as a result of the battle of Plassey in 1757. One hundred years were to complete in 1857 and the people began to feel that the British rule in India would come to an end in that year. This created the psychological background for the rising of 1857. Moreover mischievous people wanted disturbances so that they could have an opportunity for plunder.

VII. Immediate Causes

The Greased Catridges. In 1856 the Government decided to replace the old fashioned musket, 'Brown Bess' by the 'Enfield rifle.' The training for the use of the new weapon was to be imparted at Dum Dum, Ambala and Sialkot. The loading process of the Enfield rifle involved bringing the cartridge to the mouth and biting off the top with mouth in January 1857 a stroy got currency in the Bengal regiments that the greased cartridges contained the fat of pig and cow. At once a denial was issued by the military authorities without investigating into the matter. Subsequent enquiries proved that "the fat of cowas or oxen realy had been used at Woolwich arsenal." (V.A. Smith). Assurances of superior officers and slight concessions proved of no avail. Thus both the Hindu and Muslim soldiers refused to use these catridges and when forced they broke out in open rebellion at several cantonments. They were presently joined by aggrieved princes, Zamindars and other people who bad been wronged at the hands of the British and thus they adjoined together to get rid of the English tyranny.

In this way we see that the Great Rising of 1857 cannot be attributed to a single chance cause. It was the outcome of social, religious, political and economic cause all combined.

The Spread of the Great Mutiny. It was on May 10, 1857 that a Mutiny broke out at Meerut, owing to the foolish imprisonment of 85 sepoys for their refusal to use the greased cartridges. Having murdered many Europeans, the mutineers marched to Delhi where the regiments at once mutinied and proclaimed Bahadur Shah II as the sovereign, making it a seminational rising. In the same year, the Sepoys mutinied at Lucknow. Sir Henry Lawrence, the Chief Commissioner of Oudh, died after a heroic struggle for 87 days. The place was relieved by Generals Havelock of Outram. The town was completely in the hands of the mutineers. At Jhansi, the sepoys instigated by the ex- Rani shot down their officers. Similar excesses were committed at several military stations in Bengal and the North-western Provinces.

After defeating Nana Sahib, he set out for Lucknow. The mutineers re-captured the town immediately after his departure. General Nicholson relieved Delhi. Generals Havelock and Outram entered Lucknow, but were themselves besieged in the Presidency which was finally relieved by Campbell. A kind of guerrilla war continued for two years before the province returned to loyalty. On December, 6, 1857, Campbell defeated the Gwalior sepoys under Nana Sahib and captured Gwalior. Tantya Tope, Nana Sahib's Minister, fought gallantly, but was forced to retreat. He was betrayed, caught and hanged in 1859. With his fall the Mutiny came to a close. Nana Sahib is supposed to have perished in the Nepal jungles. Bahadur Shah, the last aged Mughal Emperor, was kept as a state prisoner first at Calcutta and then at Rangoon where he died at the age of 87. Rani Lakshmi Bai died in the battlefield.

FAILURE OF THE GREAT REBELLION

1. Following are the main causes of the failure of rebellion. Formidable and widespread though the, revolt was, it was yet to a great extent localised, limited and ill-brganised, The Mutiny was not universal. Dr. R.C. Mazumdar says. "It was never an all-India character but was localised, restricted and poorly organised." "The area affected was the Punjab, the United Provinces. Rohilkhand, Oudh, the Territory between the Narbada and the Chambal and the Western parts of Bengal and Bihar on the Northeast. Afghanistan was friendly under Dost Mohammad, Sindh was quiet, Rajputana was loyal. India South of the river Narbada made no movement of importance, though the native regiments mutinied at Kolhapur in the Southern Marathan country an there were also many dangerous outbrusts of feelings at Hyderabad; the Nizam's Capital. Thus the revolt was only local and not nation-wide.

2. The whole programme arranged, as it was, came to nothing on account of the rising taking place prematurely or before the date fixed for the purpose. The date fixed for the simultaneous rising in the country was 31st May, 1857. The date was known only to the leaders of each organisational centre and 3 officers of each of the regiments. But certain events.

(i) Mangal Pandey was tried and was ordered to be hanged.

(ii) The soldiers of 19th and 34th Indian regiments were disbanded.

(iii) The Subedar of 34th regiment was hanged-made the Indian soldiers impatient for the rebellion and so the revolt bagan before the appointed day. It was a serious suicidal mistake. Dr. Ishwari Prasad says. "As events proved, the Meerut accident by precipitating the revolt saved the British Raj from the ruin which Nana Sahib and his colleagues had planned. Wilson, White, Malleson, three noted historians of the revolt, agree in regarding the Meerut outbreak as fortunate for the Company and fatal to the revolt. It upset the whole plan of the rebels, deprived them of a concerted action and in many places the local leaders did not know what to do.

3. Superiority in War Weapons. The resources of the British Imperialism were unlimited. Fortunately for them, the Crimean War and other wars in which the Britishers were involved out of India had come to an end by 1856. As such, the British armies were being brought into India in large numbers from different parts of the world for; the suppression of the Mutiny. Many of the soldiers were recruited in India itself. The Indian rebels possessed only a few old rifles. They were mostly fighting with swords and spears. On the other hand, the European soldiers had new type of rifles and the new war weapons about which even Nana Sahib had said, "it pre-disposes of its victim before it is actually fired."

Superiority in the Postal and Telegraph systems of the Britishers. The British Government had the advantage of the widespread telegraph system and control of postal communication. By these means the British were able to know the movements of the Indian rebels and their tactics at once. Thus an arganised plan was chalked out by the English to suppress the mutiny. Talking of the telegraph system and its advantages for the suppression of the Mutiny the "Times", a London Newspaper, aid, "The telegraph system ever since its inception did not perform such an encouraging feat of importance up to this time as it showed in the case of India in the days of Mutiny."

Superiority in British Navy. It has already been pointed out above that the resources of the British were unlimited in India. The British had the command of the sea and, consequently, they were able to bring into Indian men, material and munitions to help them to secure victory over their opponents. It is rightly said that even if the Britishers had been pushed back on the coasts of the ocean, or had been thrown into the sea, even then they, with the aid of their naval superiority, would have been able to recover India. The resources of the Peninsula in men and women lay at the disposal of the company, in addition to those of the native states, the Punjab and the Gorkhas of Nepal. On the other hand, the leaders of the revolt had not rich territories to fall back upon, and no recruiting ground except the

Northern provinces and the regiments of the Company that promised to split their causes. Several armies of the revolt had nothing to fight with except their swords as their leaders could not provide them with guns and ammunition. The Company's forces, on the other hand, were always equipped with heavy guns.

4. The Great Mutiny of 1857 was mostly in the nature of a feudal revolt though subsequently it had assumed a national colour to a limited extent. But one conspicuous thing in the course of the Mutiny was that the native Princes did not join this Mutiny against the Britishers. Where Oudh, Rohilkhand and the rulers and Jagirdars of the Northern India had led the great rebellion, there the rulers of Patiala, Jindh, Gwalior, Hyderabad and other rulers came forward with their united co-operation to suppress the rebellion. The European historians have very much appreciated the services of Sir Dinkar Rao, the Minister of Gwalior, and Sir Sallar Jang, the Wazir of Hyderabad. Many of the Princes refused to make a common cause with the rebels; rather they joined the Britishers. It has, therefore, been rightly said that by the help rendered to the Britishers, the Punjab state proved to be most disastrous to the cause of the mutineers and Gorkha leaders also rendered a lot of help to the Britishers. In this connection Sir William Russel writes in "My Diary in India", "Yet it must be admitted that with all their courage they would have been quite exterminated if the natives had been all and altogether hostile to them. The desperate defence made by the garrisons was no doubt heroic, but the natives shared their glory and they by their aid and presence rendered the defence possible. Our siege of Delhi would have been quite impossible if the Rajas of ihind and Patiala had not been our friends and if the Sikhs had not been recruited in our battalions and remained quiet in the Punjab. The Sikhs at Lucknow did good service and in all cases our garrisons were helped, fed and served by the natives, as our armies were attended and strengthened by them in the field."

5. Lack of Unity. The Indian rebels were not properly organised or if they were at all organised their central organisation was very weak. There was no dearth of bravery and boldness in its leaders; but one thing that was very conspicuous by its absence in them was the absence of experience in organisation and concerted action. It was not possible for them to regain their lost independence by mere small depredations and sudden attacks which are specially noticed in the Guerilla tactics of war. The British Government at the Centre and the Provincial Government made an enquiry concerning the Mutiny through Commissions and Boards, but these Commissions and Boards failed to get any clue which would have enabled them to know the origin of any organised conspiracy of Mutiny. Rather, the case started against Bahadur Shah II, the Mughul Emperor, proved, on the other hand, that the Mutiny was a surprise to him as much as it was to the Britishers. The Mutiners suffered also from lack of unity of purpose. The Mutiny had broken out all of a sudden and nobody had the idea of the turn it would take; there was no understanding between the Hindus and the Muslims. They were divided in their aims with nc common political object. "There was no unity among them and they were unable to combine effectively for the execution of the common plan or common aim." A close and careful study of the Mutiny records reveals a very sad story of everyone for himself and no one for the country. The Mughul Emperor, the proclaimed head of the Mutiny, the Queens and the Princes and other leaders of the revolt—all pulled in their own directions and played a double game to secure their own ends and interests. The Sepoys of Oudh fought for the restoration of their own king, while Nana Sahib and the Queen of Jhansi, on the other hand, pressed their own claims. A number of smaller adventures, not inspired by any patriotic impluses sprang up to take advantage of the opportunity offered by the Mutiny for their personal advantage. Khan Bahadur Khan, the grandson of Hafiz Rahmat Khan, declared himself as the Viceroy or Naib Nazim of Rohilkhand. The Banjaras of Saharanpur set up a new king of their own. The Gujjars had different Rajas in different areas, Fatuna having proclaimed himself as the king of the Gujjars. One Devi Singh proclaimed himself the king of 14 villages in the Mathura district.

6. The lack of leadership amongst the rebels was another very important cause which brought about the failure of the mutiny. The only capable leaders of the mutineers were the Rani of Jhansi, Tantya

Tope and Nana Sahib. "With a few honourable exceptions of whom the most distinguished were Ahmadullah and Tantya Tope, most of the leaders who took part in the struggle did so for personal reasons. They did not rise against the British till their personal interests had been damaged by the policy of the British Government. Besides, the natives spying for the British were at work inside and outside the Fort, among whom the name of Maulvi Rajab Ali stands out as the most notorious. On the other hand the English had the advantage of having very capable leaders and tried generals like the Lawrence Brothers, Outram, Havelock, Nicholson, Neill, and Edwards. This was really fortunate for the British Government. It was these British leaders and Generals who resisted the mutineers very stubbornly in the early stage of the Mutiny and who were thus in a position to control the situation. They had received a substantial aid from their homeland in the later stages of the mutiny. Otherwise also, they were far superior to the Indian leaders in military and political qualities. All of them had only one object before them and that was the defence of the British Government in India."

7. Personal Jealousies. The leaders of the revolt were mutually jealous and continually intriguing against one another. In fact these personal jealousies were largely responsible for the Indian defeat." The personal jealousies of the Indian leaders always stood in the way of collective action under one supreme leader. As against this the English had the advantage of one supreme leadership, not less heroic and undaunted that the rebel leaders. Thus we find that the mutual jealousies among the native leaders was another cause which seriously undermined their solidarity and ultimately led to their defeat.

8. Bahadur Shah, the Mughal Emperor, was mentally ill prepared for such a great revolution as had taken place in the country. On the other hand, the mutineers had an explicit faith in the competence of the Emperor whom they wished to enthrone as Emperor of India but the turned out to be a broken reed. It has, therefore, rightly been said that for nearly two years the fight dragged on now here and now there, success sometime attaining the freedom fighters, sometime the efforts of the oppressors. It was not as the prejudiced British historian sometimes said "a Hindu movement' or as sometimes alleged "a Muslim movement." It failed because it was disorganised. It failed because some acted selfishly and some for personal reasons; they acted only when their personal interests were involved. It was Tantya Tope, Laxmi Bai and Ahmed-ullah who fought practically unselfishly. If the British won, it was through treachery, due to the personal jealousies and selfishness of the Indian rulers which they exploited to the utmost.

9. Another very important factor which contributed to the success of the English in the Mutiny was the noble efforts of Lord Canning and Sir John Lawrence in the early stages to check the outcry both in England and in India for their ruthless and indiscriminate policy of vengeance that the English in England and India advocated. On the other hand, Canning refused to show vindictive spirit and followed a mild and pacific policy towards the Mutineers. He was nicknamed as "Clemency Canning" in contempt, but it was afterwards recognized that his clemency was not only morally splendid, but also politically expedient, for it surely raised the British prestige in the eyes of the Indians and helped to create mutual confidence and goodwill. "Lord Canning never for a moment lost his balance of mind during the excitement of the Mutiny." Therefore his policy of mercy and moderation did much to hasten the end of hostillities and restoration of order. In this way we can canclude that the Great Rising of 1857 cannot be attributed to a single chance cause, there were many important and deep-rooted causes responsible for this national upheaval. The greased-cartridge affair merely precipitated the crisis, it was not the real causes. The fire had long been smouldering and the greased-cartridge affair only acted as the immediate causes of the Mutiny. There were many causes-political, economic, social and religious-which brought about the Great Mutiny. It was suppressed by the British with a great difficulty. The Mutiny failed for want of concerted aims before the mutineers, lack of organisation amongst them, lack of capable leaders and last of all on account of lack of national support.

The Main Events of the Great Rising of 1857

(1) Mangal Pande and the First Shot of the Revolt. It is generally believed that the Great Rising of 1857 began from Barrakpur in Bengal where a Brahman sepoy of the East India Company Mangal Pande refused to use the grease cartidges and invoked his other comrades to take arms against the English for the protection of their religion. When Sergeant Major Hudson ordered the soldiers to arrest him none of the soldiers stepped forward. Thereafter the Sergeant Major Hudson tried to arrest him he shot him dead. He also killed another English officer who was advancing towards him on a horse. Col. Wheeler asked the soldiers to arrest Mangal Pande, but his orders were also not complied with by sodiers. Thus, we see that the Mutiny started about two month, before the fixed date. The incident also shows that although all the Indian soldiers agreed with the views of Mangal Pande, yet they were hesitating to start Mutiny before the fixed date. Hence Mangal Pande tried to shoot himself but was made a prisoner in wounded state. The British officials decided to hang him to death of 8th April and 19th and 34th Regiments were ordered to be disbanded. In the whole Cantonment of Barrackpore, no one was ready to perform the task of hanging Mangal Pande. Hence four persons were called from Calcutta to perform this task and Mangal Pande was hanged on 8th April 1857. The news of Mangal Pande's hanging spread like wild fire throughout the country and it became impossible for the sepoys to wait till 31st May which was the date fixed to start Mutiny.

(1) Revolt in Meerut. The cantonment of Meerut was the most important cantonment in Northern India in those days. The news of the Barrackpur incident reached Meerut and the sepoys there also started revolt. On the 24th of April 1857 Colonel Smith gathered them to use the new catridge. There were 90 soldiers in that unit. Only 5 of them obeyed his orders while the rest of the 85 did not obey that order. They were punished with ten years rigorous imprisonment. On May 9, they were brought naked before the entire regiment and thus disgraced publicly. This severe punishment sent a wave of indignation in all the soldiers of the Meerut Contonment. In the darkness of the same night the soldiers prepated their plan of action.

This 10th of May was Sunday. The English officers sensed no danger and felt secure. But on the same day the Indian soldiers released the prisoners killed many English officers and civilians and marched to Delhi the same night.

(3) Out-Break of the Revolution in the Adjoining Districts of Delhi. People were greatly encouraged with the success at Delhi. Soon they rose in revolt in Aligarh, Etawah, Mathura, Mainpuri and in Quhelkhan division and the control of the government treasuries began to pass into the hands of the revolutionary forces. Everywhere the Europeans were killed. Thus very soon the green flag of Emperor Bahadur Shah II began to wave in all the destricts and territories round about Delhi. For sometime the British rule in the above mentioned places was ended.

(4) Spread of the Revolution and Role of Some Prominent Personalities in it. The Indians at different places remained in suspense for about a week but then the revolt at Meerut, Delhi, Firozepur and Muzzafarnagar inspired them and they rose in revolt at many places. Very soon the revolt covered the entire territory from Delhi to Bihar in the East. In June revolt occurred in Lucknow Kanpur and Jhansi. In Punjab, the British disarmed the Indian soldiers. The soldiers protested against it at one or two places but they were forced to yield. Some rulers of Punjab, Rajasthan and South India helped the British in suppressing the revolt. Thus Delhi, Lucknow, Bareilly, Kanpur, Jhansi and Gwalior and Arrah in Bihar remained the main centres of revolt, after the sepoy revolt of Meerut.

(5) Occupation of Delhi by the Rebel Army. On the 11th of May these Meerut soldiers reached Delhi and made an appeal to the Delhi soldiers to join their ranks to free the mother country. The Delhi soldiers were already prepared to join hands with the rebels and very soon they joined the rebel forces. Delhi was captured by the rebels on May 12, some Englishmen were killed while the rest fled away. Bahadur Shah II was proclained the Emperor of India. Then they took the Emperor in a procession round about Delhi. Thus the rebels got full control over Delhi was soon to become the centre of the Great Revolt and Bahadur Shah its great symbol. This spontaneous raising of the last Mughal King to the leadership of the country was recognition of the fact that the long reign of the Mughal dynasty had made it the traditional symbol of India's political unity. With this single act, the sepoys had transformed a munity of soldiers in a revolutionary war. This is way rebellions sepoys from all over the country automatically turned their steps towards Delhi and all Indian chiefs took part in the Revolt hastened to proclaim their loyalty to the Mughal Emperor. Bahadur Shah II, in turn, under the instingation and perhaps the pressure of the sepoys, soon wrote letters to all the chiefs and rulers of India urging them to organise a confederacy of Indian states and replace the British regime.

(6) Role of Bakht Khan and Bahadur Shah at Delhi. At Delhi the nominal and symbolic leadership belonged to the Emperor Bahadur Shah II, but the real command lay with a Court of Soldiers headed by General Bakhat Khan who had led the revolt of the Bareilley troops and brought them to Delhi. In the British army he had been an ordinary Subedar of artillery. Bakht Khan represented the popular and plebian element at the headquarters of the Revolt. The Emperor Bahadur Shah was perhaps the weakest link in the chain of leadership of the Revolt. He was not firm even in his support of the Revolt. He had little genuine sympathy for the humble sepoys who in turn did not trust him fully. He was angered by the assertion of authority by the leaders of the sepoys. He vacillated between the desire to resign as Emperor and the desire to save his skin in case of the Revolt was crushed by the British. His position was also undermined by his favourite Queen Zeenat Mahal and his sons who carried on intrigues with the enemy. His weak personality and old age his lack of qualities of leadership created political weakness at the nerve centre of the Revolt and did incalculable damage to it.

(7) Role of Nana Sahib at Kanpur. At Kanpur the leader of the Revolt was the adopted son of Peshwa Baji Rao II, Nana Sahib Dhondu Pant. Nana Sahib expelled the English from Kanpur with the help of the sepoys and proclaimed himself the Peshwa. At the same time he acknowledged Bahadur Shah II as the Emperor of India and declared himself to be his Governor. The Chief burden of fighting on behalf of Nana Sahib fell on the shoulders of Tantya Tope, one of his most loyal servants. Tantya Tope has won immortal fame by his patriotism, determining fighting, and skillfull guerilla operations. Azimullah was another loyal servant of Nana Sahib. He was an expert in political propoganda. Unfortunately, Nana Sahib tranished his brave record by decitfully killing the garrison at Kanpur after he had agreed to give them safe conduct. But the later researches revealed that Nana Sahib had no hand it there killings. Now it is accepted that when the troops took their seats in the boats and began crossing the Ganges they were fired upon by the Indian troops. Many English soldiers were killed as a result of the firing. Nana Sahib came to know of the incident when it was over.

(8) The Role of the Begum of Avadh at Lucknow. The Revolt at Lucknow was led by the Begum of Avadh who had proclaimed her young son, Birjis Kadr, as the Nawab of Avadh. Helped by the sepoys at Lucknow, and by the zamindars and peasants of Avadh, the Begum organised on all-out attack on the English. On the night of 30th May 1857, the work of the revolution began there. All the Zamindars and Tulukdars of the province took an active part in the work of the revolution there. The revolutionary armies brought to an end the rule of the English in the whole of the province and established their rule there.

(9) Role of Lakshmibai at Jhansi. The young Rani joined the rebels when the British refused to acknowledge her right to adopt an heir to the Jhansi gaddi (the throne) annexed her state, and treatened treat her as an instigator of the rebellion of the sepoys at Jhansi. The Rani vacillated for some time. But after some time when she had fully organised her armies she came to fight against the British tooth and nail. To suppress the activities of the Rani Sir Hugh Rose moved towards Jhansi in the month of March 1858. The Rani took the command of the forces in her own hands and put up a very brave fight against the British. She called Tantya Tope for her help. That brave general moved to assist the heroic Rani at the head of his troops but while on the way he was Intercapted by the forces of Sir Hugh Rose and was defeated. The position of the Rani became very critical by this defeat. But she did not lose her heart. The British mounted quick offensive against the Rani but the Rani was facing them with cool courage and displaying extreme bravery and heroism in every field. The tales of her bravery and courage and military skill have inspired her countrymen ever since. Now the English resorted to intrigues and diplomacy and won over certain people to their side. These traitors opened the southern gates of the fort of Jhansi to the advantage of the British and the British armies entered the fort through that gate. Driven out of Jhansi by the English armies after a fierce battle in which "even women were seen working the batteries and distributing ammunition," she administered the oath to her followers that "with our own hands we-shall not our Azadshahi bury." She captured Gwalior of with the help of Tantya Tope and her trusted Afghan guards. Maharaja Sindhia loyal to the British, made an attempt to fight the Rani but most of her troops deserted to her.

(10) The Role of Maulavi Ahmadullah at Faizabad. Maulavi Ahmadullah of Faizabad was another outstanding leader of the Revolt. He was a native of Madras where he had started preaching arined rebellion. In Januray 1857 he moved towards the North to Faizabad where he fought a large scale battle against a company of British troops sent to stop him from preaching sedition. When the general Revolt broke out in May he merged as one of its acknowledged leaders in Avadh. After the defeat at the Lucknow, he led the rebellion in Rohilkhand where he was treacherously killed by the Raja of Puwain who was paid Rs.-50,000 as a reward by the British. Maulavi Ahmadullah's patriotism valour, and military ability have won him high praise' even from British historicans.

(11) Role of Kunwar Singh at Jagdishpur. Kunwar Singh, a ruined and discontented Zamindar of Jagdishpur near Arrah, was the chief organiser of the Revolt of Bihar. Though nearly 80 years old, he was perhaps the most outstanding military leader and strategist of the Revolt. He faught the English forces in Bihar and later joining hands with Nana Sahib's armies, he also campaigned in Avadh and Central India.

12. Suppression of the Revolt. When the British came to know of the happenings in Meerut, Delhi and around about Delhi they felt greatly terrified. But inspite of the fear they decided to suppress the uprisings firmly and with a strong hand. It was lucky for the English that they got sometime to prepare their plan of action. In northern India the English had few English soldiers and so they got English armies from Bombay and Madras. They also detained those English armies which were being sent to China. In addition to making their position strong militarily they won over some of the native rulers to their side who helped the English greatly. At this time the English paid the greatest attention to the Punjab because there was the fear of these types of dangers from that side namely.

(i) Fear that the armies in the Punjab may also revolt.

(ii) Fear that the Afghans may invade India.

(iii) Fear from the side of the Sikhs who had been recently subjugated by the English. The English disbanded the Indian army unit and severely punished, those who revolted against the authority. Dost Mohmmed, the ruler of Kabul did not invade India and strictly adhered to the treaties which were concluded in the treaties which were concluded in between him and the English in 1855 and 1857. The Sikh armies not only remained indifferent towards the revolution but they grealty helped the English to suppress the rebellion.

In addition to this the central government at Calcutta gave special rights and powers to the English officers to deal with the rebels and these officers used these powers to great advantage and suppressed the uprisings. The English represented to the Gurkhas of Nepal that before the treaty of Sagauli the Avadh armies were responsible for all the highhandedness against Nepal.

(a) Capture of Delhi by the British. After having made the full preparation for the suppression of the Mutiny, Lord Canning ordered commander-in-chief, Anson, to attack Delhi Anson however, died of cholera while proceeding from Simla to Delhi. Thereafter, Sir Henry Barnard was appointed the Commander-in-Chief. The army of Brigadier Wilson also joined him in the way. By the end of May, this joint army reached near Delhi. In the beginning, the mutineers forced the British to withdraw back, but later on they were unsuccessful to defeat the British. In July 1857, Subedar Bakhtar Khan reached Delhi along with his Bundela soldiers. Bahadur Shah made him the Governor of Delhi and the Commander-in-Chief of the revolutionary armies.. Mirza Illahi Bux, a relation of Bahadur Shah, however, betrayed Bahadur Shah and gave his secrets to the British. In September 1857 General Nichlson reached Delhi with a big army consisting of the British, Gorkha, Sikhs Punjabi and Kashmiri soldiers. The ruler of Jind also reached Delhi to help the Briitsh. After a terrible fight which lasted for ten days, the British recaptured Delhi on 24th September. Bahadur Shah was made a prisoner and was sent to Rangoon where he died in 1873. The fall of Delhi decided the fate of revolt.

(b) **Jhansi.** Sir Hugh Rose recaptured Jhansi by assault on 3rd April 1858. The Rani of Jhansi and Tantya Tope marched towards Gwalior where they were hailed by the Indian soldiers. The Sindhia however, decided to remain loyal to the English and took shelter at Agra. Nana Sahib was proclaimed the Peshwa and plans were chalked out for a march into the South. Gwalior was recaptured by the English in June 1858, the Rani of Jhansi, died fighting clad in Soldier's uniform on the rampets of the fort. Tantya Tope escaped southward; in April 1859 he was captured by one of Sindhia's feudatory who handed him over to the British to be hanged.

(c) **Kanpur.** The military operations for the recapture of Kanpur were closely associated with the recovery of Lucknow. Sir Compbell occupied Kanpur on December 6. Tantya Tope escaped' and joined to Rani of Jhansi.

(d) **Lucknow.** The early attempts of Havelock and Outram to recover Lucknow met with no success, some relief came in November 1857 when Sir Colin Campbell, the new Commander-in-Chief, sent from England entered the city with the help of Gorkha regiments and evacuated the Europeans. In March 1858 the city was finally reduced, but guerilla activity continued till September of the same year.

(f) **Shahjahanpur and Bareilly.** Shahjahanpur by March, 1858 had become the stronghold of the mutineers. Nana Sahib and Maulvi Ahmed Ali Shah of Faizabad had also reached there. Hence Campbell, (the British armies' commander) proceeded from Lucknow towards Shahjahanpur but the two great leaders went to Bareilly where Begum Hazrat Mahal, Nana Sahib, Bala Sahib and other revolutionary leaders had also assembled. Bareilly was captured by the British in May. Ahmedshah was murdered by a traitor, Nana Sahib and Begum Hazrat Mahal and Bala Sahib fled away to the Tarai of Nepal and never returned to this country.

MILITARY CAUSES FOR THE REVOLUTION OF 1857

As a result of the British disaster in Afghanistan in the First Afghan War, the military discipline in the British army had gone down to its lowest ebb. Lord Dalhousie had written clearly to the authorities in England that "the military discipline right from the top to the bottom and from officers to soldiers was weakest and full of shame" The Bengal army was a great brotherhood, whose members used to move as a unit. The army service in Bengal army had been made hereditary. Most of the Bengal army consisted of the recruits taken from Oudh and North-western Province. Many of them belonged to high caste Brahmin and Rajput families. These high caste Indian recruits did not like that military ,discipline of the British authorities in India, which treated them as equals to the recruits of the inferior caste, be imposed upon them. I was, on account of this reason that Sir Charles Napier had said, "It have no faith in these high caste recruits and mercenary soldiers." In this connection Dr. Ishwari Prasad says. "Implicit obedience to the European commanders has been a characteristic of the Indian soldiery. Keen observers, however, had begun to notice a gradual weakening of that obedience roughly dating from the Afghan disaster. That disaster was Nature's punishment for unrighteousness and it was unrighteousness that shook the loyalty of the Indian soldiers to the Company. The annexation of Oudh finally snapped it. Individual revolts had preceded the outburst of Mangal Pandey. "The discipline of the army," wrote Dalhousie to the President of the Board of Control, "from top to bottom, officers and men alike, is scandalous." The Indian soldiers began gradually to realize that they were the instruments of English expansion and the degradation of their own people. The recruitment of the Gurkhas and the Sikhs, the raising of the irregular troops in the Punjab and the Frontier tracts-all tended to convince them that their own future was in peril. Even during the days of Lord Dalhousie, three small revolts had already taken place one after the other, first in 1849 in No. 22 regiment, second in 1850 in No. 60 regiment and, third, in 1852 in No. 30 regiment.

2. It should however, be noted here that the sentiments of the Bengal army were the same as those of the citizens of Oudh. According to Maulana Azad, "After the annexation of Oudh, in the whole of Indian army, and especially in the Oudh army, a sort of attitude of insubordination and rebellion had gained ground because of the great blow that they sustained at the hands of the British officers of the East India Company. They suddenly felt that the power that the East India Company had obtained in India through the sacrifices of the Indians was being utilised by the Englishmen against their very king, *i.e.*, the Mughul Emperor. Oudh was the home of the sepoys and when it was annexed in 1856, about 60,000 men were rendered idle on account of the disbanding of the state army. The national feelings of the sepoys were wounded. So great was the resentment among the Indian soldiers that one of them told Sir Henry Lawrence that "If the sepoy is not speedily redressed, he will redress himself."

3. General Service Enlistment Act, 1856. In the year 1856, the anning Government passed the General Service Enlistment Act. According to this, it was decided that no sepoy who was enlisted under the Act could refuse to fight across the sea. This act was not applicable in the case of old sepoys. But even then, it created a lot

of discontentment amongst them against the British people, because in Bengal army the service had almost become hereditary. Sarkar and Dutta write: "This affected the scruples of the Indian sepoys about crossing the Sea: it was soon brought in their minds under the category of the insidious measures aimed at caste: another of the items accumulating to form an avalanche."

4. With the expansion and consolidation of the British rule in India the conditions laid down on the new recruitments in their services in the army department exercised so tight and irritating a control over the soldiers that they could not further tolerate the high-handedness to which they were subjected by the British officers. The self-respect of the sepoy was trampled Upon at every step. "It is by no means uncommon for an officer to curse and swear at his men on parade and use most disgusting terms of abuse to them. The highest pay attainable by a sepoy as Subedar of the infantry was less than the minimum pay of a raw European recruit. Very often there was no promotion of an Indian soldier. He may enter as a Risaldar and retire as a Risaldar. The sepoys were disallowed Batta which they used to get while away from their homes on active duty. Further, the Indian soldier were being called Upon to fight in wars across the seas. Consequently they remembered with great pain the old privileges that they used to enjoy in service, when the Indian princes used to appreciate their services and rewarded them with gifts and presents. But, now, with the conquest of the Punjab and Sindh by the English, the Indian soldiers had to witness bad days, because of the loss of many of the old privileges which they were deprived of. Moreover, the soldiers who had gone to Afghanistan to take part in the First Afghan War, were excommunicated from their social brotherhood by their companions. The soldiers who were considered disqualified for service abroad, were not pensioned off to go to their homes; rather they were to perform their duties in the British cantonments in different places. Before this the Indian soldiers were also enjoying the privilege of sending letters, etc., to their relatives free of cost, but now with the pasing of the Post Office Act of 1854, this privilege was taken away from them. In 1824, the sepoys at Barrackpore refused to go across the sea to fight in Burma and, as a result of their

refusal, the 47th Indian regiment was disbanded by the Britishers. Similarly, in 1844, the four Bengali regiments did not yield to the pressure of the British Government to go to war towards Sindh for fighting purposes till the request for the additional grant of Batta was allowed. In other words, there was a universal discontentment among the Indian soldiers on account of the loss of the above privileges.

5. The Disparity. Between the Indian troops and British troops in India was very high this encouraged the Indians. The Indian army consisted of 2,33,000 troops and 45,322. British troops. Although Lord Dalhousie had pointed out the urgency of filling in the gap, the Home Government had slept over in the matter. The distribution of troops in India was also faulty the strength of the Bengal, army was 1,51,361. About 40,000 troops were in the Punjab. No European force existed in Bengal and Bihar, except at Cacutta and Dinapur near Patna. The Indians were well aware of the weak position of the Company at many places and would like to take advantage of the same. The absence of many British officers had made this difference even greater because with the acquisition of new states most of them had been stationed on the borders of the states as administrative officers. Apart from this, a greater part of the Indian army had gone to take part in the Crimean War, where the disaster of the British forces had considerably demoralised the British soldiers in India.

6. Circulation of Mysterious Chapatis. "The general unrest was indicated by the mysterious Chapatis or cakes which began to circulate from village to village from 1856 onwards. There was a similar circulation of lotus flowers among the regiments. Although the cause is not known, it created an atmosphere of mystery. The centenary of the Battle of Plassey was to (all on 23rd June, 1857 and the people were looking forward to the end of British rule in India after hundred years. There were meetings of the Indian soldiers against their European officers. They were thinking in terms of revenge against them. Their plan of compaign was simple. They were to strike all over India on the same day (22nd June, 1857). They were to kill all European officers, break open prisons, take over the Government treasury, cut telegraph wires and railway lines, and capture power magazines, armouries and forts. It was hoped that if all the blows were given at the same time, they were sure to shake this edifice of the foreign Government." (Mahajan).

7. Being seriously dis-affected with the British Government on account of the factors enumerated above, the native soldiers were only looking forward to an opportunity to take revenge against the British Government. The opportunity came to them when the question of greased cartridge which the native soldiers were ordered to use before firing a gun cropped up. This thing is to be remembered very clearly that the greased cartridges themselves gave no cause of discontentment to the Indian soldiers as a new cause; rather, they created an opportunity for the suppressed unrest to burst forth openly against the British Government. It was in 1856 when, according to a regulation, the sepoys were required to bite the end of the cartridge before using it. There was a rumour that the cartridges to be used with the new Enfield rifles were greased with the fat of cows and pigs. One of them was sacred to the Hindus, while the other was forbidden to the Muslims. On account of their ignorance, the British Government denied the truth of this allegation. However, on a secret enquiry, it was later on found that actually the fat of cows and pigs had been used. The result was that the sepoys got infuriated. "The fire of -vengeance once ablaze could scarcely be quelled by the representations of Lord Canning downwards that the story of the greased cartridges was untrue and was spread by mischief-mongers. English historians have themselves admitted that cow's fat and lard were used in the composition of the tallow used in the new cartridges." The native army of Bengal was in a state of restlessness. In April, 1857, some troops refused to use the cartridges supplied to them. They were court-martialled and sentenced to ten years' imprisonment. On 9th May, they were publicly degraded and deprived of their uniforms and shut up in a jail. Thus, when the Hindu sepoys were convinced of the fact that the East India Company had turned into Aurangzeb they decided to play the part of Shivaji. This was the commencement of the Great Mutiny of 1857.

❒

11

The Policies of the Associations (1851-1885)

RAJA RAM MOHAN ROY AS A SOCIAL REFORMER

Raja Ram Mohan Roy was born on September 27,1772 at Radhanagar, a small village in Bengal. His father Ramakanta Roy was a small Brahmin Zamindar. He learnt over a dozen languages including Sanskrit, Persian, Arabic, English, French, Latin, Greek and Hebrew. As a yong man he had studied Sanskrit literature and Hindu philosophy at Varanasi and the Quran and Persian and Arabic literature at Patna. He was also well acquainted with Jainism and other religious movements 'and sects of India. He was deeply influenced by English language and western culture and travelled to England. Later on he made an intensive study of western thought and culture. To study the Bible in the original he learnt Greek and Hebrew. His extensive studies freed his mind from the bigotry that characterised an average Indian. Raja Ram Moham Roy's parents were orthodox Brahmins, while he was a rationalist right from the beginning. He had to leave his house at the early age of 16/ 17 years for criticizing the idol-worship and remained away for a number of years. He returned home only after his father's death. In 1805 he joined the service of the East India Company in the Revenue Department. At Murshidabad he came in contact with a British Officers, Digby who was known for his liberal views. In 1809 he wrote in Persian his famous work 'Gift to Monothesis' in which he put forward weighty arguments against belief in many gods and for the worship of a single God. He settled at Calcutta in 1814 and soon attracted a band of young men with whose cooperation he started in 1815 the Atmiya Sabha. He published the Bengali translation of the Vedas and of five of the principal Upnishads to prove that all the principal ancient texts of the Hindus preached monotheism or worship of one God. He also wrote a series of tracts and pamphlets in defence of monotheism. In 1830 A.D. he went to England as an advocate for the Mughal Emperor Akbar 11(1816-1837 AD.) He also joined the service of the East India Company and gradually reached a high position. In 1830 A.D. he pleaded before the British Government to enhance the annual pension of the Mughal Emperor and not to lower his position.

His Contribution. Raja Ram Mohan Roy began his strugle for removing the evils prevalent in contemporary Hindu Society. His various reform activities can be studied under following heads:

(i) Religious Reforms. The credit of starting the religious and social reformation in modern India undoubtedly goes to Raj a Ram Mohan Roy. He was born at such a time when India was passing through one of its darkest period. Various evils like blind-faiths, sacrificial rituals, caste divisions, idol worship *etc.*, had greatly over-shadowed the Hindu religion. Raja Ram Mohan Roy was a man of liberal religious views and was friendly to all religions. He was influenced by monotheism of Islam and the Moral principles of Christianity. It was because of his liberal views that the Muslims regarded him a Muslim, the Christians a Christian and the Hindus a Vedantist. In reality he did not belong to any religion in the conventional sense of the term. He believed in the fundamental truth and unity of all religions. He never criticised any religion or any form of religious worship.

Raja Ram Mohan Roy tried to revive in the Hindu world the doctrine of the unity of Godhead, and devoted himself to this task after retiring from the East India Company's service, and settling down in Calcutta in 1814. His earliest attempt was the foundation of the Anniya Sabha, which lasted from 1815 to 1819. The next important step was his foundation of another organisation, which later on became famous as the Brahma Samaj. On 20th August, 1828, with Tarachand Chakravarty as its Secretary. But its new this its service soon excited the hostility of the orthodox citizens of Calcutta, who started a rival organisation named the Dhatrma Sabha, with Bhavani-Charan Banerji as the Secretary, and with its organ, the Samachar Chandrika, which opposed Raja Ram Mohan Roy's Bengalis Weekly, Samvada Kaumudi. The Trust-Deed of the Brahma Samaj was drawn up on the 8th January, 1830. Raja Ram Mohan Roy proved to be the champion of Hinduism. While he defended Hinduism against the hostile criticism of the missionaries, he sought to purge Hinduism of the abuses that had crept into it. At the early quotations from the Vedas. He re-interpreted Hindi doctrines and found ample spiritual basis for his humanitarianism in the Upnishads. He rejected Christianity, denied the divinity of Jesus Christ; but accepted the humanism of Europe. Thus Ram Mohan Roy sought to effect a cultural syntnesis between the East and the West.

He admired the moral and philosophic message of Jesus and wanted it to be incorporated in Hinduism. At one stage his missionary friends hoped that he might even embrace Christianity. But as a rationalist he was equally critical of the Trinity and miracle stories. He vigorously defended Hindu religion and philosophy from the ignorant attacks of the missionaries. At the same time, he adopted an extremely friendly attitude towards other religions.

(ii) As a Social Reformer. Ram Mohan Roy raised his voice against all sorts of social evils and oppressions. He worked very hard to stop the evil practice of 'Sati.' He wrote articles in the papers and delivered speeches in public meetings against this evil practice. Like this he prepared public opinion against this practice. He used to go to the cremation grounds in Calcutta and tried to stop 'Sati, by talking to the relatives of the woman. He worte many letters to Lord William Bentinck to resort to legal proceedings against the people who encouraged Stably quoting from the ancient scriptures he declared that even Hindu religion was against the practice of Sati. When the conservative section amongst the Hindu presented a petition to

Parliament to continue this inhuman practice, than Raja Ram Mohan Roy presented a counterpetition advocating that the custom of Sati was inhuman and unjust. His view won in this matter. It was because of his co-operation that in 1829 A.D. Lord William Bentinck could declare Sati against law. Along with the suppression of Sati he also preached in favour of the widow remarriage as of the suppression of Sati would otherwise remain meaningless. He wanted to secure a place of honour for women in the Hindu society. He quoted extensively from the Vedic literature in order to raise the status of the Hindu women. To improve the status of women he, also demanded for them the right of inheritance to property. He also condemned the practice of polygamy as it would not be possible to insure a place of respect of women unless polygamy was suppressed. The Indians were backward in respect of education and as such they fell a prey to various superstitions and useless rituals.

(iii) Rom Mohan Roy was one of the earliest propagators of modern education which he looked upon as a major instrument for the spread of modern ideas in the country. In 1817, David Hare, who had come out to India in 1800 as a watchmaker but who spent his entire life in the promotion of modern education in the country founded the famous Hindu College. Ram Mohan Roy gave most enthusiastic assistance to Hare in this and his other educational projects. In addition, he maintained at his own cost an English school in Calcutta from 1817 in which, among other subjects, mechanics and the philosophy of Voltaire were taught. In 1825 he established a Vedanta College in which courses both in Indian learning and in Western social and physical sciences were offered. Ram Mohan Roy was equally keen on making Bengali the vehicle of intellectual intercourse in Bengal. He compiled a Bengali grammar.

(iv) Political Field. It was Raja Ram Mohan Roy who writes Rabindranath Tagore, "inauguarated the modern age in India." In the political sphere, in social and religious spheres, everywhere the Raja was the first among the Indians who foughy for the advancement of this country. Politically, he believed, the British were in India by a divine dispensation. They had a mission to perform in this country, and therefore they must continue till that mission is fulfilled. He was in favour of the Indians getting political rights, but according to him only such rights should be given to them as they were competent to enjoy. He was, however, anxious that the essential conditions for the political awakening of this country must be created as early as possible. He therefore supported the introduction of English education in this country, which he believed would throw open the floodgates of English liberal and democratic thought to India. He sponsored the opening of the Hindu College in 1819, to educated the Indians on modern lines. He also helped Alexander Duff and John Wilson to start an English School. The Raja stood and fought for the freedom of speech and expression. He started the first vernacular paper in India, Sambad Kaumudi. In 1821, and he setup the first press in this country. He condemned the Press Regulations of 1823 and carried on a vigorous agitation against them. He also submitted a memorial to the Supreme Court in this respect. He was perhaps influence in his political ideas by the great English philosophers such as Bacon and Bentham. He was anxious to bring about reform in the existing administrative system of the country and was the first Indian to be consulted by the British Parliament on Indian affairs. He gave an evidence before a select committee of the British House of Commons. The Brahma Samaj also participated in building national sentiment among the Indians.

Raja Ram Mohan Roy brought out journals in Bengali, Persian, Hindi and English to spread scientific, literary and political knowledge among the people, to educate public opinion on topics of current interest, and to represent popular demands and grievances before the Government. He was also the initiator of public agitation on political questions in the country. He condemned the oppressive practices of the Bengal zamindars which had reduced the peasants to a miserable condition. He demanded that the maximum rents paid by the actual cultivators of land should be permanently fixed so that they too would enjoy the benefits of the Permanent Settlement of 1793. He also protested against the attempts to impose taxes on tax-free lands.

Mohan Roy took a keen interest in international events and every-where he supported the cause of libertry, democracy, and nationalism and opposed injustice, oppression, and tyranny in every form. The news of the failure of the Revolution in Naples in 1821 made him so sad that he cancelled all his social engagements. On the other hand, he celebrated the success of the Revolution in Spanish America in 1823 by giving a public dinner. He condemned the miserable condition of Ireland under the oppressive regime of absentee landlordism. He publicly declared that he would emigrate from the British Empire if Parliament failed to pass the Reform Bill. In joining hands in his individual capacity as well as collectively with those persons who demanded the freedom of the country and who stood for the greatness of India, Ram Mohan Roy demonstrated his greatness as a patriotic statesman. The greatness of Ram Mohan Roy close not lie in the great success that he achieved but it lies in the fact that he was the first Indian in India of those days who understood and explained to the in In lians the inter-relationship and interdependence that lay in all the reforms which concerned the society, the religion and education and he advocated an integrated approach.

BRAHMO SAMAJ AFTER THE DEATH OF RAJA RAM MOHAN ROY

Debendranath Tagore (1817-1905) was an associate of Raja Ram Mohan Roy and after his death, he took up the leadership of the reform movement. He was a man of deep learning and spiritual poise. He wielded great intellectual authority in the Brahmo Samaj. He "proclaimed the supremacy of human reason which was in its original institutions really the Eternal Light of God reflected through the mind of man over all scriptures and hallowed injunctions."

Another leader of the Brahmo Samaj was Keshab Chandra Sen. He was very much influenced by Christianity. He gathered around himself a group of younger men who were zealous not only in propagating the reform of Hinduism but also in social service such as famine relief. Gradually, a rift developed between the old conservative group of the Brahmo Samaj and the young reformers led by Keshab Chandra Seen. Ultimately there was a splie. The old party led by Debendranath Tagore came to be known as the Adi Brahmo Samaj. In 1868, Keshab Chandra Sen founded the Brahmo Samaj of India. Keshab Chandra Sen took an important part in the passing the Marriage Act of 1872. But in 1878, he married off his daughter of less than 14 years of age to the Maharaja of Cooch-Bihar who was less than 16 years of age. This action of him was condemned by the people and public meetings were held to turn him out from the Brahmo Samaj. Keshab Chandra Sen died in the year 1884. Though there were serveral branches of the Brahmo Samaj in Bengal, yet it could not become as popular as the. Arya Samaj. However, it made a significant contribution in changing the outlook of the Hindus towards Western ideas.

The Brahmo Samaj made an effort to reform Hindu religion by removing abuses, by basing it on the worship of one God and on the teachings of the Vedas and Upnishads, and by incorporating the best aspects of modern western thought. Most of all it based itself an human reason which was to be the ultimate criterion for deciding what was worth while and what was useless in the past or present religious principles and practices. For that reason, the Brahmo Samaj denied the need of a priestly class for interpreting religious writings. Every individual had the right and the capacity to decide with the help of his own intellect what was right and what was wrong in a religious book or principle. Thus the Brahmos were basically opposed to idolatry and superstitious practices and rituals in fact the entire Brahmanical system, they could worship one God without the mediation of the priests.

Under the leadership of Ram Mohan Roy the Brahmo Samaj opposed many evils of the Hindu society such as casteism, untouchability, polygamy, child marriage and the Sati system. His efforts bore fruit when the evil practices of Sati and Child marriage were abolished by law. He also advocated the freedom of the Press. The Brahmo Samaj was weakened by internal dissentions in the second half on the 19th century. Moreover its influence was confined mostly to urban educated groups. Yet it had a decisive influence on the intellectual, social, cultural and political life of Bengal and the rest of India in the 19th and 20th centuries.

CONTRIBUTION OF ISHWAR CHANDRA VIDYASAGAR

In the time of Ishwarchandra Vidyasagar, Indian society suffered from many ills. The weak sections of society, childern, women, low caste people and the poor were often the victims of those evils like infanticide, human sacrifice. Oppression of women, caste system, custom of Sati, polygamy, prohibition of widow remarriage and child marriage. The harbinger of social and cultural renaissance in India in the nineteenth century after Raja Ram Mohan Roy was Pandit Ishwarchandra Vidyasagar.

Pandit Vidyasagar was a great scholar and social reformer. He was born in an ordinary family in 1810 A.D. He was a very hardworking and brave man. He became professor in a Sanskrit College. Inspite of being a Sanskrit scholar and supporter of ancient culture of India he was impressed by the Western philosophy. His views had firmness, clarity and softness. He believed in simplicity and humanism.

Contribution Towards the Making of India

(1) In the Field of Education. He made a notable contribution towards the progress of Indian education. He gave a new form to the Sanskrit education because he developed a new technique to teach this subject. He developed a Bengali alphabet which is used till today. By means of his literary writings he contributed towards the development of modern prose in Bengali. He gave a place to western thought in his college. He put a stop to the monopoly of Brahmins in the field of studies in Sanskrit and encouraged non-Brahmins to study Sanskrit.

(2) Bethuan School. It was established by Pandit Ishwarchandra Vidyasagar in 1849, in Calcutta. Through this school he struggled for womens education, support of widow remarriage, opposition to child marriage etc. In the orthodox contemporary society of India it was believed that educated women will lose their husbands. Because of this orthodox view point the school had great difficulty in acquiring students. If a young girl dared to enter the school, her parents faced social boycott. Loud slogans were raised against those women and they were called all sorts of names. Though these schools Pandit Vidyasagar wanted the women to be educated in western learning and be conversant with western thought. The orthodox section was opposed to giving to the women western education because they thought that the family life would become peaceless and like the western women even the Indian women will try to make their husbands as their servants.

(3) Contribution in the Social Reforms. Pandit Vidyaṣagar struggled to remove the evils of Indian society. He supported widow remarriage to rescue the women from the oppressed condition. The orthodox Hindus bitterly criticised him for his advanced views, he also opposed child marriage, supported women education.

In brief, Pandit Vidyasagar made his important contribution towards making of modern India in the form that of a great educationalist and a social reformer. It was due to his efforts in 1856 that a law was made for widow remarriage. Sanskrit and Bengali languages got encouragement. He tried to uplift the women.

HENRY VIVIAN DEROZIO

Henry Vivian Derozio was a native of Scotland who primarily came to Calcutta as a dealer of watches but permanently stayed there. He was one of those great Anglo-Indians who had special love for India and her People. He joined the Hindu College as a teacher of Philosophy in 1826 at the young age of 17. Within no time he drew around him the best boys of the college whom, he constantly encouraged to think freely, and to question all authority, to love, liberty, equality and freedom, and to worship truth, Derozio, and his followers are known as the Derozians and Young Bengal, were fiery patriots. Derozio was perhaps the first nationalist poet of modern India. He expressed his love for India in his poetry. For example, he wrote in 1827 A.D.

My country! in the days of glory past
A beauteous halo circled round thy brow,
And worshipped as a deity thou Wast,
Were is that glory, where that reverence now?

And one of his pupils Kashi Parshad Ghosh, wrote in 1830 AD.

Land of the Gods and lofty name;
Land of the fair and beauty's spell;
Land of the bards of mighty fame;
My native land: for e'er farwell!

Derozio promoted radical ideas through his class lectures and by organising student societies for debates and discussions on literature, history, philosophy -and science. Through these activities Derozio practically charmed the young Hindu students of Calcutta and brought about an intellectual revolution among them. His followers, collectively, were known as Derozians or the Young Bengal. He ridiculed all kinds of old traditions, defied social and religious conventions and demanded freedom of thought and expression and education for women. The supporters of the Young Bengal Movement were influenced by the ideals of the French Revolution. They, therefore, preached the ideals of liberty, freedom and fraternity. The very strong radical views of this group and their non-conventional practices like showing no respect to religious idols, beef eating, *etc.* alarmed the orthodox Hindus of Calcutta. They thought that the teachings of Derozio were the root cause of the heretical views held by their young folk and brought pressure on the authorities of the Hindu College to dismiss him. Therefore, he was removed from service of the Hindu Colleges in 1831. The same year he died of cholera at the young age of 22.

The Young Bengal Movement. A radical trend arose among the Bengali intellectuals during the late 1820's and the 1830's. This trend was more modern that even Ram Mohan Roy's and is known as the Young Bengal Movement. Its leader and inspirer was the young Anglo-Indian Henry Vivian Derozio. He inspired these students to think rationally and freely, to question all authority, to love liberty, equality and freedom, and to worship truth, Derozio and his famous followers, known as the Derozians and Young Bengal, were fiery patriots. The Derozians attacked old and decadent customs, rites, and traditions. They were passionate advocates of women's rights and demanded education for them. They did not, however, succeed in creating a movement because social conditions were not yet ripe for their ideas to flourish. They did not take up the peasants' cause and there was no other class or group in Indian society at the time which could support their advanced ideas. Moreover, they forgot to maintain their links with the people. In fact, their radicalism was bookish; they failed to come to grips with the Indian reality. Even so, the Derozians carried forward Ram Mohan's tradition of educating the people in social, economic and political questions through newspapers, pamphlets, and public associations. They carried on public agitation on public questions such as the revision of the Company's Charter, the freedom of the Press, better treatment for Indian labour in British colonies abroad, trial by jury, protection of the ryots from oppressive zamindars, and employment of Indians in the higher grades of government services. Surendranath Banerjee, the famous leader of the nationalist movement, described the Derozians as "the pioneers of the modern civilization of Bengal, the conscript fathers of our race whose virtues will excite veneration they organised a society for the Acquisition of General knowledge. They did not; however succeed in creating a long movement.

CONTRIBUTION OF SWAMI VIVEKANAND

Swami Vivekanand was born in 1863. His life had been completely different from his Guru Ramakrishna. From his childhood itself he had a feeling of revolt against contemporary society. He had made a deep study of Western philosophy along with Indian philosophy but he could not attain mental peace.

(1) He popularized the religious message of his Guru Ramakrishna and tried to give it a form suitable to the needs of Indian society at that time.

(2) Above all, Vivekanand stressed social action. Knowledge unaccompanied by action in the actual world in which we live was useless, he said. He too, like his Guru proclaimed the essential oneness of all religious and condemned any narrowness in religious matters. Thus, he wrote in 1898, "For our own motherland a junction of two great systems, Hinduism and Islam.......is the only hope. At the same time, he was convinced of the superior approach of the Indian philosophical tradition. He himself subscribed to Vedanta which he declared to be a fully rational system.

(3) Vivekanand criticised Indians for having lost touch with the rest of the world and become stagnant and mummified. He wrote: "The fact of our isolation from all other nations of the world is the cause of our degeneration and its only remedy is getting back into the current of the rest of the world motion is the sign of life."

(4) Vivekanand condemned the caste system and the current Hindu emphasis on rituals, ceremonies, and superstitions, and urged the people to imbibe the spirit of liberty, equality, and free thinking.

(5) Regarding liberty of thought, he said: "Liberty in thought and action is the only condition of life, growth and well being; where it does not exist, the man, the race, and the nation must go down".

(6) Like his Guru, Vivekanand was also a great humanist. Shocked by the poverty, misery and suffering of the common people of the country, he wrote:

> The only God in whom I believe, the sum total of all souls, and above all, my God the wicked, my God the afflicted, my God the poor of all races.

(7) Vivekanand wanted to carry the religious message of Ramakrishna Paramhansa throughout the world. In 1893 he attended the Parliament of Religious held at Chicago

(U.S.A.) and made a great impression by his learned interpretations. He addressed the gathering as 'Brothers and Sisters's and in his address he emphasised the universal principles basic to all religions. He propounded the true meaning of Vedantas of Hinduism. He proclaimed the Vedantas as the grand universal religion of the world. Above all Vivekanand gave a social purpose to Hinduism. He openly declared that he did not believe in a religion which did not wipe out the widow's tears or bring a piece of bread to the orphans mouth. Swami Vivekanand's speeches of Chicago made a deep impression on the West. New York Herald declared Vivekanand to be "undoubtedly the greatest figure in the Parliament. "The western materialism realised its fruitlessness and nothingness as against the spiritiual glory of the Vedantas or the Hinduism. His militant presentation of the Hindu thought greatly strengthened the pride of Indians in their own culture and religion.

(8) In 1896, Vivekanand founded the Ramakrishna Mission to carry on humanitarian relief and social work. For this purpose he took upon himself the task of awakening his countrymen and reminding them repeatedly of their weaknesses. He inspired them, to struggle unto life and death to bring about a new state of things—sympathy for the poor and needy and bread to their hungry mouths, enlightenment to the people at large." A band of workers devoted to this cause were trained through the Ramakrishna Mission. He organised the disciples of Ramakrishna Mission in 1897. In 1899 he established the Belur Matha at Calcutta which became the centre of the Mission activities. In 1899 Vivekanand again visited U.S.A. He also attended the Congress of History of Religions in Paris in 1900 A.D. He died in 1902 at the age of 39. Though the span of his life was very short yet he left an endearing influence. On the succeeding generations. Though religion was mission in

life, he was keenly interested in the improvement of all aspects of national life.

Ramakrishna Mission. It was started in 1896 by Swami Vivekanand in memory of his Guru, Ramakrishna Paramhansa. It has branches all over India and has done a good deal of humanitarian work. The members of this mission do not accept, the full programme of Brahmo Samaj but they are all liberal thinkers. They do not accept the Orthodox principles of Hinduism. The followers of Ramakrishna are divided into two groups. Firstly, there are ascetics. They do not marry any dedicate their: lives to God and the service of mankind. Secondly, there are these followers who live in the world and earn their livelihood but regulate their lives according to the teachings of Ramakrishna. The Ramakrishna Mission has started a large number of schools, orphanages and dispensaries.

SWAMI DAYANAND (1824-1883)

Swmi Dayanand Saraswati (Mulshankar) was born in 1824 in a Brahmin family of Kathiawar. Even in his childhood (14 years) he had opposed idol worship. At the age of 22, he ran away from his house in search of knowledge and made a deep study of Sanskrit language and literature. In 1863 he started propagating his ideas. He got real learning from Swami Virjanand. He devoted his life to the propagation of Vedic religion and reform of Hindu society.

Swami Dayanand founded Arya Samaj in Bombay in 1 75 A.D. Through this institution he tried to propagate his ideas among the people. Swami Dayanand believed that selfish and ignorant priests had perverted Hindu religion with the aid of the Puranas which he said were full of false teachings. For his own, inspiration, Swami Dayanand went to the Vedas, which he regarded as infallible, being the inspired word of God, and as the fount of all knowledge. He rejected all later religious thought if it conflicted with the Vedas. This total dependence on the Vedas and their infallibility gave his teachings an orthodox colouring, for infallibility meant that human reason was not to be the final deciding factor. However, his approach had a rationalist aspect, because the Vedas, though revealed, were to be interpreted by himself and others, who were human beings. This individual reason was the decisive factor. He believed that every person had the right of direct access to God. Moreover, instead of supporting Hindu orthodoxy, he attacked it and led a revolt against it. The teachings he derived from his own interpretation of the Vedas were surprisingly similar to the religious and social reforms that other Indian reformers were advocated. He was opposed to idolarty, ritual, and priesthood and particularly to the prevalent caste practices and popular Hinduism ,as preached by Brahmins. He also directed attention towards the problems of men as they lived in this real world and away from the traditional belief in the other world. He also favoured the study of western sciences. Rejecting orthodoxy, he supported reasoning. He strongly opposed caste system and propagated the ending of untouchability. For women's emancipation he opposed practices like the custom of Sati and child marriage. He opposed image worship ceremonies and priestism. He concerned himself more with problems of this , life than the other. Arya Samaj started many schools and colleges 'for the promotion for education. For the protection of Hindu religion it started Shudhi movement which saved the Hindus from conversions. Converts to Christianity or Islam were remade Hindus but this practice of Arya Samaj injured the feelings of supporters of secularism. More important work of Swamiji is "Satyarth Prakash." It was published in 1874. In this book Swami Dayanand attacked child marriages as being contrary to the Vedas; In his book, he also denounced other established religions, According to Dayanand, "The Vedas were infallible and Hinduism should be purified by returning to the Vedas." For some time there was a talk between him and Madam Blavatsky, the founder of the Theosophical Society for union between the two societies. But it failed. The Swami died on 30 October 1883, at Ajmer, as a result of the slow effect of a subtle poison administered to him mixed in food, by a Muslim concubine of Maharana Sajjan Singh of Jodhpur. The Swami had gone there on the invitation of the Maharana, and had taken a strong exception to his living with the concubine.

CONTRIBUTION OF ARYA SAMAJ

The Arya Samaj undertook the task of reforming Hindu religion in North India. It was founded in 1875 by Swami Dayanand Saraswati (1824-1883). Swami travelled all over India to propagate his views and established Arya Samaj organisations at different places for the same purpose. In the beginning, the Arya Samaj kept only the following three principles:

1. The Arya Samaj would accept only the Vedas as the final truth.

2. Every member of the Arya Samaj would contribute 1/100 part of his income towards the Samaj, Arya Samaj School or the newspaper of Arya Samaj, Arya Prakash.

3. The educational institutions established by Arya Samaj would give education only in learning of the Vedas.

But in 1877 above three principles were replanced by the following ten principles:

1. Opposition to idol-worship.

2. Belief in female-education.

3. God is primary cause of all true knowledge.

4. God is all-truth, all-knowledge, unbegotten infinite and the cause of the universe. To him alone worship is due.

5. Vedas are the books of true knowledge. Every Arya must read them.

6. All should be treated with love and due regard to their merit.

7. In personal affairs, all are to have freedom, but no person is to stand in the way of the general good.

8. Ignorance must be dispelled and knowledge diffused.

9. Attempts to propagate Hindi and Sanskrit languages.

10. Primary work of the Samaj is to benefit the whole world by improving the physical, spiritual and social conditions of the people.

Every member should observe the following Mahamantaras:

1. Brahma Yajona, which is two fold:

    (a) Sandhya or worship of God every morning and every evening.

    (b) Swadhyaya or regular reading of pertions of scripture every day.

2. The day is to be began with Deva Yajona-the well known Havans or burning of ghee.

3. Pitri Yajona or some sort of daily service to parents.

4. Atithi Yajona or the feeding of some ascetic or a learned man.

5. Balivaishna Deva Yojona or a duty towards poor and helpless persons and towards domestic animals.

Main programmers and Activities:

The basic principles on which the social ideas of the Samaj were based were:

(i) Fatherhood of God and Brotherhood of man.

(ii) Equality of sexes.

(iii) Absolute justice and fair play between, man and man, and nation and nation. Equal opportunities to all according to their nature, Karma and merit.

(iv) Love and charity towards all.

Work or Contribution of Arya Samaj. The work or contribution of Arya Samaj can be divided into following four main categories:

1. Religious Field. In the field of religion, the Arya Samaj opposed idol worship, ritualism, the practice of animal-sacrifice, the idea of heaven and hell and the concept of fatalism. It claimed the supremacy of the Vedas and, on the basis of their principles, emphasized on doing on one duties Yajona, recitation of the mantras, *etc.* It simplified Hinduism and developed faith in its supremacy among the Hindus. It forbids Hindus to regard the Purnas and other such books as the sources of the development of the Hindu religion. It regards all such books as only religious and social myths, histories and some type of literature of a nation and says that they do not contain the fundamentals of the Hindu religion. It asks the Hindus to regard only the Vedas as the fountain source and the only true base of the Hindu religion. Swami Dayanand believed that selfish and ignorant priests had perverted Hindu religion with the aid of the Puranas which he said were full of false teachings. Arya Samaj inculcated a spirit of self-respect and self-reliance among the people. At the same time, one of the Arya Samaj's objective was to prevent the conversion of Hindus to other religions.

2. Social Field. Social reforms done by the Arya Samaj are most important. The Arya Samaj opposed the traditional institution of caste system. According to Arya Samaj the basis of the division of society into four castes:

(i) The Brahmins

(ii) The Kashtariyas

(iii) The Vaishyas and

(iv) The Shudras-should be the natural talent and the work done by an individual and not on the basis of heredity or birth. Inter-caste marriages and inter-dining was practical by the members of the Arya Samaj in their routine life. Arya Samaj opposed child marriages, pologamy, Parda-system and the practice of Sati. It instantly worked for uplift of the depressed classes of the society. The first Hindu orphanage was established by the Arya Samaj in the Punjab in Ferozepur during the life time of the Swamiji with a splendid and commodious building. Later on a number of orphanages on similar lines were established at different places in Northern India. In 1897-98 there were very serve famines in the country. A very commendable service was rendered by the Samaj in organising relief of distress. Thousand of children were rescued and for them several new orphanages were opened in the Punjab. In 1908, famine relief was organised in the United Provinces. The famine relief included different kinds or other social services as well, organization of medical relief in the time of pestilence, nursing the sick and helping in the disposal of the dead.

3. Educational Field. Arya Smaj is the greatest educational institutions in the country: No other organisation has so many educational institution under its control and management as the Arya Samaj has. In the provinces of the Punjab and Uttar Pradesh there are hundreds of D.A.V. Colleges, Gurukuls and Schools which impart modern education to tens of thousands of pupils. Gurukuls provide education mostly of Sanskrit, the Vedas, Ayurved *etc.*, D.A.V. Schools and Colleges provide modern education in Humanities and Sciences. These educational institutions have participated not only defending Hindu religion, society and culture but also in the growth of education, knowledge and enlightenment in general.

4. Political Fields. The Arya Samaj was mainly a Hindu reform movement and was not a political organization. But even then it played a very important part in creating national consciousness. Swami Dayanand was the first man to use the term Swaraj. He was the first to insist on people using only swadeshi things, manufactured in India and to discard foreign things. He was the first who recognised Hindi as the national language of India. The credit of the many of the national building programmes and acts of the Indian National Congress should go to the Arya Samaj because it provided inspiration for all those good things. Many national leaders like Lala Lajpat Rai, Bal Gangadhar Tilak. Gopal Krishna Gokhle *etc.* were deeply impressed by the philosophy and principles of Arya Samaj. The Arya Samaj, infact participated in building up personalities of many Indians who imbibed the spirit of militant Hinduism from it and participated actively in the national movement.

CONTRIBUTION OF MRS. ANNIE BESANT AND THEOSOPHICAL SOCIETY

Society was founded at New York in the United Sates of America by Lady Madan H.P. Blavatsky (a Russian born American citizen) and an American Colonel Henry Steel Olcott in 1875A.D. Swami Dayanand invited both these leaders to visit India and in 1883 A.D., they later came to India and established the headquarters of the Society at Adyar near Madras in 1886.

The Society believed that the source of all religions is one. It wanted to remove all discrimination of caste, colur and creed and wished to create universal brotherhood. The Theosophists advocated the revival and strengthening of the ancient religions of Hinduism. Zoroastrianism, and Buddhism. They recognised the doctrine of the transmigration of the soul. The members of the society endeavoured to attain a knowledge of God by spiritual ecstasy, direct institution or special individual relations. The society accepts the Hindu beliefs in re-carnation, Karma and draws inspiration from the philosophy of the Upanishads and, Samkhya, Yoga and Vedanta schools of thought. The founding fathers of the Society were greatly impressed by the Hindu culture. They warned the Indians not to be taken by the Christian missionaries and admitted that the Hinduism could lead the world.

In India the Theosophical movement became somewhat popular with the election of Mrs. Annie Besant as its President after the death of Col. Henry Steel Olcott in 1907 A.D, Early in her life Mrs. Annie Besant lost all faith in Christianity, divorced her husband, an Anglican clergyman, and came in contact with the of Theosophical Society in 1882 A.D. in U.S.A. In 1889 A.D. she formally joined the Theosophical Society. Mrs. Annie Besant came to India in 1893 and became the leader of the movement. She adopted India as her motherland and regarded Indian culture much superior to the western culture. Many people were attracted towards her owing to her love for Hinduism and the people. In the beginning she devoted herself to the revival of Hindu religion with its philosophy, rituals and modes of worship. Though her ideas were used by those who were opposed to social reform in their conflict with the reformers, they helped to impart to the educated Indians a sense of pride in their own country. Her activities in the field of education were more significant. She laid the foundation of the Central Hindu College in Benaras in 1898 where both the Hindu religion and Western scientific subjects were taught. The college became the nucleus for the formation of Benaras Hindu University in 1916. Mrs. Annie Besant also did much for the cause of girls education. Due to her interest in education the headquarters of the Soceity at Adyar became a centre of knowledge with a library of rare Sanskrit books. Annie Besant later threw herself into the work of social reform and politics. She raised her voice against casteism and the discrimination based on caste, religion and colour. She also formed the Home Rule League on the pattern of the Irish Home Rule movement campaigned for Home Rule for India during the First World War. After her detention, she became President of the Indian National Congress in 1918 A. D. Although the Theosophical movement did not enjoy mass popularity, its work under the leadership of Annie Besant for the awakening of Indian people was remarkable. She thus contributed great deal to the development of the national spirit of India.

The Theosophical Society provided a common denominator for the various sets and fulfilled the urge of educated Hindus. But it should be accepted that as religious revivalists, the theosophists were not very successful. But they made a pecular contribution to development in modern India. It was a movement by westerners who glorified Indian religions and philosophical traditions. This helped Indians recover their self-confidence, even though it tended to give them a sense of false pride in their past greatness.

MAHADEV GOVIND RANADE

Mahadev Govind had been a brilliant student right from Matriculation onwards, keeping first position in all examinations. He started his career as a teacher. After working as a teacher for sometime he joined the judicial service and rose to the Court Bench by sheer merit. Ranade was one of the founders of the Indian National Congress, but his greatest passion was social reform. As a judge in Poona, he took an active part in the activities of the Sarvajanik Sabha which was a leading organization making public opinion known to the Government. He joined the Prarthna Sabha and took keen interest in its social reform activities. In fact, under his able guidance the Prarthna Samaj became the active centre of a new social reformation in Western India. He was one of the founders of the Widow Marriage Association and was an ardent promoter of the famous Deccan Education Society.

Its object was to impart such education to the young as would fit them for the unselfish service of the country. An all India organization, the Indian Social Conference, was formed in 1887. made was the soul of the Conference and was its General Secretary for 14 years. Under Ranade's leadership, the Conference worked as a secular organization of Indian Society. Some of the demands of the conference were the abolition of caste, support to Inter-caste marriages, raising of the marriageable age, discouragement of polygamy, widow re-marriage, women's education, improvement in the condition of outcastes, and settlement of reolgious disputes between the Hindus and Muslims by the appointment of Panchayats. Justice Ranade believed in two basic principles so far as social reform work was concerned. First, he wanted to deal with the whole man, and not to carry out reforms on one side only. Secondly, he believed that in Social reforms long formed habits cannot be ignored so easily.

In brief, we can say that Ranade was a great intellectual and took a broad view of the problems. He was convinced that the nation needed to progress in all spheres of life—social, educational, political and economic. He said, "You cannot have a good social system when you find yourself low in the scale of political rights nor can you be lit to exercise political rights and priveleges unless your social system is based on reason and justice. You cannot have a good economic system when your social arrangements are imperfect. If your religious ideas are low and gruelling, you cannot succeed in the social, economic or political spheres. This interdependence is not an accident but is the law of our nature." Under his leadership, the work of social reform was made more broadbased and was extended all over the country. He advocated for the industrialization of the country. His slogan was "Industrialise or Perish".

SIR SAYYID AHMAD KHAN

Sir Sayyid Ahmad Khan's (1817-1898 A.D.) name stands out conspicuous among the Muslim reformers of the nineteenth century. Born in Delhi in 1817 in a respectable Muslim family, he received education in the traditional Muslim style. He joined the service of the British East Indian Company as a Judicial Officer and remained loyal to the British government during the days of the Revolt of 1857 A.D. This gave him a right to speak in favour of his community which the rulers could not long ignore. He pointed out to the British the depressed position of the Indian Muslims whom the British government had declared as its "real enemies and most dangerous rivals," After hard persuation Sayyid Ahmad Khan was able to convince the British officials of the necessity of a better undersanding of the Indian Muslims. The problem of religious and education reforms was more an up hill task before him and he took responsibility very seriously and sincerely.

His Contribution, Thoughts and Attitude

1. In the Religious Field. Sayyid Ahmad Khan made significant contribution in the direction of religion, education and social sphere to bring about awakening amongst the Muslims. He was tremendously impressed by modern scientific thought and worked all his life to reconcile it with Islam. This he did, first of all, by declaiming that the Quran alone was the authoritative work for Islam and all other Islamic writings were secondary. Even the Quran he interpreted in the light of contemporary rationalism and science. In his view any interpretation of the Quran that conflicted with human reason, science or nature was in reality a misinterpretation. He asked the Muslims to adopt the basic principles of Islam *viz*., simplicity and purity. He was a firm believer in religious toleration. He wrote many a time on the Hindu-Muslim unity.

2. In the Field of Education. Muslims Sayyid Ahmad Khan emphasized modern western education because through such progressive education only Muslims could progress like other Indian sections. Orthodox Muslim section opposed it but Ahmad Khan faced bravely all the difficulties. As a practical step towards popularising English education he started building up new schools. He was greatly impressed by modern scientific thinking throughout his life. In 1862, he founded the Scientific Society to translate and publish scientific works in Urdu to familarize people with modern science. For propagation of education amongst the Muslims he founded the "Anglo-Oriental College" at Aligarh in 1875. Later on it developed into the famous Aligarh Muslim University. It was because of this that the movement of freedom started by Sir Sayyid Ahmad is known as the Aligarh Movement. The College had a strong European staff, and Arabic and Persian were taught as optional subjects only. Aligarh Muslim University became one of the most important breeding grounds of new trends in the social and cultural life of the Muslims. In his educational and literary activities, he had served all the people of India.

3. In the Field of Society. Along with religious reform and spread of education he tried to bring about reform in the Muslim society and opposed Pardah system, easy divorce and polygamy. Sayyid Ahmad Khan also tried to reform the social abuses in the Muslim community. He condemned the system of piri and muridi. The piris and faqirs claimed to be followers of the Sufi school and passed mystic words to their disciples (murids). He aiso condemned the institution of slavery and described it unslamic.

4. In the Political Field. Sir Sayyid insisted on the co-operation of the Muslims with the British government and looked at all political movements with distrust. Thus when the Indian National Congress was formed (1885), he opposed it. He wanted more time for the Indian Muslims to organize and consolidate their position and thought.

Sayyid Ahmad Khan was patriotic and his relations with Hindus were friendly. Though Sir Sayyid opposed the Indian National Congress, he emphasized the unity between Hindus and Muslims his opposition to the Indian National Congress was not based on any belief that it was a Hindu organization but because he was opposed to all political agitations. Basically he was a secular. He held the view, "in consideration of the fact that we belong to the same country, we are a nation and the progress and usefulness of the country, and of both of us, depended on our unity, mutual sympathy and love." He believed that all religions had a certain underlying unity which could be called practical morality. Believing that a person's religion was his or her private affair he roundly condemned any sign of religions begotry in personal relations. He was also opposed to communal friction. However, the political ideas of Sir Sayyid were not liked by most of the modern progressive historians and scholars. He was opposed to all political agitation and movements. He only wanted the backwardness of the Muslim middle and upper classes to go. His politics was the result of his firm belief that immediate political progress was not possible because the British Government could not be easily dislodged. His political attitude shocked other Muslim leaders who beginning with moderate reform activities, had joined the Indian National Congress and were working for the building up of a secular movement for national regeneration. One of the reasons for his attitude was his belief that the Muslim interests should be harmed if they started taking part in political agitation. Another was the extreme upper-class attitude. On the Indian National Congress demand for having elected representatives in the Provincial Legislative Councils and for holding Civil Service examinations in India. With the members of noble families in our country like it that a person of lower class or law status even if he had taken the RA. or M.A. degree and possessed the necessary- ablity should govern them and dispose of their wealth, property and honour? Never." Inspite of these limitations, Sir Sayyid was more than any other social reformer responsible for awakening the Indian Muslims to the realities of the modern world and preparing them to meet the challenge.

MUSLIM REFORM MOVEMENT

The reform movements in the Muslim community began in the latter half of the 19th century.

(i) These movements developed at a later stage among muslims because the Muslim middle class came later was weak.

(ii) The British conquest had dispossessed most of the Muslim jagirdars. These jagirdars could not reconcile themselves to the new situation shield away from modern education.

(iii) Many Muslims were skilled workers and were ruined as a result of the economic impact of British conquest.

(iv) In the Revolt of 1857 A.D., the Muslim masses and religious leaders fought against the British. After the Revolt was crushed, the British government took repressive measures against Muslims and regarded them as its enemies, holding them responsible for the Revolt. The British government followed a deliberate anti-Muslim policy and discriminated against them.

(v) The Muslim jagirdars and other people related with the upper class of this community who still remained, suffered from a feudal outlook. They lived their lives in the old way, unmindful of the changes that were taking place.

The Muslim upper classes had tended to avoid contact with Western education and culture, and it was mainly after the Revolt of 1857 that modern ideas of religious reform began to appear and resulted in the rise of a number of movements. Most of these movements were concerned with imparting modern English education to the Muslim community, campaigning against polygamy and the Purdah system and reinterpreting religion in the light of modern ideas. Some of these movements devoted themselves to the spread of education and social reforms and some to political opposition to the British Government.

1. The Wahabi Movement. Sayyid Ahmad Brahlvi was the first Muslim thinker who felt drawn to the task of bringing about some reforms in the Muslim religion and to improve the lost of the Muslim community. He was a contemporary of Raja Ram Mohan Roy. He spread the message of the Wahabi Movement, which had been started in Arabia by Mohammad Ibn Abdul Wahab to preach oneness of God. The orignial movement in Arabia was to purify Islam and denounced the worship of graves, walis, peers, faqirs and aulias. Quran was translated in Persian for the use of common man. After the death of Sayyid Ahmad Brahlvi in 1831 Patna became the centre of the movement. A central committee was in charge of overall operations and there were also district committees and permanent preachers. It used to meet every Friday night after prayers. The Wahabi movement in its earlier phase was a purely religious one restricted to a particular section of the Muslim community. Gradually it assumed a political character and became popular with all ranks of the Mohammadan community. The leaders of the movement tried to launch angitation against the annexation of the Punjab by the British Government but their agitation was suppressed with an iron hand.

2. Ahmadiya or Qadiani Movement. Mirza Ghulam was the founder of this movement. He was born at Qadian in the district of Gurdaspur, in Punjab, so this is also called the Qadiani Movement. He was conservative and reactionary in his attitude. He believed that prophet Mohammad was not the last purports of God (or Allah). Other religions too had the prophet. They should also be respected. He was the supporter of the Islamic practice of divorce and polygamy and was opposed to the abolition of Purdah. He believed in the teachings of Quran and advocated to have a liberal attitude other religions. He was not in favour of a constant 'Jehad' (The Holy War) against the Hindus. There was a split in the movement in 1914 A.D. It was divided into two groups—the Lahore Party and the Qadiani Party.

3. Deoband Movement. Another important movement is associated with the centre of a religious school at Deoband near Saharanpur in Uttar Pradesh. It was founded by the Ulama, the Muslim theologians, and their followers who had fought against British rule in 1857. It was also a centre of political revolt against British rule and imparted to its students love for political freedom. When Sir Sayyid Ahmad Khan advised Muslims to keep away from the Congress and join the pro-government Patriotic Association, about 100 Ulama from all over the country and even from Medina and Baghdad issued a Fetwa forbidding Muslims to join the Association and permitting them to join the Congress.

4. Badruddin Tyabji. There were other more thorough going movements of social reform amongst the Muslims. These movements worked for the emancipation of women, combated the system of purdah, polygamy and child-marriage. These movements were particularly strong in western and southern India. Badruddin Tyabji (1844-1906) was the most outstanding leader of these movements. He was the first Indian bar-at-law to start practice in the Bombay High Court. Along with other social reformers and national leaders, he was active in the Indian Social Conference. This Conference was formed in 1887. The Conference worked as a secular organization and compaigned for various reforms aiming at the reform and modernization of Indian society. Some of the demands of the Conference were the abolition of caste, intercaste marriages, raising of the marriageable age, discouragement of polygamy, widow re-marriage, women's education, improvement in the condition of outcastes, and settlement of religious disputes between Hindus and Muslims by the appointment of Panchayats.

5. Muhammad Iqbal. One of the greatest poets of modern India, Muhammad Iqbal (1876-1938) also profoundly influenced through his poetry the philosophical and religious outlook of the younger generation of Muslims as well as of Hindus. Like Swami Vivekananda, he emphasised the need for constant change and ceaseless activity and condemned resignation, contemplation, and quiet contentment. He urged the adoption of dynamic outlook that would help change the world. He was basically a humanist. In fact, he raised human action to the status of a prime virtue. Man should not submit to nature or powers that be, he said, but should control this world through constant activity. Nothing was made sinful in his eyes than the passive acceptance of things as they were condemning retualism, ascestisism, another wordily attitude, he urged men of work for and achieve happiness in this world of the living.

GROWTH OF THE INDIAN RENAISSANCE IN THE 19TH CENTURY

The Indians came in contact with the Western culture when intellectualism and individualism were its dominant features. The movements were started during this period. On account of ignorance of the people many evil, unsocial cruel in human customs and traditions were prevalent in the society. Sati system, child marriage, polygamy, child infanticide, caste system, untouchability, prohibition of travelling overseas, purdah system *etc.*, were some of the social and religious evils which were prevalent in the society. The impact of western civilization roused them and forced the people to revise their orthodox ideas and to make a revolution of their old values. Indians with English education gave up their attitude of uncritical defence to authority, tradition and customs and so became the pioneers of almost all movements for social and political reforms.

The Causes. Various factors participated in the growth of Indian Renaissance some of them are given here by:

1. **Political Unification.** The British united larger part of Indian politically and administratively. The social and religious reform movements were expressions of the early beginnings of national feeling, and contributed to its further development.

2. **Recognition of the True Nature of British Rule**-The political unification of the country provided politically conscious Indians the opportunity to think about their own countrymen and provoked them to kind out the causes of their misery. The politics of the moderated nationalists

were founded on the belief that British rule could be reformed from within. But the spread of knowledge regarding political and economic questions gradually undermined this belief. The nationalist writers and agitators blamed British rule for the poverty of the people. Politically conscious Indians were convinced that the purpose of British rule was to exploit India economically, that is, to enrich England at the cost of India.

3. **Contacts with Other Countries.** The foreign contacts and the progress achieved in different countries inspired Indians to achieve similar progress for themselves. The rise of modern Japan after 1868 showed that a backward Asian country could develop itself without Western control.

4. **The Propoganda of Christian Missionaries.** The propaganda carried out in different parts of the country by Christian Missionaries to make converts in India provoked both the Hindus and the Muslims into reinforcing their efforts to defend and reform their religion and society.

5. **Rediscovery of India's Past by the Foreigners.** Certain western scholars like Max Muller and William Jones revived the past glory of Indian culture by their researches and writings. The Indians felt that their culture was in no way interior to that of the West and it needed only revival to stand upon or even surpass the Western culture.

6. **Western Thought and Education.** As a result of the spread of modern western education and thought during the 19th century, a large number of Indians imbibed a modern rational, secular democratic and nationalist political outlook.

7. **The Role of the Press and Literature.** The other chief instrument through which the nationalist, minded Indians spread the message of renaissance was the press. The press and new literary works brought Indians in close contact with the ideas of liberty, equality and fraternity *etc.*

The Growth of the Indian Renaissance. Social and religious reform movements arose among all communities of the Indian people. In religion, they attacked bigotory superstition and the hold of the priestly class. In social life, they aimed at the abolition of caste, child marriage, polygamy, purdah ,system and other legal and social inequalities.

1. **Raja Ram Mohan Roy and Brahmo Samaj.** The Central figure in this awakening was Raja Ram Mohan Roy (1772-1883), who is rightly regarded as the first leader of modern India. He was moved by deep love for his people and country and worked hard all his life for their social, religious, intellectual and political regeneration. He founded the Brahmo Samaj in 1828.

2. **Reformation Movement among Muslims.**

3. **The Akali Movement.**

4. **Religious Reforms among the Parsis.**

Effects of the Indian Renaissance (A) Good Effect. The Indian Renaissance gave birth not only to various socio-religious movements but affected every aspect of Indian life. Main effects of the Indian Renaissanced were realised in the following fields.

1. Religion. The social and religious movements revived faith among Indians in their own religion and brought forth the necessity of reforming their religion. All religions communities of India including the Hindus, Muslims, Parsis, Sikhs and Christians *etc.* attempted to modernise and simplify their religion. The best attempt in this direction was made by several Hindu reformers and institutions. Raja Ram Mohan Roy and his Brahmo Samaj, Swami Dayanand Saraswati and Arya Samaj, Vivěkanand and Ramakrishana Mission etc. aimed to reform the Hindu religion and revive its past glory. Foreign scholars like Max Muller, Sir William Jones, Charles Wilkins etc. helped in reviving the past glory of India. They translated several religious texts of the Hindus and proved these were among the bese religious treaties of the world. Many Hindus gave up superistions, useless religious rituals idol worship *etc.* Arya Samaj forbade to regard the Purans and other such books as the sources of the development of the Hindu to regard only the Vedas as the fountain source and the only true base of the Hindu religion. Swami Vivekanand placed the Hindu religion on the high pedestal of spritualism. In this way we can say the different socio-religioius reforms strengthened the Hindu Religion.

2. Society. The effects of socio-religious reform movements of the nineteenth century were not limited to religious only. Each of them made praise worthy efforts to ride the society of its evils as well. They actively opposed the caste system, untouchability, child-marriage, Sati system, Purdah system, polygamy etc. supported the general uplift of women, including widow remarriage and the spread of modern education to men and women several schools and colleges were opened by these movements and reforms. Due to efforts of certain movements inter-caste marriages and inter-dining were promoted and hospitals, dispensaries, orphanages, libraries etc. were opened.

3. Political. The social and religious reform movements of the nineteenth century contributed most to Indian nationalism though indirectly. Raja Ram Mohan Roy, Swami Dayanand Saraswati, Swami Vivekanand, Ishwarchandra Vidyasagar, Mrs. Annie Besant etc. were all great patriots. They revived the glory of ancient India, created faith among the people in their religion and culture and, thus, gave the message of self-respect, self confidence and love to their motherland and to the people of India. Swami oayanand Saraswati, founder of Arya Samaj exercised great nationalising influence upon his followers. He was the first who used the word Swaraj and declared Hindi as the national language of India. Many Arya Samajist leaders were in the forefront of the national movement and were primarily responsible for the rise of extremism in Indian National Congress. According to Mrs. Annie Besant : "It was Dayanand Saraswati who proclaimed India for the Indians."

4. Economic. The Renaissance awakened the Indians to their miserable economic conditions as well. Several reformers were convinced that the purpose of British rule was to exploit India economically, that is, to enrich England at the cost of India. They realised that India could make little progress in the economic field unless British imperialism was replaced by a government controlled and run by the Indian people. They realised that the British rule had impoverished their economy. It had destroyed their small and cottage industries leading to pressure on agriculture and the only remedy for retrieving the economy lay in industrialization.

5. The growth of the attitude of reason was the cause as well as one of the results of the Indian Renaissance. Before the beginning of the social and religious movements the Indians were largely traditionalists and lived on blind faith. The religious reform movements of modern times and an underlying unity most of them were based on the twin doctrines of Reason (Rationalism) and Humanism, though they also sometimes tended to appeal to faith and ancient authority to bolster their appeal. The reformers of the 19th century opposed the ritualistic, superstitions, irrational, and obnscuranist elements in Indian religions. Many of them abandoned, though with varying degrees, the principle of authority in religion and evaluated truth in any religion or its holy books by its conformity to logic, reason, or science. Some of these religious reformers appealed to tradition and claimed that they were merely reviving the pure doctrines, beliefs, and practices of the past. But, in fact, the past could not be revived. Western education and literature destroyed blind faith of the Indians.

6. The religious reform movements helped many Indians to come to terms with the modern world. In fact they arose to recast the old religions into a new modern world to suit the needs of new social group of society. Thus pride in the past did not prevent Indians from accepting the essential superiority of the modern world in general and modern science in particular. As a result of the reformed outlook, many Indians began to acquire a modern, this worldly, secular and national outlook in place of a narrow outlook dominated by considerations of caste and religion, though the latter tendency by no means came to an end. Moreover more and more people began to think terms of promoting their physical and cultural welfare in this world in place or' passively accepting their lot and waiting for improvement in life and after death.

7. Before renaissance of 19th century many Indians had fallen so low as to have lost confidence in their own capacity for self-government. Moreover, many British officials and writers of the time constantly advanced the thesis that Indians had never been able to rule themselves, that Hindus and Muslims had always fought one another, that Indians were destined to be ruled by foreigners, that their religion and social life were degraded and uncivilised making them unfit for democracy or even self-government. Many of the social reformers tried to arouse the self-confidence and self respect of the people by counterings this propoganda. They printed to the cultural heritage of India with pride and referred the critics to the political achievements of rulers like Ashoka, Chandragupta Vikramaditya, and Akbar. In this task they were helped and encouraged by the work of European and other foreign scholars in rediscovering our national heritage in are, architecture, literature, philosophy, science and politics. Scholars like James Forgusson, Dr. Fuller, Dr. Clart, Percy Brown and John Marshall found out the historical movements, paintings, pieces of sculpture, books etc. at different places in India, and, thus proved that India had a rich cultural heritage.

(B) Bad Effects. Some negative or bad effects of the religious reform movements may also be noted. They were:

(1) All of the religious reform catered to the needs of a small percentage of the population. The urban middle and upper classes. None of them could react the vast masses of the peasantry and urban poor, who continued by and large to lead their lives in the traditional, custom-ridden ways.

(2) The second limitation, which later became a major negative factor, was the tendency to look backward, appeal to past greatness and to rely on scriptural authority. These tended to go against the positive teachings of the reform movements themselves. They underminded to some extent the supermacy of human reason and scientific outlook. Appeals

to past greatness created false pride and smugness, while the habit of finding a Golden Age in the past acted as a check on the full acceptance of modern science and hampered the effort to improve the present. But most of all these tendencies tended to divide Hindus, Muslims, Sikhs and Parsis as also high caste Hindus from low caste. Hindus. Any over-emphasis on religion in a country containing many religions was bound to have a divisive effect.

Main features of the Socio-Religious Reform Movements in India in the 19th Century

I. Mojor Religious Reform Movements of 19th Century. In the nineteenth century Brahmo Samaj, Param Hansa Mandali. Prarthana Sabha, Ramakrishna Mission. Arya Samaj, Theosophical society, Muhammadan Literary Society, the Religious Reform Association of the Parsis and Akali Dal of Sikhs all these organizations made notable steps to bring about religious reforms in India. Though these religious movements were true to their basic principles and concepts yet by adopting reason and humanism they tried to make the Indian people adoptive to new needs and to the freedom movement. By reason they tried to remove the ills of their respective religious so that superstitions and fales customs could be done away with. Everybody was expected to become a humanist.

II. The Religious Movements were Started First of All in Bengal. It is correct that Bengal was the first province in India to have social and religious reform movements in 19th century. There were many causes for that, some of which are given below:

(i) Ram Mohan Roy, who is regarded as the first great reformer or father of Modern Indian settled permanently in Calcutta after 1814 and soon attracted a band of young men with whose co-operation he started the Atmiya Sabha. From now onwards he carried on a persistant struggle against the religous and social evils which were widely prevalent among the Hindus in Bengal. He raised his voice in favour of modern education.

(ii) In 1828 Ram Mohan Roy founded a new religious society, the Brahmo Sabha later known as the Brahmo Somaj in Bengal. The institution laid emphasis no human dignity opposed idolatry, and criticise the social evils such as the practice of Sati system, Caste system, Child marriage etc. and advocated the remarriage of widow and women education.

(iii) First of all Indian journalism was started in Bengtal by Ram Mohan Roy. He brought out journals in Bengali, Persian, English and Hindi to spread scientific, literary and political knowledge among the people.

(iv) Bengal was the province in the country where British rule was first of all established. The drain of wealth began first of all from Bengal. The province came under direct influence of western culture and activities earlier than the other regions.

(v) In India a radical trend arose among the intellectuals first of all in Bengal during the late 1820's and the 1830's. Its leader and inspirer was the young Anglo-Indian Henry Vivian Derozio. He was a teacher in Hindu College of Calcutta. He promoted radical ideas through his class lectures and by organising student societies for debates and discussions on history, philosophy, science and literature. He inspired these students to think rationally and freely, to question all authority, to love equality, liberty and fraternity, and to regard truth.

(vi) The next towering personality who devoted his whole life for the cause of social and religious reformation was Pandit Vidya Sagar. He also made Bengal the chief centre of his work. He protested against child marriage and suppprted widow remarriage.

(vii) The impact of Western ideas was felt much earlier in Bengal than in other provinces of the country. The Western education was imparted firstly of all by the Company and European missionaries in Bengal. Some Indians started modern schools and colleges first of all in Bengal.

(viii) Bengal was the first province which was occupied by the British. Before their rule it was the richest and most fertile province of India. Its industries and commerce were well developed. The abuses of the British government and the drain of wealth led to impoverishment and exhaustion of the unlucky province. Though the English had extended their dominion to other parts of our country but Bengal remained the main centre of their political, economic and other activities. They ruled over India upto 1911 from Calcutta. Therefore it became the main centre of Indians also.

(ix) Bengal was the first province where the Western missionaries launched a tirade against Indian social and religious evils in their bid to convert maximum people to Christianity. Therefore the task for social and religious reforming also started first of all in Bengal to check the increasing influence of Christian missionaries.

III. Most of the Movements were Based on Reason. Most of the modern religious reform movements were based on reason though to reach their ideas to the people they took recourse to ancient books also. But they adopted a reasoned and scientific attitude to examine the truth of the ancient scriptures. They asked the people to give up those 'ancient customs which were harmful to the society and the country *e.g.*, Brahmo Samaj opposed the custom of Sati, Justice Ranade animal sacrifice and infanticide etc. and Swami Dayanand opposed idol worship. Sir Sayyid Ahmad refused to consider any other scripture except Quran as a truly religious scripture. On the basis of reason he opposed polygamy, easy divorce etc. Brahmo Samaj denied the need of a priestly class to interpret the religious duties. Param Hansa Mandali opposed the caste system. Parsi relgious reformers also carried out a compaign against orthodoxy.

IV. Humanitarianism and the Religious Reform Movement. Almost all the religious leaders and reformers of the 19th century relized the truth of humanitarians in. They advocated that mankind can progress and it has progressed all along. They accepted those moral values which render useful service to humanity. They advised the Indians to make compromise with modern world rather than blindly praising their post all the time. They stressed that in every field modern techniques should be adoped.

V. Contribution of Religious Reform Movement Towards Making of Modern India. The religious reform movements developed the reasoning and humanitarian faculty of the people. They instilled into the mindes of the Indians the feelings of relatively more self-respect, self-confidence and patriotism. They helped the people to scheme a compromise with modern world. This made this great attempt of preparing the people to accept the basic superiority of modern science happily. They encouraged the people to develop a wider perspective in place of narrow outlook.

VI. Some Disadvantages of the Movements. But the religions reform movements had some harmful effect also.

(i) By making a reference to ancient scriptures on every issue they unknowingly harmed human reason and scientific attitude.

(ii) Because of this the followers of every religion began a search into their past and began to try to prove their superiority over the followers of other religions. This encouraged the tendency of diversities among the Hindus, Muslims, Sikhs, Parsis etc. and later on it was also responsible for encouraging communalism in India.

(iii) Other drawback of these reform movements was that it was confined only to urban areas, specially to high class urban people. They did not take into account the fact that majority of Indian population lived in villages.

REFORMS OF LORD CANNING

Lord Canning was appointed the Governor-General of India in February 1856. He was a very learned, able and industrious man. He was confronted with a terrible situation as had not been faced by any of his predecessors. Had he come in the peaceful time, he would have proved to be an ideal ruler. He was the last Governor-General under the Company and the first Viceroy under the Crown. His policy was to heal, rather than to inflame, the wounds inflicted by the late Mutiny. Hence in dealing with the mutineers he sought to temper punishment with mercy and resolutely set his face against the outcry both in England and India for a ruthless and indiscriminate policy of vengence. For this he was attacked with rabid hostility by the Europeans who in derision nicknamed him "Clemency Canning", but he maintained his view with a noble disdain of popular clamour. The most significant event of his career was the Mutiny of 1857 or the First War of Indian Independence. He was successful in suppressing the mutiny of 1857. After the uprising of 1857, the British Parliament abolished the East India Company and transferred its power to the Crown.

After the uprising of 1857, the British Parliament transferred the power of the East India Company to the Crown by the Government of India Act, 1858. In order to clarify the British Policy and to inform the Indian rulers and people, the British Queen issued a proclamation which was read at a Royal Durbar held at Allahabad on November 1,1858 by the first viceroy, Lord Canning.

The shock of the Mutiny brought home to the British Government the necessity of introducing certain constitutional changes. The most important change was transfer of the Control of the Indian Government from the Company to the Crown. But it was felt that something more was needed. The mutiny had revealed the fact that the British Government was deplorably out of touch with Indian public opinion and as a consequence there was no understanding between the rulers and the ruled. Sir Bartle Frere pointed out the danger of continuing "to legistate for millions of people with few means of knowing except by a rebellion whether the laws suit them or not." Hence it was decided to associate a few influential Indians with the legislative business of the Government. The result was the Indian Council Act of 1861. It added a fifth member to the Governor-General's Council and enlarged it for legislative purposes by the appointment of additional members, not less than six and not more than twelve in numbers of whom at least half were to be non-officials *i.e.*, outside the ranks of Civil Service. These additional members were to be nominated by the Governor-General and it was understood that most of the non-official members would be Indians. The function of this enlarged, council was strictly confined to legislation. The Act also reversed the policy of centralisation adopted by the Charter Act of 1883 by restoring to the Governments of Madras' and Bombay their legislative power. It also provided for the creation of similar Legislative Councils in Bengal, the United Provinces and the Punjab as also in any new province that might be created.

The Act of 1861 empowered the Governor-General to frame rules for the transaction of the business of the Executive Council. Lord Canning used the power thus conferred on him to introduce what is called the portfolio system. By it he delegated especial business to individual members of the Council. Thus arose the separation of departments under individual members who on their own initiative dealt with most of the matters in their departments. Only the most important subjects were placed before the Governor-General and in case of difference of opinion were considered by the whole Council. Thus each branch of the administration came to have its separate official head and spokesman and the business the Government was largely decentralised. This decentralisation of the business of their Government made for efficiency and dispatch.

Queen Victoria's Proclamation is a land mark in the History of India because by this Proclamation the British Government assumed the direct responsibility of governing India. It went long way to improve the contemporary conditions of India. It not only satisfied the Indian princes and Nawabs but also the Indian people because it assured them of peace, prosperity, religious freedom, impartiality and equality of behaviour and appointment on higher posts on the basis of ability and equality. Many scholars and historians regard the proclamation as the founder of a new age because it paved the way for the constitutional development by establishing provincial legislation and giving rights of local self government to Indians.

Lord Canning was appointed the first Viceroy of India by Queen Victoria's Prolamation. He did not follow a policy of vengence towards the Indians after the mutiny.

It was on account of this mild policy of Lord Canning that the Europeans in India even called him Clemency Canning. His liberal and tolerant policy again inculcated faith among the Indians and a new age of constitutional development, national movement and scientific and physical development began.

Lord Canning showed favours to the India Princes who had helped the British during the mutiny of 1857. Honorary titles, gifts of money and lands were conferred on them. He abolished the Doctrine of Lapse which was started by Lord Dalhousie. It was made clear to the Indian princes that the British Government would interfere in case of misgovernment but even in that case the Government would take over the administration temporarily and would withdraw after the situation became normal.

Reforms of Lord Canning

(a) **Financial Reforms.** The system of financial administration was greatly improved by the appointment of a Finance Member brought out from England. The first member so appointed was Janes Wilson. He proposed three types of taxes. But his successor Laing proposed only one tax. Thus income tax was imposed at the rate of 5 per cent on the income of five hundred rupees and more a year. Military and civil expenditure were greatly reduced. The levy on salt was enhanced. Before Canning left India, the financial condition had improved and there was no deficit that was caused by the Mutiny.

(b) **Judicial and Police Reforms.** The laws were codified. The Penal Code drafted by Macaulay became law in 1858 and was followed in the next year by the code of criminal procedure. In 1861 the Sadar Courts of the company and the Supreme Court of the Crown in India were amalgamated to form the High Court in the Presidency towns. According to Indian High Court Act 1861 High Courts were set up at Calcutta, Bombay and Madras.

Canning improved the status of the tenants by the Rent Act of 1859 which protected them against arbitrary evictions by land lords. This Act applied to Bengal, Agra and Central Provinces Inspector General was the head of the Police department. Deputy generals of Police were also appointed to assist him in his work. In each district a Superintendent was appointed in order to maintain law order and peace in the district. He was to work under the Supervision of District magistrate. Each district was divided into several circles and each circle was placed under the charge of Deputy Inspector who was assisted by several policy men.

(c) **Army Reforms.** The proportion of the European Soldiers to the Indian Soldiers was not less than one to two here after. It was decided that the Indian soldiers were never to be more than two times of the British soldiers. Artillery was put explusively in the hands of the European.

(d) **Administrative Reforms.** Pegu and Arakan provinces of British Burma were placed under the charge of a Chief Commissioner. Nagpur, Saugar and the Narbade districts were formed into central provinces and were placed under the charge of a Chief Commissioner. Sikkim was incorporated into British empire.

(e) **Agricultural Reforms.** The permanent settlement of Bengal (1793) had failed to protect the interests of the peasants and labourers who were exploited by the zamindar. Bengal rent act was passed in 1859. Farmers who had been holding lands for 20 years on the same rent were deemed to be entitled of this right since 1793. It was decided that unless an enquiry of a court was made their revenue could not be enhanced.

(f) **Educational Reforms.** Universities were set up at Calcutta, Bombay and Madras. There was only the examining universities, and were established on me model of London university.

Other Works. East India Railway was opened between Calcutta and Allahabad in 1861. In 1859-60 there were disputes between European indigo planters and the Bengal peasantry. The planters wanted to force the tenants to cultivate indigo; it led to riots. A commission was appointed to enquire into the matter.

There were severe famines in North West Provinces of Agra and Oudh and parts of Rajputana and Punjab. These famines accounted for the lives of 10 per cent of population in the famine stricken areas. A lot of money was spent on the relief measures.

Estimate of Lord Canning. Lord Canning was one of the greatest Governor-General and Viceroys of India. He was a man of versatile genius. He was highly intellectual. He worked very hard and did not care even for his physical health. He suppressed' the mutiny with great tact and energy. He did not follow the policy of vengence towards the Indians. "He was a noble man who never in the midst of greatest peril allowed his judgment to be swayed by passion or his fine sense of honour and justice to be tarnished by even a passing feeling of revenge."

In this way we can conclude with a remark of Lord Curzon that Lord Canning "Stands in Indian History as one of the most pathetic but also one of the most heroic figures that have represented the name and upheld the honour of England."

ADMINISTRATION OF LORD LYTTON

Lord Lytton, the new Viceroy, who was appointed as such by the Conservative Government of Disraeli, the then Prime Minister of

England, was the son of Sir Edward Lytton, the novelist, dramatist and politician. Lytton was a man of great ability, a poet, essayist and an eloquent speaker. He had served as a diplomatist in many Europpean courts. He came to India commissioned to inaugurate of new Afghan policy which-aimed at arresting the progress of Southward advance of Russia towards Central Asia. He was wellversed in the art of diplomacy but he had no substantial amount of experience in administration. Once before this he was offered the Governor-Generalship of Madras but he had to refuse the offer on health basis. But now this offer of the Viceroyship he accepted on the ground that the refusal of this, offer would mean avoidance of doing one's duty to Government. Robet says about Lytton, "A strictly unaggressive attitude and non-interference carried out perhaps to an extreme and a marked consideration for Afghan susceptibilities were (by Lord Lytton) replaced by spirited foreign policy, imperialistic aims, and a subtle and provocative diplomacy." Lord Lytton died at Paris where he had gone as an ambassador in 1891 at the age of 60. About Lord Lytton Mr. Zacharias has correctly said, "Lord Lytton and Lord Curzon were the two such Viceroys of India who by their policies have inflicted greater loss on India and England than any other Viceroy. The unprogressive and conservative policy of Lord Lytton produced discontent in the minds of the Indians and it was this policy which hastened the political activities of the Indians against the British Government and which also resulted in the counter-offensive Acts against Lytton's Government.

The administration of Lord Lytton can be divided into two categories. *(i)* Internal Administration and, *(ii)* Forign policy.

(I) Internal Administration

1. A famine of an unprecedented intensity broke out in 1876-78 in South India, Madras, Bombay, Mysore. Hyderabad, some parts of the Central India and the Punjab, followed by cholera and fever. Lytton's Government took measures to alleviate it with strict regard to economy in the expenditure of money. About this famine it is said that the loss of human life, in spite of strenuous efforts, was appalling

and mortality was supposed to exceed 50 lakhs. In order to avoid the repetition of the famine in future in the country, it was henceforward decided that the Indian Government should not deal with each famine when it occurred but that preventive and anticipatory measures should be taken. Consequently, two measures to accomplish this end were adopted and they form the basis of the future famine policy of the Government of India. The first was that a Famine Commission under Sir Richard Strachey was set up in 1878 which led to an extensive enquiry and the enunciation of certain rules and regulations to combat this serious menace to human life. The chief measure adopted was to find out means of employment for the able-bodied persons on relief works at a wage sufficient enough to maintain their health and the grant of gratuitous help only to helpless poor destitutes. Subsequently, it was also decided the budget for an annual surplus of £151akhs be raised over the ordinary revenues to be used in years of famine for the construction of railways and canals and this amount was to be raised by means of taxes on trades, professions and cesses on land. Lord Lytton had sound ideas about the true principles of famine relief, *viz.*, freedon of inland trade in grain, the construction of railways and irrigation works for the prevention of famine and the planning of systematic relief works.

2. The financial administration of Lord Lytton was also very sound, as we see:

(a) It was considered desirable to have an exclusive control of the Indian Government over the entire manufacture of salt in India in order to equalize the duty on it in other parts of India also, to do away with the long and extensive line of imports which had been kept up to prevent the smuggling of salt from native states into British territory. The Government of India entered into an agreement with the salt-producing states by which they gave it up in return for some compensation. This having been done, the duty was equalized in a way that the transport of salt from one part to the other ceased to be profitable and thus the customs line was swept away.

(b) It was Lord Mayo who had initiated for the first time the scheme of financial decentralisation. Lord Lytton extended and developed this scheme to a greater extent. In 1878 the provincial Governments were given a share in the local revenues instead of the fixed grants, along with responsibility for productive public works. The salt tax was in a large measure equalized. Many import duties were remitted. The object of financial decentralization was to give to province's incentive for efficiency and economy.

(c) Lord Lytton's Government removed import duties on 29 articles of consumption along with the inland custom on sugar. It was the earnest desire of Lord Lytton to abolish all import duties from most of the articles of consumption, but in view of the lean exchequer of India on account of the heavy drain of the Second Afghan War, he could not implement this desire to abolish all the import duties. Anyhow, an advance was made in the direction of free trade by remitting many import duties. "The House of Commons in England passed a Resolution declaring that the duties imposed were protective and, as such, were not to be abolished. The Manchester merchants demanded the abolition of all duties. The Viceroy's Council was against total abolition. But Lord Lytton exercised his right of veto and abolished all duties on cotton cloth which was not finer than 30 counts."

3. The Vernacular Press Act, 1878. The anti-public policy of Lord Lytton and the sufferings of the people arising out of the great famine of 1877 rendered the people of India very much discontented against the Government. Consequently, discontentment was an open expression amongst the people. Moreover, the Second Afghan War did find support in India. The expenditure incurred on the War was resented. The famine of 1878, as already pointed out, had disturbed the mind of the people. Expenditure on the Delhi Durbar in many quarters was considered unjustified. This gave an ample material to the press for criticising and consequently a violent criticism began to appear in the press. The Government, on the other hand, got alarmed and it passed the Vernacular Press Act in 1878. This Act required the editors of the Vernacular Papers to enter into a bond to publish nothing likely to excite the feelings of dissatisfaction against the Government. This measure was highly invidious and very unpopular with the Indians because the Englishmen were exempted from this Act and there was no provision for appeal. The Act being discriminatory, no wonder the Indians condemned him for that. This Act was also called as Gagging Act, and it is being remembered by the public by this name even now. One of the members of the Indian Council, Sir Erskine Parry, styled this Act as conservative and out of time which arrested the progress of India in future. According to him there could be no stronger law to suppress the Press as the present Act.

4. Lord Lytton founded the Statutory Civil Services in 1879 in order to fulfil the promise contained in the Queen's Proclamation of 1858 that "no native of India will be debarred by reason of nationality from holding office," by which he attempted to ehcourage the recruitment of Indians for positions and official responsibilities. One-sixth of the posts which had hitherto been reserved for the Covenanted Civil Service together with some of the more important posts in the uncovenanted services were combined to form the Statutory Civil Service which was entirely reserved for Indians. At the some time Indians retained the right to fill as many places in the Covenanted services as their abilities would enable them to fill. It was on the whole not a success because it failed to attract the persons from the higher classes. The Statutory Civil Service was abolished 8 years later.

5. According to this Act the possession of arms, wearing of them or carrying on trade in weapons without a due licence from the Government was considered as an offence. Huge punishments were fixed for the violators of this law. Licences were issued to a very limited number of people and that also very sparingly. The most important evil of this Act was that it created a racial hatred between the Europeans and Indians because this law was not made applicable in case of Europeans, Anglo-Indians and other officers of the

Government. By passing this Act, Lord Lytton proved as correct the British point of view that the Indians were not worthy of confidence and trust. Consequently, these two measures aroused indignant protests all over India against the British Government because they seriously curtailed the rights of the Indians.

6. Passing of the Royal Titles Act. Lord Beaconsfield's Ministry invested the Queen of England with former title of the Empress of India, though the passing of this Bill in Parliament was ridiculed by many. An assemblage of native Princes took place in Delhi on 1st January, 1877 when the new dignity was proclaimed by the Viceroy, amidst enthusiastic demonstration of loyalty. The sovereign of India got the title of Kaisar-i-Hind the presence of many native and British Officials afforded an opportunity of holding a conference on the important legislative and fiscal matters which pressed hard at this time while concessions were made, rewards for best services were granted and pensions augmented.

7. Lord Lytton also advocated the introduction of gold standard in India in place of silver. This proposal also fell through.

8. Lord Lytton's Government also planned the enrolment of an Indian peerage and suggested the formation of an Indian Privy Council of ruling Chiefs to advise the Viceroy. His suggestion was not accepted but a similar thing was later on set up in India after the passing of the Government of India Act, 1919 in the form of Narendra Mandal or Chamber of Princes.

9. Lord Lytton also insisted on a high standard of justice against Europeans guilty of assult of Indians. He foreshadowed the Ilbert Bill by trying to stop Europeans from bullying Indians by heavy punishment.

10. The Viceroy opened the Mohammedan Anglo-Oriental College at Aligarh now converted into the Muslim University. The pioneer in this direction was Sir Syyid Ahmad Khan.

(II) Lord Lytton's Foreign Policy

1. North-Western Frontier. He recommended that the North-western frontier should be placed under the Central Government and not under the Punjab Government. This proposal was materialised by Lord Curzon later on.

2. Nepal. Jang Bahadur, the virtual sovereign of Nepal, who had rendered meritorious services to the British in Indian Mutiny, died in 1887. Although he strictly excluded Europeans from his territory, be invariably maintained an amicable policy towards Indian Government and the loss of so steady a friend on the frontier was severely felt by the Indian Government.

3. Lord Lytton's Afghan Policy. The Second Afghan War. Lord Lytton's policy of aggressive interference in Afghanistan was the immediate cause of the commencement of the Second Anglo Afghan War. Lord Lytton came to India commissioned to inaugurate a new policy. He substituted a (Forward) aggressive policy for that of non-interference pursued by his predecessors. His objects were to bring about a gradual disintegration and weakening of the Afghan power and to prevent Afghanistan from falling under the control of Russia. He held that Amir Sher Ali should be treated as an open enemy if he would not declare himself an open friend of the British. He proposed to established a British Resident at Herat and to send a British Mission for the purpose. But Sher Ali declined to receive the Mission saying that he could not do so without granting similar rights to Russia. Thereupon, Lord Lytton, as a preliminary step to war-like operations, occupied Quetta in Balochistan by an amicable aggreement with the Khan of Khelat.

(a) Events of the Second Afghan War. The matters came to a head when in 1878 a Russian envoy ignoring the protest of Sher Ali reached Kabul and negotiated a treaty with him. On receiving these news, Lytton insisted that Sher Ali should receive a British envoy also but the latter refused. Thus the Amir's refusal to receive the British Mission led to the war. On the declaration of the war against Sher Ali, three expeditions advanced upon Kabul by the three great passes of Afghanistan. There was little effective opposition.

(b) The British Government then recognized Yaqub Khan, a son of Sher Ali, as the Amir of Kabul and concluded the treaty of

Gandamak with him. By it the new Amir agreed to receive a British Resident at Kabul; to submit to the control of the British Government in his relations with foreign powers and to cede certain territories including the British occupation of the passes. The British, on the other hand, engaged to support the Amir against the foreign agreession and to pay him an annual subsidy of six lakhs of rupees.

(c) But this arrangement displeased the freedom-loving Afghans who murdered the British Resident, Sir Louis Cavagnary, with the whole body of his escort soon after his arrival at Kabul. This disaster brought on the renewal of the war. British forces were set in motion; Kandhar was occupied and General Roberts defeated the Afghans at Charasiab and entered Kabul. Yaqub Khan had already taken refuge in the British camp and was removed to India as a state prisoner for his suspected connivance at the late massacre.

(d) His successor Lord Ripon hastened to make friends with the Afghans by recognizing Abdul Rahman, a nephew of Sher Ali, as the Amir of Kabul. But soon troubles arose as Ayub Khan, another son of Sher Ali and a rival of Abdul Rahman, inflicted a serious defeaton the British forces at Maiwand and compelled the vanquished army to take refuge in Kandhar. Kandhar was, however, relieved by General Roberts but the English evacuated it, after which it was seized by Ayub Khan. But later he was defeated by his rival Abdul Rahman who recovered Kandhar as well as Herat. The British Government recognized Abdul Rahman as the Amir of Afghanistan and the latter in return for an annual subsidy agreed not to have any political relations with any foreign power except the English. Thus the Russian menace was removed from Afghanistan.

Results of the Second Afghan War. The Afghan policy of Lytton was a failure except for the British occupation of Quetta. As pointed out, the spirited Afghan policy of Land Lytton proved an utter failure. His objectives, *viz.*, the breaking up of Afghanistan and stationing of a British Resident at Kabul were completely frustrated. The only useful result that followed was the British occupation and strategical position' of Quetta which secured the use of the Bolan Pass. But this result, though important, was incidental and was not the main objective of the policy which was neither just nor politically expedient. Dr. V.A. Smith, however, gives credit to Lord Lytton for a policy which ended in disgrace and which was reversed by his successor and has not since been followed.

Lord Lytton's Achievements. The estimate of Lord Lytton's achievements in India, two views of an opposite nature have been expressed by various historians and, as such, it is desirable to discuss both the points of view as follows:

(a) **First View.** Bright side. According to Lord Curzon. "A study of the papers, however, both as published at the time and later on the official records in India, led me to admire the extraordinary ability and resourcefulness with which Lord Lytton conducted his case on paper and the perfection of the English prose in which his Minutes and Despatches were clothed. Of all the Governor-General and Viceroys, he seemed to me to have the greatest literary gift, not indeed exceeding Warren Hastings or Dalhousie in lucidity of exposition or vigour of phrase, but superior to both in the artistic quality of his writing." In another connection he writes, "It has been said that this picturesque and poetic figure—for Lytton was picturesque in appearance as well as in fact—was in reality out of date and that he ought to have been born and to have lived in Elizabethan times. There is pertinence in this observation, for certainly in the picture gallery of Indian Viceroys, there is no more singular or indeed startling portrait than his. In the Embassy at Paris he found a very congenial stage in his social and diplomatic accomplishment." Though Lord Lytton was often hasty and impulsive he brought some new fruitful conception into the field of Indian politics. Though several events during the Viceroyalty of Lord Lytton forecast a shadow over his reputation as a statesman, yet he had many liberal projects in view and he brought new and fruitful conception into the field of Indian politics, as said above. He advocated the introduction of gold standard into monetary system of

India and had his plan been adopted, India would have spared a great economic loss which arose from the subsequent depreciation of silver. He suggested the creation of a North western Frontierunder the direct control of the Government of India—are form which Lord Curzon subsequently carried out. He planned the enrolment of an Indian peerage and suggested the formation of Indian Privy Council of Ruling Chiefs to advise the Viceroy. He took stern action against the tendency of the Courts to pass too lenient sentences on Europeans who had assaulted Indians.

(b) **Dark Side.** His Afghanistan policy was universally condemned not only by the people of India but also by the Leaders of the Liberal Party and a majority of Englishmen. It was undoubtedly "a calamitous and unrighteous blunder and for that alone Lord Lytton's claims to statesmanship are justly forfeit." He is held guilty for the terrible loss of life on account of the famine in 1877-78 which took away about 50 lakhs of human lives and he made insufficient arrangements to alleviate the sufferings of the people. While the people were dying of famine he was busy in holding the Durbar at Delhi. The Vernacular Press Act and the Indian Arms Act were two means which restricted not only the freedom of the Vernaculer Press and took away the liberties of the Indians but these measures marked him as one of the most reactionary rulers who had come to suppress the liberties of the people. Thus by his narrow policy and illiberal acts he made the political situation in India worse and drove the whole of India almost to desperation. Consequently, there was storm of opposition amongst Indians that led to the organization of political associations to carry on agitation and propaganda among the people in defence of their rights as citizens. Lytton was one of the most unpopular and unsuccessful rulers of India. In this connection the following lines of Dr. V.A. Smith are noteworthy. He write , "His reputation has been obscured by the lack of an adequate biography; by certain foreign peculiarities of manner and habits which offended conventional opinion; and above all, by reason of the bitter; partisan controversies aroused by his Afghan policy, executed by him under the instructions of Lord Beacons field and Salisbury. The equally venomous criticism of the Vernacular Press Act further discredited him in popular opinion. These causes have prevented Lytton from attaining the "enduring fame", promised by the Prime Minister and perhaps may be said to have left a general impression that he was a failure as a ruler of India. If such an opinion exists, it is based upon insufficient grounds. The best parts of his internal policy were of a permanent value, and served as the basis of developments effected by his successors; while the most essential measures of his Afghan policy by which mean the occupation of Quetta and the securing of the Kurram Valley, either remained undisturbed.

In this way we can conclude that Lord Lytton came to India commissioned to inaugurate a new policy, called "A spirited forward foreign policy" with reference to Afghanistan, in view of the danger of the advance of Russia towards the Central Asia. In connection with his policy towards Afghanistan, it can be said that it proved a failure. With regard to his internal administration, he took certain measures which irritated the people of India very much, and it would, therefore, not be too much to pass a final verdict about the internal and external policies of Lord Lytton that they proved a failure.

ADMINISTRATION OF LORD RIPON

Lord Lytton was succeeded by Lord Ripon as Governor-General and Viceroy of India in 1880. He was a staunch follower of the liberal policy of Gladston the Prime Minister of England. His political views were just the reverse of that of Lord Lytton. He resembled Lord William Bentinck in many ways. He had a strong faith in the virtue of place, self Government and principle of Laissez faise. He therefore, followed a very liberal policy in India. Hitherto, the British Government gave all attention and preference to her own interest and ruled with out any regard to the wishes and ideas of the Indian people. India was treated just a colony which should exist only for the welfare and prosperity of the "mother country. The Indians were not allowed to have any say in the matters of administration. According to Burke The English nation in India is nothing for a seminary for the succession of officers. They are a nation of policemen they are a republic, a commonwealth without people. They are a state made up wholly of magistrates". Montegomeay has also remarked. "In India we set aside the people altogether we device and say that such thing is a good thing to be done and we carry it out without asking them very much about it." It was Lord Ripon who for the first time attempted to give education of Local Self Government to Indians so that they might acquire knowledge of democratic and local self government institutions and take active part in the management of their local affairs and in the course of time befitted for self-government. Feelings of agitation and dissatisfaction were developing in the minds of the Indians. Inspite of their high education and qualifications even the most talented Indians were not appointed on higher posts. Lord Ripon sympathised with the aspiration of the Indians and took all possible steps to satisfy them. He declared that his object was to give popular and political education to enable them to look after their own affairs an take interest in the development programmes for the betterment of their lot. His liberal policy was disliked by most Britishers. However, he remained firm on his policy and took many steps and measure for the good of the people of India. He made sincere attempts to remove all disqualifications based upon social considerations. It was on account of this that he was able to secure an extraordinary hold on the affection of the India population and earned a popularity unequalled by and Viceroy who came to India. Ripon gained the goodwill of Indians by many useful reforms and measures.

The reign of Lord Ripon is generally called as period of reforms and his fame rests mainly upon his reforms. Here we discuss about his reforms:

(i) The development of local self government in India owes their progress to the sincere efforts of Lord Ripon in this direction. His most significant contribution was in the field of Local Self Government. He passed a resolution in 1881 which clearly stated that the time had come when further steps could be taken to develop the system of Local Self Government. The said resolution directed the Provincial Governments to transfer considerable revenue to local bodies who were of deal with matters of local importance. The next step in this direction was taken by him when he passed the famous Resolution of 1882. It was made quite clear in this resolution that the expansion of the system of Local Self Government was not to improve the effeciency of the administration. To quote Lord Ripons own words, It is not primarily with a view to improvement in administration that this measure is put forward and supported. It is chiefly desirable as an instrument of political and popular education. Most of his colleagues were of the opinion that the Indians were indifferent towards Self Government and incapable of holding posts of responsibility. He disagreed with this general view of the British Government. He believed that, in fact, the system of Local Self Government had not been properly tried in India.

The area of each Board was to be kept small so that it would know the wishes of the people and service their interests accordingly. The members of the Board as far as possible were to be not non-officials and the numbers of officials could not exceed one third of the total strength of the members of the Board. The resolution stressed the principle of election. To quote Lord Ripon, "It should be the general function of the executive officers of the Government to watch specially at the outset the proceedings of the local boards to point out to them matters calling for their consideration, to draw their attention to any neglect on their part and to check by official remonstrance any attempt to exceed their proper functions or to act illegally or in any arbitrary or unreasonable manner. "The Resolution of 1882 further suggested that the Indians should be encouraged to become the members of the local bodies. He ensured the help of the Government to do utmost to help them in the efficient discharge of their duties. While extending Local Self Government, Lord Ripon stressed its educative value also. It has been earlier pointed out that the aim of Ripon was to give popular education to the people of India. While explaining the Resolution of 1882, Ripon said "If the Boards are to be any use for the purpose of training the natives to manage their own affairs they must not be overshadowed by the constant presence of the Barre Sahib of the district."

Financial Reforms of Lord Ripon. The work of decentralisation that was started at the time of Lord Mayo was carried a step further by Lord Ripon. The whole income was divided into three heads:

(i) Imperial *(ii)* Divided and *(iii)* Provincial heads of revenue. The income from the Imperial head went direct to the Central Government. The income from the divided heads was to be divided between the Centre and the Provinces. The income from the Provincial Heads was to go exclusively to provinces. It was also decided to give a fixed percentage of land revenue by the Imperial Government in order to make good the deficit in the provincial budget.

Educational Reforms. With a view to enquire into the manner in which the principles of woods Despatch of 1854 had worked in the country and also to recommend the further course of action. Lord Ripon appointed a Commission consisting of 20 members with Sir W.W. Hunter as Chairman. The Hunter Commission recommended the withdrawal of State so far as possible from the management of the institutions of higher education. It was in favour of giving them a good deal of autonomy to manage their affairs themselves. The work of management of such institutions was to be given to Indians if there were reasonable prospects of keeping up the efficiency. Special and ordinary grants were also to be given or running of the colleges. Special steps were taken to encourage education among the Muslims. It was also decided that a fixed part of the provincial revenues was to be spent on education.

The Government promised to grant sums of money to private bodies to encourage them to open schools. The local bodies were also given encouragement to promote the cause of primary education in the country.

Commercial Reforms. Like Lord Northbrook and Lord Lytton Lord Ripon also followed the free trade policy and took further steps in this direction. He abolished import duties on several articles. Salt duty was lowered. He retained duties on arms and ammunition for purely political reasons.

Social Reforms. Lord Ripon also paid attention to improve the condition of factory workers. In order to improve to conditions of the workers in the factories the first Factory Act was passed in 1881. The Act laid down that children between the ages of seven and twelve, years could not be made to work for more than nine hours a day. Previously the child labour was exploited. The Act provided that the dangerous machinery was to be properly fenced to eliminate or atleast minimise the chances of accident.

Repeal of Vernacular Press Act. The Vernacular Press Act passed by Lord Lytton had imposed restrictions upon the news papers published in Indian languages. Vernacular news papers were not allowed to publish anything likely to cause dissatisfaction among the people against the Government. This Act was discriminatory and derogatory to the Indians because it imposed restrictions only on vernaculars news-papers and no such restrictions were imposed on newspapers published in English. Realising that the grievances of the Indians were quite genuine. Lord Ripon repealed the Act. In his letter dated 19th February 1881 to Lord Harington communicating his decision to repeal the Act Lord Ripon wrote thus, "The fact is that the officials in India regards the press as an evil, Necessary perhaps but to be kept within as narrow limits as possible. He has no real feeling of the benefits of free discussion."

Civil Service Recruitment. It Before the time of Lord Ripon civil service competitions were held in England and the upper age limit for candidates was 18 years. Thus the Indian faced great difficulties in appearing at the civil service competitions. Lord Ripon suggested that civil service competitions should be held simultaneously in England and India but his suggestion was not accepted by the Home Government.

The Ilbert Bill Controversy. Lord Ripon being a true liberal, did not like race discrimination in judicial matters. He wanted to remove this sort of disqualification based on race distinctions. He felt that the discrimination of this kind between the members of the same service had become anomalous. He, therefore, wanted to abolish it. Consequently Sir Courtney Ilbert the then Law Member of the Government of India prepared a bill in 1883 to bring the Indian and European Magistrates on the same footing. After having been approved by Lord Ripon's 'Executive Council as well as by almost all the Provincial Governments, the draft of the bill was introduced in the Imperial Legislative Council in February 1882. The British Community raised a hue and cry against this bill and denounced it very strongly. They held a great public meeting in Calcutta Tower Hall and denunced the bill in the strongest Possible terms. The organisers made fiery speeches an even went to the extent of attacking the personal integrity of Lord Ripon. He was insulted in the streets by the plotters. The news paper entitled the 'Englist man' wrote, "The only people who had any right in India are the British. The so called Indians have no right whatever." Keeping in view the growing opposition by the European community and in view also of the great increasing tension between- the two communities a sort of compromise was made which amounted to a surrender of the principles for which the bill was presented. According to the modified bill every European subject brought before the Magistrate or Session judge whether an Indian or European could claim to be tried by a jury half of whom were to be Europeans or Americans. In arriving at this compromise Lord Ripon was guided by the desire to avoid the risk of street row in Calcutta organised by the Europeans. In a letter to Lord Kumberley the admitted, "I do not deny, however, that the great weakness of the Government for dealing with the Europeans disturbance weighed with one as it did with my colleagues. I had no idea till I came to Calcutta that the European police force at the disposal of the Bengal Government was so very small.

BRITISH POLICY TOWARDS TIBET

The Table land of Tibet stretches northward from the Himalayas and its Western and Southern frontier marches with Kashmir, the Punjab, Nepal, Sikkim, Bhutan and upper Burma. The Country is almost inaccessible. The government is a monkist and aristocratic theorocracy at the head of which are the two lamas knows as the Dalai Lama of Lhassa and Tashi Lama of Tasbilhupnpo. There is an executive council and a national Assembly but the conservative influence of the great monasteries was supreme. Since the early years of the eighteen the century Tibet had been under the suzerainty of China, to Chinese officials called Amhans or Residents Controlling the policy of the Tibetan government.

Early Relation. British relations with Tibet began from the time of Warren Hastings who twice sent envoys to Tibet to open up trade with India. But his attempts failed for the Tibetain disliked the presence of foreigners in their country. For about a century the land of Tibet remained unknow. But the extension of the British prolectorate over Sikkim aroused the interest of the British Government in Tibetan affairs. In 1885-86 they extracted from China a very reluctant consent to the desptach of a British commercial mission to Lhassa but the Tibetans were determined to oppose the entry of the mission. A very awkward situation ensued. Subsequently, a new agreement was made with China but which the British Government agreed to abandon the mission on condition that the Chines waived their claims to sovereignty over Burma and offered no objection to its annexation by Great Britain. In 1887 boundary disputes led the Tibetans to invade Sikkim an independent state under British protection but they were driven out with loss. The British Government then took up the matter with China under whose sovereignty Tibeted nominally lay and in 1890 a convention was concluded which settled the Sikkim-Tibet boundary and provided for a joint commission to discuss the possibility frontier trade.

Lord Curzon's Tibetan Policy. In Lord Curzon's time two new conditions developed in Tibetan Politics which considerably influenced the British attitude. The Tibetans wanted to free themselves from Chinese Seizerainty and showed a desire to welcome Russian influences as a countee poise. Secondly the Dalai Lama unlike most of his predecessors had contrived to free himself from the bitelage of the aristocracy. In his impending struggle against difficulties external and internal, he sought the aid of Russia. Lord Curzon who feared the consequences of the consolidation of Russian influence over Tibet, pressed the British Government at home to adopt a forward policy and to allow a mission to be sent to Tibet. The Russian Government plainly declared that Russia had no designs upon Tibet but Lord Curzon persisted in believing in the existence of a Tibet Russian agreement. He found some flunsy grounds of complaints against Tibet and despatched a mission under colonel Younghusband in 1903. The Tibetans refused to meet it unless the mission should retire to the frontier and began to masstrops to expel the intruders.

The Treaty of Lhassa. The British proces then entered Lhassa. The Dalai Lama having fled away a treaty was concluded of Lhassa between the Regent and the British in 1904. The Treaty provided for the establishment of trade marts at three stations and for the appointment of a British Commercial agent. The Tibetans undertook to pay an indemnity of 75 lakhs of rupees in annual installments of one lakh and to allow the British troops to occupy the Chumbi valley till the whole sum was paid. Other provisions secured to Great Britain direct control over the foreign policy of Tibet. But in concluding these terms Younghusband had exceeded his powers. Besides, the treaty violated the pledge recently given to Russia that Great Britain would not seek to annex Tibetans territory so long as other power refrained from interfering in the affairs of Tibet. Hence although the Indian Government defended Younghusband's action, the secretary of state mrullified the terms of the treaty reducing the indemnity to 25 lakhs and the occupation of the Chumbi Valley to three years.

Criticism of Lord Curzon's Tibetan Policy. It should be noted that Lord Curzons's aggressive policy in Tibet is hard to justifiy. It was an unwarranted interference with a weak and independent state. It bears a close resemblance to Lord Lytton's

Afghan policy of 1878. The action of both Lord Lytton and Lord Curzon was the out come of a dread of Russian design and both pressed upon the reluctant. Home authorities a vigorous forward policy. Both tried to force a British agent upon a reluctant nation—Lord Lytton on the Afghans and Curzon on the Tibetans. Eventually the policy of both was disallowed Younghusband expedition failed it its main object of opening up trade between Tibet and India. Its only result was a temporary set back of the Tibetan national movement, so that the Chinese re-established their authority much more effectively than had been the case before.

Lord Morley's Policy. During Lord Minto's Viceroyalty Great Britain and China concluded a convention. Which besides conforming the Treaty of Lhasa contained two other clauses. By the first Great Britain bound herself not to annex Tibet nor to interfere in its internal administration; by the second China engaged to impose like restrictions on other foreign powers. Lord Morley, the secretary of state for India completely reversed Lord Curzon's policy by withdrawing British troops from the Chumbi Valley when the indemnity was paid off by China. Next followed the Anglo-Russian convention of 1907 which settled the integrity of Tibet. The result of the British interference in Tibet was that the whole control of the country passed into the hands of China, but the danger of Russian intervention was averted.

AFGIIAN POLICY

Lord Lawrence realised the danger of Russian expansion in Central Asia. He was of the opinion that Great Britain and Russia should come to some agreement regarding the demarcation of the line of influence of the two in Central Asia. If that was done, there would be nothing to fear from Russian expansion up to that time, Rather her civilising influence would be good for the people of Central Asia. His view was supported by Sir Herbert Edwardes, the great frontier officer. Sir Henry Rawlinson, a member of the Secretary of State's Council, in 1868 advised a more forward policy though it was—less forward than the policy tried by Lord Lytton later on. He advocated the occupation of Quetta which commanded Bolan Pass, a close alliance with the Amir of Kabul and the grant of annual subsidy to him. These suggestions were opposed by Lawrence on several grounds. Firstly, the military exports were divided as to whether Bolan Pass could best be defended from the western or the eastern end. Secondly, interference in Afghanistan would strain relations with Afghans and would only lessen Russia's difficulties in that region. In case of interference in Afghanistan, the British would be required to fight Russia near the Oxus River with hostile Afghans in the near. Lord Lawrence once aptly remarked that the first invaders of Afghanistan would be received as foes and the next would be hailed as friends and delivers. He believed that real security consisted in non-interference in Afghanistan, keeping a strong disciplined army on the frontier of India, careful management of finances and keeping the Indian princes in good mood by assuring them of their titles and possessions.

Afghan Policy of Lord Mayo. Lord Mayo (1869- 72) continued Lord Lawrence's policy of Masterly Inactivity towards Afganistan. Lord Lawrence had invited Sher Ali to visit India but the Amir has not been able to come due to internal troubles in Afghanistan. He came to India after the arrival of the new Viceroy. Lord Mayo held a grand Durbar in his honour at Ambala. The Amir expressed desire to enter into much closer relations with the Indian Government. He asked for a definite treaty, a fixed annual subsidy assistance in arms and men whenever he should feel its necessity an obligation on the part of the British to support his throne and dynasty, and the recognition of his favourite younger son, Abdulla Jan, as heir to the throne in preference to the eldest son, Yakub Khan, who had helped him to become the ruler of Afghanistan Lord Mayo felt that the acceptence of these terms would commit the Indian Government to a policy of interference in Afghan affairs at a later date and would imply reversal of the policy of Masterly Inactivity. Lord Mayo diplomatically declined these terms but gave a written promise of moral support to be followed by gifts of money, arms, ammunition whenever the British Government deemed it desirable. Sher Ali was further told that the Government of India would view with severe displeasure any attempt to dethrone him. Thus Lord Mayo did not commit Indian Government to interference in Afghan affairs and at the some time sent Sher Ali charmed by his geniality.

Lord Mayo continued his predecessor's policy of trying to arrive at some understanding with Russia regarding the boundary of her sphere of influence in Central Asia. Negotiations were started between the British Foreign Secretary, Lord Clarendon, and Prince Gortschakoff in Europe. Dougals Forsyth was sent by the Indian Government to St. Petersburg in 1869 to lay its view points before the Russian Government. Russian agreed to recognise Sher Ali's rule south of the Oxus River, provided he respected the integrity of Bokhara, north of that River. The northern frontier of Afghanistan was not demarcated in detail.

General Kaufmann, Governor of Russian Turkistan, started writing lctters of complimentary nature to Amir Sher Ali The latter went on passing all these to the Indian Government. Lord Mayo did not attach much importance to these and told the Amir that the letters were merely of a complimentary nature and he need not feet perturbed.

Afghan Policy of Lord Northbrook. Lord Northbrook also continued the policy of Masterly Inactivity Russia was making steady advances towards the northern frontier of Afghanistan. In June 1873, she occupied Khiva in Central Asia. This alarmed Sher Ali and his envoy met the Viceroy next month at simla. He told the Viceroy that Sher Ali wanted a closer alliance with the Government of India due to the uneasiness caused by the Russian expansion. Lord Northbrook considered such a request reasonable and wanted to agree to help the Amir with money, arms and troops in case of unprovoked invasion. The British were to be the judge of such a necessity. The British Cabinet did not agree to make such a commitment. It would have been a wise step to make an agreement at this stage In 1869 Sher Ali had not been long enough on the throne to inspire confidence that he would be able to maintain his position but by 1873 he had stabilised his position. A binding agreement with the Amir at this stage would not have been a reversal of the policy of Lord Lawrence and Lord Mayo, but only its modification to suit the altered circumstances. The Amir felt disappointed. Lord Northbrook further irritated Sher Ali by addressing to him a mild rebuke for treacherously arresting his eldest son, Yakub Khan, and proclaiming the younger son, Abdulla Jan, as heir.

In 1874 Disraeli became the Prime Minister of England and he appointed Lord Salisbury as the Secretary of State for India. They were afraid of Russian expansion towards Afghanistan. The best thing for them was to insist on an assurance from Russian Foreign Office that the integrity of Afghanistan would be respected and the Russian officers should stop all communications with Sher Ali Unfortunately they decided to exert pressure at Kabul and not at St. Petersburg Lord Salisbury told Northbrook that Sher Ali should be asked to admit a British Resident in Afghanistan.

RESULTS OF LYTTON'S POLICY TOWARDS AFGHANISTAN

Lord Lytton was sent as Viceroy at Governor-General by the imperialist Prime Minister, Disraeli. He totally reversed the policy of Masterly Inactivity which had been followed by his three predecessors. He had instructions for a definite alliance with Sher Ali. He was authorised to offer most of the terms to Amir which he had asked for in 1873 namely, a fixed subsidy, the recognition of his favourite son, Abdulla Jan, as heir to the throne and to agree to defend. Afghanistan against aggression. These terms, however, were to be granted if Sher Ali allowed a British Resident in Afghanistan. The condition was reasonable as a preliminary to a defensive alliance but the Viceroy had no right of force an alliance or an envoy if Sher Ali was opposed to it. Lord Lytton took a few steps which ultimately led to the Second Afghan War.

(1) Non-Acceptance of Complimentary Mission. Sher Ali was asked in 1876 to receive a Complimentary Mission which was to announce to him the assumption of the title of Empress of India by Queen Victoria. The Amir feared that it might be a prelude to the establishment of a permanent British mission is Afganistan. He courteously declined to receive the complimentary mission on the ground that it was unnecessary. The British Muslim agent at Kabul, obviously with Amir's permission, reported that among other causes for refusal was the fact that the Amir could not guarantee to protect the envoy against the fanaticism of his subjects. Moreover, if he permitted a British mission, he could not refuse the same privilege to the Russians.

(2) Acquisition of Quetta by the British. Lord Lytton made a treaty with the Khan of Kalat in 1876 by which the British got Quetta. It is a place of great strategic importance because it commands Bolan Pass, one of the gates to Afghanistan. The Amir remembered that the British forces had attacked Afghanistan through Bolan Pass during the Afghan War.

(3) Establishment of a British Agency at Gilgit. Lord Lytton made a confidential arrangement with the ruler of Kashmir and established a British agency at Gilgit. Even Captain Cavagnari the agent chosen by Lytton, warned the Viceroy that such a policy would further annoy the Amir. Sher Ali felt that this had been done to keep watch over his dominion and to establish relations with his subjects.

(4) Entry of Russian Envoy and the Counter-Demand of Lytton. The Relations of Great Britain and Russia became highly strained in Europe when Russia imposed the Treaty of San Stefano on Turkey in 1877. The Congress of Berlin was held to revise this treaty. The Russian Government sent General Stoletoff to Kabul, Sher Ali told the Russian Governor of Turkistan that the Russian envoy need not come to Kabul. He would send one of his own ministers for talks. Sher Ali was simply told by the Russian Governor that the envoy would go to Kabul and the Czar would hold the Amir responsible for any harm happening to the envoy. He was further threatened that powerful rival (Abdur Rehman) to his throne would be set up. The Russian envoy reached Kabul. Lord Lytton made certain demands on Sher Ali. He must receive a British envoy, should not enter into negotiations with other powers without the permission of the British, cede the right to send British officers to Kabul for a conference whenever the British considered it necessary and allow a permanent British Resident at Herat.

The demands were unjust. Russia was responsible for sending the envoy to Kabul and Sher Ali had agreed under threat only to let him come to Kabul. Russia, not the Amit, should have' been called to accounts for this. Whatever justification existed from the point of view of Lytton, that also disappeared. The Russian agent was recalled from Kabul after the Treaty of Berlin. Thus a golden bridege was built for retreat from an untenable position. The proper course was to befriend the Amir again. But Lord Lytton thought that the Treaty of Berlin had freed his hands, since Sher Ali could not expect Russian help. It was decided to send a Muslim envoy to announce the approach of the British mission. The Afridis of the Khyber Pass owed allegiance to the Amir and they were bribed to allow the Muslim envoy and his bodyguard to pass. Sher Ali resented this bribing of his subjects. The advance guard of the British envoy was checked by an Afghan officer at Ali Masjid and was told plainly that it would not be allowed to proceed further without orders from Kabul. The envoy ascertained that the Afghans were prepared to use force to stop him and returned to Peshawar. The Viceroy declared that the mission had been forcibly repulsed and sent an ultimatum on the second of November demanding a full and suitable apology and the acceptance of a permanent British Resident in Afghanistan. It was to expire on 20th of November. The death of Amir's favourite son, Abdulla Jan, delayed the reply and it was received on 30th of November.

Events. The British forces attacked Afghanistan through Khyber Pass, Kurram Valley and Bolan Pass. There was very little effective opposition Sher Ali fled away to Russian Turkistan where he died. The British made the Treaty of Gandmak in May 1879 with Yakub Khan, son of Sher Ali. The following were its clauses:

(a) The Amir was to conduct his foreign policy according to the advice of the British.

(b) The Amir was to give Kurram Pass along with Pishin and Sibi districts to the British.

(c) There was to be a permanent British Resident at Kabul with agents at Herat and other places on the frontier.

(d) The British troops were to be withdrawn from Afghanistan, except at Kandhar which was not to be evacuated tell autumn.

(e) The British were to support the Amir at their discretion, with money and men against foreign agression.

(f) The Amir was to be given subsidy of six lacks of rupees a year.

The Treaty of Gandmak was the Highest Watermark of Lord Lytton's Afghan policy. Disraeli declared that the British in India had secured the scientific frontier. The triumph, however, was shortlived. Only a month later the mutinous Afghan troops murdered the envoy and the whole of his bodyguard. Yakub Khan was either powerless to intervene or in secert sympathy with the mutinous troops. Nothing was done to save the envoy. The British forces marched again and occupied Kabul. Yakub Khan abdicated and was sent to Dehra Dun. Lord Lytton decided to separate the provinces of Kandhar from the rest of Afghanistan. It was given to an Afghan chief, Sher Ali Khan, and he was to be protected by the Indian Government.

There was a change of ministry in England and Gladstone became the Prime Minister and sent Lord Ripon to India. The new viceroy recognised Abdur Rahman as Amir of Kabul. The only conditions were that the Amir was to have no political relations with any foreign power except the English. The English were to retain the districts of Pishin and Sibi. So long as the Amir fulfilled the first condition, the English were to defend him against unprovoked foreign agrression. The demand for resident was given up Sher Ali Khan was to hand over Kandhar to Air and come to India.

Ayub Khan, son of Sher Ali, was at Herat. He defeated the British troops at Maiwand and beseiged them in Kandhar. General Roberts came from Kabul and defeated Ayub Khan. Kandhar was handed over to Abdur Rahman and the British forces returned to Indian. Ayub Khan again captured Kandhar but Abdur Rahman defeated him and recovered Kandhar. Ayub Khan fled to Persia and Abdur Rahman became the Amir of the whole of the Afghanistan.

❐

12

The Growth of Nationalism

The national feeling began to grow in India during the second half of the nineteenth century. It was not the result of a single factor. It was the product of a number of factors operating during the period extending over several decades.

The history of Indian nationalism suggests three well marked phases according to Dr. Raghuwansi. They are as follows:

(a) The first is the period of the ascendancy of liberalism lasting till the stormy regime of Lord Nathaniel Curzon. This period witnessed the growth of nationalist agitation on constitutional lines.

Political agitation during this period lacked vigour and effectiveness and was exclusively on upper middle class agitation. The spirit of nationalism was especially marked in Bengal, Bombay and Madras.

(b) In this phase nationalism acquired a more dynamic and threatening character. There was reaction against westernisation, which was intensified by economic factors. The Swadeshi and Boycott movements, following the partition of Bengal in 1905, produced a tremendous convulsion of patriotic spirit.

(c) In the final phase, the Gandhian epoch (1920-1947) Indian nationalism acquired greater vitality and adaptability. The World War turned the scales against liberalism for ever and prepared the ground for the bloodless victories of Gandhism. In 1920-22 was launched the non-cooperation movement for the redress of Punjab and Khilafat wrongs. Simon Commission came in 1927.

The most important factors which contributed to the growth of national feeling are:

(a) Conquest of India by the British. The Indians had not enjoyed long periods of political unity before the coming of the British. Even when it was achieved under rulers like Ala-ud-Din, it was shortlived. The British conquered the whole of India and kept it under control for along time. It enabled people to think in terms of the unity of the country. British Imperialism made the people of the whole of India feel that they, were one.

(b) Contact with the West. The establishment of British rule brought the Indians in intimate contact with the West. Nineteenth century in Europe was the century of nationalism and the educated Indians imbibed these ideas. Italy and Germany achieved national freedom in the second half of the nineteenth century. This gave encouragement to the educated Indians to achieve freedom 'and become a free nation. The Western literature had also a nationalist tone and its study developed the feeling of nationalism among the Indians.

(c) Improved Means of Communication. The means of communication also began to improve about the middle of the nineteenth century. Grand Trunk Road was completed and railways were introduced in the time of Lord Dalhousie. The improved means of communication enabled people of the different parts of the country to come in intimate contact with one another. It created a feeling of oneness among them. The Indian leaders could easily move to different parts of the country, come in contact with one another and address the people.

(d) English Language. India is a vast country and its people speak different languages. Hence it was difficult for the people of different parts of the country to understand one another. The British rule in India led to the introduction of the English language. Many people began to study this language in different parts of the country. English language enabled the educated persons of different provinces to understand one another. It became the lingua franca of the educated class in Indian and enabled the educated people of different parts to communicate their thoughts with one another.

(e) Scholars and Reformers. Many scholars carried out researches into the history and culture of ancient India. Some of them were Max Muller, Monier, Williams, Colebrooke, Ranade, R.G. Bhandarkar. Their writings revealed the greatness achieved by the Indians in the past. It created among the people of India feelings of pride in the past and a faith in the future. The religious and social reformers like Raja Ram Mohan Roy, Devendra Nath Tagore, Ishwar Chandra Vidyasagar, Swami Dayanand, Ramakrishna Paramhansa, Vivekanand presented a glorious picture of India's past and appealed to the people to revive those good old days. Col. Olcott was of the opinion that Swami Dayanand exercised 'great nationalising influence upon his followers. In the words of Mrs. Annie Besant, "It was Dayanand Saraswati who proclaimed Indian for the Indians." Swami Vivekanand also inspired self-confidence among the Indians. The Queen of his adoration was Mother India.

(f) Discontent of the Indians. Before the outbreak of the Mutiny in 1857, there were many Englishmen who worked for the good of India. There was a lot of bloodshed on both sides during the Mutiny. The Europeans wreaked vengeance afterwards. The policy of repression created discontent in the country. The Europeans began to behave arrogantly towards the Indians. The Indians had to make way for the Europeans even in the railway compartments. The assaults on Indians by the Europeans were common. The latter were tried by European judges and were either let off free or were given very mild punishments. The Europeans believed that the life of a European was worth the lives of many Indians.

(g) Indian Press. The Indi.an Press, English as well as Vernacular, aroused national consciousness among the people of India. Newspapers like 'The Indian Mirror', 'Bombay Samachar'. 'The Amrit Bazar Patrika. 'The Hindu Patriot', 'The Bengalee', 'The

Kesari', 'The Hindu', had strong nationalist tone and diffused ideas of nationalism among the people.

Many literary figures also contributed to the growth of nationalism. The writings of Din Bandhu Mitra, R.C. Dutt, Hem Chandra Banerjee, Bankim Chandra Chatterjee and Rabindra Nath Tagore also made people national minded.

(h) Anti-Indian Policy of Lord Lytton. Lord Lytton followed an anti-Indian policy. He held the famous Dehi Durbar in 1877 when several parts of India were in the grip of a terrible famine. It was even remarked. "Nero was finding while Rome was burning." The unjust Second Afghan War was costing the Indian treassury good deal. The Indian Press bitterly criticised this policy and Lord Lytton passed the Vernacular Press Act in 1878 to stop this criticism. It placed restrictions on the Vernacular Press, and not on the newspapers published in English. This discriminatory Act was universally condemned by the Indians. The Indian Arms Act was passed in 1878. The Indians had to get licence to keep arms but no such licence was needed for the Europeans. This Act made invidious distinction between the Indians and the Europeans. It imposed a badge of racial inferiority on the Indians.

(i) Bad Economic Condition. The economic condition of the Indians was very bad. The English education was becoming widespread and many educated Indians were unemployed. The Indians felt that the British were exploiting their country and that was the cause of the poverty of India. According to Blunt, the Finance Minister of India looked more to the interests of Great Britain that to those of India. The free trade policy of the Government of India stood in the way of the development of the country. The Indian cotton industries were not able to withstand competition from the machine made goods of England.

(j) Ilbert Bill Controversy. Lord Ripon tried to remove some of the grievances of the Indians but, before he could do that, the famous Ilbert Bill controvesy started. This Bill aimed at giving authority to the Indian Judges to try the Europeans even in non-

Presidency towns. The Anglo Indians and the Europeans rased great hue and cry against this. A compromise was at last made. It was agreed that a European could claim trial by a jury consisting of at least half the Europeans and Americans, if his case was before an Indian judge. Such an attitude of Europeans was derogatory to the self-respect of the Indians. The Indians had already formed national organisations of provincial character in some provinces. Now they felt the need of having an all-India national organisation. Such an association called Indian National Congress was founded by A.O. Hume, a retired British civilian officer, in 1885.

(k) Indian Press and Literature. The Indian press (Hindi and English) gave a fillip to national consciousness. There was the Anglo-Indian press also which was anti-nationalist. The Indian press was critical of government measures. It advocated racial equality and wanted the government of the country to be managed by the Indian themselves.

The shortage of national platform was supplied by the Press. It awakened the educated classes and inculcated in them patriotic sentiments and national consciousness. In this context, popular literature was developed in the Indian languages, especially in Bengali. Bankim Chandra's "Anand Math" is the Bible of modern Bengali patriotism. 'Bande Mataram' song first appeared in this book.

STRUGGLE OF LIBERAL NATIONALISM

The history of the Congress in Indian can be divided into four stages. The first stage lasted from 1885 to 1905. The second stage lasted from 1906 to 1918. The third stage was from 1919 to 1928 while the fourth stage was from 1921 to 1947.

Aim of A.O. Hume. The Congress was founded by A.O. Hume, a retired British civilian officer, in 1885. It is said that he first idea of Hume was to have a body to discuss social matters of the country. He changed his original idea at the suggestion of Lord Dufferin. The idea in founding the Congress was to have an organisation which was to perform the same functions which Her Majesty's Opposition performed in England. Lord Dufferin wanted that this body should meet every year and point out to the government its shortcomings. The Congress was to act as a safety value for popular discontect. It was to provide a peaceful and constitutional channel for the expression of Indian unrest so that it might not drift towards terrorism. This is not correct. The aim of Hume was not to save British Empire from disruption. His object was to provide the Indians with an organisation which would make them fit for liberty and self-government in the long run.

Attitude of the Congress Before 1905. The first period of the development of Indian National Congress extends from 1885 to 1905. It was the period of moderate nationalism. The Congress was not a revolutionary body during this period. Its leaders declared loyalty to the British Government several times. Its leaders during this period believed that the British Government would do justice and redress their grievances. They spurned the idea of agitation and unconstitutional means. They carried on their work by debates, propaganda petitions and deputations. They adhered to the policy of appeals. Their methods have been described as political mendicancy. According to G.N. Singh, the Congress during this period did the spade work.

Attitude of the Government. The attitude of the Government towards the Congress was friendly in the beginning. Lord Dufferin gave a party to the delegates of the second session of the Congress. The Governor of Madras entertained the third session of the Congress. The attitude of the Government changed after a short time. Lord Dufferin condemned the Congress in 1888 and called it "microscopic minority" of educated Indians. A circular of 1890 forbade Government employees from attending the meetings of the Congress.

Some Important Congress Sessions. The first session of the Congress was held at Bombay under the Presidentship of W.C. Bannerji, a leading barrister of Calcutta. The most important delegates were Pherozshah Mehta, Dadabhai Naoroji, Dinshaw Wacha and K.T. Tilang. It was attended by people from different parts of the country.

The second session was held in Culcutta in 1886 and its members were entertained at a garden party by Lord Dufferin. The third session was held at Madras in 1887 and the members were entertained by the Governor of Madras.

The friendly attitude of the government changed after this because the Congress leaders started a strong propaganda among the masses. Hume, in a pamphlet, appealed to the prosperous people of England-not to forget the starving Indians. He made arrangements for carrying on propaganda through the Press in England. He was able even to enlist the support of a few members of the British Parliament.

The Congress of 1888 was held at Allahabad and the site for the holding of the ongress session was purchased by the Maharajadhiraj of Darbhanga. The Congress session of 1889 was held at Bombay and was attended by Charless Bradlaugh, a Member of Parliament. The Congress wanted the government to introduce further reforms. It was partly due to the agitation carried on by the Congress that the Indian Councils Act of 1892 was passed.

Dadabhai Naoroji, a member of the House of Commons, was the President of the Lahore session of the Congress in 1893. He was heartily welcomed by the people on his way from Bombay to Madras. He brought a message of co-operation and encouragement from the Irish Members of Parliament. The Congress session of 1894 held at Mardas was presided over by Alfred Webb, an Irish Member of Parliament. Surendra Nath Bannerjee presided over the Poona session of the Congress in 1895. Gopal Krishna Gokhale presided over the Banaras session of the Congress held in 1905. The session of 1906 held at Calcutta was presided over by Dadabhai Naoroji and he unfurled the Swarajya flag.

NATIONAL MOVEMENT

Many factors contributed towards the growth of the nationalist movement in India, some of them were as follows:

(1) **British Imperialism.** The most important factor was British Imperialism. It was British imperialism that brought about the unification of the country and enabled the people to think as one nation. Before the advent of the British the people of the South were usually separate from the rest of India except for some short intervals. British imperialism made the people of the whole of India think as one nation. According to Prof. Moon, "British imperialism in India gave her a political unity under a third party inspite of many discardant elements in Indian Society."

(2) **Impact of the Western Civilisation.** The establishment of British Supermacy in India brought the Indians into intimate contact with the European Countries and the latters influenced them immensely. Nineteenth Century in Europe was the century of nationalism and liberalism and the Indians learnt their lessons from the Europeans on both these points, Indians learnt a lot from the Western Countries particularly from Germany, Italy, Greece and Belgium. A wave of nationalism and liberalism was prevalent in Europe in 19th Century. This influenced the Indians also and they also began to aspire for achieving independence. The Indian students studying in European Universities started thinking that if Germany and Italy could become independent why not India could do the same. Besides this the writings of western thinkers such as Macaulary Burks Mill and Herbert Spencer also encouraged the feeling of independence nationalism and liberalism among the minds of the Indians. According to Coupland, the Indians lerned from British history that British Liberalism and backed the cause of nations rightly struggling to be free in South America in the Balkoms in Italy and in Ireland.

(3) **Spread of English Language.** After the mutiny of 1857 English education made rapid progress, specially in Bengal and the Indian intelligentsia began to draw upon the store house of western culture. The latter half of the nineteenth

century was the golden age of Liberalism in Europe particularly in England. The study of the political classics of English literature from Milton to Mill planted in the minds of English educated Indians seeds of Liberalism in its two aspects—nationalism and democracy.

The British had introduced English language in India with their own selfish interest. It was mainly to get Indian clerks in order to stregthen the British rule in India. But it proved to a great boon for the Indians. In his book "India Today" R. Palm Dutta writes: "when Macaulay... imposed, the system, his object was not to create national consciousness but to distroy it down to the very deepest root of its being his object was to train up a stratum of decite executants of the English wills cut off from everyline of watch with their people." English education enabled people of different provinces to came close to one another. Thus helped to develop national feeling and political consciousness. The educated Indians read the works of Mazzini of Italy, Roussaeu and Voltani of France, Macaulay, Mill etc., of England. The works of these champions of liberty, liberalism and nationalism further developed political consciousness and unity among the Indians. Rabindra Nath Tagore observed:, "we had come to know England through her glorious literature which had brought new inspiration to our young lives. The English authors whose books and poems we studied were full of love, of humanity, justice and freedom. Sardar Panikar wrote: "The mining of ancient fortress of Hindu custom was a major achievement for the reason that it was uniformly speard all over India. Had the education been through the Indians languages, the emphasis of the movement would have been different from province to province according to the development, flexibility and character of the language used.

(4) Scholars. The contribution of scholars, poets and religious reformers contributed towards the progress of the nationalist movement in the country. They emphasised the past glory and the rich heritage of India. Among such great scholars who showed the past glory and interpreted the hidden treasure of our glorious heritage were Ranade, Har Prasad Shastri, RG. Bhandarkar, Rajendra Lal Mittra and foreign Scholar Maxmuller, Monier. Williams and Colebrooke. They revealed to the people of India, the majesty of the Sanskrit language and also inculcated among them the feelings of pride in their past and a faith in the future.

(5) **Means of Communication.** The improvements in the means of transport and communication also quickened the pace of nationalism movement in the country. The Indian leaders found themselves in a position to carry on their national propoganda in every mole and corner of the contry. Without these means of communication and transport things would have been unthinkable. The frequent meeting of the leaders among themselves and their direct personal contact with the people in different to parts of the country gave a momentum to the nationalist movement in the country.

(6) **Social and Religious Reformers.** Religion has always played a significant part in India from time immemorial. After the establishment of the British rule when the Christian missionaries started converting Hindus to Christianity. Many social and religious and social reformers came on the field and started reminding the people about their glorious part. In order to save Hinduism from the attacks of the Christian missionaries they started several movements to reforms the social and religious evils of Hinduism. Swami Daya Nand Sarswati, founder of Arya Samaj exercised great nationalising influence upon his followers: According to Mrs. Annie Besant: "It was Daya Nand Sarswati who proclaimed India for the Indians." According to Sister Naviditta Swami Viveka Nand was also a great patriot and the queen of his adoration was his motherland. Thus we

see that these social and religious reformers made a significant contribution in the development of national movement.

(7) **Economic Exploitation.** From the very beginning the British aimed at the economic exploitation of India. They took away raw materials from India and brought here their manufactured goods. The policy of economic exploitation of the Indians ruined the Indian industries and the wealth of India was being taken away by the British to their own country. Even after the British established their rule in India, they did not make any change in their attitude and policies. They adopted a free trade policy which proved to be ruinous for Indian trade and industries. Indian industries failed to compete with those of the British because the British and all the advantages and privileges on their side. The British officials working in India were a very heavy drain on the Indian resources. The economic system of Indian was adjusted to the needs of the people of England. The interests of the Indians were completely ignored. According to Mrs. Blund : "The vice of the Indian finance was that the Finance Minister of India looked more to the interests of Great Britain than to those of India." Sir Henry Cotton also condemned the exploitation of Indian and the subsequent miseries of the people of India. The Indians resented the attitude of the Englishmen towards them. The Europeans in India were aerogant. They had a very low opinion of the Indian character. They took pleasure in calling the Indians the creatures of an inferior breed, "half Gorilla half Negro." They ridiculled the Indian black heathens worshipping stocks and stones and swinging themselves on bamboo trees like bees." The European masters regarded the Indian as "the helots of the land, the hewers of the wood and the drawers of water." No wonder the relations between the Indians and Europeans became strained.

(8) **Development of Indian Press and Literature.** The Indian Press and literature both English and Vernacular also aroused national consciousness among the people of the country. Great was the influence of the papers like the Indian Mirror. 'Bombay Samachar', 'The Hindu Patriot', 'The Amrit Bazar Patrika', 'The Hindu', 'The Kesri', 'The Bengalee' etc., on the political life of the country. The writings of Den Bandhu Mitra, Hem Chandra Banarjee, Navin Chandra Sen, Bankim Chandra Chaterjee, R.C. Dutta an Rabindra Nath Tagore also affected the minds on the people. The 'Anand Math' of Bankain Chandra Chaterjee has rightly been regarded as "the Bible of modern Bengalee patriotism Tagore and D.R. Roy gave people lot of nation poetry, songs and plays. The writings of these patriots and scholars brought about a revolution in the minds of the Indians.

(9) **Racial Jealoucies.** During the mutiny the relations of the Europeans and the Indians were greatly embittered. A large number of Britishers were killed in the Mutiny. Now the Britishers were also full of venguence and the helpless and innocent Indians became the victims of their vengeance. According to Zakarias : "The light of distrust had begun to fall upon England's relations with India; these people had mutinied once and committed dreadful atrocities; how could one trust them not to plan further sedition? After the mutiny testified an eyewitness, the old sympathy with India changed to feeling of repugnance: the old spirit of content with life and work in India, the old inclination to regard things in and India rather an English light gave place to a reluctance to stay in Indian longer than needs must, and a disposition to judge things by an emphatically English standard." The English killed their prisoners without trial and in a manner held by all Indians to be the height of barbarity. General Neil gave orders that certain villages were marked out for distruction and all the men inhabiting there were slaughtered and indiscriminate burning of

inhabitants occurred wherever the English armies moved. These atrocities aroused discontent and unrest among the people of India. No doubt the Mutiny was suppressed for the time being, but they were not able to suppress the feelings of nationalism among the people of India. Travelling in the upper class railway compartment was not for the Indians. Even the ruling Chiefs were bullied into unlacing the boots and shampooing the weary legs of the Sahibs just back from hunting expeditions.

(10) **Discrimination with the Indians for Appointment in Government Services.** In the beginning no Indians were appointed on high posts. The British thought the Indians were not capable of any trust or faith. The Proclamation of Queen Victoria in 1858 declared that hence farward Indians would be appointed on high posts on the basis of their merit irrespective of their caste religion or race. Inspite of this proclamation this policy was not properly implemented. In 1868 Surendra Nath Banerjee passed the L.C.S. Examination yet he was not given any high position. When Queen's Bench Division gave its decision in his favour he was appointed an Assistant Collector in November 18-71. But two years after this he was removed from service. This discriminatory, arbitrary and unrust policy of the Government created a great discontent and unrust among the educated people of India.

(11) **Events of the Reign of Lord Lytton.** Lord Lytton was an imperialistic Governor-General and some of the events of his reign gave further impetus to the national movement. His imperialistic policies accelerated the nationalist movement. The following events of Lord Lytton's reign gave impetus to the nationalist movement :

(a) For employment in Civil Service the minimum age was reduced from 21 to 19 years. This aroused discontent and unrest of the Indian.

(b) He held a magnificent Durbar at Delhi when a severe famine was raging in different parts of the country. It showed that he had no sympathy for the people who were suffering on account of the famine. It was rightly remarked: "Nero was fiddling while Rome was burning."

(c) The Vernacular Act of 1876 was passed imposing restriction upon the press.

(d) The Arms Act of 1876 further increased the discontent of the Indians. Indian could no longer keep any arms without obtaining licences for the same. According to Surendra Nath Banerjee the Arms Act "imposed upon us a badge of racial inferiority."

(e) The Seun Afghan War put heavy strains on the Indian treasury. Lord Lytton's Afghan policy was subjected to severe criticism by the Indians.

(f) In order of please the English merchants of Lancashire he abolished export duty on cotton. The measure dissatisfied the Indian merchants. The Indian industries suffered irreparable loss.

Reaction of the Indians. In view of the reaction any attitude of the British Government the educated Indians realised the necessity of organising their political life. The lead in this matter was taken by Surendra Nath Banerjee who has been rightly discribed as the father of nationalist agitation in India. When he passed the I.C.S. Examination attempts were made to remove his name from the list. Soon after his appointment the Government dismissed him on inadequate grounds. This dismissed member of the "Heaven born" service was destined to be the most popular among the pioneers of national movement. He took to politics and journalism and in 1876 founded the Indian Association with the object of making it centre of an all India movement. This Association animated as it was by the vision of a United India, proved to be the precursor of the National Congress. It focused public attention on India's problems and thereby helped to create a body of public opinion.

Civil Service agitation started when the Secretary of state reduced the maximum age limit for the Civil Service Examination from 21 to 19. This measure as Surendra Nath Saird was a deliberate attempt to blast the prospect of Indian candidates for the Indian Civil Service." The Indian Association organised a national protest against this measure. Surendra Nath took a where wind tour of Northern Indian in the cours of which he addressed crowded meetings at important places. His superb oratory deeply moved the audience and everywhere he was received with great enthusiams. His tour in the words of, Sir H. Cotton "assumed the character of a triumphal progress."

The Association next organised an all India memorial to the House of Commons with a praper not to lower the age for the Civil Service Examination and to hold simultaneous examinations in England and in India. Mr. Lal Mohan Ghose, a barrister was deputed to England to present to memorial in person. His speeches made profound impression the British audience and the result was the creation of Statutory Civil Service for India. The Civil Service Agitation was soon followed by agitations for the repeal for the Vernacular Press Act and Arms Act the two measures of Lord Lytton which made an invidious distinction between Indians and Europeans.

Birth of the Congress

Preceiving the increasing intensity of the Indian feelings A.D. Hume a retired civilian wanted to divert them into a constitutional channel. He feared that unless a safe out let was found the discontent of the people would fester beneath the surface and will eventually lead to dangerous consequences In a letter addressed to the graduates of Calcutta University, he exhorted them to found an organisation for the moral, material and political progress of their motherland. He enlisted official support for his proposal. Lord Dufferin encouraged the formation of some responsible organisation through which the "Government might be kept informed regarding the best Indian public opinion." He was convinced that India needed a political organisation "which would perform the function which Her Majesty's opposition did in England." According to Mr. Hume's plan was taken up by some prominent Indians and the Indian National Congress was ushered into existence in December 1885. It met at Bombay under the Presidency of Mr. W. C. Banerjee a prominent Bengalee barrister and was attended by only seventy two delegates. The pancity of attendence was due to the fact that Surendra Nath and other prominent leaders could not attend the Congress because of the simultaneous Session of the Indian National Conference in Calcutta. As the two organisation had the same objects in view, the separate existence of the Indian national conference was no longer necessary and so it merged itself into the National Congress.

Objects of the Congress. The first session of the Indian National Congress was attended by prominent persons like Pherozshah Mehta, Dadabhai Naoroji, K.T. Telang, Dinshaw Wacha etc., while delivering the Presidential address W.C. Banerjee the President of the first session of the Indian National Congress laid down the following as the object of the Congress:

(a) The promotion of personal intimacy and friendship amongst all the most earnest workers in our Country's cause in the various parts of the empire.

(b) The authoritative record of the matured opinions of the educated classes in India on some of the most important and pressing social question of the day.

(c) The eradication by direct friendly personal intercourse of all possible race, creed or provincial prejudices amongst all the lovers of the country and the fuller development and consolidation of those sentiments of national unity that took their origin in our beloved Ripon's ever memorable reign.

(d) The determination of the methods by which during the next twelve months it is desirable for the native politicians to labour in public interest."

The Congress was an All India Institution and had the support and Co-operation of the Hindu's, Muslims, Parsees, Sikhs, Christian Anglo-Indians and Europeans. W.C. Banerjee the first President of the Indian National Congress was an Indian Christian. Its next President was Dadabhai Naoroji who was a Parsee. The third President was Badruddin Tayabji who was a Muslim.

FIRST PHASE (1885-1905)

During this period the Congress though a national body mainly represented the educated middle class intelligensia, men of legal, medical; engineering and literary professions. It deligates were mostly drawn from the cities who had hardly any contact with the masses.

The organisation had been launched with the blessings of Lord Dufferin. The Congress took pride the British connection and looked upon the British Government not as an ananlgomist but as an ally. In 1886 Dadabhai Naoroji Presiding over the Calcutta Session dwelt at length on the "blessing of British rule" and his remarks were cheerd by the audience. Mr. Hume moved resolution for three times three cheers for the most Gracious Majesty the Queen Empress and a further resolution for long life of the Queen. Shri Anand Mohan Bose as Congress President declared in 1898: "The educated classes are the friends and not the foes of England her natural and necessary allies in the great work that lies before her."

There was implicit faith in British sense of justice and fair play. The Congress Leaders believed that all they had to do was to prepare their case and present and plead it before the English Government and Nation and their grievances would be redressed and justice done. With a view to educating the English people about the real needs of Indian in 1890 a decision was taken to hold a session of the India National Congress in London in 1892 but owing to the British elections of 1891 the proposal was postponed and afterward never revived S.N. Banerjee explained that the object of the Congress was, "not the supression of British rule in India, but the broadening of its basis, the liberalising of its spirit, the enabling of its character and placing it on the unchangeable foundation of a Nation's affections."

In the first phase of its life the Indian National Congress simply demanded a few concessions and not liberation for the nation. True. Lokmanya Tilak used the word Swaraj or self government towards the last decade of the nineteenth century but if did not become popular. The period may be called the period of moderate Nationalism. In was not a revolutionary body and its leaders declared loyalty to the British Government several times. They were against the idea of agitation and unconstitutional means and preferred to carryout their work by debates propoganda, petitions and deputations. They mostly adopted the policy of appeals. In 1890 a deputation of the Indian National Congress went to England and demanded representation of 50 percent elected candidates in the Legislative Assemblies slowly and gradually more and more youths joined Congress. There was an increase in self-confidence among the Indians and after 1905, the ultimation of the Congress became the attainment of independence. The achievements of the period were decried by the Progressive otherwise called the Extremist leaders of the early twentieth century. The policy of the moderate leaders or the 'Old Guards' was criticised as 'political mendicancy. In all fairness it must be said that men like Dababhai Naoroji, Sir Pherozshah Mehta, Sir Den Shah Wacha, Gopal Krishna Gokhle, Surendra Nath Benerjee etc., were the most progressive elements in Indian Society and true patriots. They earnestly wished the betterment of Indian Society and worked to lessen the harshness of British Rule. They did a lot of spade work.

❐

13

India and Neighbours (1818-1884)

King Mindon (1853-78) was a different man from his predecessors. He tried through various friendly means to get back Pegu. When in 1854 he sent envoys asking Dalhausie to restore Pegu the Governor-General remarked pungently. "Tell the envoys that so long as the sun shines which they see those territories will never be restored." Mindon wisely pursued a policy of friendship with the Government of India. In 1862 a commercial treaty was concluded with the British. It opened up British trade with China through Burma by authorising British steamers to proceed up the Irrawedy. The British secured further commercial advantages in 1867.

Mindon's diplomatic relations were not confined to the British alone. He tried to establish diplomatic contact with other European powers as well. In 1873 Burmese mission visited Paris and concluded a commercial treaty. Another treaty was concluded with Italy. In 1874 the state of Persta welcomed a Burmese envoy but the Czar of Russia refused to accept a Burmese mission. Mindon also tried to open direct negotiations with Queen Victoma as he considered beneath his dignity to treat on equal terms with a viceroy who was a mere official.

Signs of estrangement began to appear between Mindon and the British. In 1876 a dispute arose over court eliquatte. According to the Burmese custom the British Resident including the Chief Commissioner when attending the Court had to take off his Shoes Kneel before the king. The Government of India tried to stop this inconvenient practice. Mindon would not give way and reportedly said that he would fight for 'Shoe' though he had not fought for Pegu.

Mindon died in 1879 leaving behind 48 sons and 62 daughters. He intended that the three most efficient should succeed him and rule as joint Kings. But the ministerial party in the state placed a younger son Thihaw on the throne. The new King was weak and vicious. In February 1879 he cruelly massacred eighty members of the royal family who could prove to be his possible rivals. The British Resident protested but was curtly told that Burma was a sovereign state. In October, 1879 the Britsh Residency was withdrawn from Mandalay. Tension began to develop between the two governments when the crew of a British steamer were assaulted by some Burmese and a British Vessel Yunan was forcibly detained. Negotiations for renewed treaty in 1882 between the two Governments came to nothing British merchants in Rangoon and Lower. Burma began to urge the annexation of Thibaws domimors. But the Chief Commissioner, Bernard was advised to avoid annexation as this would lead to infinite trouble. The Viceroy Lord Mayo had strenly warned the officials in Burma not to interfere in the affairs of Upper Burma. Northbrooke took care to avoid intervention.

Annexation of Upper Burma. It was the French action which hastened the annexation of Upper Burma. France having won an empire in Cochin China and Tonkin now tried to dominate Upper Burma by peaceful penetration. The Burmese Government was anxious for friendship with France. Burmese Missions visited France in 1878 and 1883. In January 1885 Ferry, the Foreign Minister signed a trade treaty and secretly promised to allow importation of arms into Burma through Tonkin. France followed up the treaty the stationing a Consal Haos, at Mandalay. Negotiations began for the establishment of a France bank at Mandalay, construction of a railway from Mandalay to the rail head in British Burma and the management of the royal monopolies.

Immediate Cause of War. The immediate cause of war was the fine imposed by the Government of Burma on the Bombay Burma Trading Corporation an English firm which extracted timber over half the kingdom. The underlying motive was to hand over the forests to a French Syndicate after evicting the Corporation. The London agent of the corporation approached and secretary of state. On arrival the Viceroy Lord Dufferin found the situation opportune. France having suffered reverses in Tonkin withdrew from Upper Burma. Thibaw was incapable of firm resistance. The Burmese refusal to submit the corporation case to the Viceroy's arbitration reached Rangoon on 13th October 1885. Where upon the viceroy with the permission of the Government in England, despatched an ultimatum to Thibaw on 19th October. It deserted the Burmese king to receive a permanent Resident giving him free access to the king without humiliating ceremonies to submit the corporation case to the Viceroy's arbitration, to submit their foreign relations to English control and to grant the British the right to trade with the Chinese through his dominions. Dufferin, now, decided to force the issue.

On Thibaws rejection of the ultimatum, British troops under General Prendergost were ordered to move in early November. The Burmese hardly made any resistence. Thibaw surrendered unconditionally and the first stage of the war was over within a fortnight. On 1st January 1886, by a proclamation. Upper Burma, kingdom larger than that of France was annexed. The majority in the Government and Parliament Warmly Supported Dufferin.

But the end of War did not mean the extinction of law less bands of armed men who continued harassing guirilla warfare against the British. It took five years pacify and consolidate the kingdom of Upper Burma and another six years to bring under effective control the border tribes such as sharn and chins.

In 1885 the Province of Burma was formed by the combination of upper and Lower Burma with headquarters at Rangoon. It was governed by Chief Commissioner upto 1897 when it was placed under a Lieutinant-Governor. The Government of India exercised legislative power till 1897 when the Burma Legislative Council was constituted as a small body with an official majority and limited powers. A special committee with Sir Fredrick Whyte as its President, visited Burma in 1921. As a result of its recommendations Burma was constituted as a Governors province in 1923.

BRITISH INDIAN GOVERNMENT WITH BURMA

The British Indian Government thrice came in conflict with the Burmese Government in the nineteenth century. These three conflicts resulted in the defects of the Burmese and the whole of Burma passed into British hands.

(a) First Burmese War (1824-26). It was in the year 1823 that Lord Amherst on the soil of India as Governor-General. He had not yet made himself familiar with the political conditions of India that he was compelled by the force of circumstances to wage war against Burma. The natives of Burma were making roads in the British territory without any impediment.

A Government of India has to take into account the political importance of the North-Eastern frontier as well Mughal Imperialism especially in the times of Aurangzeb tried to push its limits towards these eastern frontiers; and the British Empire in India was in the course of its territorial expanison, also drawn towards it.

The eastern boundary of Bengal, in which was included the district of Chittagong, for long remained 'very ill-defined, and variable'. Immediately south of Chittagong lay the kingdom of Akakan, south of that Pegu and south of that again the coastland of Tenasse rim. In the later half of eighteenth century the history rapidly brought Arakan, Pegu, Tenass rin and the whole basin of Burma underwent dramatic changes.

The region of Pegu was conquered by a Burman chief, named Tampora, from the Talaings in the delta of the Irrawaddy, and thus was established a strong monarchy in about 1750 AD. In 1766, Burmese attacked Siam and captured Tenasserim. In 1784, Tampora captured the independent State of Arakan and thus the Burmese established their control equally over upper and lower Burma, by 1793, and next pushed on close to Surma valley in 1813. These Burmese conquests made it necessary for the English to open political intercourse with the Burmese; and their Government in Calcutta accordingly sent envoys to Burma-Captain Symes in 1795 and 1802; Captain Cox in 1797, Captain Canning in 1803, 1809,

1811. But the envoys were not favourably treated and the mission proved unsuccessful, while the contemporary mission to the north-western Asiatic States produced better results.

The advance of Burmese on the Chittagong frontier made an ultimate collision with British inevitable. Fugitives flying from the territories conquered by the Burmese took shelter if the British border and used their new quarters as a base of inroads into the conquered provinces the British Government steadily declined to surrender them to the Burmese in spite of repeated demands to this effect on the part of the latter. So, when the British were engaged in the large-scale campaign against the Pindaris, the king of Ava in 1818 sent a letter to Lord Hastings demanding the surrender of Chittagong, Dacca, Murshidabad and Kassim Bazar on the ground of these being andent dependencies of Arakan, and hence part of the Burmese dominions. But before the letter reached Calcutta, the British had been relieved of pressures from other qurters, and the Governor-General returned the communication to the king of Burma with the remark that it was perhaps forgery.

After a temporary respite the Burmese resumed their role of conquest and annexation. In 1822, their able General Mahabanduk captured Assam which brough Burmese into contact with the whole of north-eastern frontier of British India. Manipur was also captured by the Burmese.

In 1823, the Burmese captured Shahpuri, a small island near Chittagong and the Burmese threatened an invasion of interior Bengal. Lord Amherst tried to establish peace with the Burmese, but the Burmese replied by turning out the British forces from an outpost near Shahpuri.

P.E. Roberts has pointed out. "The physical features of Burma which was one vast expanse of forest and morass, located longitudinally by mountain ranges and the valleys of the Irrawaddy. Sittang and Salween", afforded the best defence to the Burmese. As a military force in open fighting the Burmese could not be certainly compared with the British troops of that time, but the former possessed considerable skill in building stockades of timber with great rapidity, or in throwing up earth works and sinking rifle pits.

Organizing the plan of operation against the Burmese, the British Government decided that on the frontier, "operation should be in a great measure defensive; but not so exclusively as to prelude the expulsion of the Burmese from territories in which they had recently established themselves by usurpation." The main blow was to be struck through an expedition by sea to Rangoon with the idea that it could then proceed up the Irrawaddy, Bengal Presidency supplied a part of the force required for the expedition, the remaining part was chiefly recruited from Madras.

Capture of Rangoon. The British Armeda under the command of Major-General Sir Archibald Camphell occupied Rangoon on 11th May, 1824. But the entire population had disappeared into the jungles of Pegu leaving Rangoon denuded of every kind of supplies. The expedition had been undertaken in a wrong season and without any satisfactory arrangement for securing supplies. Soon after the occupation of Rangoon, the rains started and with them fever and dysentery; while their troops had to depend on the provisions supplied irregularly by the Calcutta contractors.

Bandula proceeded to invade Bengal in the month of May. He repelled a British detachment at Ramu on the Chittagong frontier; but now he was recalled for meeting the counter invasion of Pegu. On 1st December. 1824, the Burmese Army, 60,000 in number, appeared in front of the British position at Rangoon and threw up entrenchments with great rapidity.

Sir Archibald Campbell then decided to advance upon Prome, the second city of the Burmese Empire, and after whiling away some time in dilatory preparations, he commenced his march on February 13, 1825. But Bandula held out bravely for a month before the column sent against him, and the general advance was delayed till 1st April, when Bandula was killed by a rocket and his troops consequently demoralised beat a haty retreat during the night abandoning every thing including a store of grain. Three weeks later

Cambell occupied Prome, the capital of Lower Burma, on 25th April without any resistance, but as the rains started further operations had to be stopped.

Negotiations for peace started which proved futile and hostilities were resumed. But all the attempts of the Burmese to repulse the British troops remained unsuccessful. The Burmese now opened negotiations for peace, The last and desperate attempt was made by the Burmese with a force of 10,000 men, but they were repulsed. The British forces now advanced upto Yandaboo within sixty miles of their capital.

Terms of the Treaty of Yandaboo

(a) The king of Ava agreed to surrender Arakan and Tenasserim to the British.

(b) He agreed to pay heavy war indemnity amounting to a million sterling.

(c) He also agreed not to interfere in any way in Assam.

(d) He agreed not to interfere in Cachar and Jaintia and to recognise Manipur as an independent State.

(e) The king of Burma also agreed to enter into a commercial treaty upon principles of reciprocal advantage. Accordingly a commercial treaty was signed in November.

(f) The king of Burma did not accept a British Resident upto 1830.

The first Burmese war has been criticised for the manner in which it was conducted. According to Innes, "The war had been in many respects a disastrous one." The expeditions had been, dispatched on almost entire ignorance of the circumstances of the country to which it was to proceed, and without any adequate preparations for securing supplies, it meant a grossly needless waste of life and wealth.

But this fact cannot be denied that this war proved advantageous for the British. With Bengal and Assam they got the priceless sea-coast and Cachar and Manipur.

The Burmese made peace by the Treaty of Yandaboo in 1826. Its most important provisions were the following:

(a) The Burmese gave the provinces of Arakan and Tenasserim to the Company.

(b) The Burmese Government had to pay indemnity of one crore of rupees.

(c) The Burmese were not to interfere in Assam, Cachar, Jaintia and Manipur. These place thus passed under the control of the Company.

(d) A commercial treaty was to be concluded between the Company and the Burmese Government.

(e) A British Resident was to be posted at Ava, the Burmese Capital.

The First Burmese War put an end to Burmese aggression. The rich provinces of Arakan and Tenasserim were secured. Assam, Cachar, Jaintia and Manipur passed under Company's control. Thus the war gave valuable territories to the Company.

(B) Second Burmese War (1852). The Second Burmese War was fought in the time of Lord Dalhousie in 1852. The following were its important canses:

(1) Lord Dalhousie feared that France or some other European power might not establish itself in Burma. In order to root at such a possibility, he wanted to bring Burma under his control. This was the real and underlying cause and he wanted an excuse to go to war with Burma.

(2) By the Treaty of Yandaboo, the English merchants had been permited to settle in Burma and carry on trade. Their commercial rights were not clearly defined and each party interpreted these in its own way. The English merchants

were ill-treated but they continued to trade because of high profits. They complained to Lord Dalhousie about the bad treatment meted out to them by the Burmese Government. Dalhousie wanted an excuse to go to war with Burma and be seriously took up the cause of the English traders. He wrote to the Government of Burma that it had violated the Treaty of Yandaboo and must pay damages to the English merchants for the wrongs done to them. Commodore Lambert was sent to Rangoon. He captured a ship belonging to the Burmese king. This led to the exchange of gun-fire and Lord Dalhousie declared war.

Events. The British forces were sent under General Godwin. Martaban and Rangoon were captured. This was followed by the occupation of Prome. Thus the whole of Lower Burma fell into the hands of the British. The Burmese Government refused to negotiate a treaty and Lower Burma was then annexed by a Proclamation.

The Second Burmese War resulted him the annexation of Lower Burma. It brought great commercial advantages to the British. The war reduced the possibility of the occupation of Burma by a European power because Upper Burma was now cut off from the sea.

(C) Third Burmese War (1885). The Third Burmese War was fought in the time of Lord Dufferin. The following were its most important causes:

(1) Lower Burma had passed into the hands of the British as a result of Second Burmese War but Upper Burma was still independent. Thebaw, the new king of Burma, did not like that the British should trade with Upper Burma and adopted a stern -attitude. The English merchants complained to the Governor General that they were ill-treated.

(2) Thebaw, the king of Burma, began to negotiate commercial treaties with Germany. "Italy, and specially with France when possessions in Indo-China were near his eastern frontier. A Burmen Mission went to Paris in 1868 and a

French envoy proceeded to Mandalay in 1885. He made arrangement to establish a French bank there. The French Government disclaimed all knowledge of his proceedings and recalled him, but Lord Dufferin wanted to root out any possibility of French influence by occupying Upper Burman and wanted an excuse to do so.

(3) The king of Burma imposed heavy fine on the Bombay and Burma Trading Company and ordered the arrest of its officials. Lord Dufferin insisted an inquiry into the matter but the Burmese king refused to reaopen the question. The Governor-General sent an ultimatum that the king should admit a British envoy at Mandalay, suspend proceedings against the Company till the arrival of the envoy, have no relations with any power except on the advice of the Government of India and permit the British to trade with the Chinese through his dominions. The king refused and war was declared on Burma.

The British had already collected troops in Lower Burma and a swift attack was made. The Burmese got no time to prepare and were taken by surprise. Upper Burma was overrun and the Burmese king was sent to India. The Burmese continued guerrilla warfare for about two years.

Upper Burma was now annexed and that completed the conquest of the whole of Burma. The Burmese policy of Lord Dufferin has been criticised on several grounds. Firstly, it is said that King Thebaw was a tyrant. It was an internal affairs of Burma and was no concern of the British. Secondly, it has been said in defence of the British that the English merchants were not properly treated. This, however, was no justification for war. If they could not put up with the treatment, they were free to stop trade with Burma. Thirdly, the princip grievance of the British was that the king was in communication with the French. This was no justification for interference and annexation. The Burmese king was a sovereign prince and was free to have relations with any foreign power.

❐